utopia

Published on the occasion of an exhibition organized
jointly by The New York Public Library and the
Bibliothèque nationale de France

Paris, Bibliothèque nationale de France
Utopie. La quête de la société idéale en Occident
Site François-Mitterrand
April 4 through July 9, 2000

New York, The New York Public Library
Utopia: The Search for the Ideal Society in the Western World
Humanities and Social Sciences Library
D. Samuel and Jeane H. Gottesman Exhibition Hall and
Edna Barnes Salomon Room
October 14, 2000 through January 27, 2001

utopia

The Search for the Ideal Society in the Western World

Edited by
Roland Schaer, Gregory Claeys, and Lyman Tower Sargent

The New York Public Library/Oxford University Press

New York Oxford
2000

Oxford University Press

Oxford New York

Athens Auckland Bangkok Bogotá Buenos Aires
Calcutta Cape Town Chennai Dar es Salaam Delhi
Florence Hong Kong Istanbul Karachi Kuala Lumpur
Madrid Melbourne Mexico City Mumbai Nairobi
Paris São Paulo Shanghai Singapore Taipei Tokyo
Toronto Warsaw

and associated companies in Berlin Ibadan

Most of the texts in this work are also published in French in
Utopie. La quête de la société idéale en Occident, Bibliothèque
nationale de France/Fayard, 2000.

Library of Congress Cataloging-in-Publication Data

Utopia : the search for the ideal society in the western
world / edited by Roland Schaer, Gregory Claeys, and
Lyman Tower Sargent.
    p. cm.
  Includes bibliographical references and index.
  ISBN 0-19-514110-5—ISBN 0-19-514111-3 (pbk.)
    1. Utopias. I. Schaer, Roland, 1947– II. Claeys, Gregory.
III. Sargent, Lyman Tower, 1940–

HX806.U7918 2000
016.321'07—dc21
                    00-042781

Printed in Hong Kong on acid-free paper.

Karen Van Westering, Manager of Publications
Anne Skillion, Senior Editor
Barbara Bergeron, Editor
Ken Benson, Warren Platt, Researchers

For their advice and assistance with the American catalogue, our
special thanks go to curators Roland Schaer, Gregory Claeys, and
Lyman Tower Sargent, as well as to Pierrette Crouzet, Jacqueline
Michelet, and Francoise Avril in the publications office of the
Bibliothèque nationale de France.

Designed by Ann Antoshak

www.nypl.org   www.oup-usa.org

Photo Credits

© 2000 Artists Rights Society (ARS), New York/ADAGP, Paris:
239, 283, 328–29.

© 2000 Artists Rights Society (ARS), New York/SIAE, Rome: 279,
280 top, 281.

© 2000 Artists Rights Society (ARS), New York/VG Bild-Kunst,
Bonn: 286–87, 294–95.

Courtesy of Avery Architectural and Fine Arts Library, Columbia
University in the City of New York: 307 bottom.

California Historical Society, all photos © Gene Anthony: 344
(FN-31965, Acc-80-31-2); 345 top left (FN-26073, FS-01966,
Acc-80-31-53); 345 top right (FN-31964, Acc-80-31-80).

Collection Cinémathèque française–Musée du Cinema.
All Rights Reserved: 283.

Columbia University, Rare Book and Manuscript Library,
Plimpton MS 17, f. 3 (detail): 66.

Henry Dreyfuss Collection, Cooper-Hewitt, National Design
Museum, Smithsonian Institution: 309.

Stiftung Deutsches Hygiene-Museum, Dresden: 324.

Courtesy of the Estate of Buckminster Fuller: 310 top.

Copyright 1964 GM Corp. Used with permission of GM Media
Archives: 310 bottom.

By permission of the Houghton Library, Harvard University: 223.

Courtesy of the Donald E. Janzen Collection: 340–41.

Courtesy of MCA Records/Universal Music Group: 345 bottom.

Courtesy of Bert Miles: 336–37.

The Pierpont Morgan Library, New York: 238 top (PML 76952,.4);
238 bottom left (PML 76952,.7); 238 bottom right (PML
76952,.5A).

© Musée des Arts et Métiers, Paris/PHOTO STUDIO CNAM: 199.

Copyright the Dorothea Lange Collection, The Oakland Museum
of California, City of Oakland. Gift of Paul S. Taylor: 231 bottom.

© PMVP: 205 top (Photo Ph. Joffre); 205 bottom (Photo I.
Andreani).

Copyright © 1931 and renewed 1959 by Random House, Inc.
Reprinted by permission of Random House, Inc.: 254.

© Leni Riefenstahl: 326–27.

© Estate of Alexander Rodchenko/Licensed by VAGA, New York,
NY: 290 top.

© Varvara Stepanova/Licensed by VAGA, New York, NY: 288.

© 1958, 2000 The Frank Lloyd Wright Foundation, Scottsdale,
AZ: 308.

The Exhibition

Organizing Committee

Curator

Roland Schaer
Délégué à la diffusion
culturelle, Bibliothèque
nationale de France (BNF)

Curatorial advisors

Gregory Claeys
Professor of the History of
Political Thought, Royal
Holloway and New Bedford
College, University of London

Ruth Eaton
Architectural historian

Danielle Lecoq
Professeur d'histoire médiévale, chargée de cours à
l'université de Paris VII –
Denis Diderot

Lyman Tower Sargent
Professor of Political Science
at the University of Missouri,
St. Louis

Curatorial research

Holland Goss
Research Curator,
The New York Public Library
(NYPL)

Coordination

David Cronin
Manager,
Public Programs, NYPL

Anne-Françoise
Leprévots-Bonnardel
Conservateur en chef,
département des Estampes et
de la Photographie, direction
des collections, BNF

Laurent Portes
Conservateur, service de
l'Inventaire rétrospectif,
direction des collections, BNF

Additional advice

Denis Bruckmann
Conservateur en chef, adjoint
au directeur du département
Littérature et Art, direction
des collections, BNF

Bernard Vouillot
Conservateur en chef,
responsable du service de
l'Inventaire rétrospectif,
direction des collections, BNF

Laurent Gervereau
Directeur du musée d'Histoire
contemporaine (Paris)

Didier Ottinger
Conservateur, musée national
d'Art moderne, Centre
Georges Pompidou (Paris)

**Staff of The New York
Public Library who participated in the development
and implementation of the
exhibition:**

Exhibitions Program Office

Assistant Manager:
Susan Rabbiner

Research Coordinators:
Jeanne Bornstein, Meg Maher

Registrars: Jean Mihich,
Caryn Gedell

Exhibitions Conservator:
Myriam de Arteni

Installation Coordinator:
Russell Drisch

Exhibitions Assistant:
Jeanne Stehr-Jahn

Intern: Anne Dressen

Editor: Barbara Bergeron

Graphic Design:
Marc Blaustein,
Kara Van Woerden

Public Relations:
Herb Scher, Sabina Potaczek,
Liz Smith

Website: Renee Roberts,
Michelle Misner, Jane Moffitt

Digitization: Anthony Troncale,
Danielle Mericle

Digital recording for audio
stations: Adrian Cosentini

*For their assistance with the
planning and implementation
of the New York exhibition,
special thanks to Viviane
Cabannes, Nadine
Marienstras, Anne-Hélène
Rigogne, and Catherine
Geldof in the Service des
expositions at the BNF.*

Installation and
Casework Design:
Tim Culbert + Celia Imrey,
INLINE Studio

**The Library wishes to
thank the following
institutions and individuals
for their generosity in
making items from their
collections available for
use in the exhibition:**

Bibliothèque nationale de
France, Paris

The California Historical
Society, San Francisco

Centre historique des
Archives nationales, Paris

Francis P. Chinard, M.D.

Cinémathèque française, Paris

Rare Book and Manuscript
Library, Columbia University,
New York

Fellowship for Intentional
Community, Rutledge,
Missouri

Special Collections, Harvard
Law Library, Harvard
University, Cambridge,
Massachusetts

Houghton Library, Harvard
University, Cambridge,
Massachusetts

Institut Claude-Nicolas
Ledoux, Arc-et-Senans, France

Donald E. Janzen Collection,
Danville, Kentucky

The Pierpont Morgan Library,
New York

Musée Carnavalet, Paris

Musée des arts et métiers,
CNAM, Paris

The Museum of Modern Art,
New York

Yad Tabenkin Archives, Israel

Private Collection

Major support for the exhibition *Utopia: The Search for the Ideal Society in the Western World* has been provided by The Florence Gould Foundation.

Support for The New York Public Library's Exhibitions Program has been provided by Pinewood Foundation and by Sue and Edgar Wachenheim III.

Additional support for this exhibition has been provided by Delta Air Lines.

▲ **Delta**

Support has also been provided by Andreas C. Dracopoulos, Grand Marnier Foundation, and The Cultural Services of the French Embassy.

Support for this exhibition has been provided by a grant from the New York Council for the Humanities, a state affiliate of the National Endowment for the Humanities, as part of State Humanities Month.

Official Partner of the Millennium Council

Acknowledgments

WE WOULD like to express our gratitude first
of all to Paul LeClerc, President of The New York
Public Library; Jean-Pierre Angremy, President
of the Bibliothèque nationale de France; and
Philippe Bélaval, former directeur général, who
gave the first impetus, as well as encouragement
and support, to this project.

Other individuals in the two libraries who
played key roles in bringing this exhibition to the
public include, at the Bibliothèque nationale de
France, Jacqueline Sanson, directeur des collections,
and François Stasse, directeur général; and at
The New York Public Library, William D. Walker,
Andrew W. Mellon Director of The Research
Libraries; Jean Bowen and her successor, Rodney
Phillips, Director, Humanities and Social Sciences
Library; and H. George Fletcher, Brooke Russell
Astor Director for Special Collections. We are
grateful to the chiefs, curators, and staff of all divi-
sions of The Research Libraries of The New York
Public Library who provided ideas and information
during the planning of the exhibition.

Editors

Roland Schaer

Director of Cultural Development at the Bibliothèque nationale de France from 1994 to 2000. He was the organizer in 1996–97 of the exhibition *Tous les Savoirs du monde. Encyclopédies et bibliothèques de Sumer au XXIe siècle* and editor of its catalogue (Paris: BNF/Flammarion, 1996), and the author of *L'Invention des musées* (Paris: Gallimard collection "Découvertes," 1993). He is now Professor of Philosophy in Rouen.

Gregory Claeys

Professor of the History of Political Thought, Royal Holloway and New Bedford College, University of London, a specialist in the intellectual history of Great Britain in the nineteenth century and a leading expert on British utopian thought. His publications include *Citizens and Saints: Politics and Anti-politics in Early British Socialism* (Cambridge, England: Cambridge University Press, 1989) and, as editor, *Utopias of the British Enlightenment* (Cambridge, England: Cambridge University Press, 1994). He is a Consulting Editor for the *Journal of the History of Ideas*.

Lyman Tower Sargent

Professor of Political Science at the University of Missouri, St. Louis, and one of the foremost anglophone experts on the literature of utopias. Among his many publications are *Contemporary Political Ideologies: A Comparative Analysis* (11th ed., Fort Worth, Texas: Harcourt Brace College Publishers, 1998), a widely used text in American colleges, *British and American Utopian Literature, 1516–1975: An Annotated, Chronological Bibliography* (New York: Garland, 1988), and, with Gregory Claeys, *The Utopia Reader* (New York: New York University Press, 1999). He is the editor of the journal *Utopian Studies*.

Contributors

Bronislaw Baczko

Historian, honorary professor at the Faculty of Letters at the University of Geneva. His books include *Lumières de l'utopie* (Paris: Payot, 1978), *Les Imaginaires sociaux. Mémoires et espoirs collectifs* (Paris: Payot, 1984), and *Job, mon ami. Promesses du bonheur et fatalité du mal* (Paris: Gallimard, 1997), among others.

Françoise Choay

University professor emerita, a specialist in the history and theory of space planning and historian of ideas. She is the author of *Urbanisme, utopies et réalités* (Paris: Le Seuil, 1965), *La Règle et le modèle* (Paris: Le Seuil, 1980), and *L'Allégorie du patrimoine* (Paris: Le Seuil, 1992).

J. C. Davis

Professor of English History, University of East Anglia, a specialist in modern political and utopian thought. His extensive publications on utopian thought include *Utopia and the Ideal Society: A Study of English Utopian Writing, 1516–1700* (Cambridge, England: Cambridge University Press, 1981–83), "The Millennium as the Anti-Utopia of Seventeenth-century Political Thought," *Anglophonia: French Journal of English Studies*, no. 3 (1998), and "Utopia" in *Encyclopedia of the Renaissance*, Paul F. Grendler, Editor in Chief (New York: Scribner's, in association with the Renaissance Society of America, 1999).

Ruth Eaton

British urban and architectural historian. She has participated in the preparation of several exhibitions and publications, contributing most notably to *La Ville: art et architecture en Europe, 1870–1993* (under the direction of Jean Dether and Alain Guilleux; Paris, Centre Georges Pompidou, 1994), *Archaeology of the Future City* (under the direction of Takashi Uzawa; Tokyo, Museum of Contemporary Art, 1996), and *Living Bridges: The Inhabited Bridge: Past, Present and Future*, ed. Marianne Steens and Peter Murray (Munich and New York: Prestel, 1996).

Laurent Gervereau

Curator of the musée d'Histoire contemporaine in Paris, director of the journal *L'Image*, and President of the Association internationale des musées d'histoire. He has curated numerous exhibitions including, with Wladimir Berelowitch, *Russie URSS, 1914–1991. Changement de regards* (musée d'Histoire contemporaine, BDIC, 1991), and is the author of *Voir, comprendre, analyser les images* (Paris: La Découverte, 1994; 1997), *Rêver demain. Utopies, science-fiction, cités idéales*, with Yolène Dilas and Thierry Paquot (Paris: Alternatives, 1994), and *Les Images qui mentent. Histoire du visuel au XXe siècle* (Paris: Le Seuil, 2000).

Krishan Kumar

Formerly Professor of Social Thought at the University of Kent, Canterbury, England, currently Professor of Sociology at the University of Virginia, a specialist in political and social thought. His notable publications include *Utopia and Anti-Utopia in Modern Times* (Oxford and New York: Blackwell, 1987) and *Utopianism* (Milton Keynes: Open University Press, 1991) and, as editor with Stephen Bann, *Utopias and the Millennium* (London: Reaktion Books, 1993).

Danielle Lecoq
Historian, Professor at the Lycée Janson de Sailly and at Université de Paris VII – Denis Diderot, specialist in representations of the world, especially in the medieval period. She is the author of "L'image d'Alexandre à travers les mappemondes médiévales," in *Geographica antiqua*, no. 2 (1993); "Des Antipodes au Nouveau Monde ou de la difficulté de l'Autre," in *La France-Amérique (XVIe–XVIIIe siècle)*, proceedings of the XXXVth international colloquium on humanistic studies (Paris: H. Champion, 1998); and, with Antoine Chambard, *Terre à découvrir, terre à parcourir. Exploration et connaissance du monde XIIe–XIXe siècle* (Paris: Université de Paris VII – Denis Diderot/L'Harmattan, 1998).

Frank Lestringant
Professor at the Université de Paris IV – Sorbonne; his research, on the confluence of literature and history, bears in particular on the cosmographer André Thevet and on French attempts to colonize America in the sixteenth century. In addition to a dozen essays and editions of Marot, d'Aubigné, Léry, Palissy, Thevet, and Vestegan, his publications include *L'Atelier du cosmographe ou l'Image du monde à la Renaissance* (Paris: Albin Michel, 1991), *L'Expérience huguenote au Nouveau Monde (XVIe siècle)* (Geneva: Droz, 1996), and *Une sainte horreur ou le Voyage en Eucharistie (XVIe–XVIIIe siècle)* (Paris: Presses Universitaires de France, 1996).

Alain Milhou
Director of the Department of Spanish at the University of Rouen, a corresponding member of the Royal Academy of History at Madrid, and a specialist in Iberian studies. He is the author of *Colón y su mentalidad mesiánica en el ambiente franciscanista español* (Valladolid: Universidad de Valladolid, 1983) and *La Destruction des Indes de Bartolomé de Las Casas (1552)* (Paris: Chandeigne, 1995).

Yaacov Oved
Professor of history emeritus at Tel Aviv University, executive director of the International Communal Studies Association, head of the department of communitarian studies at the research center Yad Tabenkin, and a specialist in modern history (the history of communitarian movements and of utopian anarcho-communist thought). He is the author of *Two Hundred Years of American Communes* (New Brunswick, N.J.: Transaction Books, 1988) and *The Witness of the Brothers: A History of the Bruderhof* (New Brunswick, N.J.: Transaction Books, 1996).

Laurent Portes
Curator of the retrospective cataloging service at the Bibiliothèque nationale de France. He has contributed to the exhibition catalogues *Voltaire et l'Europe* (Paris: BNF/Editions Complexes, 1994) and *Tous les Savoirs du monde. Encyclopédies et bibliothèques de Sumer au XXIe siècle* (Paris: BNF/Flammarion, 1996). He also directed, with Bruno Blasselle, *Mélanges autour de l'histoire des livres imprimés et périodiques* (Paris: BNF, 1998) and is the author of "Sciences, politique et science politique dans la France du XIXe siècle: leur rapport à l'utopie," *Revue de la Bibliothèque nationale de France*, 5 (June 2000).

Jean-François Pradeau
Historian of ancient philosophy, he teaches the history of philosophy at Université Marc Bloch in Strasbourg. He is the author of *Platon et la cité* (Paris: Presses Universitaires de France, 1997) and *Le Monde de la politique. Sur le récit atlante de Platon, Timée (17a–27b) et Critias* (Sankt Augustin: Academia Verlag, 1997). He has translated the *Critias* of Plato (Paris: Les Belles Lettres, 1997) and, with Chantal Marbœuf, the *Alcibiade* of Plato (Paris: Flammarion, 1999).

Frédéric Rouvillois
Professor of Law at the University of Caen. He is the author of *L'Invention du Progrès, aux origines de la pensée totalitaire (1680–1730)* (Paris: Kimé, 1996), the preface to Daniel Halévy, *Histoire de quatre ans (1997–2001)* (Paris: Kimé, 1997), and *L'Utopie* (Paris: Garnier Flammarion, 1998).

Alain Touraine
Sociologist, director of studies at the Ecole pratiques des hautes études en sciences sociales in Paris. He is the author of *Production de la société* (new ed., Paris: Le Seuil, 1993) and *Pourrons-nous vivre ensemble? Egaux et différents* (new ed., Paris: Le Livre de Poche, 1997).

Caption Writers
Paris
Marie Avril
Ruth Eaton
Marianne de Fleury
Catherine Hofmann
Danielle Lecoq
Anne-Françoise Leprévots-Bonnardel
Mathieu Lescuyer
Emmanuel Pernoud
Laurent Portes
Anne Sanciaud-Azanza
Roland Schaer
Bernard Vouillot

New York
Jeanne Bornstein
Holland Goss
Anne Skillion

Translators
Nadia Benabid
Susan Emanuel
Richard Howard

A Note on This Edition

Illustrations in this volume are drawn primarily from
materials included in the exhibition *Utopia: The Search
for the Ideal Society in the Western World* and its French
counterpart, *Utopie. La quête de la société idéale en Occident.*
Some of these materials, particularly those represented
in the essay "Utopia and Twentieth-century Avant-gardes,"
were not exhibited at The New York Public Library; others
were displayed there in different editions or formats.

Contents

THIS EXHIBITION began with a friendship between two libraries, the Bibliothèque nationale de France and The New York Public Library. Earlier cooperation between the two institutions resulted in numerous cultural exchanges and several collaborations, and especially in a common commitment to making the fullest possible use of new digital technologies to preserve important national cultural resources – the materials for research – while at the same time increasing access to these materials by users worldwide. This digital initiative was perhaps a first shared utopia, bringing together practical expertise and public readership.

Despite the difficulties of the exercise, it seemed natural for our two libraries to jointly organize an exhibition, and to cross the threshold of the millennium together. And the theme of utopia seemed an appropriate one, affording the opportunity to speculate on the role of the imagination, and even of fiction, in the construction of the future, to consider the pleasures and uses of the utopian model, and to explain its history, all the while drawing lessons from the century just ended.

Above all, the links between New York and Paris, between the United States of America and Europe, have found ideal expression in the theme of utopia. If the invention of utopia – both the word and the literary genre – in 1516 was contemporaneous with the "invention" of the New World, it was because these inventions corresponded with the emergence of modern humanism, and they shared a confidence in the human capacity to explore and invent new forms of social living. This is what made America, in the eyes of those wanting to come to its shores as well as of those already there, the utopian land *par excellence*, an emblematic figure of the promises of modernity.

In these circumstances, it is more than symbolic that the Bibliothèque nationale de France is exhibiting in Paris, among many treasures from The New York Public Library, a copy of the Declaration of Independence in Thomas Jefferson's hand, on its first visit to Europe; and that in return, among the many treasures from the Bibliothèque nationale de France on view in New York – including illuminated manuscripts and rare items relating to the French Revolution and to the social utopias of the

Romantic Age – is the Green Globe, on which for the first time, at the very beginning of the sixteenth century, the New World figured as a continent.

The joint production of a great exhibition is an extremely rich adventure that allows a cross-fertilization of different sensibilities, cultures, and national patrimonies. This collaboration has strengthened the ties between our two institutions. We hope that visitors and readers in our two countries and throughout the world will find in the result much matter for pleasure, reflection, and imagination.

JEAN-PIERRE ANGREMY
de l'Académie Française,
Président, Bibliothèque nationale de France

PAUL LECLERC
President and Chief Executive Officer,
The New York Public Library

Utopia: Space, Time, History

IN THE strict sense of the word, utopia came into being at the beginning of the sixteenth century. In 1516, Thomas More devised the rhetorical conceit that gave rise to this

1

literary genre, which would flourish, with periods of fruitfulness, off and on, from the seventeenth to the twentieth centuries. When Classical authors relied on fictional means to depict ideal societies, they did so, in part, to foil the censors; further-more, by deliberately positioning themselves in imaginary realms where all things are permitted, they could make full use of their descriptive talents to endow their made-up societies with all the attributes of a material, manifest, and not just theoretical reality – qualities that befit a politics of literature.

Sir Thomas More invented the word: the island where the society was founded was a "non-place" and a "nowhere." The negation can be interpreted in several ways: Are we to understand that this form of society is imaginary, unprecedented, or even impos-sible? How can we conceive that it exists even so on the perimeter of the New World? And if More's *Utopia* was intended as a complement to Erasmus's *The Praise of Folly*, is it then nothing more than one of those humanist rhetorical exercises in which a fabricated upside-down world shows up the sense-lessness of the world we choose to put our faith in?[1]

If the history of utopia necessarily begins with Thomas More, it is not only because he coined the word and invented the genre. Rather, it is because this English humanist, good Christian though he may have been, described an ideal society achieved solely by human means: evil and vice are ousted after "the best state of a commonwealth" has been instituted in the here and now, taking, in other words, the human condition as it is. Unlike mil-lenarian visions and eschatological promises, More's Utopia does not call for the intervention of divine providence. Nor does it rely, like Golden Ages and Lands of Cockaigne, on nature's supernatural bounty to exonerate people from labor. Nor are

1 Thomas More
Libellus vere aureus nec minus salutaris quam festivus de optimo reip[ublicae] statu, deq[ue] nova Insula Utopia
[Louvain, Belgium]:
Thierry Martin, [1516]
NYPL, Henry W. and Albert A. Berg Collection of English and American Literature

The first edition of Thomas More's *Utopia* juxtaposes an illustration of the island of Utopia with a sample of its alphabet, both of which add a sense of exotic reality to More's fictional country. The alphabet is accompanied by a poem in Latin, which reads in English: "Utopus, my ruler, converted me, formerly not an island, into an island. Alone of all lands, without the aid of abstract philosophy, I have represented for mortals the philosophical city. Ungrudgingly do I share my benefits with others; unde-murringly do I adopt whatever is better from others." More entrusted the publication of his work to his friend, the philosopher Desiderius Erasmus, sending him the text and the prefatory mate-rials in September 1516. By November, Erasmus had enlisted Thierry Martin of Louvain to print it, and in December, the first copies were distributed.

2 Conradus Schlapperitzi [Bible History]
Germany, [1445]
NYPL, Manuscripts and Archives Division

This fifteenth-century manu-script shows Adam and Eve before the fall, about to eat from the Tree of Knowledge, an act whose consequences have inspired innumerable quests throughout Western history for a return to a lost paradise.

3 I. N. [Ignacy Nivinsky?]
Zhenshchiny, Idite v Kooperatsiiu [Women, Go to the Cooperatives]
N.p.: Izdanie Vserossiiskago TSentral'nago Soiuza potrebitel'n[ykh] obshchestv [Publication of the All-Russian Central Union of Consumer Societies], 1918
Poster, color lithograph?
NYPL, Manuscripts and Archives Division

The promise of a better life under communism is depicted in this 1918 poster from the Soviet Union. Plentiful food, comfort, leisure, education, and the joy of work are sig-nified by the hearty factory worker bearing a basket laden with food and new boots, while her smiling child carries school books and a jump rope. The Soviet experiment with communism from 1917 to 1989 has been seen as one of the greatest political utopias ever attempted. But it has been estimated that millions died through starvation, forced labor, and imprisonment during the Stalinist period.

Utopians, unlike other heroic and Golden races, exempt from the traits and flaws of their mortal natures. It suffices that they are human. "He would bid you regard as praiseworthy in humanity's name that one man should provide for another man's welfare and comfort – if it is especially humane (and humanity is the virtue most peculiar to man) to relieve the misery of others and, by taking away all sadness from their life, restore them to enjoyment, that is, to pleasure."[2] Utopia's first prerequisite, therefore, is *humanitas*, humanity as a virtue. The uncompromising severity of the critique More levels at the reigning order in the England of his day is matched by his equally uncompromising faith in the ability of human beings to overcome the ills he so condemns. It must also be added that the exceedingly radical measures for the foundation of a new political community, the diametric reversal of reality he proposes, are in fact ways of rehearsing the organizing principles of a polis that is utterly different from anything we know. More's maneuver consists in showing the ways in which the other world pertains to this one – hence the many paradoxes and ruses of this reasoned utopia, this realist fiction, this serious fantasy. This purported relation serves, moreover, as a backdrop to More's launching of one of the essential motifs of modernity, one that bespeaks the courage or the recklessness of the moderns and that is rooted in what the Enlightenment will later call human "perfectibility."

By consigning his invention to the literature of travel, in which the political imaginary, assisted by fiction, can freely roam, More had endowed the literary genre with a formal matrix. In an era of *curiositas* and exploration, anticipated worlds, inspired by the actual discoveries of different worlds and principally the New World, gave rise to

a fantastic and archipelago-studded geography.[3] It would not take long for this geography to exhaust the globe and sweep past the Western isles and the Southern continent to plummet to the depths of the earth or cast its sights on the moon and sun. When it came to representing the experience of otherness, all parts, including the most improbable places, were fair game.

BEFORE DELVING further into modern utopia's onward course, we must first reexamine the ancient and biblical traditions that came before it.[4] The reason for this is twofold: on the one hand, the explicit ways in which utopia set itself apart from its precursors will become more apparent; and on the other hand, ironically, we cannot even begin to broach post-Morean utopian thought without highlighting the motifs it borrowed from the Classical mythology, Greek philosophy, and Christian doctrine that were its wellspring and matrix.

Utopians lay ready claim to Plato, especially to the "ideal city" set forth in the *Republic*. It cannot be denied that Humanism ushered in a powerful rereading of the political texts of the Ancients and that the utopian texts of the classical age borrowed heavily from the Platonic teachings of the guardian class. The dialogical form, as practiced by More, was Platonic, to be sure, and more significantly, the utopian project sought to reassert its bond to political philosophy, which had been eclipsed by theology. True to form, however, utopia was not deterred from providing a simultaneous critique of political philosophy's canonical form in the late Middle Ages and early Renaissance, namely *The Mirror of Princes,* which derived from the Platonic idea of the prince turned philosopher as a requisite criterion for the foundation of the ideal city. Utopia took exception to all of that; consequently, Thomas More's protagonist, the traveler and observer Raphael Hythlodaeus, supplements his passionate account of the wondrous things he has witnessed with a protestation against ever again serving monarchs, as all counsellors are, in the end, servile. Utopia, by and large, turned away from moral judgments of power to pursue the prospect of recasting the political and social order.

Similar polarities apply to the Christian frame of reference. It goes without saying that life without vice and evil finds its Christian expression in images of paradise, the irretrievably lost beginning from which we've been severed by original sin and that can be regained only beyond the confines of earthly existence, in the promised heavenly Jerusalem that awaits the elect. The doctrine invokes a transcendental temporality and spatiality. Those who set their sights on paradise, even when it was to be found on earth, discovered, upon reaching its gates, that first they had to die. Utopia's departure from this tack is a profound one, a rupture that is comparable to the contemporaneous crisis surrounding the Greek and Christian conception of the cosmos wherein all values were organized around the alleged separation between the celestial and terrestrial. This crisis resolved itself, as we know, in the birth of a homogeneous and, before too long, "disenchanted" physical space.[5] The island of Utopia is the site, therefore, where this paradoxically terrestrial and nowhere place is found; while it retains the essential otherness and irremediable separation of celestial latitudes, it is anchored in an earthly here and now, in the precise place where fiction saw fit to fix it.

All the same, true continuities do exist between Christianity and utopia. The prophetic tradition for one, millenarianism in particular, is a case in point. A century after Thomas More, Francis Bacon together with later disciples of the "new philosophy" systematically attributed their utopias, built, like "Houses of Salomon," on the advancement of knowledge and the power of learned men and in which the mastery of nature ensured abundance and harmony, to the prophecies of Daniel or Isaiah – as though the Kingdom of God could be resuscitated through the agency of the advancement of human knowledge. Here is to be found, no doubt, one of the major sources of modernity, a subject to which we shall return. The intersections between millenarian derivations of the Apocalypse of Saint John and utopia have frequently been pointed out, whether the examples be the Lollards and Taborites or the most recent New Age avatars.[6] These movements, by virtue of their literal interpretation of the thousand years of earthly bliss, have in effect been consigned to the margins of the orthodoxy that was to gain acceptance through the Augustinian reading of this text. That being said, the profound affinity between Judeo-Christian eschatology and utopia cannot be avoided, especially when it has been organized around the firm and action-inducing conviction that history is nearing its end and that the advent of a new world and a new man must of necessity follow. And we are again referred to modernity, when utopia is repeatedly enlisted by philosophies of history.

Utopia brings to the fore a specific relationship between literature and politics, or perhaps more precisely between fiction and action. On the one hand, utopia is an imaginary projection onto a fictitious space created by the text

3

of the narrative; on the other hand, the project it sets forth assumes implementation and as such it veers toward the side of history while simultaneously drawing its sustenance from fiction. For this reason, after the revolutionary upheavals of the end of the eighteenth century, we must address literary as well as social and political dimensions – both in the history of the genre, which endures today as the political novel, and as one of the recurring motifs of political discourse and social movements – at the risk of using a less sharp and more debatable definition of utopia.[7] Utopia in the first half of the nineteenth century, for example, clearly seems to withdraw from the literary terrain to massively invest itself in political and social practice and to join forces with reality or aspiring reality. In the centuries that followed, utopian practice envisaged experiments on the local scale, as well as sweeping global reforms; while the former sought to reinvent social relations by founding communities on the outskirts of prevailing opinion, the latter construed all struggles as part of humanity's quest for emancipation and for a time when freedom would rule.[8]

Another parallel dialectic, which to a degree encompassed the first one, was also at work. In the literary utopias that abounded throughout the eighteenth century, space was at issue: utopia played with possible geographies, and utopians were essentially explorers. But then time became the principal arena for the staging of utopias. This essentially literary innovation, readily attributed to Louis-Sébastien Mercier's *Memoirs of the Year Two Thousand Five Hundred* (1771), may, in fact, date as far back as 1659, the year in which the Abbé de Pure published *Epigone, Story of the Future Century*. Time travel became the prevalent form of the utopian novel in the last third of the nineteenth century, especially with the revival that was occasioned by the works of Bellamy and William Morris.[9] Utopia established itself as a prognostic genre, capable of anticipating a history that had yet to come; in no time, these anticipatory visions took on a vacillating quality as they alternated between the dream and the nightmare, paradise and disaster, "eutopia" and "anti-utopia."

Anticipation, in this case, is not to be confused with the earlier mode of prophecy, especially as the aftermath of the revolutionary upheavals ushered in an era, encompassing Condorcet and Marx by way of Comte and Hegel, of philosophies of history and "grand narratives" that sought to bring rationality to bear on historical time and to explain instability and irreversibility through logical causality. While some endowed history with transcendence under the insignia of Progress and Reason, and others, like the materialist philosophies, professed the scientific status of their discipline, all of these rationalized conceptualizations of time and history altered utopian stakes by, in effect, situating utopia within a historical chronology, usually as the final act. Utopian society was no longer to be found, as it had been in the traditional novels, at the end of a propitious journey, or as the result of a chance encounter, or in the happy contingency of a shipwreck that turned out well. Rather, it was to await us at the end of a process of rational discourse like a vista or the final destination of a history governed by meaning, not to say necessity.

The utopian dimension of modernity exploded and evolved, as the nineteenth century turned into the twentieth, into the religion of the future, the all-out predisposition for the future expressed in the era of the avant-gardes.[10] Ernst Bloch would attempt a theory of the headlong drive toward all things new by showing, in a sumptuous fresco wherein all the figures of hope are called into play, that modern history has given rise to a rigorous kind of dream, a "robust dream," that is totally purified of memory, of nostalgia, and of flight, and which is incarnated in the construction of socialism, wherein immemorial hope and historical necessity are united.[11]

To these utopia-bearing avant-gardes of the first half of the twentieth century, Progress was also no longer the joyous and inevitable boon of a science majestically marching to the beat of time: the utopia to come could only be brought about by violence, by subverting the past and destroying the old tenacious ways. This is why absolute faith in the historical necessity of a radiant future always had to go hand in hand with the most radical political voluntarism, from which it drew its strength. The Soviet Union of the 1920s and 1930s was the very embodiment of this.

Nevertheless, the twentieth century makes Progress appear what it really is: a belief. A necessary belief, perhaps, as on more than one occasion it served to cement the collective will, but a belief that history, by dint of retrogressive disasters and modern barbarity, has taught us to reject. The utopian literature of this period is caught between dream and nightmare and intersected by a utopian and anti-utopian dialectic. The dialectical arc, in this instance, opens wide to include the best as well as the worst of all possible worlds; its deconstruction of the illusions of Progress transforms

expectation into lucid forewarning.[12] At the same time, utopia is thus revealed as a double object, and the countenance of utopian achievement is by definition radiant and somber. This inevitably brings us to the difficult contemplation of those aspects of the modern utopian tradition that contained the seeds of its totalitarian version.[13]

Finally, this crisis of faith in Progress also calls into question what was without a doubt the common basis for every kind of utopia the century had to offer: adherence to technology, human mastery of nature, and the exaltation, fanatical at times, of instrumental and mechanical reasoning. While the radical offensive against tradition, particularly with regard to the forms of power underlying social relations, gained greater depth and continuity in the 1960s and 1970s, utopias characterized by their critique of productivism and ways of life in the industrial cities were resurrected.[14] These instances are proof that utopia can, if necessary, survive the loss of faith in Progress, that it can be reborn at the very core of a critique of technology, that it can forego "grand narratives" and the myth of the end of history, that it can be accompanied by what Hans Jonas has called "the principle of responsibility."

It would be pretentious to conclude with a summary assessment of the twentieth century. All the same, an examination of the ends to which utopia has been used and an exposition of utopia in the context of its historical, religious, and philosophical roots, would go a long way toward giving such an assessment substance, since utopia is a motif that powerfully reveals certain trends of our modernity.

Our situation could very well be a paradoxical one: we know that, in actual fact, we do construct the future; whether we like it or not, we know that the purely human choices we make today will have lasting consequences for the world for generations to come. Unless we are willing to accept that these are blind choices and that the destiny of the world we are constructing is subject to laws that are entirely beyond our grasp, we have no choice but to opt for utopia, in the spirit, as it were, of Sartre's statement, "We are condemned to be free." Utopia, one might say, is the measure of how far a society can retreat from itself when it wants to feign what it would like to become.

Translated by Nadia Benabid

1 See J. C. Davis, "Utopia and the New World, 1500–1700," pp. 95–118 below.

2 Thomas More, *Utopia*, trans. Edward Surtz (New Haven, Conn.: Yale University Press, 1964), 93.

3 See Davis, "Utopia and the New World, 1500–1700"; Frank Lestringant, "Utopia and the Reformation," pp. 161–79 below; and Alain Milhou, "*Mundus novus et renovatio mundi*: Messianic and Utopian Currents in the Indies of Castille," pp. 140–60 below.

4 See Danielle Lecoq and Roland Schaer, "Ancient, Biblical, and Medieval Traditions," pp. 35–82 below.

5 See Rémi Brague, *La Sagesse du monde* (Paris: Fayard, 1999).

6 See Jean Delumeau, *Mille Ans de bonheur: Une histoire du Paradis*, vol. 2 (Paris: Fayard, 1995).

7 See Gregory Claeys, "Socialism and Utopia," pp. 206–40 below, and Bronislaw Baczko, "Fin-de-siècle Landscapes Against a Background of Ruins," pp. 201–5 below.

8 See Michelle Riot-Sarcey, *Le Réel de l' utopie* (Paris: Albin Michel, 1998).

9 Edward Bellamy's *Looking Backward, 2000–1887* was published in 1888, and William Morris's *News from Nowhere, or an Epoch of Rest*, in 1890.

10 See Roland Schaer, "Utopia and Twentieth-century Avant-gardes," pp. 278–97 below.

11 Ernst Bloch, *The Principle of Hope*, 3 vols., trans. Neville Plaice, Stephen Plaice, and Paul Knight (Cambridge, Mass.: MIT Press, 1986).

12 See Krishan Kumar, "Utopia and Anti-Utopia in the Twentieth Century," pp. 251–67 below.

13 See Frédéric Rouvillois, "Utopia and Totalitarianism," pp. 316–32 below.

14 See Lyman Tower Sargent, "Utopia and the Late Twentieth Century: A View from North America," pp. 333–45 below.

Lyman Tower Sargent

Utopian Traditions: Themes and Variations

THE WORD *utopia*, the genre of utopian literature, and the phenomenon of utopianism have been used in many ways for many purposes throughout history.[1] This essay examines this history and explores some of those purposes. In what follows I present the various forms or subgenres that have been used to present eutopias or ideal societies and discuss the changing content with which those forms have been filled over time. Certain forms have been more in favor at particular times, and some have disappeared altogether, but many of them have remained roughly the same from their invention to the present. The content of a few of the forms, those most reflective of fantasy and least responsive to contemporary social and political forces, has been fairly consistent, but in most it has varied considerably. Over time, the social dreams produced have differed sufficiently from each other that the history of the utopia reflects the whole range of human experience and desire.

Utopias are generally oppositional, reflecting, at the minimum, frustration with things as they are and the desire for a better life. Many utopias remain little more than expressions of such frustrations, while others directly challenge the current state of affairs with proposals for how it should be changed. The former tend to edge off into fantasy; the latter sometimes resemble reform tracts, treatises of political theory, or calls for revolution.

Although the word *utopia* and the literary genre resulted from the book now known as *Utopia*[2] by Thomas More, the phenomenon long predated the book. It is not possible to specify the first appearance of utopianism, but early expressions are found on Sumerian clay tablets, in the Old Testament, and in the poetry of Hesiod in the eighth century B.C.E., and utopian speculation played a central role in the philosophic and political debates of fifth-century B.C.E. Athens.

As early as these debates, utopian literature had separated into two main strands: utopias brought about without human effort, such as Hesiod's Golden Age or Eden, and utopias brought about through human effort, such as the *Laws* of Plato.[3] Every culture that has ever been studied has had utopias brought about without human effort. Not every culture appears to have utopias brought about through human effort that predate knowledge of More's *Utopia*, but such utopias do exist in China, India, and various Buddhist and Islamic cultures. This demonstrates that the traditional notion that utopianism is the peculiar creation of Christian culture is simply wrong.

Utopias Brought About Without Human Effort

The earliest utopias were myths of an unrecoverable earthly paradise or golden age in the past. They generally had similar characteristics: abundance, unity, and ease. Life was simple; there was security, expressed negatively as an absence of conflict and positively in images of abundance and little or no work. People did not age, and they either did not die or had an easy death. Greek and Roman myths contain similar descriptions of the resting places of heroes or the heroic dead, called the Isles of the Blest, the Fortunate Isles, Elysium, or the Elysian Fields. Hell was available as a contrast.

With the development of Christianity, heaven became a central part of the utopian lexicon, and hell became more important than in the pre-Christian myths. While utopian descriptions of heaven exist throughout the tradition, they became particularly important in the nineteenth century in the novels of Elizabeth Stuart Phelps and her many imitators.[4] Utopian heavens are less common today but continue to be written, the most recent significant one being *Happiness* (1988) by Theodore Zeldin. Hell, the archetypal dystopia or bad place, has not played as central a role in utopianism.[5]

From Greek and Roman mythology and to the present, myths of Noble Savages depict the usually romanticized, simple life of peoples living outside civilization. This myth became particularly important in the period of the settlement of North and South America. A subset of these peoples is the Wild Man (there are very few Wild Women) who appeared in the Middle Ages living in the forests of Europe and were depicted as savage savages, often with aggressive sexuality. They continue to exist in images of the elusive Yeti and Big Foot. Sometimes they became fertility symbols such as The Green Man. In North and South America and Australia, settlers often presented the natives as Wild Men to justify killing them. After their slaughter they often reappeared as Noble Savages.

Related to both the Golden Age tradition and the Noble Savage is Arcadia, first described by Virgil. While the Arcadians labor, they do not work hard because their simple lives do not require much effort. In essence, they are romanticized peasants, but in the sixteenth century the peasants became nobles in *The Countesse of Pembrokes Arcadia* (1590) by Sir Philip Sidney.

Another variation on the utopia without human effort is the Cockaigne. Although there is a clear resemblance between the Golden Age and the Cockaigne, the latter usually goes a step further. There is no hunger because there is a surfeit of food and drink. There are no sexual problems because sexual desire is immediately gratified, and there is no work. The Cockaigne is much more explicitly political than is the golden age. As A. L. Morton argued, the Cockaigne is a "people's utopia,"[6] in the sense that it specifically says that the rich will never enter it; it can be entered only after years of the worst kind of work.

Generally identified with the Middle Ages, Cockaignes are found throughout Greek literature. The focus of most of them is food. The Cockaigne continues into the twentieth century, particularly in folk songs like "The Big Rock Candy Mountain" and, possibly, in science fiction like the Culture series by Iain M. Banks, in which the people of the rarely mentioned eutopia have the power to create at will almost anything they want.[7]

The Old Testament prophets, apocalypses, and descriptions of the Millennium provide yet other variations. The prophets and most apocalypses stress the troubles to come, with only a brief description of a better society to come. But both the Apocrypha and the Pseudepigrapha contain many apocalypses that include at least brief utopian visions.

Revelation or the Apocalypse is the major canonical example. The opening of the seven seals and the blowing of the seven trumpets is a catalogue of horrible punishments. The punishments go on and on until the entire earth and all its inhabitants are destroyed. But after the thousand-year rule of the righteous and the final Armageddon,

Then I saw a new heaven and a new earth; for the first heaven and the first earth had passed away, and the sea was no more. And I saw the holy city, new Jerusalem, coming down out of heaven from God, prepared as a bride adorned for her husband; and I heard a loud voice from the throne saying, "Behold, the dwelling of God is with men. He will dwell with them, and they shall be his people, and God himself will be with them; he will wipe away every

tear from their eyes, and death shall be no more, neither shall there be mourning nor crying nor pain any more, for the former things have passed away." (21: 1–4 R.S.V.)

This is followed by a description of the new Jerusalem, emphasizing that it is built out of precious metals and jewels. "The wall was built of jasper, while the city was pure gold, clear as glass" (21: 18).

The non-canonical apocalyptic books tend to describe the messianic kingdom in terms reminiscent of the Golden Age. For example, the Book of Enoch describes the future kingdom as follows: "And then shall the whole earth be tilled in righteousness, and shall all be planted with trees and be full of blessing. And all desirable trees shall be planted on it, and they shall plant vines on it: and the vine which they plant thereon shall yield wine in abundance, and as for all the seed which is sown thereon each measure (of it) shall bear a thousand, and each measure of olives shall yield ten presses of oil" (En. 10: 18–19; trans. R. H. Charles).

The Middle Ages are generally thought to have been without serious expressions of utopianism, but in reality they were rife with utopian imagery. In addition to continuing all the variations so far mentioned, others were added. Designs for the City Four Square, expressions of the desire for the rebuilt Temple in Jerusalem, and the search for the location of the actual Eden were common themes; the last of these continued well into the period in which the New World was explored. Later, this concern produced descriptions of imaginary gardens supposed to be modeled on Eden, and the creation of actual gardens intended as representations of Eden.[8] In addition, there were tales of the land of Prester John, the islands discovered by St. Brendan and Hy Brasail in medieval Irish literature, the Feast of Fools, and discussions of the Perfect Prince and the Last World Emperor.

Two individuals contributed imagery that strongly influenced both the Middle Ages and many later writers. The discussion by Saint Augustine in *De Civitate Dei* of the relationship between the City of God and the Earthly City is important to utopianism within orthodox Roman Catholicism, and the writings of Joachim of Fiore provided the basis for much heretical utopianism.

Most of the forms taken in the Middle Ages by utopias brought about without human effort disappeared with the waning of that period. A few continue in the beliefs of some religious sects, but some, like the Cockaigne, have remained part of popular culture. The belief in the Second Coming of Christ and the expectation of a millennial age have become stronger in response to the year 2000.

On the whole, utopias brought about without human effort have not directly challenged the status quo, and some are the inchoate dreams of the most oppressed members of society. But at the end of the Middle Ages and during the early years of the Reformation, such dreams became embodied in heretical movements.[9] In addition, the festivals of Saturnalia and Carnival and the Feast of Fools, which were attempts to temporarily bring about the overturning of the established order, were prefigured in these utopias. In a few cases, they led to serious attempts to bring about such changes, but most often such festivals were suppressed or taken over by those in power.

Utopias Brought About by Human Effort

The origins of the utopias brought about by human effort are as lost in the mists of time as are those of utopias given by the gods. Various parts of the Old Testament, the Eloquent Peasant of Ancient Egypt, Solon, the *Lycurgus* of Plutarch, the *Cyropaedia* of Xenophon, Aristophanes, and Plato are all early examples of such utopias. And Solon, Plato (if we accept the "Seventh Letter"), and the Essenes are early attempts to bring the vision into being.

The relationship of the individual to society, gender relations, economic relations, political power, and the roles of education and law in bringing about eutopia were all aired in Greece during the fifth century B.C.E. Plato wrote two major works that have been called eutopias, his *Republic* and *Laws*, which together introduce themes that continue throughout the history of utopianism. These works represent the two most important means of bringing about the transformation necessary to create eutopia, education and law.

The *Republic* has a system of economic equality for the Guardians, and such equality can also be found in the Sparta of Lycurgus; reform in that direction was undertaken by Solon in Athens; and Aristophanes satirizes it in *Plutus*. Thus, eutopias of economic equality were part of early Greek political debate.

Also in the *Republic*, Plato raises the issue of female-male relations in terms of education, power, and sexual relations, together with questions about the institutions of marriage and the family. These issues were obviously on the agenda at the time. Plato's own position in the *Republic* is still open to debate, but within what he defines as limits of strength, he appears to suggest that women should be educated, and there is no obvious bar to a

woman as Philosopher-King. Aristophanes satirized all aspects of the debate a number of times but also presented empowered women positively in both *Lysistrata* and *Ecclesiazusae*.

The Essenes, the early church in Jerusalem, or the earliest withdrawn communities of Christians can be seen as the first in a nearly continuous tradition of intentional communities established to practice a particular vision of a better life. Some of the withdrawn communities of Eastern religions may have developed earlier, but they do not appear to have influenced the Western utopian tradition until the twentieth century.

In the Middle Ages, the withdrawn Christian communities of early Christianity were recreated in the monastic orders. The elaboration of rules of living for such communities by, for example, St. Benedict and St. Francis make the connection to utopianism clear, as does the explicit utopianism of some monastic architecture.[10]

One of the major sources for More's *Utopia* was almost certainly monasticism, and one need only read one of the rules of the orders alongside the *Utopia* or almost any early post-More eutopia to see the similarity. Convents provided one of the few places in the Middle Ages in which women could be both educated and empowered, and a tradition of withdrawn communities for women figures in the earliest eutopias written by women, such as *Le livre de la Cité des Dames* (1405) by Christine de Pisan and *A Serious Proposal to the Ladies* (1694) by Mary Astell.

The monastic orders were clearly a major source of the whole tradition of intentional communities, initially developed by heretical Christian sects and later secularized. Although there were a few early studies, this connection has only recently been recognized by students of intentional communities.[11]

But for all of this, Thomas More invented the genre of literature that we call the utopia.[12] The great and frustrating thing about the *Utopia* is that even after almost five hundred years, there is very little agreement about its meaning. The use of words like *Anydrus* – no water – for the main river may be a simple play on the "no" in the "no place" that is Utopia, or it could be a signal to us to tread very carefully in taking all of this seriously.

Everyone wants to interpret More from his or her own point of view. For some, as a good Catholic, St. Thomas More simply cannot have meant some of the things practiced by the Utopians. Marxists want him to be a good forerunner of Marx. Feminists note his decision to educate his own daughters and want him to be much more of an egalitarian than he actually was. Unfortunately, too many people expect a saint rather than a man – and, of course, their own version of what it means to be a saint. We should also remember the More that did not want *Utopia* translated because he thought it might be corrupting.

Both the man More and the book *Utopia* provide the basis for many readings. Perhaps that is how one invents a genre: leave it so open-ended that other creative minds can play with it. In *Utopia*, More gave us the isolated island on which a group of people have developed a better social order than that in the contemporary world. In so doing he gave us the mechanism of satirizing contemporary society by holding up a better example for comparison. And at least in this first entry in the utopian literary genre, the differences between the contemporary world and the better one are not so great that becoming better is unimaginable. Today much of More's *Utopia* is clearly dystopian, but with some historical imagination, we can see that life in this law-ridden, patriarchal, hierarchical society would have looked like heaven to the poor of 1516, if they had been able and allowed to read about it.

The immediate post-More eutopias in England are closest to what J. C. Davis calls a "perfect moral commonwealth,"[13] in which everyone behaves in the best manner expected of their role in society. Thus *A Pleasant Dialogue betweene a Lady called Listra, and a Pilgrim* (1579) has a godly prince ruling by divine right, a humble nobility, obedient citizens, and a good clergy. It emphasizes simplicity, learning, and honesty. But being fallen Christians, the people do not live up to the perfection expected, and a quite vicious legal system is needed to make sure they do. For example, a judge found to have taken a bribe has his leg sawn off with a wooden saw. While there are other perfect moral commonwealths, and many eutopias present perfectibility as an ever-receding goal,[14] this form appears only intermittently.

The importance of these early post-More works is found not in the details but in the fact that they are explicitly Christian, and deal with the problem of how to create a better society for the fallen. This becomes a major theme in utopianism and is a central reason that some theologians treat utopianism itself as heretical.[15]

The novel as a common type of literature began to emerge in the seventeenth century, and as a result, the utopian novel became the most common way of presenting a utopia. There were no other major changes in the way utopias were presented until the twentieth century, but in the interval the novel changed in many ways and the utopian novel changed with it. In particular, in the nineteenth century, the sentimental novel was effectively combined with the more traditional eutopia to produce a more palatable and better-selling product. *Looking Backward, 2000—1887* (1888) by Edward Bellamy was the most successful such combination. Also in the nineteenth century, Samuel Butler reinvented the utopian satire with his *Erewhon* (1872), which has had many, less successful, imitators.

In the seventeenth century, the most common literary form taken by the utopian novel was the imaginary voyage, but golden ages, noble savages, Arcadias, and depictions of paradise and the millennium continued. But the content of the utopias changed dramatically from that of the previous century, and the seventeenth century produced both the first in a continuing tradition of feminist eutopias and the first eutopia set in the future.

Also, the first eutopias using science and technology were published, although science and technology are less important in these eutopias than has often been argued because the science normally plays a quite small role in the eutopia. Even in *New Atlantis* (1627) by Francis Bacon, which is most often read as a great tract on the importance of science and may have helped bring about the creation of the Royal Society, the science is actually a quite small part of a patriarchal, Christian eutopia. And others that are often cited as part of the growth of the scientific outlook, like *A Description of the famous Kingdom of Macaria* (1641) by Gabriel Plattes, barely mention science. The Manuels[16] argue that *Macaria* represents the English face of pansophia, the integration of all knowledge; and the intellectual circle to which Plattes belonged, generally called the Hartlib circle (after Samuel Hartlib, once thought to have been the author of *Macaria*), was involved in such a project. There were eutopias written as part of this, most notably *Reipublicae Christianopolis Descriptio* (1619; known as *Christianopolis*) by Johann Valentin Andreae and the various works of Comenius (Jan Amos Komensky). Comenius, Andreae, and the others that the Manuels discuss (Giordano Bruno and Tommaso Campanella most notably) do not seem to support the hypothesis that science was a primary seventeenth-century route to eutopia. In the seventeenth century, science was in the process of being freed or differentiated from magic and religion, but at this time the split was only beginning; science, religion, and magic were still very much part of each other, even in those writers we tend to think of as the scientists of the age.[17] And for these people, alchemy, millenarian expectations, science, and social improvement were all mixed together. It is only as these become differentiated that eutopias based on science and technology in our sense become possible.

For the historian of English political thought, the seventeenth century is immensely important, and that importance is reflected in its eutopias. From this perspective, James Harrington's *The Commonwealth of Oceana* (1656) is the central text. Eutopias were used in seventeenth-century political debate by republicans like Harrington, monarchists like Francis Lee, Anthony Le Grand, and Margaret Cavendish, and radicals like Pieter Plockhoy and Gerrard Winstanley. Problems of political organization and the locus of power are probably the dominant themes, followed by the need for greater economic equality.[18]

The eighteenth century adds two major subgenres, Robinsonades and Gulliveriana. One can argue at great length about whether *Robinson Crusoe*[19] (1719) by Daniel Defoe should be called a eutopia. The crux of the question is whether or not a solitary eutopia is possible. Certainly Crusoe does not think so, and while the arrival of Friday helps, he is not sufficient to change the situation. While it might be possible to construct a solitary eutopia, Defoe did not do so.

Still, *Robinson Crusoe* gave rise to a genre of literature we call the Robinsonade (even though there were, as always, earlier models, such as *Hayy Ibn Yaqzan* [1150] by Ibn Tufayl), which has been extremely popular. The Robinsonade, utopian or not, is a reflection of a worldview based on the voyages of exploration. The world is a vast place with many unexplored, perhaps empty, perhaps eutopian islands left to discover. Therefore, one of the typical utopian forms includes a shipwreck and the accidental discovery of an isolated island including a people who are better, in at least some ways, than those landing on the island. This form, which increasingly strained credulity, lasted well into the twentieth century; science fiction writers then adopted it, using unknown planets instead of unknown islands.

Aside from those works that merely appropriate the name, the most common appropriations of *Gulliver's Travels*[20] (1726) by Jonathan Swift take one of two forms. Either they use one of the countries Swift described – Lilliput being the most popular, followed by the Houyhnhnmland, with Brobdingnag and Laputa much less popular – or they use the Houyhnhnms as a rough model and endow some animal or plant (science fiction has even extended this technique to minerals) with speech and, sometimes, reason. Many also followed Swift in comparing humans unfavorably to their invented character.

In addition, Samuel Johnson's *Rasselas* (1759; first published as *The Prince of Abissinia. A Tale*) is, among many other things, an early, utopian version of the Oriental tale. A favorite trope of utopian literature, particularly in France, during this period was the invention of a new language.[21]

There is one dominant thread running throughout eighteenth-century eutopias – the concern with human reason, its potential and its problems. Few eighteenth-century eutopias ignored it altogether, but no conclusions were drawn. While the proponents of rationality probably dominate, it is its attackers who are mostly remembered today.

North America in the seventeenth and eighteenth centuries raises the question of the relationship between colonialism and utopianism. Both North and South America became locations for traditional utopian dreams and practices.[22] Both were the locus of descriptions of the earthly paradise and savages noble and wild, and the millennium is to come in North America (usually after the conversion of the Indians).

In the United States, some of the colonies were explicitly utopian, and the process of separation from the colonial power led to revolution, too often thought of solely as a limited political revolution rather than as a social one. While it is true that on the whole the same people held power before and after the revolution, the period between 1776 and 1787 was one of considerable social and political turmoil, attempts to change daily practice in many areas of life, the re-creation of thirteen state governments, and the establishment and rejection of the Articles of Confederation. During this period many activists hoped to shift power from the states, where it generally resided under the Articles, to local governments. In the North, this culminated in Shays's Rebellion, the first attempt to secede from the Union. Those involved in the Rebellion contended that the Revolution had simply reinforced the power of the rich and hoped to empower the poor. If we look at these events through the lens of utopianism, we see the emergence of a very active utopian tradition based on colonialism and the struggle to get rid of it. The same thing occurs, albeit in different form, in New Zealand.

The nineteenth century is a complex one in the history of utopianism. First, in large part due to the growing ease of publication, many more utopias were published. Second, the publication in the

United States of Edward Bellamy's *Looking Backward, 2000—1887* in 1888 produced a worldwide upsurge in the publication of utopias, although we now know that there were many more pre-1888 utopias than we once thought. Third, after 1895, when H. G. Wells published *The Time Machine*, science fiction becomes a major form for publishing utopias. Fourth, the utopian socialists, Robert Owen, Charles Fourier, Henri de Saint-Simon, and Etienne Cabet, produced both a number of attempts to establish eutopia by withdrawing from society and building new communities and a flourishing literature about utopian schemes of all sorts. Fifth, Australia and New Zealand began to produce a substantial utopian literature that differed significantly from that of other countries. And sixth, Karl Marx and Friedrich Engels attacked utopianism at the same time that there was a rapid growth in explicitly Communist utopianism, which they presumably rejected.[23] The dominant theme of the nineteenth century is socialism in all its varieties. In the United States, religion is still of central importance, but it has faded in British eutopias. In New Zealand, the dominant theme is the possibility of creating a eutopia in New Zealand. In all countries, the most important second theme is women's rights.

The twentieth century has seen significant changes in the forms in which utopias are present. First, science fiction developed into the most common subgenre, or, as some would prefer to think of it, utopias became a subgenre within science fiction.[24] Second, film became a major means for presenting both eutopias and dystopias. Third, architecture reemerged as a major utopian form. And fourth, the "critical utopia," or a utopia that is open-ended, self-reflective, and with identifiable problems yet to be solved, developed as an identifiable subgenre.[25]

The beginning of the century saw the continuance of the resurgence of utopian writing stimulated by *Looking Backward*, but that is best thought of as a reflection of the end of the nineteenth century and the hopes engendered by the turn of the century. But even in his earliest novels, such as *The Time Machine* (1895) and *When the Sleeper Wakes* (1899), H. G. Wells offered a mixed message on the future by presenting both positive and negative images. The intellectual turn of the century was World War I and the successful Bolshevik revolution in Russia. While World War I produced a widespread loss of hope, the Russian Revolution produced hope followed, for many, by rapid disillusionment. For some the hope remained, but the disillusionment combined with the hopelessness produced by the war

led to the creation of the modern dystopia, its first manifestation being *We* (1924) by Evgenii Zamiatin, an explicit attack on Soviet Communism but also a satire of the time-management systems developed by industrial capitalism. Two other exceptional dystopias followed: *Brave New World* (1932) by Aldous Huxley, an attack on the consumption ethos of capitalism, and *Nineteen Eighty-four* (1949) by George Orwell (Eric Blair), a general attack on totalitarianism. Huxley reinforced the negative message by publishing a "Foreword" to *Brave New World* in 1946 and *Brave New World Revisited* in 1958, in both of which he argued that the dystopia described in *Brave New World* was approaching much faster than he had expected. These three dystopias gained such recognition that many people came to believe that the eutopia had disappeared.

But the reality is that in the twentieth century there has been a dialectic between eutopia and dystopia, with the eutopian hopes of social movements being created as dystopias and then being overthrown by the belief in a new eutopia. The most obvious recent case is communism, in which the dream of a classless society – reflected in many literary eutopias and satirized in many literary dystopias – is actualized in authoritarian regimes that are ultimately overthrown in part because of a belief in the eutopia of the free market.

Eutopias and dystopias have reflected the major social and intellectual movements of the twentieth century, including communism and fascism and National Socialism, as well as the movements for rights for the poor, women, and racial, sexual, and ethnic minorities. The most common contemporary eutopia is feminist.

Plans for ideal cities have existed from the Middle Ages to the present, and architects regularly produce utopian schemes. In the twentieth century, architects from Le Corbusier, Bruno Taut, and Frank Lloyd Wright to R. Buckminster Fuller and Paolo Soleri thought of themselves as utopians creating better places in which people could live and in which they would live better lives. Soleri is still at work creating a community in Arizona called Arcosanti. Throughout the century, architecture journals have been full of utopian proposals.

The communal movement, which had never disappeared, was revived in the twentieth century. Until the revival of the 1960s, these communities were frequently called "utopian" communities. Today they are mostly called intentional communities, but many members of these communities explicitly connect them to utopianism, and a number of communities (such as Twin Oaks and East Wind in the United States and Los Horcones in Mexico) explicitly drew their inspiration from *Walden Two* (1948) by B. F. Skinner. All three are still in existence, and Twin Oaks is more than thirty years old.

Interpretations of the History of Utopianism

The range and variety of utopian literature makes it difficult to capture within one interpretive framework. These variations reflect two situations. In the first, they reflect the differences brought to the eutopia by differences in class, gender, nationality, religion, sexual orientation, etc., and exist alongside the main theme or themes, possibly slowly changing it or them. In the second situation, sometimes but not always derived from the first, the differences reflect emerging issues that might eventually supplant the dominant theme or themes. An example of the first sort of variation is the feminist eutopia, which has existed virtually throughout the history of utopianism but has seriously changed the dominant modes of utopianism only in the past thirty years. An example of the second sort is the emergence of industrialism, which ultimately completely supplanted the dominant modes of utopianism and is now itself being supplanted by post-industrial or post-Fordist modes.

One of the commonplaces of utopian interpretation is that there is a great divide in utopian literature between the classical utopias (from the beginning until the late nineteenth or early twentieth century) and the modern utopia, that divide being between the essentially static nature of the classical utopia and the recognition of change in the modern utopia.[26] While there is no neat chronological break in the history, there clearly has been a gradual change in the dominant modes of presentation.

Another commonplace of interpretation is that Lycurgus's Sparta is the source of much Western utopianism. While there is certainly a degree of truth in the claim, Sparta was a totalitarian system based on slavery, and I think it is more accurate to look at the specific Spartan ideas and institutions used and transformed by later utopians. Sparta is presumed to have influenced Plato, who was fed up with the Athens that had put Socrates to death, and certainly the fact that the egalitarian Guardians depended on a lower class, but not slaves, parallels Spartan egalitarianism. Also, Lycurgus abolished money to create a more egalitarian society, as had Solon in Athens, who forgave debts and outlawed the practice of selling oneself into slavery to pay off debts. Lycurgus also aimed at greater equality

between men and women, but it is worth noting that he also institutionalized a system in which marriage took place through a process that is best described as rape. But the central Spartan practice of importance to the history of utopianism is the relationship between the individual and society. In Sparta, society was primary and the individual secondary. Clearly this influenced later utopianism, but much, perhaps even *as* much, utopianism has been developed in opposition to this position as has been developed in support of it.

There are two questions the answers to which make it possible to better understand utopias. The first is: What needs to be changed to bring about a better society? Is it the economic system or the political system? And do changes in these create changes in other parts of society?

The second question is: How is the change brought about? Overwhelmingly in utopian traditions, the mechanism of change is either law or education. But what makes these changes possible? Revolution is the less common option; evolution, as in *Looking Backward*, is more common, but frequently we simply aren't told. Still, evolution produces revolution in the social order. In Marx's terms, the political revolution has been replaced by evolution, but the more important social revolution has still taken place.

In the twentieth century, there were three primary interpreters of utopianism – Karl Mannheim, Frederick L. Polak, and Ernst Bloch. In *Ideology and Utopia* (first published in German in 1929 but better known in its much expanded 1936 version),[27] Mannheim argues that identifiable social groupings (no more precise word being possible) produce thought systems. The social origins of thought systems can be studied and the ways in which social status and mobility have determined the thought can be known. The two most important mental sets are ideological and utopian. The ideological mentality reflects dominant social groupings that are unconsciously obscuring the fragility of their position. The utopian mentality reflects subordinate social positions and escape from the mental bonds of current reality. The utopian mentality is at the base of all serious social change.

Ideology is, for Mannheim, an almost wholly negative concept. It is backward looking, oriented to an outmoded status quo. On the other hand, he is ambivalent about utopia and argues that the loss of utopia would be a disaster since it is essential for social change. Still, utopia is oriented not to reality but to a vision of a better life. Mannheim wants both the reality and the vision.

Frederick L. Polak's argument is that the image of the future affects the actual future. "We will view human society and culture as being magnetically pulled towards a future fulfillment of their own preceding and prevailing, idealistic images of the future, as well as being pushed from behind by their own realistic past."[28]

Polak goes on to argue that "if Western man now stops thinking and dreaming the materials of new images of the future and attempts to shut himself up in the present, out of longing for security and for fear of the future, his civilization will come to an end. He has no choice but to dream or to die, condemning the whole of Western society to die with him."[29]

Polak also says that utopia encourages efforts toward the development of human dignity.[30] For Polak, utopia means choice, freedom, and creativity. It is a constant mirror held up to the present, showing the faults of contemporary society. Utopia rightly upsets people because it constantly suggests that the life we lead, the society we have, is inadequate, incomplete, sick.

Today the most-quoted interpreter of utopianism is Ernst Bloch, whose three-volume *Das Prinzip Hoffnung* (1955–59) [*The Principle of Hope* (1986)] and many other writings on utopia explore both the concept and its history. Bloch concludes that utopia pervades human experience, saying, "So far does utopia extend, so vigorously does this raw material spread to all human activities, so essentially must every anthropology and science of the world contain it. *There is no realism worthy of the name if it abstracts from this strongest element in reality, as an unfinished reality.*"[31]

But, more importantly, Bloch argues that the idea of the "Not-Yet" in the form of the "concrete utopia" provides the basis for positive social change, saying:

Concrete utopia is therefore concerned to understand the dream of its object exactly, a dream which lies in the historical trend itself. As a utopia mediated with process, it is concerned to deliver the forms and contents which have already developed in the womb of the present society. Utopia in this no longer abstract sense is thus the same as realistic anticipation of what is good; which must have become clear.[32]

It is this declaration of the importance of utopian thinking for creating the space in which a better reality can be created that has made Bloch's work so important.

Utopianism Social dreaming.

Utopia A nonexistent society described in considerable detail and normally located in time and space.

Eutopia or **positive utopia** A nonexistent society described in considerable detail and normally located in time and space that the author intended a contemporaneous reader to view as considerably better than the society in which that reader lived.

Dystopia or **negative utopia** A nonexistent society described in considerable detail and normally located in time and space that the author intended a contemporaneous reader to view as considerably worse than the society in which that reader lived. The first use of this word is usually ascribed to Glenn Negley and J. Max Patrick in the "Introduction" to their anthology *The Quest for Utopia* (New York: Henry Schuman, 1952). While this certainly appears to be the first modern use of the term, I once came across it in a seventeenth-century text. I sent a note regarding it to *Alternative Futures*, but the journal collapsed before the note was published and it was lost in the cleaning-up process. I had stupidly not kept a copy, and I have yet to find the reference a second time. A history of terms used to describe negative futures (John Stuart Mill used "cacotopia") would be useful.

Utopian satire A nonexistent society described in considerable detail and normally located in time and space that the author intended a contemporaneous reader to view as a criticism of that contemporary society.

Anti-utopia A nonexistent society described in considerable detail and normally located in time and space that the author intended a contemporaneous reader to view as a criticism of utopianism or of some particular eutopia.

Critical utopia A nonexistent society described in considerable detail and normally located in time and space that the author intended a contemporaneous reader to view as better than contemporary society but with difficult problems that the described society may or may not be able to solve and which takes a critical view of the utopian genre.*

Intentional community A group of five or more adults and their children, if any, who come from more than one nuclear family and who have chosen to live together to enhance their shared values or for some other mutually agreed-upon purpose.**

* For a discussion of this definition, see Lyman Tower Sargent, "The Three Faces of Utopianism Revisited," *Utopian Studies* 5, no. 1 (1994): 9.

** For a discussion of this definition, see Sargent, ibid., 14–15.

Notes

1 For an explanation of some of the terms used in this essay, and throughout this volume, see the Glossary on page 15. See also Hans-Günter Funke, "Utopie, Utopiste" in *Handbuch politisch-sozialer Grundbegriffe in Frankreich, 1680–1820*, ed. Rolf Reichardt and Eberhard Schmitt in collaboration with Gerd van den Heuvel and Anette Höfer (Munich: Oldenbourg, 1985–), 11: 6–104; Lucian Hölscher, "Utopie" in *Geschichteliche Grundbegriffe: Historisches Lexikon zur politisch-sozialen Sprache in Deutschland*, ed. Otto Brunner, Werner Conze, and Reinhart Koselleck, 8 vols. (Stuttgart: Klett-Cotta, 1990), 6: 733–88 [translated by Kirsten Petrak with French quotations translated by Nancy Sloan Goldberg and Latin quotations translated by Annette Giesecke-Dunham, in *Utopian Studies* 7, no. 2 (1996): 1–65]; and Ruth Levitas, *The Concept of Utopia* (Hemel Hempstead, England: Philip Allan/Syracuse, N.Y.: Syracuse University Press, 1990).

2 Original title: *Libellus vere aureus nec minus salutaris quam festivus de optimo reip[ublicae] statu, deq[ue] nova Insula Utopia.*

3 For a discussion of these categories, see Lyman Tower Sargent, "The Three Faces of Utopianism Revisited," *Utopian Studies* 5, no. 1 (1994): 1–37.

4 See Colleen McDannell and Bernhard Lang, *Heaven: A History* (New Haven, Conn.: Yale University Press, 1988).

5 See Alice K. Turner, *The History of Hell* (New York: Harcourt, Brace, 1993).

6 A[rthur] L[eslie] Morton, *The English Utopia* (London: Lawrence & Wishart, 1952), 11–12.

7 Books in the series include *Consider Phlebas* (London: Macmillan, 1987; reprinted London: Orbit, 1991); *The Player of Games* (London: Macmillan, 1988; reprinted London: Orbit, 1989); *Use of Weapons* (London: Macmillan, 1990; reprinted London: Orbit, 1992); *Excession* (London: Macmillan, 1996; reprinted London: Orbit, 1997).

8 See Max F. Schulz, *Paradise Preserved: Recreations of Eden in Eighteenth- and Nineteenth-century England* (Cambridge, England: Cambridge University Press, 1985).

9 See Norman Cohn, *The Pursuit of the Millennium* (London: Secker & Warburg, 1957); 2nd edition with the subtitle *Revolutionary messianism in medieval and Reformation Europe and its bearing on modern totalitarian movements* (New York: Harper & Row, 1961).

10 See Wolfgang Braunfels, "The St. Gall Utopia" in his *The Monasteries of Western Europe: The Architecture of the Orders* (London: Thames & Hudson, 1972), 37–46; and Walter Horn and Ernest Born, *Plan of St. Gall: A Study of the Architecture and Economy of a Paradigmatic Carolingian Monastery*, 3 vols. (Berkeley: University of California Press, 1979).

11 See George A. Hillery, Jr., and Paula C. Morrow, "The Monastery as a Commune," *International Review of Modern Sociology* 6, no. 1 (Spring 1976): 139–54. Reprinted as only by Hillery in *Communes: Historical and Contemporary*, ed. Ruth Shonle Cavan and Man Singh Das (New Delhi, India: Vikas Publishing House, 1979), 152–69.

12 For genre studies, see Raffaella Baccolini, "Breaking the Boundaries: Gender, Genre, and Dystopia" in *Per una definizione dell'utopia: Metodologie e discipline a confronto. Atti del Convegno Internazionale di Bagni di Lucca 12–14 settembre 1990*, ed. Nadia Minerva (Ravenna, Italy: Longo Editore, 1992), 137–46; Raffaella Baccolini, "Journeying Through the Dystopian Genre: Memory and Imagination in Burdekin, Orwell, Atwood, and Piercy" in *Viaggi in Utopia*, ed. Raffaella Baccolini, Vita Fortunati, and Nadia Minerva (Ravenna, Italy: Longo Editore, 1993), 343–57; Artur Blaim, *Early English Utopian Fiction: A Study of a Literary Genre* (Lublin, Poland: Uniwersytet Marii Curie-Sklodowskiej Wydzial Humanistyczny, 1984); Robert C. Elliott, *The Shape of Utopia: Studies in a Literary Genre* (Chicago: University of Chicago Press, 1970); Vita Fortunati, *La letteratura utopica inglese: Morfologia e grammatica di un genere letterario* (Ravenna, Italy: Longo Editore, 1979); and Gary Saul Morson, *The Boundaries of Genre: Dostoevsky's Diary of a Writer and the Traditions of Literary Utopia* (Austin: University of Texas Press, 1981; reprinted Chicago: University of Chicago Press, 1991).

13 See J. C. Davis, *Utopia and the Ideal Society: A Study of English Utopian Writing 1516–1700* (Cambridge: Cambridge University Press, 1981), 26–31.

14 See John Passmore, *The Perfectibility of Man* (London: Duckworth, 1970).

15 See, for example, Thomas Molnar, *Utopia: The Perennial Heresy* (New York: Sheed & Ward, 1967).

16 Frank E. Manuel and Fritzie P. Manuel, *Utopian Thought in the Western World* (Cambridge, Mass.: Belknap Press of Harvard University Press, 1979).

17 See Keith Thomas, *Religion and the Decline of Magic: Studies in Popular Beliefs in Sixteenth- and Seventeenth-century England* (London: Weidenfeld and Nicolson, 1971).

18 See Davis, "The Full Employment Utopia of Seventeenth-century England," pp. 299–367 in his *Utopia and the Ideal Society.*

19 Original title: *The Life and Strange Surprizing Adventures of Robinson Crusoe, of York, Mariner: Who lived eight and twenty Years all alone in an un-inhabited Island on the Coast of America, near the Mouth of the Great River of Oroonoque; Having been cast on Shore by Ship wreck, where-in all the Men perished but himself. With An Account of how he was at last strangely deliver'd by pyrates. Written by Himself.*

20 Original title: *Travels into several Remote Nations of the World.*

21 See Paul Cornelius, *Languages in Seventeenth- and Early Eighteenth-century Imaginary Voyages* (Geneva: Librairie Droz, 1965); James Knowlson, *Universal Language Schemes in England and France, 1600–1800* (Toronto, Ontario, Canada: University of Toronto Press, 1975); Edward D. Seeber, "Ideal Languages in the French and English Imaginary Voyage," *PMLA* 60 (June 1945): 586–97; M. M. Slaughter, *Universal Languages and Scientific Taxonomy in the Seventeenth Century* (Cambridge, England: Cambridge University Press, 1982); and Marina Yaguello, *Lunatic Lovers of Language: Imaginary Languages and Their Inventors*, trans. Catherine Slater (Cranbury, N.J.: Fairleigh Dickinson University Press, 1991).

22 See the essay by J. C. Davis in this volume (pp. 95–118); Lyman Tower Sargent, "Utopianism in Colonial America," *History of Political Thought* 4, no. 3 (Winter 1983): 483–522; and Joel Nydahl, "From Millennium to Utopia Americana" and "Early Fictional Futures: Utopia, 1798–1864" in *America as Utopia*, ed. Kenneth M. Roemer (New York: Burt Franklin, 1981), 237–91.

23 See Vincent Geoghegan, *Utopianism and Marxism* (London: Methuen, 1987).

24 See Darko Suvin, *Metamorphoses of Science Fiction: On the Poetics and History of a Literary Genre* (New Haven, Conn.: Yale University Press, 1979).

25 Tom Moylan, *Demand the Impossible: Science Fiction and the Utopian Imagination* (London: Methuen, 1986).

26 See, for example, Elisabeth Hansot, *Perfection and Progress: Two Modes of Utopian Thought* (Cambridge, Mass.: MIT Press, 1974) and Judith Shklar, *After Utopia: The Decline of Political Faith* (Princeton, N.J.: Princeton University Press, 1957).

27 Karl Mannheim, *Ideology and Utopia: An Introduction to the Sociology of Knowledge*, trans. Louis Wirth and Edward Shils (New York: Harcourt, Brace & Co., [1936]; new edition, London: Routledge, 1991).

28 Fred[erick] L. Polak, *The Image of the Future: Enlightening the Past, Orientating the Present, Forecasting the Future*, 2 vols. (New York: Oceana Pub., 1961), 1: 15.

29 Ibid., 1: 53.

30 Ibid., 1: 445.

31 Ernst Bloch, *Das Prinzip Hoffnung*, 3 vols. (Berlin: Aufbau-Verlag, 1955–59); trans. Neville Plaice, Stephen Plaice, and Paul Knight as *The Principle of Hope*, 3 vols. (Oxford, England: Basil Blackwell, 1986), 624; emphasis in the original.

32 Ibid., 623.

Alain Touraine

Society as Utopia

FOR SOME time now, the theme of utopia seems to have lost all mystery, even though utopias flow from an imagination that is always surprising in its precision and meticulous delirium. As so many remarkable writers from Marx to Bloch have noted, utopia is the representation of a necessary yet impossible society. It is the Land of Cockaigne dreamt of by the hungry, who in this image combine social critique and mirage. From the critics of utopian socialism to Karl Mannheim, utopia has been defined as *anticipation*, as thinking that is in advance of history. Therefore, it is both tempting and prudent to consider and to illustrate this long-established kind of analysis, even though, as we shall see, the fertile work of Ernst Bloch has enabled the idea of utopia to overflow the riverbanks by which its follies were formerly contained.

Thus it is prudently but resolutely that I propose here another interpretation of utopia. It will not contradict the classic one, but will take another point of view, perhaps surprising at first encounter: while people agree almost spontaneously about what makes a thought or action "utopian," and about the gap (sometimes extreme) between utopia and reality, I will be suggesting that utopia may be defined by a specific content that opposes it to other forms of dreaming, anticipation, or denunciation that arise when people lose hope in a paradise in some world beyond, and therefore seek it on earth. Utopia gives form to the idea that the human being is entirely social, that a person has neither supernatural nor individual reality, even if the social order is often conceived of as part of a wider natural order. Utopia is a plea for a society that creates itself, imposing freedom or servitude on its members, pushing away any nonsocial principle of the legitimacy of the social order. The utopian world always rests on equality, never on liberty or even on justice. Utopias often confuse the liberating affirmation of citizenship with the imposition of order, of which Plato gave the oldest and strongest image in the *Republic* and the *Laws*. One might add that this purely political conception of society, which since Machiavelli has unrelentingly progressed by suppressing the religious order, was at first, in the time of Thomas More, endowed with hope, before becoming more constraining, and then transform-

ing itself into a denunciation of totalitarianism in all its forms. The tenor of a utopia brings forth the confidence or the fear that societies have placed in themselves. Finally, whether luminous as a golden age or dark as a concentration camp, utopian society has generated either belief in an entirely social being or, inversely, fear of a destructive control by society over people considered to be no more than its limbs or organs.

Utopia was really born only when the political order separated from the cosmological or religious order, when the elements of society no longer corresponded to the functions of a body, as with Plato himself. The very fact of defining society as a hierarchical ensemble of functions – religious, military, economic – gave birth to a very important mode of conceiving of social life, but one that was alien to the spirit of utopia. Saint Augustine's *City of God* is not a utopia but rather the image of an order founded in God that is present – but never completely so – in the Church. The city of God is the work of divine grace, uniting the predestined elect. This city, ideal and real at the same time, whose history corresponds to the ages of life, cannot be a real utopia, since it is not the work of men but of God. Moreover it will triumph only at the end of time, when the earthly city melts into the reign of God, whose city is its prefiguration within human history. To the same set of conceptions belong socio-religious movements that engage in a struggle for the transformation of society, so that it might be inhabited by the spirit of God.

Thomas More

Three books written almost at the same time strikingly mark the rise of modern political thinking, and even the birth of the idea of society. In 1511, Erasmus published *The Praise of Folly*, dedicated to his friend Thomas More, who issued his *Utopia* in 1516. Between these two dates appeared Machiavelli's *The Prince*. *Pantagruel* and *Gargantua* by Rabelais appeared in 1532 and 1534. It was much later, in 1576, that Jean Bodin's *Six Livres de la République* defended an absolute monarchy without a religious foundation.[1] This historical reminder situates Thomas More's book as giving rise to a whole literary genre, and also shows that the idea of utopia, far from defending unrealizable forms of social life, from the start (and, as I shall try to show, throughout its history) referred to the affirmation that society is its own foundation, freed from any religious legitimization. Since Machiavelli, society has often been identified with the State; often, too, it has been animated by an evangelical spirit that is opposed to the follies of the highborn, which gave Erasmus's book a tone more moral than political. Thomas More's *Utopia* proposes, on the contrary, a specifically social theory of society. The grand category of modern times is the idea of society, founded both on the law and on equality, as removed from the traditional community as it is from absolute monarchy, even when the latter presents itself as a state of rights (*Rechsstaat*). The time of More's utopia is that of the reign of Henry VII – who had succeeded the violent Richard III – and the accession of Henry VIII, still the young humanist, before he became involved in constructing a tyrannical monarchy. Between the Wars of the Roses and Henry's break with the Pope, the very Catholic Thomas More, who would pay with his life for his attachment to his faith, believed in the possibility of constructing a *res publica* – neither Society nor State but what links the two, the submission of each person to laws, and, above all, the absolute triumph of the citizen over the individual, translated into the holding in common of all goods, according to a principle enunciated by Plato. More, so close to Erasmus that it was the latter who had suggested to More that he write *Utopia*, was by contrast distant from Machiavelli, whose conception of the state gives the arts of war a central place in the sovereign's activity. His life also contrasts with that of Cardinal Morton, to whom he remained so attached after having been educated in his household, and who was the very example of a permanent conspirator under Richard III, before becoming Henry VII's chancellor and receiving the Archbishopric of Canterbury and a cardinal's hat. Such was the meaning of utopia: the invention of a society that was indeed possible, but for which there was little real room between the convulsions of a waning feudal system and the formation of absolute monarchies.

The idea upon which this model society was constructed is that the same moral principles should govern both individual life and public life. While the separation between public and private, and consequently the need for pluralism and tolerance, today appears to us indispensable to democracy, More's utopian thought rests on the complete integration of the individual and government, itself governed by moral principles that should also be applied in private life. This leads a utopian government to condemn to forced labor and slavery those who steal and thus sin, instead of making them galley slaves in the service of the prince or condemning them to death. "This is the law and this the procedure in the matter. . . . The object of public anger is to destroy the vices but to save the persons and so to treat them that they necessarily become good and that, for the rest of their lives, they repair all the damage done before."[2] It is not virtue but wisdom and well-understood interest that should guide kings; wars ruin them, and arbitrary rule weakens them. Concern for the well-being of their people should dominate their conduct. Utopia almost fades away in what More expects from the philosopher king (whom he takes from Plato and who is also close to the idea he had once formed about the young Henry VIII). There is no need whatever to refer to utopia in condemning the king's issue of counterfeit money or the cruelty and arbitrariness of the absolute monarch. But Thomas More's moral discourse is revealed in his evocation of the Macarians, whose king, on the day of his coronation, swears not to have more than a thousand pieces of gold in his treasury. His thinking becomes utopian – that is to say, it affirms the preeminence of the principle of organization over personal motivations – when his Utopia offers two absolute principles: a communal holding of goods and isonomy (the equality of everyone before the law). One might think that in any society (or at least in modern ones that are detached from an entirely sacred order) power should be limited by a nonsocial principle, which might be equality among all divine creatures, or else an appeal to reason, progress, or – quite differently – to personal interest. But what is specific to utopia is that it subjects social life only to itself. Its interest is conceived as the two principles of justice and especially of equality. Nothing is more social than equality, as Norbert Bobbio has reminded us by making it the principle of any leftist politics, that is, of progress.[3] But a society founded on equality (and even commonality of goods) imposes upon individuals in an absolute manner a principle that they are in fact pushed by everything – their interest but also the defense of their liberty – to reject: a total submission to what the utopian philosopher or absolute prince considers to be for their good – or rather, for the common good. Utopia is the image of society's complete hold over those who belong to it. Society is the body social, for the survival and health of which individuals and groups perform their functions.

If More's book is the most beautiful expression of the utopian spirit, it is because he is the wisest and least frightening, and above all the most liberal – as well as the sharpest – social critic. Thus some hasty Marxists have seen his text as pre-revolutionary, defending the people against kings and combating social inequality. An admirable man, as moral as he was religious, and the victim of the king whom he had advised, Thomas More well exposes the double face of a utopia that imposes equality by suppressing liberty, but without having aimed at repression or the exercise of arbitrary power. In his Utopia it is the law alone, voluntarily accepted, that defines constraints as extreme as those exercised by the Leviathan in Hobbes or imposed by the general will in Rousseau, but constraints that should also lay the basis for personal liberty. It is a society of equals, but a total society. The term "communism" has often served to designate those representations of society that, in order to fight against inequality, personal enrichment, and the exploitation of others, construct a power that might be – and that in fact has been – destructive of freedoms and has created new inequalities, more political than economic. But More's Utopia is instead a society where everything is public service, while he adds that this perfect society has been created by a conqueror, Utopus, and not by a popular decision; created perfect, it has no history and consequently no mechanism for change. Utopia is *u-chronic*, meaning it eliminates human activity and innovation as well as conflict. Even if, for More, the essential thing was to criticize the belligerent and prodigal nobility, the bourgeois utopia could be just as oppressive as royal arbitrary power, whose clutches were greater. Even if More's intentions are as removed as possible from what is described in Michel Foucault's *Surveiller et punir* [*Discipline and Punish*],[4] his *Utopia* well illustrates a movement toward the growing interiorization and precision of dependence described by Foucault. The power in Utopia is that of reason, but it cannot determine directly the content of decisions. Thus it is defined as in accord with nature, which condemns luxury just as much as personal initiative. And it defines a natural and therefore just society as being both conforming to the needs and even the pleasures of its inhabitants as well as implacable in its desires.

The modern rise of rationalization provoked a multiplication of utopias, from those of More and Rabelais to that of Tommaso Campanella and the social criticism of Swift. Utopia is by no means the revenge of the imagination on reason; it imposed the reign of reason on a society still dominated by the nobility and by the king's good pleasure. The voluntarism of utopia is absolute; it is as full of confidence in reason as it is critical of power and wealth. In terms of a somewhat shopworn Marxism, one could say that utopia manifests the dictatorship of the bourgeois spirit while struggling against the merchant bourgeoisie. Thus it is more exactly a civic dictatorship. Our century, filled with totalitarian illusions and horrors, has difficulty perceiving social critique within what sometimes appears to us as an arbitrary construction of the imagination – which is a mistake – or as the unlimited power of a law identified with the community and thus with its leaders, as a decree of history and the condemnation of all freedom. Therefore it is necessary to reread Thomas More and his friend Erasmus's *The Praise of Folly* in order to find in utopia at once a critique of the feudal order and of the absolute monarchies then in formation, as well as the call for equality that gives *Utopia* its scent of anticipation, particularly concerning women, who have in Utopia the same rights and the same access to education as men. The great utopias of the sixteenth century have the vigor of the rising bourgeoisie, still more concerned with destroying the power of princes than with imposing its own. Thomas More, while being of a profoundly religious mind, a Catholic, respects religious freedom in Utopia, where the most common belief is in Mithras, the principle of the creation and unity of the world, but where Christianity has penetrated and spread – without, however, forbidding other beliefs.

Because the utopia of Campanella's *Civitas Solis* [*The City of the Sun*], written a century after the texts of More and Erasmus, has no social content that is both imperative and critical, it is merely an intellectual construction without a contemporary echo, since the reign of the Priest-metaphysician governing Pan, that is to say, *potestas*, Sin, who is *sapientia*, and Mor, who is *amor*, springs more from the "pansensism" of the Calabrian's diverse works and dramatic life than from a tradition of thought linked to the hopes and temptations of the modern world. Campanella is perhaps an expression of the absolutism being established in Europe, but his vision is above all religious and he subjects the social order to higher exigencies, which is the opposite of More's intention. The possession of women in common (often associated with his name) is in fact a frequent element in utopias, but its interest does not lie in its apparent pansexualism; it is simply part of a will to transform society right down to its foundations. Thomas More, by contrast, defended monogamy.

As modern times begin, utopia is not an extravagance of the imagination, but rather the affirmation of a social morality, inspired by the Roman idea of *pietas*, according to which the search for one's own advantage is wisdom when that activity is in the service of the public good, which is a sacred duty. Utopia is turned toward neither the past nor the future: it is a will toward the present, a program for re-creating society by means of government. More precisely, it constructs a society that is its own raison d'être. Even as convinced a believer as Thomas More wants society to rest not on religion or faith, but only on itself, which leads him to join Erasmus's great call for tolerance. But the central idea is truly that society should be its own raison d'être, and this idea appears at a moment in history when societies – especially great cities – are being constituted that are not yet under the direct domination of absolute monarchs. Henry VIII will quickly bring his weight to bear upon London, so recognizable in the image More gives of Utopia, even though he says that all the cities of his country are similar.

This conception of utopia drawn from More's book obliges us to contrast utopia with millenarianism, although the Anabaptists and particularly Thomas Münzer[5] and Melchior Hoffmann are often cited, for example in German thought, as the first utopians of the modern world. The "Allstedt League" organized by Münzer was so closely linked to the peasants' revolt that Münzer was decapitated in 1525. Religious spiritualism, associated with social critique and thus with the nostalgia of the Christian community, precipitated in Munster, Strasbourg, and Holland a mobilization that was sometimes violent, sometimes peaceful (such as the one leading to the creation of the Mennonites, who relied on a refusal of society in the name of personal will and religious order, but without violence).

Long before the Anabaptists, Joachim of Fiore in the twelfth century had announced the third kingdom, that of the Holy Spirit, after the kingdoms of the Father and Son. With Joachim, Messianism was associated with a strong social critique attacking princes and the Church. But there was no question of a utopia here; rather, it was a movement designed to prepare the new Pentecost, the reign of the *Societas amicorum*. It is impossible to use the same term for ideal societies created and

described by utopians as for visions both eschatological and militant that announce the kingdom of God, that is to say, that subject the social order to a religious, and hence nonsocial, order; that replace the disorder of society with the triumph of divine love. From Joachim of Fiore to the Anabaptists and the agrarian communism of the English Diggers, anti-authoritarian Messianism turns its back on utopia. Brazilian millenarianisms, inspired in the beginning by Portuguese Sebastianism, were also the reaction to a breakdown in rural society taking place at the end of the nineteenth century, when the abolition of slavery and then, soon after, the fall of the Empire marked the triumph of the urban bourgeoisie (supported by the republican and positivist army) over the great northeastern landowners. Driven from their region by drought and poverty, led on by prophetic preachers, the Canudos ended up creating, under the inspiration and direction of Antônio Conselheiro, a community of refuge as well as an ideal city. The republican army destroyed this communitarian city with extreme brutality. This movement and numerous others that followed in Brazil, from Father Cicero to the agrarian leagues of Francisco Julião, were both social and spiritual, but in the name of defeated classes or categories rather than of an "ascendant class." These movements did not call for a new society against the old power but, on the contrary, launched an appeal to the millennium and to faith, and they were animated by a desperate struggle against the social order then being created, which was for them not a liberator but a dominator and destroyer. Millenarian movements are the opposite of utopias; socio-religious movements, from Joachimism to the Anabaptists in particular, arise from social movements contesting authority, as Engels emphasized in discussing the peasants' revolt.[6]

Utopia, as Thomas More constructed it, is not an imaginary society created in opposition to a real society, but corresponds to the awareness that a society must constitute its own raison d'être, that good is the common good, that the individual must submit entirely to society in order to attain happiness and self-realization. This idea carries within itself the hopes of nascent modernity. It will never disappear but will change color. Brilliant in the time of Machiavelli, Erasmus, and More, it will become as dark as night by the middle of a twentieth century haunted by totalitarianisms and, to a lesser extent, by the fear of the sorcerer's apprentice that he is no longer master of his creation. The history of the utopia is that of a faith in a society that emancipates itself, a faith that is succeeded by fear of *Megalopolis* and *Animal Farm*. Midway along this road, the idea of a self-founding society triumphed in the great works of political philosophy, in those of Hobbes and Locke and in Rousseau's *Social Contract*.

Charles Fourier

Between the beginning and the end of this history, the utopia had an intermediary stage, that of the beginnings of industrial society, the utopia of progress. More than the beginning of European modernity, this moment also represented its triumph, as Victor Hugo describes it at the end of his life in *Actes et Paroles* (1875). He announces the realization of the hopes placed in the French Revolution, "when utopia will be consolidated in progress, when the sketch will have resulted in the masterpiece, when the coalition of kings will have been succeeded by the fraternal federation of peoples." Innumerable indeed are the representations of progress as a route advancing toward the sun. But this image is more prophetic than utopian. In fact, two imaginary realms are opposing each other: one that dissolves society in progress, order in movement, and which also enters into the reality of class struggle; and one that by contrast conceives of a perfect, natural society, which is therefore no longer solely founded on itself. The idea of utopia thus breaks into two camps. On one side, Saint-Simon is the ideologue of nascent industry; several of his disciples, from Talabot and Enfantin to Ferdinand de Lesseps, will be great entrepreneurs. Robert Owen, on the other hand, is more a social reformer than a utopian or prophet. His disciples were the first to call themselves socialist. It is true that at the center of Owen's life stands the creation and failure of the New Harmony colony in North America, but previously this self-made man had transformed his factory at New Lanark into a model establishment and, after his return to England, he had created a network of cooperatives and even a union, the Grand National Consolidated Trades Union, which heralded the First International although it existed only a short time. The anti-religious passion that led him to create a sect and his commitment to social struggle both make him an important figure in the social history of the beginnings of the Industrial Revolution, even if the *Book of the New Moral World* (1834–45) presents a doctrine in which utopian aspects are everywhere present.

But what advantage is there in extending the idea of utopia to include social movements like those of the Anabaptists or the English Levelers or the union of California grape-pickers created by Cesar Chavez?

By contrast, Charles Fourier tried to escape movement, but since society itself was in motion, he sought the natural foundations of social order. This was at a time when the utopia was at its most inward-looking, lacking a vision of society, since it opposed nonsocial (natural and scientific) principles to the organization of society. Fourier's work has had great intellectual influence, particularly in Russia, where it directly touched Dostoyevsky, who was arrested and exiled to Siberia with a group that was following Fourierist ideas, as well as Nikolay Gavrilovich Chernyshevsky. That influence was far-reaching, especially because Fourier constructs a detailed and complete model of society rather than simply borrowing the principal traits of the dominant order and inverting them in a critique of the existing society. The utopia proliferates but loses its realist aspect as a diagram of a society in formation whose success is still far from certain. Fourier describes not a simultaneously ideal and real society, but rather a sort of counter-society, which would become natural the moment real society became artificial.

Fourier's work is difficult to read since it is so full of categories and typologies that are endlessly combined in an arithmetic as arbitrary as it is precise, free from any concrete social reference. But beyond this "mania" – a word he uses often, especially in the amorous domain – what springs from his work is his effort to provide an entirely non-social image of society. He places characters, types, and passions in relation to the natural and even mathematical order of things. It is true that his elementary societies, the phalansteries, made up of 810 men and an equal number of women, are meant to be capable of fulfilling all functions, but this construct rests on a psychological and not a social principle. The requisite number arises from the combination of twelve primitive passions, of which five are sensory and correspond to each of the five senses, four are affective – friendship, ambition, love, and "familism" (or parenthood) – and the remaining three are distributive and hence more directly social – the "Composite," which tends to unite, the "Cabalist," which creates school or party spirit, and the celebrated "Butterfly" passion, which has a need for variety. What strengthens the non-social character of this construction even more is that these passions all derive from a central principle, "Unityism," since the individual and human society are both made in the image of the universe. The unity of man with himself, with God, and with nature is the principle of analysis and the goal of action. "If one presupposes a social order in which the seven missions I have just explained are fulfilled, then man finds himself in accord and unity with the system of the universe, which is organized in diverse series (simple, mixed, composite, power-giving, infinitesimal) – all moved by sheer attraction."

Newton's discovery of the principle of universal attraction is here amplified and enlarged to encompass all realms of existence and in particular human relations: this is the ambitious goal set by Fourier. And at a time when social ruptures (those resulting from the French Revolution as well as those caused by the rise of industry) were being accentuated, Fourier sought a "societary" principle; his words of association, attraction, harmony, and socialism indicate this obsession with an order to be re-created: the "root of all social evils, namely, INCOHERENT INDUSTRY, or non-associated labor, . . . is the very opposite of the economic designs of God."[7] Harmony can be reestablished: "The two sexes, women and neuters, become in Harmony supporters of the authorities, because they form part of them. The great art of politics is to interest each member of the body social in the maintenance of the established order." This is why Fourier's most original ideas bear on education and on love. It is true that he says of children that "the Societary Order wants to make them heroes with social virtues, beings devoted to sustaining universal unity."[8] Here, again, it is the unity of body and mind, the combination of the complementary and the contrary, that is essential. Very soon the reader comes to a surprising discourse, particularly on the dirtiness of children, which must be respected and utilized in training the "Little Hordes" to take care of dirty and repugnant work.

Fourier's ideas on love best show the nonsocial but combinatory character of a kind of thinking that in the name of harmony is very distant from the praise of familial and conjugal virtues. The more complex the sexual combinations, the more useful manners are to harmony, which leads to a search for a complex kind of liaison between "celadony" (céladonisme) (that is to say, Platonic love) and lubricity. Taking for granted that the great majority of sexual relations take place outside marriage, Fourier praises all manias and perversions, and gives particular importance to "pivotal" affection, "the one that binds the whole, to which one returns periodically and which is sustained in competition with other loves that are newer and more ardent."[9] Simone Debout-Oleskiewicz, who edited Le Nouveau Monde

amoureux (which did not appear in French until 1967),[10] has correctly underlined the central importance of the conception of sexuality in Fourier's system and his enthusiasm for "omnigamous" loves and for orgies. This conception is the most evident proof that Fourier is developing not the portrait of an ideal society or of a counter-society, but, in a quite opposite way, a project for a combinatory of passions that gives social life a properly nonsocial foundation. While the ideology of progress traversed the whole nineteenth century and spread the idea of the modern and ideal society, Fourier's kind of thinking, which is not isolated and was exalted (with reason) by the Surrealists – and also by the Giangiacomo Feltrinelli Foundation in Italy – actually represents an anti-industrial counter-utopia. From the saltworks of Arc-et-Senans built by Claude-Nicolas Ledoux to the "Familistère" (workers' cooperative association) at Guise, whose existence was brief but telling, the utopias of the beginning of the industrial era, which had so many applications, especially in North America, were not only defensive reactions to growing social differentiation – which led in Brazil to the messianisms that aimed to salvage the communitarian link – but, more profoundly, were an attempt to create, at the very moment of the Industrial Revolution, a society founded not on work and technology but on social exchanges, passions, and cultural complementarities.

After Fourier, who invented a nonsocial society constructed on the basis of nonsocial forces and constraints, many people turned their backs on the urban and industrial society then in formation and sought, in a way different from Fourier's, to unite the individual directly with nature, beyond and against society. Can we still speak of utopia here? We are even beyond Fourier's counter-utopia. The central theme in Henry David Thoreau, for example, first explored in his Journal and in A Week on the Concord and Merrimack Rivers (1845), and best expressed in Walden (1854), is the search for intimate experience through an encounter with the original inhabitants and pioneers. Thoreau sought ecstatic experience in order to overcome the death of his brother; his extreme individualism led him, after his period of voluntary solitude at Walden Pond near Concord, to take stands against the Mexican War and against slavery. Thus he was an inspiration to Martin Luther King, Jr. But Walden was not a perfect community: it was a solitude in which he lived for two years in a cabin built with his own hands. It was both a call to discover the virgin frontier and a rejection of "civilization." Thoreau heralded the hippies more than he did the social reformers. Walden is not a counter-society but a mystical and ascetic experience outside of society. The Transcendentalism of Emerson in the village of Concord near Boston, one of the birthplaces of American Independence, became with Thoreau both closer to the study of nature, which increasingly occupied him, and more focused on the search for the self.

This is the reason one might defend the idea that utopia, defined as the self-legitimization of the social, has corresponded above all with pre-industrial modernity, when urban and administrative integration was breaking down social particularisms and traditional privileges. After the start of industrialization, on the contrary, utopias combatted what one might call the socialization of social life; it is understandable that the partisans of historical materialism and of a kind of progress that has been freed of capitalist obstacles should condemn utopian socialism while paying it great heed, as Marx did in the Fourierist analysis of the "Series." To speak of utopian socialism in the name of scientific socialism can only distort understanding – as if the former could perceive only certain real elements that could assume meaning only within the perspective of the latter. In reality, the judgment of Marx, whose Hegelian training made him sensitive to any search for the unity of social life, ought to have been more negative: first because the world of Fourier is a world without social actors, and especially because it is a noneconomic world, and still less a capitalist one, in which the technical division of labor rests on a psychological analysis, and in which the social hierarchies – at the top of which reign "sybarites" and, even higher, "passionate maniacs" who are in a "perpetual composite" state[11] – have no relation to classes or even socio-economic or socio-professional strata. Fourier's utopia is not a social utopia, while Owen's is. And Fourier's influence, even when converted by Victor Considérant into an orthodox and expurgated version,[12] shows that utopia during the century of the first great industrial modernization was far from an assertion of society by itself and its utilitarian and hedonistic thinking, and that in fact it presented a rupture between a natural order (both of the universe and of feelings and passions) and a social order that was defined by Fourier (like many others up to Georges Sorel) as the rupture of unity of both society and the individual being. Today one might add the rupture of the unity between human beings and nature. The creative and confident utopia that is close to reality,

the utopia of Thomas More and Erasmus, has now become distrustful and systematic, often to the point of appearing delirious, as the prisoner of categories that are arbitrarily constructed and imposed.

The more society takes control, the more it is swept along by economic forces that are little or poorly controlled, such as those of capitalism, and the more utopia becomes distant from that impotent and fragmented society and concentrates upon constructing another world, a collective life that responds not to the needs and logic of society, but on the contrary to the natural requirements of the human being. And a rupture that had been brewing since the start of the nineteenth century would explode in the second half, starting with Nietzsche and Freud, between the actor and the system, between order and the libido, between morality and the will to power, between mechanical time and the lived duration of people – and also between rational, legal authority and charismatic authority, as in the work of Max Weber.

Utopia would never return to an image of society making explicit the sociocentric logic of modern societies in formation, as it had done during the brief period separating feudal society from absolute monarchies.

George Orwell

In our century dominated by totalitarianisms still more than by the rapid increase in new technologies, we have lived under the black light of utopias describing the destruction of social life and its liberties by a pseudo-natural power, one that is scientific and in fact totalitarian. Faust's fear in selling his soul to the devil and the sorcerer's apprentice's fear of losing control over his creation have spread to a general crisis within progress, which is translated sometimes into a resort to older orders, religious or political, that people try to resuscitate, and sometimes, in an opposite way, into the analysis of self-destructive societies that are close to the sinister reality that has conquered ever larger parties in Europe.

George Orwell is a utopian in the sense that Thomas More is, but that Fourier in fact is not. Orwell, too, gives a social explanation for social life, even if his model is as negative as More's was positive. It is really a question of political analysis in both cases, and neither one was looking for the nonsocial raison d'être that they imagined. How they differ – or, rather, what makes them complementary – is that Orwell's world is that of a systematic de-socialization, a destruction, a cannibalism of society by an absolute power that is in fact impersonal even though he is called Big Brother. Orwell is saying that this world is beyond Nazi and Communist totalitarianisms. "The command of the old despotisms was 'Thou shall not.' The command of the totalitarians was 'Thou shalt.' Our command is *'Thou art.'*"[13] The last part of the book is in effect the transformation of the very being of Winston Smith who, after having renounced his ideas and his feelings, ends up betraying the love of his life, from the bottom of his heart and at the moment when his torturer is going to have him devoured by rats. All that he has left is to love the Big Brother whom he has hated all his life.

This hyper-totalitarian society recognizes no external reality. It can impose the statement that the earth is flat or that 2 + 2 = 5. But what is this society? It is the Party. Orwell, who had fought with the anarchist brigade Partido Obrero de Unificación Marxista (P.O.U.M.) during the Spanish Civil War, and who died early of tuberculosis, was thinking above all of the Communist Party – which redounds to his glory at a time when European leftists (especially the French) were blinding themselves in the name of anti-fascism to the true nature of Communism. And what is the Party's goal? "The Party seeks power entirely for its own sake."[14] And absolute power can exist only if "the thought police" manage to conquer, occupy, and reconstruct minds. "Power is in tearing human minds to pieces and putting them together again in shapes of your own choosing."[15] Orwell analyzes at length this domination of minds and its principal instruments: "crimestop," "blackwhite," and "doublethink."[16] Subjectivity must be entirely under the Party's mastery; any hope that social integration might be the other aspect of individual happiness has disappeared. The revolutionary and democratic ideas of the early nineteenth century (like those of Owen) have vanished and been replaced by the taste for suffering and the call to hate. Any confidence in society has disappeared. But the continuity with Thomas More is undeniable: the utopia is a social fiction but wants to be a model of reality. Nobody thinks Orwell invented the complete totalitarianism he is describing. This regime is real, even if the characters in the fiction are unreal, in the same way that More's cities were London, Amsterdam, or Hamburg.

It is this that distinguishes Orwell from Aldous Huxley or H. G. Wells, who extended scientific and technological evolution in order to imagine its unreal and even improbable consequences, as Jules Verne had done long before them; they were still carried away by belief in science. The world of

Nineteen Eighty-four is not founded on science, on an extreme mastery of nature by science and technology; it has entirely to do with power and dehumanization. Orwell's work is a utopia for still more specific reasons. It is a society without time, in which memory is abolished and history is constantly rewritten. It is a society without space, since the world is divided into three great powers: Oceania, Eurasia, and Eastasia, which is to say, the Anglo-American world, a Soviet Union that has swallowed Europe, and a China or Japan that has absorbed the Far East. These three regional blocs have analogous regimes that are equally totalitarian: the neo-Bolshevism of Eurasia, the "Death-worship" of Eastasia, and the Ingsoc of Oceania. The Evil world does not confront the Good world; Evil has triumphed everywhere. In a way unforeseen by Hegel, it is the end of history, and the single force that was able to resist totalitarianism before it was vanquished and liquidated was love: "Not merely the love of one person, but the animal instinct, the simple undifferentiated desire: that was the force that would tear the Party to pieces."[17]

Orwell, like Hannah Arendt, thought the totalitarian system was as crushing as More had thought bourgeois society was liberating. Beyond the immense differences that separate a positive model from a negative one, we find on both sides the equally strong figure of a being who is entirely social, which for both of them means an entirely political being. But whereas for More the political creates the social, as the Greeks (Aristotle as much as Plato) thought, for Orwell and for those who were witnesses of the totalitarianism of this century, politics can completely destroy collective freedoms, and bring social life down to a mechanical or organic level by suppressing (almost) completely the gaze and voice of the human subject.

Is this the end of the history of the utopia? On the contrary, we have probably already entered a new era of utopia, born of the new technologies of communications, space exploration, and genetics, whose originality is to be both exalting and frightening and whose power is so immense that it provokes strategies of retreat, a return to the mystery of origins, which the exploration of the future and of prehistory will perhaps allow us to discover.

Utopia is not present everywhere; it is not humanity's unconscious that can be said to reveal itself in personal and collective dreams and nightmares that are only too real. Utopia is the recurrent attempt to completely explain society by itself. It is thus the temptation par excellence of modernity, which wants to push to the limits the secularization and disenchantment of the world of which Max Weber spoke. It places paradise – or hell – upon earth. It removes any religious principle, as is best shown in the example of More (although he was a devout Catholic) or the vaguely cosmic references of Fourier to a God more mathematician than divine. The force of utopia comes from this: utopians were and are those who have willed a person to be entirely a citizen or a worker or a legislator, all those who have thought that education should socialize and transform a natural being, a savage, into a social being, all those who are completely dissatisfied by the word "civilization," that is to say, by an identity between social life and moral life. Utopians are those who believe neither in the individual nor in any of the individualist moral theories, of which faith in the rights of man is the most living form these days, moral theories that depend on the idea of the subject. Utopia is, above all, a will to destroy the subject and all attempts to give a nonsocial background to social life, or at least to recognize in the social arena the presence of a subjective logic, which one might call humanist were that word not so vague. Utopia, when it is important, does not aim at the margins of society, does not try to imagine a niche that is protected from society's tumults and violence. It aims at the center; this is why it is a total vision and why its authors aimed so much at describing their utopias in a manner as detailed as that of Fourier in discussing his phalanstery, his program of education, or his conception of the liberated erotic life. Utopia is the religion of society; this is why it has accompanied modernity, but veering from lightness to dark, from blazing sunlight to the night of concentration-camp universes.

Karl Mannheim

I have chosen to analyze certain books, and first of all, Thomas More's *Utopia*, in order to extract a general interpretation of utopia, its nature and its historical transformations. But it would be difficult not to consider now some other interpretations and to decide if one of them is better than another, or if they simply pertain to different objects. The most celebrated interpretation is found in a small book by Karl Mannheim, *Ideologie und Utopie*, published in 1929, hence well before the exile to which the Nazi regime consigned the Frankfurt professor. The principal originality of this now-classic book is to define ideology and utopia in relation to each other. But this is also what weakens his analysis of utopia. Although Mannheim's reflections on ideology,

nourished by the German intellectual tradition from Kant to Hegel and then Marx, form the veritable foundation of the sociology of knowledge, which has opened up debates that have never been concluded, his analysis of utopia is weak, in the first place because the separation between ideology and utopia is not clear – which Mannheim recognizes at several points. His first definition of utopia is that "A state of mind is utopian when it is incongruous with the state of reality within which it occurs."[18] But this definition applies equally well to all ideologies, which leads Mannheim to complete it as follows: "Only those orientations transcending reality will be referred to by us as utopian which, when they pass over into conduct, tend to shatter, either partially or wholly, the order of things prevailing at the time."[19] The passage from ideology to utopia takes place, then, as soon as an action follows the thought. In a word, utopia is revolutionary; it is borne by the refusal of reality and by a desire to transform that will really overthrow reality, even if the utopia or the charismatic prophet fails. Utopia is thus propagated especially by dominated groups, as we have noted in the extreme form of anarchists opposed to all forms – *topoï* – of social organization. This conception was spread in the nineteenth century. Alphonse de Lamartine (quoted by Mannheim) had already said: "Utopias are often only premature truths."[20] It is this historicism that makes it difficult to separate utopia from ideology. It is "extremely difficult to determine what is to be regarded as truly utopian (i.e. realizable in the future) in the outlook of a rising class, and what is to be regarded as merely the ideology of dominant as well as ascendant classes."[21]

Let us first note that these definitions by Mannheim directly clash with the work of Thomas More and his successors; Mannheim recognized this, but it left him in a quandary. In the second place, Mannheim himself admits there is a continuity more than an opposition between ideology and utopia. There is no ideology that is not oriented toward action, which is a purely cognitive operation. And when Mannheim speaks (in his third example) of conservative utopia, most of his readers would instead write "conservative ideology." Finally, it is arbitrary to assert that utopia prepares a future; it often refers to a past, in order to defend it or reestablish it. Such is in fact the case with numerous religious utopias that have, in effect, mobilized collective movements primarily to resist modern society and to return to a religious one. There are many examples of summoning the past, as with

Cargo Cults and in all the expectations of the return of a liberator who has disappeared.

Inversely, why call a revolutionary or prerevolutionary movement a utopia? It is impossible to separate real social relations from a cultural gambit that is most often defined in "utopian" terms in relation to reality. The indispensable concept here is that of social movement, not of utopia. An ideology is easier to integrate into a properly sociological analysis than a utopia would be.

What remains of Mannheim's analysis, dating from the period between the wars, is the use of the utopian idea from a Marxist perspective, that is to say, as the preparation, in a still-deformed way that is blind to social relations of domination, of scientific socialism. This vision refers exclusively to the Hegelian idea of historical ensembles, stages in the dialectical development of the spirit, but reinterprets it in specifically economic terms. Ideology is the interpretation by the dominant class of the situation in which its domination is established, and which it tries to define in absolute and nonsocial terms, whereas utopia is the action and thought that prepare the swing from one type of society to another, without the utopian force's being able to affect the capacity to direct this new historical order.

This evocation of a long historical period now ended does allow us to see Mannheim's weakness: can the Communist utopia be separated from the ideology of the new anti-capitalist regimes created by socialism, from German National Socialism to Leninist Bolshevism, or, equally, German or Swedish Social Democracy? At this century's end, when we are speaking once more of social democracy, is it not clear that political parties of this type in fact form the new managerial elites rather than represent the mass of the marginal and unemployed? What Mannheim thought was that there was an inevitable break between the passage from one society to another. From the old society rises a radical critique that is projected toward the future, but which will not enter it – any more than Moses could enter the Promised Land, which for him remained a utopia. The swing, due also and especially to other technical, economic, or even political causes, allows, in the new situation, the appearance of new ideologies that are often the reverse of utopias that disappeared or were destroyed before entering into the new world. This justifies the central role of the new ideology of a prince or a party, which gives birth to a history that advances not gradually but by a series of ruptures and dialectical reversals. There is then a discontinuity (and even

conflict) between a popular and prophetic utopia that is oriented toward a present that denies the dominant evolution, and the ideology borne by the masters of power and used by them to give legitimacy to their domination. Thus utopia, defined by Mannheim as the force that prepares and makes possible the birth of the future, is instead the force that cannot inspire the future and tries to control a dangerous evolution by stopping history, in the name of a transcendent principle or of a necessary return to a Golden Age.

Thus we must do the inverse of Mannheim's operation: not separate utopia and ideology, but rather leave open the possibility of a certain continuity among a refusal of the past, a construction of the future, a refusal of the future, and an appeal to the past. This combination of four opposite and complementary orientations is what allows social movements to be the actors of history instead of being completely split between the impotent dynamism of the dominated and the imperious justification of the new order by the dominant. The word "ideology" better suits the study of social actors. On the contrary, the idea of utopia (as I have analyzed it here through the classics of utopian literature) may be defined by the negation of actors and even of the processes of historical change. We are reminded of this by the quasi-identity between utopia and u-chronia, but the latter is different from millenarianisms, which Mannheim considered as utopias of time, since they indicate an accelerated movement toward the end of the world. While it may be convenient to keep the negative connotations of the word "ideology," utopia may be considered as both positive and negative, since it describes an ideal city but one in which, as in Rousseau's republic, the general will simultaneously melts and threatens personal freedom. The two conceptions might be brought closer to each other historically, now that Mannheim's thought belongs to a period whose special character appears more obvious than in 1929, when his book was published. Between the Morean utopia of the model society and the Orwellian utopia of absolute totalitarianism lies the utopia of progress, that is to say, the utopia of society-history, engaged in self-transformation through the contradictions made passé by dialectic. It was in this long period, during which Enlightenment philosophy was replaced by the philosophy of progress (and Kant's influence was replaced by Hegel's and then Marx's), that utopia itself became historical, inseparably mixed up with ideology. Meanwhile, models of counter-society like Fourier's shut themselves outside the social order, in the properly delirious (that is, lacking in objective references) construction of a combination of forces of the universe and of passions, of the human mind and body. The Marxist and Mannheimian conception is thus inscribed within the general definition I have given of utopia as a diminution of actors and their relation to the internal logic of the social order.

Ernst Bloch

The work that dominates more than a half century of our reflections on utopia is not so much Mannheim's as that of Ernst Bloch, especially if one adds to the three huge volumes (in the U.S. and editions) of *Das Prinzip Hoffnung* [*The Principle of Hope*][22] other works written between 1938 and 1947 in the United States and published in 1959, especially *Geist der Utopie* [*The Spirit of Utopia*],[23] which was in fact written from 1915 to 1917, at the height of World War I. Bloch's central idea is that we have privileged in our consciousness and our actions what comes from the past, from knowledge to tradition and to all that is established, and that we have left in the shadows what is turned toward the future, "The Not-Yet-Conscious, Not-Yet-Become, although it fulfils the meaning of all men and the horizon of all being."[24] But the project is so vast that the theme of social utopias occupies only Part Four of *The Principle of Hope*,[25] whereas the fifth and final part of the work[26] is mostly a reflection on religion, while the first volume, after having evoked psychological experiments on the waking dream, is devoted to the philosophical analysis of what one might call hope, that is to say, the constant anticipation, whether subconscious or unconscious, of a future that wishes to be the realization of self.[27] Even though this book refers constantly to Marxism (and in fact belongs to it), we may consider it original, because although it adopts Marxist hopes, it follows a path opposite to the one that led Marx to give growing importance to the internal analysis of capitalism. Bloch repeatedly states that his object of study is the anticipatory consciousness. His approach is better defined by his opposition to Freud than by his agreement with Marx, since he tries to understand the present through the future it carries within it rather than through the past that supposedly determined it by means of an "act of repression." But what makes Bloch's work the most complex vision of utopia is that it ends not with the hope for a better world beyond struggle and liberation, but on the contrary with the double search for

the *Heimat* (home) and hope in the *hic et nunc*, in lived experience (particularly, but not solely, religious) – which is perceptively analyzed by this atheist thinker. As Bloch says in the introduction: "The Here and Now, what is repeatedly beginning in nearness, is a utopian category, in fact the most central one; even though, in contrast to the annihilating circulation of a Nothing, to the illuminating circulation of an All, it has not yet even entered time and space. Instead, the contents of this most immediate nearness still ferment entirely in the darkness of the lived moment as the real world-knot, world-riddle. Utopian consciousness wants to look far into the distance, but ultimately only in order to penetrate the darkness so near it of the just lived moment, in which everything that is both drives and is hidden from itself."[28]

Nothing is simultaneously closer to and more distant from Karl Mannheim than the thought of Ernst Bloch. Both gaze into the future and find meaning in the relationship to the future; they seek in the present for movement toward the future outside individual consciousness. But for Mannheim, anticipation is the society of the future, a new stage of progress and hence in the development of the human spirit or in the hold of humanity over its environment, and his vision is historical; the future is in the present, as communism arose from capitalism, according to Marx. Bloch is Marxist enough to share this conception at first. He constantly contrasts thought turned toward the past with anticipatory thought, the Not-Yet-Conscious, which "*as a whole is the psychological representation of the Not-Yet-Become in an age and its world, on the Front of the world*" (Bloch's emphasis).[29] He gives many examples of this, of *Sturm und Drang* in particular, which heralded a liberalism still hindered in Germany by outmoded social structures. As with Mannheim, he also contrasts utopia with ideology,[30] defining the latter as an "embellishment of what exists"[31] that produces archetypes, ideals, allegories, and symbols. No one has highlighted more than he, within a Hegelian and Marxist perspective, the presence of the future within the past and also the transformation of anticipatory thought into hope and will. Utopia is allied, too, with interest, as the bourgeoisie crammed itself with utopia during the French Revolution while preparing the triumph of its interests. Marx wrote to Ruge in 1843: "The world has long possessed the dream of a matter, of which it must only possess the consciousness in order to possess it in reality."[32] But Bloch's movement carries him in a different direction: he parts with individual consciousness and rises toward the movement of society, but then goes beyond it by returning to the *hic et nunc,* by seeking in the present for the presence of what goes beyond it, a presence that many have called the divine and which he tries to attain at the level of the present, in knowledge and not in the recesses of the unconscious. Not in the sense of empirical knowledge, but rather in the sense that what is not yet acknowledged by the individual becomes hope, the movement toward the future. After this, the effort falls down and breaks apart. Bloch detects the presence of this hope in the folk tale, in the arts, and especially music, as he had already done in *The Spirit of Utopia*. This discovery culminates in wisdom. Here he wants to be close to the *New Atlantis* of Francis Bacon, whom he thinks went further than Thomas More. It is art, whether by Dante or Shakespeare, that best reveals the possibility of going beyond existing reality.

Bloch's approach is much more different from Marx's than he says it is, since his end point is linked to the present: "The final will is that to be truly present. So that the lived moment belongs to us and we to it and 'Stay awhile' could be said to it."[33] It is a strange ending to a voyage into hope that ends in the present, in possession and complete belonging. Is this not the most general definition of utopia? And is not Bloch someone who has traversed the hopes of the century of progress and Marxist thought in order to come back to this image of perfection? But how can we define this perfection in terms of movement? First of all, by his being rooted in Marxist thought, which is more a thinking of *Wohin* ("toward which") than of *Woher* ("from whence"); then by his seeing in Eros the source of any "Novum," any "Front" activity, that is to say, the emergence of meaning and of the future in the present. It is with this declaration that Bloch ended the preface to his book: "Essential being is not Been-ness; on the contrary: the essential being of the world lies itself on the Front."[34]

But is it possible to combine a principle of hope and a focused attention on the present? Bloch's work is animated by a social and Marxist eschatology as much as by a mystical or religious vision, a tear in the fabric of social time and a dazzling seizure – not of meaning, but of what projects the present outside itself. Philosophically, this thought is rich and powerful, since it is located at the juncture of two opposing currents: confidence in progress, and the necessity of the struggle to overcome social constraints. Nevertheless, histori-

cally, it is difficult to bring together forces that have fought each other and that are increasingly lived as contradictory. Belief in progress has been combatted by the movement for the direct discovery of intentional action; one cannot be simultaneously centered on history and centered on the knowing and acting subject. It is perhaps this historic rupture that prevented Bloch from being recognized by non-Marxists and Marxists alike, and which made him a figure at once so important and yet so fragile in intellectual life. It is because he has this double attachment that Bloch is a utopian, because he is enthusiastic about social utopias, especially the Anabaptists, and, even beyond literary utopias, about all the images of ideal society offered us by urban planning, the art of gardens, painting, or music, which make the modern world, in all its aspects, into a production of utopia or even a world utopian in itself, always out of balance with itself, never attached to order, always dreaming of movement.

But Bloch went so far, wanted so strongly to transform order into movement, into innovations, into conquests and conflicts, that we might ask if his analysis of society still rests on an entirely social principle, our hallmark of utopian thought. More, Fourier, and Orwell constructed in their minds a social, psychological, or political order, and their mood varies from optimism to the greatest pessimism via refusal of the social order; but they all three wanted to transform society in the name of a positive or negative image of this society. Bloch tries to find his place in this great family, while criticizing his predecessors, More in particular; but he seems swept along toward the opposite of utopian thought, that is, toward opposition to social organization or to the progress of some properly nonsocial principle, whether religious, economic, or political, which not only gives its legitimacy to a social order but, more importantly, constitutes a principle of appeal against the decisions of power and of organization in society.

THE HISTORY of utopia began only when society abandoned the image of paradise. Utopia is one of the products of secularization. These days, the virtual is richer than utopia, and the very idea of a perfect society has decomposed in the torrent of change or the terrorizing immobility of totalitarian regimes of all types. What outstrips the social can no longer be the social itself, and must become nonsocial again. This leads to the resurgence of religious images, most often based not on the affirmation of a god but rather on a kind of thinking we might call liberal in the sense that it escapes social controls; the idea of the rights of men was and still is its main manifestation. The utopia is no longer possible when the idea of a perfect society is rejected, when completeness and perfection can be found only in absolute Evil, and when the search for the social person rests on an idea of democracy that is as distant as possible from any utopia since it destroys any stable and central principle of power, and since it no longer assigns a place to an idea of society lost in the changing relations among social actors, their interests, ideologies, and modes of expression and action.

Utopia is not present in all stages and forms of modernity. It was formed at the start of this modernity, at the moment when the Nation, the absolute State, and the Nation-State were being organized, at the moment when the representation of social life was highly political. It became a model of counter-society when capitalist industrialization removed from political power the control over economic and social life. It was transformed, finally, into a nightmare at the moment when the Party-State devoured society and removed all freedom. It is this nightmare, so close to reality, that George Orwell described. We do not see any paradise being reborn except artificial paradises, but we do see a growing distrust of society, which often leads ecologists as well as lawyers and educators to reject the idea of social utility. Protest replaces participation, and litigation is substituted for integration.

Utopia is only one of the two faces of modernity, the one that asserts the hold of society over itself, but it is constantly fought by that other aspect of modernity that is less conquering than iberating. The latter asserts moral individualism and turns back to a non-social principle of action in order to limit the domination of a power that scientific and technical developments may yet render more and more total.

Translated by Susan Emanuel

1 See Jean Bodin, *Les Six Livres de la République* (first published in 1576), 6 vols. (Paris: Fayard, 1986). A facsimile reprint of the first English translation (1606) appeared as *The Six Books of a Commonweale*, ed. with an introduction by Kenneth Douglas McRae (Cambridge, Mass.: Harvard University Press, 1962); this in turn was reprinted by the Arno Press in 1979.

2 Thomas More, *Utopia*, Book I, trans. Edward Surtz (New Haven, Conn.: Yale University Press, 1964), 33.

3 See Norbert Bobbio, *Thomas Hobbes and the Natural Law Tradition*, trans. Daniela Gobetti (Chicago: University of Chicago Press, 1993).

4 Michel Foucault, *Discipline and Punish: The Birth of the Prison*, trans. Alan Sheridan (New York: Pantheon Books, 1977).

5 Thomas Münzer, *The Collected Works of Thomas Muntzer*, ed. and trans. Peter Matheson (Edinburgh, Scotland: T. & T. Clark, 1988).

6 Friedrich Engels, *The Peasant War in Germany*, trans. Moissaye J. Olgin (New York: International Publishers, 2000).

7 Charles Fourier, *Œuvres complètes*, 12 vols. (Paris: Editions Anthropos, 1966–68), 2: 21; trans. in *Harmonian Man: Selected Writings of Charles Fourier*, trans. Susan Hanson; ed. with an introduction by Mark Poster (Garden City, N.Y.: Doubleday, 1971), 29. Other selections from Fourier's voluminous writings are available in English in *Design for Utopia: Selected Writings of Charles Fourier*, trans. Julia Franklin; with an introduction by Charles Gide (New York: Schocken Books, 1971), and in *The Utopian Vision of Charles Fourier: Selected Texts on Work, Love, and Passionate Attraction*, trans., ed., and with an introduction by Jonathan Beecher and Richard Bienvenu (Columbia: University of Missouri Press, 1983).

8 Fourier, 5: 159.

9 Ibid., 5: 468.

10 In vol. 7 of the *Œuvres complètes. Le Nouveau Monde amoureux* was reissued by Editions Slatkine (Paris) in 1984.

11 Fourier, 5: 552.

12 Victor Considérant, *Exposition abrégée du système phalanstérien de Fourier*, 3rd ed. (Paris: Librairie Sociétaire, 1845).

13 George Orwell, *Nineteen Eighty-four*, vol. 9 of *The Complete Works of George Orwell* (London: Secker & Warburg, 1997–98), 267.

14 Ibid., 275.

15 Ibid., 279.

16 See ibid., 220–26 for Orwell's explanation of these three key "Newspeak" words.

17 Ibid., 132.

18 Karl Mannheim, *Ideology and Utopia: An Introduction to the Sociology of Knowledge*, trans. Louis Wirth and Edward Shils; with a preface by Louis Wirth (London and New York: Routledge, 1991), 173.

19 Ibid.

20 Ibid., 183.

21 Ibid., 184.

22 Ernst Bloch, *The Principle of Hope*, 3 vols., trans. Neville Plaice, Stephen Plaice, and Paul Knight (Cambridge, Mass.: MIT Press, 1986).

23 Ernst Bloch, *The Spirit of Utopia*, trans. Anthony Nassar (Stanford, Calif.: Stanford University Press, 2000).

24 Bloch, *The Principle of Hope*, 1: 5–6.

25 Ibid., 2: Part Four – "Outlines of a Better World."

26 Ibid., 3: Part Five – "Wishful Images of the Fulfilled Moment."

27 Ibid., 1: Part One – "Little Daydreams"; Part Two – "Anticipatory Consciousness"; Part Three – "Wishful Images in the Mirror."

28 Ibid., 1: 12.

29 Ibid., 1: 127.

30 Ibid., 1: 153–58.

31 Ibid., 1: 149.

32 Quoted in ibid., 1: 156.

33 Ibid., 1: 16. The quotation in this passage is from Goethe's *Faust*, Part I (1700).

34 Ibid., 1: 18.

See pp. 52, 70, 56.

Ancient, Biblical, and Medieval Traditions

The Golden Age and Paradise: The Time of Innocence

The Golden Age: Humans at the Table of the Gods
First of all the deathless gods who dwell on Olympus made a golden race of mortal men who lived in the time of Cronos when he was reigning in heaven. —HESIOD[1]

IN THE beginning of *Works and Days*, Hesiod evokes the existence of a "golden race" still dining with the gods, still carefree, nourished by an earth that spontaneously produced "fruit abundantly and without stint," and spared from suffering, old age, and fear of death. These "golden men" were ruled by justice and did not know war or any form of violence. Under the benevolent reign of Kronos, they were representatives of the royal principle, knowing only sovereign activity. Ever young, they led a free and happy existence, in a time inalterably new, and close to that enjoyed by the gods.

In Hesiod's poem these races[2] succeed each other cyclically. The golden race comes first, less in the chronological sense than because it incarnates the excellence of human virtue and the proximity of the divine.[3] Thus the sequence of races – gold, silver, bronze, and iron, with the age of heroes between the last two – could correspond to a hierarchy of qualities, but this does not imply an inevitable succession, leaving open the realm of aspirations.

In the great political dialogues in which he undertakes to define the ideal city, Plato revisits this myth in the guise of "the reign of Kronos." As in Hesiod, the golden race lives at a time when the generous earth exempts men from productive labor, when peace and justice rule, and property does not exist.[4] The foundation of this excellent state is a just subordination; the divine element effectively governs each of the world's components:

For then the god began to rule and take care of the rotation itself as a whole, and as for the regions, in their turn, it was just the same, the parts of the world-order having everywhere been divided up by gods ruling over them. As for living things, divine spirits had divided them between themselves, like herdsmen, by kind and by herd, each by himself providing independently for all the needs of those he tended, so that none of them was savage, nor did they eat each other, and there was no war or internal dissent at all.[5]

As for men, a "god tended them, taking charge of them himself, just as now human beings, themselves living creatures, but different and more divine, pasture other kinds of living creatures more lowly than themselves. . . ."[6] Destined to recall the happiness of the community first allied with the divine order, before the world started going "backwards," the myth of the golden race was transformed into a metaphor and also historicized, so that the theme of the Golden Age gradually supplanted that of the golden *race*.

It was in Rome, during the period from the end of the first century B.C.E. to the first part of our era, that the term "Golden Age" really appeared (*aurea ætas, aureum sæculum*). It conferred a chronological dimension on what at first was merely a structural kind of classification.[7] The reign of Kronos shifted from myth to history. Thanks to historical events – the end of the Roman Republic, the civil war, the reign of Augustus – the Golden Age took on both moral and political value in the writings of poets, from Lucretius via Virgil[8] to Ovid,[9] and among historians like Tacitus, and moralists like Seneca. The Golden Age now evoked a prestigious past, the happy times when men and gods shared the same table and lived in perfect harmony in the bucolic surroundings of lush prairies and fertile plains full of trees dripping with honey and bushes bent under the weight of ruby grapes, alongside burgeoning flocks of sheep with multicolored fleece. Abundance was offered to and shared by everybody. It was a time of *otium*, when people lived as equals, far from vain curiosities, unconcerned with what lay elsewhere, in an eternal springtime.

For the moralists, who present history as a decline in manners and an estrangement from the divine, the Golden Age is thus the benchmark by which contemporary depravity may be judged. As Catullus put it:

For the gods would frequent the worshipful homes
    of heroes
and show themselves present wherever men
    were assembled

before contempt had become the response
　　to religion. . . .
But after the earth had been imbued with hideous evil,
and men had abandoned all their desire for Justice,
when one brother had soaked his hands in the blood
　　of another,
when children no longer wept at the death of their parents,
when a father could wish for the death of his very
　　own son,
for the new stepmother seems to have found him
　　attractive;
when an unwitting young man lay with his impious mother,
who had no fear of the shades of her deified parents,
then good & evil were confused in criminal madness,
turning the righteous minds of the gods from our behavior.
So they no longer appear now when mortals assemble,
and shun the light of luminous day altogether.[10]

A favorite and almost commonplace motif among pagan authors, the Golden Age was rapidly adopted by Christian writers. They had been molded by Virgil, Ovid, and Lucretius, and by a tradition[11] that one could trace back to the second century B.C.E.; they were concerned to make biblical history coincide with ancient mythology, and so they borrowed from this genre while renewing it.

For the apologists of the time of Constantine, when Christianity became the state religion, the Golden Age corresponds to the first age of the world described in Genesis. Lactantius situates it between the expulsion from Eden and the Flood or, more exactly, before Ham's sin and exile, which marks the definitive breakdown of the original community, a rupture in the first stock, the arrival of "the first people which did not know God."[12]

The Golden Age

Aubry after J. W. Baur
Aetas Aurea
From *Ovidii Metamorphosis oder Verwandelungs Bücher*
Nuremberg: Paul Fürst, [1680s]
NYPL, Miriam and Ira D. Wallach Division of Art, Prints and Photographs

The most important source for the myth of the Golden Age, in which the first "race" of men lived in peace and pleasure, is Hesiod's *Works and Days* (eighth century B.C.E.). Later, in the first century, Ovid described the Golden Age in Book I of his *Metamorphoses*: "That first age was golden: all was then fresh and new / and so arranged that out of spontaneous goodness, men, / without the compulsion of laws or fear of punishment, kept / their faith with one another, behaving with decency, / fairness, justice and generosity. . . ."

The artist and engraver Johann Wilhelm Baur was born in Strasbourg in 1607, spent much of his life in Italy, and moved to Vienna shortly before his death at the age of thirty-four. In his last years in Vienna, he created 150 plates illustrating Ovid's *Metamorphoses*, the first of which is shown here in a later edition engraved by Aubry.

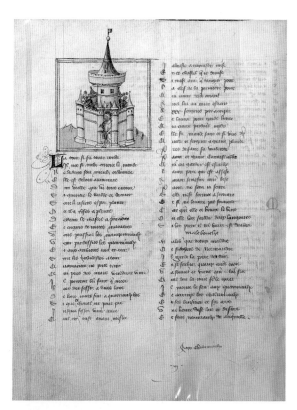

**Guillaume de Lorris and
Jean de Meun
[Roman de la Rose]**
[France, 15th century]
NYPL, Spencer Collection

The Dream and the Quest

"In the twentieth year of my life, at the time when Love exacts his tribute from young people, I lay down one night, as usual, and slept very soundly. During my sleep I saw a very beautiful and pleasing dream; but in this dream was nothing which did not happen almost as the dream told it."

The most famous work of the Middle Ages, the *Roman de la Rose* is constructed around the themes of the dream and the quest, and takes place in an allegorical universe, the center of which is an orchard or a paradise of love. This long poem is really two separate works. The first part, written by Guillaume de Lorris around 1237, represents the epitome of the courtly tradition and portrays the author as a dreamer and lover in quest of a rose; the second part, added by Jean de Meun between 1275 and 1280, is a philosophical digression on love, in which Aristotelian naturalism, reason, and satire replace the courtly tone of the earlier text.

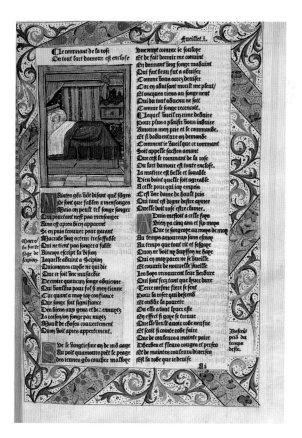

**Guillaume de Lorris and
Jean de Meun
*Cy est le Romāt de la Roze***
Paris: Galliot, 1526
NYPL, Spencer Collection

Saturn, who reigned over this age, was held not as a god, according to Euhemerus, but as a good king who was honored much later as a god. He makes *communitas* rule, which is in fact what Christians tried to practice in those days, founded on the justice that alone allows the recognition of God as Father and of men as brothers. Then "That one [Ham], exiled, settled in a part of that land which is now called Arabia. . . . This was the first people which did not know God because its leader and founder did not receive the worship of God from his father when he was cursed by him, and so he bequeathed an ignorance of the divinity to his posterity. . . . [And] torn from the stock of a holy root, they established for themselves new customs and institutions arbitrarily."[13]

Christian poets of the fifth century like Dracontius,[14] Sedulius, and Avitus, Bishop of Vienne, took the Golden Age theme as a backdrop for a description of paradise that promised to become the model for all the gardens of Edenic virtues in medieval literature,[15] whether gardens of love or monastic ones, or Mother Nature's garden, site of the creation of the "perfect man," described in the twelfth century by Alanus de Insulis in *Anticlaudianus*.[16]

The Garden of Eden
And the Lord God planted a garden in Eden, in the East. –GENESIS 2: 8

The original site of which Genesis speaks is a garden, a "paradise." To translate the Hebrew *gân*, the authors in fact chose the term *paradeisos*, borrowed from the Persian by Xenophon in the *Anabasis*, which originally referred to the secluded parks of the Achemenide princes. If the word still served in the Hellenistic period to characterize the gardens of Ptolemy at Alexandria, it also referred to a well-irrigated place, an orchard planted with fruit trees and vines.[17] An expression charged with princely recollections of abundance and sumptuousness, bubbling brooks in the middle of the desert, and also evocative of nature tamed, cultivated, and humanized, the common noun would be transformed in the Vulgate into a proper noun, "Paradise," the site of humanity's origin. As for Eden, sometimes considered a toponym (place name), it was also a common name signifying "luxury," "delicacy," "delights." It is this last meaning that was consecrated by Saint Jerome, who translated it as *hortus voluptatis* or *hortus deliciarum*.[18] Henceforth, for commentators on the first chapters of Genesis,

the place of beginnings that had been arranged by the Creator for Adam and Eve would take on the bucolic character that had been adopted by Latin poets, particularly Virgil and Ovid, to describe the Golden Age. The terrestrial paradise became a *locus amœnus*,[19] a place full of charm, a temperate climate, an eternal spring full of flavors and scents. It is planted with trees that simultaneously bear flowers and fruits, which in iconography often constitute the only décor in paradise. It is a dream of self-sufficiency delivered from the tyranny of material needs, which later will come to convey the myth of the country of Cockaigne.

At the center of the garden rise two remarkable trees, the tree of life and the tree of knowledge of good and evil. "And out of the ground the Lord God made to grow every tree that is pleasant to the sight and good for food; the tree of life also in the midst of the garden, and the tree of the knowledge of good and evil. . . . '[B]ut of the tree of the knowledge of good and evil you shall not eat, for in the day that you eat of it you shall die'" (Genesis 2: 9, 17).[20] To the sylvan charms of paradise is added living water, the fountain flowing in its midst. This unique river soon divides, as maps of the world show, into four: the Tigris, the Euphrates, and two others, early identified with known rivers, the Gihon with the Nile and the Pishon with the Ganges,[21] tangible links between the original paradise and the human earth.

The ideal vision of the shady garden with living waters is sometimes replaced by a city, a citadel, a castle, the earthly replica of the celestial city, reminiscent of the citadel of the Old Testament but also connected with urban resurgence – as if, after the twelfth century and the height of clearing for cultivation, the idea of original happiness could only spread inside a city, eminent sign of protection and civility.

In this site of delight, whichever it is, God "put" Adam – man was created, according to certain traditions,[22] from red clay in Hebron, to which, 930 years later, after having rested a moment at Calvary,[23] he was supposedly transported. All kinds of qualities are attributed to Adam: "It is reported that he was thirty when he was created, that he had the wisdom of Solomon, the strength of Samson, the beauty of Absalom."[24] The first being endowed with speech, he was entrusted by God, by virtue of his perfect knowledge of the visible universe that was made for him and with him, to name the animals, to keep the garden, and (along with his companion Eve, created by God in paradise, flesh

The Creation

**Bible historiée
et vie des Saints**
[France, ca. 1300]
NYPL, Spencer Collection

"In the beginning God created the heavens and the earth. The earth was without form and void, and darkness was upon the face of the deep; and the Spirit of God was moving over the face of the waters. And God said, 'Let there be light'; and there was light. . . ." – Genesis 1: 1–10

This illuminated Bible from northern France is one of the most beautiful manuscripts of its time. The work of at least eight people, 846 of its original 1,034 illustrations have survived. Before the manuscript came to The New York Public Library in 1929, it was in the collection of Sir George Holford in England, and a 1924 catalogue of his collection stated: "This was the book that [the Pre-Raphaelite artist, Edward] Burne-Jones used to come frequently to see, but never got through the whole of the pictures. He said that if a new flood came and submerged the earth, this book saved would serve to regenerate Art."

The Peaceable Kingdom

Nicolas de Lyre
Postilla in Genesim
Mantua, between 1395 and 1400
BNF, Département des Manuscrits

The Franciscan Nicolas de Lyre, who died in 1349, was the author of a biblical commentary that was so universally successful that it replaced the works of previous interpreters, and continued to be authoritative even beyond the medieval period. This copy offers an unusually well-developed series of images; of great refinement, it was produced for the sumptuous library of the Duke of Milan, Giovanni Galeazzo Visconti. The artist, probably Mantuan, delights in rendering naturalistic details, of which we catch only a glimpse in the profusion of animals that inhabit the scene of Creation.

The Garden of Eden

**Horae Beatae Mariae
Virginis as usum Ecclesiae
Gallicanae, cum Calendario**
[Franco-Flemish, late 15th century]
NYPL, Spencer Collection

". . . therefore the LORD God
sent him forth from the garden of Eden, to till the ground
from which he was taken. He
drove out the man; and at the
east of the garden of Eden
he placed the cherubim, and a
flaming sword which turned
every way, to guard the way
to the tree of life." – Genesis
3: 23–24

of his flesh)[25] to people the earth. Adam figures as the "re-creator" of the world, the legislator, giving through words a form to the universe, at the same time that he represents the unique man from whom the human species is to be propagated. Saint Augustine, in *The City of God*, explains how the Creator willed that the "purpose was . . . to ensure that unity of fellowship itself and ties of harmony might be more strongly impressed on him, if men were bound to one another not only by their similar nature but also by their feeling of kinship. For not even woman herself, who was to be joined to man, did he choose to create as he did that very man, but he created her out of that man in order that the human race might derive entirely from one man."[26] Perhaps we should see behind this keen desire for unity, the reactivated dream of a primitive androgyny, a quest for an initial perfection, about which Johannes Scotus Erigena speculated in the ninth century, and which was fractured by the split of sexualities.[27] In any case, "if man and woman had remained in paradise they would have reproduced without concupiscence, and the woman would have given birth without pain and without stain, and, barely born, the child would have walked and talked."

This original happiness was short-lived: according to Honorius Augustodunensis in the twelfth century, "At the beginning of the day, Adam was created and he gave names to all the animals. But in the middle of the day, woman was created and she ate at once of the forbidden tree. She gave some of the fruit to her man and he ate also. So in the evening of that day God drove both out of Paradise."[28] Just as the Golden Age had once been broken by the daring of Prometheus,[29] Adam and Eve, united in carnal love,[30] would, like all their descendants, know exile and be separated from the site of origin and divine proximity, the restoration of which would command all Messianic hopes.

*The Terrestrial Paradise:
A Very Real Place on Earth*
Now empty and surrounded by flames, inaccessible except to those rare elect, like Elijah and Enoch, who were spared from death, removed from living and "in reserve" for the combat of the final days, paradise remained present on the earth's surface.

Of course, in the fourth century Origen had developed an allegorical interpretation of the Genesis text:

And who will be found simple enough to believe that like some farmer, "God planted trees in the garden of Eden, in the east" and that He planted the "tree of life" in it that is a visible tree that could be touched, so that someone could eat of this tree with corporeal teeth and gain life, and further could eat of another tree and receive knowledge "of good and evil" (Gen. 2: 8–9)? Moreover, we find that God is said to stroll in the garden in the afternoon and Adam to hide under a tree. . . . Surely, I think no one doubts that these statements are made by Scripture in the form of a type by which they point toward certain mysteries.[31]

Origen is followed in the ninth century by Johannes Scotus Erigena (the translator into Latin of *De caelesti hierarchia* [*The Celestial Hierarchies*] of Pseudo-Dionysius the Areopagite):

Paradise is not a place on some part of the earth, covered with trees, but something spiritual, sown with the seeds of virtues, planted in human nature and, as it is clearly said, nothing other than human substance itself, made in the image of God, in which dwells the tree of life, that is to say, the Word of the Father, Wisdom.[32]

However, this purely spiritual exegesis remained marginal. Soon, Epiphanius, Bishop of Constantia in Cyprus, attacked Origen's interpretation:

If there is no sensible paradise, there is no spring; if there is no spring, there is no river and no four beginnings; if there is no Pishon, there is no Gihon; if there is no Tigris, there is no Euphrates; if there is no Euphrates, there is no fig tree, no leaves, no Adam, nothing to eat, no Eve and she did not eat from the tree; there is no Adam. If there is no Adam, there are no men, and the truth is now myth and everything is allegory. But there is Adam, we are all descended from him, and through multiplicity, in succeeding generations, we see that.[33]

To the spiritual conception of paradise, he opposed the testimony of the senses:

Myself, I have seen the waters of Gihon, waters I could contemplate with my fleshly eyes. . . . I have also drunk the waters of the great river Euphrates, waters that quite simply my hand could touch and my mouth absorb, not spiritual waters.[34]

It was Saint Augustine, in *De Genesi ad litteram* and in *The City of God*, who would strike a balance between the allegorical and literal interpretations:

No one therefore prevents us from understanding paradise allegorically. . . . There is one condition, however:

we must also believe in the actual truth of the story which is presented to us in a most faithful record of events.[35]

Once it is admitted that the original paradise is really on earth, it must still be located. This is a risky investigation, as Sir John Mandeville stressed in his *Travels*:

You should realize that no living man can go to Paradise. By land no man can go thither because of the wild beasts in the wilderness, and because of the hills and rocks, which no one can cross; and also because of the many dark places that are there. No one can go there by water either, for those rivers flow with so strong a current, with such a rush and such waves that no boat can sail against them. There is also such a great noise of waters that one man cannot hear another, shout he never so loudly. Many great lords have tried at different times to travel by those rivers to Paradise, but they could not prosper in their journeys; some of them died through exhaustion from rowing and excessive labour, some went blind and deaf through the noise of the waters, and some were drowned through the violence of the waves. And so no man, as I said, can get there except through the special grace of God. And so of that place I can tell you no more; so I shall go back and tell you of things that I have seen. . . .[36]

Such uncertainty led some to situate paradise on another earth, different from the one inhabited by humankind. This theory, developed in the sixth century in the East by Cosmas Indicopleustes,[37] is not totally absent from Western thought. One finds it in the oft-repeated assertion that paradise is "very far from our orb," separated by the double obstacle of the ocean and the mountains, that it is *secretum*, removed from regions where people dwell. Gervase of Tilbury, in *Otia imperialia* at the beginning of the thirteenth century, suggested prudently that it was perhaps beyond the torrid zone: "It is not something I affirm, but it is an opinion that may be defended because it is said that it is a place that is inaccessible to us by reason of the heat of the interposed sun."[38]

Displaced in the Middle Ages to a position in the Orient, paradise was in the sixteenth century again situated outside the ecumenical world, from a desire to reorganize space and time that resulted from the great explorations and discoveries.[39] Thus, for Duarte Pacheco Pereira, in *Esmeraldo de situ orbis* (ca. 1508), the ocean did not circle all the earth but rather constituted a sort of "mediterranean" between the Old and New Worlds, and paradise

was to be found in the newly discovered Western Indies.[40] It was also understood thus, in the middle of the seventeenth century, by Antonio de León Pinelo, in *El Paraiso en el Nuevo Mundo* (1650–56):

And although today a third continent has been discovered, Australia or Antarctica, it is excessively cold and by its natural position unsuitable for this privilege, as has been remarked concerning the Arctic and Septentrional on the opposite side. So if of the three, Australia is excluded, and if bar Kēphā, Saint Ephraem, and the ancient Church Fathers exclude the one we inhabit, it follows necessarily that paradise was situated in the Indies then imagined and today discovered.[41]

In the medieval West, this remained an isolated opinion. Most commentators, based on the translation of the Septuagint, placed paradise in the Levant. This was an ancient tradition already mentioned in the *Book of Jubilees*, which goes back to the second century B.C.E. Also accepted by the Greek Orthodox patriarchy, this thesis would win over most Western commentators. Thus Saint Isidore of Seville: "Paradise is a place in the east. . . ."[42]

East is where the light comes from, where the sun rises each morning with new glory, and seems each evening to want to die and disappear when setting: it is the image of Christ, the true light, sun of justice, promise of resurrection; the oriental lateral, on the right of heaven, as Saint Thomas Aquinas wrote in the *Summa Theologica*: "It was fitting that it should be in the east, for it is to be believed that it was situated in the most excellent part of the earth. Now the east is the right hand of the heaven . . . and the right hand is nobler than the left; hence it was fitting that God should place the earthly paradise in the east."[43] The East of beginnings, where space and time coincide, marking the earth with the seal of the Providence that rules the course of the world.

Placed in the east, paradise was suspended between insularity and *terra firma*. It was an island, the archetype of all islands, as represented by Lambert of Saint-Omer in the *Liber Floridus*'s world maps as if the secluded world of an island, closed in upon itself and playing on the ambiguity of appearance and dissembling, might better than any other signify the double nature of this place, as well as convey an image and matrix of purity and perfection. For others, the location of paradise corresponded to a large space on a continent, a land that Honorius Augustodunensis (following Saint

The Promised Land

Monteville compose par Messire Jehan de Monteville chevalier natif dangleterre de la ville de Saint alain lequel parle de la terre de promission . . .
[Lyons: Claude Nourry, ca. 1509]
NYPL, Spencer Collection

Composed in the mid-four-teenth century, *The Travels of Sir John Mandeville* chronicled the wanderings of an English knight throughout the Middle East and Asia over the course of thirty-five years. The richly detailed narrative was probably written by someone who never left Europe but compiled most of his information from existing sources. The first part is a guide to the sights of the Holy Land, while the second describes the wonders of Asia, including strange peoples, Prester John's kingdom, and the Garden of Eden. Mandeville's insistence that the world was round and fully inhabited inspired the explorers of later centuries.

Mahomet's Paradise

Markus Paulus Venetus [Marco Polo]
Reisen, en Beschryving Der Oostersche Lantschappen . . .
Amsterdam: Abraham Wolfgang, 1664
NYPL, Rare Books Division

The tales of Marco Polo's thir-teenth-century travels and adventures in China, India, and Persia have inspired explorers, writers, and readers for cen-turies. His descriptions of gold, jewels, and spices give the East an air of Paradise on Earth. This engraving from a German edition of the seven-teenth century shows a view of "Mahomet's Paradise."

Isidore of Seville) defined in *Imago mundi* as the first region of Asia, thus inaugurating the long string of principal divisions of the *orbis terræ*.[44] But if in Asia, was it actually in India, in Armenia, or in fact in Babylon, as Calvin thought?[45] The controversy continued until the eighteenth century and even beyond. So paradise still had to find its place, a conjectural and thus inaccessible space, no doubt on the borders of the world, on "that thin line where it stops being a world and where it starts being one."

The Golden Age in Greece having passed, happiness had taken refuge somewhere on earth, trading its temporal identity for a territorialized myth. Here we reach the source of utopia, somewhere between myth and fable, as these uncertain places inspire (especially among historians) tales describing, in these unverifiable elsewheres, societies heir to the original happiness, places to which some voyager has supposedly strayed. Herodotus, the first, evokes the country of the Sun, a land of abundance where Ethiopians live:

It is a meadow in the skirts of their city full of the boiled flesh of all manner of beasts, which the magistrates are careful to store with meat every night, and where whoever likes may come and eat during the day. The people of the land say that the earth itself brings forth the food. Such is the description which is given of "the Table of the Sun."[46]

Much later, the country of the Sun would reappear in Diodorus of Sicily (80–30 B.C.E.), who summarizes the history of Iambulus, a third-century voyager transported despite himself beyond the country of the Ethiopians, to an island in the ocean.[47] It is a circular island, geometrically perfect, populated with men who "differ greatly both in the characteristics of their bodies and in their manners from the men in our part of the inhabited world," but who are beautiful and "well-proportioned in the outline of the body." They benefit from a temperate climate because "they live at the equator, and they suffer neither from heat nor from cold,"[48] and day and night are of equal length. The land spontaneously produces more than the necessities, and the inhabitants nourish themselves from the fruit of a reed they crush and grind: "skilfully with their hands, they mould it into loaves, which are baked and eaten, and they are of surprising sweetness." Springs of warm water furnish them plentifully for "bathing and the relief of fatigue."[49] Everything is held in common, including women and children. "[W]hile the children are infants those who suckle

the babes often change them around in order that not even the mothers may know their own offspring."[50] The absence of rivalry lets them live in concord, since although they "enjoy an abundant provision of everything from what grows of itself in these islands," these men seek simplicity "and take for their food only what suffices for their needs." To clothe themselves, they make use of "a certain reed which contains in the centre a downy substance that is bright to the eye and soft, which they gather and mingle with crushed sea-shells and thus make remarkable garments of purple hue."[51] "Moreover, the inhabitants give attention to every branch of learning and especially to astrology. . ."; [52] they have an alphabet and a system of writing. As for their government, it is divided into groups of four hundred members: "In each group the oldest man regularly exercises the leadership, just as if he were a kind of king, and is obeyed by all the members; and when the first such ruler makes an end of his life in accordance with the law upon the completion of his one hundred and fiftieth year, the next one succeeds to the leadership."[53]

Their whole life is regulated with precision:

. . . they do not all take their food at the same time nor is it always the same. . . . They also take turns in ministering to the needs of one another, some of them fishing, others working at the crafts, others occupying themselves in other useful tasks, and still others, with the exception of those who have come to old age, performing the services of the group in a definite cycle.[54]

During festivals and feasts, they honor the gods "with hymns and spoken laudations," especially the Sun, "after whom they name both the islands and themselves,"[55] meaning the seven islands, "and they are very much the same in size and at about equal distances from one another, and all follow the same customs and laws."[56] Free of disease, they live a very long time, until the age of 150: "[T]here is also a law among them that they should live only for a stipulated number of years, and that at the completion of this period they should make away with themselves of their own accord, by a strange manner of death; for there grows among them a plant of a peculiar nature, and whenever a man lies down upon it, imperceptibly and gently he falls asleep and dies."[57] The dead are buried in the sand when the tide is out, perhaps to avoid any stain.

This tale is constructed from many borrowings in which reminiscences of the Golden Age mingle with the ideal Platonic city, organized into a mathematical perfection where space, resources, and population are voluntarily balanced, since the inhabitants practice a form of eugenics by selecting the most resilient and courageous children and by setting the date of their own deaths. These characteristics will recur in Tommaso Campanella's *Civitas solis* [*The City of the Sun*].

Apart from the country of the Sun, there were many other marvelous lands that seemed each to contain traces of the happiness of another age: the islands of Hiera and Panchea,[58] also described by Diodorus; the city of Pious (Eusebes), whose existence is recorded by Aelian[59] following upon an account by Theopompus of Chios; and the country of the Hyperboreans,[60] beyond the Aquilon, recalled by medieval maps of the world. But more than these fragments of earth, it was on the Islands of the Blessed that the Golden Age took refuge. It is there, at the earth's extremities, that Zeus established the heroes, according to Hesiod: "[T]hey live untouched by sorrow in the islands of the blessed along the shore of deep swirling Ocean, happy heroes for whom the grain-giving earth bears honey-sweet fruit flourishing thrice a year."[61]

With Pindar, these islands become the recompense of virtuous men:

[T]hose with the courage to have lived
. . . while keeping their souls
free from all unjust deeds, travel the road of Zeus
    to the tower of Kronos, where ocean breezes
blow round
the Isle of the Blessed, and flowers of gold are ablaze,
some from radiant trees on land, while the water
    nurtures others; with these they weave
garlands for their hands and crowns for their heads,

in obedience to the just counsels of Rhadamanthys,
whom the great father keeps ever seated at his side
the husband of Rhea, she who has
    the highest throne of all.[62]

These places, preserved from human blemish and time's erosion, heirs of ancient mythology, were transmitted to the Middle Ages through such intermediaries as compilers, Latin lexicographers, and Church Fathers; they also figured on world maps. The assimilation of classical culture by Christianity in effect allowed the latter to include "fable," either explicitly, as a tale that is neither true nor plausible, or as an *integumentum*, that is to say, a screen that reveals truths otherwise hidden or difficult to grasp. Integrated now into medieval rhetoric, this

fable will feed into imaginary narratives.[63]

Apart from these borrowings, other happy lands arose, emanating from the memory of the aspirations of the Middle Ages. For example, in the middle of the twelfth century there appeared, first in the *Chronicle* of Otto I, Bishop of Freising,[64] mention of the kingdom of Prester John.[65] This had an uncertain location, migrating over the years from India, where Sir John Mandeville situated it,[66] to Ethiopia, close to the Mountains of the Moon, near the presumed source of the Nile. This kingdom, well known from the letter from its sovereign to the Byzantine Emperor Manuel I Comnenus, which was widely circulated and interpolated, is the model for the Christian kingdoms. Placed under the protection of Christ and Saint Thomas and the prophet Daniel, there reigned neither lust nor deceit:

Let it be known to you that nobody in our land dares to commit the sin of lechery, for at once he would be burned, because the sacrament of marriage has been ordained by God; nor does anybody dare to lie in our country, for he would be hanged [immediately].[67]

A kingdom of abundance with no poverty thanks to the prince's largesse, it is governed by a person who is both king and priest, uniting in a single being spiritual and temporal authority (a perfect union ardently desired):

We also sing there [at the altar of St. Thomas] on the annual feast days, and on account of this we are called Prester John, for we are a priest because of sacrificing at the altar, and we are a king because we are just and upright.

Know that I had been blessed before I was born, for God has sent an angel to my father who told him to build a palace full of God's grace and a chamber of paradise for the child to come, who was to be the greatest king on earth and to live for a long time. And whoever stays in the palace will never suffer hunger, thirst, or death. When my father had woke up from his slumber, he was overly joyful and he began to build the palace which you will see.[68]

This kingdom possessed all marvels, including a tree of life:

There grows in our country also the tree of life from which the holy oil is coming. This tree is completely dry and a serpent is guarding and watching it day and night, all the year round, except on Saint John's day, when it is fast asleep, and this is the time when we approach it. . . . This tree is only a day's journey from the earthly paradise.[69]

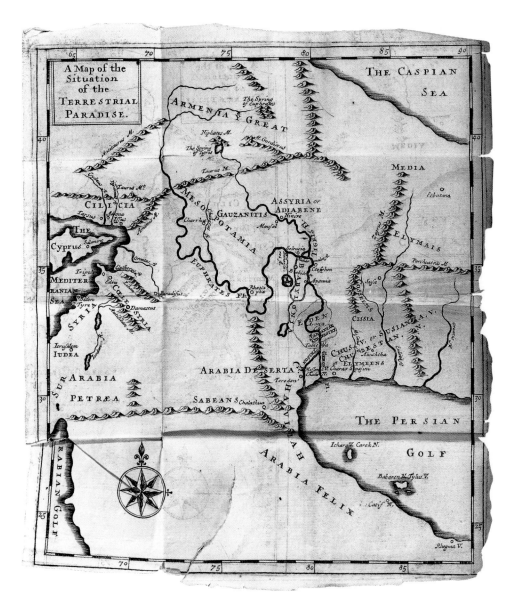

The Place of Paradise on Earth

P[ierre] D[aniel] Huet
"A Map of the Situation of the Terrestrial Paradise"

In *A Treatise on the Situation of Paradise* (London: Printed for James Knapton, 1694)
NYPL, General Research Division

Father Daniel Huet, one of the great savants of his time, presented this brief treatise on the location of the earthly paradise to his academic colleagues, a difficult task, given the "obscurity of the material." People had "placed it in the third Heaven, in the fourth, in the Orb of the Moon, in the Moon it self,

upon a Mount near the Orb of the Moon, in the middle Region of the Air, out of the Earth, upon the Earth, under the Earth, in a hidden place and far beyond the Knowledge of Men. They placed it under the artick Pole, in *Tartaria*, in the place where now is the *Caspian* Sea. Others have placed it as far as the extremity of the South, in the Land of Fire. Many will have it to be in the East, either along the sides of the River *Ganges*, or in the Isle of *Ceilan*, deriving also the name of *Indies* from the word *Eden*, which is the name of the Province where

Paradise stood. They have placed it in *China*, and beyond the East also, in a place uninhabited. Others in *America*, others in *Africa* under the *Æquator*, others in the *Æquinoctial-East*, others upon the Mountains of the Moon, from which they thought the *Nile* sprung. The greatest part in *Asia*, some in the great *Armenia*, others in *Mesopotamia*, or in *Assyria*, or in *Persia*, or in *Babylonia*, or in *Arabia*, or in *Syria*, or in *Palæstina*. Some also would have honoured with it our *Europe*, and which is beyond the greatest Impertinency,

placed it at *Hedin* a City in *Artois*, upon no other ground than the Affinity of that name with the word *Eden*. I do not despair, but some Adventurer, to have it nearer to us, will one day undertake to place it at *Houdan*."

Huet himself chose to place the earthly paradise "upon the Canal which the Tigris and Euphrates joined together do make, between the place of their coming together, and that of their going one from another, before they fall into the Persian gulf."

The Kingdom of Prester John

Abraham Ortelius
"Presbiteri Johannis Sive
Abissinorum Imperii
Descriptio"
In *Theatrum Orbis Terrarum*
(Antwerp: Christopher
Plantin, 1584)
NYPL, Rare Books Division

Prester John's kingdom haunted the Western imagination
until the sixteenth century and
even beyond. Located sometimes in India, sometimes in

West Africa (as the cartogra-
pher Ortelius does here, by
placing it in Abyssinia), this
Christian kingdom surrounded
by pagan lands was conceived
as a bastion against the Infidel
and was sought by the Crusaders; others perceived it as
a second Garden of Eden. The
entire genealogy of Prester
John's kingdom, beginning
with King David, is provided
in the cartouche in the upper
left-hand corner of the map.

It is a veritable antechamber of paradise and a typo-logical prefiguration of another kingdom to come, that of the priest-king par excellence, who will put an end to the turbulence of evil by restoring eternal stability. Far from a willful mystification, the *Letter of Prester John*, whoever the author might be, wishes to be a document that is both a moralizing model for the princes of this world and a message of hope.

Quests

Against the backdrop of a nostalgia for origins, for the lost paradise, the Christian Middle Ages developed a whole literature of the quest: voyages in search of places where a new life could be found, the promised city, the celestial Jerusalem. These peregrinations functioned, too, as metaphors for an earthly life wandering in exile, where hope becomes the obverse of nostalgia.

Jerusalem, the Promised Land

First among these places, because it was formerly the theater of the Passion and Resurrection, was Jerusalem.[70] For a long time, the Christian tradition had appropriated Judaic speculations about Jerusalem, considered the earth's navel. But what had been a pure spiritual exercise became a reality after the twelfth century – a time when the pres-ence of the city became more tangible. In a desire to make the visible correspond with the invisible, Jerusalem took its place at the astronomical and geometrical center of the *orbis terræ*. Invested with a sacred power, the little city in Judea dilated to the dimensions of the whole cosmos. In a sermon written in honor of the exaltation of the Cross, Peter the Venerable (ca. 1092–1156), Abbot of Cluny, insisted on this identity, presented as a revelation, between the mystical center and the geographical center of the world:

Certainly the All Powerful author of salvation, to realize his work could have chosen the outer recesses, the extreme limit of Gaul, the torrid parts of the South or the frozen ones of the North, or any other immense place on this orb; but since the fruit of this salvation concerned all of humanity equally, and He had no intention of saving just one part of the world but the world as a whole, He preferred not to exercise the work of Redemption in a distant corner of the orb, but in the very middle. . . . This place, situated almost at the very middle of the orb, the Savior called "the heart of the world."[71]

At the same time, a city that had until then appeared only on the periphery of world maps became the point of convergence of the three parts of the earth, where everyone endeavored to identify the center. In the twelfth century, Saewulf, an English pilgrim, located, in front of the Church of the Holy Sepulchre not far from Calvary, "the place called 'Compas,' where Our Lord Jesus Christ with his own hand marked and measured the *centre of the world*."[72] It was there that Christ after his Resurrec-tion appeared for the first time to Mary Magdalene. For John of Würzburg (fl. ca. 1162), the place, now integrated into the new constructions erected by the Crusaders, also commemorated the site where Joseph of Arimathea washed and anointed Christ's body before wrapping it in the white shroud and burying it in the tomb dug in the rocks.[73]

It was in this mysterious interval between Christ's death and Resurrection, between the Old and New Law, corresponding to the space between the Temple, Calvary, and the Sepulchre, that the image of the city was developed. The "Temple of the Lord" was raised on the eastern extreme "in the lower part that overhung the valley of Josaphat," the octagonal building surmounted by a cupola sup-ported by "a dozen monolithic columns and eight in stone . . . arranged in a circle under the roof."[74] It was built around a hollow rock, in the most secret part of which was sealed the ark containing manna, Aaron's rod, the Tablets of the Law, and other sacred objects. The Temple thus figured as the point of crystallization of Old Testament memory, which it recapitulated. It held the history of Israel as well as the first theophanic manifestations of the Messiah, and it opened a new era that would culmi-nate in the perennial image of celestial Jerusalem.

A most venerable place, the Temple was never-theless obscured by the more immediate images of the sites of the Passion and Resurrection. Pilgrims were directed to the Anastasis built around the Sepulchre, the veritable heart of the city, to the point that going to Jerusalem amounted to "walking to the Sepulchre."[75] Not far away was the image of death and the Cross, a death that was affirmed as more triumphant than suffering, a glorious death in which the Cross was less an instrument of torture than a sign of victory over the abyss.[76]

For masses of pilgrims, to go to Jerusalem was first of all to search for the traces, the *vestigia*, that (despite the successive modifications of a city said to have been razed seven times since the Passion) still preserved the imprint of Christ's feet rising in the dust to the summit of the Mount of Olives, the *below and opposite*

**Heinrich Bünting
*Intinerarium sacræ Scrip-
turæ, das ist ein Reisebuch
über die gantze heilige
Schrifft, in zwey Bücher
gethellt . . . Auffs new
mit Fleiss übersehen und
gemehret mit einem Büchlin
"De monetis et mensuris"***
Helmstadt: chez
J. L. Siebenbürger, 1582
BNF, Réserve des Livres Rares

"So that the disposition of
the whole extent of land may
be more easily perceived, I
have placed as preface [to my
book] a universal cosmography in the form of a cloverleaf,
seal of the celebrated city
of Hanover, my sweet and
beloved homeland. The grain
or seed of this cloverleaf is
the site of the Church, Judea,
with the very holy city of
Jerusalem at its center.
The three leaves, extending
toward the Levant [rising],
the West [setting], and the
Middle [noon], represent the
three principal parts of the
world – to wit, Europe, Asia,
and Africa." Thus, Heinrich
Bünting, a Reformation pastor,
explained the two-page representation of the world that
appeared at the beginning of
his *Intinerarium sacræ Scrip-
turæ*. Composed in Latin and
German, this collection gathers
together from "sacred texts
of the Bible, all the routes
of the patriarchs, judges,
kings, prophets, princes, of
Christ himself and the apostles, who were all unhappy
pilgrims in this world."

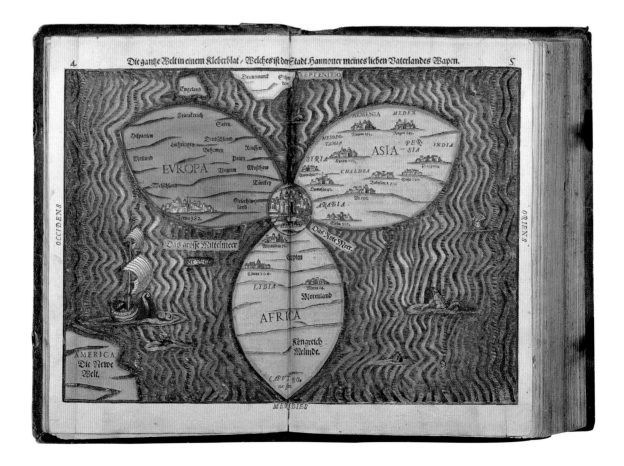

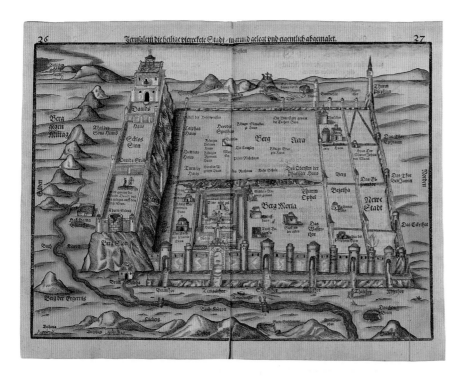

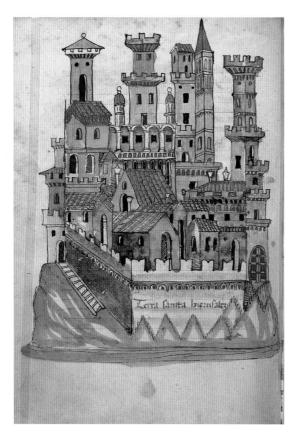

traces of blood in the praetorium, where Jesus was scourged, and, especially, great relics, most extraordinarily the Cross and the empty Sepulchre. For pilgrims it also meant, mimetic of the agony of the Passion and the glory of the Resurrection, walking in the footsteps of Christ, the apostles, and martyrs. Finally, it meant rising toward the Light by means of the *via ascetica*, entering into the Promised Land, which was described by Pope Urban II (in the words attributed to him by the twelfth-century chronicler Robertus Remensis) as Jerusalem, "the navel of the world, the land fruitful above all others, like another paradise of delights."[77] Saint Bernard of Clairvaux echoed this: "Hail promised land, source of milk and honey for your ancient inhabitants, now become the source of healing grace and vital sustenance for the whole earth!"[78] The Promised Land achieved, Jerusalem is the "eye" from which "grace, salvation, life" stream over all nations.

However, the pilgrimage to Jerusalem is only the secular version of another quest, the superior form of which was for Saint Bernard the monastic life: "The goal of monks is to search for not an earthly Jerusalem but the celestial one, and not by advancing with their feet but by progressing with their heart."[79] Beyond the actual city was hidden a much greater hope for paradise and the other heavenly Jerusalem.

Saint Brendan's Voyage:
Paradise Emperilled by the Sea
The *Navigatio*[80] dramatizes the story of Saint Brendan and his companions. Born in County Kerry around 484, the historical Saint Brendan belongs, like Saint Columba, to a generation of Irish monks of the sixth century who were cultivated men, pioneers of an ascetic and missionary monasticism in Anglo-Saxon England and the Continent. The story, written sometime between the end of the eighth and the beginning of the tenth centuries, is presented from the start as a *peregrinatio*. It narrates a voyage over the ocean by Abbot Brendan and his fourteen (two times seven) monks – plus three more who join at the last moment and for whom a tragic destiny is foretold – in search of the *terra repromissionis sanctorum*, the earthly paradise, a combination of nostalgia and hope that is described at the beginning and end of the story.

The Fish Island

**Honorario Philopono
[Caspar Plautius,
Abbot of Setenstetten]**
***Nova Typis Transacta
Navigatio***
N.p., 1621
NYPL, Rare Books Division

Of Irish origin, the legend of
the voyage of Saint Brendan
has been called a Christian
Aeneid, mixing pagan and
Christian, Celtic, and Classical
elements. It tells of an Irish
abbot who journeys with fourteen brother monks for seven
years among the magical
islands near Ireland in a quest
for the Promised Land of the
Saints. Divine guidance leads
them to wondrous islands,
including one populated by

sheep, one replete with white
birds, a crystal pillar in the
sea, and an island with three
choirs. Each year they are led
back to the same place for
the celebration of Easter. Their
Easter vigil is always held
on the back of a great fish
named Jasconius (sometimes
referred to as a whale). At
the end of their seven-year
spiritual and nautical quest,
Brendan and his monks arrive
at a fog-encircled island of
light and fruit and precious
stones, the Promised Land of
the Saints. After forty days, a
young boy tells them to leave
and promises Brendan that
he will return to the island
paradise upon his death.

At the beginning of the text lies the paradise lost by Barrind, a hermit who, accompanied by Mernóc, his spiritual son, has discovered on the Western side of the world the Promised Land, in the form of an island guarded by an angel of the Lord and hidden behind a thick curtain of fog: a land flooded with constant light, blanketed with fruit trees and flowers, where the commonest pebble is a precious stone, where the erosion of time and bodily necessities are abolished. The island has remained as "it has been from the beginning of the world"; Barrind and Mernóc must leave it with regret, carrying with them only its fragrance, which permeates their clothing.

Instructed by this tale, Saint Brendan decides to set sail, and he discovers at the close of his long *peregrinatio* the island for which he has been searching seven years. The description of paradise regained ends a tale that began with paradise lost. The paradisiacal space that the Latin text presented as a garden of delights becomes, in the version by a twelfth-century Anglo-Norman cleric (who, it should be added, drew on a reading of the Apocalypse), a citadel, a fortified city, enclosed by walls that, were it not for sin, would have been merely protective but instead have become fearsome:

The monks set course directly for the entryway, but it is very difficult for them to cross because it is guarded by dragons that burn everywhere as if they were made of flames. Above the place where one enters, a sword is suspended, the hilt on high and the point below; the one who is not afraid of it is truly foolhardy.[81]

Only the angel of the Lord can hold back the dragons and the sword. Only the monks can penetrate the paradise of delight, where the vision of Eden and heavenly Jerusalem are mixed:

They see a land very fertile in beautiful woods and prairies. The splendid fields are constantly in flower and form a garden. . . . [T]here are no trees or plants that do not exude a marvelous fragrance. . . . [I]t is always summer and the weather is mild. . . . Rivers everywhere flow with milk. This abundance is everywhere: rose bushes exude honey, thanks to the dew that descends from heaven. There is no mountain that is not made of gold, no stone that is not worth a treasure. The sun does not stop shining with all its might, no wind or gust shakes the smallest lock of hair, no cloud in the sky masks the light of the sun. The inhabitant will suffer from no misfortune, he will know no storm, he will be sheltered from heat, cold, affliction, hunger, thirst, privation.[82]

As they prepare to leave, Saint Brendan and his companions load their ship with fruits and precious stones as souvenirs and for consolation, armed with the promise that another *peregrinatio* will bring them back, while they await the Judgment.

Between these two terms in paradise unfolds an initiatory voyage of seven years, during which the small crew, sailing on a fragile craft, is exposed to the perils of land, sea, and hell. Their wandering from island to island is less linear than circular, making them return on fixed dates to the same places. Thus they celebrate Easter night each year on Jasconius, the fish island (this is one of the most popular episodes of the *Navigatio*). In this Easter period, commemorating Jonah's stay in the belly of the whale and that of the three children in the furnace, and the descent of Christ into hell, Jasconius (a ring-shaped monster who tries in vain to bite his tail and whose name recalls the Celtic root *Iasc,* fish) is assimilated, by a sort of return to chaos, to the swaying of the world on its foundations that accompanied the Crucifixion, before Christ's definitive triumph over death in the Resurrection. This same fish-island, gigantic and monstrous, conquered by divine grace after seven years have passed, will lead them to the banks of the paradise of birds, breaking the circle of their peregrinations, signifying that the end of their adventure is at hand.

Punctuated by liturgical time, this initiatory voyage, a metaphor for progress in monastic and ascetic life, met with extraordinary success, not only in clerical circles but in the secular world of princes, townspeople, mariners, and cartographers. In the twelfth century, the island where Saint Brendan landed was described in the *Imago mundi* of Honorius Augustodunensis, alongside the *insula magna*, the great island mentioned by Plato:

There was in the ocean a certain island, agreeable and fertile among all others, unknown to men, discovered by chance, then sought without being able to be found, and finally called Lost: it was, they said, where Saint Brendan had come.[83]

It figured again in the thirteenth century on Ebstorf's map of the world, off Africa, opposite Mount Atlas – *insula perdita. Hanc invenit Sanctus Brandanus . . . a nullo hominum postea invenita.* The unattainable island, that which can never be possessed, became on Hereford's map, again in the thirteenth century, one of the Fortunate Islands – *Fortunate insule sex sunt. Insula sancti Brandani* – as it was on Sideri's nautical chart. Finally, on the map

[Pseudo-Callisthenes]
Das Buch der Geschicht des
Grossen Allexanders
Strasburg: von Marten Schotten,
1488
NYPL, Spencer Collection

The hero of this narrative is
one of the great figures of
Western culture, Alexander
the Great. Alexander's quest
brings him to the "spring
of immortality" (from which
he does not drink), the trees
of the Sun and the Moon,
which foretell his death by
poison, and the land of the
Apple-eaters. Translated from
Greek into Latin in the fourth
century, the *Alexander
Romance* was translated into
at least fifteen languages
during the Middle Ages. Much
of its popularity was due to
the fact that with each translation, the story was adapted
to a particular audience, with
large and small variations
on Alexander's adventures
and heroic exploits.

attributed to Christopher Columbus or his brother
Bartolomé, it is no longer a single island, but, in a
direct reference to the *Navigatio*, a series of islands
that one can see on the northern side, on the route
that leads to earthly paradise.[84]

The Alexander Romance *or*
Paradise at the End of the Road
Barely revealed to the gaze of the saints, paradise
obstinately evades the quests of heroes. In Pseudo-
Callisthenes' *Historia Alexandri magni* (the *Alexander
Romance*), written between 200–100 B.C.E. and
200–300 C.E., the conqueror makes several painful
attempts to find it. Reaching a region of shadows
while trying to find the country of the Blessed,
Alexander unwittingly comes upon the fountain
of Immortality:

We came to a place where there was a clear spring,
whose water flashed like lightning, and some other
streams besides. The air in this place was very fragrant
and less dark than before. I was hungry . . . [Andreas,
the cook] took a dried fish and waded into the clear water
of the spring to wash it. As soon as it was dipped in the
water, it came to life and leapt out of the cook's hands.[85]

Another time, having reached what he thinks are
the limits of the earth, "where the sky touched the
earth," Alexander tries with an ingenious mechan-
ic's help to rise into the air until "a flying creature
in the form of a man" stops him: "O Alexander,
you have not yet secured the whole earth, and are
you now exploring the heavens? Return to earth as
fast as possible, or you will become food for these
birds."[86]

Elsewhere, in the *Letter to Aristotle About India*,
after having seen "next to the ocean, in Ethiopia,
promontories reaching to the sky," "the Enesian
(Enesios) mountains," and "the cave of Dionysus
(Liber)," Alexander inquires about the possibility of
seeing some other thing "worthy of admiration and
history."[87] Then, on the advice of two old Indians,
he decides to consult the oracular trees of the sun
and moon:

. . . one of them said, "King, whoever you are, you will
see the two trees of the sun and the moon which speak
Indian and Greek. The male tree is the tree of the sun,
and the other, the feminine tree, is the tree of the moon.
From these you will be able to learn what good or evil
impends for you."[88]

The Trees of the Sun and Moon

Jean Wauquelin
Chroniques d'Alexandre
Bruges, 1448–49
BNF, Département des Manuscrits

Composed at the request of the Duke of Burgundy, Philippe le Bon, and sumptuously illuminated, *The Chronicles of Alexander* offers a representation of the celebrated scene of the king's meeting with the trees of the Sun and Moon during his fantastic Indian adventures. Endowed with the power to reveal the future, the trees announce the conqueror's coming death. While within the tale this scene reflects a sovereign will to dominate space and time, it also arises more generally from the flourishing literary genre of Oriental marvels, through the charms of which the West discovered a dream world.

After an exhausting march, Alexander and a few companions arrive at the sacred spot:

The grove was luxuriant, full of frankincense and opobalsam. Very much of this develops on the branches of these groves and the inhabitants of this area were accustomed to eat it. . . . They lie down and sleep without any pillows and blankets, using only the hides of animals. Clothed with these, they live the same way for almost three hundred years.[89]

In this paradise, at the crossroads of the Golden Age and the Garden of Eden, Alexander is confronted with his destiny. Asked three times (at sunset, moonrise, and sunrise), the trees can tell him only of his coming death – which even his possession of the universe cannot spare him. He can only return to Babylon and continue to the end of the road.

According to another story inserted into the *Faits des Romains*, two of Alexander's companions are sent up the Nile in search of paradise. They reach "a small manor beautifully decorated and enclosed by a high wall and possessing a beautiful orchard." On the other river stands a mountain so high that it seems to touch the sky. An old man with a white beard tells them there is a rich orchard nobody may enter. "You are not wise to want to inquire into the secrets of the Lord of the world."[90] Obliged to go back, they carry away with them, as enigmatic as the enclosed garden, a stone in the form of an eye. As in the consultation with the trees of the sun and moon, Alexander is trapped by his condition as a mortal who is forbidden entry into paradise – where reside Enoch and Elijah, the only two people who did not know death. The story ends with the announcement of the Redemption and the end of time.

The Pilgrimage of Human Life

All the texts that recount voyages back to paradise – whether novelistic, dream-like, or metaphoric – end in failure in some way. Paradise, even for the best, is merely glimpsed. Nothing can totally dissipate the fog or shadows that surround it, nor pierce the secrets of space and time. The passage through death is the condition of access to the world beyond, where reconciliation is promised to the just; in this example, Godefridus of Sancto Victore's soul bids farewell to his body:

You who are my flesh, you were born with me, you developed with me. You were the companion of my exile while waiting to share heaven with me. We have long lived and worked together. We have been together for the best and the worst. We would have wanted to go together to the Lord but we cannot. Our union weighs us down. I sometimes blame you for being dark, earthly, and made of dust. You find me hard when I make you fast and keep vigil. Let us break an association that is onerous for us both. I will go first to the Lord. But I promise you that in time I will come back to you and take you with me. Then you will be luminous, strong, and splendid. You will find me peaceful and kind.[91]

This recurrent theme of life's voyage is developed in an allegorical fashion after the fourteenth century in a particular literary genre. It is no longer, as previously, a case of relating an initiatory or novelistic voyage, but rather one of describing in the first person a voyage in which the author is directly implicated and during which he must make choices in his life that involve his salvation. Begun in the impetuousness of youth, the peregrination culminates in the arrival of sickness and old age, the heralds of death.[92]

One of the first stories in this genre is *The Pilgrimage of Human Life* by Guillaume de Deguileville, first published in the 1330s. Everything begins with a dream that invites the author to undertake the pilgrimage to Jerusalem.[93] The dreamer starts his walk dressed in the pilgrim's habit and attributes given him by Grace Dieu: the scrip "made of green silk," which hung "from a green sash," and the staff "made of the wood of Sethin," emblem of hope, topped by a "pommel with a round mirror"[94] that allows the far-off holy city to be seen. The pilgrimage begins but is laden with traps: the seven deadly sins, temptations, heresies, and the seductions of pleasure. Twice the pilgrim is in grave danger, saved finally by Grace Dieu, who leads him onto the ship called Religion:

At this point, I saw a wonderful great ship floating on the sea, very near the shore, ready to go across the sea. . . . [Grace Dieu said:] "If you want to go to Jerusalem quickly, you must enter and lodge in one of the castles there, either Cluny or Citeaux. . . . They are all defensible and strong places for keeping both soul and body."[95]

At the end of his voyage, after many travels, the pilgrim perceives the end of time. But the dreamer must awaken. *The Pilgrimage of Life* is thus followed by *The Pilgrimage of the Soul* once the gates of death are crossed. Guided by an angel, he follows another path, this time toward celestial Jerusalem, the visible translation of an ineffable desire; it alone

can satisfy the quest and put an end to agitation
and traveling. It is the same motif of the ultimate
anabasis, or voyage into the interior, already found
in Boethius's *Consolation of Philosophy*,[96] where the
Platonic figure of the soul's voyage is crossed with
the Christian theme of ascension toward God.

Apocalypse and Millenarianism

The quest literature anticipates the geography of
utopias, a matter of space. The eschatological and
millenarian themes announce another motif, the
coming of utopia in historical time. With the development of philosophies of history in the nineteenth
century, many writers posited that the Golden Age
was not to be located at the origins, but at the end,
as if one had to invert the sense of time in Greek
myth. In fact, as we have seen, Hesiod's time is a
cyclical time. The idea of a great cycle, announcing
the return of the golden race, is taken up by Plato
in the *Statesman*[97] and the *Timaeus*[98] in the form of
the great cosmic revolution, a turning of time upon
itself produced each time the stars take up exactly
their original position. Cyclical time in the created
world is "the mobile image of eternity." The theory
of the "Great Year," probably marked by Pythagorean influences, became widespread, not only by
means of Greek thought, but also in Rome, particularly around the first century B.C.E. We find it in
Seneca and Lucan, and Cicero develops it in *The
Dream of Scipio* (in Book VI of his *Republic*), which

was influential in the Middle Ages thanks to
Macrobius's *Commentary*.[99] For a long time it
would feed astrological speculations – right up
to recent New Age developments. Among many
other Latin writers, the return of the Golden
Age can be produced not by the completion
of a cosmic cycle, but rather by the intervention
of sage legislators or the advent of a providential
emperor. Greco-Roman antiquity above all
conceived of time in a circular form, subject to
a cycle of rebirths and declines.

   To this model, the Church, triumphant beginning in the fourth century, opposed a linear time:[100]
only at the end will the doors "of a new heaven and
a new earth" open. The Church's official version
was simple: the world has only one time and it will
end with the return of Christ, and the end of time
will mark the last stage of a history that has been
punctuated since Creation by the Fall and by Salvation. This doctrine was founded on a solid biblical
tradition drawing on Hosea, Zechariah, Isaiah,
Ezekiel, and Daniel, which can be traced forward to
the New Testament in the Gospel of Saint Matthew
and the second Epistle of Paul to the Thessalonians,
and which is completed by apocryphal writings
ascribed to Esdras, Enoch, Peter, and Paul. To
these internal influences may be added Sibylline
writings[101] inherited from classical antiquity, often
reworked by Jewish or Christian writers. As for
the end of time, the major text is the Revelation of
Saint John, which prophesies first, in Chapter 20,
an initial resurrection of the just for a happy reign

The Anabasis of the Soul

Boethius
De Consolatione Philosophae
France, 1450
NYPL, Spencer Collection

"Now since through my earlier instruction you glimpsed the shape of true blessedness, and further recognized where it lies, once I have run through all of the preliminaries which I think are necessary, I shall show you the way which will bring you back home. I shall also equip your mind with wings to enable it to soar upward. In this way you can shrug off your anxiety, and under my guidance, along my path, and in my conveyance you can return safely to your native land."

Widely read during the Middle Ages, *The Consolation of Philosophy* was written in 523–524 and represents Boethius's reflections on the reconciliation of divine providence and human freedom. It is unusual in that it makes no reference to Christian faith or dogma. It was Boethius who made the goddess Fortuna and her turning wheel, which symbolizes the mutability and transience of success, one of the key images of medieval culture. In this rendition, each of the four figures on the wheel bears a scroll with a descriptive word: "Regnabo" (I shall reign); "Regno" (I reign); "Regnavi" (I have reigned); and "Sum sine regno" (I am without a kingdom).

This manuscript was once owned by Cardinal Charles de Bourbon, Archbishop of Rouen (the uncle of Henry IV of France).

Apocalypse

Apocalypses
[England, ca. 1280]
NYPL, Spencer Collection

"Then I saw an angel coming down from heaven, holding in his hand the key of the bottomless pit and a great chain. And he seized the dragon, that ancient serpent, who is the Devil and Satan, and bound him for a thousand years, and threw him into the pit, and shut it and sealed it over him, that he should deceive the nations no more, till the thousand years were ended. After that he must be loosed for a little while." – Revelation 20: 1–3

This thirteenth-century manuscript of English origin contains the Book of Revelation, also known by its Greek name, Apocalypse, which means "revelation." The illustration shows the angel locking up the beast for a thousand years, ushering in a millennium of peace and joy.

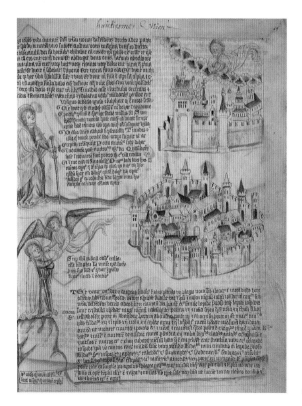

Apocalypsis
[Germany?, early 15th century]
NYPL, Manuscripts and Archives Division

"And in the Spirit he carried me away to a great, high mountain, and showed me the holy city Jerusalem coming down out of heaven from God, having the glory of God, its radiance like a most rare jewel, like a jasper, clear as crystal. It had a great, high wall, with twelve gates, and at the gates twelve angels, and on the gates the names of the twelve tribes of the sons of Israel were inscribed. . . ." – Revelation 21: 10–12

This manuscript contains the Apocalypse, or the Book of Revelation. Shown here is the descent of New Jerusalem, symbolizing the start of a new millennium of happiness. Made in Germany in the early fifteenth century, this manuscript is identified by its bookplates as having been a part of the library at the Cistercian Abbey of Cîteaux in France and later in the collection of James Lenox, one of the founders of The New York Public Library and an avid collector of early Bibles.

of a thousand years on earth, and then, in Chapter 21, the end of time and the advent of celestial Jerusalem.

A Thousand Years of Happiness

Then I saw an angel coming down from heaven, holding in his hand the key of the bottomless pit and a great chain. And he seized the dragon, that ancient serpent, who is the Devil and Satan, and bound him for a thousand years. . . . Then I saw thrones, and seated on them were those to whom judgment was committed. Also I saw the souls of those who had been beheaded for their testimony to Jesus and for the word of God, and who had not worshiped the beast or its image. . . . They came to life, and reigned with Christ a thousand years.

—REVELATION 20: 1–4

For a long time, these thousand years were understood by the Church in a realist manner as the immanence of the end of time, as the promise of an earthly, paradisiacal kingdom in which the returned Christ's authority would chase away evil and recompense the just:

. . . it behoves the righteous first to receive the promise of the inheritance which God promised to the fathers, and to reign in it, when they rise again to behold God in this creation which is renovated, and that the judgment should take place afterwards. For it is just that in that very creation in which they toiled or were afflicted, being proved in every way by suffering, they should receive the reward of their suffering; and that in the creation in which they were slain because of their love to God, in that they should be revived again; and that in the creation in which they endured servitude, in that they should reign. . . . It is fitting, therefore, that the creation itself, being restored to its primeval condition, should without restraint be under the dominion of the righteous.[102]

One finds an analogous reading in Tertullian:

But we do confess that a kingdom is promised to us upon the earth, although before heaven, only in another state of existence; inasmuch as it will be after the resurrection for a thousand years in the divinely-built city of Jerusalem, "let down from heaven" (Revelation 21:2). . . . We say that this city has been provided by God for receiving the saints on their resurrection, and refreshing them with the abundance of all really spiritual blessings, as a recompense for those which in the world we have either despised or lost; since it is both just and God-worthy that His servants should have their joy in the place where they have also suffered affliction for His name's sake.[103]

For Lactantius, the incarnation of Christ has already inaugurated the return of the Golden Age, marked by the fraternal charity that reigns in the Church and corroborated by the peace of Constantine; it announces the millennium, an era of peace when the just will rediscover earthly paradise,[104] before the devil is unleashed once more, but then his ruin is consummated when God finally transforms his elect into angels. The return to the Golden Age and to earthly paradise is thus a sort of obligatory passage before the final resurrection, a moment that will not be long in coming because the dénouement is near:

. . . since He rested on the seventh day from His completed labors and blessed that day, so it is necessary that, at the end of the six thousandth year, all evil will be abolished from the earth, and that justice reign for a thousand years, and that there be tranquility and rest from the labors which the world is now enduring for so long.[105]

For the next two hundred years at most, this world will go through torment. Wars will annihilate Roman power, the sword will strike the whole universe. Then will come natural plagues, the corruption of the air and waters, the death of all animals, the appearance of comets, a darkening of the sun and moon, the fall of stars, the leveling of mountains, as well as famine and epidemics,[106] all before the liberator arrives, "brilliant with light." Idols will then be burned, the earth will open, and God will judge the world. Then will begin God's Sabbath and the millenarian reign of justice, the construction of the celestial city, in which "the stars shall be more brilliant, and the brightness of the sun increased," and a new Golden Age, when rivers of milk and honey will flow, when the wolves will lie down with the lambs.[107]

This vision prevailed in the early Church, but Saint Jerome and Saint Augustine substituted a purely symbolic interpretation. They are decided adversaries of literal millenarianism. The Jerusalem announced by Zechariah is not an earthly reign to come, but the Church itself. One should not dream of a gleaming Jerusalem covered with gold and precious stones. The goods promised are celestial goods, and everything should be understood on a spiritual plane. While waiting for the millennium, Jerome and Augustine see the remains of paganism as traces of the Golden Age of Saturn, or even as the dangerous flavor of Judaism. They especially fear that, lulled by these fables,

Christians will forget that the true food and drink are of a spiritual order, that the capital event, the foundation of the Church, is already accomplished, and that this instituted Church is henceforth the kingdom of Christ on earth. The very name of the Apocalypse, meaning Revelation, indicates its mystical content. The ascetic and the exegete agree on this.

While the most authoritative voices urged patience, explained the delays, and insisted on the impossibility of fixing the date and hour, they had a hard time balancing underlying desires and worries, which were sometimes insistent and expressed on several levels, whether through popular movements, echoed more or less objectively in narrative texts, or through prophetic texts, often written in relation to contemporary events, and finally through scholarly speculations on what the Book of Revelation was about. Because the text retained its ambiguity, official doctrine and its symbolism were never in agreement.

Since the eighth century, some brief, precise works on the modalities of the last days had circulated in the West. One was attributed to Bishop Methodius of Patara, but was in fact just the Latin version of a Syriac text from the end of the seventh century: the *Apokalypsis* offered a scenario that would have a lasting influence. Arab invasions, threats weighing on the Eastern empire, were only the prelude to still greater catastrophes. Soon the gates of the North would open and the peoples of Gog and Magog, held back since Alexander, would swarm over the West. Against them would rise up the emperor of the last days, who would leave his crown at Golgotha:

. . . the Lord will send one of the princes of his host and strike them down in a moment. After this the king of the Romans will go down and live in Jerusalem. . . . [T]he king of the Romans will ascend Golgotha upon which the wood of the Holy Cross is fixed, in the place where the Lord underwent death for us. The king will take the crown from his head and place it on the cross and stretching out his hands to heaven will hand over the kingdom of the Christians to God the Father.[108]

This figure of the emperor of the last days opens the way to pseudo-prophecies of a political kind, a well-known literary genre already used by Virgil, lists of which were circulating in the oracles of the Tiburtine Sibyl.

Joachim of Fiore and the
Advent of the Reign of the Spirit
One of the most astonishing of these exegetes, whose thought goes beyond speculation about signs and dates, is the Calabrian monk Joachim of Fiore (ca. 1135–1202). A Cistercian who entered the faith around 1159, and became abbot of the Corazzo Monastery in 1177, he was fascinated by hermitism, to the point of spending a year (1188–89) on the high arid plateau of Calabria. Joachim was an exegete of Holy Scripture. In 1198, after the election of Pope Innocent III, he told Adam of Perseigne, who had asked him about his terrible prophecies:

God, who once gave prophets the spirit of prophecy, gave me the gift of the spirit of discernment, to understand clearly, in the spirit of God, all the mysteries of Holy Scripture, as the holy prophets understood them, they who once published Scripture by the spirit of God.[109]

God had given him the gift of discernment, *intelligentia*, allowing him, thanks to assiduous reading of the text, to understand the meaning of contemporary events and thus to apprehend the future:

[The prophets too] saw only partially and prophesied only partially; and we also, until now, saw only partially, that is to say, as an enigma as if through a mirror (1 Cor. 13: 9–12). . . . In fact it is one thing to see a great number of things, and another to see the whole. One thing, to see the city while still walking toward it; another thing to arrive before its gate; another thing, to go inside. We who find ourselves in front of the gate are in a position o say many things that formerly remained hidden, all or in part. But we are not like those who will be inside and see face to face.[110]

His conception of history brought him to the threshold of the radical renewal that marked the advent of the Age of the Spirit; Joachim undertook a rigorous, calculated, and visual exegesis:

That the pleasures of the world have reached their end, that tribulations are imminent, that the reign of heaven is at hand, I try to prove even in a contemplative and incomplete form, by testimony that is both certain and necessary.[111]

The cornerstone of Joachim's system, developed in particular in the *Expositio in Apocalypsim*, is a division of historic time into three ages or states:

The Common Lineage

**Conradus Schlapperitzi
[Bible History]**
Germany, [1445]
NYPL, Manuscripts and Archives
Division

This image, showing Adam tilling the soil and Eve spinning
wool, illustrates a popular saying of the fourteenth century:
"When Adam delved and Eve
span, Who was then the gentleman?" The adage appears
in German at the top left of
the page, and a third line has
been added: "In whom from
God such honor ran." The
widely known folk saying,

suggesting that all people are
equal since all share a common lineage, beginning with
Adam and Eve, gained popularity when the priest John
Ball included it in a passionate
sermon in 1381. Ball reportedly shouted out the verse to
incite the wrath of the English
peasantry and stir them to
revolt against landowners.
Throughout the centuries, the
rhyme has been repeated by
many utopian thinkers, including especially William Morris,
as an appeal for class and gender equality.

There are three states of the world . . . that the mysteries
of Holy Scripture attest to us: during the first we were
under the law; during the second we were under grace;
during the third, which we are expecting very soon,
we will enjoy a more perfect grace. . . . More precisely,
science was characteristic of the first state; the regime
of wisdom of the second; the plenitude of intelligence
of the third. The first was placed under the auspices of
servile dependence; the second under filial dependence;
the third under liberty. The whip for the first; action for
the second; contemplation for the third. Successively . . .
the state of slaves, the state of free men, the state of
friends. Winter, the start of spring, summer. Nettles,
roses, lilies. Herbs, ears, wheat. Water, wine, oil. . . . In
effect, the first state is related to the Father, the author
of all . . . the second to the Son, willing to assume our
shape in which he could fast and suffer to reform the status of the first man who had fallen by eating the fruit; the
third to the Holy Spirit, of which the apostle says "where
the spirit of the Lord is, there is freedom" (2 Cor 3: 17).[112]

The teaching of Joachim is a jumble of schemas[113]
supposed to invite contemplation and to serve as a

step toward interior perception, toward insight
using the eyes of both the body and the soul.
The way in which the images are incorporated into
the principal texts indicates that these figures
must have been drawn by Joachim himself to teach
his disciples or readers, in order, as he says in the
Expositio, to avoid any controversy. The images are
a dynamic synthesis of his teaching, a visual translation of this anxious wait for the advent of the
third state of the world, the grand revolution of
the Spirit, the eternal Pentecost:

As for the third state, it will open around the end of our
current century, not under the veil of the letter, but in
the full liberty of the Spirit, when the false gospel of the
son of perdition and his prophets has been revoked and
destroyed, then those who will give instruction in justice
to many people will appear, similar in splendor to the
firmament, and they will shine like stars for all eternity.[114]

Joachim of Fiore died in 1202, but his *Everlasting
Gospel*, after 1254 preceded by an introduction
by Gerard of Borgo San Donnino, guaranteed the

propagation of his theses, in particular as relayed by Franciscan spiritual movements that considered themselves the foremost apostles of the Age of the Spirit, founders of a "spiritual church." Stengthened at the end of the thirteenth century by the activity of three strong personalities, Pierre Jean Olivi (1248–1298), Angelus Clarenus (1247–1337), and Ubertino da Casale (1259–1328), the movement would spread in Tuscany and in the south of France. Some, like Gerard Segarelli, who was burnt in 1300, or Fra Dolcino, executed in 1307, thought they were invested with the duty to purify the Church by any means, so as to hasten the advent of the Holy Spirit, awakening millenarian expectations that were always more or less latent.[115]

This obsession with the end of time, combined with an evangelical current that preached asceticism and purification, might in part explain "panic movements" among the poorest and most deprived in the direction of Jerusalem, where the judgment was to take place, a prelude to the advent of celestial Jerusalem, such as the "Children's" or "Shepherds" Crusades[116] in 1212, 1251, and 1320. But this obsession could also engender bloody and devastating movements like the pogroms that accompanied the first crusades or the ravages perpetrated by the troops of Peter the Hermit in the Holy Land.

With the deadlines passed, military and political realities quickly took over from eschatological hopes and life resumed its course. However, the unassuaged and deeply rooted desire for a new reign might be reborn at any moment, since "he will wipe away every tear from their eyes, and death shall be no more, neither shall there be mourning nor crying nor pain any more, for the former things have passed away" (Revelation 21: 4).

Tabor, or Millenarianism in Action
In 1381 in England, at a time when John Wycliffe[117] in Oxford was distinguishing forcefully between the official Church, hierarchical and corrupt, and the invisible Church (no less real) of the *congregatio prædestinorum*, meaning the reunion of souls destined by the Lord for paradise, there burst out the peasant revolt known as Tyler's Insurrection. Even if some of its leaders like John Ball called themselves disciples of Wycliffe, whose doctrine had been spread since 1380 by the "poor priests," the Lollards, their dream owed less to the doctrine professed by the great theologian than to the desired return to paradise:

When Adam delved and Eve span,
Who was then the gentleman?[118]

The phrase well expresses hostility to the dominant classes and to Church dignitaries, as well as the aspiration to another model of society. Even more than in England, though, it was in Bohemia that a questioning of the Roman clergy, a challenge to monks and prelates, and an aspiration to establish the celestial Jerusalem here and now would crystallize.

Since the middle of the fourteenth century, a vigorous reformation movement[119] had been arising around Jan Milíc of Kromeríze and Matej of Janova (died 1394). Both saw the Great Western Schism that was then tearing the Church apart as the activity of the Anti-Christ, the antithesis of the *corpus mysticum*, the invisible but true Church, the communion of saints that encouraged the faithful to read the Bible and come to the communion table as often as possible. But it was left to Jan Hus (1369–1415) to spread these ideas by the fiery language of his preaching. His condemnation and death in Constance in 1415 would ignite, at the very core of the revolt in Bohemia, one of the most important millenarian movements in size and duration.

In 1419, after four years of popular struggle by the nationalist movement, King Wenceslas undertook to restore traditional Catholicism. The radical wing of the Hussite movement felt excluded and organized gatherings on hilltops in southern Bohemia; priests continued to distribute communion, in both bread and wine, and to preach against the abuses of the Church. Soon, assemblies modeled on the primitive Evangelical community were established, laying the foundations for a totally new life, of fraternity, peace, and sharing. The most celebrated was that of Mount Tabor – a hill near the chateau of Bechyne on the Luznice River – named after the mountain where Christ appeared to his disciples after his death (Matthew 28: 16), where he announced his second coming (Mark 13), and where his return was awaited. Soon rejected by moderate Hussites, particularly in the capital, the persecuted Taborites began to preach the advent of the end of time, encouraging the faithful to find refuge in the five cities that, according to Isaiah (19: 18), would alone be spared the wrath of God:

During this time certain Taborite priests were preaching to the people a new coming of Christ, in which all evil men and enemies of the Truth would perish and be exterminated, while the good would be preserved in five cities. . . . These are the names of the five: Plzeň, which they called the city of the sun, Zatec, Louny, Slaný, and Klatovy. . . . [M]any simple folk, accepting these frivolous doctrines as true, and having zeal, as the Apostle says, but not acting through knowledge, sold their property, taking even a low price, and flocked to these priests from various parts of the Kingdom of Bohemia and the Margravate of Moravia, with their wives and children, and they threw their money at the feet of the priests.[120]

In the five towns, safe from God's wrath, the elect lived in the expectation of the end of time, announced between February 10 and 14, 1420, in resistance to and the struggle against the Anti-Christ:

We do not think that it is just a fable, but the truth, that a century of happiness will be established, in which people will know no evil, no suffering, but rather an ineffable joy.[121]

Inspired by the preachings of Scripture, many thought that Christ was already among them, having entered "like a thief in the night," and that he had come back to "separate the good grain from the chaff," to "chase the thieves and demons from the house of the Lord." They were the arm of God launched into the world to cry vengeance. Liberated from all human laws, they could plunge their swords into the bodies of their enemies, and "wash their hands in their victims' blood" as a punishment for sin, as the Spirit willed. After this extermination, the old "century" would yield to another one, radically different and founded on a new relation between God and humankind. In this renewed kingdom, Christ descending in glory would reign over the saints who "will shine like so many suns in the kingdom of their Father, living radiant as the sun, wholly without stain." Full of the Spirit, purged of sin forever, the elect would be able to taste a state of innocence close to that of the angels or Adam before the Fall. The union of the faithful to the Father would be such that the mediation of the Church could disappear. With the law of the Lord henceforth inscribed in their hearts, books would become useless:

Those who remain alive in that time will be brought to a state of innocence, like Adam and Enoch and Elijah in paradise, and no one will suffer hunger or thirst or have any physical pain or any sorrow. . . . In that time there will be no kingship or dominion on the earth, nor any subjection. All rents and dues will cease. No one will compel another to do anything, but all will be equal brothers and sisters.[122]

Already in Plzeň, Pilsek, and elsewhere, all property was held in common, in great casks into which new arrivals – peasants and craftsmen – poured the sums produced by the sale of their goods, each receiving according to his needs.

This increasingly narrow dream would linger until 1434 when it was definitively killed at Lipany with the defeat of the last partisans of an ascetic religion, living by the model of the primitive community Church under the leadership of Bishop Mikuláš of Pelhrimova, one of the last disciples of Jan Hus. But from the Shepherds Crusade through the apocalyptic Taborite movement, via the pantheism of the Brethren of the Free Spirit,[123] characteristic features recur. One always finds a charismatic leader, a prophet who designates roles. The Anti-Christ and his troops are identified with the rich, the powerful, the Jews, the clergy. A "day of wrath" with an effusion of purifying blood is foreseen, to be followed by the earthly reign of a good emperor, of a mystic chief, or of Christ himself, the millenarian prelude to the advent of celestial Jerusalem.

The Celestial Jerusalem

When a thousand years have gone by, with the world purified and judgment passed, then the Holy City will descend, "prepared as a bride adorned for her husband" (Revelation 21: 2).

She is the true bride of Christ:

"Behold, out of the land of Syria I will begin to call a new Jerusalem, and I will subdue Zion and it will be captured; and the barren one who has no children will be fruitful and will be called the daughter of my Father, but to me, my bride; for so has it pleased him who sent me."[124]

A protective city with high walls, as paradise once was, it is the Mother who "brings you forth joyously, joyous and free, and puts you into the world free of the ties of sin."[125]

Tradition assures us that the heavenly Jerusalem that is above is built up of holy gems and we know that the twelve gates of the heavenly city, which signify the wonderful beauty of the apostolic teaching, are compared to precious jewels.[126]

Metonymy for the cosmos, it is the city of perfect proportions, measured by the angel with a golden measuring rod (Revelation 21: 15). Facing the East, flooded with its own light, "the city has no need of sun or moon to shine upon it, for the glory of God is its light, and its lamp is the Lamb" (Revelation 21: 23).

Aristotle
Ethica Nicomachea,
Politica, Economica
Venice, 1393
Columbia University, Rare Book
and Manuscript Library

This portrait of Aristotle
appears in a manuscript containing Latin translations of
three of Aristotle's works, The
Nicomachean Ethics, *Politics*,
and *Economics*. Signed and
dated by the copyist Johannes
de Francis, the volume also
contains Boethius's *De Consolatione Philosophiae*. Notes
and commentary from a
humanist scholar, Francesco
Barbaro, and his grandson,
Ermolco Barbaro, appear
throughout the volume. One
of the notes indicates that
Ermoleo Barbaro used this

manuscript as the basis for a
course of lectures on Aristotle
at the University of Padua in
1475–76.

These works rank with those
of Plato (who was Aristotle's
teacher) as among the most
important foundations of
later political utopian thinking.
Aristotle was particularly
concerned with the human
potential for improvement,
both moral and political.
In the *Nicomachean Ethics*,
Aristotle is concerned with
the development of virtue
as it leads to moral perfection
and a happy life, and in the
Politics, he examines political
systems, both real and imagined, in an effort to determine
the ideal political and social
arrangement.

It is the land of repose, the country of exiles:

Who will give us wings like the dove, and we shall fly
across all the kingdoms of the world, and we shall
penetrate the depths of the eastern sky? Who will then
conduct us to the city of the great king in order that what
we now read in these pages and see only as in a glass,
darkly, we may then look upon the face of God present
before us, and so rejoice?[127]

A Mother-Wife, round and yet square, spiritual and
yet abundantly represented, she is the desired city
to which all aspire, in the sweetness of the cloister
or in vengeful fury, the enigmatic city where dreams
exhaust themselves.

The Order of the City

Mythological motifs, biblical references to lost
paradise, and the millenarian tradition might be
considered retrospectively as the matrices of utopian thought. As such they are indispensable to the
understanding of utopias. However, utopia properly
speaking is clearly separate from this heritage –
and Thomas More's text in some sense represents
this separation – in that the appearance of the ideal
society no longer comes out of an eschatological
perspective, nor does it issue from a providential
event or an idealization of nature, but rather is

presented as a human construction, in which social
organization achieves the ideal through its own
means. In this sense, utopia is a theme of modernity.

We also gather why the first authors of utopias
– More, Campanella, and Bacon – explicitly refer,
in the context of humanism, to specifically political
thinking inherited from Greek and Roman antiquity, to texts in which a philosophy concerned with
politics devotes itself to the constitution and legislation of the city, chief among which are works by
Plato and Aristotle.

The Republic *of Plato*
The treatment of the "good city" in Plato's works,[128]
considered schematically, takes three forms: an
apparently "historical" story in the *Timaeus* and the
Critias, a detailed legislative and legal work in the
Laws, and a dialectic inquiry on justice and the art
of governing in the *Republic* and the *Statesman*.

At the wellspring of utopia, the *Republic* occupies the central place, since the dialogue itself has
some of the formal appearance of a utopia. Thus,
Socrates agrees that the foundation of the city,
as described in the dialogue, takes place "only in
discourse": it exists in the *logos*, not on earth; this
is so primarily in the sense that it is "ideal," that it
forms a "model." However, this sphere of existence
is that of neither fiction nor the imaginary, but of
the intelligible. In addition, this city is the *just* city;
more exactly, its construction by and through the

dialogue proceeds from a search for justice; it is in order to make justice apparent[129] that Socrates proposes to build a representation of the just city, as a readable modeling of justice in itself.

Under what conditions is a city just? To answer that, it is necessary "in discourse" to represent its birth: the true discourse on the city is a foundational discourse, a discourse that founds.

How is the city composed at its birth? Plato's answer is simple: it is composed of all kinds of men, different in nature; it is composed of differences. There is, originally and irreducibly, diversity in the city, which permits within itself the totality of this diversity, across the whole scale of values from the most noble to the most vile, from golden races to iron races. Here there is a kind of Platonic realism: for the city to be just, it is not necessary that each of its members be just; in more modern terms, in order for the general interest to triumph, it is not necessary that each have the general interest in view or take as his goal the good of all; as we shall see, it suffices that one party "safeguards" the common good.

So there *are* parties; one can go even further: there is a city because there is diversity in nature or in birth; the social exists only because tasks are diverse, split, and hence divided up, and because abilities, too, are diverse, split, and divided up. The idea of the city includes the principle that its members do different things; it is naturally advantageous for different men to perform different tasks; this is the raison d'être for their association, and this advantage is the city itself. It follows that the city demands that each do the task that belongs to him, that the city is just when each occupies the place that is his own, and that it is unjust as soon as some people change places with others. The misfortune of the city occurs when the carpenter wants to become a boilermaker, when each wants to try everything and become "a multiple of himself," and, more seriously still, when the hierarchy of classes is turned upside down. Each occupying his own place is the precondition for justice, because it is the condition in which natural diversity is gathered into unity, the condition requisite for the city to form a totality. The idea of the city, the just city and the one city, is really the same object, a multiplicity brought into unity.

Now for this unity to be safeguarded, a particular class must be constituted, that of the guardians, whose task is precisely to take upon itself the interest of the whole, a class of men, therefore, capable of renouncing their particular interests; to consti-

tute this class, one must resort both to the selection of the best natures and to education. All consequences follow from its members being at the service of the collectivity as a whole. From among them will emerge the perfect guardians, philosopher-kings[130] called to exercise power.

In the city, each is only a part of the whole. But for those who must act consciously as guardians of all, for those whose role that is, particular dispositions must be put into effect. Here the city is like a flock, as Plato says: the guardians are like dogs, guarantors of the flock under the shepherd's staff. In order for any rivalry or violence among the guardians to be impossible, so that with regard to the rest of the city the dogs do not become wolves, it is necessary that they possess nothing of their own, that they get rid of any private attachment: in this superior part of the city, property and family are abolished, each possesses only his own body. To say that the guardians act in the name of all means for Plato that their whole existence is an affair of state, which regulates mating, has recourse to abortions, organizes selection, sees to education. In the class that lifts itself above the rest – the class necessary for the social totality to be constituted – each person forgets about himself. This wrenching is nothing other than philosophy itself, a turning away from the attractions of the sensible world in order to contemplate the heaven of Ideas. Hence the ultimate condition of the just city: philosophers must exercise political power. This condition is paradoxical, if not an aporia: for this city to be realized in this world, it must be governed by those who turn away from it.

Plato's *Republic* is not strictly a utopia, in that it is not a case of constructing a city by the exercise of human domination over nature but, on the contrary, of submitting to a transcendent nature, which consigns the historicity of real cities to inevitable decline. On the other hand, this text will become a major reference for utopian thinking to come because it poses in the most radical terms the question of the constitution of the city as a coherent totality, as a single multiplicity. Above all, Plato's thought, along with Aristotle's,[131] mediated by Cicero's *Laws* and *Politics*, would furnish the bases for that of Saint Augustine, and through him for the whole political thought of the Middle Ages.

Saint Augustine and the Reign of the Two Cities
Saint Augustine erected the immense theoretical and theological edifice that constitutes *The City of God* at a time when the Roman Empire, become

Christian, was being undermined by internal division and menaced by invasion from outside. In a troubled political situation, what meaning could be given to the Christian community on earth with regard to the expectation of the celestial city, and how could that be combined with a Christian's belonging to society? These were the questions facing the Bishop of Hippo.

Nourished on Plato and Aristotle, Augustine postulated the social character of human nature. Made to live in the company of other men, men took peace as their goal:

For so great a good is peace that even where earthly and mortal affairs are in question no other word is heard with more pleasure, nothing else is desired with greater longing, and finally nothing better can be found.[132]

But what is peace?

The peace of the body, therefore, is an ordered proportionment of its components. . . . [D]omestic peace is an ordered agreement among those who dwell together concerning command and obedience; the peace of the heavenly city is a perfectly ordered and fully concordant fellowship in the enjoyment of God and in mutual enjoyment by union with God; the peace of all things is a tranquillity of order. Order is the classification of things equal and unequal that assigns to each its proper position.[133]

This harmony, wholly inspired by Plato, is the state that would have prevailed without sin:

This is the prescription of the order of nature, and thus has God created man. For, he says: "Let him have dominion over the fish of the sea, and over the birds that fly in the heavens, and over every creeping thing that creeps upon the earth." (Genesis 1: 26) For he did not wish a rational creature, made in his own image, to have dominion save over irrational creatures: not man over man, but man over the beasts. So it was that the first just men were established as shepherds of flocks, rather than as kings of men.[134]

But now, with the harmony broken, men dominate men, and the actual economy is governed by the anarchy of inferior appetites that put selfish interests above the common good. There is an evident violence in institutions like private property, slavery, and even government – all purely human creations made necessary by the inaptitude of men to live according to the commands of reason. In the pres-

ent state, dominated by death and sin, two cities co-exist: on the one hand the city of men, and on the other "the camp of the saints," the "well-loved city," which is just "the Church of Christ" spread across the whole world:

The two cities then were created by two kinds of love: the earthly city by a love of self carried even to the point of contempt for God, the heavenly city by a love of God carried even to the point of contempt for self.[135]

The two cities in the actual time of the "first advent" of Christ are inextricably mingled to the point that the celestial city, or at least that part of it that is in exile in the world, does not shrink from obeying the earthly city. But the earthly peace that it does respect, it brings back to the peace of heaven:

. . . it must be deemed and called the only peace, at least of a rational creature, being, as it is, the best ordered and most harmonious fellowship in the enjoyment of God and of one another in God. And when we arrive thither, there shall be no mortal life, but a life indeed; no animal body to burden the soul with its corruption, but a spiritual body that wants nothing and is subdued in every part to the will. This peace the heavenly city during its pilgrimage enjoys by faith, and by this faith it lives justly when it makes the attainment of that peace the goal of every good action in which it engages for the service of God and one's neighbour; for the life of a city is certainly a social life.[136]

To the contradictions between political action and philosophical practice, between the real city and the ideal city, raised by the classical tradition, Saint Augustine responds with the idea of a double membership, a double citizenship that means each member of the City of God orders his temporal life within the framework of the earthly city, while finding in the Church community the expectation of the city to come.

Nourished by classical tradition and enriched by theological reflection, as well as by the meditations of Pseudo-Dionysius the Areopagite[137] – who was held to be an Athenian disciple of Saint Paul's, the evangelist of the Gauls, as well as the founder of a celebrated abbey – on the *Celestial Hierarchies*, Saint Augustine's thought bequeathed to medieval philosophers and theologians the bases of a doctrine founded on order and hierarchy, upon which Christian princes would draw in abundance.

Good Government

It was on the basis of Augustinian formulations that thinking about the relations between temporal and spiritual power was organized, as theorized about in a letter sent in 494 by Pope Gelasius I to Anastasius, Emperor of the East. The emperor was subject to the bishops for divine affairs, *res divinæ*, in particular for his own salvation, but on the other hand, his own imperial power, his *potestas*, was in no way subject to their *auctoritas*. Together, *auctoritas pontificum* and *regalis potestas* represented the "duality divinely established to govern the world side by side."[138] This duality would find its political metaphor in the image of two swords taken from Luke 22: 38 – "Look, Lord, here are two swords" – but the two swords would soon become rivals due to the hegemonic drives of their respective wielders, with each claiming to be head of the body that according to theologians constitutes the Church.

In the twelfth century, Hugh of Saint-Victor as holder of pontifical supremacy asserted:

That there are two lives [the one earthly, the other heavenly] and, according to the two lives, two peoples and in the two peoples two powers . . . one superior to the other. . . . Now the more worthy the spiritual life is than the earthly and the spirit than the body, so much does the spiritual power precede the earthly or the secular in honor and in dignity.[139]

Before triumphing in 1302 in the papal bull *Unam sanctam* of Pope Boniface VIII, this theory became more precise and refined; it was asserted by means of two types of works: legal texts like the *Decretum* by Gratian and theoretical texts like *De ecclesiastica potestate* by Giles of Rome. Unlike Roman law, which firmly leaned on the Justinian code, canon law was merely a miscellaneous assemblage of precepts taken from the Old and New Testaments, pontifical decrees, conciliars, and more or less apocryphal documents. It was a Benedictine monk, Gratian,[140] who produced around 1140 the best and most complete summation of canon law, in *Concordantiæ discordantium canonum*, or the *Decretum*, which along with Peter Lombard's *Sententiarum Libri IV*, written slightly later, would long endure as the standard reference as well as the point of departure for a school of exceptionally brilliant and productive canonists up until the 1350s, furnishing the papacy with a solid basis in which to ground its political reflections.

For its part, royal power did not remain at a standstill. The fifty-year standoff between the papacy and the Holy Roman Empire known as the "Investiture Controversy" gave rise to a whole polemical literature, and the development of national monarchies (particularly the French monarchy) between the twelfth and fifteenth centuries encouraged princes to seek solid foundations on which to rest their pretension to the best possible government.

In the twelfth century, John of Salisbury supplied what is often considered the first political treatise in the classic sense. A former pupil of the most famous teachers of his era, including Peter Abelard, Thierry of Chartres, William of Conches, and Robert of Melun, he was secretary to Thomas à Becket, the Archbishop of Canterbury, and was entrusted with numerous missions to Rome. Exiled to France from 1163 to 1170, he became the Bishop of Chartres from 1176 to 1180. In 1159 he published the *Policraticus*, a heterogeneous work of political theory that brings together pieces written years before, and is profoundly influenced by reading Plato, via glosses or perhaps either Chalcidius's *Commentary on the Timaeus* or Macrobius's *Commentary* on Cicero's *Somnium Scipionis* [*The Dream of Scipio*]. After a virulent critique of the court in Books I to III – a satirical target that would become commonplace in the fourteenth and fifteenth centuries – John tries to show in Book IV what the royal function should be, producing a veritable program for good government founded on Deuteronomy, which ends with the distinction between monarchy, in which the king is the image of God, and tyranny, in which he is the image of Lucifer or pride, and he goes so far as to justify tyrannicide by leaning on Cicero and Matthew's Gospel (26: 52). Finally, in the two following books, V and VI, John takes up and develops the metaphor of the political body. The State is compared to a human body whose members assist each other. The feet represent the people who tread the earth and enrich it with their labor. The arms are men of war devoted to the defense of the country. The eyes and ears are the magistrates, alert to repress abuses and to render justice to all. Finally, the head is the king. But a living body requires a soul, and this soul is religion, personified by the sovereign pontiff. The book offers the image of a good prince with a great love of justice who should be a mirror for his subjects:

This valiant doctor [John of Salisbury] considered that great men, kings, dukes, counts and other grand lords, who are examples to others and govern them so that

The City of God

**St. Augustine,
Bishop of Hippo**
De Civitate Dei
[Florence, ca. 1470]
NYPL, Spencer Collection

St. Augustine is shown here as a Renaissance scholar writing at his desk while contemplating a city floating overhead. Scholars have seen this celestial city as both the City of God in Augustine's great book as well as the city of Florence, identifying the dome as

Brunelleschi's masterpiece atop the cathedral of Santa Maria del Fiore. The dome had been completed only a few years before this manuscript was painted, and the artist of this miniature, Zanobi di Strozzi, had been working in and near Florence for many years. The ornament around the border, a style called "white vine," was most likely painted by another Florentine artist.

none dare question them, so dutiful are their deeds, words, and kindness, especially their hospitality, so sagely do they govern and rule by true philosophy, that each must see there his own reflection, to follow the virtues and amend the faults.[141]

It is not surprising that Charles V had John of Salisbury's book translated into French by Denis Foulechat in 1372.

Before him, Philip IV had benefited from the advice of Giles of Rome (1243–1316).[142] An Augustinian brother and master of theology in Paris, head prior of his order in 1292, and Bishop of Bourges in 1295, he was also the tutor of the young king, to whom he dedicated *De regimine principum,* translated into French by Henri de Gauchy in 1282 under the title *Du gouvernement des princes.* Here again, it is less as a preacher than as a philosopher converted to Aristotelianism that the author addresses his pupil. Enlightened and guided by divine law and natural reason, a king (like Aristotle's legislator) is his own master, master of his house and his kingdom: "demi-god and very much like God," exemplary mirror for his subjects, "right rule of human works," "Sergeant of God," on whom depends "the life and safety of the kingdom." The book was a milestone in the genesis of the ideology of absolute power and of the divine right of the monarchy.

John of Salisbury and Giles of Rome were pioneers in a vast body of reflection, from Brunetto Latini's *Livres dou tresor* (ca. 1266)[143] and Dante's

De monarchia (1309),[144] which would culminate in Marsilius of Padua's *Defensor Pacis* (1324).[145] It was at this time that in Siena on the walls of the Sala della Pace in the Palazzo Pubblico, Ambrogio Lorenzetti[146] completed painting the image of "Good Government," one that makes peace reign on earth and assures the common good through concord and equity:

All lordships and all high positions are given to us by the Sovereign Father, who among the holy establishments of the world wanted the government of the cities to be founded on three pillars, that is, justice, reverence and love.[147]

*From Universal Peace to
Withdrawal from the World*
While some resorted to polemics, others preferred to embrace a dream of universal peace. Ramon Llull (1235–1316), a Catalan contemporary of Dante's, shared with him the sentiment that the emperor was the leader of temporal society and that "the people's peace resides in the king's justice." In *Blanquerna,*[148] he envisaged the pope's convening an assembly of representatives of the world's powers, Christian or not, in order to keep peace between peoples. This assembly would examine the reports of envoys sent to inquire into the reasons behind conflicts. To make its decisions respected, the assembly would elect an executive council charged with imposing sanctions and levying fines on recalcitrants.

"Two loves have thus made two cities..."

Saint Augustine
***Le Cité de Dieu*, translated by Raoul de Presles**
Paris: maître François, between 1469 and 1473
BNF, Département des Manuscrits

The availability of the French translation by Raoul de Presles of *De Civitate Dei* gave rise to the production in France of a number of large, deluxe, richly illuminated manuscripts. Perhaps the most celebrated is the one for which Robert Gaguin, a general of the Trinitarians, a preeminent theologian and humanist, personally planned the series of images, in collaboration with the best Parisian illuminator of his day, known as "Maître François." A full-page miniature depicts the celestial city above, and the earthly city below – a visual translation of natural subordination, the source of peace and harmony. And while the Virtues lead the elect in a procession toward the celestial city, the earthly city, encircled by demons, must still wage war against the Vices.

*A Mirror for the
Instruction of Princes*

Gilles de Rome
*Le livre du gouvernement
des princes*
Bourges, 16th century
BNF, Bibliothèque de l'Arsenal

De regimine principum, a treatise on the education of
princes, written around 1280
for Philippe le Bel (later King
Philip IV) by Giles of Rome,
Archbishop of Bourges, met
with great success, attested
to by the numerous extant
manuscripts and the many
translations, including this
one, completed at Vannes in
1433, by an anonymous
Dominican friar at the request
of Count de Laval. A disciple
of Saint Thomas Aquinas,
Giles of Rome adapted Aristotelian ethics to Christian pre-
scriptions in order to instruct
the future king on the principles of ideal government. The
second chapter opens with a
miniature representing the
"powers of the soul" that the
future sovereign must possess: Justice, Strength, Prudence, Sympathy.

La Cité des Dames

Christine de Pisan
Le Livre de la Cité des Dames
Paris: maître de la Cité des dames, 1405
BNF, Département des Manuscrits

Christine de Pisan is celebrated today as the first woman in the West to live by her pen. Essentially her own publisher, she worked closely with a renowned Parisian illuminator who has become known as "the master of the *Cité des Dames*"; four copies of this work from his studio – two of which were originally presented to the dukes of Berry and Burgundy – have survived. Here, the double image that introduces the manuscript is an almost literal depiction of its origin. Distressed at reading so many negative comments about women from "philosophers and poets and from all the orators," Christine has a vision of "three crowned ladies": Reason, in whose mirror people see themselves with "clear self-knowledge"; Rectitude, possessing "the straight ruler which separates right from wrong and shows the difference between good and evil"; and finally Justice, who has in her right hand a gold goblet that "serves to measure out to each his rightful portion." These women invite the author to build a fortified citadel so that henceforth virtuous women may have "a refuge and defense against the various assailants." With the help of Reason, who gives her "durable and pure mortar," Christine undertakes to lay the foundations for her metaphoric city with its "lofty walls all around . . . with mighty towers and strong bastions." Here, a world is invented through the words and hands of women.

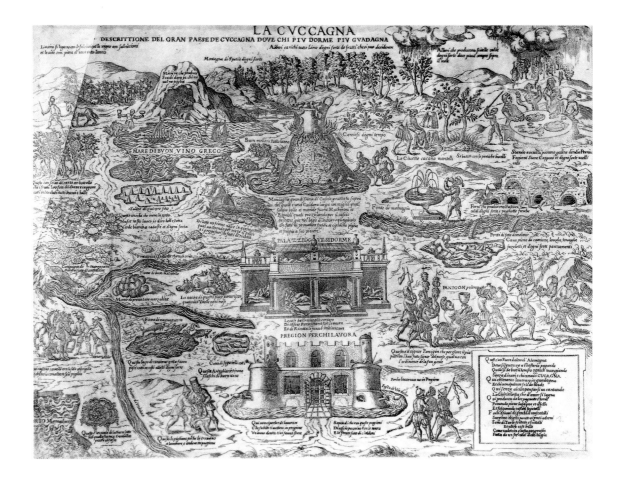

The Land of Cockaigne

La Cuccagna: Descrittione des gran paese de cuccagna dove chi piu dorme piu guadagna

Engraving, [Rome or Venice, late 16th century]
NYPL, Miriam and Ira D. Wallach Division of Art, Prints and Photographs

In this Italian depiction of the land of Cockaigne (also called Schlarraffenland, or "land of milk and honey," by the Germans, and Luilekkerland, or "lazy luscious land," by the Dutch), feasting, sleeping, and pleasure are the main activities, and "the more you sleep the more you earn." Mountains of grated cheese sit in a sea of Greek wine, roasted birds fall from the sky like rain, trees produce ripe fruit all year round, owls lay fur coats, artichokes are always ripe for picking, and people are arrested for working.

The Land of Cockaigne was a medieval peasant's dream, offering relief from backbreaking labor and the daily struggle for meager food. In eighteenth-century Naples, it also provided an ideal theme for festivals. On numerous feast days, residents erected a large Cuccagna arch made of meats, cheese, bread, fruits, and vegetables given by the King. When the King gave the signal, the residents scrambled to destroy the arch, grabbing as much food as possible for themselves along the way and providing an entertaining spectacle for the court watching from above.

. . . once in every year each power should come to a safe place whither all the other powers should come likewise, and that, after the manner of a chapter, they should hold discussion in all friendship and make correction each of the other, and that they that refused to abide by the decisions of the definitors of the chapter should be fined.[149]

The project also imagined direct negotiations between opponents under the mediation of a third power. Within the curie, a "cardinal of peace" would be assigned to facilitate travel and assure the protection of ambassadors and preachers circulating among the various nations. Rather than sanctions, Llull believed in discussion and negotiations conducted in a universal language, Latin. Since Babel, it had been the diversity of languages that had made "men make war with each other; and through this war and this diversity of tongues there was likewise diversity of beliefs, and there were created opposing sects. . . . [I]f there be no more languages than one, men will grow to understand each other, and through understanding they will love each other more, and adopt the more readily the same customs wherein they will agree."[150] There would henceforth reign "one language, one belief and one faith."[151] Llull exhibits a keen desire to return to unity, guarantor of peace and harmony, the only means of escaping the state of "dissimilarity" humankind has suffered since the Fall, similar to what one finds in Dante:

. . . if we review the ages and the dispositions of men from the fall of our first parents (which was the turning-point at which we went astray), we shall not find that there ever was peace throughout the world except under the immortal Augustus, when a perfect monarchy existed. That mankind was then happy in the calm of universal peace is attested by all historians and by famous poets; even the chronicler of Christ's gentleness deigned to bear witness to it. . . . Truly that time was "full," as were all temporal things. . . . What the state of the world has been since that seamless garment was first rent by the talon of cupidity . . . – would that we might not witness it.

Oh human race, how many storms and misfortunes and shipwrecks must toss you about while, transformed into a many-headed beast, you strive after conflicting things.[152]

But unlike Dante, who summons the reign of a universal monarch in the person of Emperor Henry VII, and unlike Pierre Dubois, who in *De recuperatione Terræ Sanctæ* (ca. 1305) implores Philip IV to arbitrate peace, Ramon Llull introduces his scheme in a novelistic world, perhaps in order to preserve, by distancing it from the real world, its impact as fiction, that is to say, its force.

In the same way, a century later, Christine de Pisan (1364–1430), excluded by her status as a woman and strengthened by her "usual habit" of studying "the weighty opinions of various authors," resorted to the stratagem of a waking dream and of allegory in order to integrate women into an ideal government. In a vision, three women – Reason, Rectitude, and Justice – announce that they have chosen her to erect the City of Ladies, "so that from now on, ladies and all valiant women may have a refuge and defense against the various assailants":[153]

Thus, fair daughter, the prerogative among women has been bestowed on you to establish and build the City of Ladies. For the foundation and completion of this City you will draw fresh waters from us as from clear fountains, and we will bring you sufficient building stone, stronger and more durable than any marble with cement could be. Thus your City will be extremely beautiful, without equal, and of perpetual duration in the world.[154]

They all four set out for the Field of Letters "on a flat and fertile plain, where all fruits and freshwater rivers are found and where the earth abounds in all good things,"[155] and each applies herself to the task. Little by little the city is built; the women are simultaneously supervisors, workers, raw materials, and hostesses. It becomes the living memory of women:

. . . all of you who love glory, virtue, and praise may be lodged in great honor, ladies from the past as well as from the present and future, for it has been built and established for every honorable lady.[156]

But even to stand apart is perhaps still too much for some, who prefer to withdraw from the world altogether, either to dream like Boccaccio[157] of a government as ephemeral as it is perfect, or to join a monastic community, that collective solitude under the protection of the "father" abbot, alone able to overcome ever-changing contradictions by pushing them to the extreme. The monastery seems to be an oxymoron in William of Malmesbury:

In the middle of wild swampland where the trees are intertwined in an inextricable thicket, there is a plain with very green vegetation which attracts the eye by reason of

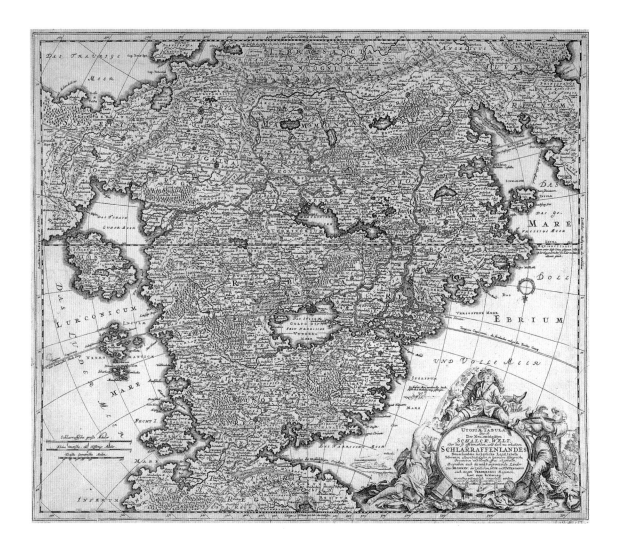

A Map of Schlarrafenland

Accurata Utopiæ tabula Das ist. Der Neu-entdekten Schalck-welt oder des so offt benanten, und doch nie erkanten Schlarraffenlandes Neu erfundene lächerliche Land-tabelle . . .
[Nuremberg]: Prostat in
Officina Homanniana, [17–]
Map, engraving with faint color
NYPL, Map Division

This satirical map of Schlaraffenland (Land of Cockaigne), issued in the eighteenth century by the noted publisher Homann and respecting the cartographic conventions of its time, depicts an imaginary empire of pleasure, debauchery, and excess. The Kingdom of the Golden Calf, the Empire of the Stomach, the Land of Drink, and the Republic of Lust (among others) are filled with sites such as the city of Blasphemy, the house of the Mad, and the district of Laziness. The title is engraved in a cartouche reminiscent of paintings by Breughel: two cardplayers, flanked by a gigantic cook and a pair of debauchees, throw money in the air. The country of Cockaigne offers a topography dominated by earthly paradise, where the trees of life and of knowledge are planted; it extends to the north in the *terra sancta incognita,* with "the Church of the new Jerusalem" in the center, rising on the *mons Christus,* while below reigns "the kingdom of shadows," an inferno surrounded by the flames of Gehenna, which one reaches through Charon's gate, reminding us that it is desire, concupiscence, and inconstancy that separate the angelic kingdom from that of the fallen angels. What had been a mere diversion becomes the pretext for a sermon. From the age of myth, we slowly slip into one of criticism.

The Abbey of Thélème

François Rabelais
Oeuvres
Paris: Chez Ferdinand Bastien,
an VI [1797]
NYPL, Rare Books Division

A law student, a monk, and a
practicing physician, as well
as a writer, François Rabelais
was the epitome of the Renaissance man. He is best known
for his *Pantagruel* and his
Gargantua, the story of a giant
and his son, which is a study
in contrasts – both supernatural
and realistic, solemn and
comic, lofty and bawdy. The
content of the work is reflected in its style, which shifts
between erudite and colloquial.

The Abbey of Thélème at the
end of *Gargantua* (1534) is the
best example of Rabelais's
notion of an ideal society.
Thélème is an inverted monastic society, without walls or
regulations, whose nobles are
so carefully selected that they
all agree with one another
just because they are so much
alike. The only rule is "Do
what you will"; therefore,
to keep everyone happy, if
anyone said "'Let's drink,'
everyone drank."

Rabelais knew Thomas More's
Utopia well; Gargantua's wife,
Babedec, is "the daughter
of the king of the Amaurotes,
in Utopia" and Pantagruel,
their son, is "the Prince of
Utopians." A famous letter
at the end of *Pantagruel* by
Gargantua to his son is dated
from Sir Thomas More's land
of Utopia.

its fertility; no obstacle impedes the walker. Not a particle
of the soil is left to lie fallow; here the earth bears fruit
trees, there grapevines cover the ground or are held on
high trellises. In this place cultivation rivals nature; what
the latter has forgotten the former brings forth. What
can I say of the beauty of the buildings whose unshak-
able foundations have been built into the marshes? This
incomparable solitude has been granted the monks so
that they may grow more closely attached to the higher
realities for being the more detached from those of
mortal life. . . . Truly this isle is the home of chastity, the
dwelling place of probity, the school of those who love
Divine Wisdom. In short, this is an image of Paradise; it
makes one think already of heaven.[158]

The existence one leads there is the regimented
and crazed realization of unanimity, unity and
hierarchical equality. The *Book of the Constitutions
and Ordinations of the Dominican Order* comes back
constantly to this:

As we were warned by the Rule, our first reason for
being assembled into a community is to live together and
to have in God a single soul and a single heart. . . . The
unanimity of our life, rooted in God's charity, should set
an example of universal reconciliation in Christ . . . in Him
we form a single body, we who share the same bread; in
Him, finally, we hold everything in common.[159]

If rules, discipline, and tears are necessary, it is in
order to accede to happiness:

What more shall I say of you, O solitary life, blessed life,
pleasure-garden of souls, holy life, angelic life, hall of
heavenly jewels, court of the senators of heaven? . . .
Those who know you love you; those who have rested
in the delight of your loving embrace know the merits
of your praise.[160]

This excess is answered by the dream of the country of Cockaigne.[161] This maniacal asceticism is
echoed in the chateau of Dame Tartine, the seas of
milk, the roasted chickens, the strings of sausages
hanging from posts, trees bearing "larded capons,
rabbits, fresh eggs," the dream of a sated world
painted by Brueghel, liberated for a moment from
racking hunger. At the same time, though, Rabelais
was dreaming for the Abbey of Thélème of impossi-
bilities finally reconciled.

Translated by Susan Emanuel

Notes

1 Hesiod, *Works and Days*, 109–10, in *Hesiod. Homeric Hymns; Epic Cycle; Homerica*, trans. Hugh G. Evelyn-White (Cambridge, Mass.: Harvard University Press, 1936), 11.

2 On the myth of metallic "races," see Bodo Gatz, *Weltalter, goldene Zeit und sinnverwandte Vorstellungen* (Hildesheim: Ed. G. Olms, 1967).

3 On the interpretation of the Hesiodic myth, see Jean Pierre Vernant, *Myth and Thought Among the Greeks* (London and Boston: Routledge & Kegan Paul, 1983).

4 On utopian communism in Greek thought, see Doyne Dawson, *Cities of the Gods: Communist Utopias in Greek Thought* (New York: Oxford University Press, 1992).

5 Plato, *Statesman*, 271d–e, in *Complete Works*, ed., with introduction and notes, by John M. Cooper (Indianapolis: Hackett Publishing Company, 1997), 313.

6 Ibid., 271e.

7 On the Roman notion of the Golden Age, see Jean-Paul Brisson, *Rome et l'âge d'or: de Catulle à Ovide, vie et mort d'un mythe* (Paris: Editions la Découverte, 1992).

8 On the Golden Age in Virgil, see Brisson, and J. Perret, "Daphnis pâtre et héros: perspectives sur un âge d'or (Virgile, "Buc.," V)," *Revue des études latines* 60 (1982): 216–34.

9 On the importance of Ovid in the Middle Ages, see *Colloque Présence d'Ovide* (1980), ed. Raymond Chevallier (Paris: Les Belles Lettres, 1982).

10 Gaius Valerius Catullus, LXIV, in *The Poems of Catullus*, trans. Charles Martin (Baltimore: Johns Hopkins University Press, 1990), 91–92.

11 See Arnaldo Momigliano, "Daniele e la teoria greca della successione degli imperi," in his *Settimo contributo alla storia degli studi classici e del mondo antico* (Rome: Edizioni di storia e letteratura, 1984), 297–304.

12 Lactantius, *The Divine Institutes*, Book II, Chapter 13, in *The Divine Institutes, Books I–VII*, trans. Sister Mary Francis McDonald (Washington, D.C.: Catholic University of America Press, 1965), 151. With reference to Lactantius, see René Pichon, *Lactance: Etude sur le mouvement philosophique et religieux sous le règne de Constantin* (Paris: Hachette, 1901).

13 Lactantius, *The Divine Institutes*, Book II, Chapter XIII, p. 151.

14 Blossius Aemilius Dracontius, *De laudibus Dei*, trans. as *Louanges de Dieu. Livres I et II*, ed. and trans., with commentary, by Claude Moussy and Colette Camus (Paris: Les Belles Lettres, 1985).

15 On the evolution of the paradise-orchard, see J. V. Fleming, "The Garden of the *Roman de la Rose*: Vision of Landscape or Landscape of Vision," in *Medieval Gardens*, ed. Elisabeth B. MacDougall (Washington, D.C.: Dumbarton Oaks Research Library and Collection, 1986), 201–34.

16 Alanus de Insulis, *Anticlaudianus; or The Good and Perfect Man*, trans. with commentary by James J. Sheridan (Toronto: Pontifical Institute of Mediaeval Studies, 1973).

17 On the meaning of the word "paradise," see F. Vigouroux, "Paradis," *Dictionnaire de la Bible*, general editor Louis Pirot (Paris: Librairie Letouzay et Ané, 1928–), 4: 2, cols. 2119–20. See also Jean Delumeau, *History of Paradise: The Garden of Eden in Myth and Tradition*, trans. Matthew O'Connell (New York: Continuum, 1995).

18 On the ambiguity of the world "Eden," see Vigouroux, cols. 2120–28, and Monique Alexandre, *Le Commencement du Livre: Genèse, I–IV: La version grecque de la Septante et sa réception* (Paris: Beauchesne, 1988), 244–46.

19 On the definition of *locus amœnus*, see Ernst Robert Curtius, *European Literature and the Latin Middle Ages*, trans. Willard R. Trask (New York: Pantheon Books, 1953), 192–93, 195–201.

20 See Saint Gregory of Nyssa, *On the Making of Man*, Chapters XIX–XX, in *A Select Library of Nicene and Post-Nicene Fathers of the Christian Church. Second Series*, vol. 5 (Grand Rapids, Mich.: Wm. B. Eerdmans Publishing Co., 1961), 409–10.

21 Regarding the identification of the rivers of paradise with known rivers, see Monique Alexandre, "Entre ciel et terre: les premiers débats sur le site du paradis (Gen. 2: 8–15) et ses réceptions," in *Peuples et pays mythiques: Actes du Ve Colloque du Centre de Recherches mythologiques de l'université de Paris X, Chantilly, 18–20 Septembre 1986* (Paris: Les Belles Lettres, 1988), 187–224, esp. 199.

22 On the creation of Adam, see Louis Pirot, "Adam et la Bible," *Dictionnaire de la Bible*, 1: cols. 86–101. Also see Alexandre, *Le Commencement du Livre*, 174–75. Adam is a generic name referring to human beings (Genesis 5: 2).

23 The tradition that Adam was buried in Hebron has its source in Saint Jerome, *De situ et nominibus locorum hebraicorum liber*, in *Onomastica sacra*, ed. Paul de Lagarde (Göttingen: L. Horstmann, 1887). According to another tradition, Adam's sepulchre was placed at Calvary.

24 Honorius Augustodunensis, *Elucidarium*, I, 68, in *L'Elucidarium et les lucidaires: Contribution, par l'histoire d'un texte, à l'histoire des croyances religieuses en France au Moyen âge*, ed. Yves Lefèvre (Paris: De Boccard, 1954), 117.

25 "Disciple: 'Where was woman created?' Master: 'In Paradise from the rib of man while he was sleeping.' Disciple: 'Why was woman created from man?' Master: 'So that they could be one in their love as they are one in body.'" See Honorius Augustodunensis, *Elucidarius*, I, 70–71, in *The Old Norse Elucidarius: Original Text and English Translation*, ed. Evelyn Scherabon Firchow (Columbia, S.C.: Camden House, 1992), 19. On the creation of Eve, see Alexandre, *Le Commencement du Livre*, 282–88.

26 Saint Augustine, *The City of God Against the Pagans*, trans. George E. McCracken, et al. (Cambridge, Mass.: Harvard University Press; London: W. Heinemann, 1957–72), Book XII, Chapter 22, in 4: 111; see also Book XII, Chapter 28, in 4: 129.

27 Johannes Scotus Erigena, *De divisione naturæ*, Book IV, in *Patrologiæ cursus completus. Series secunda* [Latin] (Paris: J. P. Migne, 1850–64), 122: col. 799. On this dream of a primitive androgyny, see Georges Duby, *The Knight, the Lady, and the Priest: The Making of Modern Marriage in Medieval France* (New York: Pantheon Books, 1983), 50–51.

28 Honorius Augustodunensis, *The Old Norse Elucidarius*, I, 91, p. 23.

29 For Hesiod, the end of the Golden Age is explained by Prometheus's sin: "[T]herefore [Zeus] planned sorrow and mischief against men. He hid fire." See *Works and Days*, 45–50, pp. 5, 7. This punishment is aggravated by the creation of woman; see *Works and Days*, 90–95, p. 9.

30 Regarding the love uniting Adam and Eve, see Hildegarde of Bingen, *Causæ et curæ*, 104a, in Peter Dronke, *Women Writers in the Middle Ages* (Cambridge: Cambridge University Press, 1984), 244.

31 Origen, *On First Principles*, Book IV, 3, 1, in *Origen*, trans. Rowan A. Greer (New York: Paulist Press, 1979), 189. On Origen and paradise, see Reinhold R. Grimm, *Paradisus coelestis, Paradisus terrestris* (Munich: Fink, 1977), 33–43. On Origen's influence, in particular in the twelfth century, see Jean Leclercq, *The Love of Learning and the Desire for God: A Study of Monastic Culture*, trans. Catharine Misrahi (New York: Fordham University Press, 1982), 91–96. See also Henri de Lubac, *Exégèse médiévale: Les quatre sens de l'Ecriture. 1re partie. I–II* (Paris: Aubier, 1959), I, 1: 198–304; I, 2: 586–99.

32 Erigena, *De divisione naturæ*, Book IV, 21, in *Patrologiæ cursus completus. Series secunda* [Latin], 122: col. 841B.

33 Saint Epiphanius, Bishop of Constantia in Cyprus, *Ancoratus*, 58, in *Patrologiæ curus completus. Series Græca* (Paris: J. P. Migne, 1857–80), 43: col. 120BC, quoted in Alexandre, "Entre ciel et terre," 187.

34 Ibid.

35 Saint Augustine, *The City of God*, Book XIII, Chapter 21, 4: 217, 221; see also Saint Augustine, *On the Literal Interpretation of Genesis, An Unfinished Book*, in *On Genesis*, trans. Roland J. Teske (Washington, D.C.: Catholic University of America Press, 1991). See Jean Delumeau, *Sin and Fear: The Emergence of a Western Guilt Culture, 13th–18th Centuries*, trans. Eric Nicholson (New York: St. Martin's Press, 1990), 245–81.

36 Sir John Mandeville, *The Travels of Sir John Mandeville*, trans. with an introduction by C.W.R.D. Moseley (Harmondsworth: Penguin Books, 1983), 185. See Ch. Deluz, "Le paradis terrestre: Image de l'Orient dans l'Occident médiéval," *Sénéfiance* (Aix-en-Provence: Centre universitaire d'études et de recherches médiévales d'Aix-en-Provence) 11 (1982): 145–61.

37 On the land beyond, see Cosmas Indicopleustes, *Topographie chrétienne. 1, Livres I–IV [Christiana topographia]*, ed. and trans., with introduction and notes by Wanda Wolska-Conus (Paris: Editions du Cerf, 1968), Book II, 24 and 43–44. See K. Kitamura, "Cosmas Indicopleustès et la figure de la terre," in *Moïse géographe: Recherches sur les représentations juives et chrétiennes de l'espace* (Paris: J. Vrin, 1988), 80–98.

38 Gervase of Tilbury, *Otia imperialia*, I, X, in *Scriptores rerum brunsvicensium*, 1, ed. Gottfried Wilhelm Liebniz (Hanover: Sumptibus Nicolai Foersteri, 1707–11), 892. This opinion was known to Pierre d'Ailly, who expressed it several times in *Imago mundi* but ultimately refuted it. It is also found in the jottings of Christopher Columbus.

39 See W.G.L. Randles, *De la terre plate au globe terrestre: Une mutation épistémologique rapide* (Paris: A. Colin, 1980).

40 Duarte Pacheco Pereira, *Esmeraldo de situ orbis*, trans. George H. T. Kimble (London: Printed for the Hakluyt Society, 1937), Book I, Chapter 4.

41 Léon Pinelo, quoted in Randles, 24.

42 Saint Isidore of Seville, *Etymologiæ*, quoted in Delumeau, *History of Paradise*, 44.

43 Saint Thomas Aquinas, *Summa theologica*, I, 102, trans. Laurence Shapcote, in *Great Books of the Western World*, Mortimer J. Adler, editor in chief (Chicago: Encyclopaedia Britannica, 1990), 17: 524.

44 Honorius Augustodunensis, *Imago mundi*, I, 8, ed. Valerie I. J. Flint, in *Archives d'histoire doctrinale et littéraire du moyen âge* 57, 1982 (Paris: J. Vrin, 1983), 7–153, esp. 52.

45 Jean Calvin, *Commentaries on the First Book of Moses Called Genesis*, trans. from the original Latin, and compared with the French edition, by John King (Edinburgh: Calvin Translation Society, 1847–50), 1: 115, 119–22. Calvin situated paradise in Mesopotamia. His map of Eden is reproduced on p. 120 of the *Commentaries*. On variations in the location of terrestrial paradise, see E. Cothenet, "Paradis," *Dictionnaire de la Bible*, 6: cols. 1181–90; and François Dupuigrenet Desrousilles, *Dieu en son royaume: La Bible dans la France d'autrefois, XIIIe–XVIIIe siècles* (Paris: Bibliothèque nationale; Editions du Cerf, 1991).

46 Herodotus, *History*, III, 17, trans. George Rawlinson, in *Great Books of the Western World*, 5: 93. See Jean-Pierre Vernant, "Food in the Countries of the Sun," in Marcel Detienne and Jean-Pierre Vernant, *The Cuisine of Sacrifice Among the Greeks* (Chicago: University of Chicago Press, 1989), 164–69.

47 Diodorus of Sicily, *The Library of History*, in vols. 1 and 2 of *Diodorus of Sicily, in twelve volumes*, trans. C. H. Oldfather (Cambridge, Mass.: Harvard University Press; London: W. Heinemann, 1933–67), Book II, Chapters 55–60, 2: 65–83.

48 Diodorus, Chapter 56, pp. 69, 71.

49 Ibid., Chapter 57, p. 73..

50 Ibid., Chapter 58, p. 75.

51 Ibid., Chapter 59, pp. 77, 79.

52 Ibid., Chapter 57, p. 73.

53 Ibid., Chapter 58, p. 77.

54 Ibid., Chapter 59, pp. 79, 81.

55 Ibid., p. 81.

56 Ibid, Chapter 58, p. 77.

57 Ibid., Chapter 57, pp. 73, 75.

58 On Hiera and Panchea, see Y. Vernière, "Iles mythiques chez Diodore de Sicile," in *Peuples et pays mythiques*, 159–67.

59 Aelian, *Historical Miscellany*, trans. N. G. Wilson (Cambridge, Mass.: Harvard University Press, 1997), Book III, 18, pp. 145, 147.

60 On the Hyperboreans, see Diodorus, Chapter 47, pp. 37–41.

61 Hesiod, *Works and Days*, 170–75, p. 15.

62 Pindar, *Olympian Odes*, II, 4, 68–77, in *Pindar*, trans. William H. Race (Cambridge, Mass.: Harvard University Press, 1997), 71.

63 An example of this assimilation is the history of the Rechabites, the clan of the sons of Rechab who live virtuously, without houses, without sowing, vines, or possessions, and who are faithful to a prohibition to drink wine proclaimed by their ancestor, transported on a cloud to an Oceanic island protected by a wall of fog, rich in beautiful and fragrant fruit trees. See Alexandre, "Entre ciel et terre," 198.

64 Otto I, Bishop of Freising, *Ottonis episcopi Frisingensis Chronica sive historia de duabus civitatibus*, ed. Adolf Hofmeister and Walther Lammers (Berlin: Rütten und Loenig, 1960). For an English edition of the *Chronicle*, see *The Two Cities: A Chronicle of Universal History to the Year 1146 A.D.*, trans. Charles Christopher Mierow (New York: Octagon Books, 1966). On Otto I, see M. Gosman, "Otton de Freising et le Prêtre Jean," *Revue Belge de Philologie et d'Histoire*, 61 (1983): 270–85.

65 See Malcolm Letts, "Prester John: Sources and Illustrations," *Notes and Queries*, 188 (1945): 178–80, 204–7, 246–48, 266–68; 189 (1945): 4–7; and Jean Richard, "L'Extrême-Orient légendaire au Moyen Age, roi David et Prêtre Jean," *Annales d'Ethiopie*, 1 (1955): 225–42.

66 Mandeville, Chapter XXIX, p. 177.

67 Vsevolod Slessarev, *Prester John: The Letter and the Legend* (Minneapolis: University of Minnesota Press, 1959), 77.

68 Ibid., 77–78.

69 Ibid., 75–76.

70 Among the many books and articles on Jerusalem, see A. I. Galleti, "Gerusalemme o la citta desiderata," *Mélanges de l'Ecole française de Rome. Moyen Age, Temps Modernes*, 96, no. 1 (1984): 459–87.

71 Peter the Venerable, *Sermo vir laudem Sepuleri Domini*, in *Patrologiae cursus completus. Series secunda* [Latin], 189: cols. 978D–979A.

72 The pilgrimage of Saewulf dates from 1101–3. The text was translated into English in *Jerusalem Pilgrimage, 1099–1185*, ed. John Wilkinson, with Joyce Hill and W. F. Ryan (London: Hakluyt Society, 1988). For the position of the "compass," see 103.

73 See John of Würzburg, *Descriptio locorum terre sancte*, in *Peregrinationes tres: Saewulf, John of Würzburg, Theodericus*, ed. R.B.C. Huygens (Turnholti: Brepols, 1994). The pilgrimage of John of Würzburg was translated into English in *Jerusalem Pilgrimage*, 244–73; see esp. 260.

74 One of the best descriptions of the sanctuaries of Jerusalem in the beginning of the twelfth century is that of Abbot Daniel, who made a trip to the Holy Land around 1106. This account was translated into English in *Jerusalem Pilgrimage*, 120–71.

75 See Alphonse Dupront, *Le mythe de croisade*, 4 vols. (Paris: Gallimard, 1997), esp. 3: 1361–84, and in particular 1374–75.

76 On the "talismanic" significance of the Cross, see Dupront, 1300–12. The link between paradise and the Cross is all the stronger because at that time there were in circulation a number of apocryphal tales about the wood of the Cross being made from the tree of life, and of Adam buried at the foot of Calvary, so that the blood of the New Adam bathed the skull of the first man.

77 Quoted in Norman Rufus Colin Cohn, *The Pursuit of the Millennium: Revolutionary Millenarians and Mystical Anarchists of the Middle Ages* (London: Maurice Temple Smith Ltd., 1970), 64. On the content of what is attributed to Urban II, see Dupront, 1368, and André Vauchez, "Les composantes eschatologiques de l'idée de croisade," in *Le Concile de Clermont de 1095 et l'appel à la croisade: Actes du colloque universitaire international de Clermont-Ferrand (23–25 June 1995)* (Rome: Ecole française de Rome, 1997), 233–43.

78 Saint Bernard of Clairvaux, *In Praise of the New Knighthood*, Chapter V, in *The Works of Bernard of Clairvaux*, trans. R. J. Zwi Werblowsky (Spencer, Mass.: Cistercian Publications, 1970–): 7: 144–45.

79 Letter from Saint Bernard of Clairvaux to the Abbot of Saint-Michel-en-Thiérache, ca. 1129–30, quoted in Giles Constable, "Monachisme et pèlerinage au Moyen Age," in his *Religious Life and Thought (11th–12th Centuries)* (London: Variorum Reprints, 1979), 1–27, esp. 21.

80 The best Latin edition of Saint Brendan's *Navigatio* is *Navigatio Sancti Brendani Abbatis: From Early Latin Manuscripts*, ed. Carl Selmer (Dublin: Four Courts, 1989). For the early twelfth-century Anglo-Norman version, see *Le Voyage de Saint Brandan / Benedeit*, ed. Ian Short (Paris: Union générale d'éditions 10/18, 1984).

81 Ibid., 123.

82 Ibid., 125–27.

83 Honorius Augustodunensis, *Imago mundi*, I: 35, esp. 66.

84 See Danielle Lecoq, "Saint Brandan, Christophe Colomb et le paradis terrestre," *Revue de la Bibliothèque Nationale*, 45 (1992): 14–21.

85 Pseudo-Callisthenes, *The Greek Alexander Romance*, trans. Richard Stoneman (London and New York: Penguin Books, 1991), Book II, Chapter 39, p. 121.

86 Ibid., Chapter 41, p. 123.

87 Lloyd L. Gunderson, *Alexander's Letter to Aristotle About India* (Meisenheim am Glam: Hain, 1980), 150.

88 Ibid., 151.

89 Ibid., 151, 154.

90 *Alexandri magni iter ad paradisum*, ed. Julius Zacher (Königsberg: T. Theile, 1859).

91 Godefridus de Sancto Victore, "Discours d'adieu de l'esprit à la chair" ["The Mind's Farewell to the Body"], *Microcosmos*, Chapter CCXX, quoted in Philippe Delhaye, "Le Microcosme de Godefroid de Saint-Victor et sa vitalité morale dans le macrocosme," in *L'Homme et son univers au Moyen Age, Actes du septième Congrès international de philosophie médiévale, 30 août–4 septembre, 1982* (Louvain-la-Neuve: Editions de l'Institut supérieur de philosophie, 1986), II: 769–75, esp. 773.

92 On the general theme of life's voyage, see Siegfried Wenzel, "The Pilgrimage of Life as a Late Medieval Genre," *Medieval Studies*, 35 (1973): 370–88. See also Dupront.

93 See Edmond Faral, *Guillaume de Digulleville, moine de Châalis* (Paris: Imprimerie nationale, 1952). See also Joseph Delacotte, *Guillaume de Digulleville, poète normand. Trois romans-poèmes du XIVe siècle. Les "Pèlerinages" et la "Divine Comédie"* (Paris: Desclée de Brouwer, 1932).

94 Guillaume de Deguileville, *The Pilgrimage of Human Life*, trans. Eugene Clasby (New York: Garland, 1992), Book I, pp. 45, 46.

95 Ibid., Book IV, pp. 171, 172.

96 Boethius, *The Consolation of Philosophy*, trans V. E. Watts (Harmondsworth: Penguin Books, 1988), Book IV, Chapters I–II, pp. 116–23. On the importance of Boethius as a link between Antiquity and the Middle Ages, see Alain de Libera, *L'Art des généralités: Théories de l'abstraction* (Paris: Aubier, 1999), 159–280.

97 Plato, *Statesman*, 270b et seq., pp. 311–13.

98 Plato, *Timaeus*, 39d, in *Complete Works*, 1243.

99 On the "Great Year," see Pierre Boyancé, *Etudes sur le Songe de Scipion (essais d'histoire et de psychologie religieuses* [Bibliothèque des Universités du Midi. Fasc. XX] (Bordeaux: Feret et Fils, 1936), esp. 160–61. *The Dream of Scipio* was well known in the Middle Ages thanks to Macrobius's *Commentary*. See *Commentary on the Dream of Scipio*, trans., with an introduction and notes, by William Harris Stahl (New York: Columbia University Press, 1952).

100 See Auguste Luneau, *L'Histoire du salut chez les Pères de l'Eglise, la doctrine des âges du monde* (Paris: Beauchesne et ses fils, 1964).

101 On the Sibylline writings, see Valentin Nikiprowetzky, *La Troisième Sibylle* (Paris/The Hague: Mouton, 1970).

102 Saint Irenaeus, Bishop of Lyon, *Against Heresies*, Book V, Chapter 32, p. 1, in *The Ante-Nicene Fathers: Translations of the Writings of the Fathers Down to A.D. 325*, ed. Alexander Roberts and James Donaldson (Edinburgh: T&T Clark; Grand Rapids, Mich.: W. B. Eerdmanns, 1989–94), I: 561.

103 Tertullian, *Against Marcion*, Book III, Chapter 24, in *The Ante-Nicene Fathers*, III: 342, 343.

104 On the return to the earthly paradise in Lactantius, see *The Divine Institutes*, Book II, Chapter 12, p. 149.

105 Lactantius, *The Divine Institutes*, Book VII, Chapter 14, p. 510. On Lactantius and millenarianism, see Pichon, esp. 127–29, 211–12. See J. Daniélou, "La Typologie millénariste de la semaine dans le christianisme primitif," *Vigiliæ christianæ*, 2 (1948): 1–15.

106 Lactantius, *The Epitome of the Divine Institutes, Addressed to His Brother Pentadius*, Chapter LXXI, in *The Ante-Nicene Fathers*, VII: 254.

107 On the return of the Golden Age, see ibid., Chapter LXXII, pp. 254–55; a return to the Golden Age must precede the Last Judgment. On Lactantius and the Golden Age, see Lactantius, *The Divine Institutes*, Book V, and J. L. Swift, "Lactantius and the Golden Age," *American Journal of Philology*, 89, no. 354 (1968): 144–56.

108 Pseudo-Methodius, *Apokalypsis*, Chapters XIII and XIV, quoted in Bernard McGinn, *Visions of the End: Apocalyptic Traditions in the Middle Ages* (New York: Columbia University Press, 1979), 76. See also Claude Carozzi, *Apocalypse et salut dans le christianisme ancien et médiéval* (Paris: Aubier, 1999).

109 A statement reported in 1208 by Ralph of Coggeshall, quoted in Henry Mottu, *La Manifestation de l'Esprit selon Joachim de Fiore: Herméneutique et théologie de l'histoire d'après le "Traité sur les quatre Evangiles"* (Neuchâtel [etc.]: Delachaux & Niestlé, 1977), 24.

110 Joachim of Fiore, quoted in Mottu, 25.

111 Ibid., 26.

112 Ibid., 233.

113 On these schemas, see Marjorie Reeves and Beatrice Hirsch-Reich, *The "Figuræ" of Joachim of Fiore* (Oxford: Clarendon Press, 1972).

114 Joachim of Fiore, quoted in Mottu, 289.

115 On the followers of Joachim of Fiore, see Francis Rapp, *L'Eglise et la vie religieuse en Occident à la fin du Moyen Age* (Paris: Presses universitaires de France, 1971), 186.

116 On these eschatological movements, see Paul Alphandéry and Alphonse Dupront, *La Chrétienté et l'idée de croisade* (Paris: Michel, 1954), I: 43–57 and II: 115–48. See also Dupront, *Le mythe de croisade*.

117 On Wycliffe's theories and the Lollard movements, see Rapp, 188–96.

118 Quoted in Albert B. Friedman, "'When Adam Delved . . .': Contexts of an Historic Proverb," in *Wise Words: Essays on the Proverb*, ed. Wolfgang Mieder (New York: Garland, 1994), 495. This is from a sermon by John Ball, but this maxim was already commonplace at the time, since one finds it quoted in a religious poem from the beginning of the fourteenth century; much later, it was taken up throughout Europe. On this English revolt of 1381, see R. H. Hilton, *Bond Men Made Free: Medieval Peasant Movements and the English Rising of 1381* (London: Temple Smith, 1973), 206–7.

119 On the reformation in Bohemia before Jan Hus, see Rapp, 196–206. On Jan Hus and the Taborite revolt, see Josef Macek, *Jan Hus et les traditions hussites: XVe–XIXe siècles* (Paris: Plon, 1973), and Cohn, 205–22.

120 Master Laurence of Březová, note of January 1420, quoted in Howard Kaminsky, "Chiliasm and the Hussite Revolution," *Church History*, 26 (1957): 43–71, esp. 47.

121 From a Taborite commentary on the Apocalypse, ca. 1425, quoted (in Latin) in Kaminsky, 43.

122 Ibid., 58.

123 On the Brethren of the Free Spirit, see Rapp, 182–83.

124 Jesus Christ, quoting an unknown prophet in *The Epistle of the Apostles (Epistula Apostolorum)*, in *The Apocryphal New Testament: A Collection of Apocryphal Christian Literature in an English Translation*, ed. J. K. Elliott (Oxford: Clarendon Press; New York: Oxford University Press, 1993), 577.

125 Saint Zeno, Bishop of Verona, quoted in Dom O. Rousseau, "Quelques textes patristiques sur la Jérusalem céleste," in *La vie spirituelle*, 381.

126 Saint Clement of Alexandria, *Pædagogicon*, Book II, Chapter 12, in *Patrologiæ cursus completus. Series Græca*, 8: cols. 540–42; published in English as *Christ the Educator*, trans. Simon P. Wood (New York: Fathers of the Church, 1954), 191. On the description of celestial Jerusalem, see Mireille Mentré, *Création et Apocalypse: Histoire d'un regard humain sur le divin* (Paris: O.E.I.L., 1984), 179–91.

127 "Une élévation sur les gloires de Jérusalem" by an anonymous cleric of the Benedictine Abbey of Bèze, beginning of the twelfth century, quoted in Leclercq, 65.

128 On the political ideas of Plato, see *History of Political Philosophy*, 3rd ed., ed. Leo Strauss and Joseph Cropsey (Chicago: University of Chicago Press, 1987), 33–89.

129 Plato, *Statesman*, 297b, p. 341.

130 See Michel-Pierre Edmond, *Le Philosophe-roi: Platon et la politique* (Paris: Payot, 1991).

131 On Aristotle's political thought, see Strauss and Cropsey, 118–54.

132 Augustine, *The City of God*, Book XIX, Chapter 6, 6: 163. On Saint Augustine's political thought, see Henri Xavier Arquillière, *L'Augustinisme politique: Essai sur la formation des théories politiques du Moyen Age*, 2nd ed. (Paris: J. Vrin, 1955), and Strauss and Cropsey, 176–205.

133 Augustine, *The City of God*, Book XIX, Chapter 13, 6: 175.

134 Ibid., Book XIX, Chapter 15, 6: 187.

135 Ibid., Book XIV, Chapter 28, 4: 405.

136 Ibid., Book XIX, Chapter 17, 6: 199.

137 Pseudo-Dionysius the Areopagite, *Pseudo-Dionysius: The Complete Works*, trans. Colm Luibheid; foreword, notes, and trans. collaboration by Paul Rorem (New York: Paulist Press, 1987).

138 Pope Gelasius I, *Epistola XII*, in *Patrologiæ cursus completus. Series prima* [Latin] (Paris: J. P. Migne, 1844–49), 59: col. 42, quoted in Marcel Pacaut, *La Théocratie, l'Eglise et le pouvoir au Moyen Age* (Paris: Editions Montaigne, 1957), 275.

139 Hugh of Saint-Victor, *De sacramentis christianæ fidei*, Book II, Part 2, Chapter 4, in *Patrologiæ cursus completus. Series secunda*, 176: col. 418; trans. Roy J. Deferrari as *On the Sacraments of the Christian Faith* (Cambridge, Mass.: Mediaeval Academy of America, 1951), 256.

140 On Gratian and the composition of the *Decretum*, see *The Cambridge History of Medieval Political Thought, c. 350–c. 1450*, ed. J. H. Burns (Cambridge: Cambridge University Press, 1988), 269, 276–77, 286–89, 314 ff. Also see Gratian, *Gratiani Decretum: La traduction en ancien français du Décret de Gratien: édition critique*, ed. Leena Löfstedt, 4 vols. to date (Helsinki: Societas Scientiarum Fennica, 1992–).

141 Denis Foulechat, Préface" to his translation of John of Salisbury's *Policratus*, *Le Policratique de Jean de Salisbury (1372), Livres I–III* (Genève: Droz, 1994), 87. For an English translation, see *Policraticus: Of the Frivolities of Courtiers and the Footprints of Philosophers*, ed. and trans. Cary J. Nederman (Cambridge: Cambridge University Press, 1990). On John of Salisbury, see *The Cambridge History of Medieval Political Thought, c. 350–c. 1450*, 325–29.

142 On Giles of Rome, see *Histoire culturelle de la France*, ed. Jean-Pierre Rioux and Jean-François Sirinelli (Paris: Éditions du Seuil, 1997–98), I: 290–92, and Giles of Rome, *On Ecclesiastical Power*, trans. Arthur P. Monahan (Lewiston, N.Y: E. Mellen Press, 1990).

143 Brunetto Latini, *The Book of the Treasure (Li Livres dou Tresor)*, trans. Paul Barrette and Spurgeon Baldwin (New York: Garland, 1993), esp. Book III.

144 Dante Alighieri, *Monarchy*, trans. and ed. Prue Shaw (Cambridge: Cambridge University Press, 1996).

145 Marsilius of Padua, *Marsilius of Padua: The Defender of Peace*, Vol. 2: *The Defensor pacis*, trans. with an introduction by Alan Gewirth (New York: Columbia University Press, 1951–56).

146 On the frescoes of the "Good and Bad Government," see Quentin Skinner, "Ambrogio Lorenzetti: The Artist as Political Philosopher," *Proceedings of the British Academy*, 72 (1986): 1–56; Nicolai Rubinstein, "Le allegorie di Ambrogio Lorenzetti nella Salla delle pace e il pensiero politico del suo tempo," *Rivista storica italiana*, 109, no. 3 (1997): 781–802; Ernst Hartwig Kantorowicz, *The King's Two Bodies: A Study in Mediaeval Political Theology* (Princeton, N.J.: Princeton University Press, 1997), 112–13.

147 Latini, Book III, pp. 74, 354.

148 Ramon Llull, *Blanquerna*, trans. from the Catalan by E. Allison Peers (London: Dedalus; New York: Hippocrene Books, 1987).

149 Ibid., Book IV, Chapter 95, p. 400.

150 Ibid., Book IV, Chapter 94, pp. 396, 398.

151 Ibid., p. 396.

152 Dante, *Monarchy*, Book I, Chapter 16, p. 28.

153 Christine de Pisan, *The Book of the City of Ladies*, trans. Earl Jeffrey Richards (New York: Persea Books, 1982), Part I, Chapter 1, p. 3; Chapter 3, p. 10.

154 Ibid., Part I, Chapter 4, p. 11.

155 Ibid., Part I, Chapter 8, p. 16.

156 Ibid., Part III, Chapter 19, p. 254.

157 Giovanni Boccaccio, *The Decameron*, trans. Mark Musa and Peter Bondanella (New York: Norton, 1983).

158 William of Malmesbury, *De gestis pontificum Angliæ*, IV, in *Patrologiae cursus completus. Series secunda* [Latin], 179: cols. 1612D–1613A, quoted in Leclercq, 130.

159 *Livre des constitutions et ordinations de l'Ordre des frères prêcheurs* (Toulouse: Secrétariat provincial de la Province dominicaine de Toulouse, 1979).

160 Saint Peter Damian (1007–1072), *The Book of "The Lord Be With You,"* Chapter XX, in *Selected Writings on the Spiritual Life*, trans. with an introduction by Patricia McNulty (London: Faber and Faber, 1959), 80.

161 On the country of Cockaigne, see *Les Malheurs des temps: Histoire des fléaux et des calamités en France*, ed. Jean Delumeau and Yves Lequin (Paris: Larousse, 1987), 169, and Anna Birgitta Rooth, *Från lögnsaga till Paradis* (Uppsala: Universitetet; Stockholm: Distributor, Almqvist & Wiksell International, 1983).

Plato's Atlantis: The *True* Utopia

THESE DAYS, the definition of the genre known as "utopia" is debated by historians of ideas as well as of literature,[1] and yet most comparative studies or anthologies devoted to this genre and its history recognize Plato's *Critias* as the inaugural, and sometimes archetypal, utopian story. That the author of this short and incomplete tale is a philosopher complicates the task of anthologists and historians from the start. In fact, it is astonishing that a tradition of fiction should be seen as having originated with a writer who made true knowledge of the real world the defining characteristic of what he undertook to establish as "philosophy." Yet this is the philosopher who defended the necessity for and possibility offered by one myth, the myth of Atlantis, whose legacy has been immense, and which still today has its enthusiasts, believers, and priests.[2]

If one hesitates to place the extraordinary fiction of the *Critias* within the philosophical mission of his complete works, this is largely due to Plato himself. The inclusion of a tale, the mythos, does not in itself distinguish the *Critias* from his other dialogues; most of them have recourse to myth in dealing with the world or with the destiny of souls after death. Plato, justly considered a "mythologue," constantly underlines the pedagogic and ethical importance of Greek tales, which he appropriates and adapts for his persuasive or heuristic purposes.[3] But the myth of the *Critias*, by recounting a war that supposedly occurred nine thousand years previously between ancient Athens and the island empire of Atlantis, partially departs from his customary usage, for the very simple reason that it is declared "true" by the characters who relate it. Far from being a plausible tale that, in Plato's hands, could be immediately distinguished from rational, explanatory, and scholarly discourse (*logos*), the myth is presented as a true discourse, a *logos alêthinos*,[4] whose subject is government and political constitution. Plato's story represents in fictional form the reasons for the ruin of the Athenian empire, which is described in the guise of an Atlantis that fails in its invasion of the virtuous Athens of ancient times. It is the Athens of his own time, defeated after the Peloponnesian War, whose fatal imperialist excesses the philosopher is really describing. Moreover, this description of distant cities and events allows him to say something true, not only about Athens's recent history, but about that of any city, whether corrupt or virtuous.

This is one of the reasons why all readers of the *Critias*, whether classical or modern, whether lovers of mythology, literature, or philosophy, have taken such pains to assign the Atlantis tale to a category (is it myth or rational discourse?), a genre (fiction or historical testimony?), or a function (historical analysis in disguise or utopia?). And this is one of the reasons why, still today, they give it high status but have difficulty placing it within the literary history of utopia. Raymond Trousson, in the first pages of his *Voyages aux Pays de nulle part*, states that "Plato is considered the true creator of the utopian genre, and this is correct, but in fact his is a very singular case that obliges us to disregard the established principles of theoretical discussion."[5] The creator of the genre thus seems to escape that genre's rules. If Trousson's judgment is well founded, it is because the *Critias* is not so much the first example of the utopian genre but rather the very precondition of its existence, the pretext, or "hypotext," for it. We have to recognize that Plato's tale is a literary hybrid, and a philosophical hybrid, too. As I shall try to show, this is because it is effectively a utopia in itself.

The study of the immense legacy of Atlantis reveals a great disparity in the uses to which it is put, which corresponds to a diversity in the readings that have been made of the *Critias*'s text and audience. It has been cited variously by different traditions: as a pretext for literary ramblings on imaginary worlds, as a source of fictional examples of political conflicts and the vanity of empires, and as a model of political organization for modern utopians. One can distinguish roughly three sorts of readings of the tale, according to whether it is used for ends that are ideological (as when it stands for the first testimony to the existence of Atlantis),[6] or literary (when it is placed in the tradition of imaginary voyages and Cockaignes), or philosophical (when one simply asks how it functions within Plato's works). Since the fourth century B.C.E., these three types of readings have not had the same reception. The legacy of the *Critias* was first apparent within literature and, much later, within ideology. But philosophy was the poor relation of this heritage. The conception of a fictional city, while it found favor among Hellenistic authors (especially the Cynics and Stoics), did not arouse in ancient philosophers the same interest that Plato had shown in the *Critias*, as well as in the *Republic* and the *Laws*, to which I shall return. It is really only among modern utopians that we find a similar philosophical desire to say something "absolutely true" by means of a fable about a city and its constitution. But this is what makes for a utopia, which we may consider the constitutional form of the political mythology of philosophers.

The Shipwreck of Plato's Atlantis

The *Critias* is the sequel to the cosmology of Plato's *Timaeus*, a tale whose purpose is a plausible explanation of the genesis and nature of the world, with the help of a myth telling how a divine artisan fashioned the world's soul and body, before causing the birth of all living beings. The two dialogues are two parts of the same conversation, in the course of which Timaeus and then Critias expound before Socrates the nature of the world, then of man, and finally of the city. Critias's discourse, to the extent that he deals with the excellent and virtuous city, should be seen as complementary to, or even a correction of, the speech Socrates had made "the day before" on the city and its constitution (the *politeia*, or a very artificially summarized *Republic*). To play his dual role of saying something about the ideal city and of giving life and movement to the constitution forged by Socrates, Critias undertakes to tell how, nine thousand years earlier, the city of Athens had undergone attacks from the island of Atlantis, which in defeat was soon entirely drowned in a flood, while the Athenian army, for its part, disappeared as a result of an earthquake (*Timaeus* 24e–25d). But the ancient conflict is not the subject of the announced tale; incomplete, the story from the *Timaeus* here in the *Critias* merely takes the form of a minute description of two rival powers, with particularly meticulous attention paid to the Empire of Atlantis. *Critias* describes its site, geography, town planning, population, and certain of its institutions and customs. Plato's Atlantis tale, therefore, consists only of a brief summary followed by a minute description. And classical readers, if contemporary testimony can be trusted, never possessed a text different from ours: the *Critias* is an incomplete dialogue, not one that has been partially lost or suppressed. This is surely the reason why it has so spontaneously served as a palimpsest, or even

as an incipit waiting to be completed by all "seekers after Atlantis."

At the end of the classical period, the first book of the *Commentary on the Timaeus* by the neo-Platonist philosopher Proclus (412–485) reviewed the principal classical interpretations of Plato's tale. Proclus distinguished between those that considered the story to be a fable (*muthos*) and those that considered it authentic testimony, an inquiry (*historia*). From the first reader named, the academician Crantor (fl. 335 B.C.E.), who believed in the historical accuracy of the ancient events reported by Plato, to the neo-Platonists Amelius (third century) and Iamblichus (ca. 240–325), who took it as an allegorical expression of the cosmic opposition that constituted the universe, the authors mentioned by Proclus appear to have sought to relieve the *Critias* of the annoying ambiguity conferred by its double genre, by choosing between myth and truth. But the truth was not necessarily historical in their eyes; Crantor, who two generations after Plato maintained that the *Critias* was "mere history,"[7] was the only classical interpreter known to have defended *Critias*'s "authenticity." If certain testimony can be believed,[8] ambiguity about this has persisted since Aristotle, for the simple reason that classical readers all recognized that the ostensible subject of the Atlantis story, the retelling of an ancient conflict situated between the cosmology of the *Timaeus* and the recollection of the political project of the *Republic*, could not be unduly extracted from its doctrinal context. Analysis of the literary genre as well as of the real function of the story thus seemed suitable. When no other historical or literary testimony seemed to corroborate the existence of Atlantis, or even of archaic Athens, some classical readers (and even more contemporary commentators) wondered if Plato had not committed in the *Critias* a work of dissimulation, prudently choosing to disguise some other conflict as a fable. The neo-Platonic commentators thus maintained that the archaic conflict mimicked a conflict between opposing cosmic principles, by relating the *Critias* to the cosmological argument in the *Timaeus*, in which Plato had just explained that the rational determination of the universe always ran up against a principle of indetermination and trouble; other classical and modern readers chose to insist instead on the political and pamphleteering mission of a fable that described the fatal excesses of a bellicose maritime empire, and which had been composed by an Athenian who was hostile to his own city's maritime imperialism.

We should remember, though, that the *Critias*'s legacy among the classics cannot be confined to cosmological or political interpretations offered by philosophical commentators. Historians, geographers, and naturalists, more interested in its descriptions than in the conflict summarized in the *Timaeus*, found in it original and useful material for an investigation into Atlantis, which many of them stressed as plausible and precise. Far removed from cosmological, symbolic, or allegorical interpretations, then, one could make documentary use of the *Critias* and regard the island described by Plato as a "curiosity." Thus, among others, Strabo (first century B.C.E.), who showed no interest in Plato's doctrine, or in the war recounted in the *Critias*, underlines the great interest of the geographical descriptions of Atlantis and Athens and the plausibility of the seismic phenomena mentioned by Plato. A century later, in his *Natural History*, Pliny too mentions the *Critias* in order to attest to the antiquity of earthquakes.[9] Both the geographer and the naturalist, while they held Plato's story to be a fiction, still thought it was fabricated on the basis of an exact knowledge of nature and its history. As fantastic as was the existence of the island of Atlantis, nevertheless its botany, zoology, geography, and the phenomena that would swallow it up were indeed real: Plato had described a false object by true means. Hence one had to distinguish between the *Critias* and what arose, at least for the Poets, from the tradition of "marvels," imaginary lands, enchanted places, and those voyages beyond the Pillars of Hercules whose tradition went back at least to the Hyperboreans of Hecataeus.[10] Of course, the Platonic story remained a fable, a composition as fictional as the "*périples*," or discovery voyages,[11] but its geographical material, its reality effects, and its concern with exactitude prevented its being attached from the start to the tradition of marvelous countries. It was something else, another kind of literature.

The strangeness of the Atlantis story and its incompleteness (it was so tempting to remedy that) did much to produce offspring. The choice of a distant and insular habitat, beyond the traditional frontiers of the known and inhabited world, the description of powerful and rich Atlantians who performed immense and incredible things, evidently struck a chord in a great number of readers. And not only when they recognized in the Atlantis of the *Critias* the already Homeric motif of the insular and fantastic elsewhere,[12] but also and more especially when they tried to pursue, complete, or transform Plato's tale. Atlantis then became in turn the destination of marvelous voyages; it was revisited. Thus we find it in Plutarch (a Platonist), in his dialogue *Concerning the face which appears in the orb of the Moon*, where the Homeric island of Ogygia is re-viewed and augmented in the light of Atlantis; Plutarch borrowed from the *Critias* the theme of an island as big as a continent, situated west of the Pillars of Hercules, as well as geographical elements (the alluvial deposits, the depths), the sign of Taurus, and the abundance of resources.[13] Plato's Atlantis finds itself serving the elaboration of a distant and fantastic place, despite the moral lesson of the *Critias* (121),[14] which denounces the corruption of the Atlantians. In this sense, with Plutarch (or Lucian),[15] it is no longer a matter of borrowing from Plato the most extraordinary elements of his fable. The interest of this literary heritage consists, despite Crantor's judgment, in the recognition of the fictional character of the Platonic tale. The Atlantis that impresses writers is a Platonic construction, a city made by Plato; thus one encounters again, now from a very different perspective, the idea that the cities described by Critias are artifices designed to represent something other than themselves. The question overlooked by the writers is posed anew: what does the Atlantis of the *Critias* designate?

A contemporary and denigrator of Plato, Theopompus of Chios[16] composed a comic voyage that was a pastiche of the Atlantis story, describing the fabulous Meropis, with its grand cities, two rivers, eternally young inhabitants, and then a conflict that pits the city of Saintsbury (Eusebe) against the city of Wartown (Machimon). The former is a peaceful town, whose inhabitants are freed from any labor by the prodigality of the land (they are thus happy and "die laughing"), while the latter is a bellicose city, immense (populated by more than two million men), whose inhabitants are "extemely warlike. Born fully armed, they subjugate their neighbors."[17] Theopompus's pastiche, as we see, acknowledges the fictional character of Plato's invention, but he grants its political function, which he mocks by caricaturing it. Thus both the fictional character and the political purpose of the tale seem to have been evident in the years immediately following the writing of the *Timaeus* and the *Critias*. Doubts arose only in the next generation (Crantor's), when the most surprising chapter of the *Critias*, the long description of Atlantis, began to command readers' attention.

To Describe a City

The *Critias* could be summarized as the description of archaic Athens and then of the island of Atlantis, considering successively the situation and geography of the belligerent powers, then their citizens. The descriptions cover, in the case of both powers, five distinct rubrics: the birth of citizens (anthropogony), their manners and functional roles (ethnography), their resources and means (economy), the borders and features of their country (topography), and, finally, the division between territory that is cultivated (*khôra*), or urban (*astu*).

Plato devotes the most care to the description of the metropolis of each of the two archaic powers; the cities he invents consist above all of a certain urban development of the territory. The *Critias* distinguishes clearly between the general and geographic situation of the two territories together (their topography and borders), and the urban and architectural disposition of the cities; more precisely, Plato describes three types of geographic space: the regional "allotment" chosen by the founding god, then the city, and then its terrain, which differ, not only in relation to development (structures and architecture differ from one space to another) but also in relation to civic functions, labor, and use of the land. These distinctions follow the characteristic divisions within the Greek representation of political space. Traditionally, in historical inquiries as well as in political treatises, city space is conceived on the basis of a distinction between the single urban metropolis (called either *polis* or *astu*), and its territory, usually agricultural. In describing a city, the ancient authors always took pains to observe this distinction, to trace the borders between the town and its countryside, as does Critias (110d–112d, 113b–d, 115c–117e). However, the urban and geographic type of metropolis, established on an elevation and possessing arable land (as is the case here with archaic Athens), is not typical of all archaic or classical cities. Along with Roland Martin, we can distinguish between two forms of urban grouping, which correspond "to two modes of occupation and exploitation of the land. On one side we find cities without territory for exploitation, oriented to commercial exchange, which are merchant cities . . . ; and on the other stand cities with vast territory, whose activity is essentially agricultural, depending closely on their *khôra*."[18] The territorial and urban contrast between the maritime type and the agricultural type suggest that the Platonic story does not oppose two singular and antithetical cities so much as two *types* of cities.

The chthonic agrarian type and the bellicose maritime type are two generic and apparently antithetical types of civic grouping: Athens and Atlantis represent two distinct models of organization of the political community.[19] But these types, and the development of the land and the urbanization that distinguish them, remain Greek.[20] So if Atlantis is really described in terms of foreign ornamentation (vaguely Egyptian, Persian, Syracusan, or Cretan), it is according to the geographical and urban disposition of the classic Greek city. The inhabitant of Atlantis, despite his gigantic size and his luxurious way of life, is a Greek inhabitant. Moreover, archaic Athens and Atlantis, as unlike as they are, figure as two kinds of a similar form of civic occupation of the land: they are thus not opposite or excessively contrasted regimes, as a democracy and an aristocracy might be, but two sister constitutions that enter into conflict because one of them did not know how (or was not able) to conserve the divine excellence that it had when it was founded.

To Inhabit a Fictional City

Describing the different groups of citizens according to whether their function is artisanal, agricultural, or military (*Timaeus* 24a–b), Plato links this tripartite approach with a strict division of civic territory, with each group separated from the others. His precision is even weightier in that Athens in the fourth century B.C.E. was distinguished by the relative confusion of its social urban space. While the Acropolis and the Agora indeed played the role of civic centers, urban balance was not thereby ensured, not only because a division of functions and authorities was blurred by the distance and conflict between central sites (the town around the Acropolis), between the north (the Agora) and the south (the Olympieion and the Python), but also and especially because no structured and systematic organization of urban space had been imposed on Athens while the city was growing.[21] This absence of topographical and functional control over the urban territory is caricatured on Atlantis, which figures as an exaggeration of the confused evolution of Athens toward its harbor zones. There is no form of zoning on the island, nor any urban plan for the sharing and separation of construction zones for different purposes.[22] On the contrary, religious, military, commercial, and residential buildings had indistinctly multiplied all over the city, in outlying areas, on the plains, and in the mountains. In a general way, the separation between town and territory, while it ruled the descriptive map of the two archaic cities, did not give rise, on Atlantis, to a separation between urban habitat and cultivated zones. Rather, these spaces were mixed up, and the slowly urbanized land welcomed haphazardly all civic activities. The former urban zone (the metropolis) became the terrain of disparate activities; even around the sanctuary of Poseidon there was a mixture of shrines, orchards, gymnasia, and tracks for horses (*Critias* 117b–c). The principle of Atlantian urbanism is a repetition and multiplication of the same functions and same constructions. Far from a particular space being prescribed for a single function, each part of the territory hosted all religious and political functions. Atlantian civic groupings, or districts, were not distinguished by function, but were all conceived on the same demographic and geographic model: they were the same size and had the same army, they were like so many multiplications of the same place. But Atlantian royalty did not believe that it was simply multiplying as its territory was being extended. *Critias* 118a–119b is the clearest illustration of this, indicating that the mountains and central plain each possessed (indiscriminately) villages, temples, armies, and towns, because the island was considered a city by the king. Therefore Athens is never contrasted with an Atlantis city, because one no longer existed. Athens was confronting an empire, because the conditions for the existence of a city, from an urban and political standpoint, were not present in Atlantis.

The urban space of Atlantis has the peculiarity of being quite regular and geometrical, composed of equal quadrilaterals and of concentric circles. The extreme density of the urban and territorial population is grouped into spaces that are either analogous (precincts) or identical (districts). We noted above that Athenian urbanism was meant to resolve the difficulties linked to the gradual extension of the town, the aggregation of agricultural and peripheral populations pushing into the city as it extended itself toward the sea. While the map of Athens remained confused, important accomplishments in urbanism took place in Piraeus. The geometric checkerboard of Atlantis seems to be evidence of a polemic allusion to these developments, no doubt particularly to those attributed to the architect Hippodamus of Miletus. Sorry geometricians, the Atlantians multiplied spaces that were identical but lacking in proportion. Their empire possessed no defined limit (the metropolis grew by endlessly repeating itself), and a relation was lost between the population of citizens and their places of habitation; in effect, they were obliged to limit population for want of being able to limit the territory.

The Utopian Production of the City

According to Plato, the city grew up at the same time that it took shape within a region, whose resources it either benefited from or transformed by technological projects. Considered from this perspective, Critias's descriptions distinguish between two kinds of relation to the territory: that of Athens, content to receive and profit from excellent natural resources; and that of Atlantis, less well off, which exploits them excessively for the sole purpose of indefinite enrichment. The localization of the town in both cases presupposes a political shaping that situates the dwellings and circumscribes the activities so that they may conserve a certain regularity. Thus, an order, morphology, and boundaries were established, as Critias never fails to explain. This is another way the two powers differ, since Athenian simplicity and strict limits contrast with Atlantis's disordered multiplication of structures and civil, religious, and military locales.

While politics does not produce its raw materials (whether natural resources or human population), it must achieve their combination and direct their usage. The tale of Atlantis, read from this point of view, insists quite particularly on the principles and political instruments that make possible this ordering of the city's materials, always stressing the importance of political instruments capable of ordering things as they should be. (Does one impose urban planning on the city and privilege certain buildings in relation to others? What are the civic functions that should be exercised? What kinds of customs or economy should be encouraged?) The story's function is thus to examine the choices, some of which have been made to represent hypotheses and others of which could be made to do so. Through the story and the detailed description of fictional cities, Plato thus conceives a form of simulation (*mimêsis, Critias* 107b), both restricted and schematic, whose function is to make intelligible, to analyze and criticize a plurality of existing or possible political regimes.

If one sticks to the most probable chronological hypotheses, the *Critias* is the first of Plato's dialogues, apart from the *Laws*, to make use, for the purpose of political arguments, of urban and geographical descriptions and city maps. This peculiar recourse to geographical description defines a new form of political narrative, a method mixing analysis and critique to explain city things.

The privileged relation these cities enjoy with their territory is a relation of use and production; in the *Critias*, the way in which the political community inhabits, manages, and exploits the territory that is its own seems to suffice, much more than would ethical or constitutional information, to characterize the nature and value of its political regime. The detail of the urban map and architectural buildings of Atlantis is no doubt what strikes most readers. As I have suggested, the precision and strangeness of the fictional descriptions had an important influence on fictional journeys to the antipodes and "discoveries" of unknown peoples.[23] But retrospectively compared to the *Critias*, these tales manifest no political mission. One could therefore show again how impoverished the legacy of Plato's story was from a philosophical and political point of view; in Aristotle's great treatise *Politics*, a model fictional constitution occurs only in the optative book on political inquiry (VII, 4–12). Recourse to the fiction of an island city for the purpose of political reflection scarcely seems to find an equivalent, or offspring, except in the philosophy of the Renaissance.

Thomas More's *Utopia* (1516) and then Tommaso Campanella's *Civitas Solis* [*The City of the Sun*] (1602) include the Platonic dialogue among their direct sources; a concern for geographical description, for a map of the city, for descriptions, and for a division of classes and tasks is common to them. But the kinship remains too allusive, even from the philosophical aspect, for one to conclude immediately that there is a commonality of genre, or to grant archetypal status to Plato's tale. On the other hand, it is on the basis of Renaissance works that people have retrospectively characterized the Atlantis story (and the *Republic* or the *Laws*) as a "utopia." This comparison is of great importance, not in order to appreciate the literary or philosophical posterity of the Atlantis story, because that is manifestly not at issue here, but in order to define the very particular rationality applied there. Giving to the Athenian disaster the exaggerated face of Atlantis allows Plato to retain and privilege certain aspects of Athenian excess (imperialism, rural overpopulation, and a kind of sabotage produced by imbalances), so as to assemble them into a political type whose story might represent what it is becoming, its history. It is precisely this form of rationality (the restriction of the political community to a few criteria for the fictional composition of a program-

matic city) that Renaissance utopians put to use. To the extent that the comparison here is merely indicative, one might turn to the main conclusions of Pierre-François Moreau's *Récit Utopique*. Dealing notably with More, Moreau has defined the three characteristic discourses of the modern utopian genre: "a critical discourse, through which the situation of England and other European states is sifted; a descriptive discourse, which contrasts this disorder with the social life of the utopian island; and a justifying discourse, which enunciates under what conditions such a social life is possible. The relations among these three discourses, as they are established in the course of the text, will set the functioning and limits of the genre for nearly three centuries."[24] The interest of this definition rests on the importance it grants to description, which allows Thomas More (like Tommaso Campanella or Francis Bacon) simultaneously to make a critique and to offer a rational political ("justified") alternative, without being obliged to abandon his fictional subject or renounce the purpose of his description. Such a concern can be read in the Platonic tale, and it is this mixed intention that has been ignored in the recent debate over the "utopian" character of the Platonic dialogues. This debate has been distorted, both by the anachronism of the adjective "utopian," rather risky when applied unequivocally to Plato,[25] and by the frequent confusion between what might be termed, in Plato's doctrine, notions of the "ideal," which refers to intelligible reality, and the "model," which refers to the paradigmatic artifice designed to make sensory reality intelligible. This is why it seems more prudent to refer to the two forms of political organization described by the *Critias* as "constitutional types," as cities constituted by the discourse and defined as such, whose function is both explanatory (to understand and expound the nature of various existing cities) and, once again, programmatic (a use of these explanatory types is possible). This is also why, in quite another sense than the inaccessible ideal or simple model, one may quite rightly call this philosophical fiction "utopian," but only to the extent that one understands utopia as a theoretical elaboration, for analytical and tactical ends, of cities conceived and described on the basis of a finite number of restrictive hypotheses.

Plato's *Republic* introduces for the first time in Greek political reflection a fictional hypothesis, that of an excellent city, and undertakes to define its constitution, some of its magistrature, institutions, and functional forms of citizenship.[26] His concern is not to describe an existing city, nor even to imagine, for example, what might be the conditions for actually reforming such a city, but rather to conceive, by means of and within a discourse (*en logô*), a constitution, a city deprived of terrestrial existence. What is founded by and in the *Republic* is a city, as Glaucon says, "that exists in theory, for I don't think it exists anywhere on earth." "But perhaps," replies Socrates, "there is a model of it in heaven, for anyone who wants to look at it and to make himself its citizen on the strength of what he sees. It makes no difference whether it is or ever will be somewhere, for he would take part in the practical affairs of that city and no other."[27] Such a hypothesis, common to the *Republic* and the *Laws*, is the foundation in philosophy of a genre of constitutional treatise (an inquiry *peri politeias*) that one may legitimately designate by the name "utopia," as will modern utopians from the sixteenth century onward.[28] That utopia thus has an ancient, philosophical, and political origin, however, does not allow us to conclude immediately that there exists a continuous and homogeneous history of a utopian tradition that, via More and Campanella, will run from Plato to the Saint-Simonians and Fourierists, embracing in passing all that literature has produced about imaginary cities and ideal constitutions. Still, a comparison between the Platonic dialogues and modern utopian constitutions at least has the merit of allowing us to perceive the interest, if not the necessity, of a recourse to an island fable, which is one of the distinctive signs of utopia for philosophers who deal with the city, communal life, and its government. The hypothesis that presides in philosophy over the writing of a utopia is really that the fiction of an excellent constitution is the sole means of having a true discourse about communal life.

The descriptions in the *Critias* – the principal reasons for the text's ambiguity and for its great "mythic" heirs – are plausible descriptions; they describe known objects in known terms. In order to describe the two archaic powers, Plato appropriates the vocabulary and method of discourses on the city that were then current, to make them serve the presentation of the different characteristics (geographical, institutional, economic, or civic) of the two belligerents. This descriptive genre is so surprising in Plato's work, which until then had been distinguished by its aptitude for mediating knowledge of the community (by means of the soul and technical paradigms), that this recourse to historical and geographical descriptions was long held to be a

simple pastiche of historical tales. To understand it otherwise presupposes that one explains why the story uses real materials, enumerates known vegetal resources, and even submits its descriptions to architectural rules and political institutions already observed elsewhere. Critias is merely describing, even when he mentions Atlantian "*oreichalkos*" [mountain copper] (114e), familiar objects that were commonly known. All the originality of the story consists instead in elaborating, starting from these objects, fictional and unprecedented case studies of regimes and political communities. The representation and knowledge of cities, which speeches or historical and constitutional expertise gather and develop, is thus put at the service of an invention, of a fictional conception. This is what explains why we find, in the *Timaeus* and the *Critias*, the Herodotean historical inquiry, the classical periegesis, or certain themes of the *Politeiai*, placed in a configuration that no longer describes a reality. The cities Critias describes do not exist "on earth" but are described as one ordinarily describes existing cities. To what purpose? The most immediate political function of the Platonic story is quite evidently polemic, and one may legitimately take the *Critias* as a pamphlet directed against the most recent imperialist inclinations of Athens. Because of the defeat promised to a corrupt Athens, the Atlantian shipwreck is a sort of bad omen, a lesson that is also a threat addressed to Plato's fellow citizens. So that things might be clear enough to the reader, it was essential that Atlantis be identified with the Athenian city, and that the reasons for its defeat be apparent there. This is precisely what Plato was trying to do by "composing" Atlantis from a small number of hypotheses and distinctive traits. These characterize it as a maritime power, bellicose and imperialist, carried away by an indefinite and overreaching expansionist movement. The set of documentary materials that are borrowed to realize the portrait of Atlantis is designed to accentuate and condemn this overreaching, while, by privileging some of them (maritime power, urbanism, certain customs), allowing Athens to be recognized in Atlantis. But they also give rise to a certain number of political hypotheses. In effect – and this is the "utopian" particularity of the Atlantis story – the nature, suitability, and value of these distinctive traits are examined *in situ*, in the framework of a rational fiction that tests them as hypotheses. It is really the particularity of utopia, as Jacques Lévy recently defined it, to be "founded on a restrictive hypothesis of the type 'all other things being equal.' . . .

Its function is to evaluate in a systematic manner the effects on the whole society of a particular type of transformation."²⁹ This is a type of reasoning "by hypothesis" (*ex hupotheseôs*) that Plato in the *Meno* had already maintained was appropriate for conceiving how excellence might be acquired or not (86e–87b).³⁰ The descriptive choice of the *Critias* is all the more appropriate for this political rationality, both fictional and hypothetical, because the dialogue proceeds precisely by linking to each other the distinctive traits of the two archaic powers. Thus Athens's excellent land explains the freedom of action of its army, and its strict limitation of territory accords with the physical and social separation of its citizens; and Atlantis's territorial extension is associated with architectural and decorative profusion, then with a population increase. The correlations pointed out this way constitute effectively the political hypotheses that the fiction tests: describing the topographical alienation of the Atlantian population outside the initial limits of Poseidon's theocratic sovereignty, Critias can legitimately draw the conclusion of a loss of the divine element in the nature of its inhabitants.

With the Atlantis story, Plato writes a political text that does not satisfy the narrow requirement of accounting for relations among inherent forces: there is no question here of *Athenian* politics, institutions, and conflicts; the demonstration is not premised on the examination of Athenian politics. This by no means precludes its producing – this is the poetic effect of the tale – the conditions for this examination. The "rational fiction" of the utopian story thus keeps a programmatic function, to the extent that it produces and tests the conditions of political understanding of what an excellent or corrupt city is, even while its subject, the fictional product of a simulation, of course remains by definition "unrealizable."³¹ That there is no direct realization to expect from rational fiction, however, in no way suggests that it is a useless fiction: there is a possible use for it, a use "with a view to action" ("epitactical"). It is addressed to the one who must rule the city, and know what is best for that. In this sense, as Socrates and Critias suggest, the memory of the archaic conflict might be called "true."

Translated by Susan Emanuel

Notes

1 On the utopian literature of the ancient world, philosophical or not, see especially Lucio Bertelli, "L'utopia greca," in *Storia delle idee politiche, economiche e sociali*, vol. I: *L'Antichità Classica* (Turin: Unione Tipografico–Editrice, 1982), 463–581, including a full bibliography; and Doyne Dawson, *Cities of the Gods: Communist Utopias in Greek Thought* (New York: Oxford University Press, 1992). The most complete literary history remains Raymond Trousson, *Voyages aux Pays de nulle part: Histoire littéraire de la pensée utopique*, 2nd ed. (Brussels: Editions de l'Université de Bruxelles, 1979).

2 Pierre Vidal-Naquet in several indispensable studies has reconstructed the modern history of the Atlantis myth. See his "Athens and Atlantis: Structure and Meaning of a Platonic Myth" (1964), revised and reprinted in *The Black Hunter: Forms of Thought and Forms of Society in the Greek World*, trans. Andrew Szegedy-Maszak; with a foreword by Bernard Knox (Baltimore, Md.: Johns Hopkins University Press, 1986), 263–84; "Hérodote et l'Atlantide: Entre les Grecs et les Juifs. Réflexions sur l'historiographie du siècle des lumières," *Quaderni di Storia*, 16 (1982): 3–76; "Atlantis and the Nations" (1987), reprinted in *Politics Ancient and Modern*, trans. Janet Lloyd (Cambridge, England: Polity Press, 1995), 38–65. Philanthropic "societies" and archaeological "studies" are still devoting efforts to the search for the lost continent. The most recent of these quests for the history of the island, Richard Ellis's *Imagining Atlantis* (New York: Alfred A. Knopf, 1998), gives a fair idea of the rather disconcerting tenor of the "Atlantis fascination."

3 On this question, see Luc Brisson, *Plato the Myth Maker*, trans., ed., and with an introduction by Gerard Naddaf (Chicago: University of Chicago Press, 1998).

4 This happens several times: see Plato, *Timaeus*, 20 d 9, 21 a 3 and 6, 21 d 1–3, 22 e 5, and 23 d 2–3, in *Complete Works*, ed., with introduction and notes, by John M. Cooper; associate ed. D. S. Hutchinson (Indianapolis: Hackett Publishing Co., 1997), 1224–91. See my commentary on these passages in Jean-François Pradeau, *Le Monde de la Politique: Sur le récit atlante de Platon, Timée (17–27) et Critias* (Sankt Augustin: Academia Verlag, 1997), 22 ff.

5 Trousson, 33.

6 It is "ideological" in the sense that the myth of Atlantis is made to serve the constitution of national mythologies, most often when they try to represent their origins. See the studies by Vidal-Naquet cited in note 2 above.

7 Quoted by Proclus, in *Proclus' Commentary on the Timaeus of Plato*, Book I, 76, 1, trans. Thomas Taylor (Frome, Somerset, England: Prometheus Trust, 1998), 77. See also Book I, 129, 10 et seq. and 177, 10 et seq. (pp. 123 ff. and 166 ff.), where Proclus concedes in turn that an island the size of Atlantis really once existed.

8 In his *Geography*, Strabo observes that Posidonius (ca. 135–51 B.C.E.) prefers to believe "that Atlantis did once exist, but disappeared." This was a "better way" than stating (Posidonius here recalls Aristotle's comment on Homer) that "Its inventor caused it to disappear." See Strabo, Book II, Chapter 3, 6, in his *Geography*, trans. Horace Leonard Jones, 8 vols. (Cambridge, Mass.: Harvard University Press, 1917–49), 1: 391–92.

9 Describing ancient floods as the origin of the separation of continents, Buffon did the same in his *Histoire Naturelle*, willingly citing the tradition that "the old and new worlds were formerly but one continent, and that, by a violent earthquake, the antient Atalantis of Plato was sunk," and that this was a trustworthy explanation of the opening of the Strait of Gibraltar. See Georges Louis Leclerc, Comte de Buffon, *The System of*

Natural History, 2 vols., compiled chiefly from Swammerdam, Brookes, Goldsmith, etc. (Edinburgh: J. Ruthven and Sons, 1800), 1: 7.

10 For a presentation of all this "geography of the outer limits" literature, to which Herodotus greatly contributed, see Christian Jacob, *Géographie et Ethnographie en Grèce Ancienne* (Paris: A. Colin, 1991); and, for borrowings from Plato through Herodotus, see Pradeau, 156–85.

11 Thus Strabo deals with Plato's Atlantis immediately after having denounced the perfectly fictional character of the "voyages" of Antiphanes, Pytheas, and Euhemerus. See Strabo, Book II, Chapter 3, 5; 1: 391.

12 See the island of Ogygia in the *Odyssey* VII, 244, among others.

13 See Plutarch, *Moralia*, Chapter XXVI (940f–942c), in *Plutarch's Moralia in Sixteen Volumes*, trans. Frank Cole Babbitt et al. (Cambridge, Mass.: Harvard University Press; London: W. Heinemann, 1927–76), 12: 181–93. In Section 5 of his introduction to this dialogue (p. 22 of the volume cited), Harold Cherniss shows how Plutarch conceived of this episode as "an imitation of Plato's Atlantis in the spirit of Hecataeus' story of the Hyperboreans, Theopompus' Meropis, and the Sacred Records of Euhemerus."

14 Plato, *Critias*, in *Complete Works*, 1292–1306.

15 Whose voyage to the moon is also reminiscent of Plato's isle: see his *Vera historia* (*A True Story*) in vol. 1 of *Lucian*, trans. A. M. Hartman et al., 8 vols. (Cambridge, Mass.: Harvard University Press, 1913–67). With regard to fantastic voyages, the most interesting text, prior to Plutarch and Lucian, is one that Diodorus of Sicily devoted to the voyage of Iambulus (who supposedly lived in the third century). He came to an island in the ocean and discovered an extraordinary civilization populated by large

humans with huge ears. One finds here the motifs of abundance, the community of women and children, and moral excellence. See his *The Library of History*, vol. 2 of *Diodorus of Sicily, in twelve volumes* (Cambridge, Mass.: Harvard University Press; London: W. Heinemann, 1933–67), Book II, Chapters 55–60. Along with Theopompus of Chios's pastiche, the Diodorus text is the first source for the Hellenistic literature, often of Stoic inspiration, that associates the marvelous voyage with what Louis Gernet calls "social utopia"; see his "The City of the Future and the Land of the Dead" (1933), reprinted in his *The Anthropology of Ancient Greece*, trans. John D. B. Hamilton and Blaise Nagy (Baltimore, Md.: Johns Hopkins University Press, 1981), 112–24, in which the author explains how this new tradition uses mythological voyages for the purpose of social critique. This literature has been widely studied, and Bertelli's bibliography mentions the principal works.

16 Theopompus of Chios, born in 378, was a historian. In Felix Jacoby's *Die Fragmente der griechischen Historiker* (Berlin: Weidmannsche, 1923–69) see fragments 75 and 259. These are translated in Gordon Spencer Shrimpton, *Theopompus the Historian* (Montreal and Buffalo: McGill–Queen's University Press, 1991), 226–27 and 272.

17 Ibid., 226. See also Aelian, *Historical Miscellany*, Book III, 18, trans. and ed. N. G. Wilson (Cambridge, Mass.: Harvard University Press, 1997), 145, 147.

18 Roland Martin, "Rapports entre les structures urbaines et les modes de division et d'exploitation du territoire," in his *Architecture et Urbanisme*, preface by Jean Pouilloux and Georges Vallet (Rome: Ecole Française de Rome, 1987), 583.

19 Two other Platonic dialogues take up, in a very different fashion, the same contrast, again in order to condemn the maritime imperialism of which

the best (or worst) representative is Athens: *Menexenus* and the *Laws*, in *Complete Works*, 950–64 and 1318–1616. See especially the *Laws*, Book IV, 705c–707d.

20 See the introduction to: Plato, *The Atlantis Story: Timaeus 17–27; Critias*, with introduction, notes, and vocabulary by Christopher Gill (Bristol, England: Bristol Classical Press, 1980).

21 On this subject, and the confusion of zones of Athenian civic space, see Martin, "L'espace civique, religieux et profane dans les cités grecques de l'archaïsme à l'époque hellénistique," in *Architecture et Urbanisme*, 549–79.

22 On classic urban *zoning*, see Martin, "Rôle des principes fonctionnels dans l'urbanisme de la Grèce antique," in *Architecture et Urbanisme*, 89–117; and also his *L'Art Grec* (Paris: Librairie Générale Française, 1994), 251–67.

23 Because of this literary influence, people have sometimes called the *Critias* one of the first sketches of the "novelistic" genre that grew out of the travesty of historical narration (a genre that includes, for example, the oldest Greek novel, Chariton's *Chaereas and Callirhoe*). See B. E. Perry, *The Ancient Romances: A Literary-Historical Account of Their Origins* (Berkeley: University of California Press, 1967), 168–71; and, more convincingly, Massimo Fusillo, *Naissance du Roman*, trans. Marielle Abrioux (Paris: Editions du Seuil, 1991), 56–66, published originally as *Il Romanzo Greco: Polifonia ed Eros* in 1989.

24 Pierre-François Moreau, *Le Récit Utopique: Droit Naturel et Roman de l'Etat* (Paris: Presses Universitaires de France, 1982), 11. Moreau's definitions are more convincing than those proposed by Françoise Choay in her *The Rule and the Model: On the Theory of Architecture and Urbanism*, ed. Denise Bratton (Cambridge, Mass.: MIT Press, 1997), originally published as

La Règle et le modèle: Sur la théorie de l'architecture et de l'urbanisme in 1980.

25 As Victor Goldschmidt stresses in his *Platonisme et pensée contemporaine* (Paris: Aubier, 1970), 165–68.

26 As unlikely as it is that Plato was the first to conceive of an excellent or "ideal" *politeia* (this genre had precursors in the fifth century B.C.E.), the way in which his *Republic*, *Critias*, and *Laws* defend its philosophical and political necessity does appear inaugural; see Bertelli and Dawson.

27 Plato, *The Republic*, Book IX, 592a–b, in *Complete Works*, 971–1223. See the remarks on this passage by Bertelli, 472 ff.

28 The first of them, Thomas More, refers explicitly to his debt to Plato (see, among others, *Utopia*, Book I, 39, 50, 52–54; and Book II, 104).

29 Jacques Lévy, "La libération de l'utopie," in Patrick Garcia, Jacques Lévy, and Marie-Flore Mattei, *Révolutions, fin et suite* (Paris: Centre Georges Pompidou, Bibliothèque publique d'information, 1991), 299–314; quotation on 308. With reference to More's *Utopia*, from a perspective analogous to the way we are considering the Platonist text, see Louis Marin, *Utopics: Spatial Play*, trans. Robert A. Vollrath (Atlantic Highlands, N.J.: Humanities Press, 1984), 33–60.

30 Plato, *Meno*, in *Complete Works*, 870–97.

31 Lévy insists on this; see 308–9. Moreau also mentions the "justificatory" aspect of the utopian discourse, distinguishing between the enunciation of the conditions of a possible social transformation, and what would be the plan for an exhaustive and immediate transformation of society. What had appeared determining in Plato, from the *Republic* on, was that the "excellent" constitution had no earthly reality, and the *Laws* would say just that.

See pp. 135, 97, 146.

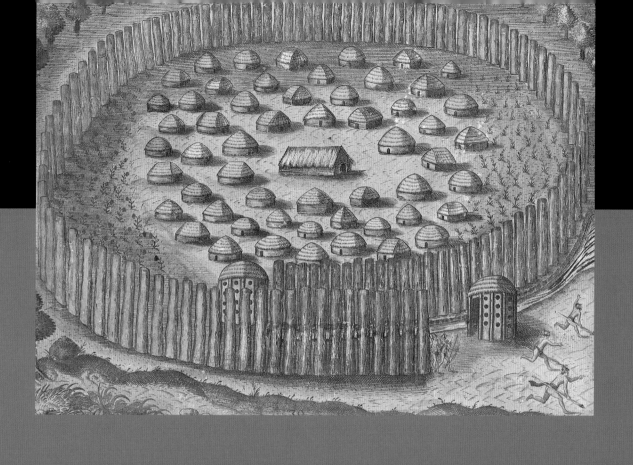

Utopia and the New World, 1500–1700

AS WE look back over the last millennium, it is hard not to be struck by a number of generations whose lives appear to have been lived in the context of dramatic, pivotal change. The generation of Europeans coming to maturity around the turn of the sixteenth century, half a millennium ago, surely has this sort of claim to our attention. Among the many events shaping their experience between 1492 and 1516, they found themselves confronting new and unexpected worlds. The geographical discoveries of Columbus and the explorers who followed him and the inauguration of a new genre of literary and political expression in More's *Utopia* appear, at first glance, to be poles apart: the first, an encounter with what, in the long term, turned out to be a stubborn reality to which Europeans had to accommodate themselves; the other, a conceptual

leap that would free their minds for fantasies ultimately capable of accommodating all human desire.

That the re-inauguration of utopian writing owed something to the discovery of the New World is an orthodoxy whose premises have barely been questioned, but the contrast between the gritty realities of new landfalls and the escapist reverie of utopian imaginings will not withstand scrutiny. Both the New World and Utopia remained for this generation, and many to follow, fictive, mythic constructs, and the ghosts of Europe's past dreams haunted them both. The discrimination between Old World and New had itself fictional dimensions, as was quickly recognized by the Inca Garcilaso de la Vega: "There is only one world and although we speak of the Old World and the New, this is because the latter was lately discovered by us, and

Arcadia

Sir Philip Sidney
Arcadia de Gräffen
von Pembrock
Frankfurt: Anthony
Hummen, 1643
NYPL, Rare Books Division

First published in 1590, *The Countesse of Pembrokes Arcadia* is an instructive tale of a king hoping to escape the dire prophecies of an oracle; in this work, Sir Philip Sidney creates a world of conflict between those blessed with reason and willing to accept divine providence and the laws of nature, and those who act out of uncontrolled passion. Sidney's Arcadia is full of fertile fields, gentle shepherds, and beautiful princesses, but the king's defiance of his own destiny sets in motion a series of actions that create a gulf between the Arcadia of the story and the Arcadia of legend. Only at the end, when divine providence sorts everything out and proves its power, does hope for achieving the idyllic, perfect Arcadia return.

not because there are two."[1] Much the same might be said about the distinction between utopia and the "real" world. Both were articulations of perceived worlds that drew on a stock of inherited concepts and were constrained by the vocabularies and linguistic conventions they used. If utopia is a shimmering mirage on the edge of our consciousness, it is worth reminding ourselves that, as David Riesman once observed, "the status quo proves the most illusory of goals."[2]

So it is that the newly discovered Americas were first seen through the eyes of Old World perceptions, dreams, and images of ideal societies or nightmares of howling wildernesses and plague-infested deserts. ". . . for not in vain," wrote Vasco de Quiroga (the would-be transporter of More's Utopia to New Spain) in 1535, "but with much cause and reason is this called the New World, not because it is newly found, but because in its people and in almost everything it is like as was the first and golden age."[3] The dream of the New World remained, as John Elliott has observed, a European dream.[4]

1492 was the year both of Columbus' first voyage and of the recovery of Granada from the Moors. The military and territorial triumph of Iberian Christendom in Europe appeared to be but a precursor to its evangelical and territorial triumph in the New World. But while some explored geographical new horizons, others sought to reestablish contact with past experience and achievement on a fresh and more direct basis. Humanistic studies, the recovery of classical Latin and Greek, became for the generation of Desiderius Erasmus, Thomas More, and their friends, a means by which the *philosophia Christi* and the practical wisdom of the ancients could be brought to bear on the problems of contemporary life. In Erasmian humanism, the renaissance of learning and the renewal of morality and society converged. Such convergence was not unproblematic. To see afresh the practical wisdom of classical philosophy or the teachings of Christ, revealed through the Greek New Testament, was to realize the degree to which ideals had been corrupted, the extent to which wisdom had been ignored or neglected. In the last decades of the fifteenth and the first of the sixteenth century, the mood of many humanists was one of conflict between hope and bitterness. In their darker moments, faith in the *studia humanitatis* and human *virtu* was shaken. Moral renewal might not be enough. Ortensio Lando, who with Anton Francesco Doni produced the first Italian edition of More's *Utopia*, lamented in his *Paradossi* that men were so unhappy when they saw all the evil around them that it was better to be blind than to see. It was a mood reinforced by the late Renaissance fear that history itself might be no more than an endless and meaningless flux. The renewal of the Old World was an aspiration faced with complex and daunting problems. Might the New World offer a cleaner sheet on which to design more perfect worlds?

New World/New Worlds
In the mind of Columbus himself, the act of discovering the New World had been prefigured in ancient prophecies and he was merely the chosen agent. "God made me the messenger of the new heaven and the new earth, of which he spoke in the Apocalypse of Saint John after having spoken of it by the mouth of Isaiah; and he showed me the spot where to find it."[5] Like scriptural images of Eden, Heaven, or the Millennium, so too classical images of Arcadia, the Golden Age, Atlantis, and the Isles of the Blest could be transported to the New World. For de Quiroga, the simplicity, equality, and goodness of the indigenous peoples combined with the fertility of the soil contrasted sharply with the restlessness, competitive emulation, "greed, ambition, arrogance, ostentation, boasting, . . . toil and anxiety" of the Europeans. The Golden Age of the pre-Columbian Americas was "seemingly immune from the hazards of fortune";[6] that is, until the footfall of the Europeans.

But before we read this situation as providing the required stimulus for the revival of utopian thought in the Old World, some cautions are necessary. First, Thomas More established an agenda for the utopian imagination that was far removed from this scripturally or classically inspired primitivism. Second, the revival of classical and scriptural learning in themselves promoted a greater interest in the social ideals of the Judeo-Christian tradition and those of antiquity. They did not have to be refracted through the prism of the New World to attract attention. Third, while the idealization of the Americas was a strain running through European perceptions and culture to the eighteenth century and beyond, it was an America invented by Europeans. The real America was slow to impinge on European consciousness, even that of the intellectuals. Thomas More was not entirely typical in finding a place for the New World on his conceptual map. Before the end of the sixteenth century, cartographers and cosmographers could continue to ignore the new continent altogether.[7]

The Green Globe

The Green Globe
Wood, hand-labeled
and -painted, ca. 1506
BNF, Département des
Cartes et Plans

Long attributed to Johannes
Schöner's Nuremberg studio,
this globe is very close in
nomenclature and certain
design elements to the world
map drawn in 1507 by the
humanist geographer Martin
Waldseemüller. This was the
first globe to designate the
new-found lands as "America" (for Amerigo Vespucci).
Perceiving before anyone else
the true significance of these
discoveries, Vespucci was the
first to identify them as a new
continent, a "*Mundus Novus*,"
which was, he noted in the
letter describing his third
voyage, "richer in peoples and
animals than all of Europe or
Asia or Africa."

The New World

Sebastian Munster
***Tabula Nouarum
insularum, quas diuersis
respectibus occidentales &
Indianas vocant***
Woodcut map from Ptolemy,
Geographia Universalis (Basel, 1540)
NYPL, Miriam and Ira D. Wallach
Division of Art, Prints and
Photographs

This is one of the earliest maps
to show the Americas as a
continent separate from Asia,
thus establishing them as a
truly "new" world for European explorers. One of the
great cartographers of the
sixteenth century, Sebastian
Munster faithfully depicted the
Japan ("Zipangri") described
by Marco Polo as an island
within an archipelago of 7,448
others. He also included the
legendary Fortunate Islands
off Africa, as well as the less
desirable "Ins. Infortunatae"
in the Pacific. As was common
on early maps, the presence of
cannibals in South America is
indicated by a leg on a bonfire.

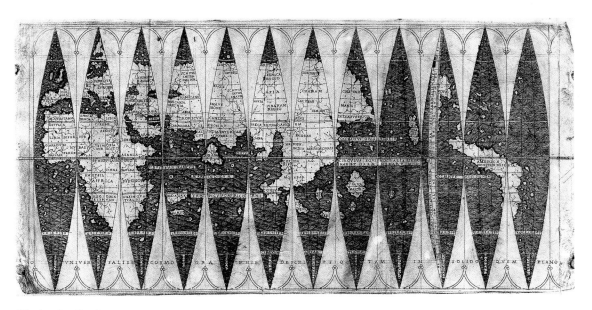

The American Continent

Louis Boulengier
***Universalis Cosmographia
Descriptio Tam in Solido
Quem Plano***
Engraving, ca. 1517
NYPL, Rare Books Division

Although the exact date of
publication of these globe
gores is not known, they
were found inserted into
a copy of Martin Wald-
seemüller's *Cosmographia
Introductio* printed in Lyons
in 1517 or 1518. They were
probably printed no earlier
than 1514, and appear to be
a close replication of those
that accompanied the first
edition of *Cosmographia
Introductio* (1507). In that text,
Waldseemüller suggests that
the newly discovered lands
be named after Amerigo
Vespucci, and on the large-
format map that was printed
with the volume, the name
"America" appeared over
what is now Brazil. These
globe gores show a slightly
simplified version of that
world map. This is the only
copy of these gores in existence today.

America

**Theodore Galle after
Johannes Stradanus**
America
Engraving from *Nova Reperta*
(Antwerp: C. de Mallery, 1580–90)
NYPL, Miriam and Ira D. Wallach
Division of Art, Prints and
Photographs

In this engraving, a European
explorer, probably Amerigo
Vespucci, awakens an allegorical America from her slumber;
their postures clearly establish
the balance of power. The
naked inhabitants of America
fascinated the European
explorers, for whom nudity
was both shameful and a
sign of people unaware of
Christianity. In the background,
other intriguing elements of
the New World are depicted,
including exotic animal life
and a group of cannibals.

Not only was the New World engaged in an unequal struggle with antiquity and the East for a place in the European imagination, but more perceptive commentators could, as the sixteenth century unfolded, perceive new worlds being generated close to home. The dynastic monarchies, establishing their courts and governing capacities, prompted – intentionally or otherwise – secular worlds of competing, emulative calculations of interest. Alongside them came new orders of commercial and state finance, stumbling toward new instruments and a new order, vulnerable to crisis but responsive to an unremitting need. The bounds of the city-state, the guild, and the regulated market were being tested and almost, but not quite, everywhere would ultimately be found wanting. Experience and observation were beginning to be incorporated into languages that would in time lead to new claims of "scientific" authority. Within a generation of the triumph of Western Christendom over Islam, the unity of Christendom was formally broken. Almost a century and a half of murderously fratricidal, confessional conflict followed. This was the anvil on which new states, new military regimes, new fiscalities, and new administrative orders were to be hammered out in the process we frequently describe (with perhaps a whiff of slightly too much teleology) as early modern statebuilding. But the Reformation/Counter-Reformation divide produced not only civil and physical conflict; it also produced wars of words. It functioned as a fracturer of discourses, a centrifuge of consciences. The new technology of the movable type printing press greatly accelerated this process and exposed in stark form the problem of how in a new world of decentralized communication a social consensus sufficient for stability was to be managed. All of these processes exposed deep-seated dilemmas for existing moral and social orders. They pressed on received wisdom and, in their novelty, asserted a right to new solutions.

The Ideal Society Responding to New Worlds

The discontented philosopher unwilling to settle for a nostalgic rehash of old values had to reach out for a social idealization that would embrace these observed and worrying new currents. Utopia could be the result but it was not the only, not the most common, nor the most readily absorbed form of social idealization through which social commentators responded. Exhortations to the moral renewal of all men, women, and children in the offices assigned to them, their stations and classes in life, were common. A variant on this perfect moral commonwealth tradition focused on princes and through exhorting them to ethical heroics sought to change the moral tone and performance of society as a whole. This reliance on individual and collective moral renewal was not alien to the

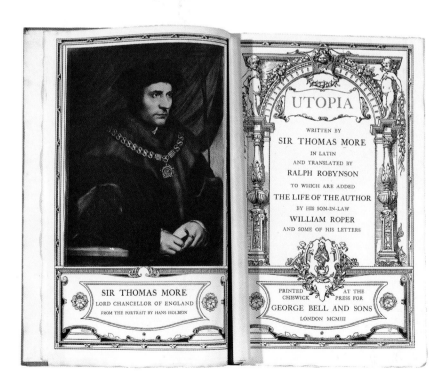

Thomas More

Thomas More
Utopia
London: Printed at the
Chiswick Press for
George Bell and Sons, 1903
NYPL, Rare Books Division

This early twentieth-century edition of More's *Utopia* was printed by an English private press in an edition of 200 copies. The frontispiece portrait of More is based on the famous 1527 portrait by Hans Holbein, now in the Frick Collection in New York City.

A Map of Utopia

Abraham Ortelius
***Utopiae Typus,
ex Narratione Raphaelis
Hythlodæi, Descriptione
D. Thomas Mori***
Copper engraving, [Antwerp,
1595–96]
Private Collection

This is the only extant copy of the map of Utopia drawn by Abraham Ortelius after the work of Thomas More and at the request of More's friends J. M. Wackher à Wackenfels and Jacob Monau. It was engraved in Antwerp around 1595 during a time of turmoil (several years before, in 1586, Ortelius was harassed for his contacts with Peter Heyns, a well-known Calvinist); most likely, very few copies were printed and distribution was minimal. Respecting the geographic conventions of the time, the map offers a free interpretation of More's *Utopia*: although fifty-four cities (plus one), including the famous Amaurotum, are represented in accordance with More's narrative, the island drawn by Ortelius does not closely resemble the shape of a new moon, and the large interior bay, faithfully depicted in the first engraving of 1516, has completely disappeared.

The choice of names for cities and rivers was inspired by the literal meaning of the term "u-topia" (no-place), which made possible the creation of place names in ten different languages (Utopian, Latin, Greek, Italian, Spanish, etc.). For example, in French there are three cities – Horsdumonde ("out of this world"), Nulleville (no place), and Sansterre (lack of land) – and two rivers, Sans-poisson fleuve (river without fish) and Sanseau fleuve (river without water). The abundance of ships and topographical details on the island itself – mountains and forests, towns and rivers, wheatfields and vineyards, animals – all suggest the prosperity of this ideal island kingdom.

Christian humanists, and the contribution of Erasmus to the Mirror of Princes tradition, his *Institutio Principis Christiani* [*Education of a Christian Prince*], was published in the same year as More's *Utopia*, 1516. The arcadian myth of the Golden Age was also alive and well, and frequently shaped perceptions of and aspirations for the New World. At a more popular level, a dream of gross abundance and social inversion survived in the legends of the Land of Cockaigne, Lubberland, or Schlaraffenland. But the context of problems and aspirations to which we have referred also stimulated a major outpouring of millennial expectation. Echoed in Columbus' view of his own mission, it reached new scale and intensity in the verbal and military conflicts associated with the religious struggles of the sixteenth and seventeenth centuries.

The importance of these distinctions is not simply as a means of formal categorization. They represent conscious alternative choices for many of those who went on to describe utopias, and in that respect, some clarity about them can help us to understand the significance of utopian writing and thought in the early modern world.[8] The perfect moral commonwealth rested on a vision of society perfected by the perfect moral and social performance of its members; the flaws of an imperfect society would be overcome by Christian moral renewal. In the millennium, reliance on human moral effort was replaced by the this-worldly intervention of divine grace. The prophesied second coming of Christ would lead to a thousand years of rule by King Jesus and/or his saints, a reign of justice and peace. The arcadian vision built on the combined premises of temperate abundance in nature and moderate appetites in men and women. Cockaigne assumed a relaxation of both: natural abundance and the satiation of the senses. These traditions of discourse about social idealization were quantitatively more important than utopian speculation throughout this period. Arcadianism revived classical values of civility and calm felicity that could be seen as reference points appropriate to newly discovered societies prior to their conversion to Christianity. Cockaigne, the reverie of a society on the margins of subsistence, wished away moral choices in a dream of material superfluity. For all their varying popularity, none of these ideal society forms engaged overtly with the problems of the "new worlds" of the sixteenth century. In order to do so, the utopian writer had to break with their assumptions, to build on different premises.

Utopia, as re-inaugurated by Sir Thomas More, envisaged an ideal society of fallen human beings coming to terms with an imperfect world of scarce resources and without benefit of divine assistance. Such a society might have to contain divergent discourses, potentially conflicting opinions. The individuals and groups within it would be pursuing their own interests and calculating appropriate strategies for their fulfillment. Such a society might exist in an unstable environment of competing, predatory, and aggressive neighbors. How were such competing opinions, interests, and pressures to be reconciled? The utopian answer is *not* through the idealization of human nature nor of the natural environment, nor through divine grace, but through the idealization of social organization. Social structures, regulations, rituals, sanctions, and institutions must be devised to reconcile and stabilize competing interests and opinions within a framework of justice. Perfection, in an absolute sense, might not be a defining characteristic of utopia[9] but a species of perfection is: the ideal form of social and political organization congruent with the deficiencies of man and nature. It is perfection in a fallen world; the best we can do in a state of sin.

It is in terms of this characterization that we can understand the nature of the relationship between utopia and the New World. The discovery of a Golden Age or arcadian society in the New World was of little immediate interest to the utopian imagination since it built on different premises. Indeed, as the discussions of Spanish jurists and philosophers in the sixteenth century reveal, the right, in a more immediately practical sense, to European dominion over what was found in the newly discovered lands was by no means taken for granted.[10] Utopias too had many more geographical settings than the Americas in this period: Madagascar, the eastern Mediterranean, Jerusalem, just south of the equator, and Terra Australis being among the most favored.

More's *Optimo Reipublicae*, 1516

Nevertheless, Hythlodaeus, the character who provides the description of Utopia in Thomas More's book, had "accompanied" Amerigo Vespucci on three of his four voyages. It was while on the last of these that he left most of his companions, traveled on farther, and "discovered" Utopia.[11] This has been the basis for much assertion that More's fiction was deeply influenced by the accounts of Vespucci's voyages and the New World, and *Utopia* clearly has links with those discoveries and the contrast they might imaginatively offer with a familiar and flawed

Utopia Illustrated

François van Bleyswyck
Etchings, 1715
BNF, Département des Estampes
et de la Photographie

These loose illustrations,
prepared for the 1715 Leyden
edition of Thomas More's
Utopia, make it possible to
envisage, as if we were leaf-
ing through the work itself,
some of the conventions
of life in Utopia, which are,
in turn, austere, innovative,
and even outrageous.

a. "How the island of Utopia
is shaped like a crescent"

b. "How the king of Utopia
distinguishes himself from
other citizens"

c. "How engagements
are made in Utopia"

d. "How Utopians breed
chickens by incubation"

e. "How the ambassador
received the Anemolians"

f. "How justice is
administered among
the Polylerites"

g. "How death is a
celebration rather than a
bereavement in Utopia"

h. "How thirty Utopian families eat in each refectory"

a

b

c

d

e

f

g

h

The First English Edition

Thomas More
***A fruteful and pleasant
worke of the beste state
of a publyque weale . . .***
London: Abraham Bele, 1551
NYPL, Henry W. and Albert A. Berg
Collection of English and American
Literature

Utopia was so well received that
just three months after its initial
printing, Erasmus encouraged
More to reprint it. Between
1516 and 1689, twenty-four Latin
editions were produced, and
in the sixteenth and seventeenth
centuries, it was also widely
translated into German (1524),
Italian (1548), French (1550),
English (1551), Dutch (1553), and
Spanish (1637). This is the first
edition in English, translated by
Ralphe Robynson.

society. The organization of *Utopia* into two books –
the first on the ills of the Old World, the second
on the virtues of Utopia – would appear to support
such a reading. But we need to read what is an
exceptionally subtle work more carefully. More
deliberately plays down the newness, and to some
extent the virtue, of the New World. Toward the
end of the first book, Peter Giles, who with a fictional "More" was one of the principal characters
engaged in the text's dialogue with Hythlodaeus,
challenged the latter: how could there be a better
society in the *New* World with all its lack of experience? Hythlodaeus responded by asserting that the
New World was older than the Old World: "there
were cities amongst them before there were men
amongst us." Furthermore, they had historical
records of stages even before the development of
this urban civilization. In the past they had learned
and absorbed all that the Egyptians and Romans
had known (107, 121, 181–83 [40, 47–48, 77–79]). More
repeatedly undermined the contrast between the Old
World and the New, between Europe and Utopia,
and suggested continuities and affinities between
them. The appetite of the Utopians for the Greek
literature and philosophy made available to them by
Hythlodaeus and his companions was one indication
of this underlying compatibility. There were good
things to be discovered in the old Europe and bad
things to be found in the worlds newly discovered.
More promised that, on a future occasion, he would
give a fuller account that would include descriptions
of the many ill-advised customs to be found among
these "new nations" (21, 53 [12]). So Utopia was an old
civilization in a region of the world where we might
encounter old vices in abundance. Despite its antiquity, it could still learn much from Europe.

None of this should obscure the seriousness
with which More laid bare the failings of contemporary European society in his "Truly Golden
Handbook," nor the care which he took in showing
how the "Best State of a Commonwealth" was
maintained in Utopia. Book I's remorseless analysis
revealed Tudor society to be avaricious, sycophan-
tic, unjust, and hypocritical. Christian morality,
any morality, was a negotiable code. The room
for goodness and wisdom in the operation of
its politics was nugatory. Utopia, by contrast,
was a society of open minds in which wisdom was
valued. It was caring, unmaterialistic, within
the constraints of a hierarchical and patriarchal
mindset, egalitarian, just, open, and sincere.
And yet we will miss More's meaning if we ignore
the continuities he chose to maintain between

the two societies. Principal amongst these was the way in which human beings would calculate and pursue their rational interests according to the circumstances in which they found themselves. At the end of Book II, when Hythlodaeus concludes his account of Utopian society, he summarizes both the contrast and the continuity between that happy place and elsewhere:

Outside of Utopia, to be sure, men talk freely of the public welfare – but look after their private interests only. In Utopia, where nothing is private, they seriously concernthemselves with public affairs. *Assuredly in both cases they act reasonably.* (237–39 [107])

Underlying the contrast between the two societies is the continuity of the rational calculation of interests in accordance with circumstances. From its title page onward, *Utopia* reminds its readers to calculate their interest in reading this book which is, in turn, much concerned with what in the Latin text are the key terms of *commodum, commoditas, beneficium,* and *utile, utilis, utilitas.* In a pair of complementary observations incorporated in the letters accompanying the text, More places the work of writing *Utopia* directly in the context of his daily pursuit of his and his family's interests, and William Budé locates the act of reading the same text in exactly the same context (39–41 [4, 116]).

More also had an ambitious intellectual agenda, which he shared with his friends. One aspect of this was the desire to find an institutional context for virtue. The limitations of the Church and of monastic institutions had been exposed by Erasmian satire just as the limitations of law were exposed in More's description of contemporary Europe. Moral exhortation and satire were, More implied, not enough. He turned to a staple Renaissance debate: the discussion of what constituted the best state, one in which the citizens could live well and enjoy the benefit of just laws. Like other Renaissance debates, this one polarized around classical protagonists. The Platonic/Petrarchian solution was to leave the business of rule (*negotium*) to a guardian class or philosopher prince so that subjects might enjoy a life of contemplation (*otium*). The Ciceronian response was that it was never wise to entrust our happiness to others and that all citizens must be active in ensuring the rule of good laws and the pursuit of the good life. As Quentin Skinner has argued, it is possible to see Hythlodaeus in *Utopia* as the defender of the Platonic position, while "More" advocated the Ciceronian "ideal of civic

self-government, based on an active and politically educated citizenship."[12] A second debate into the context of which *Utopia* must be set is that over what constituted true nobility (*vera nobilitas*). Was it inherent in lineage and wealth, liberality and honor, as Aristotle, Aquinas, and their sixteenth-century followers argued? Or was it, as Erasmus was arguing, virtue alone that was the test of true nobility? Again, Skinner is right to see *Utopia* as intervening on Erasmus' side by showing what a society of true nobility would look like (Book II) in contrast to one based on a false ideal of nobility (Book I).[13] But while this goes some way to contextualize the themes pursued in *Utopia*, it does not provide the key to its details or its proposed solutions, in particular the overriding features of More's ideal social structure: community of goods, equality, and the universal obligation to labor. For that we need to understand the significance of friendship in the thinking of More and his mentor, Erasmus, as well as to return to the calculation of interests.

David Wootton has shown that a key impetus to the writing of *Utopia* in 1515–16 was the publication in 1515 of a new edition of Erasmus' *Adages* with several additional political adages.[14] The *Adages* was a massive and apparently ramshackle collection of ancient wisdom, collecting and tracing fragments of ancient sayings, proverbs, nostrums, and maxims that had come down into contemporary usage or recovering those that had got lost along the way. Like an archaeologist's report, the *Adages* laid out the recovered fragments as part of a greater whole. As Erasmus's Greek New Testament recovered the *philosophia Christi*, so the *Adages* was an exercise in recovering the practical wisdom of the ancients. Plato was a central figure in this for Erasmus, but Pythagoras was probably even more important, and it is, according to Wootton, the pythagorean theory of friendship that, via Erasmus, provided the critical inspiration for the writing of *Utopia*. The hallmarks of true friendship, as displayed in the *Adages*, were community of goods, equality, and shared work – exactly the qualities that underpinned the social organization of Utopia. The first of the adages in Erasmus' collection was the pythagorean observation that "Between friends all is common." The second adage was "Friendship is equality. A friend is another self." Others deal with the obligation of all to work. So, Wootton argues, More took the sustaining themes of the *Adages* and showed in Book II of *Utopia* what a society based on pythagorean friendship would look like. Book I shows the social consequence of putting self

The Third Edition of Utopia

Thomas More
De optimo reip. statu, deque nova insula Utopia . . .
Basel: Io. Frobenium, [1518]
NYPL, Rare Books Division

This third edition of Thomas More's famous work includes the same alphabet as the first edition but contains a much more elaborate and detailed depiction of the island. The woodcut is by Ambrosius Holbein, the older brother of the artist Hans Holbein the Younger.

The man gesturing in the lower left corner is Raphael Hythlodaeus, the sailor who reportedly told the tale of the marvelous island discovered on Vespucci's fourth voyage to the Americas. One of many plays on words found throughout the book, Hythlodaeus means "well-versed in nonsense." The name More gave to his imaginary island is also a pun: the prefix "u-" comes from the Greek *eu-* meaning "good" as well as from *ou-* meaning "not." Consequently, More burdened his own and all future utopias with being both a good place and no place at the same time.

above "friends" and, of course, looks uncannily like contemporary society. As the *Adages* was the work of an archaeologist of ancient wisdom on the theme of friendship, so *Utopia* is a study of the social meaning of that wisdom in its application (Book II) and its absence (Book I).

There were, of course, affinities between pythagorean friendship and Christian love, but in a world where the gravitational pull of human motivation was toward the pursuit of interests rationally calculated in accordance with circumstances, it is the nature of those circumstances that becomes crucial. The key variant between the circumstances of Utopia and those of the world as we know it rests in the role allowed to pride. In a striking phrase that puts the pursuit of interests, properly calculated, on a par with Christ's will for us, Hythlodaeus concluded, "Nor does it occur to me to doubt that a man's regard for his own interests or the authority of Christ our Savior . . . would long ago have brought the whole world to adopt the laws of the Utopian commonwealth, had not one single monster, the chief and progenitor of all plagues, striven against it – I mean, Pride." And the cardinal characteristic of pride was that "Pride measures prosperity not by her own advantages but by others' disadvantages" (243 [109]). So human beings are constant in their reasonable inclination to pursue their own interests as they calculate them in accordance with the circumstances in which they find

themselves. In Utopian circumstances, such a calculation will be compatible with a society based on the values of friendship and/or Christian charity. In the world as we know it, the same inclination will reasonably lead to a calculation of interests that is competitive and mutually destructive. The essence of pride is, in a word, emulation, for pride is interested only in its own advantage as seen in light of the comparative disadvantage of others. It distorts the rational pursuit of interests into an emulative devotion of energies to ensuring that others do not realize their interests. The essence of its evil is in its emulative destructiveness, its hostility to the community and equality of friendship. To realize the best state, to provide an appropriate institutional context for virtue, was to establish circumstances that worked against pride and eliminated emulation.

With Thomas Hobbes, More is one of the two great commentators on the socio-political impact of emulation in early modern England. Tudor society was presented by him as an arena in which it was rational to seek to outdo others in reputation, wealth, idleness, numbers of retainers, and attention; where in the emulative theater of the court, each courtier will play down the role and arguments of others in order to seek his own advantage. For in this context, "it is but human nature that each man further his own discoveries most" (59 [14]). At the centers of power, emulative responses and calculations drive out wisdom, and princes themselves vie

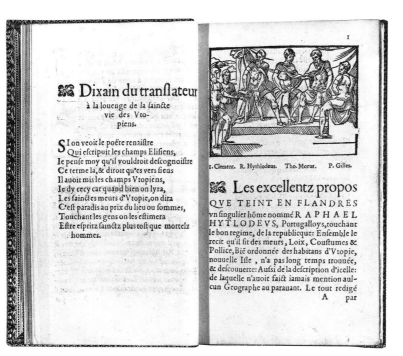

The First French Edition

Thomas More
La description de l'isle d'Utopie . . .
Paris: Charles L'Angelier, 1550
NYPL, Henry W. and Albert A. Berg
Collection of English and American
Literature

The first edition in French was translated by Jean Leblond, the Norman poet and translator, in 1550. Another French edition was published in Lyons in 1559, followed by five others in the seventeenth and eighteenth centuries. This woodcut depicts Raphael Hythlodaeus recounting his adventures to Thomas More, his friend Peter Giles, and John Clement, the tutor to More's children.

for domination. Within such a milieu it is folly to be high-minded or disinterested, or to expect the values of friendship to withstand the rational imperatives of rivalry.

In More's hands, the utopian exercise was one in the construction of an alternative milieu – one which blocks emulation and forces pride to wither. Central to that design was community of goods. Those things in the conspicuous consumption or possession of which some had triumphed over others were made common possessions. So land, houses, horses, food became communal assets. Clothing was uniform. Travel was closely regulated. Contempt for gold, silver, and jewels was encouraged. No one had more leisure than another. All had to work. What we regard as positional goods had no meaning in Utopia. The social environment of that happy place was structured around the values of pythagorean friendship: community of goods, equality, and the sharing of labor. Power ceased to be associated with lineage. Indeed, on occasion the family had to give way to the values of friendship. Hence the regulation of households meant their negotiability as kinship groups. Those who could not respect the values of friendship were reduced to slavery. The beliefs of the Utopians underwrote all of this. They believed in a benign creator, the immortality of the soul, and judgment after death for conduct in this life. Beyond that, they could accept a plurality of religious expression provided that it was based on mutual respect, equality (221 [97]). Similarly, they pursued pleasure in a rational way and were concerned that all men should equally have that right. Among other things, openness to euthanasia and divorce followed from this. Within the institutional, legal, and conventional codes of Utopia there was nothing for emulation to take hold of. Private interest had become the public interest and it was therefore reasonable for all to pursue the common good. Outside of this framework, Utopians found themselves back in a context of competition, the quest for domination and superiority, the familiar world of international rivalry. It followed that, in an international context, it was reasonable for them to pursue their narrow national interest to maximum advantage by such means as cost them least.

Utopia was a playful work, laced with puns, jokes, and satirical sketches. But this is not the same as saying that it was not a serious work. In grappling with the best-state exercise, tackling the problem of true nobility, exploring the social meaning of friendship, and founding a better

society on a human motivation steered by the calculation and pursuit of individual interests, More's project went to the heart of the Erasmian humanist agenda. In that sense it is one of the great achievements of the late Renaissance. But it also marked the reemergence and, to some extent, the reshaping of a genre of political analysis and speculation. *Utopia* is a book about the calculation of our interests. It is rational for us to pursue them in ways appropriate to the circumstances in which we find ourselves, and, on the whole, we are rational. Society is like a theater with conventions, scripts, expectations, and roles. It is in our interests to act within those conventions and to calculate our particular advantage in terms of them. If we want a more just world or a society in which the virtues of true friendship are realized, it is not enough to appeal to virtue or sentiment alone. This was the shortcoming of the Erasmian agenda. Rather, More was suggesting that we must alter the conventions, rewrite the scripts, and redefine the roles. We must redesign the theater. But an underlying continuity will be our calculation and pursuit of our interests. Human nature remains the same. The utopian exercise is one about social reprogramming and was to remain so for the two centuries after More produced his "Golden Handbook."

Emulation, Reason, and Religion in the Century After *Utopia*

By the mid-sixteenth century, More's *Utopia* had appeared in ten further Latin editions and in French, Dutch, English, German, and Italian translations. In due course, it also spawned imitators who were well aware of the key themes and strategies displayed in the work.

One of these was Robert Burton, an Oxford academic, who first published his *Anatomy of Melancholy* in 1621. Ostensibly a treatise on what had become a fashionable malady, the work was actually an exploration of the social, individual, and psychological consequences of sin, of the Fall of Man. It was an enormously successful work, and as it went through successive editions, Burton increased the length of the text by almost two-thirds. In his preface he described "an Utopia of mine own," and as the text grew, the length of this section tripled.[15] Like More, Burton saw emulation as both a symptom and a cause of the sick society, the melancholia, which he observed around him:

Scarce two gentlemen dwell together in the country . . . but there is emulation betwixt them and their servants,

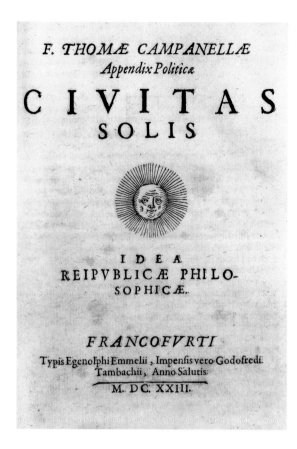

F. THOMÆ CAMPANELLÆ
Appendix Politica

CIVITAS
SOLIS

IDEA
REIPVBLICÆ PHILO-
SOPHICÆ.

FRANCOFVRTI
Typis Egenolphi Emmelii, Impenſis vero Godofredi
Tambachii, Anno Salutis.
——————————
· M. DC. XXIII.

some quarrel or some grudge betwixt their wives or
children, friends and followers, some contention about
wealth, gentry, precedency etc. (I: 69–70; see also 74,
160–62, 269)

Whereas More saw a maladjusted society compelling
men to act counter to conscience, antisocially but
still rationally, Burton saw a maladjusted society
forcing men to act contrary to reason, as enemies
to themselves and ultimately as self-torturers and
self-destroyers. In considering the form of ideal
society that might escape all of this, Burton examined – and rejected – a number of alternatives. One
was the descent of a *deus ex machina* who by miraculous grace would "alter affections, cure all manner
of diseases . . . and reform all distressed states and
persons. . . ." But these were "vain, absurd, and
ridiculous wishes not to be hoped: all must be as it
is . . ." (I: 96–97). Another alternative that had to
be rejected was the perfect moral commonwealth:
"we converse here with men, not with gods" (I:
106). Similarly, fallen nature was so degenerate as
to rule an arcadian vision of natural harmony out
of the question (I: 130–36; see also II: 189). A utopia
of legal, bureaucratic, and institutional regulation

offered the only strategy. Because, unlike More, Burton could not rely on human rationality to operate
in appropriate circumstances, such regulation had
to be all the more detailed. The managed society he
envisaged had a planned and regulated economy, a
controlled and supervised market, public provision
against personal misfortune, elaborate civic ameni-
ties, and state control of leisure, dress, and work.
It was managed through a hierarchy based on a
combination of birth, virtue, and merit. Regional
administration would be in the hands of noblemen
or gentlemen chosen on merit through a system of
examination, subject to annual reports and mutual
inspection. There were few laws. They were strictly
kept. Lawyers were few and maintained as public
servants. Burton's answer to the malaise of an emulative society was a system based on merit and close,
effective regulation. "We have excellent laws enacted, you will say, severe statutes, houses of correction,
etc., to small purpose it seems; it is not houses will
serve, but cities of correction" (I: 92–93).

More's exercise in the reconciliation of interests and their individual calculation had a certain
subtlety. A key to that was the Utopians' openness
to a variety of forms of religious expression while

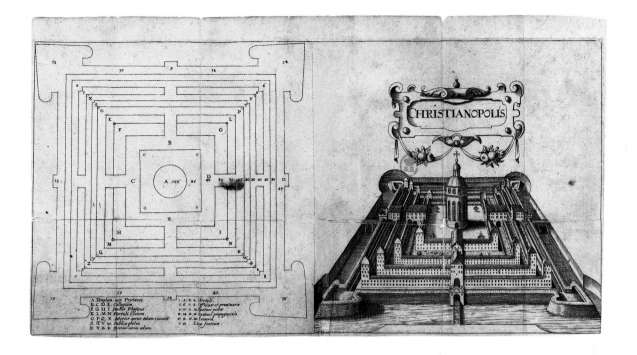

insisting on a required core of belief. The sharpness
of post-Reformation religious divisions, as More's
own practice as a persecuting Lord Chancellor
bears witness, made that virtually impossible to
sustain. The assumption that a dangerous fracturing
of discourses, a multiplicity of consciences, had
to be contained insistently informed the utopian
agenda from the mid-seventeenth century. A seminal approach to the problem was that of Tommaso
Campanella in his *City of the Sun* (1623). A Dominican by training, Campanella defended open-ended,
empirical scientific inquiry as exemplified by
Telesio and Galileo but, without apparent paradox,
also advocated a universal Catholic monarchy under
the Papacy, Spain, or France. His publishing of
both positions resulted in long periods of imprisonment and torture. Campanella's utopia, like More's,
sought to reconcile private reason and public good.
In both, a central feature of the solution was the
abolition of private property, since both Utopians
and Solarians believed that private property,
by privileging the personal over the communal,
prevented reasonable men from pursuing the
common interest. "When self-love is destroyed,"
Campanella concluded, "only concern for the
community remains."[16] In *The City of the Sun*, as in
Utopia, physical property was communally owned,
but Campanella extended community ownership
and control to sexuality and to personal attributes
such as generosity, fortitude, and diligence. The

means by which reason, in a new context, led to the
pursuit of the common good were to be carefully
monitored. The most significant contrast with
More, however, was in relation to the problem of
knowledge of the natural world in an ideal society.
In *Utopia* there was belief in miracles "which
occurred without the assistance of nature" and
therefore remained incomprehensible.[17] For
Campanella's Solarians, nature was not only entirely
comprehensible but already fully comprehended.
All scientific knowledge was recorded in carvings
on the seven concentric walls of the City of the
Sun, forming a huge memory system or database.
Scientific knowledge was already complete and
could be contained in "only one book," the city
itself. Campanella associated science with astrology,
the knowledge of natural law and regularity. There
was no room for miracles and, since knowledge was
complete, no room for scientific research. There
was nothing for reason to do, in the study of nature,
but to contemplate the divine order. Science was
public knowledge but the stamp of the city on the
mind brought an end to disputes about it.

It was believed that *The City of the Sun*
influenced the Jesuit communities, or *reducciones*
("reductions") in Paraguay. For Francis Bacon,
however, the discovery of the New World had to
be seen in the context of the potential discoveries
to be made by a science based on a new method:
"the new found world of land was not greater

addition to the ancient continent than there remained at this day a world of inventions and sciences unknown. . . ."[18] The geographical discoveries of the explorers could be dwarfed by the intellectual ones of the scientists, but only if the researches of the latter were properly organized and conducted. Bacon knew that knowledge, like virtue (to which it was closely related), was problematic if it was too violently contested or so dynamic as to destabilize the foundations of society. It is this awareness, rather than any simple acknowledgment of the importance of scientific inquiry,[19] which gives Bacon's *New Atlantis* some claim to be considered one of the most significant of early modern utopias.

First published in 1627, the year after its author's death and six years after his long political career ended in disgrace, the *New Atlantis* is more than an unfinished setting for a scientific academy. It has a great deal to say about the utopian family, about fecundity, and about both domestic and civic ritual. The New World, in this case Peru, was not the terminus but the point of departure for the voyage that led to the discovery of New Atlantis. It was "beyond both the Old World and the New" (14–17). Nevertheless, the core of the work remains the scientific establishment of the House of Salomon, whose Fellows are dedicated not only to the collection of all existing knowledge but to the pursuit and collation of new knowledge, to scientific discovery. As Bacon, in writing his utopia, recognized, this was to let freedom, contingency, and the power of scientific discovery loose within a social framework designed to eliminate moral contingency and to perpetuate a stable social order. Since knowledge, science, was power, the men of science were the controllers of power. At this point, ambiguity took over, and Bacon was unable to complete the design. The scientists of New Atlantis were pictured, on the one hand, as moral paragons, charged with distinguishing the immediate works of God, miracles, from those mediated through nature. On the other hand, they were also human – capable of cheating and lying – and must therefore be subject to the same controls and scrutiny as other citizens (43). The Baconian dilemma is one that has dogged the scientific utopia ever since; either utopia controls science or scientific discovery subverts utopia.[20] The degree, nevertheless, to which utopian writing, rather than any other form of late Renaissance political or social thought, brought about an engagement with the problem of scientific power is striking.

For many of those who admired and shared Bacon's scientific aspirations, the central problem of his utopia could be escaped by relocating to a millennial, rather than a utopian, context. This is, to a large extent, true of the Baconian scholars and idealists of the network extending out from Samuel Hartlib in mid-seventeenth-century England and Europe.[21] Equally, the pansophist aspirations of a sequence of social idealists who looked to an alliance of science and religion in the reconquest of man's dominion over fallen nature – from Giordano Bruno, through Christopher Besold, Johann Heinrich Alsted, and Johann Valentin Andreä to Gottfried Wilhelm Leibniz – shared this tendency. However, when the emphasis shifted to a pre-millennial godly discipline, this could lead to utopian outcomes, especially on the Protestant side of the Reformation divide. There were parallels between godly and scientific elites since both possessed privileged enlightenment and their utopias were equally problematic. Andreae's *Christianopolis* (1619), written by a prominent Lutheran pastor, confronted the problem faced by a maturing religious movement: how could a godly community be built in a fallen world? His answer shared some of the features of enclosed monastic households and some of those, as Andreae saw it, of Geneva under the discipline of John Calvin. Greatest priority, however, was given by Andreae to the socially integrative capacities of education. "The College" was at once the physical and the social center of the community. Under the influence of the great Czech pedagogue Jan Amos Comenius, this theme was again to flourish in mid-seventeenth-century England. Samuel Gott's *Nova Solyma* (1648), a Latin work intended for a European audience, was a utopian exercise in a millennial setting. It described an idealized society of Christianized Jews located in the Holy Land. Both an attempt to reconcile millennial and utopian aspirations, and to place a religious elite within a social setting, *Nova Solyma* hesitated uncertainly between the self-rule appropriate to the saints and the godly discipline appropriate to a world of fallen humanity. Gott's vigorous attempt to devise an educational system and theory that would free the former while restraining the latter ended in debate rather than conclusion.[22]

War, Revolution, and Utopia

War was an important aspect of the context in which these works were produced: the fratricidal religious wars between Catholics and Protestants, fellow Christians; the devastation of the Thirty Years War (1618–48) and the English Civil Wars (1642–51). How could Christian liberty and the godly discipline of all be reconciled in a world of relentless internecine conflict? One of the most brilliant and illuminating exercises in response to this question came in the work of Gerrard Winstanley (1609–1676) and culminated in his utopia, *The Law of Freedom* (1652). Born in Lancashire, Winstanley served an apprenticeship in London before becoming a freeman of the Merchant Taylors Company in 1637. By 1643, the onset of civil war had brought his business down and reduced him to agricultural employment. In 1648, he began to publish a series of writings that together represented a major attempt to come to terms with the economic and social consequences of war, with a Protestant reformation collapsing into an anarchy of competing authorities, and with a rhetoric of revolution that appeared increasingly to be devoid of substance. Central to Winstanley's analysis was a contrast between an old world of covetousness and a new world of community, but this was not a matter of geographical displacement but of the reorientation of the social order. How was that to be brought about? In his early writings Winstanley envisaged a universal redemption and the dissipation of the forms of social control in a millennial moment. "There shall be no need of Lawyers, prisons, or engines of punishment one over another, for all shall walk and act righteously in the creation, and there shall be no beggar, nor cause of complaining in all this holy Mountain."[23] Like a true chiliast, at this stage Winstanley saw Christ, and his spirit rising in all men, as the sufficient means by which this transformation would be brought about. "The swords and counsels of the flesh shall not be seen in this work, the arm of the Lord only shall bring these mighty things to passe, in this day of his power . . . yet wait patiently upon your King, he is coming, he is rising, the Son is up and his glory will fill the earth" (153).

As the rule of earthly powers, Kingly government was replaced by commonwealth's government, so an old world of covetousness would be replaced by a new world of community. Like More, Winstanley saw the old world as one in which human rationality had been distorted by the social pressures upon it. These had originated at the Fall when covetousness led to the private expropriation of goods out of what was created as a "Common Treasury." Such expropriation, and the injustices attendant upon it, could be maintained only by a system of rule that amounted to conquest, although rulers soon realized that lawyers could be used to veil injustice in the language of law and that clergy could be hired to distort the gospels and preach up the rights of

private property. A system based on the buying and selling of all commodities – including human labor – sustained exploitation and injustice. The poor man hiring out his labor was therefore complicit in the maintenance of the system that exploited him. The famous "digging" experiments of 1649 and 1650 were attempts to establish alternative communities where the poor could withdraw from selling their own labor and yet sustain themselves. Winstanley believed that without the labor of the poor the economy of the private landlord would collapse, and he would find it reasonable, in these circumstances, to abandon covetousness and throw in his lot with the digging communities. Violence was unnecessary (487).

From 1648 to 1650, therefore, Winstanley was expecting a social transformation to be brought about by the power of Christ. Men and women could help and begin to act out a new morality by following the divine injunction to "*Worke together. Eat bread together,*" and by giving up the cheating art of buying and selling (190). Between 1650 and the publication of *The Law of Freedom* in 1652, Winstanley's cast of mind shifted. In this work he looked to Oliver Cromwell, not Jesus Christ, as the agent of change, and the design moved from a millennial to a utopian one. Since Kingly government had been overthrown, Winstanley proposed that the Commonwealth's land – by which he meant common land, waste lands, and land confiscated as a result of the Civil Wars – should form the basis upon which a new social order would be constructed. Private landlords could choose to remain on their estates, but they might find their laborers choosing not to remain in an exploitative situation and leaving to join the new society (513).

The Law of Freedom presented sixty-two laws by which that society would be governed. These laws were to be read to the people four times a year. The letter of the law was to be rigidly enforced although no one could be punished for their beliefs. Those who administered the law for profit would be executed (Laws 1–9). Violence and disorder were to be vigorously curbed. Gossips, rumor mongers, and those who used "reviling and provoking words" could be dealt with severely. Resistance to an officer or the usurping of his authority was punishable by slavery (Laws 10–14). All households had obligations to work the land. Persistent idleness could be punished by flogging or slavery (Laws 15–17). Buying and selling was illegal and a capital offense. Working for hire or hiring labor resulted in slavery. Money was abolished and all goods were held in

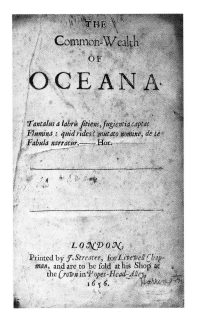

Oceana

James Harrington
The Common-Wealth
of Oceana
London: Printed by J. Streater
for Livewell Chapman, 1656
NYPL, General Research Division

Perhaps the last great flowering
of the late Renaissance utopia,
Harrington's *Oceana* was
addressed to Oliver Cromwell
and offered solutions both to
the most pressing problem of
the Cromwellian Protectorate
and to the long-term instability
of English politics that were
to have considerable influence
on American constitutionalist
debates in the late eighteenth
century. This first edition was
printed by John Streater, a former colonel in Cromwell's army.

Like More, Winstanley saw the old world as
one that encouraged men to see their interests
as residing in the exploitation of others. But that
world of buying and selling, of some expropriating
others, seemed to him not to embody a form of
rationality but to breathe "the spirit of unreason-
able ignorance." To break that pattern and to bring
society back into clear alignment with what "the
great Creator Reason" had intended, it was necessary that "There must be suitable Laws for every
occasion and almost for every action that men do;
for one Law cannot serve in all seasons, but every
season and every action have their particular laws
attending thereupon for the preservation of right
order" (515, 528). Winstanley's thought, therefore,
moved from the idea that all would be redeemed
and consequently free, to a vision of a society
locked in continuing battle with covetousness
and waywardness, comprehensive in its pursuit of
godly discipline. Others would pursue his theme
of comprehensive godly discipline; some would
even link it to addressing the problem of the poor;
but none would link it so radically to the establishment of communal ownership and the eradication
of commercial values.

Constitutionalism and the Best State
In its more scholastic form, the Renaissance
best-state exercise emphasized law and institutions,
constitutionalism, rather than education. The
devising of an ideal education for the prince and
his advisors, as in Antonio de Guevara's *Relox de
les principes* (1529) or Erasmus's *Institutio Principis
Christiani* (1516), gave way to a concern with the
constitutional constraints upon them. Similarly, the
ideal aristocracy, frequently a feature of portraits
of idealized republics, such as those of Venice –
as described, for example, by Traiano Boccalini[24] –
were exchanged for Polybian balances of governmental forms designed to prevent the degeneration
of aristocracy into oligarchy. The ultimate expression of this development was James Harrington's
Oceana of 1656, a complex exercise in political
architecture or overt constitutionalism. A second
impetus toward constitutionalism was the desire
to regularize the relationship that powerful and
increasingly militarized states might have with their
subjects. The "profound Peace" of the idealized
Formosa depicted by George Psalmanazar at the
opening of the eighteenth century was based on
violent and harsh punishments severely executed.[25]
It looked too like the warfare of a militarized state
upon its own people: government by continuous

communal storehouses from which households met
their needs in a controlled way (Laws 18–21, 27–33).

All public officials were elected annually by
all men over twenty except those disqualified
by criminal conviction. Men over forty years old
were eligible for election, although younger men
of exceptional ability or virtue could be chosen.
Canvassing was not permitted. Hypocrites were
not allowed to hold office; rather, "rational men of
moderate conversation" were preferred. Overseers
were to regulate the production and distribution
of goods and to enforce the obligation of all to
work (Laws 34–41). Slavery or bondage – for which
the minimum sentence was twelve months –
was an important sanction in the new society. It
was used against a wide variety of offenses: striking
an officer, failing to assist an officer, acting in a
socially disruptive manner, neglect of agricultural
equipment, idleness, neglect of duty by a waiter
in a storehouse, enticing others to buy or sell,
claiming a property in the earth, giving or taking
labor for hire, attempted abduction of another
man's wife, and wasting food (Laws 42–51). There
was no provision for a legally supported church,
and preaching for hire was a capital offense. The
patriarchal household remained the basic social
unit in Winstanley's utopia. Although marriage
was a matter of mutual consent, the non-kin
membership of the household was not determined
by the patriarch. He was, in effect, a civic official
with both educational and disciplinary duties
(Laws 52–62).

internal conquest. The utopian agenda extended from preventing imperfect individuals from constituting an imperfect society, to controlling the relationship between imperfect rulers and imperfect subjects. An engagement with constitutionalism and, to some extent, with the impersonalization of politics followed. Paolo Paruta, a Venetian writing in the late sixteenth century, defined the ideal government as that "by which people living in peace and union, may work righteously and obtain civil Felicity." But "immoderate Authority" and violent sanctions would only, according to Paruta, unbalance the commonwealth if the problem of custom were not addressed; "good institutions of life" were therefore necessary, and for Paruta this involved the establishment of a commonwealth constitutionally well balanced in the Polybian sense.[26] Such an ideal constitution could resist the closure of utopian perfection by stabilizing the framework in which politics and the development of policy might be pursued. The consequence was always to expose the commonwealth to the possibility of corruption. Typically, the utopian response was to reach beyond this, to embrace immortality, eliminating corruption and integrating the machinery of state with the fabric of society in such a way that there was no longer any role for politics or policy. This fusing of the social and the constitutional, with its attendant termination of politics, is best exemplified in *Oceana*, perhaps the last great flowering of the late Renaissance utopia.

Harrington's *Oceana* was addressed to Oliver Cromwell and offered solutions both to the most pressing problem of the Cromwellian Protectorate and to the long-term instability of English politics. The Cromwellian regime had been developed in the aftermath of the military coups of December 1648 and April 1653. It was dependent on a standing army, which appeared indispensable both to the security of the nation and to the security of the regime, but it could not command the whole-hearted support of the political nation. In those circumstances, moves were made in 1656 and 1657 to persuade Cromwell that a return to the ancient constitution and his own assumption of the Crown were required in the name of stability. Harrington's argument was that escape from dependence on a standing, mercenary army was essential but also that to return to monarchy would be to reinvest in instability. What was required was a much more thoroughgoing and elaborate republican constitution than had been seen in England – or any extensive nation – before. His work therefore operated

on two levels of analysis. One was an exploration of the long-term trends of history and politics; the other, a prescription based on "political architecture" or constitutional design. The aspiration behind it was the utopian one of establishing a perfect and immortal commonwealth, inured against instability and immune to corruption.

Like More, Harrington believed that in the long run, men acted reasonably or prudently in pursuit of their interests. But, equally, in the long run the key to those interests lay in the possession of land and therefore of the capacity to feed oneself and others on a continuing basis. Where one person owned all the land, the interest of all would be identified with that one individual, and therefore absolute monarchy, on what Harrington thought of as the Turkish model, would be possible. But because the sole ruler would be dependent on a mercenary army (in the Turkish example, the janissaries), his power would be prey to military coups and therefore unstable. If a few possessed all the land, aristocracy would be the result, but as baronial conflict was endemic to such a sharing of dominion, the aristocrats needed an umpire, a monarch, to prevent their mutual destruction. In such a situation, regulated monarchy was the norm, and this was typical of the gothic or feudal balance that had persisted throughout the Middle Ages in much of Europe. In the early sixteenth century, Harrington argued, the balance of landownership in England had begun to tip from an aristocratic to a popular basis. The secularization of Church lands in the Reformation had merely accelerated the process of transferring land from the possession of the few to that of the many. In such a situation, a popular government or republic became not only possible but desirable if stability were to be achieved without military force. To escape the cul-de-sac of arbitrary military rule in England, therefore, Cromwell had to be the agent of a utopian experiment: recasting the government of England on a properly constituted, popular – and therefore legitimate – basis. Material circumstances now made it in the national interest of the English to have a genuine republic.

However, as Harrington was well aware, other constitutional proposals, specifically the Levellers' *Agreement of the People*, had been made to establish a popular form of government in England.[27] To him these proposals were flawed because they lacked the comprehensiveness and skill in political architecture that would render his utopian republic immune to corruption, immortal. The key feature of his design, of his political architecture, was what he called the "equal commonwealth." This had four necessary features: an "equal Agrarian"; the secret ballot; a bicameral legislature (with the functions of debate and decision separated and a dependent executive); and rotation of office. The Agrarian Law was designed to control the distribution of property in land so as to maintain the popular basis of its ownership *while* maintaining an aristocracy (into whose hands the balance of property could *not* fall) to provide political leadership and wisdom. Both houses of parliament were elected on a popular, manhood franchise. The upper house, or Senate, had a preponderance of gentry/aristocracy among its membership and it alone had the function of legislative proposal. The lower house, or Assembly, had a preponderance of popular representatives and it alone could approve or reject the proposals put to it by the Senate. In this way, Harrington hoped to reconcile political leadership and insight with popular sovereignty. This depended, in turn, on measures to avoid the development of party affiliations. One of these measures was rotation of and vacation from office; the other was the secret ballot.

Provision was made for something like this system to be replicated at the local and regional levels and, most important, for a citizen militia to be run parallel to it. All males over thirty – with limited exceptions – were enfranchised for participation in civil government. So, too, all males between the ages of eighteen and thirty were enfranchised to participate in the organization of a national, regional, and imperial citizen militia and were obligated to serve in it. Indeed, only if they had honored their military obligations would they be qualified for full citizen status. The Harringtonian republic was deliberately equipped, in Machiavellian fashion, to be "a commonwealth for expansion" and Harrington extended his republican model to incorporate colonies as they were acquired. The extent to which Harrington was successful in maintaining the freedom of participatory citizenship has been a matter of debate, but his preoccupation with reconciling power and authority, the few and the many, the bearing of arms and popular sovereignty in a framework of durable stability led to a constitutional apparatus of such complexity that the mechanics began to dominate. Later in the seventeenth and eighteenth centuries, those who admired his restatement of classical republicanism – those whom John Pocock calls the neo-Harringtons – tried to free his thought from the machinery and to give new priority to the participatory ideal. In doing so, they contributed much to both Whig and Tory ideologies in terms of theories of corruption and participation. Others, however, engaged in further elaboration of the machinery and so kept Harrington's utopian aspirations alive.

In large measure, Harrington's problem and his response to it could be seen as that of achieving a Polybian balance of governmental forms in an extensive agrarian society where a king had been executed for attempting to subvert the laws, where the threat of a military-based oligarchy was real, and where the specter of popular anarchy or antinomian excess appeared equally threatening. A more aristocratic, if equally utopian, version of the classical republic could be pursued in the narrower confines of the Italian city-states. Francesco Patrizi's *La Città Felice* (Venice, 1553) limited citizenship to the leisured – military commanders, magistrates, and priests. Slaves and the common people were to be carefully controlled. But the perfect nobility was equally a feature of the closest thing we can get to a royalist utopia – Francis Lee's *Antiquity Reviv'd* (London, 1693) – which built heavily on Sir Robert Filmer's theories of political patriarchalism. It was at this point that utopia, focusing on the moral virtues of an idealized aristocracy, began to merge with the perfect moral commonwealth and in some respects functioned as an extension of the municipal courtesy book, weaning aristocrats from a community of emulative honor to one of civility. The military virtues associated with codes of honor were also being transmuted from the personal (or those of lineage) to the regimental, were being institutionalized and bureaucratized in accordance with the neo-stoic values associated with the standing armies emerging from the military revolution and almost continuous warfare of the seventeenth century. The anonymous French utopia of 1616, *Histoire du Grand et Admirable Royaume d'Antangil*, attempted to reconcile Protestant aspirations with the Polybian balances of a classical republic, both set firmly on a foundation of detailed military organization. Antangil, an island south of Java, was divided into 120 provinces, each further subdivided into regular groups of towns, parishes, and households. A Council of State, consisting of three wise and experienced men from each province, advised the king and a senate. The wickedness of men made a monarch necessary, but kings themselves could be corrupt and vicious. Balance was therefore necessary: a monarch to act as a check against oligarchy, a senate as a check against tyranny. The system was described in enormous detail with special emphasis on military and judicial organization as well as on education and training.

America Delineated

Jodocus Hondius
America Noviter Delineata
Engraved map, ca. 1590
NYPL, Miriam and Ira D. Wallach
Division of Art, Prints and
Photographs

The detailed coastlines and
indications of towns, rivers,
and mountains on this map
reflect the huge increase in
knowledge that had occurred
in the fifty years since the
appearance of Sebastian
Munster's 1540 map (see
page 97). Additional information about what explorers
might find in these new lands
is given in the elaborate
border decorations depicting
cities, towns, and indigenous
peoples. None of these views
are original to this map; they
are all reproductions of images
that were circulating widely in
other works.

Jodocus Hondius, one of the
most important cartographic
engravers of the late sixteenth
century, is best known for
his editions of Gerardus
Mercator's famous atlas.

Utopia in the New World: Colonial Utopia

It was Harrington's admirers in North America who were instrumental in preserving several features of the "perfect and immortal commonwealth" in the constitution of the United States. But the Americas and, as the seventeenth century wore on, geographical discoveries elsewhere stimulated not only the "discovery" of ideal societies but the sense of a *tabula rasa* on which new forms of ideal society could be both imagined and built. The initial formulation was almost always Arcadia. Columbus, Peter Martyr Vermigli, Bartolomé de las Casas, all expected to encounter Golden Age societies, whose noble simplicity was to be contrasted with European decadence and corruption. At the moment when *Utopia* was being published in 1516, de las Casas was planning the final perfection of Cuba, Hispaniola, San Juan, and Jamaica through their conversion to Christianity. In the 1530s, Vasco de Quiroga recommended More's utopian design as an appropriate alternative for New Spain since contemporary European customs were clearly inappropriate for the Golden Age. In Brazil, Uruguay, Argentina, and Paraguay in the early seventeenth century, the Jesuits in the reductions attempted to maintain the innocence of the natives through a paternalistic and morally controlled communism. Spain's first fictional utopia, *Sinapia* (ca. 1682), still reflected this belief in a paternalistic, primitive communism, with a purified Christianity providing strong moral guidance. But in the same work, mixed forms of government were embodied in an elected prince and magistracy balanced by a careful separation of judicial, military, and religious functions.

The colonial setting became a stage for a variety of depictions of social idealization in which the competing themes of arcadian primitivism and utopian constraint dominated. By the later seventeenth century, mixed government forms were coming to be the hallmarks of the latter. Addressing the problems of England's "first colony," Ireland, Richard Beacon engaged in a Machiavellian meditation on the reform of the Irish that was in several ways a remarkable anticipation of Harrington.[28] Colonies of the exogenous came to be seen as presenting more complex challenges and sometimes evoked harsher responses. Nowhere is the transition in terms of ideality better expressed than in the early history of Virginia, described by Michael Drayton in 1606 as "Earth's only Paradise."[29] The colony's arcadian status was soon damned through the sinfulness and willfulness of its human materials. By 1609, quarreling, faction, disorder, disease, famine, and retaliation by the natives had reduced the colony to anarchy. Of nine hundred who had emigrated, only sixty survived. From 1609 to 1611, Sir Thomas Gates, Thomas West, and Sir Thomas Dale elaborated a series of rules for the colony; they were codified and edited by William Strachey in 1612 under the title of *Lawes Divine, Morall and Martiall*. The imposition of order involved making impiety, blasphemy, and insubordination capital offenses. Sabbatarianism and a regime of daily worship were strictly enforced. Rigid controls over the disposition of property, prices, and hygiene were established. Work, the care of tools, trade with the natives, and the moral behavior of individuals were closely regulated and monitored. A similar pattern may be observed in Peter Cornelius Plockhoy's 1660s scheme for the Dutch colony of the New Netherlands.[30] After the restoration of the monarchy in 1660, English commentators took a more aristocratically informed view of the possibilities of colonial government. The constitutions devised for New Jersey in the 1660s and 1670s, for example, were all continuations of Harringtonian and Leveller ideas.[31] The Carolina constitution of 1669, which may have been drafted by John Locke, was more directly Harringtonian in inspiration, but the most elaborate exercise in adapting the Oceanic utopia for the colonies was the 1683 scheme for the government of Pennsylvania.[32] Even imaginatively, then, to populate the blank sheet of the New World with recognizable human beings bearing some resemblance to their counterparts in the Old World meant the replication of old social problems, and it should come as no surprise to find utopian projectors resorting to established languages and established solutions.

A New World of Full Employment?

Another way of viewing colonization was through the establishment of self-supporting communities or colonies within the Old World itself. Winstanley's digging communities – colonizing the wastelands of England – might be seen as examples of this. Where such communities were geared to the full exploitation of all available resources, including human capacities – in other words, to full employment – the effect was akin to an imperial extension of those resources. John Bellers likened the effectiveness of his proposed "Colledge of Industry" to the colonization of a new land: "as if going to plant a new Country, which would be the gaining of several new provinces to the Kingdom. . . ."[33] "The Labour of the Poor, being the Mines of the Rich," discovering a way to provide labor for the poor was equivalent to discovering a new land rich in mines.[34] A succession of utopian projectors in seventeenth-century England shared this aspiration. Equally, they shared confidence in the potential success of their projects and awareness of the two great problems attendant upon such success: what to do with the traditional leisured class and how to consume the abundance that full employment would create without succumbing to the corrupting effects of luxury. In 1610, Rowland Vaughan proposed siphoning off the surplus from such a project to the gentry who would have contributed the original capital and who possessed the second merit of being inured to affluence.[35] Gabriel Plattes, who placed his *Macaria* (1641) self-consciously within a tradition of utopian writing, envisaged a state-managed economy dedicated to the maximization of production and commercial advantage. The freedom of the propertied to leave under-utilized land in parks and chases would not be allowed to withstand that objective.[36] In *The Poor Mans Advocate* (1649), Peter Chamberlen proposed setting colonies of the poor on what Winstanley had called "Commonwealths Land." The benefit to the nation from the maximized utilization of this public resource, the elimination of waste and the full employment of the unemployed, would be in the form of the reduction, even elimination, of taxes on the propertied classes. Writing in England in 1659, the Dutch Mennonite Peter Cornelius Plockhoy proposed setting up integrated communities of the middling sort – artisans, tradesmen, and husbandmen – based on the model of a regulated trading company. By withdrawing "Husbandmen, Handy-crafts people, Marriners and Masters of Arts and Sciences" from society at large, he would liberate them from the problems of the leisured, parasitic class and those of the indigent poor, ensuring that the productive enjoyed the full fruits of their labors and resourcefulness.[37] Nevertheless, the problem of prosperity and the attendant temptations of luxury remained a dilemma for Plockhoy's proposed communities. As his approach had been based on the regulated company, so that of John Bellers, writing in the 1690s against the backdrop of the first joint-stock company boom, was the new form of company. With the investment of the rich, the poor would be set to work in organized and efficient communities of three hundred inhabitants. The poor would gain a self-sufficient plenty, investors would be enriched by the profits of the enterprise, and the nation, as we have seen, would gain the equivalent of a number of colonies in the New World.

Conclusion

Utopia in the sixteenth and seventeenth centuries could be a startling and unsettling phenomenon. Like the New World, it challenged the political imagination to transcend time and place in new ways. It suggested that the most intractable social problem might not be inherent in ourselves or in our stars, but, more prosaically, in the way we organize things. Its liberation from existing custom required a lawgiver, frequently a fictional one like Utopus or Salomona, who rose above everyday limitations not only to legislate but also to design social arrangements and rituals, institutional mechanism and constitutions, bureaucracies and means of enforcement that would contain and shape that second nature that was prone to ignore, break, or undermine codes of conduct or the rule of law. Utopian writing showed the capacity to absorb the classical aspirations of humanism and the desire for a more godly community on both sides of the Reformation divide. Equally, it went on to absorb the military, bureaucratic, and fiscal aspirations of the neo-stoic state born, in part, out of the warfare engendered by those divisions. Where it hesitated was in respect of three "New Worlds." The New World of geographical discovery continued, in this period, to retain the potential to surprise, the contingent capacity to produce the unexpected and the unplanned. It is understandable that the response was to export to the colonies the designs already elaborated as "solutions" for the Old World. The second problematic "continent" was that of "discoveries" latent in the activity of scientific research as it was coming to be understood in the age of the "Scientific Revolution." It was, again, the contingency, but also the power, of such discoveries that was menacing to utopian stability. Finally, the vision of full employment began to be thought about systematically for the first time in these years. It brought with it a worrying prospect attendant upon success: an intolerance for idleness coupled with a fear of affluence. The world of geographical discoveries – at least as far as this globe is concerned – has gone. Science and full employment remain with us: the one advancing by disconcerting leaps; the other, for the most part, frustratingly out of reach. The utopian tradition, in the meantime, continues to make us "look at the real world with new eyes."[38] It continues to offer us, in return for our imaginative effort, a new perceptual world.

Notes

1 J. H. Elliott, *The Old World and the New 1492–1650*, Cambridge Studies in Early Modern History (Cambridge: Cambridge University Press, 1970), 102; quoting Garcilaso de la Vega, el Inca, *Royal Commentaries of the Incas*, trans. H. V. Livermore, 2 vols. (Austin: University of Texas Press, 1966), I: 9.

2 David Riesman, *Individualism Reconsidered and Other Essays* (Glencoe, Ill.: Free Press, 1954), 70.

3 Quoted in Silvio Zavala, "Sir Thomas More in New Spain," in R. S. Sylvester and G. P. Marc'hadour, eds., *Essential Articles for the Study of Thomas More* (Hamden, Conn.: Archon Books, 1977), 304.

4 Elliott, 26.

5 Christopher Columbus, *Book of Prophecies*, quoted in Mircea Eliade, "Paradise and Utopia: Mythical Geography and Eschatology," in Frank R. Manuel, ed., *Utopias and Utopian Thought* (Boston: Houghton Mifflin, 1966), 262.

6 Silvio Zavala, *Recuerdo de Vasco de Quiroga* (Mexico: Editorial Porrúa, 1965).

7 Elliott, 8. See also 12, 14.

8 For further development of these categories and their implications, see J. C. Davis, *Utopia and the Ideal Society: A Study of English Utopian Writing 1516–1700* (Cambridge, England: Cambridge University Press, 1981), Chapter 1.

9 Lyman Tower Sargent, *British and American Utopian Literature 1516–1975: An Annotated Bibliography* (Boston: G. K. Hall, 1979); and his "Utopia: The Problem of Definition," *Extrapolation* 16, no. 2 (1975). The denial of the "closure" of perfection is pushed to an extreme (and, in my opinion, ends in incoherence) in Lucy Sargisson, *Contemporary Feminist Utopianism* (London and New York: Routledge, 1996).

10 Anthony Pagden, "Dispossessing the Barbarian: The Language of Spanish Thomism and the Debate over the Property Rights of the American Indians," in Anthony Pagden, ed., *The Languages of Political Theory in Early-Modern Europe* (Cambridge, England: Cambridge University Press, 1987), 79–98.

11 Edward Surtz and J. H. Hexter, eds., *The Complete Works of St. Thomas More*, vol. 4; Utopia (New Haven, Conn., and London: Yale University Press, 1965), 51 [10]. Hereinafter cited as *Utopia*. For convenience, I also give in square brackets [ ] the page reference to George M. Logan and Robert M. Adams, eds., *More: Utopia* (Cambridge: Cambridge University Press, 1989) though I have preferred the Yale translation in the text.

12 Quentin Skinner, "Sir Thomas More's Utopia and the Language of Renaissance Humanism," in Pagden, ed., *Languages of Political Theory*, 134. This is an important essay in the modern contextualization of Utopia and establishes a very strong case for treating More's intention in devising Utopia as "serious."

13 Ibid., 141–56. Skinner offers a valuable discussion of utopian communism but it needs to be supported by Wootton's work discussed below.

14 David Wootton, ed., *Thomas More's "Utopia" with Erasmus' "The Sileni of Alcibiades"* (Indianapolis: Hackett, 1999).

15 Robert Burton, *The Anatomy of Melancholy*, ed. Holbrook Jackson, 3 vols. (London: Dent, 1932), I: 266–69; II: 186–89.

16 Daniel J. Donno, ed., *The City of the Sun: A Poetical Dialogue* (Berkeley: University of California Press, 1981), 39. The work was written in 1602 and first published in 1623.

17 *Utopia*, 225 [100].

18 Francis Bacon, *Valerius Terminus*, in James Spedding, Robert Leslie Ellis, and Douglas Denon Heath, eds., *The Works of Francis Bacon*, 14 vols. (London: Longmans, 1868–90), III: 223.

19 [Francis Bacon], *New Atlantis: A Worke Unfinished written by the Right Honourable Francis Lord Verulam, Viscount St. Alban*, ed. William Rawley (London, 1627), 7.

20 J. C. Davis, "Science and Utopia: The History of a Dilemma," in Everett Mendelsohn and Helga Nowotny, eds., *Nineteen Eighty-four: Science Between Utopia and Dystopia, Sociology of Sciences Yearbook*, 8 (Boston: Reidel, 1984), 21–48.

21 See Charles Webster, *The Great Instauration: Science, Medicine, and Reform 1626–1660* (London: Duckworth, 1975); J. C. Davis, "The Millennium as the Anti-Utopia of Seventeenth Century Political Thought," *Anglophonia* 3 (1998): 57–76.

22 The most accessible version of Andreä's utopia is still F. E. Held, ed., *Christianopolis an Ideal State of the Seventeenth Century translated from the Latin of Johann Valentin Andreä with an Historical Introduction* (New York: Oxford University Press, 1916). For Gott, an even older edition does service: Walter Begley, ed., *Nova Solyma, the Ideal City: or Jerusalem Regained*, 2 vols. (London, 1902).

23 Gerrard Winstanley, "The New Law of Righteousness," in G. H. Sabine, ed., *The Works of Gerrard Winstanley* (Ithaca, N.Y.: Cornell University Press, 1941), 183.

24 Traiano Boccalini, *Advices from Parnassus*, trans. Henry, Earl of Monmouth (London, 1656).

25 George Psalmanazar, *An Historical and Geographical Description of Formosa* (London, 1704).

26 Paolo Paruta, *Politick Discourses*, trans. Henry, Earl of Monmouth (London, 1657), esp. 1, 3, 11.

27 This account follows that in Davis, *Utopia and the Ideal Society*, Chapter 8.

28 Richard Beacon, *Solon his Folie* (Oxford, 1594).

29 Michael Drayton, *Ode to the Virginia Voyage* (London, 1606).

30 L. and M. Harder, *Plockhoy from Zurik-Zee: A Study of a Dutch Reformer in Puritan England and Colonial America* (Newton, Kans.: Board of Education and Publication [General Conference, Mennonite Church], 1952).

31 J. P. Boyd, ed., *Fundamental Laws and Constitutions of New Jersey 1664–1964* (Princeton, N.J.: Princeton University Press, 1964).

32 *The Two Charters granted by King Charles IId to the Proprietors of Carolina* (n.d.), British Library 1061 g 10; Benjamin Franklin, ed., *A Collection of Charters and Other Publick Acts relating to the Province of Pennsylvania* (Philadelphia, 1740).

33 John Bellers, *Essays About the Poor, Manufactures, Trade, Plantations and Immorality* (London, 1699), 4.

34 John Bellers, *Proposals for Raising a Colledge of Industry* (London, 1696), 2.

35 Rowland Vaughan, *Most Approved and Long Experienced Waterworks* (London, 1610).

36 [Gabriel Plattes], *A Description of the Famous Kingdom of Macaria* (London, 1641).

37 Peter Cornelius Plockhoy, *A Way Propounded* (London, 1659), 3.

38 George Kateb, ed., *Utopia* (New York: Atherton Press, 1971), 19.

The City as an Intellectual Exercise

I N *U TOPIA*, published in 1516, Thomas More's
Portuguese voyager, Raphael Hythlodaeus, fictional
companion to Amerigo Vespucci, recounts a dinner
conversation at the Archbishop of Canterbury's
table, the pretext for a scathing critique of the
institutions and condition of modern England,
before relating his sojourn on the crescent-shaped
island of Utopia, home to "what is now, perhaps, the
most civilised nation in the world."[1] Criticism of the
status quo, coupled with a contrasting projection
of a model arrangement not only of society but also
of space, achieved without divine assistance, are the
elements that characterize the utopian genre.

More describes Utopia's geography, its towns,
its peoples, its laws, informing us that "There are
fifty-four splendid big towns on the island, all with
the same language, laws, customs, and institutions."[2]
In emphasizing the urban environment of his
alternative world, More suggests that the cradle of
society can mirror, and perhaps even determine, its
social organization and the behavior of its citizens.

Alberti's satire, *Momus* [*The Prince*], conveys this
notion clearly: when Jove seeks to install a new
order into a world in which the capricious son of
Night has wreaked havoc after being expelled from
the heavens, he finds inspiration not in the advice
of philosophers but in the vision of a magnificent
theater of perfectly harmonious proportions
and design. This concept was far from new in the
Renaissance – classical Greece had already bound
the body politic and the urban organization inextricably in the word *polis*, "city-state." The majority of
utopian societies are imagined as residing in urban
environments, the cities themselves indicating
humankind's domination of the forces of nature,
their frequently geometrical layouts subliminally
conveying the rational design that regulates their
social and political organization. More's fifty-four
towns, spaced out regularly across the territory, are
"all built on the same plan, and, so far as the sites
will allow, they all look exactly alike."[3] One feels
that, while he contained his project within the con-

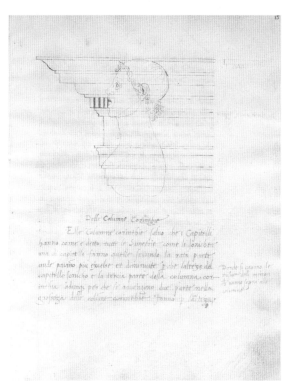

The Human Analogy

**Francesco di Giorgio Martini
[Opera di Architectura]**
[Siena, Italy, 1479–80]
NYPL, Spencer Collection

In this work, the Renaissance
architect Francesco di Giorgio
Martini draws heavily from the
newly rediscovered ideas of
the first century B.C.E. Roman
architect and engineer Vitruvius. Francesco translated
selected passages from Vitruvius's writings and developed
them into his own theories
of "human analogy." While
Vitruvius suggested the proportions of the human body
as a source for architectural
proportions, Francesco tried to
explain in words and illustra-

tions how this could work,
particularly in terms of
columns. Here he demon-
strates the theory that in
the same way that a man's
shoulders support his neck
and head, a column's archi-
trave should support the
cornice and the frieze; he
goes so far, in fact, with his
analogy that the teeth of the
man correspond exactly to
the dentils (teeth-like decorations) on the column. The text
and drawings in this manuscript were most likely executed by a professional scribe
in the Italian city of Siena
around 1479 or 1480, when
Francesco was living there.

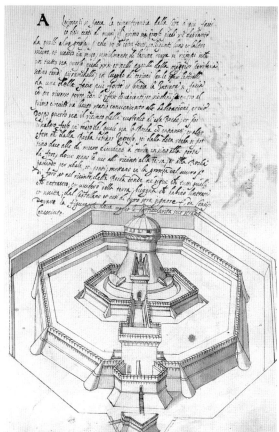

Ideal Architecture

Francesco di Giorgio Martini
***Trattato di Architettura
Civile e Militare***
[Siena, 1530s]
NYPL, Spencer Collection

Francesco di Giorgio Martini's second *Treatise on Civil and Military Architecture* considers many aspects of ideal architecture and city planning, and illustrates the growing interest in military matters. As a witness to the French invasion of Naples in 1494, Francesco was able to evaluate the precise ways in which existing fortifications had become obsolete. His text, illustrated with numerous plans for fortified towns, takes into account social and political issues as well as defense considerations.

At least four scribes are thought to have collaborated on the transcription of this copy from a manuscript in the Monte Oliveto Maggiore monastery in Siena; none of the scribes have been identified. Many of the drawings have been attributed to the sixteenth-century Sienese artist Domenico Beccafumi, the brother-in-law of Pietro Cataneo; others are thought to be the work of numerous other artists in Siena.

fines of a fictitious island about the size of England (in order to stress the contrasts between the two while minimizing the risk of losing his head because of this work), had he been writing in the twentieth century he might have covered the surrounding territories with thousands of similar towns, and the oceans and outer space would surely not have escaped either.

Running parallel to the utopian literary genre is that of the ideal city. In the former, the social arrangement appears to be of primary concern and the urban of secondary; in the latter, this is usually reversed. The former is described in words (predominantly, though not exclusively), the latter in words and/or images and/or three-dimensional models. In the ideal city tradition, criticism of the existing urban situation is expressed explicitly on occasion but often merely implied. A new, contrasting, urban model is projected: it may aspire to creating a spatial framework that is considered better adapted to the social, political, and economic change that has already occurred (independently of the ideal city designer), or is currently occurring, or indeed to actually provoking such transformation.

While earlier centuries set precedents that have been demonstrated in this exhibition, the Renaissance gave birth to full-fledged ideal cities and utopias. At this time, the city and society came

to be considered as objects that could be invented intellectually, and a number of factors contributed to this phenomenon. The ties of the church and of the feudal structure were loosening, heralding in the system of wage labor and unemployment but also enabling greater individual freedom and the possibility of a degree of self-determination without divine assistance. Horizons opened and other worlds, distant in time and space, were (re)encountered, providing points of comparison with the familiar one. Scholars, mainly Greek, immigrating from the East, refugees from the Ottoman Turks, brought with them learning and manuscripts of the ancients. The classical world provided an endless – and idealized – source of inspiration as the new humanists scoured archaeological remains and ancient texts such as Vitruvius's *De architectura*, the only complete architectural treatise to survive from the ancient Roman empire. The year 1492 saw both the completion of the Christian *reconquista* as the Moors were ousted from their final foothold in Granada, and Christopher Columbus's voyages and "discovery" of the New World. Surveying techniques developed as too did those of drawing – particularly with Brunelleschi's invention of the linear perspective in or before 1413 – thus greatly facilitating the depiction of a building or urban composi-

Mathematical Order

Albrecht Dürer
Etliche Underricht, zu Befestigung der Stett, Schloss und Flecken
Nuremburg, 1527
NYPL, Spencer Collection

By resurrecting Classical ideas of architecture, Albrecht Dürer played an essential role in creating the dominant architectural vocabulary of the Renaissance. He interpreted and explained the rules and calculations founded upon the conviction of the Ancients that the divine order of the universe was mathematical in nature. In this treatise, Dürer focuses on the question of city planning. His text testifies to the influence of contemporary ideas; his plan for a fortified citadel, reproduced here, resembles the descriptions of the newly "discovered" Mexican town of Tenochtitlán, published three years earlier by Cortés (see page 123), and the plan illustrating Andreae's *Christianopolis* (see page 109).

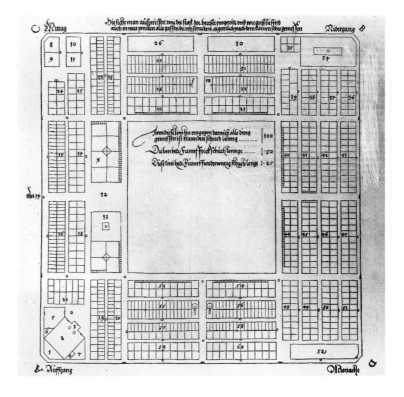

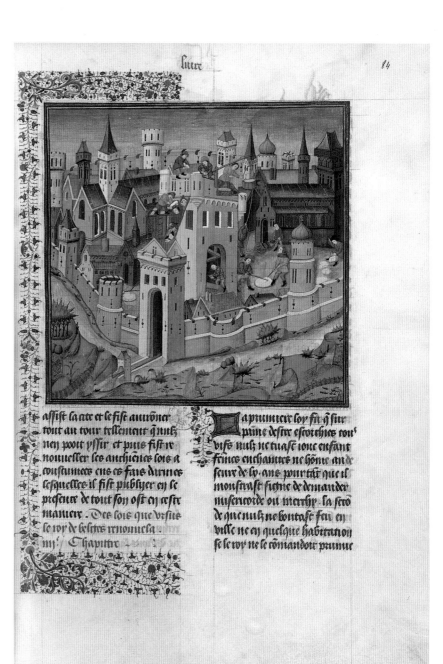

A Renaissance Myth

Jacques de Gulse
Chroniques de Hainaut,
translated and compiled
by Jean Wauquelin
Mons, ca. 1470
BNF, Département des Manuscrits

Jean Wauquelin, who was a
translator, scribe, bookseller,
and author frequently in the
employ of Philippe le Bon,
undertook the translation and
compilation of this work at
the request of one of the
duke's advisors, a native
of Hainaut. The *Chronicle*,
based on a Latin text by
Jacques de Guise, was written in 1446–48, soon after
the province of Hainaut
was incorporated into the
Burgundian state.

The miniature and accompanying text shown here tell the
story of the founder of the
first city of the Belgians, king
Ursus (bear), whose body was
covered with fur, like that of
a wild man. The book, which
includes many of the myths
concerning the origins of
the Belgians, belongs to the
popular genre of the national
historical epic, of which the
*Grandes Chroniques de
France* is another example.

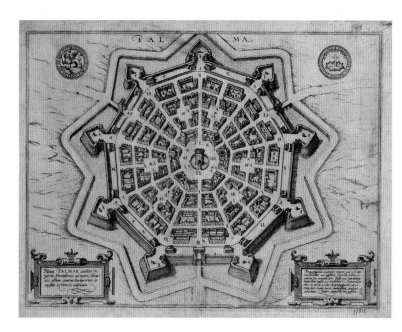

Palmanova

Georg Braun and Frans Hogenberg
***Nova Palmae civitas in patria
Foroiuliensi ad maris Adriatici
ostium contra Barbarorum incursum
à Venetis ædificata***
Engraving from *Civitates Orbis Terrarum,*
vol. V (Cologne, 1598)
BNF, Département des Cartes et Plans

The rules governing the creation of architecture and ideal cities of the fifteenth and sixteenth centuries were rarely applied, except to isolated buildings or in limited urban contexts. The construction of Palmanova, near Venice, is a major exception. This fortified city was conceived by a military architect, probably Giulio Savorgnano in collaboration with Vincenzo Scamozzi. Despite a somewhat free interpretation of the details, his spider-web layout conforms, on the whole, to the period's concept of an ideal fortified city.

The six volumes of *Civitates Orbis Terrarum,* the first atlas of city plans, were published in Cologne between 1572 and 1617; they appeared as the complement to the first atlas of the world, the *Theatrum Orbis Terrarum,* published in Antwerp by Abraham Ortelius in 1570.

The Aztec Capital

Hernán Cortés
***Praeclara Ferdinandi
Cortésii de nova
maris oceani Hyspania
narratio sacratissimo . . .***
Nuremburg:
Frederic Arthemesium, 1524
NYPL, Rare Books Division

This anonymous woodcut of Tenochtitlán, the Aztec capital, after a drawing probably commissioned by Cortés, accompanies the text, translated into Latin, of the conquistador's second letter from Mexico, October 15, 1520. Cortés was very impressed by the magnificence of the city, constructed in the center of a lake and accessed by four artificial dikes. Traversed by long straight streets, the city had a central plaza with temples where human sacrifice was practiced. As with many representations of the New World, it is difficult to know to what degree European ideals influenced the accuracy of this image.

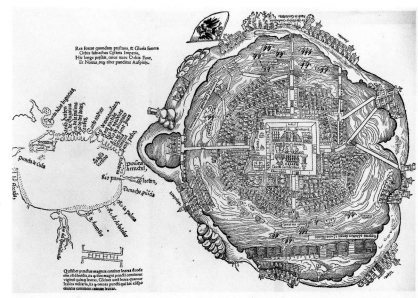

tion. The distribution of ideas was further aided by the more widespread production of paper and the introduction of printing. Art and architecture were elevated to veritable sciences, relying on mathematical rules, and the artist's status in society improved greatly. The architect, inventing and depicting buildings and urban designs away from the contextual constraints of site, distinguished himself from the master builders of the Middle Ages. Piero di Cosimo's painting *The Building of a Double Palace* (ca. 1510–15) can be interpreted as symbolizing this change, its palace in the background representing the idea of the architect, the object that it is the task of the craftsmen in the foreground to realize.

Signs of this increasing objectivization of the city were already apparent in Leonardo Bruni's *Laudatio florentinae urbis* of 1403, which broke ground by methodically describing a town, albeit an extant one, Florence, extolling its merits as the physical representation of the city-state. By the middle of the Quattrocento, humanist architects, working independently of the church but dependent instead upon the powerful merchant families, began to depict not existing cities, but products of their own imagination, places that might be built by their patrons in contrast to the medieval urban environment they had inherited and that might reflect the new political, economic, and social system over which these figures ruled. These cities employed the classical vocabulary of the Renaissance whereby space was rationally organized, mirroring the arrangement of the universe, and

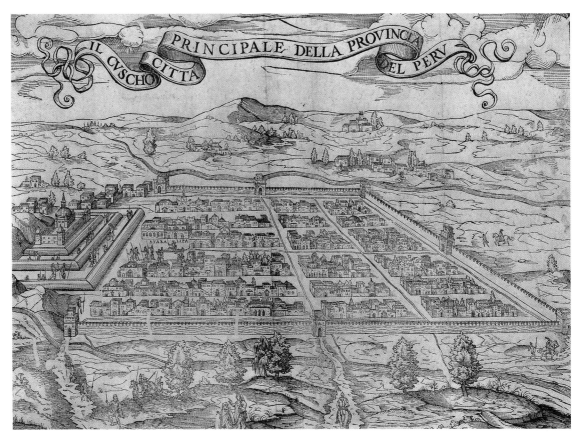

Cuzco

Giovanni Battista Ramusio
Il Cuscho Citta Principale
della Provincia del Peru
Venice, 1606
NYPL, Map Division

The Spanish conquistadors were particularly impressed by the discovery of the splendid capital of the Aztec and Inca empires. The beauty of Cuzco, Peru, with its gold-covered buildings and its solid stone walls, was described by Francisco Pizarro and by Miguel de Estete, who accompanied Pizarro on his expedition to Pachacamac in 1533.

Leon Battista Alberti set out the principles guiding the achievement of the ideal order in *De re aedificatoria* in the middle of the century. The three famous *Città Ideale spalliere*, painted at the close of the fifteenth century and now housed in Baltimore, Berlin, and Urbino, convey handsomely the type of city the humanist architects had in mind. Many of the plans were orthogonal, but circular and/or radial schemes, which Vitruvius had suggested (contrary to current Roman practice) and Filarete proposed for Sforzinda, gained favor progressively. Variations on the circular form satisfied not only symbolic requirements – the focal seat of power reflecting both the microcosm (the human heart) and the macrocosm (the sun) – but also military ones.

The first complete program for an ideal city was invented by Antonio Averlino, known as Filarete: named Sforzinda in honor of his patron Francesco Sforza, the scheme was described in detail in a lengthy treatise that dates from 1457–64. Francesco di Giorgio Martini's *Trattato di architettura*, completed late in his life, in 1495, paid great attention to matters of fortification along with advice on city building, an aspect that was increasingly to dominate social or aesthetic concerns during the bellicose sixteenth century, which saw methods of warfare change (following, in particular, the invention of the modern cannon). Leonardo da Vinci was horrified by the filth and promiscuity of medieval towns of the Italian peninsular, a reality underlined by the death toll resulting from the

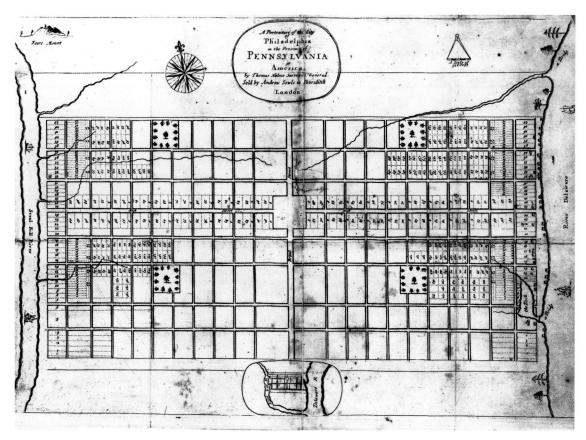

Philadelphia

After Thomas Holme
A Portraiture of the City of Philadelphia in the Province of Pennsylvania
Engraving from *A Letter from William Penn Proprietary and Governour of Pennsylvania . . . to the Committee of the Free Society* (London, 1683)
NYPL, Miriam and Ira D. Wallach Division of Art, Prints and Photographs

Unlike earlier colonial settlements, Philadelphia, founded in 1682, was completely planned out in advance by its founder, the Quaker William Penn, and his surveyor, Thomas Holme. This map, from a prospectus aimed at would-be purchasers, shows a well-organized, gridded rectangle, featuring house lots of uniform size, a central square with a marketplace and town hall, and four square public parks.

Penn envisioned a city free from disease and the threat of fire, and open to all religions. In a radical departure from other settlements in Europe and America, his plan incorporates wide, straight streets, and plenty of open space for gardens and orchards; it includes neither city walls nor a fortress. But despite rapid growth, the "City of Brotherly Love" did not fully live up to Penn's ideals. Lots were subdivided by owners for more housing, and a network of narrow alleyways developed between them.

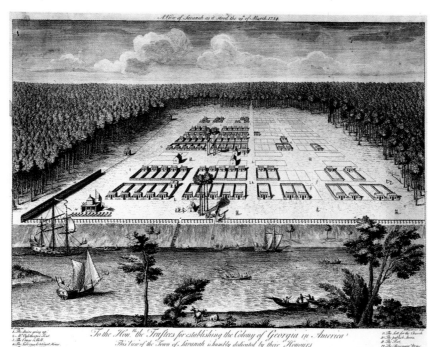

Savannah 1734

**Paul Fourdrinier after
Peter Gordon
*A View of Savanah
as it Stood the
29th of March, 1734***
Etching, 1734
NYPL, Miriam and Ira D. Wallach
Division of Art, Prints and
Photographs

James Oglethorpe's plan for
Savannah, Georgia, offers
an interesting variation on the
grid model so often used in
North America. He invented
the ward, made up of a public
square with four plots for public buildings and four groups
of lots with ten houses each.
The residents possessed
triangular plots of land outside
the town limits and agricultural lands beyond those.

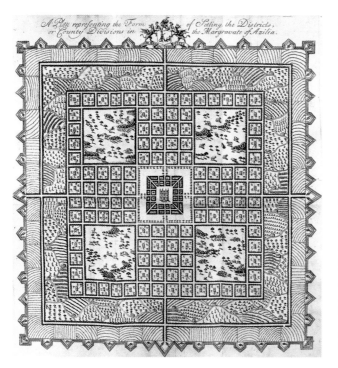

An Ideal Colony

**Sir Robert Montgomery
*A Discourse Concerning the
Design'd Establishment
of a New Colony to the South of
Carolina, in the most delightful
country of the Universe***
London, 1717
NYPL, Rare Books Division

The Lords Proprietors of Carolina tried
to attract colonists by instituting religious freedom and tax exemptions.
In 1717, the Englishman Robert Montgomery was granted the land between
the Savannah and Altamaha rivers in
what is now northern Georgia, and
in this pamphlet he presents his plan
for an ideal colony. Four large forests
are surrounded by 116 plantations.
The residence of the Margrave is at
the heart of the town. Fortified walls,
buffered by a band of countryside,
surround and protect the entire settlement. Montgomery himself never
reached America, and his plan was
never realized.

Vue perspective de la Ville de Chaux

Ledoux's Ideal City of Chaux

Pierre-Gabriel Berthault after Claude-Nicolas Ledoux "Vue perspective de la Ville de Chaux"
In *L'architecture considérée sous le rapport de l'art, des moeurs et de la législation*, vol. 2 (Paris: Chez l'auteur, 1804)
NYPL, Miriam and Ira D. Wallach Division of Art, Prints and Photographs

The elliptical arrangement of buildings, constructed by Ledoux when he was inspector of the Royal saltworks in Franche-Comté in the 1770s, became the basis for his ideal city of Chaux (the name is derived from the forest adjacent to the saltworks). This view of the city, combining constructed and unconstructed elements, appeared in a 240-page compilation of his work that Ledoux published at his own expense in 1804. Although his dream of a city that would house a morally and socially better world was never realized, the independent and singular character of various parts of his project – in contrast with Baroque style – represented a decisive breakthrough, considered the architectural embodiment of the late eighteenth-century social revolution.

The Cenotaph of Newton

"Sublime mind! Vast and profound genius! Divine being! Newton!
Accept the homage of my weak talents. . . . O Newton! . . .
I conceived the idea of surrounding thee with thy discovery,
and thus, somehow, surrounding thee with thyself." These two
drawings, taken from a series of plates devoted to Newton's
cenotaph, illustrate the philosophy of Boullée who, like his contemporaries, was fascinated by Newtonian physics. They also
express Boullée's approach to architecture; he loved the sphere,
the purest of "circular bodies," which unites symmetry and
variety, the two golden rules of architecture. In his artistic, innovative, and philosophical research, Boullée deemed architecture
superior to the other arts, since it permitted him to achieve a
realism that he believed could not be attained in painting.

His work marvelously illustrates the characteristics of late eighteenth-century architecture – large, simple constructions with
no unnecessary decoration – as well as the principles emblematic
of an *architecture parlante* (speaking architecture) whereby the
purpose of a building is expressed by its exterior form. Newton's
sarcophagus rests on a raised catafalque. The feeling of night
is created by the beams of natural light that filter through its
pierced vault to give an impression of starlight. The effect of day
is created by a lamp placed on an ancillary sphere suspended
in the center of the globe.

**Etienne-Louis Boullée
[Newton's Cenotaph]**

opposite: **A Newton
elevation. Perspective**

below: **Cross-section of
Newton's Cenotaph with
interior nighttime effect**

Watercolor drawings, ca. 1785?
BNF, Département des
Estampes et de la Photographie

"I wanted to situate Newton
in the sky." Perhaps this was
Boullée's answer to Diderot's
1763 challenge: "I defy the
boldest from amongst the
artists to select his sky as
nature does, strewn with
brilliant stars as on the most
serene of nights."

plagues (for instance, Milan lost one-third of its inhabitants in the plague of 1484–85). He sought hygienic, orderly, rational alternatives in a number of intriguing and farsighted drawings bequeathed to posterity from the late fifteenth and early sixteenth centuries: some deal with specific locations, such as Milan, while others appear to be ideal schemes worked out *in absolu*, perhaps with no particular site in mind. Among the latter we find sketches for a city of different levels in which an intricate technical but also social vertical segregation is depicted. His proposal to reduce the Milanese population and rehouse the surplus in a series of ten satellite towns with populations of thirty thousand each was to be echoed directly in schemes put forth many centuries later. The most important treatises of the sixteenth and early seventeenth centuries to consider ideal fortified cities in depth include Albrecht Dürer's *Etliche Underricht zu Befestigung der Stett, Schloss und Flecken* (1527), Pietro Cataneo's *I quattro primi libri di architettura* (1554), Iacques Androuet du Cerceau's *Livre d'architecture* (1559), Girolamo Maggi and Iacomo F. Castriotto's *Della Fortificatione delle Città* (1564), Buonaiuto Lorini's *Delle Fortificationi Libri Cinque* (1592), Francesco de Marchi's *Della Architettura militare* (prepared from 1540 but published posthumously in 1599), Jacques Perret's *Des Fortifications et artifices* (1601), Vincenzo Scamozzi's *L'Idea della Architettura Universale* (1615), and Robert Fludd's *Utriusque cosmi, majoris scilicet et minoris, metaphysica, physica atque technica historia . . .* (1617–18).

The Italian ideal city designs of the Renaissance were produced, as is often the case, at a time that combined great change with a degree of frustration for architects, who were unable to actually build entire cities in accordance with the ideal criteria due to demographic and financial limitations. As the military domain progressively monopolized the field on paper, it was also to provide an opportunity at last to turn the drawings into reality. In 1593, the Venetian senate decided to protect its eastern frontier against the potential attacks of the archduchies of Trieste and Gorizia locally and the Turkish enemy abroad by building the most advanced fortress city of its day. Palmanova, with its massive protective walls, still stands in a kind of time bubble, which curiously satisfies the utopian characteristic of resistance to change.

Though one might of course debate the seriousness of as playful a character as More in his desire to see his alternative environment actually realized, most utopians and designers of ideal cities – elaborated *in absolu*, with little or no concern for local geographical, cultural, social, or environmental conditions – dream of their implementation. The

Old World in the sixteenth century provided little scope for such action, but the New World was truly a land of opportunity on this count. Despite the contribution of the encounter with the Americas to the dethroning of former certitudes, the vision of the foreign lands was filtered through European glasses, and peoples and towns were often depicted according to Europeans' ideals. While many felt that here at last Paradise or the Golden Age had been found, the New World nonetheless provided less an example to be emulated at home than a blank page upon which ideas invented in the Old World could be put to the test. Traditional forms of settlement, in the town as in the countryside, with their panoply of spiritual and cultural significance for the indigenous populations, were systematically abandoned in favor of, most frequently, the rational, planned grid layout.

Santo Domingo, founded in 1496 and refounded in 1502, is the oldest of the American cities to have been created by the Europeans: blocks of buildings are laid out upon a gridiron plan with a large rectangular plaza, site of the principal church and numerous religious celebrations, occupying the center. This pattern dominated throughout New Spain, and the Iberian authorities issued a series of instructions concerning the ideal planning of new towns from 1513 on, culminating in Philip II's set of *Royal Ordinances concerning the laying out of the New Towns* of 1573. These dealt with colonial towns but not with military establishments or the religious *reducciones* (reductions), the villages into which the indigenous populations were herded. An essential element of the process of evangelization, they were initiated early in the sixteenth century, and the motivations of the *conquistadores* and the methods they employed varied greatly. Vasco de Quiroga, sent to Mexico in 1531 by the Emperor Charles V to temper the excesses committed by Cortés's successors, was influenced by his reading of More's *Utopia* in his creation of hospitality villages. The reductions founded by the Jesuit missionaries from 1609 and grouping the Guarani Indians are perhaps the most famous. Their regular orthogonal plans, which barely differed from one village to another, represented a sharp contrast with the Indians' traditional settlements and caused severe disorientation among peoples who lived in a profoundly symbiotic relationship with their environment. The procedures practiced by the Society of Jesus in their "civilization" of the Indians were nonetheless "softer," more gradual, than those of many of their predecessors: the physical aspect of the reduction thus paid

lip service to Indian custom by initially allowing the villagers to live polygamously in the dwelling houses until monogamy was established and internal walls introduced.

The grid layout presents a practical way of arranging territories and is particularly appreciated in cases of arm's-length planning such as the Spanish colonization of America. It had been employed by the Greeks and Romans who, upon the creation of their new colonies, measured not only the urban but also the surrounding rural land and even, for divinatory purposes, the air, as Aristophanes mockingly recorded in *The Birds*. Early North American cities like Boston contain small areas that follow an organic pattern, but the grid quickly came to dominate both urban and regional planning in the United States. The Land Ordinance of 1785 split territories into townships, each six miles square and subdivided in turn, a pre-urban cadastre resembling that suggested by Thomas More in *Utopia*. For the new North American capital, Jefferson had proposed a straightforward grid plan that was condemned in the following terms by Pierre Charles L'Enfant, the planner of Washington, D.C.: "Such regular plans indeed, however answerable they may appear upon paper or seducing as they may be on the first aspect to the eyes of some people must even when applyed upon the ground the best calculated to admit of it become at last tiresome and insipid. . . ."[4] (Instead, L'Enfant rejected simple geometrical ideal patterns in a plan that was sympathetic to the context, responding to the site and conveying the appropriate symbolic message by combining grandiose diagonals linking the symbols of power – revealing the influence of his childhood years spent in Versailles – with the grid.) For More, checkerboard land division represented equality. For Thomas Jefferson, it was the concretization of a democratic ideal, as he hoped citizens (then restricted to white males) would all be landowners and hence voters. For others, one of the principal attractions of the grid was that it facilitated (like the panoptical scheme) surveillance: the ideal city tradition also treads the tightrope between utopia and dystopia.

Europe entered the eighteenth century in the throes of the Baroque with political/urban patterns set from the Renaissance culminating in grandiose schemes such as Versailles or Karlsruhe. By its close, however, the certainties of the Old World had been shaken profoundly. It is a curious paradox of history that it is the architect imprisoned in 1793 by the French revolutionaries for nurturing royalist sympathies, Claude-Nicolas Ledoux, who is considered one of the key protagonists of the major changes in architectural practice that accompanied the profound social and political changes of the period.[5] He designed the unrealized ideal city of Chaux, published in *L'Architecture considérée sous le rapport de l'art, des moeurs et de la législation* (1804). The work of Ledoux and certain of his contemporaries, such as Etienne Boullée, is considered the very embodiment of the transition from an architecture and town planning that privileged the *enchainement* – the flow of a dominant movement through an urban composition, a building and every component thereof – and used visual ploys to reflect a social hierarchy. Instead, they ushered in the modern era by creating autonomous architecture – freestanding, determined by function, devoid of superfluous ornament, and so forth – the built framework for a new society that promised liberty, equality, and fraternity.

Ledoux's words concerning the architect testify to an immodest ambition shared by many an ideal city planner: "Everything is within his realm – politics, morality, legislation, worship, government."[6] An ideal city is an intellectual design for an urban, but also social, alternative to the status quo, usually invented away from the context of site. It may be a compact unit, as in the Athens that Plato retrospectively idealized in opposition to his Atlantis, a module relentlessly cloned across the territory like More's fifty-four identical cities. Or it may take the form of a continual urban sprawl, a pattern that has developed with industrialization and the automobile. These two systems (and variants thereof) will be seen competing in the ideal city designer's imagination in later centuries. These two alternative groups of rational spatial projects share a common ambition: tentacular global domination. Yet the twenty-first century perhaps would benefit from the utopians and the ideal city designers changing course completely, replacing fifty-four identical cities by a constellation or patchwork of different ones.

1 Thomas More, *Utopia*, trans. with an introduction by Paul Turner (London: Penguin Books, 1961), 70.

2 Ibid.

3 Ibid.

4 Undated communication by L'Enfant entitled "Note relative to the ground lying on the eastern branch of the river Potomac and being intended to parallel the several positions proposed within the limits between the branch and Georgetown for the seat of the Federal City"; quoted in Elizabeth Sarah Kite, *L'Enfant and Washington, 1791–1792* (Baltimore, Md.: The Johns Hopkins University Press, 1929), 47–48.

5 Emil Kaufmann, *Von Ledoux bis Le Corbusier. Ursprung und Entwicklung der Autonomen Architektur* (Vienna-Leipzig: Editions Rolf Passer, 1933).

6 Quoted in Jean-Claude Lemagny, *Visionary Architects: Boullée, Ledoux, Lequeu* (Houston: University of St. Thomas, 1968), 109.

Voyages to the Lands of Nowhere

More had imagined a New World island. Utopian literature was to find other places in which to locate its imaginary worlds: the moon, the center of the earth, undiscovered continents. The invention of extraordinary machines would produce a new utopian theme, the fiction of scientific foresight. And then came the theme of time-travel, which would persist as a recurring motif in nineteenth- and twentieth-century utopian literature.

Subterranean Worlds

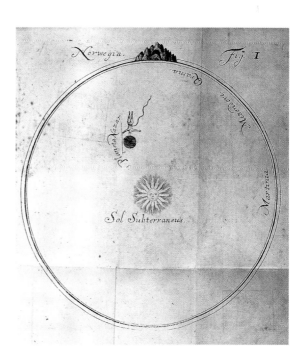

right

[Ludvig Holberg]
Nicolai Klimii Iter Subterraneum Novam Telluris Theoriam ac Historiam Quintae Monarchiae adhuc Nobis Incognitae Exhibens e Bibliotheca B. Abelini
Copenhagen: sumtibus Iacobi Prevssii, 1741
NYPL, General Research Division

The Dane Ludvig Holberg introduced the theme of a voyage to the center of the earth in a Latin text that was almost immediately translated into a number of languages.

His hero, Niels Klim, falls into an abyss and discovers another universe, the planet Nazar, which revolves inside the earth around a central sun. He encounters the Potuans – mobile, softspoken trees – who are models of wisdom and restraint. The author's abundant imagination takes precedence over satire in his description of the planet's twenty-seven different peoples.

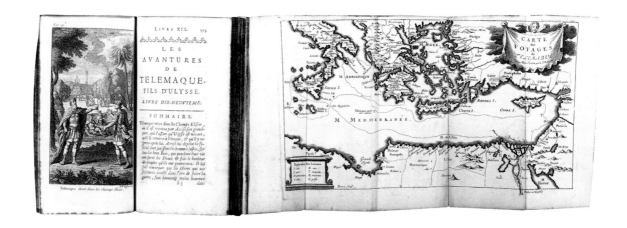

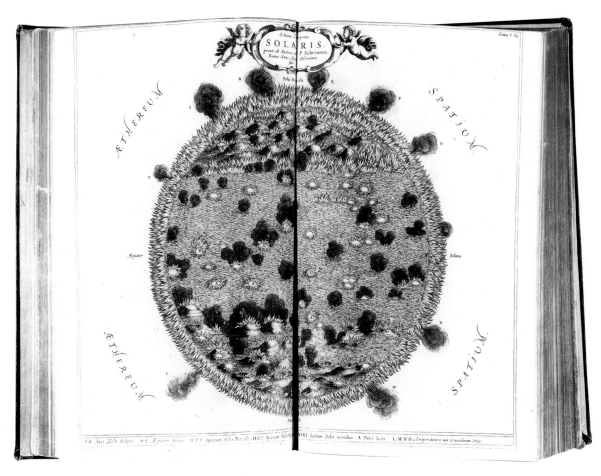

opposite

**François de Salignac
de la Mothe Fénelon**
***Les Avantures de
Télémaque fils d'Ulysse***
Paris: Jacques Estienne, [1717]
NYPL, Rare Books Division

The Adventures of Telemachus,
first published in 1699, is a
work of political theory dis-
guised as a work of fiction. The
young Telemachus embarks
on a journey throughout the
Mediterranean, guided by his
tutor, Mentor (the goddess
Minerva in disguise). During
the journey (plotted on the
map), he is instructed on the
best way to rule and shown
the virtues of simplicity, peace,
fairness, and hard work.
Considered an attack on the
extravagant lifestyle and

belligerent rule of Louis XIV, the
publication was condemned.
Nevertheless, after the Bible,
it was the most-read book
in eighteenth-century France.

The plate shows Telemachus
visiting the Elysian Fields,
where he hopes to find his
father, whom he believes
to be dead. His father is not
there, but his grandfather
shows him the two realms of
past kings. Those who were
greedy, indulgent, and evil
on earth are condemned to a
hellish place of darkness and
struggle, but those who had
led simple lives and exercised
their power fairly live in a heavenly garden, laden with fruit
and flowers, spending their
afterlife in pleasure and peace.

Athanasius Kircher
***Mundus Subterraneus,
in XII libros digestus . . .***
Amsterdam: apud Joannem
Janssonium a Waesberge & filios, 1678
NYPL, Science, Industry and
Business Library

Few scientists have been inclined
to embellish their research with
fictional conjectures. Of these
few, the German Jesuit scholar
Athanasius Kircher was among
the first. His *Subterranean World*,
a long reflection on underground
forces, is more closely related
to the genre of esoteric and
mystical treatises than to that
of utopian narratives. This is a
view of the subterranean sun.

[Robert Paltock]
***The Life and Adventures of
Peter Wilkins, a Cornish man.
Taken from his own mouth,
in his passage to England,
from off Cape Horn in
America, in the ship Hector.
By R. S. a Passenger in
the Hector. In two volumes***
London: Printed for Harrison
and Co., 1783
NYPL, General Research Division

Originally published in 1751,
the story of Peter Wilkins
tells of a shipwrecked young
man who finds himself on
an island populated by winged
people, the Glumms and the
Gawreys. Clearly influenced
by Enlightenment ideals,
Wilkins convinces the population to abolish slavery and
encourage education. Upon
the death of his Gawrey wife,
Wilkins is so overcome with
melancholy that he flees the
island on a contraption built
to be piloted by the winged
Glumms. He does not make it,
however, and instead crashes
into the sea.

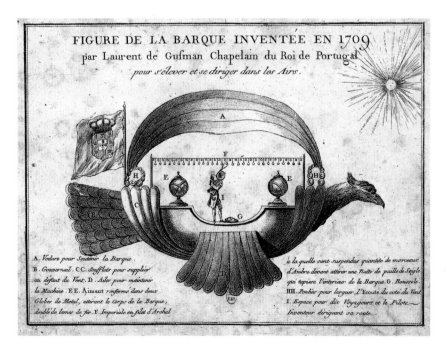

***Figure de la Barque
Inventée en 1709 . . .***
Etching and aquatint, n.d.
BNF, Département des Estampes
et de la Photographie

In 1709, the Brazilian Bar-
tolomeo-Lorenzo de Guzmán,
Chaplain to the King of
Portugal, invented a small
bird-shaped boat to allow
levitation and travel through
the skies. In this depiction
of his invention, the aeronaut,
or "flying man," appears
inside the boat. The various
parts of the apparatus are listed at the bottom of the print.

Watercolor drawing, n.d.
BNF, Département des Estampes
et de la Photographie

EXPÉRIENCE DU VAISSEAU VOLANT DE M.ᵈ BLANCHARD.
Enlevé au Champ de Mars près Paris entre Midi et 2 Heures, le 2 Mars 1784. par M.ʳ Blanchard

*Expérience du vaisseau
volant de M. Blanchard,
enlevé au Champ de Mars
près Paris entre Midi et
2 heures, le 2 mars 1784,
par M. Blanchard*
Etching with watercolor, 1784
BNF, Département des Estampes
et de la Photographie

Jean-Pierre Blanchard was
the first aviator to use a balloon with propellers and to fly
above Holland, Switzerland,
Belgium, and Poland. In 1785,
he successfully crossed the
English Channel from Dover
to Blanay (between Calais
and Boulogne). Struck by
apoplexy in his balloon near
La Haye, he crashed in 1808
and died the following year.

The Southern Land

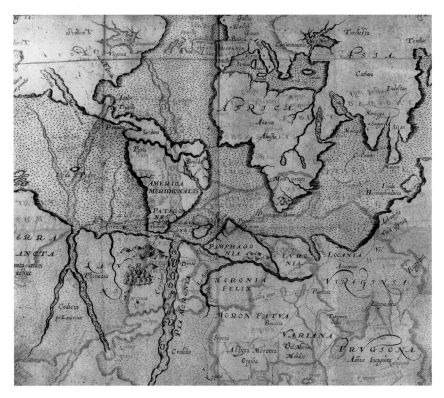

[Joseph Hall]
***Mundus Alter et Idem
sive Terra Australis ante
hac semper incognita
longis itineribus peregrini
Academici nuper rime
lustrata***
Frankfurt: Haeredes Ascany
ac Rinialme, [1605]
NYPL, Rare Books Division

Bishop Joseph Hall's *Another
World and Yet the Same*,
clearly influenced by François
Rabelais, is a satire of the
vices of his time in the form
of an imaginary voyage to
the various provinces of the
antipodes, including Crapulia
(land of gluttons and drunk-
ards), Moronia (land of fools),
and even Amazonia, where
"the women attend to military
affairs and farming" and
"wear the breeches and sport
long beards." Jonathan Swift's
Gulliver's Travels, published a
century later, was inspired by
this work, but Hall's characters
are less cynical. The theme
of Terra Australis, which will
play an important role in
seventeenth- and eighteenth-
century narratives of imaginary
voyages, makes its first
appearance here.

**[Nicolas-Edme Restif
de la Bretonne]**
***La découverte australe par
un Homme-volant; ou le
Dédale français; nouvelle
très-philosophique: suivi
de la lettre d'un singe, &ca.***
Leipzig, [1781]
NYPL, Rare Books Division

This long, dense work
combines a boundless
novelistic imagination with
moral, philosophical, and
scientific reflections. The
hero, Victorin, has invented a
system of wings that enables
him to fly to the southern
land, where he meets all
kinds of fantastic beings.

CANDIDE,

O U

L'OPTIMISME,

TRADUIT DE L'ALLEMAND

D E

MR. LE DOCTEUR RALPH.

MDCCLIX.

**Jean François Marie
Arouet Voltaire**
*Candide; ou, l'optimisme,
traduit de l'allemand
de Mr. le Docteur Ralph*
[Geneva], 1759
NYPL, Rare Books Division

When, in the first chapter of
this novel, Candide is expelled
from his castle in Germany
for making advances to his
patron's daughter, his travels
around the world begin. In
Peru, he and his valet, Cacambo, encounter the fantastic
city of legend, El Dorado.
A composite of Cockaigne,
Eden, the Golden Age, and
Utopia, El Dorado has streets
paved with gold and jewels,
no organized religion, a constitutional monarchy headed by
a benevolent king, fountains
running with liqueurs, the
fragrance of spices wafting
through the air, no prisons,

and no previous contact with
the outside world. After one
month, Candide and Cacambo
decide to leave, in part to
continue their quest to find
Candide's lost love, Cune-
gonde, and in part because
they consider El Dorado not
terribly interesting if they
cannot brag about it to others.
Having loaded up some
sheep with gold and jewels,
they depart.

The end of the book finds
Candide in another sort of
ideal world. He is in Turkey,
living a sort of communal
life with his friends, in which
each does what he or she
enjoys most, and everyone
benefits from the contributions of the others. After all
his wanderings, it turns out
that "the best of all possible
worlds" is, in fact, right in
his own backyard.

William Shakespeare
The Tempest
In *The Works of Mr. William Shakespear*
London: Printed for Jacob Tonson, 1709
NYPL, Rare Books Division

O, wonder!
How many goodly creatures are there here!
How beauteous mankind is! O brave new world,
That has such people in't!
(Act 5, Scene 1)

In Shakespeare's play, a shipwreck does not
lead to the discovery of a utopian island (the
action takes place on Bermuda), but rather sets
off a chain of events that results in love, apology
for past wrongs, a kingdom rightly restored to
a good man, and a reuniting of brothers. The pain
of the past is obliterated, and forgiveness reigns
in order to make way for a "brave new world"
of restored order and peace.

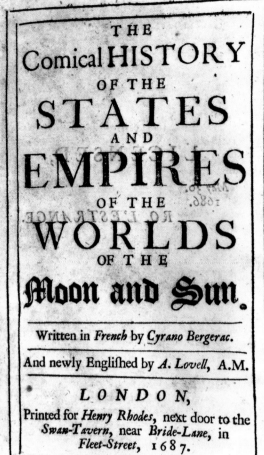

Savinien Cyrano de Bergerac
The Comical History of the States and Empires of the Worlds of the Moon and Sun

London: Printed for Henry Rhodes, 1687
NYPL, Rare Books Division

In this novel, a forerunner of the science fiction genre, Cyrano demonstrates the full measure of his abundant imagination, inquiring mind, and creativity. Through a narrative mixing fantasy, scientific realism, and poetry, he propounds a group of philosophical, scientific, and religious theories inspired by Tommaso Campanella, René Descartes, Galileo, and Michel de Montaigne that were very daring for the time.

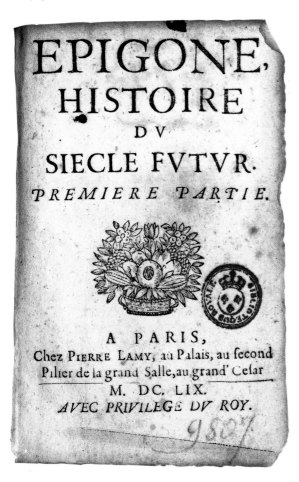

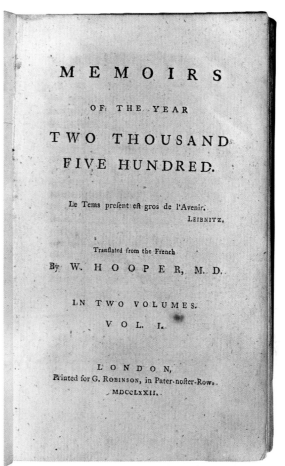

Michel de Pure
Epigone, histoire du siècle
futur. Première partie
Paris: Pierre Lamy, 1659
BNF, Département de Littérature
et Art

This is the first uchronia
(utopian story of the future).
The hero, Epigone, travels
from unknown land to
unknown land. In the Empire
of the Clodovists (France),
he is told the story of the
kings from Henrique le Grand
(Henry IV) to Clodovée XVIII,
two centuries later. Long
attributed to Jacques Guttin,
because his name appears
on the *privilège* (royal permission to publish), this work,
of which only the first part
was published, has now been
ascribed to Michel de Pure.

[Louis-Sébastien Mercier]
Memoirs of the Year Two
Thousand Five Hundred
London: Printed for G. Robinson,
1772
NYPL, The Carl H. Pforzheimer
Collection of Shelley and His Circle

Although the first utopian
story of the future (or uchronia) was written by Michel
de Pure in 1659, it was only in
the following century that the
traditional utopian theme of
peregrinations over the earth,
over the sea, or in space
began to give way to the
theme of voyaging in time.
The Enlightenment confidence
in progress promised a future
rich in possibilities: Leibniz's
observation that "the present
is pregnant of the future"
served as the epigraph to
Mercier's utopia. Overcome
with the vicissitudes of his
day, the narrator falls asleep
and dreams that he awakens
at the age of 700 in a Paris

transformed according to
his wishes. He will gradually
discover that all humanity
is now guided by reason.
Although Mercier remained
silent on the causes of this
extraordinary transformation,
he boasted of having predicted the Revolution in *L'an*
deux mille quatre cent
quarante, which appeared
in a single volume in 1771
and was then revised and augmented in 1786 in the definitive three-volume edition.
This is the first English edition,
translated by W. Hooper,
who changed the title year
from 2440 to 2500. In his
preface to the translation,
Hooper acknowledged making
the change, but he offered
no explanation for it. In 1795,
Hooper's translation was
published in Philadelphia by
Thomas Dobson, making
Mercier's book the first utopia
to be published in translation
in America.

Alain Milhou

Mundus novus et renovatio mundi

Messianic and Utopian Currents in the Indies of Castille

The Eternal Lord revealed to his beloved
Son his plan and design for America: the
renewed existence He had prepared for
the human race, in that part of the world.
—CHATEAUBRIAND, *LES NATCHEZ*[1]

"New Heaven and New Earth,"
New World and the End of the World

THE CRUSADERS, as we well know, had set their sights on the Levant, toward Jerusalem. Eschatologically inspired medieval movements, as well as those that aspired in a less anguished and more spiritual way to a *renovatio mundi*, all looked toward the Promised Land. Christopher Columbus changed all that and reversed the direction of the gaze. In fact, the Discoverer himself was torn between his obsession with the Crusades and celebration of the newly discovered lands. This New World, situated in the West, was henceforth to emerge as the new Promised Land, a land of utmost possibility. Upon completing his third ocean crossing in 1498, the Admiral made land on the Venezuelan coast and finally reached the new continent that lay facing the island that, with his unfailingly acute sense of religious symbolism, he had named Trinidad. Columbus must have fathomed the immensity and novelty of this southern land, of which the Ancients had no knowledge and which was distinct from the Asian continent he thought he had already located while navigating off the coast of Cuba. He summoned up the most extraordinary attributes to describe the new-found territory, referring to it as a "Holy Isle" and an "Isle of Grace," before surmising that it was in fact a new continent that harbored the Earthly Paradise in some inaccessible place deep within it. We need only look to his writings to uncover references to "the new heaven and . . . the new earth, which Our Lord made, as St. John writes in the Apocalypse, after He had spoken of it by the mouth of Isaiah."[2] Columbus's messianic celebration of the southern continent introduces what would become a major theme in the history of humanity – America as a Promised Land, as a substitute and New Jerusalem. Indeed, the theme would endure, pervasively present throughout the history of the New World. Columbus, merchant and Crusader, emerged out of the Middle Ages to found modernity.

Thirty years had to elapse, however, and Hernán Cortés had to conquer central Mexico (1519–22) and Magellan to cross the Strait to which he gave his name (1520) before the New World emerged in all the immensity and novelty of its geography and inhabitants. In his letter to the Council of the Indies of 151, Bartolomé de Las Casas claimed that this New World was, in fact, larger and richer by far than the old one and that it contained "the major part, indeed almost all of mankind."[3] All the more reason, therefore, for the Crown, after its failure to put an end to the brutalities and massacres, to shoulder its moral and spiritual responsibility in the face of the untold numbers of unbaptized Indians condemned to eternal Hell together with those other mortal sinners, their exploiters.

During the same period, the Franciscans of New Spain, the name by which Cortés had designated Mexico, came to regard the evangelization of countless and seemingly receptive populations in a land where demonic idolatry had reigned as a sign of the imminent eschatological times that corresponded to Christ's pronouncement on the last evangelization, which would coincide with the end of time.[4] For many of the friars, the New World and the end of the world were one and the same. After all, did not the Latin word *novissima* refer to the final days?

Millenarianism, Joachimism, Edenism, and Utopianism

From the start, the discovery of the New World lent itself to the development of the most diverse modalities of flight from the calamities of history. Let us leave to one side the marvelous world of legends that took hold of the conquistadors' imaginations, in order to focus on the most telling religious and political currents that shaped the search for an ideal society: Millenarianism, Joachimism, Edenism, and Utopianism. It is sometimes difficult in practice to arrive at definitive characterizations of the term "utopia," created by Thomas More in 1516 in response to the discovery of the new Western continent, so difficult, in fact, that the term has come to designate in its current usage all dream forms of the perfect society. All the same, as Gilles Lapouge has demonstrated to great effect, distinctions do apply.[5]

The discovery of America would as a matter of course invigorate Christian millenarianism and its somewhat subversive belief in the advent of the thousand years of earthly bliss prophesied in Apocalypse 20. Could not this very continent be the place for the establishment of a latter-day Christian republic where life would be simultaneously opulent and simple and a perfect equilibrium struck between egalitarianism and peacefully accepted hierarchies in surroundings of spiritual and material bliss? For while the Church may have disapproved of a material millennium, its tolerance of mitigated millenarianism – the belief in a thousand years of spiritual bliss that coincide with the actual reign of Christ on earth – was not denounced by Rome until 1944.

The New World was equally susceptible to currents that grew out of Joachimism. At the end of the twelfth century, Joachim of Fiore, an Abbot from Calabria, set forth a theory that divided the progress of human history into three ages (*status*) that corresponded to the three figures of the Trinity: the Age of the Father and servile obedience had,

with the birth of Christ, given way to the Age of the Son and filial obedience; as to the third age, the Age of the Spirit, it would usher in a time of freedom and spiritual enlightenment, and where would it flourish but in this New Land under the aegis of the Holy Church served by humble missioners? In the third *status*, the "spiritual Church" would rise up against the "carnal Church" that had been perverted by riches and pomp and privilege; God would henceforth be worshiped in a purely spiritual and contemplative manner free of sacraments and hierarchical organization. In this new-fledged Pentecost, rekindled Christianity would receive the *Evangelium aeternum* or the "Spiritual Gospel": this would be the living spirit freed from the letter, too intangible for the material bounds of a book, that would bestow absolute understanding of the sacred texts of both Testaments. Recent studies have helped separate the essentially spiritual aims of Joachim of Fiore's teachings from the political and millenarist efforts that arose in his wake.[6] We must not overlook Joachim of Fiore's clear-cut condemnation of millenarianism, based on a literal reading of the Book of Revelation, in his *Expositio in Apocalypsim*.[7] Furthermore, his claim had been that the third *status*, the Age of the Spirit, would be one of interiority and inner illumination that would result in a full understanding of the divine message (*intelligentia spiritualis*), allowing the transformed soul to enter a

Christopher Columbus Reaches America

Adriaen Collaert after Johannes Stradanus (Jan van der Straet) *Christophorus Columbus Ligur terroribus Oceani Superatis . . .* Engraving from *Americae Retectio* (Antwerp: Philippe Galle, ca. 1585) NYPL, Miriam and Ira D. Wallach Division of Art, Prints and Photographs

Christopher Columbus stands at the prow of his ship holding a banner depicting Christ on the cross; the banner and the dove perched at the tip of the prow are meant to indicate the peaceful and evangelical mission of his voyage. He is accompanied on this expedition by marine creatures, as well as classical Nereids and Tritons and the pagan gods Diana and Neptune.

beatific state that would be a foretaste of the bliss to come (*sabbatismus*). The new Age of the Spirit would be the *renovatio mundi*; as for the sixteenth-century Reform movements that would affect both the Catholic and the Protestant church, whether or not they were influenced by Joachimism, they too had aspirations to "renew the world."

Aside from a handful of coincidences, the evidence for attributing the themes of Joachimism to Christopher Columbus is slim. A more serious, albeit more controversial, approach is to follow the impact Joachim of Fiore may have had on Franciscan missionaries in Mexico. Be that as it may, what we cannot disregard is the influence of Joachimism on a fringe of the Society of Jesus, at least at its inception. In 1550, an anonymous Jesuit, in all likelihood Andrés de Oviedo, addressed a messianic treatise in honor of the very recently formed *Societas Iesu* to Francis Borgia on the occasion of his initiation into the order. The society had just embarked on a labor of Catholic reform that would encompass Europe as well as the missions of the Portuguese Empire in Asia (1542) and Brazil (1549). The text, which remained in manuscript form, attests to a short-lived and quickly repressed Joachimite

". . . these islands are very beautiful, and . . . full of a great variety of trees stretching up to the stars . . ."

Christopher Columbus [Letter to Sanchez]
Basel, 1493
NYPL, Rare Books Division

In Columbus's first report to King Ferdinand and Queen Isabella, he attempted to make sense of the people and places he encountered. He remarked that he had "so far found no human monstrosities, as many expected," and he observed that the native populations seemed to share most of their property. He also reported rumors of an island with unending supplies of gold. The search for cities paved in gold, inhabited by people who did not recognize private property, encouraged explorers and exploiters in the Americas for hundreds of years following Columbus's first voyage.

Columbus's news of the New World spread rapidly throughout Europe. His letters were translated into many languages and printed in numerous cities. This edition, of which The New York Public Library has the only known complete copy, is in Latin and includes woodcut illustrations. The letter was addressed to Gabriel Sanchez, Treasurer General of the kingdom of Aragon.

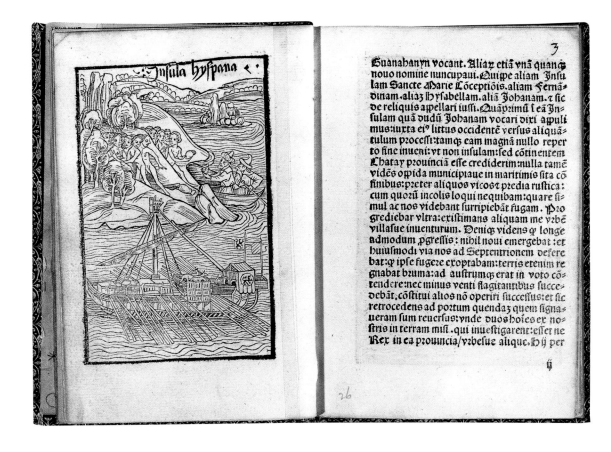

*Amerigo Vespucci Sails
Toward America*

**Adriaen Collaert after
Johannes Stradanus
(Jan van der Straet)**
***Americus Vespuccius
Florentinus portentosa
navigatione ad Occasum . . .***
Engraving from *Americae Retectio*
(Antwerp: Philippe Galle, ca. 1585)
NYPL, Miriam and Ira D. Wallach
Division of Art, Prints and
Photographs

Amerigo Vespucci, his armor
at his feet, sails toward the
shore and the setting sun.
This engraving, with its
ocean filled with allegorical
creatures and figures, features symbolism similar to that surrounding
the voyage of Columbus.
The flag shows the Cross of
Saint George, and the banner
depicts the Vespucci coat of
arms. The broken ship mast in
the foreground was included
as a symbol of Christianity's
dominance over paganism.

AMERICVS VESPVCCIVS FLORENTINVS *pertentosa nauigatione ad . Occasum assignesad Austrum duas Orbis terrarum partes, nostris oris quas incuimus maiores, te nullas ærtea nobis nitas, fæculis, aperuit, quarum alteram de sue nomine* AMERICAM *mortalium consensis nominauit. An. sal. ∞ IIID.*

New World

**Amerigo Vespucci
*Mundus Novus***
[Paris: Felix Baligault and Jehan
Lambert, 1503]
NYPL, Rare Books Division

Amerigo Vespucci firmly
believed that the land he was
exploring (Brazil) was not
Europe, Africa, or Asia, but
an entirely new world. His
assertion, along with a lengthy
description of the land and
people he encountered, was
published in this letter under
the title *Mundus Novus*.
He included this diagram to
show that he had ventured

one-quarter of the way around
the globe. The accompanying
text explained that when Europeans ("nos" or "us") and the
inhabitants of Brazil ("illi" or
"them") were both standing
upright, a line drawn from the
top of the head of one to the
top of the head of the other
would form the hypotenuse
of a right triangle. Like most
reports of the new lands,
this work was reprinted many
times throughout Europe in
the months following its first
publication, in 1503.

noctibus in illa celi parte difcurrūt inumeri vapores & ardentes faces. Dixi paulo ante in illo hemifperio/ ꝗ tamen proprie loquendo non eft ad plenum hemifperium refpectu noftri, quia tamen accedit ad huiufmodi formam/ fic illud appellari licuit. Igitur vti dixi ab olyfippo vnde digreffi fumus quod ab linea equinoctiali diftat gradibus trigintanouemfemis nauigauimꝰ vltra lineā equinoctiale per quinquaginta gradus/ qui fimul iūcti efficiunt gradus circiter nonaginta, que fūma cū quartaꝫ partem obtineat fūmi circuli fecundūverā menfure rationem ab antiquis nobis traditam manifeftum eft nos nauigaffe quartā mūdi partem. Et hac ratione nos olyfippum habitantes citra lineā equinoctialem gradu, trigefimononofemis in latitudine feptentrionali fumus ad illos qui gradu quingentefimo habitant vltra eandem lineā in meridionali latitudine angulariter gradus quiꝗ in linea tranfuerfali. Et vt clarius intelligas Perpendicularis linea que duꝫ recti ftamus a puncto celi iminente vertici noftro depēdet in caput nfum illis depēdet in latus fi coftas. Quo fit vt nos fumus in linea recta/ ipfi vero in linea tranfuerfa & fpecies fi at trianguli orthogonii cuius vicem lineꝗ tenemus cathete ipfi autem bafis & hipotenufa a noftro ad illorū protenditur vertice vt in figura patet; & hec de cofmographia dicta fufficiant

vertex capitis noftri

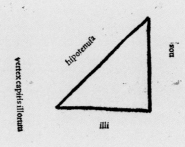

vertex capitis illorum   sou   hipotenufa

illi

temptation among the early Jesuits.[8] The author hails the advent of the third *status* of human history, the Age of the Spirit. In these aging times, as the second *status* draws to an end, the Society, the spiritual order predicted by Joachim of Fiore, would be the instrument of rebirth, of *renovatio mundi*. European Christianity experienced the interiorization of religion and of universal meditation that was taught by the Jesuits in accordance with the method of the *Spiritual Exercises*. The advent of the third *status* was to be marked equally by universal evangelization, especially in the New World, where the effort would fall to the Society. Evangelization in the previous phase, pertaining to the second *status*, had been merely superficial; it had come on the heels of armed conquests, terrible but necessary measures to defeat the Devil, absolute master of the New Continent. The conquistadors, who were guilty of both cruelty and greed, had nonetheless played their part, the part of divine wrath, of *flagellum Dei*. The sufferings to which the Indians were subjected, notably the demographic catastrophe of which the author was fully aware, were inflicted by God as a punishment for the monstrous sins they had committed: idolatry, cannibalism, human sacrifices, and

Heroic Savages and Cannibals

Dise figur anzaigt uns das Folck und Insel die gefunden ist durch den christenlichen Kunig zu Portigal oder con seinen Underthonen
Hand-colored woodcut,
[Germany, 1505]
NYPL, Spencer Collection

One of the earliest images of the inhabitants of the New World, this woodcut reveals some of the Europeans' complex and contrasting attitudes toward the peoples they encountered. The men on the right appear admirable and heroic as they pose proudly by their weapons, and the women and children to their left form a loving family scene. In the center of the image, however, a human head, leg, and arm roast over a fire, while on the far left, a woman bites into a wrist. The caption, based on Amerigo Vespucci's description in the *Mundus Novus* of the people he encountered in Brazil, is translated below. It presents a

mixture of repulsion and attraction to this strange new society, adding anarchy and incest to the more commonly observed phenomena of nakedness, common property, and cannibalism.

Translation of the Woodcut's Caption: "The people are thus naked, handsome, brown, well shaped in body, their heads, necks, arms, private parts, feet of men and women are a little covered with feathers. The men also have many precious stones in their faces and breasts. No one also has anything, but all things are in common. And the men have as wives those who please them, be they mothers, sisters, or friends, therein make they no distinction. They also fight with each other. They also eat each other even those who are slain, and hang the flesh of them in the smoke. They become a hundred and fifty years old. And have no government."

The New World Eden

a
Theodore De Bry
Adam and Eve,
from ***America,*** **Part 1**
Hand-colored engraving,
Frankfurt, 1590
NYPL, Rare Books Division

In choosing this illustration
to preface his edition of
engravings after John White,
De Bry clearly sought to
appeal to the popular idea
of the New World as a potential paradise. The abundant
wildlife and lush landscape
contribute to the idea of
Virginia as a peaceful land
of plenty, and it is easy to
see how this might serve
to entice settlers. Here,
Adam and Eve, like America
herself, are on the brink of
a cataclysmic change.

a

America, by Theodore de Bry

The majority of the images shown here are based on the eyewitness drawings of two artists, John White in Virginia and Jacques
Le Moyne de Morgues in Florida. They comprise the first two
volumes of *America*, first published in Frankfurt in 1590 and 1591
by Theodore De Bry, who devoted his life to depicting discoveries
and travels around the world. Later volumes of the series, published from 1592 to 1596, include images by De Bry based on
descriptions of the New World by the Italian Girolamo Benzoni,
the German Hans Staden, and the Frenchman Jean de Léry.

The engravings after White were made to illustrate the
1590 folio edition of Thomas Hariot's *Briefe and true report of
the new found land of Virginia*, first published without illustrations
two years earlier. In 1585, Hariot and White had accompanied
Sir Richard Grenville on a voyage to Virginia to prepare a written
and pictorial record of the landscape, natural resources, and native
inhabitants of the lands claimed for the English by Sir Walter
Raleigh. It was hoped that this combination of text and illustration
would entice prospective investors and settlers to the region.
Hariot's description and White's drawings are generally considered to be among the most accurate records of the appearance
and habits of the populations of the Southeast Coast. Although
he often made the faces and poses of the Indians appear more
European, De Bry was quite faithful to White's drawings.

De Bry's engravings after Le Moyne were first published
with Le Moyne's narrative in 1591 as *A Brief Narrative of the
New Found Land of Florida in America*. The drawings, made on
a French expedition to Florida in 1564, depict the social and religious lives of the Timucuan Indians and frequently include views
of the French settlers as well. They are considered to be slightly
less accurate than the White drawings, since Le Moyne was
reportedly eager to perpetuate the myth of the New World as a
pre-Christian Golden Age.

b

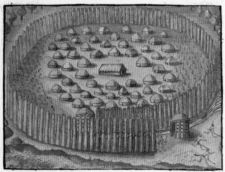

c

b
Theodore de Bry after
Jacques Le Moyne
They Reach Port Royal,
from *America*, Part 2
Colored engraving, Frankfurt, 1591
NYPL, Rare Books Division

This image shows the French
explorers arriving in Florida
and reflects their first impres-
sions of the land: oversized
melons and grapes, abundant
turkeys and deer, and wide,
easily navigated rivers. Upon
catching sight of the French
ship, the Indians flee, leaving
behind a roasting lynx; this
incident was memorialized in
the name given to the area:
"Prom. Lupi" or "Lynx Point."

c
Theodore de Bry after
Jacques Le Moyne
A Council of State **and**
A Fortified Village, **from**
***America*, Part 2**
Colored engravings, Frankfurt, 1591
NYPL, Rare Books Division

The top engraving depicts a
Timucuan council meeting at
which the men of the tribe
gather to discuss current concerns. The women are preparing a drink called "casina,"
which was passed around in
a shell for the men to drink.
Considered strengthening and
nourishing, it was also quite
strong and was used as a
test for assuming military
responsibilities. Those who
could not keep it down (note
the two vomiting men) were
exempted from particularly
difficult military undertakings.
At the lower left, a number
of Frenchmen observe the
council meeting.

The lower engraving shows
a fortified Timucuan village.
Designed for protection and
efficiency, these towns were
occupied for all but the winter
months, when the Timucuans
lived in the forests. For defensive reasons, the entrance
allowed no more than two
people to pass through at
once, and the chief's house
was located in the middle,
surrounded by huts. The circular fence rose to the height
of two men. Some crops
grow within the fence and
the stream runs just outside
the entrance, ensuring the
availability of food and water
at all times.

"How They Till the Soil"

d
**Theodore de Bry after
Jacques Le Moyne**
*How They Till The Soil
and Plant* **and** *Storing Their
Crops in the Public Granary,*
from *America,* **Part 2**
Colored engravings, Frankfurt, 1591
NYPL, Rare Books Division

The Timucuans of Florida are
here shown planting and storing their crops. The accompanying narrative explains that
in the planting, the men break
up the soil with hoes made
of fish bone and wood, after
which the women make
holes for corn and bean
seeds. These are then left
for the winter months, while
the Timucuans retreat to the
woods. In March, they return
to see their crops ripen, to
gather up the harvest, and
to store the crops in "low
and roomy" granaries whose
contents are freely available to
everyone. Le Moyne remarks,
"Indeed, it would be good if
among Christians there were
as little greed to torment
men's mind and hearts."

Prisoners in America

e
Theodore de Bry
*How They Deal with
Prisoners,* from *America,*
Part 3
Colored engraving, Frankfurt, 1592
NYPL, Rare Books Division

Hans Staden spent nine
months as a prisoner of the
Tupinamba Indians of Brazil,
and immediately after his
release wrote an account of
his captivity, which was published in 1557 with fifty-three
woodcuts. In Part 3 of
America, Theodore De Bry
reproduced Staden's narrative
and created thirty-four new
engravings based on details in
the account, the earlier woodcuts, and the descriptions of
the Tupinamba found in a narrative by a Frenchman, Jean
de Léry, which had been published in 1577. This engraving
is the last in a series depicting
the Tupinamba methods of tor-
turing and killing their enemies. The elaborate ritual
included shaving the prisoner,
painting his face, tying him up,
clubbing him over the head,
skinning him, chopping him
into pieces, and finally, as seen
here, roasting and eating him.

The Legend of El Dorado

f
Theodore de Bry
*How They Make
Objects of Gold in Quito,*
from *America,* **Part 6**
Colored engraving, Frankfurt, 1596
NYPL, Rare Books Division

Part 6 of De Bry's *America*
was illustrated with engravings based on the descriptions
of an Italian explorer, Girolamo
Benzoni, who traveled
throughout the New World in
1541. The legend of El Dorado
told of New World cities
paved with gold and precious
stones, and the hope of finding these treasures motivated
many voyages to the New
World. The narrative accompanying this engraving tells of
the gardens in Quito that once
were filled with gold statues
made with no tools other than
stones for pounding.

d

e

f

g

Two by Two

g
Theodore de Bry
[Noah's Ark], from *America,*
[Part 1?]
Colored engraving, Frankfurt,
[1590?]
NYPL, Rare Books Division

This image of Noah's Ark
lends religious overtones
to the discovery of the
New World. Perhaps it even
suggested the feeling of
the explorers as they set
foot on dry land after months
of being on the open sea.

"... without envy or greed ..."

h
Theodore de Bry
after John White
The Town of Secota,
from *America,* **Part 1**
Colored engraving, Frankfurt, 1590
NYPL, Rare Books Division

This image of the town of
Secota shows a garden paradise of abundant food and
merriment. Fields of tobacco,
corn, and pumpkins lie adjacent to special areas set aside
for ceremonies, prayer, and
feasting. The structure marked
"A" is a tomb for kings and
princes. In his caption,
Thomas Hariot remarks on
the character of the inhabitants
of Secota: "These people
live happily together without
envy or greed. They hold their
feasts at night, when they
make large fires to light them
and to show their joy."

sodomy. By adapting Joachimism to the current climate of Church reform and geographic expansion,
our anonymous author limited himself to invoking
the Age of the Spirit, while avoiding any mention
of the millennial kingdom. Beyond the pseudo-
Joachimism of medieval prophecies, he uncovered
the true spiritual message of Joachim of Fiore, who
had remained aloof from millennial beliefs.

We could, for the sake of brevity, define
Edenism as the aspiration to a natural ideal over
and against a decadent and perverted culture.
In the late Middle Ages, Edenism took as many
diverse forms as the resurrected ancient myth of
a Golden Age – such as we encounter it in Jean de
Meun's *Roman de la Rose*, in the Celtic myth that
searches for an Earthly Paradise on Saint Brendan's
Island that so fascinated Portuguese navigators
and Christopher Columbus himself, and, finally,
in Adamism, particularly as it figured among the
Brethren of the Free Spirit sect and their belief in
a Garden of Delights. The discovery of America
and the rise of new myths about Paradisiacal tropics
and noble savages would bring a new vitality to
Edenism. Was not this New World the new Canaan,

h

and were not the Indians a replica of Iron Age Europeans? We see the emergence of the myth of the noble savage in the first shipboard Journal (1492–93), in Columbus's letter to Santángel (1493), in Pero Vaz de Caminha's letter announcing the discovery of Brazil to King Manuel (1500), in Amerigo Vespucci's accounts of the *Mundus novus* (1503?) and in his *Quatuor navigationes* (1504), as well as in the *Decades de Orbe novo*, compiled at the Spanish court between 1493 and 1525 by the Milanese humanist Pietro Martire d'Anghiera.[9] The theme of the naked and innocent gentle Indian, who could not distinguish between mine and thine, was, in varying degrees, frequently mentioned in these works and would, in short shrift, serve to bolster utopian and millenarian theories. The Western Indies appeared as a new world inhabited by malleable and innocent souls, a ready ground for the creation of a utopian Christian republic and an ideal Christianity that would be the equal of that of the early Church – in short, of a spiritual and millenarian latter-day church. Thomas More's *Utopia* (1516), a communitarian model to counteract an Old World that had been distorted by selfishness, unjust hierarchies,

and incipient capitalism, takes the early accounts of the American discoveries as its point of departure. The English Chancellor imagined his countermodel of European society on an island somewhere in the vicinity of the New World. His Spanish disciple, Juan Maldonado, followed More's geographic lead when he wrote his *Somnium* (1541), chronicling an Indian republic that after a brief period of evangelization began to practice a natural but profound Christianity far beyond the sphere of Spanish dominion. Maldonado's Indians, no more real than More's Utopians, nonetheless represented Maldonado's Erasmist nostalgia for a Christian humanism that was being stifled by traditional, inquisitional, and hierarchical Catholicism in Spain.

We see here the first, "Adamic," modality of the noble savage as naked, gentle, peaceful, and "nonsectarian," that is to say, free of idolatrous beliefs and believing in a primitive and natural monotheism. But, as ethnology has shown, this so-called natural religion was little more than a myth that had grown out of the medieval religious typology codified in the last third of the thirteenth century by the great Mission theologian Ramon Llull from Mallorca to include, in addition to true Christianity and its schismatic variants, the two false "sects" of Judaism and Islam as well as barbarian factions that shunned both "faith and law." These factions were in turn subdivided into idol worshipers and disciples of natural religion. Columbus and the many others who came after him saw this "noble savage" as an easy mark not only for conversion but also for exploitation. So the Arawaks, for example, were also seen as "good servants," unlike their traditional enemies the cannibalistic Caraibe Indians, referred to by Columbus as the "Cannibals," who became the very symbol of the "bad savage" contemptuous of both divine and natural laws. If innocence and docility could justify subjugation, how much more powerfully could savagery and cannibalism bolster the argument that the New World was the Devil's territory peopled by born savages who had to be subjugated, policed, and evangelized by European Christians. Thus, despite the positive evocations we encounter in certain texts, it was virtually impossible for sixteenth-century Christians, both Catholic and Reformed, to see America as a prelapsarian world.

While the Amazon warrior, rebellious against all natural orders, became the emblem for savage America, the New World was generally perceived as chaos that was at one and the same time paradisiacal and unformed; it was a place that clamored for order, and its natural but barbarous inhabitants were like a putty to be molded with varying degrees of ease and difficulty. This was the task that fell to the hundreds of mostly Jesuit missionaries in the artificial villages, templates in voluntary urbanism, to which Indians were relocated so as to be better controlled and evangelized. This missionary utopia served both as an extension of and a counter-example to Edenism, insofar as the project had the double aim of "civilizing" and evangelizing Indians while safeguarding them from the noxious influence of corrupted Europeans. If we are to take Lapouge's lead and emphasize the correlations between urbanism and utopia, then the Spanish conquistadors, administrators, settlers, and missionaries accomplished an extraordinary feat of urban utopianism in America. In his *Diccionario geográfico-histórico de las Indias Occidentales ó América* of 1789, Antonio de Alcedo lists no fewer than 474 cities founded by the Spanish in the New World, not to mention the countless abandoned settlements as well as thousands of Spanish-Indian villages that, for the most part, followed the norms – grid plan, central *plaza mayor* – that had been set in Santo Domingo as early as 1504, well before the influence of Italian

Searching for Paradise

Mattias Quad
Typus Orbis Terrarum ad imitationem universalis Gerhardi Mercatoris
Hand-colored engraving,
Cologne, [1596?]
NYPL, Map Division

Early maps often depicted cannibals, sea monsters, and native inhabitants in order to prepare explorers for what they might find. On this map, the mapmaker has placed a portrait of Jesus above America, which emphasizes the religious motivations of many of these early explorers, some of whom were actively searching for the Earthly Paradise. A century before this map was printed, Christopher Columbus reported that he had found the Earthly Paradise on a mountaintop in present-day Brazil. The coloring on this map was most likely added in the twentieth century.

Renaissance architecture had made itself felt anywhere in the Spanish world.[10] The authorities saw the foundation of a *ciudad* or Spanish city as an assertion of Hispano-Christian identity and order over the "disorder" of a savage and pagan world. Urbanism, therefore, was promoted to defy the disorder of a world that had yet to be built; the same reasoning applies to the system by which the mendicant orders, and later Jesuits, relocated and confined Indians to designated villages called reductions. Its purpose was to police them (the *darles policía* that is such a ubiquitous refrain of the Spanish texts), or, where nomadic groups were concerned, to "humanize" them (*hacerlos hombres*/ make human beings of them), the better to evangelize them. The model of urban civilization was put into effect in what Spanish legislation had dubbed as the two "republics" – the Spanish as well as the Indian one.

Regardless of whether they were conquistadors, colonists, missionaries, Indian or Spanish Americans – that is to say Creoles – every socioracial category was implicated, either as subject or object, in the many messianic and utopian currents that seized colonial America, engaging it in a continuous dialectic between Old and New Worlds. Nor should the libertarian and utopian aspirations of Mestizos and Black Americans, the two groups that emerged to stretch the original boundaries of the European-American encounter, be overlooked; as it transpired, these groups had to resign themselves to finding a place in the interstices of a legislation that rested on the distinction between the "two republics."[11]

The Conquistadors' Dream:
Earthly Paradise, Cockaigne, Land of Freedom
His anxious religiosity and his pronounced eschatological sense make Christopher Columbus an exception to the legion of conquistadors and colonists who had put their faith in a simple religion, characterized by exteriority. The centuries of battle in the *Reconquista* against the Moors had endowed them with an extraordinary assurance in their messianic mission. One could say they saw themselves as representatives of the chosen people; they were confident about their salvation in the struggle against the Other – yesterday's infidel had simply been replaced by today's pagan. Until such time as the missionaries interceded with their prophetic message and imposition of a Christian ethic, these conquerors, whose relationship toward the Indians was free of moral concerns, were first

and foremost interested in acquiring riches, a life of ease, and rank in the social hierarchy.

The pursuit of riches and ease also took on a messianic character, albeit a degraded one. With news of the new-found riches in Peru, the New World was definitively transformed in the popular imagination into an ideal realm, a combined Earthly Paradise and Cockaigne. Here is what a peasant from the area of Toledo had to say in May 1534, a mere year after Atahualpa's ransom – the incident of the Inca, imprisoned by Francisco Pizarro, who had his subjects amass an astronomical quantity of precious metals in a vain effort to buy back his freedom: "While I was at the village blacksmith's with some friends discussing the news of Peru and of all these amounts of gold and silver that were brought back from there, one of them said that this was the country where Our Lord Jesus Christ had lived, since the grass where he walked had changed into gold and silver this was why there was so much of it to be found."[12] In the heated imagination of this Sancho Panza, gleanings from the apocryphal gospels mix willy-nilly with folkloric tradition. Shortly thereafter, however, the Spanish would equate Cockaigne with a Peruvian valley they called the "land of Jauja."[13] The legend of Eldorado also arose around this same period. Earthly Paradise was now contaminated by a pagan Garden of Earthly Delights.

There is sometimes an almost messianic dimension of liberation from the restraints of the Old World in the desire for social ascent exhibited by the conquistadors and first colonists. As we see in Las Casas's *Historia de las Indias*, the view of the New World as a "free and regal" and "fortunate" land, where the King of Spain would be the only master, was prevalent early on among peasants wishing to free themselves from feudal rule.[14] The tragedy of it, however, as Las Casas bitterly observed, was that conquistadors and colonists, nobles and commoners alike, were all bent on becoming *encomenderos* – in other words, Lords of the Indians. Only a minority would succeed in this aim; hence, the ensuing frustration that gave rise to new expeditions, troubles, and even rebellions.

After the conquest, Peru became, from 1537 to 1561, the theater of long civil wars between conquistadors. The so-called *soldados*, that is to say, the proletarians of the Conquest, played a particularly significant role in the rebellion of Francisco Hernández Girón (1553–54).[15] This wealthy *encomendero* from Cuzco raised the banner of revolt against the authorities in Lima who were aiming to apply the royal prohibition against using

Indian forced labor. At the beginning, therefore, he was nothing more than a representative of the oligarchy, even though he may have promoted himself as the "Captain of the Kingdom's Freedom." The famous rebel Lope de Aguirre was to take on the same title a few years later (1561) when he proclaimed himself the defender of all the Spaniards of Peru, from *encomenderos* to *soldados*. The former, however, having learned their lesson from Gonzalo Pizarro's great, failed revolt (1544–48), and having their self-interest at heart, took a neutral position, while continuing to benefit from the inevitable concessions made by the royal authority in an effort to calm tempers. The defection of the elite would leave Hernández Girón with a following made up primarily of *soldados* and marginal elements; his entourage also included several sorcerers and diviners and, most notably, a Morisco woman who interpreted dreams. In an effort to expand his army, he offered to emancipate any black slave who joined his ranks. He also fueled many of the millenarian dreams of poor *soldados*; he sported a medallion that bore the inscription *Edent pauperes et saturabuntur*, a phrase taken from a messianic psalm on the trials of the just and traditionally associated with the suffering Christ succoring the hungry.[16] He posed as the defender of the *pobrecitos*, a term derived from the Franciscan (*poverello*), and went so far as to claim that Francis of Assisi, the most cherished saint of Christian millenarianism, had appeared to encourage him in his endeavor. There was also a rumor afoot claiming that he had set fire to the silver mines of Potosí. This rumor was the sign of the bucolic dream of certain *soldados* who, perhaps as a result of their thwarted desire or under the influence of a handful of religious zealots who thundered against the "hell mouth" of Potosí, ended up setting fire to the very thing they had adored.

The Indianist Dream of the Missionaries: From Latter-Day Christianity to the Catholic Utopia of the Reductions?

Reflecting on Thomas More's message, Vasco de Quiroga, auditor of the *audiencia* that governed Mexico at the time and future bishop of Michoacán, imagined, as early as 1532–35, the creation of a Christian society among the Indians of New Spain, which would combine the resurgence of Apostolic times with the Golden Age of the Greco-Roman poets and philosophers of antiquity. In addition to being a disciple of More, Quiroga had also been, through a text of Saint Antonino of Florence, indirectly influenced by Joachim of Fiore.

Quiroga understood these teachings to mean the following: the Church now shows the marks of age, but from its ruins a "Renascent Church" will rise under the guidance of a Reformed clergy whose calling it is to raise the church anew amidst these Indians, who have not strayed as far from the Golden Age as the Europeans who concern themselves with power, pomp, and wealth.[17]

Like Vasco de Quiroga, the Franciscans of New Spain also had dreams of a Church with a congregation of poor, humble, and obedient Indians, separate from the greedy, violent, and arrogant colonists. In June 1524, the "Twelve" (the first Franciscan "apostles") made their entry into Mexico City, where they were solemnly welcomed by Cortés. Led by Martín de Valencia, their Father Superior, an ascetic who was given to frequent apocalyptic visions of universal evangelization, this strict order of Franciscans wished to reenact the gesture of the apostles. Their conviction that the world was in its last days lent an apocalyptic dimension to their struggle against the demon of idolatry. They supported the providential armed conquest as an extension of their own effort. Could a Christianity purified of the vices of Europe and worthy of the primitive Church be founded among the Indians of Mexico? This "Franciscan" view of the Indian is found in the writings of Toribio de Benavente, who, it could be said, wished to be the reincarnation of his master Saint Francis, the *Poverello*, when he took on the name by which the Indians had designated the pauperized cohort of the Twelve; he became *Motolinía* ("the poor one" in Nahuatl). We find the same view in the work of his disciple Gerónimo de Mendieta, who lamented the failure of the Franciscan dream in the *Historia eclesiástica indiana*, completed at the end of the century.

Are we, therefore, to take at face value the account of Georges Baudot and John L. Phelan of a "millennial kingdom" project, inspired by Joachimism in Mexico? Qualification, it seems to me, would be in order here.[18] Joachim of Fiore and his disciples believed that the third state (*status*) of the world, the Age of the Spirit, would witness the rise of filial, altruistic love and of *intelligentia spiritualis* over servile obedience, fear, and outward ceremony. This is not to be confused with the subversive millenarian anti-hierarchical movements that deformed Joachimism to other ends. The Mexican Franciscans did not once invoke a millennial kingdom. While Martín de Valencia, the leader of the Twelve, was profoundly preoccupied by eschatology and in all likelihood influenced by

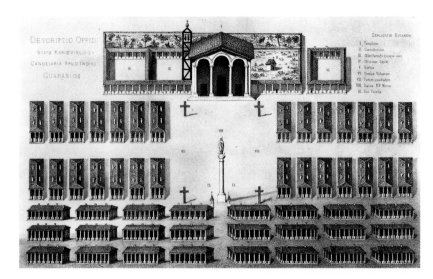

Joachimism, much like Motolonía and Mendieta, neither he nor any of his disciples for that matter could qualify as millenarian. Brother Francisco Jiménez, who was one of the Twelve and Martín de Valencia's first biographer, described a man who "doubted that the New Church could be solidly grounded among these natives." Despairing of the Indians and of the endless coercions with which they had to be wooed, he was making preparations, as early as 1532, to depart to found the ideal Church in China, whose inhabitants were demonstrably "of greater capability" and had a greater predisposition to prayer and meditation, a feature that was sorely lacking in the barbarians of New Spain, who would never become "spiritual men."[19] While it is true that Motolinía viewed the humble Indians with far more favor, the overall perception of this humility was equivocal. Neither Motolinía nor Mendieta called the power of the *encomenderos* into question as Las Casas had. Nor did they have any quarrels with the dominion of Spain over the indigenous peoples, whose permanent paternal guardianship by mission-aries they saw as a foregone conclusion. The Indians would always come in last, even when they were the first in the Kingdom of God. In an effort to jus-tify the denial of ordination to Indians, Mendieta maintained that "They are not fit to command or lead, but to be commanded and led."[20]

We would be wrong to conclude that the Franciscans were the only ones with aspirations to create a model Christianity in the New World. The Dominican Las Casas drew on Columbus's diaries and on his own experience to become the most eloquent bard of the natives' pre-Christian virtue.

He not only praised the Indians, but, extraordinari-ly for the colonial period, he even went so far as to contemplate a model Mestizo Christian Republic.

The Jesuit reductions, especially in Paraguay (1609–1767), present a more complex case. They are undeniably part and parcel of a Catholic utopia, dis-guised by the Jesuits, for the purposes of propagan-da, in the colors of the primitive Church, to offset the societal counter-model of the Spanish and their Creole and Mestizo descendants.[21] The reductions, for members of the Society, did not correspond to a latter-day church founded on the virtue of innocent savages. In fact, the Jesuits, rational and efficient instruments of the Counter-Reformation, were uni-formly hostile, aside from a few notorious examples like Andrés de Oviedo and the Portuguese António Vieira, to Joachimite and millenarian illusions.[22] They had also shed their illusions about the myth of the noble savage. Considering the Moxos, Chiqui-tos, Tupis, and Guaranis that surrounded them to be barbarians, they sought, by methods both pater-nal and severe, to make of them the best possible Christians. We get a better sense of the Catholic discipline they sought to instill when we compare their missions with the millenarian and libertarian aspirations of the nativist movements in Brazil and Paraguay. Whereas these nativist movements may be seen as resisting colonization and evangelization, they owe much to the internal, cyclical, and apoca-lyptic logic that informed indigenous ideas of time. If we are to understand the search for a "Land-with-out-Evil" of the Tupis of Brazil and their Brazilian and Paraguayan cousins, the Guaranis, we can only do so in light of this logic.[23] In other words, the

European presence may very well have increased native fears, but it did not create them. These two great ethnicities, who shared a similar language and mythology, were haunted by their own apocalyptic fears that the world would end by fire or water. But, periodically, *karaï*, or prophets – emissaries of the civilizing heroic deity – would suddenly appear to lead the community in sacred dancing and then to the "Land-without-Evil," the ancestral paradise where there is no death and the elect are saved from universal destruction, where the earth yields harvests of its own accord and where human beings become gods and are freed of all social restraints. The Portuguese chronicles recorded numerous Tupi migrations between 1539 and 1609. The great success of the Jesuit missions in Paraguay was in their ability to Christianize the Guarani dream of immortality. The Jesuits, who were seen as *karaï*, successfully convinced the Indians that had been assembled in their reductions that the "Land-without-Evil" was not located in the here and now but in the hereafter. The missions of Paraguay were neither messianic dominions nor were they millennial kingdoms; rather, they were the antechamber of Paradise. The Indian Apocalypse did not pass into Christian messianism but died in the Catholic utopia of the reductions, with the exception of those tribes that did not come into contact with evangelization and who in the nineteenth and early twentieth centuries set forth on long migrations toward the "Land-without-Evil."

The Hispano-Creole Dream:
The New World, Refuge and Hope of Europe
Fear that Spain would be destroyed anew, in a repetition of the eighth-century Muslim invasion, helped reinforce the messianic vision of the New World. Throughout the sixteenth century and even

The Christian
COMMONVVEALTH:
OR,
The Civil Policy
OF
The Rifing Kingdom of Jefus Chrift.

Written

Before the Interruption of the Government, by Mr. *John Eliot*, Teacher of the Church of Chrift at *Roxbury* in *New-England*.

And

Now Publifhed (after his confent given) by a Server of the Seafon.

LONDON:
Printed for *Livewell Chapman*, at the Crown in Popes-Head-Alley.

The First American Utopia

John Eliot
The Christian Commonwealth: or, The Civil Policy of the Rising Kingdom of Jesus Christ. Written Before the Interruption of the Government
London: Printed for Livewell Chapman, 1659
NYPL, Rare Books Division

Best known for his translation of the Bible into the Algonquin language, John Eliot worked ceaselessly to bring Christianity to the Algonquin Indians of Massachusetts in the seventeenth century. Eliot believed strongly that the "civilization" of the Indians would best be accomplished through the establishment of self-governed towns populated solely by Indians. In 1651, he arranged the purchase of six thousand acres near Natick and set about building the town with the Algonquins. When the question of governing the town arose, Eliot turned to the Bible and proposed the system of rule offered by Jethro to Moses: "choose able men from all the people, such as fear God, men who are trustworthy and who hate a bribe; and place such men over the people as rulers of thousands, of hundreds, of fifties, and of tens" (Exodus 18: 21). In this way, Jethro reasoned, the burden of ruling would be divided among different levels of authority, and smaller problems could stay within the group best able to handle them. This structure was adopted by the Algonquins of Natick, and shortly thereafter they elected rulers of tens, fifties, and hundreds.

The Christian Commonwealth expands on this idea of government, and was most likely written before Natick was established; it was not published, however, until 1659. While the structure Eliot proposes seems very logical (and indeed forms the basis for most modern bureaucracies), it was considered a direct affront to the King of England, and shortly after publication, it was banned, most copies were destroyed, and Eliot was required to make a public retraction.

Although Eliot was born in England, he had been in the American colonies for thirty years when *The Christian Commonwealth* was published. Therefore, this work is often considered the first utopia by an American.

into the early seventeenth, numerous apocalyptic prophecies warned of a "destruction" at the hands of the Turks and the peoples of the Barbary Coast, aided from within Spain by those flawed converts of Muslim ancestry, the Moriscos. Spain, under the rule of Philip II and Philip III, seemingly so proud and sure of itself, was, in fact, troubled by a latent anxiety in the face of increasing external perils – Islam, Protestantism, French power – as well as internal ones: the Moriscos, the crypto-Protestants, the crypto-Jews, a presumed fifth column inside the fortress of besieged Catholicism. After 1640, these fears were exacerbated by the specter of the possible collapse of the Spanish empire, then in crisis. In the face of these Old World perils, many turned to the New World as a last refuge for menaced Catholicism. Some even wrote of an eventual transmigration of the Catholic Church to the Indies, after its destruction in Europe.[24]

The noted Dominican Bartolomé de Las Casas is well known for his stance in defense of the Indians; his eschatological and messianic tendencies, however, are less familiar. In fact, these two facets of his complex personality are connected; Las Casas established an apocalyptic causality between the "destruction of Spain," when it fell into Muslim hands at the beginning of the eighth century; the "destruction of the Indies" at the hands of the armed conquests, which he describes as "Mohammedan"; and the renewed "destruction of Spain" that God would certainly condone as a punishment for the sins that had been committed in the Indies, if colonial abuses of justice were not rectified. Las Casas held to this conviction, expressed in the famous 1542 *Brevísima Relación de la destrucción de las Indias*, until his death, as evidenced by his last will and testament of 1564. But this apocalyptic vision contained yet another element. The heresiarch Francisco de la Cruz invoked the authority of Brother Bartolomé to lend credence to his belief that Christianity would be transplanted to the Indies after its destruction in Europe. This idea is expressed as a possibility in the *Historia de las Indias*; the Indies, we read, comprise "apparently the major part of the universe . . . where God must extend his Holy Church and, perhaps, transfer it altogether, while enabling his holy faith to shine among so many infinite nations who will know about it."[25] If this idea follows logically from the anxieties expressed by Las Casas on the subject of the possible destruction of European Christianity, it is also marked by his commendatory stance toward the Indies and its inhabitants. His apologia for the

Indians and their aptitude to accept the faith is well known. As for his descriptions of America, they abound with messianic epithets, such as "God's paradise" or "Blessed Country." It seems very likely that Las Casas did dream of founding an ideal Christianity in this paradisiacal New World, a mixed Church that would include Indians and Spanish "farmers": "with both groups united through the bonds of marriage, these two republics could be turned into a single one, one of the best, one of the most Christian and one of the most peaceful of the world."[26]

Relying on a number of Lascasian themes that he distorted with a view to justifying colonial society, the Dominican Francisco de la Cruz was the first to systematize the wide-ranging messianic tendencies of nascent Creole society. In Spain, he had been heavily swayed by "the defender of the Indians" and his ideas on peaceful evangelization and agrarian colonization as well as by his prophecies warning of the "destruction" of Spain as a supernatural consequence of the "destruction" of the Indies.[27] These predictions, together with the tragic events of 1559 – the arrest of Archbishop Carranza, accused of Lutheranism, and the auto-da-fés of the "Protestants" of Seville and Valladolid – must have had a profound impact on him. They may even explain why he set off for Peru in 1561. It may be safe to assume that he was fleeing from European Christianity, whose imminent demise he feared; he was also leaving behind a Spain that was set on a course of inquisitional intolerance. Upon reaching Lima, he achieved renown as a theologian and preacher, but before long, he was won over by the Creole mentality. He eventually abandoned Lascasian rigorousness and accepted the legitimacy of the armed conquest and the *encomienda*. The lax ways of Liman society proved too irresistible, and he fathered a son from his secret liaison with a penitent noblewoman. But there would be worse: namely, his participation, together with other prestigious men of the cloth, in an enlightened and millenarian group that was organized around the revelations of a young Creole woman.[28] This alliance would lead to his 1572 detainment by order of the Holy Office; the charge was illuminism, Lutheranism, and subversion, for which he was condemned to burn at the stake in 1578.

Francisco de la Cruz believed in the necessary destruction of European Christianity by the Turks. Thereupon, the Church would be transplanted to the Indies and the Pontifical Seat to Lima – New Jerusalem, where the Temple of Solomon would be rebuilt, and New Rome, over which he would reign as Pope and King of the New World. Francisco de la Cruz announced the advent of a millennial society that would prosper far from the siege of Satan, who would, in keeping with the classical image in Chapter 20 of the Apocalypse, be kept in chains for a thousand years. The millennium, in his view, would offer the ideal model of colonial society dominated by the Creole aristocracy and prove lenient in matters relating to social and domestic mores. The system of the *encomiendas* was to remain in place, civil and ecclesiastic authorities ratified, polygamy permitted for the general populace, and marriage permitted for priests, the descendants of the Inca dynasty permanently stripped of their possessions, the Indian masses paternalistically subjugated and the Blacks enslaved. To his dream of an ideal and hierarchical society, Francisco de la Cruz also appended the Lascasian theme of a gentle colonization carried out by Spanish peasants who would intermarry with the Indians and prepare the way for general miscegenation. Merchants and mine proprietors would become obsolete in this new Edenic and self-sufficient Peru, where all would be bent on "tilling, breeding of livestock, and artisanal crafts." Brother Francisco's millenarian system could have found great favor among Creole society because, if we disregard the mines, it essentially justified colonial interests and it recast the New World as a truly chosen land. The vice-king of Peru, Francisco de Toledo, took the potential political dangers of this Americanist heresy very seriously and pressured the Holy Office for a harsh response. In truth, however, it would have been unthinkable for the Creole aristocracy to follow Francisco de la Cruz in his separatist delirium. On the other hand, there were large numbers of poor wanderers in dire need of reconverting, unclaimed stragglers from the conquest who had nothing to lose and were ready to follow the first inspired *caudillo* who appeared to promise them heaven on earth, as had been the case earlier when the "Captains of Liberty" Francisco Hernández Girón and Lope de Aguirre arrived on the scene.

A similar triumphalist Creole spirit, also based on the idea of the transference of Christianity to the New World, is present in the work of the Franciscan Gonzalo Tenorio, a seventeenth-century Peruvian Creole.[29] His sixteen-volume manuscript, written before 1663, is a monument to the glory of the Immaculate Conception and America, chosen land of the Virgin Mary. By God's design, the Virgin, conceived without sin, was reclaimed as the figure that embodied the primitive innocence of Earthly

Paradise. Mary became the *Paradisus restitutu*, an annunciating image of the messianic Christianity that the New World was to launch. In one of his many eschatological scenarios, Brother Gonzalo imagined the transposition of European Catholicism, after its destruction by Protestants, to America. The Pope, driven out by extreme persecution, would seek refuge in America; he would exercise his spiritual authority from his new homeland and rule together with a king who was preordained to become the universal monarch and who would be none other than a secret heir of the blessed Hapsburg dynasty. But for Tenorio, the New World would be more than a mere refuge; America, with its prospering New Jerusalem, would be the place from which a final evangelizing surge would set out to secure the triumph of Christ and Mary everywhere in the world.

Gonzalo Tenorio's theories were, in addition to being the outgrowth of Creole pride, a response to troubled times: the Spanish Empire, unnerved by the crisis of 1640, was in a grave state of decadence. In Brother Gonzalo's case, the decline elicited an attitude of compensatory messianism that was favorably inclined toward Spanish America. Together with Francisco de la Cruz, Gonzalo Tenorio is an extreme, not to say pathological, example of Hispano-American messianism. The excessiveness of these views, however, does not make them any less representative of the Creole consciousness that, through the entire colonial period, advocated the dignity of the New World in defiance of the Old, thereby setting the stage for political independence if not spiritual emancipation. The theme of the transposition of Christianity to the Indies served as a sacred metaphor in their discourse; it expressed a latent desire that Spanish America would, in time, take up where Spain and Europe had left off. This theme was interconnected with the theme of a Promised Land, which, in turn, could present itself in a variety of modalities. Making its first appearance in the guise of an Earthly Paradise, in keeping with Christopher Columbus's imaginings, it persisted well into the middle of the seventeenth century, as seen in *El Paraíso en el Nuevo Mundo*, a lengthy and erudite treatise written by Antonio de León Pinelo, learned jurist and famous descendant of a Portuguese family of converts from Judaism who sought asylum in Peru.

While these are some of the more telling examples of the forms faith took in the anticipated American New Jerusalem or New Rome, a number of Creole authors refrained from such messianic extremes and were content to describe their new home as a lush and beautiful Canaan. Far from confining themselves to the biblical celebration of their beautiful tropical lands, Peruvians and Mexicans saw in the mineral wealth of their respective countries a sign of divine election. This theme of "plutolatry" was often linked to that of Mariolatry in a strange spiritual alchemy. The same imagery resurfaces in the rhetoric surrounding the Virgin of Guadalupe, proclaimed Patron Saint of Mexico in 1737 by Mexico City's civil and religious authorities on "behalf of the Mexican nation"; Papal approval followed in 1754. Members of the cult of Guadalupe, with the backing of Creole Franciscans and Jesuits, believed that Mexico, land of Mary and mineral riches, was destined to become the seat of New Jerusalem and New Rome and consequently the center of the world and the capital of Christendom. In 1749, the Jesuit Francisco Javier Carranza published the significantly titled *Transmigration of the Church to Guadalupe* in Mexico. In it he included an exegesis of Apocalypse 12 that identified the Virgin Mary being pursued by a dragon both with the Virgin of Guadalupe, who chose Mount Tepeyac as the site of her apparition, and with the Church that in the Last Days would come to seek refuge from the persecution of the Anti-Christ in New Spain.[30]

From Religious Messianism to the Messianism of Freedom

In what ways did the theme of the transposition of the Church to the Indies persist and emerge in the struggle for Independence? In his prophetic "Jamaica Letter" (1815), Simón Bolívar spoke of the transplantation of European civilization to America in what is undoubtedly a secular version of the Christian transposition: "Then will those sciences and arts which, born in the East, have enlightened Europe, wing their way to a free Colombia, which will cordially bid them welcome." In the same letter, he predicted that Panama will be the future "emporium of the world" and the future "capital of the world." In his 1819 "Angostura Speech," he introduced Great Columbia, the new nation over whose birth he had presided, as the "very centre of the world." At a time when reaction was triumphing in Europe, he summoned an image of his homeland, model among nations, "seated on the throne of freedom, grasping the sceptre of justice, crowned with glory, displaying the majesty of the New World to the Old."[31] This allegorical vision of the Home-land joined with Liberty seems to foreshadow

another allegory – the Statue of Liberty that would later be built at the gateway of New York. This brings us to the end of a long journey that began with the Judeo-Christian conception of Jerusalem as the navel of the world and passed through to the utopia of a *libertador* who had a dream that Panama of Greater Columbia would become the center of a secular universe where the old restraints would be replaced by Liberty.[32]

We should not conclude, however, that this image of the Throne of Liberty signals the triumph of secularization in the America of the *libertadores*. Another image, religious this time, also comes to the fore in the figure of the Virgin of Guadalupe, wearing the face of the Virgin of the Apocalypse, which appeared on the banners that the priests Hidalgo the Creole and Morelos the Mestizo distributed to their largely Indian armies. This religious image, apocalyptic as well as maternal, was far more eloquent on the union between elites and illiterate masses than any abstract symbol would have been. The power of this Marian cult rested on its Indian origin and Creole resuscitation. The legend, dating most certainly from the mid-seventeenth century, recounts how in 1531, the Virgin Mary appeared on Mount Tepeyac to a poor Indian; she appeared in the guise of the Virgin of the Apocalypse, who was venerated in the Spanish Monastery of Guadalupe in Estremadura; but here, on the hills that surround Mexico City, Tonantzin, the mother of the gods, was venerated long before the Spanish had set foot in the place; and in time, as the cult grew larger, in the seventeenth and eighteenth centuries, Mary-Tonantzin became the mother of all Mexicans.

Land of Freedom, God's Chosen Land, Civilization's Refuge, Utopian Land – these themes that today have been confiscated by the Anglo-Saxon country that annexed, to the great detriment of the Latin countries, the name of America, were at the beginning Hispano-American themes, too.

Translated by Nadia Benabid

Notes

1 François-René de Chateaubriand, *Les Natchez* (1826), Book V, 1st phrase, in *Oeuvres romanesques et voyages*, ed. Maurice Regard, 2 vols. (Paris: Gallimard, 1969): 2: 227.

2 Christopher Columbus, letter to Doña Juana de la Torre, nurse of Prince Don Juan, 1500, in *Select Documents*, 1: 48 (see bibliography).

3 Bartolomé de las Casas, *Obras completas* (see bibliography), 13: 68.

4 Matthew 24: 14. All biblical references in this essay are to the Douay-Rheims Bible.

5 Gilles Lapouge, *Utopie et Civilisations* (Paris: Albin Michel, 1990).

6 In his *La Postérité spirituelle de Joachim de Flore*, 2 vols. (Paris: Lethielleux; Namur: Culture et Vérité, 1978–81), Father Henri de Lubac initiated the theological revisionism of Joachimism. See especially the publications of the Centro Internazionale di Studi Gioacchimiti, which is headquartered at San Giovanni in Fiore (Calabria); since 1987, the center has published the review *Florensia*, a collection of Joachimite texts and studies (see, for example, Francesco D'Elia's very thorough anthology, *Gioacchino da Fiore: Un maestro della civiltà europea: Antologia di testi gioachimiti tradotti e commentati* [Soveria Mannelli: Rubettino, 1991]), as well as the proceedings of five international congresses. See also *Les Cahiers de Fanjeaux* (Toulouse: E. Privat), especially no. 27 (1992), devoted to the *Fin du Monde et signes des temps. Visionnaires et prophètes en France méridionale (fin du XIII–début du XV-siècle)*. The North American academics John J. Collins, Bernard McGinn, and Stephen J. Stein have edited the three-volume *Encyclopedia of Apocalypticism* (New York: Continuum, 1998); Joachimism occupies an important place in vols. 2 and 3; my chapter, "Apocalypticism in Central and South American Colonialism," which was translated from the French by Nikita Harwich, appears in vol. 3: 3–35. All quotations in the present essay, except for those by Columbus and Bolívar, are taken from Harwich's translation.

7 D'Elia, 78–80, 109-11, 166–67, and 180–91.

8 The manuscript is preserved at the Biblioteca Nacional in Madrid. Extensive excerpts from it are included in my paper "La tentación joaquinita en los principios de la Compañía de Jesús . . ." (see bibliography).

9 See the bibliography. On the subject of the Golden Age and its application to the Indians, see Pedro Mártir Anglería, *Décadas*, vol. 1, Déc. I, Book 2 (written in 1494), 121; Book 3 (written in 1500), 141–42. The first *Década* was published in Latin in Seville, in 1511.

10 Among the many valuable studies on Hispano-American urbanism, Francisco de Solano's collection of essays merits particular attention. See the bibliography.

11 See vol. 2 of *Histoire du Nouveau Monde* by Carmen Bernand and Serge Gruzinski. which is devoted to miscegenation (see bibliography). The masterpiece on the African American situation, Roger Bastide's *Les Amériques noires*, has thankfully been reissued (Paris and Montreal: L'Harmattan, 1996).

12 Archivo Histórico Nacional de Madrid, *Inquisición* (leg. 47, exp. 14).

13 See the study by François Delpech, "La légende de la Tierra de Jauja dans ses contextes historique, folklorique et littéraire," pp. 79–98 in *Texte et Contexte: Actes du XVe Congrès (Limoges, 1979) de la Société des hispanistes français* (Limoges: U.E.R. des lettres et sciences humaines, 1981).

14 Bartolomé de Las Casas, *Historia de las Indias*, Book III, Chapter 105, in *Obras Completas*, 5: 2210.

15 Alain Milhou, "Du pillage au rêve édénique. Sur les aspirations millénaristes des *soldados pobres* du Pérou," *Cahiers du Monde Hispanique et Luso-Brésilien* (Toulouse: Institut d'Etudes Hispaniques, Hispano-Americaines et Luso-Brésiliennes), no. 46 (1986): 7–20.

16 Psalms 21: 27.

17 Carlos Herrejón Peredo, "Fuentes patrísticas, jurídicas y escolásticas del pensamiento quiroguiano," pp. 9–23 in vol. 1 of *Humanistas Novohispanos de Michoacán* (Morelia, Mich.: Universidad Michoacana de San Nicolás de Hidalgo, 1982).

18 The positions taken by John L. Phelan and Georges Baudot have been the subject of an ongoing critique by Josep I. Saranyana and Ana de Zaballa. My own position ("Apocalypticism in Central and South American Colonialism"; see above, note 6) is closer to that of the more nuanced critique by Elsa Cecilia Frost (see bibliography).

19 Francisco Jiménez, O.F.M., "Vida de Fray Martín de Valencia, escrita por su compañero Fray Francisco Jiménez (h. 1537)," ed. P. Atanasio López, *Archivo Ibero-Americano*, 1st series, 26 (July–August 1926): 45–83, esp. 74–75. Alain Milhou, "América frente a los sueños orientales (1492–principios del siglo XVII)," pp. 141–211 in *España y América en una perspectiva humanista: Homenaje a Marcel Bataillon* (Madrid: Casa de Velázquez, 1998); esp. 190–98.

20 Gerónimo de Mendieta, *Historia eclesiástica indiana*, Book IV, Chapter 23.

21 A good example of this Jesuit propaganda can be seen in the work the Society commissioned from an enlightened Italian priest, Ludovico Antonio Muratori: *Il Cristianesimo felice nelle missioni de' padri della Compagnia di Gesù nel Paraguai*. Published in 1743 (Venice: Giambatista Pasquali), the book met with great success and was translated into French, in the Jesuit adaptation by Félix Esprit de Lourmel, in 1754, and into English in 1759 (see bibliography). Comparisons to the primitive Church are constant throughout.

22 Father António Vieira had strong ties to Judeo-Portuguese circles in Amsterdam and was, from 1634 until his death in 1697, the great figure of Portuguese millenarianism. See Raymond Cantel, *Prophétisme et messianisme dans l'oeuvre d'António Vieira* (Paris: Ediciones Hispano-Americanas, 1960).

23 See especially Hélène Clastres (see bibliography), and Maria Isaura Pereira de Queiroz, *Réforme et révolution dans les sociétés traditionnelles. Histoire et ethnologie des mouvements messianiques* (Paris: Editions Anthropos Paris, 1968).

24 Alain Milhou, "De la destruction de l'Espagne à la destruction des Indes: histoire sacrée et combats idéologiques," in *Etudes sur l'impact culturel du Nouveau Monde* (Paris: Editions L'Harmattan), vol. 1 (1981): 25–47, and vol. 3 (1983): 11–54.

25 Bartolomé de Las Casas, *Historia de las Indias*, Book I, Chapter 29, in *Obras Completas*, 3: 507. On this subject, see Marcel Bataillon, "Estas Indias . . ." (see bibliography).

26 Bartolomé de Las Casas, *Historia de las Indias*, Book 3, Chapter 102, in *Obras Completas*, 5: 2193.

Bibliography

27 The Inquisition's trial of Francisco de la Cruz has been published under the direction of Vidal Abril Castelló. See the works by Marcel Bataillon and Jean-Pierre Tardieu (see bibliography).

28 The *alumbrados* (literally, "the enlightened") believed in the achievement of inner light through meditation, and they took exception to all forms of ecclesiastic mediation. The first *alumbrados* were condemned by an edict of the Inquisition in 1525. The movement persisted in a less radical and less theological but more sentimental form until somewhere around 1630.

29 See the study by Antonio Eguiluz (see bibliography).

30 Jacques Lafaye, *Quetzalcóatl and Guadalupe . . .* (see bibliography), passim, esp. 379–84.

31 Simón Bolívar, *The Hope of the Universe*, introduction, selection, biographical notes, and chronology by J. L. Salcedo-Bastardo; prologue by Arturo Uslar Pietri (Paris: UNESCO, 1983), 115, 113, 155, 156. The Spanish version of these texts can be found in Simón Bolívar, *Escritos políticos* (Madrid: Alianza Editorial, 1969), 79 and 84 (*Carta de Jamaica*), 123 (*Discurso de Angostura*).

32 Alain Milhou, "De Jérusalem à la Terre promise du Nouveau Monde," pp. 187–207 in *Le Mythe de Jérusalem du Moyen Age à la Renaissance,* ed. Evelyne Berriot-Salvadore (Saint-Etienne: Université de Saint-Etienne, 1995).

This list provides complete bibliographical information; references to these works in the footnotes appear in abbreviated form.

Primary Sources

Anglería, Pedro Mártir (hispanized form of Pietro Martire d'Anghiera). *Décadas del Nuevo Mundo*, critical edition by Edmundo O'Gorman, Latin to Spanish translation by Agustín Millares Carlo. 2 vols. Mexico: J. Porrúa, 1964–65.

Caminha, Pero Vaz de. *Carta de Pêro Vaz de Caminha a el-rei D. Manuel sobre o achamento do Brasil* (1500), ed. Maria Paula Caetano and Neves Aguas. Lisbon: Publicações Europa-América, 1987.

Columbus, Christopher. *Textos y Documentos completos*, ed. Consuelo Varela; *Nuevas Cartas*, ed. Juan Gil. 2nd ed., revised. Madrid: Alianza Editorial, 1992. English edition: *Select Documents Illustrating the Four Voyages of Columbus*, trans. and ed., with additional material, an introduction, and notes, by Cecil Jane. 2 vols. London: Printed for the Hakluyt Society, 1930–33.

Cruz, Francisco de la, O.P. *Inquisición, Actas*, ed. Vidal Abril Castelló. 2 vols. in 3. Madrid: Consejo Superior de Investigaciones Científicas, 1992–97.

Las Casas, Bartolomé de, O.P. *Obras completas*, 14 vols. to date (Madrid: Alianza, 1988–). The works that best illustrate the apocalyptic and messianic spirit of the "defender of the Indians" are: *Historia de las Indias* (vols. 3, 4, and 5), *Brevísima Relación de la destrucción de las Indias* and *Octavo Remedio* (vol. 10: *Tratados* de 1552), as well as a certain number of documents that appear among the *Cartas y memoriales* (vol. 13).

León Pinelo, Antonio de. *El Paraíso en el Nuevo Mundo. Comentario apologético, Historia natural y peregrina de las Indias Occidentales, islas de Tierra Firme* [sic] *del Mar Océano*, ed. Raúl Porras Barrenechea. 2 vols. Lima: Impr. Torres Aguirre, 1943.

Maldonado, Juan de. *Quaedam opuscula nunc primum in lucem edita*. Burgos, 1541. Among the five opuscules appears the *Somnium*, which has been translated and analyzed by Miguel Avilés Fernández in *Sueños ficticios y lucha ideológica en el Siglo de Oro* (Madrid: Editora Nacional, 1981), 107–78.

Mendieta, Gerónimo de, O.F.M. *Historia eclesiástica indiana*, ed. Joaquín García Icazbalceta. Facsimile of the 1870 edition. Mexico: Editorial Porrúa, 1971.

Motolinía, Toribio, O.F.M. *Historia de los indios de la Nueva España*, ed. Georges Baudot. Madrid: Castalia, 1985.

Muratori, Ludovico Antonio. *Relation des missions du Paraguay*, trans. in 1754 from Italian by Félix Esprit de Lourmel. Reprint. Paris: Maspero, 1983. English edition: *A Relation of the Missions of Paraguay*. London: J. Marmaduke, 1759.

Quiroga, Vasco de. *Don Vasco de Quiroga y su "Información en derecho,"* critical edition by Paulino Castañeda Delgado. Madrid: J. Porrúa Turanzas, 1974.

Quiroga, Vasco de. "Reglas para el gobierno de los hospitales de Santa Fe de México y Michoacán" and "Testamento." Pp. 27–77 in vol. 1 of *Humanistas novohispanos de Michoacán*. Morelia, Mich.: Universidad Michoacana de San Nicolás Hidalgo, 1982.

Vespucio, Américo (hispanized form of Amerigo Vespucci). *El Nuevo Mundo. Cartas relativas a sus viajes y descubrimientos*, texts in Italian, Spanish, and English, ed. Roberto Levillier. Buenos Aires: Editorial Nova, 1951.

Secondary Sources

Armani, Alberto. *Ciudad de Dios y Ciudad del Sol: El "Estado" jesuita de los guaraníes (1609–1768)*, trans. from the Italian original *Città di Dio e Città del Sole* (Rome: Studium, 1977). México: Fonda de Cultura Económica, 1982.

Bataillon, Marcel. *Etudes sur Bartolomé de Las Casas*. Paris: Centre de Recherches de l'Institut d'Etudes hispaniques, 1966. On Las Casas's messianism and on his heterodox disciple Francisco de la Cruz, see "Estas Indias (hipótesis lascasianas)," 249–58, and "La herejía de Fray Francisco de la Cruz y la reacción antilascasiana," 309–24.

Baudot, Georges. *Utopia and History in Mexico: The First Chroniclers of Mexican Civilization (1520–1569)*, trans. Bernard R. Ortiz de Montellano and Thelma Ortiz de Montellano. Niwot: University Press of Colorado, 1995.

Bernand, Carmen, and Serge Gruzinski. *Histoire du Nouveau Monde*. Vol. 1, *De la Découverte à la Conquête, une expérience européenne, 1492–1550*; vol. 2, *Les métissages, 1550–1640*. Paris: Fayard, 1991–93.

Clastres, Hélène. *The Land-without-Evil: Tupi-Guarani prophetism*, trans. Jacqueline Grenez Brovender; foreword by Jonathan D. Hill. Urbana: University of Illinois Press, 1995.

Cro, Stelio. *The American Foundations of the Hispanic Utopia (1492–1793)*. 2 vols. Tallahassee, Fla.: The DeSoto Press, 1994.

Duviols, Jean-Paul. *L'Amérique espagnole vue et rêvée: Les livres de voyage de Christophe Colomb à Bougainville*. Paris: Promodis, 1985.

Eguiliz, Antonio, O.F.M. "Fr. Gonzalo Tenorio, O.F.M., y sus teorías escatológico-providencialistas sobre las Indias," *Missionalia Hispanica*, no. 48 (1959): 257–322.

Frost, Elsa Cecilia. "Milenarismo mitigado o milenarismo imaginado?" Pp. 73–85 in *Memorias del Simposio de Historiografía Mexicanista*. México: Comité Mexicano de Ciencias Históricas: Gobierno del Estado de Morelos: Instituto de Investigaciones Históricas, UNAM, 1990.

Gil, Juan. *Mitos y utopías del Descubrimiento*. Vol. 1, *Colón y su tiempo*; vol. 2, *El Pacífico*; vol. 3, *El Dorado*. Madrid: Alianza Editorial, 1989.

Gomez, Thomas. *L'invention de l'Amérique: Rêve et réalités de la conquête*. Paris: Aubier, 1992.

Lafaye, Jacques. *Quetzalcóatl and Guadalupe: The Formation of Mexican National Consciousness, 1531–1813*, trans. Benjamin Keen; foreword by Octavio Paz. Chicago: University of Chicago Press, 1976.

Milhou, Alain. *Colón y su mentalidad mesiánica en el ambiente franciscanista español*. Valladolid: Casa-Museo de Colón: Seminario Americanista de la Universidad de Valladolid, 1983.

Milhou, Alain. "La tentación joaquinita en los principios de la Compañía de Jesús. El caso de Francisco de Borja y Andrés de Oviedo." Pp. 193–239 in *Florensia. Bollettino del Centro Internazionale di Studi Gioacchimiti*, 8–9 (1994–95).

Milhou, Alain. "Variations sur les thèmes du bon et du mauvais sauvage de Colomb à l'Inca Garcilaso de la Vega (1492–1609)." Pp. 49–63 in *La Conquête de l'Amérique espagnole et la question du droit*, ed. Carmen Val Julián. Fontenay-aux-Roses: ENS éditions, 1996.

Phelan, John L. *The Millennial Kingdom of the Franciscans in the New World*. 2nd ed., revised. Berkeley: University of California Press, 1970.

Sanchez, Jean-Pierre. *Mythes et légendes de la conquête de l'Amérique*. 2 vols. Rennes: Presses Universitaires de Rennes, 1996.

Saranyana, José, and Ana de Zaballa Beascoechea. *Joaquín de Fiore y América*. 2nd ed., revised. Pamplona: Ediciones Eunate, 1995.

Solano, Francisco de. *Ciudades hispanoamericanas y pueblos de indios*. Madrid: Consejo Superior de Investigaciones Científicas, 1990.

Tardieu, Jean-Pierre. *Le Nouveau David et la réforme du Pérou. L'affaire Maria Pizarro-Francisco de la Cruz (1571–1596)*. Bordeaux: Maison des Pays ibériques, 1992.

Utopia and the Reformation

The Reformation as Utopia

THE REFORMATION, it is often pointed out, contained a strong utopian dimension. If, as Karl Mannheim[1] suggests, we should understand utopia as a permanent mental attitude, as a dynamic force contesting the static nature of ideology and system, then the Reformation at its inception was profoundly utopian: it shook the institutionalized church from the bottom up; it liberated individual conscience from submission to and obedience of tradition and authority, and even went so far as to extol the virtue of rebellion in the name of the irrevocable rights of conscience. Its most radical fringes segued into social revolution and, ultimately, the peasant revolt of 1524–25 led by Thomas Münzer.

The profound harmony that initially prevailed between Luther and the preachers of the peasant communities has been duly noted, and Jean Wirth is quite right in saying that "the great majority of peasants were Lutheran, if we understand this to mean that they accepted the religious ideas of Luther and not that Luther lent them his approval."[2]

Allegiance to the Gospels, with their simultaneously social and religious appeal, was in itself a utopian slogan. By its reversion to Scripture, through the triple affirmation of *sola gratia, sola Scriptura, sola fide* ("by grace alone, by Scripture alone, by faith alone"), Lutheran reform proclaimed universal unmediated salvation and bypassed the interpretations and suffocating tutelage of a clerical class that was deemed parasitic. Adherence to the Gospel, a rallying cry that cradled a considerable variety of religious values and an even greater range of interpretations and practical consequences, proved to be an eminently mobilizing theme and an efficient agent for the reconciliation of spiritual and temporal, for proclaiming emancipation in the here and now, not from the Commandments, but from the servile state in which the nobility and the clergy abusively held the people.

Thomas Münzer (1488–1525) – a priest and theologian and an early disciple of Luther who rapidly became his principal adversary – was an heir to medieval millenarianism. Acting on the conviction, shared by Luther, that the end of the world was imminent, Münzer used the Scriptures, and to a greater degree the apocalyptic writings of John and

Daniel, to reach conclusions with immediate political application. From a the principle of communal ownership by the "elect," he advocated a State wherein all would be equal and each would receive according to his needs. He preached violence against the inherently "impious" nobility and clergy, who were the illicit holders of a power that belonged solely and directly to God, and he called for their extermination. For Münzer, social revolution was a necessary preamble to salvation: "One can't speak to you about God so long as they are reigning over you," he wrote to his disciples in Allstedt, in April 1525.[3] Certainly, Münzer's principal merit consists in his attempt to translate into reality the eschatological myths that haunted him by exploiting the discontent of the peasants, whose rebellion was motivated not so much by penury as by the obstacles that had been placed in the path of their social ascent and their will to autonomy.[4]

Luther's scathing response (to Münzer) was not primarily doctrinal. His brutal denial concerned, instead, the fact that these were *peasants* claiming Scripture and showing their readiness to use force to impose negotiations through armed action.[5]

Indeed, Luther's theology, in its early phase, had justified religious violence, even in its most spectacular forms in iconoclasm and profanation and, by extension, social subversion. Later, the swift "recatholicization" of the Reformation by Luther, and especially by his disciples, would powerfully thwart this dangerous dynamic. The extremely brutal condemnation of the peasants and their leaders, coming as early as 1526 in the tract *Against the Robbing and Murdering Hordes of Peasants*, and their final crushing defeat, went hand in hand with the reconstitution, on other foundations, of the social hierarchy and the ecclesiastical apparatus. The principle of authority was no longer based on the Gospels, with their liberating impetus, but more generally on the Bible, and the Old Testament in particular. The Ten Commandments were once again the order of the day.

This retreat from faith to law should, however, be qualified, even though it is true that Luther urged his followers to stop preaching the Gospel to peasants and to preach the judging God of the Apocalypse and the "Moses with horns" of the ancient Alliance instead. It fell to Melanchthon, the *praeceptor Germaniae*, educator of Germany, to carry out this role. Melanchthon was in reality, as Jean Wirth has shown, "the counterweight that Luther imposed on himself."[6] For Luther was loathe to play the policeman himself and, in any case, reluctant to revise his theology of salvation. Lutheranism, therefore, called for the effective coexistence of one religion for the people, founded on passive observance and belief in the law, and another religion for the elite, affirming Christian freedom in an effusion of faith. In this instance, utopia became a kind of social privilege.

As to revolutionary peasant utopia, it too had its nuances. There, the old order, as manifested in mentalities and even in the execution of warfare, endured throughout the troubles. Their historic hope, following in the footsteps of ancient millenarianism, would be brought down in the peasant defeat of 1525 by their paradoxical conservatism.

Finally, the utopian potential of the Reformation did not altogether disappear but instead lived on in the Anabaptist movement, as attested to by the founding of New Jerusalem at Münster in Westphalia in 1534–35, barely a decade after the peasants' crushing defeat. The supposed communism of the primitive Church became the ideal of this authentically Christian society. At Münster, the communal ownership observed by the Apostles was rigorously applied; it soon grew to include the community of women. Money was forbidden and polygamy made compulsory, on the model of the patriarchs of Israel. Ancient authority was abolished, replaced by a theocracy resulting in the proclamation of John of Leyden as the new Messiah and a reign of terror that would last for over a year and end in disaster. Throughout this time, books, with the exception of the Bible, over whose interpretation religious leaders had sole control, were forbidden; streets and gates were renamed; a new calendar without Sundays or holidays that arranged the days of the week alphabetically was circulated. "Even the names of new-born children were chosen by the king according to a special system."[7] Purely ornamental coins inscribed "The Word was made flesh and and dwelt among us" were introduced. Münster's revolutionary episode, notable for its duration and impact as well as the spectacular excesses of its leader, is largely in keeping with the violent tradition of medieval millenarianism, but it also allows us to measure the immensity of the hope raised by the Reformation and outlines some of the solutions adopted by the "real utopias" of the future.

Utopia as Declamation

We shall now move from the utopian mode to the utopian genre. The two need to be distinguished in every respect.[8] Whereas the utopian mode is a state of mind, a regimen of thought, a projection of humanity toward the future, the utopian genre is circumscribed by a far more precise definition. It pertains to literary history and emerges from the outset as a rigorously codified object. The utopian genre, founded and named by Thomas More's *Utopia*, falls under another genre, namely the genre of "declamation" as it had previously been illustrated by Erasmus's *The Praise of Folly*.

Declamation, in the rhetorical sense of the word, is an exercise: an exercise in speech and thought. As a term, it is at once broader and more technical than "paradox";[9] it signifies an exercise of oratorical development on a chosen theme, a format recommended by rhetoricians for the training and formation of orators. "'Unreal reality' was the psychological, judicial, and rhetorical object" of the orator: a legal fiction and an imaginary case yielded a fake procedure; the writer Pascal Quignard has very recently used the semi-invented example of Albucius to illustrate the "outrageousness" and surrealism (*ante litteras*) that such exercises could produce.[10]

From Erasmus to Montaigne,[11] and from the birth of humanism to its crisis, declamation experienced an undeniable vogue in the European literature of the Renaissance. *The Praise of Folly*, ranked by Erasmus among his declamations, sets the tone and rules of the genre. Rabelais's praise of debts at the beginning of the Third Book and his eulogy to the herb known as Pantagruelion at the end of the same book are true-to-form declamations. Later in the century, Montaigne attributed the *Discours de la servitude volontaire* by his friend La Boétie to the same tradition: "He wrote it by way of essay in his early youth, in honor of liberty against tyrants."[12] And Montaigne also added this fundamental detail: "I have no doubt that he believed what he wrote, for he was so conscientious as not to lie even in jest."[13] While declamation may be given to humor, it also seems to demand the utmost seriousness. Fiction is not always an untruth. And utopia follows suit; it may seem to jest, but "seem" is the key word.

Several chapters and chapter fragments in Montaigne's *Essays* also fall under the category of declamation. The chapter "Of Cannibals,"[14] an apologia for the free anthropophagous tribes of Brazil and an occasion to revisit both the Golden Age of Antiquity and the ideal republic imagined by Plato and Plutarch, is undoubtedly the most famous example. "Exercise and fiction are the two essential notions that are linked" in a declamation.[15] The genre is moreover defined by the absolute freedom that makes it a privileged instrument for unbiased moral reflection. Released from historical contingencies and exempt from dogmatism as much as from any didactic purpose, it can "affect a certain detachment from immediate reality so as to better consider and evaluate it."[16]

Remote and rarely visited lands are declamation's ideal setting, and More's *Utopia* is true to form. Erasmus has Folly hail from the Fortunate Isles, where "all things grow 'unsown and uncultivated,'" and where, just as in Montaigne's Brazil, work, old age, and disease are nonexistent.[17] This long view of things, eventually tinged with irony, coincides in "Of Cannibals" with the geographic distancing of the Cannibals, who are relegated to the farthest corners of the antipodes.

The author is unmistakably present behind this mask, even if it is difficult to assess the degree to which he stands behind the arguments he presents.[18] Declamation's volatile point of view means that the speaker's identity is destabilized by a constant flux. "Essay," here, should be understood in the strict sense of the word – a thought piece without restraints or boundaries, a ludic and rigorous experiment in the risks of freedom.

Utopia as declamation, therefore, brings us back full circle to Raymond Ruyer's definition of utopia-as-genre: "a mental experiment of lateral possibilities";[19] an experiment, in other words, that poses no physical risks but that is not without its dangers; an adventurous journey for the mind where there's no risk of getting one's feet wet. This is the promotional argument of authors of encyclopedias or accounts of far-off places, as it turns up, for example, under the pen of André Thevet, cosmographer to the kings of France, at the beginning of his *Grand Insulaire et Pilotage*, written around 1588: "reality is represented here so ingenuously, that without getting your feet wet, and from the comfort of your cabinet you can learn the most beautiful and remarkable secrets about seafaring and the art of navigation and piloting."[20]

Neither More nor Erasmus nor Rabelais nor Montaigne, all of whom authored declamations, can be accused of crossing the threshold separating traditional religion from Reformation; not one can be said to have transformed social and philosophical critique into rupture and revolt. Thomas More provides us with an exemplary case in point. He ended his life as a martyr of the Counter-Reformation and

a Catholic saint, a victim of his own devotion to the spiritual power that Henry VIII, by dint of force, would first subdue and then annex. More, who was a reader of Plato and Plutarch and a friend to Erasmus, found himself, as Rabelais would soon thereafter and as countless other utopists have since, caught between two systems of thought, on the fault line that suddenly broke open between two religions. The attitude of irony and critical distance that characterizes his literary project was resolved, to very tragic effect, in his life. In other cases, this same attitude engendered an "intellectual schizophrenia," as Claude Lévi-Strauss has discussed with regard to Montaigne.[21] This destabilized mental state, uncomfortable on many fronts, produced by the uneasy marriage of an outward conservatism and an inner intellectual daring, of public conformism and freedom of conscience, is characteristic of utopia-as-genre, at least during the Classical period. There is more at stake here than finding ways of resisting censorship and intolerance or of ensuring a safe space for freedom of thought, shielded from the apparatus of Church and State, whose oppressive power was making itself felt more and more during this period. Of rather greater significance is utopia's ability, one it shares with the declamatory genre that contained it from the start, to overcome the inherent rupture that separates knowledge from action and the ideal from the real. Utopia is the thought not of the threshold, opening into metaphysical futurity (locked shut in any case), but of the border. It follows, then, that utopian thought did not arise from the heart of a well-established and institutionalized Reform, but from its margins – inner, radical margins in the case of the Peasant Revolt and Anabaptist Münster in 1535, and outer margins, into which were woven, from More to Montaigne and in the apparent folding of the humanist consciousness into itself, the infinitely varied motifs of declamation.

Utopia and the Renaissance Island
In Utopia, declamation encounters topography. Between the sixteenth and eighteenth centuries, the printing of large-scale maps and especially of island topographies, an entire subgenre of the discipline of geography, was on the rise. Venice, in particular, was responsible for the production of Atlases exclusively composed of island maps, known as *isolarii*.

A number of historians have suggested an association between Thomas More's Utopia and Portugal's feats of discovery. Thomas More had read not only Amerigo Vespucci's *Quatuor navigationes* but also the *Itinerarium Portugallensium*, a compilation printed in Milan in 1508 that included accounts of the voyages of Ca' da Mosto, Vasco da Gama, and Cabral. The island of Utopia would seem to be Indian, borrowing from India the astrological cult of heavenly planets, a meatless diet, joyous funeral rites followed by incineration of the corpse, the peaceful coexistence of diverse religions, and a caste system.[22] Not that any of it is of much significance. Of far greater importance is the fact that the island is located in the universal archipelago as revealed to Europe by the great seafaring exploits of the day.

And yet, this newly expanded world was fragmented; a broken archipelago world. It is no an accident that Utopia is an island. Islands had emerged as a privileged element of the new malleable geography that could be reconstructed and reshaped to suit the aims of specific political projects. The inconstant island, with its inherent inability to anchor itself permanently to a determined point of the *mapa mundi*, lent itself well to serving the divergent interests of rival colonial powers. The example of the Moluccas, simultaneously claimed, through the Treaty of Tordesillas, by both Spain and Portugal, is a particularly luminous case in point. In an age when, for lack of instruments, the calculation of longitude was far from exact, cartographers in both kingdoms humored their respective sovereigns by steering the entire archipelago away from either side of the famous meridian that divided the world in two.

When all is said and done, such island manipulations only served to further the latent possibilities of a system of cartographic representation inaugurated by medieval world maps. Relying on the island groupings that interrupt its vastness, the oceanic expanse lends itself to an imaginary cabotage, so that knowledge could be gained one step at a time and always within sight of the familiar landmark of a cape or reef. From the vantage point of the tall sailing ships, islands could be seen and understood at a glance. Their multiplicity meant that the globe's totality could be increased incrementally and seized one island at a time in a progressive maneuver, soon completed. And in this way, if we are to believe Francis Bacon, the advancement of knowledge progressed.[23]

The era of the Great Discoveries witnessed the emergence of a plethora of islands: Cape Verde, St. Thomas, Quiloa, Mombasa, Zanzibar, Goa on the eastern spice route; the archipelagoes of the Antilles and Bahamas where Columbus docked,

Cabot and Cartier's New World; but also Peru, Brazil, and California, long thought to be islands, and even America itself, described in many of the *isolarii* of the day as the largest island in the world. The world, which had heretofore been an inhabited monolith, would, as a consequence of the earliest transoceanic crossing, be transformed into a fragmented version of itself. The rejoining of the northern and southern parts of the American continent would occur many decades later. Until then, all the navigators in turn – Columbus, Vespucci, Verrazano, Cartier – searched in vain, from the St. Lawrence River to the Strait of Magellan, for the passageway that, aside from securing direct access to the riches of the Orient, would locate the break in the long barrier of islands that stopped their way.

The unity of the Christian West was shattered, giving way to an archipelago of denominations, especially in the confusion that reigned in the Germany and Switzerland of the early years of the Reformation and in the South of France. This dismemberment of the body universal of the Church coincided with the geographic disintegration of a world that had lost its unity and its traditional boundaries. This moment marks the almost formal convergence of these two phenomena of disintegration. The new spaces served as an allegorical support for the new fragmentation of churches and beliefs. Moreover, a sporadic and incredible experiment in alterity was taking place through diverse but concomitant paths. The utopian archipelago, in both its exotic and religious manifestations, raised the following questions: How does one understand the other and, should the occasion arise, how can one live side by side with him? Are there indeed naked peoples living without faith or law or monarch? How is it possible to be a papist? or a so-called reformed person? All these queries would eventually be joined into a single question.

This new space would make it possible for utopia, as *eu*topos or ideal place, to exist side by side with counter-utopias, execrable islands or regions where the faults and vices of a given society were exacerbated rather than rehabilitated. The archipelago of new oceans provided satire with an unprecedented vigor; various peoples, along with the groups, sects, or faiths one chose to discredit, could be reified, not to say petrified. In the Rabelaisian odyssey described in the Fourth and Fifth Books, we are not at all surprised to discover that a mere day of serene sailing separates the Island of the Popefigs from the Island of Papalmaniac.

Rabelais's Utopias:
From Thélème to Ringing Island

In keeping with the geographic upheavals of the day, Rabelais's world is mobile and full of surprises. Book 2, Chapter 32 of *Pantagruel*, "How Pantagruel Shielded an Entire Army with His Tongue, and What the Author Saw in His Mouth," has long been acknowledged as the most famous illustration of the instability of the new cosmography. The episode is a retelling from Lucian of Samosata's *A True Story*. Upon looking inside the mouth of a sea monster, Lucian's hero discovers a new world replete with mountains, forests, a temple, a fountain, vineyards. Using the unexpected uncovering of a "new world" in the mouth of a giant and the lesson in relativism it suggests, Rabelais links the Great Discoveries of his day to a folkloric theme that had already been introduced in the anonymous *Chroniques gargantuines*.[24] The macrocosm that had, thanks to Columbus and Magellan, loomed ever larger was poured into the microcosm of a disproportionately enlarged body.

Rabelais's work makes more than one reference to Thomas More's *Utopia*. Gargantua's wife and Pantagruel's mother Babedec is the "daughter of the king of the Amaurotes, in Utopia."[25] Pantagruel is the leader of the Utopians. And he has imagined a utopia of his very own: the Abbey of Thélème is a landlocked utopia situated in Touraine, "alongside the river Loire, two leagues from the great forest of Port-Huault."[26] But Thélème reminds one less of a republic than of a convent. In fact, it is a new kind of monastery where the sole rule is to "Do what you will," as its name, from the Greek *thélémé*, Will, reveals.

A more convincing and complex relationship to the allegorical archipelago comes to the fore in the last books of *Pantagruel*. The destabilized world of the early parts of *Pantagruel* and *Gargantua* tends toward fixity, much like the frozen words of the Glacial Sea. In contrast to the open-ended world of the expansion at its inception, these islands are locked onto themselves and lack mouths and orifices. The most evocative example of this is the "admirable" island of Maître Gaster, "the first master of arts graduate in the world," which resembles the Rock of Virtue described by Hesiod in *Works and Days*. Its terrain was "rugged, rocky, mountainous, and non-arable all around, unpleasant to look at, hard on the feet," but once one is up and inside, it is a place "so pleasant, fertile, healthful, and delightful that I thought this must have been the true Garden of Eden, the earthly paradise."[27]

The strange world of Ringing Island, the first port of rest in Book Five, is a world of bells that double as cauldrons, of pots and pans where the Pope's fatty soup simmers – a reference to the 1562 Protestant satiric illustration "The Overturning of the Big Marmite," an image of an upside-down, cracked bell from which seeps a soup, with floating miters and crucifixes, boiling atop a fire fueled by the bodies of three martyrs of the Reformation. Above, Truth, armed with the sword of the Holy Gospel, descends from the heavens to overturn everything.[28]

This upside-down world that is also a world of the dead, this perverted and infernal world that terrifies more than it amuses, is encountered again, a mere five years later, in the ambitious Protestant cartographic fiction published in Geneva under the title *The New Papist Mappe-Monde*. Authored by the Italian Jean-Baptiste Trento and the Frenchman Pierre Eskrich, this work consisted of a text, or a *history,* and a map of vast dimensions, or *mapa mundi.*[29] The *history* is organized by chapters and rubrics and provides a land-survey of a new world that is analogous in every aspect to the one the kings of Spain and Portugal have discovered and conquered on the other side of the ocean. But, in fact, this "other world" as depicted on the map is really Rome – its "ramparts," the Aurelian Wall together with the Pyramid of Caius Cestius, are instantly identifiable. This new *mapa mundi* constitutes, therefore, like Ringing Island, a cosmographic allegory of the Catholic Church. And also like Ringing Island, this *new* world is "monstrous" – the terms are more or less interchangeable here[30] – and it is situated in hell, inside the disproportionately enlarged mouth of Satan. The city of Rome is circumscribed by the voracious oval of Satan's lips. It, too, like Ringing Island, functions as "the other world" in both the cosmographic and eschatological sense, the new world and the world beyond simultaneously converging in the imminent end of the world.

The Utopias of the Militant Reformation:
Bernard Palissy, Jacques Perret,
the *Kingdom of Antangil*

Utopia in the Garden:
Bernard Palissy's Recette véritable

Not more than a thousand leagues from this infernal archipelago, we find Bernard Palissy, potter, "inventor of rustic ceramic wares for the King," and the designer of a dream garden of utopian conception and strong religious connotations. Palissy modeled his vision on the work of the Italians – Alberti, Serlio, and of course Francesco Colonna, author of the *Songe de Poliphile*. The work of their

French emulators and counterparts, Androuet du Cerceau and Philibert de l'Orme, also served him well.

Palissy was not first and foremost a writer. He was an artisan, a "mechanical" as they were then called, who labored with his hands and made his living by the sweat of his brow. Books had little to do with his knowledge of gardening, and he never tired of saying that his learning had been imparted to him by his art, "the art of the earth," the potter's art, in other words. Gardening, it seems, was the natural and almost necessary culmination of his craft.

Eden was the inevitable font of Palissy's endeavor. Serving doubly as a starting place and a destination, it prompted his meditation in the form of a stroll in a dream garden; Eden is, by Palissy's own admission, the "model" for his imaginary paradise. Mortal architects, after all, should not hope for anything more than the ability to copy the design of the original and quintessential Divine Architect. Naturally, this model was somewhat theoretical. Still, the central fountain and the four rivers of Paradise lend themselves well to a "quadratur," a squared design that frames a circular island where foliage flourishes. Beyond the sketchy details furnished in Genesis, the layout relies on additional passages from the Bible, notably the Psalms. Psalm 104, "How Manifold Are Thy Works," for example, is a wellspring for Palissy's garden.

If we are to take the *Recette véritable* at its word, then it was this psalm, in the French translation by Clément Marot, that served as the source and origin of Palissy's vision. In Saintes as everywhere else, the first War of the Huguenots had just ended to the temporary advantage of the Protestants, and a brief period of peaceful coexistence between both faiths was in effect. Palissy, who had had reason to fear for his life, had recently been released from prison. It was the spring of 1563, and a beautiful Sunday found Palissy deep in thought while strolling along the banks of the Charente. Suddenly, the familiar words of the prophet king came into his mind. A "choir of virgins" sat beneath the sapwoods and sang Psalm 104. "And their voices were so gentle and harmonious," writes Palissy, "that all earlier thoughts were driven from my mind,"[31] those dark, melancholic thoughts in remembrance of the civil war. And then and there, he felt the heavens opening up in his soul. The horrific spectacle that had been haunting him was replaced with a green vision of Paradise with its "fountains and brooks," its "stony mounds" and its lush grasses, its flitting birds, its fauna running free, and even whales tossing in its vast seas. His only thoughts were of capturing the miraculous vision that had appeared to him as if by magic from the verses of the Psalm. At first, he thought of a painting, but then "paintings are so short-lived." No, a garden would be the thing. A garden that would be a miniature of the world, but the world as it had been at the outset, when it was still spared from human malice and basking in the peace of the beginning.

The many themes touched upon in succession by the *Recette véritable* all converge in the "admirable design" of a garden, a refuge for Reformed believers in times of persecution. The book itself is a hodge-podge of facts and technical advice addressed to a pell-mell audience of surveyors and agronomists, enamelists and well-borers. For precarious human peace to become everlasting, human beings had to renew their bond with God by communing with his creation. And what better vehicle than a garden? A garden where man need not fear his neighbor and where animals – foxes and birds and wild hares – could freely roam and trees would not be subject to the excessive torments and tortures of the brutal and profit-hungry forester, but would be grafted and pruned in accordance with the rules of art.

Palissy's garden reestablishes a pure transparency between man and the Creator, whose glory shall henceforth be continually sung by the unhampered ascent of this verdant hymn of thanksgiving. In this garden, this scaled-down model of Creation, artificial grottoes bear enameled inscriptions that seem to have spontaneously appeared in the stone, and the tree branches that form the pavilions are cleverly grafted and tweaked to spell verses from the Bible. Fragments gleaned from biblical books of wisdom, especially from Proverbs, the Song of Solomon, and Ecclesiastes, also appear, inscribed in living nature. The primordial simultaneity of the divine Word and Creation, such as it had existed in the time of Eden, is reborn in these speaking stones and woven branches that transcribe the Word and erupt in new greenery at each consecutive spring.

Palissy's garden speaks without tropes or figures of speech. It is meant to be read literally. Insofar as it rejects images and relies on the direct application of texts on a vegetable or mineral canvas, it is typically Protestant, or Calvinist to be precise. There are no detours via allegory or the human figure. Neither statues nor hieroglyphs, such as those we encounter in the *Songe de Poliphile* or in sixteenth-century Tuscan and Latin gardens, grace this place. Furthermore, Palissy chose rugged stones and living trees over hewn stone and planed wood. His garden is a gallery of legible signs, instantly accessible to the community of believers who would have come to stroll, work, or pray in it. To recall an image from Paracelsus, to whom Palissy is in many ways akin, a garden, like the world it summarizes, is a book that one leafs through with one's feet.[32]

The Holy Book and the Book of Nature, these twin paths of access to the divine, are reunited and merged in the myth of a garden that exists outside history and its recent disasters. But it did not take long for the dream to jump the garden wall and set itself a double course, toward both the future and the past. On the one hand, we read about a truly impassable "fortress city," helical in shape like the shell of a murex, described by Palissy in the appendix to his treatise; and on the other hand, there is the evocation of the towns of Saintes and Saintonge during the short-lived Reformation spring of 1562, when a radiant future seemed in store for the community of the faithful. Suddenly, we find ourselves in Saintes, and never was a name better suited to a place: there, choirs of young girls sing psalms by the riverbank and groups of strolling workers discuss the Bible out loud. On that fateful Sunday when divine harmony descended to grace mankind, Saintes emerged transformed into an ideal vision or a dream. This real utopia and Protestant version of a millenarianist dream would last for only a brief season until the declaration of the Wars of the Huguenots would irremediably destroy it. From that point on, it withdrew into the protected enclosure of the mystical garden and garrisoned itself behind the walls of the "fortress city," the helical construction with its blurred interior and exterior, the impregnable city that "topographically expresses the unanimous will of a soldered social body" and is structurally solid.[33]

An artist whose aesthetic was shaped by the "anti-Renaissance,"[34] Palissy was a visionary, on equal footing with the greatest figures the tradition came to offer, even though he may have relied on the humble tools of the gardener, the surveyor, and the potter to reach his ends.

The Architectural Utopia of Jacques Perret
Whereas Palissy imagined the Holy Book enclosed in a garden like a jewel in a casket, Savoyard Jacques Perret imagined the exact opposite. At the turn of the seventeenth century, Perret, an architect and engineer in the service of Henry IV, published his *Des fortifications et Artifices: Architecture et perspective* together with twenty-two plates engraved by Thomas de Leu (five of which were plans for fortified cities accompanied by perspective views).[35]

Holy Scripture had found its way onto the triangles, squares, even five- and six-pointed stars that overran the bulwarks. Biblical verse was divided into ten-, twelve-, and sixteen-line segments that were closely molded to the architectural drawing; the barrier of stone, water, and earth had been augmented and reinforced by an outer shield of words written in capital letters.

God's word was the only true defense, far stronger than the most ambitious ramparts, curtain walls, or fortifications. And good architecture was yet again equated with a strict imitation of the divine order; as with Palissy, we see an unmediated and absolute conflation of the Word and those spaces inhabited by the community of believers. Unlike Palissy's garden, however, Perret's military and civilian architecture did not aim to reproduce a simulacrum of nature. More rigorously utopian than the Eden of the *Recette véritable*, Perret's ideal city belongs to the Renaissance imaginary tradition of such cities, especially as it manifested itself in Italy in the works of Luciano Laurana, Piero della Francesca, and Leonardo da Vinci.

Perret, like Palissy before him, insisted on the novelty of his enterprise and refrained from invoking the debate between the Ancients and the Moderns, with the single exception of Vegetius, whose *De re militari* was widely read during the Renaissance. Such bypassing of humanist authority to privilege the sole Word of God was rather typical of Protestant literature's efforts to reduce to *tabula rasa* all traditions that were alien to the Bible. This, however, should not be taken to mean that Perret was not profoundly conversant with the classics, starting with Vitruvius's *De architectura*. He assiduously applied himself to studying the Italians, Alberti and his successors, and was directly influenced by Pietro Cataneo, whose *L'architettura* was published in Venice between 1554 and 1567. Cataneo's reunification of military and civilian architectures, branches of the discipline that earlier treatises had seen fit to dissociate, had an undeniable impact on Perret's vision.[36]

The architectural plates that expressed this vision are, in fact, rather banal and would not qualify as utopian if they had not integrated into the drawing biblical inscriptions drawn for the most part from the Psalms. Palissy's garden, as we recall, emerged fully formed from a sung rendition of Psalm 104 delivered by a choir of virgins on the banks of the Charente. In Perret's *Des fortifications*, the quadrilateral city appeared shielded on all four sides by Psalm 91, "He who dwells in the shelter of the Most High." The pentagonal city was guarded by Psalm 127, "Unless the Lord builds the house, those who build it labor in vain." The hexagonal city was protected by Psalm 33, "Rejoice in the Lord, O you righteous! Praise befits the upright." The twenty-three-sided city had Psalm 117 as its Palladium: "Praise the Lord, all nations! Extol him, all peoples!" For its part, the sixteen-sided city was safeguarded by commandments drawn from Exodus 20 and Matthew 22: "You shall love the Lord your God with all your heart, and with all your soul, and with all your mind. This is the great and first commandment. And a second is like it, You shall love your neighbor as yourself. On these two commandments depend all the law and the prophets."[37]

Such a marked preference for the Psalms was not incidental. In the verse translations by Clément Marot and Théodore de Bèze, *Psalms* was the vehicle of choice for spreading the Reformation throughout France and was espoused by the minority church in the ensuing years of persecution and resistance. Protestants adopted the Psalms as rallying songs of gratitude and as a symbol of religious affiliation.

By immuring his ideal projections with inscriptions from the Psalms, Jacques Perret no doubt wanted to invoke the age-old malediction that weighed on the city, from the Babel and the Sodom of the Old Testament to the Great Babylon of the Apocalypse. The Psalms, lined up along the bastions to form an ultimate rampart against the outside world, played a kind of talismanic role. Not only were the five ideal cities sheltered by the Word, but their outer walls were an uninterrupted public appeal for benediction. This armor of words, however, was not endowed with magical properties nor was it understood as a guarantor of heaven-sent protection. Rather, the Psalms were selected as a reminder of the terms of a contract, of an Alliance freely accorded by God to his people, with the proviso that they follow the Commandments and show themselves worthy of such an ally. Grace, for Calvin, did not translate into dispensation from the law. Hence, the calling up of the Ten Commandments and Evangelical law to complement the message of the Psalms. The sixteen-sided city, girdled with a citation from Exodus 20 and Matthew 22, is a cautionary case in point.

But all cities did not perforce descend from Cain and his progeny. After all, had not Saint Augustine made a distinction between the City of Man and the City of God, between a worldly and a heavenly city? The first was built by the descendants of Cain, whose hope was entirely dependent on earthly possessions, while the second belonged to the followers of Abel, the first victim and martyr, whose kingdom was all spiritual.[38] Inscribing the word of God on the surrounding walls of an edifice that had been constructed by human beings with the help of compass and bevel was tantamount to building the City of God in the here and now, to furnishing an image and model that anticipated the Heavenly City on this very earth. This was the authentically visionary aim of Jacques Perret's enterprise, the utopian ambition of a project that sought to link heaven and earth and man's labor with God's design.

In Palissy's enclosed garden as much as in Perret's fortified cities, on which the city of Henrichemont in Sologne was modeled, Reformation utopias must comply with the compromised settlement of the Edict of Nantes. While these cities opened up toward the heavens, they were sealed off from mankind or designed to be speedily secured at the first sign of danger. The archipelago, or the nebula, is a rather apt metaphor for the extraordinary dispersal – not to mention the uncertain perpetuity – of Protestantism, especially in the provinces of Normandy and Aquitaine. The reformed community was protected, but isolated in island pockets – lost in the Catholic immensity of a France that had emerged as the eldest daughter of the Church. Only God and his Earthly lieutenant, the King, could safeguard these parcels of land and bliss, limited in space and, as history would eventually show, in time.[39]

The next-to-last plate in Jacques Perret's compilation is an image of the "Great Royal Pavilion"; the design, true to the overhead aperture motif, was intended to grace the geometric center of the twenty-three-sided city. The Pavilion, which could "comfortably accommodate 500 persons," stood seven stories tall and was augmented by two additional terrace levels with a portico surmounting the whole. Above this portico there stood a kind of triumphal arch in the form of an obelisk with a circular base on which rested a terrestrial sphere flanked by the moon and the sun and surrounded by a field of stars. Looming above this structure, the word "God" appears in a corona of rays. The following words, written in capital letters, appear around the base: "Only by scaling the highest summit can one contemplate the sky and the earth and the things to be found therein and thereby worship God, the one and only Father and Son and Holy Spirit in spirit and in flesh. Glory unto heaven for all time. Amen."[40]

Interestingly, Perret's tower did not borrow the segmented or helical plan that Palissy favored for his "fortress city." Palissy's helix, unreservedly soaring toward the heavens, was, no doubt, too reminiscent of traditional depictions of the Tower of Babel. The famous painting of the Tower as a symbol of excess and arrogance by Pieter Brueghel the Elder dates from 1563, the year of publication of the *Recette véritable*. By opting for a square-shaped structure, Jacques Perret foils a priori any comparison that may be drawn between his architectural vision of spiritual communion and the sacrilegious temptations of Babel.

The Kingdom of Antangil
The *Histoire du grand et admirable royaume d'Antangil*, published in Saumur by the bookseller Thomas Portau in 1616, exactly a century after Thomas More's *Utopia*, is, strictly speaking, the first French-language utopia. Whereas Palissy's *Recette* and Perret's *Des fortifications* were utopian only in spirit, *Antangil* specifically fits the definition.[41] It may even be a somewhat scholarly example. We know almost nothing about its author, except that he or she signed his work with the initials I. D. M. G. T., was a Protestant, may have been a native of Touraine, and had ties to the Low Countries. The work has been attributed by some to Pastor Joachim du Moulin and by others to Jean de Moncy.[42] In any case, this work was the first utopian text to engage with the mythical *Terra Australis*, that vast continent extending from Java to Tierra del Fuego and larger by far than both Americas combined – an object for the imperial dreams of Northern European powers and of fixation for the utopian narratives of the Classical Age. The myth of *Terra Australis* had been launched some thirty years earlier by La Popelinière's book *Trois Mondes*. La Popelinière, also a Protestant, had envisioned an area of colonial expansion for the countries of the Reformation, the Huguenots of France, England, and Holland, that would rival, if not surpass, the New World territories conquered by Spain and Portugal.[43]

Antangil is addressed to "Messrs. the States of the United Provinces of the Low Countries" and organized into five books. Books Two through Five set forth a detailed outline of the utopian program proper, classified under the following rubrics: "On the excellent policy of this Empire," "On the military police," "On diet and the instruction of the young," "On the religion of this nation." The first book, accompanied by a map that includes a list of 129 place names and inverts north and south, is essentially the geographic tableau of a vast empire, located between 30° and 50° latitude of *Terra Australis*, somewhere to the south of "Greater Java." It extends vertically,

spanned by a wide range of climates, and is bordered by the Indian Ocean "on our polar side" and "by tall snow-covered mountains" on the Antarctic side.

While the Kingdom of Antangil is said to be on "continental land," it in fact subtly reproduces the island configuration of More's Utopia. The empire is flanked by two rivers, Iarrit to the east and Bachil to the west, that outline the *Terra Australis* continent as a south-north rectangle that is amusingly described as "an elongated square." This rectangle, formed by natural boundaries, is split down the middle by the Great Pachinquir Gulf, a hundred leagues deep and seventeen leagues wide. The gulf, occupying the same longitudinal axis as the two border rivers and located exactly at the midpoint between them, is also the place where the four rivers "that have coursed throughout the better part of this Kingdom pour forth." Whereas this topography may recall the four rivers that course through the Earthly Paradise, these rivers do not issue from the Fountain of Life at the center of the garden, but come from every extremity, meandering and emptying into the very heart of the Kingdom – into this vertical Mediterranean expressed in the figure of the Gulf of Pachinquir. The capital, Sangil, where the seat of government and principal church are housed, is quite naturally situated "at the far end of the Gulf of Pachinquir," in other words at the exact center of the map. More's Amaurotum is situated likewise in the middle of the bay that indents the insular circle and gives it its crescent form. A similar crescent shape can be glimpsed, almost like an after-image, in the approximate shoe that is embedded in the seemingly square geography of Antangil.

The Kingdom of Antangil, like all utopias, closes in upon itself and is difficult to approach from the outside. Except for the natural harbors formed by the mouths of the two border rivers, the surrounding ocean is so fraught with reefs and boulders that access is all but impossible. The entrance to the Gulf of Pachinquir – "as gentle and tranquil as its name proclaims" – is the only safe ingress into the Kingdom, despite the nearby encroaching Island of Corylée obstructing three-quarters of the passageway. The remaining two narrow passes on the Kingdom's other flank are easily guarded. A volcano, "or a Vesuvius," in a state of perpetual eruption sits on the edge of the island as a convenient substitute lighthouse.

The Kingdom's vertical span, a longitudinal replica of the continent, allows for the simultaneous presence of all climatic conditions, from the coldest and driest to the warmest and most humid,

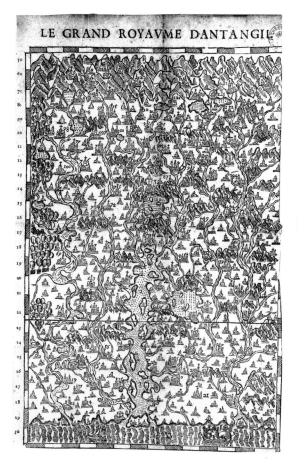

The First French Utopia

Histoire du grand et admirable royaume d'Antangil incogneu jusques a present à tous historiens et cosmographes: composé de six vingts provinces tres belles et tres fertiles. Avec la description d'icelui et de sa police nompareille, tant civile que militaire. De l'instruction de la jeunesse. Et de la religion. Le tout compris en cinq livres, par I. D. M. G. T
Leyden: Jean Le Maire [Saumur, Thomas Portau], 1616
BNF, Réserve des Livres Rares

The author of the first French Utopia, which appeared a century after More's, has never been identified. Voyages to the East Indies form the framework of the novel; the narrator, finding himself in Bantan on the island of Java in 1598, receives the ambassador of a mysterious Christian kingdom located on the southern part of the island. The major part of the rest of the work is devoted to a detailed description of the institutions, education, military, and religion of the inhabitants, revealing the reformist ideas of the author, which were inspired by the situation in France shortly after the assassination of Henry IV. This engraved woodcut depicts the capitals of the kingdom's 120 provinces, identified by number in a separate key.

"thereby making this land all the more rich and delectable, as it possesses in and of itself what other lands have only in part."⁴⁴ In variety, if not in its breadth, Antangil is an entire universe. Four climatic zones are stacked south to north: the low-lying slopes of the Sariché Mountains, cold and opulent in grassland and livestock; next, a temperate zone; then an extremely hot and dry area, marking off the lower third of the map, around the Tropic of Capricorn; and finally an area, temperate at first but rainy, because of its proximity to the sea and the sea-winds ("contrary to what the Ancients believed," the author informs us), which extends beyond the Tropic of Capricorn in the direction of the Equator. Such climatic diversity translates into an abundance of riches – from the minerals that are extracted from the southernmost mountains to the pearls that are fished out of the Gulf of Pachinquir, "some of which are pale and white like our European ones and others that are crimson and brilliant like garnets and rubies."⁴⁵ Elsewhere, we find the most exotic and varied bounty, "such as coconuts, pineapples, bananas, mangoes, betel nuts, myrobalans, cinnamon, pepper, cloves, ginger, gum Arabic, benzoin, guaiacum grains, brazil nuts and many other exquisite fruits and woods and elixirs."

It is, in other words, heaven on earth. So it should come as no surprise that of all the animals that roam the Kingdom, the winged ones far outnumber the others. Not only are there birds from both the Old and the New World, but we also find the truly marvelous and legendary bird of paradise who lives on manna, dew, and aromatic scents, and perches on clove and cinnamon trees.⁴⁶

Once every detail of this wondrous geography has been inventoried, then the relentless utopian project can begin to take shape. In *Antangil*, More's principle of equality is replaced with a clear-cut class structure: the rich and the nobles on the one hand, and the people on the other. The Senate, elected by the Council of States, is formed by delegates from the twenty-six provinces, and is the true seat of power. The king, although elected to a life term, is always subject to dismissal and has a merely theoretical function. The State has exclusive ownership of all lands and mines, but it can lease them at three-year intervals to the highest bidder. Although there may very well be no poor in Antangil, just as there are none in Utopia, a strict hierarchy is enforced in all the civil, military, and ecclesiastic facets of society.

As one would expect, the author's Protestant background makes itself felt when he turns his attention to the religion of the Kingdom. The chosen faith here is an undeniable offshoot of Reform culture, although the utopian fiction allows certain liberties. In contrast to More's Utopia, the Kingdom of Antangil has the signal privilege of being Christian. A Brahmin from India, who was personally converted by St. Thomas, brought the gospel with him many years before. The man had miraculous powers that succeeded beyond all hope, and with the guidance of the Holy Spirit, he healed "the sick, the lame, the blind, those who suffered from dropsy, paralytics, epileptics" with the touch of his hand. Thus "verified by miracles," the Christian doctrine became the official religion and within eighteen months had spread to all the Kingdom's provinces. Temples were emptied of "idols" and images, just as many churches had been during the Reformation; inscriptions honoring false gods were erased and replaced by the "most meaningful passages of Scripture." The iconoclasm of these new converts is reminiscent of that of French and Flemish crowds in the early 1560s. In an effort to temper this enthusiasm for self-denial, the Lords of Antangil rush in to salvage "countless beautiful forms and paintings that could be used for the ornamentation of public buildings and private homes." Much as in England or the Low Countries, the museum steps in for the church.

Temple interiors are refurbished, a detail underlining the deep bond that links the Reformation to the utopian spirit. The spaces are cleansed by being emptied of adornments and furnishings; henceforth, there will be more room for the Word. Wooden benches are built to line the walls in a twelve-deep, tiered formation that recalls "the in-the-round mode of amphitheaters."⁴⁷ The floor pews, "interrupted by passageways," are reserved for the women. The Bishop sits at the top of the oval, raised above the twelfth row and facing the doorway. As in the first temples built by the reformed, this new cult forbids the cruciform layout with its suspect anthropomorphism. The figure of the temple makes sense only in terms of the living community reflected by the oval formation, the community gathering in a circle to contemplate itself united in Christ and joined by the Word. This temple without altar or holy sacrament or images is empty only in appearance; in fact, it is filled with the truth, inhabited by the spiritual Presence carried by each individual and made manifest by the assembly.⁴⁸

As the "true" religion had been established from the Kingdom's early days, Antangil need not grapple with the problem of ecclesiastic institutions.

Nonetheless, this Australian Christianity has a number of original characteristics. Whereas it purports to distance itself from the corrupted Catholicism of the West and be more closely allied to the early Evangelical teachings, it nonetheless harbors dogmas that stray from strict Calvinism. As we have seen, the images were cast out of the temples, and the cult is centered on sermons. Services begin and end with the singing of Psalms. The only sacraments are baptism and holy communion. At communion, worshippers receive the full grace of the sacrament, receiving the bread from the bishop's hand. They do not pray to the saints, "as there is but one Advocate of the Father who will intercede on our behalf," and they do not pray for the dead "as we absolutely deny that chimera known as Purgatory."[49] Instead, this church flagrantly contradicts the reform doctrine of *sola fide*, and places great weight on good deeds: "They believe that without good deeds none will be saved." Meat is allowed on fast days as well as on Fridays and Saturdays, "meat and fish vendors are open at all times, in keeping with the Apostle's doctrine." Abstinence and fasting are practiced only on the eve of high holy days – the Annunciation, Easter, Pentecost, Christmas, and the first day of the year. In an additional twist, this religion has a clergy and a well-defined hierarchy, distinguished by vestments in different colors: the bishops wear a narrow-sleeved robe of reddish violet serge that bears a "cross of palm and olive branches embroidered in silk, silver, and gold." The mores and doctrines of the clergy are supervised by the ministers or archpriests, who are given ten parishes apiece to oversee, whereas a bishop, in keeping with his higher office, oversees twenty-six provinces. This Protestantism tempered by Catholic pomp and hierarchies is reminiscent of Episcopalianism and other forms of Anglicanism.

Utopia and Colonization, from Antangil to Eden
Antangil represents every aspect of the transition from the early utopias of the Reformation to the imperiled utopias of the early German Enlightenment. The utopian model has found its geographic home on the mythic *Terra Australis*, and only on rare occasions will it venture elsewhere. Utopia no longer applies to a beleaguered minority ensconced inside a larger, dominant society, but to a society that resides in a vague and distant beyond. This vague and distant beyond is, nonetheless, part and parcel of the imperial dream of emerging colonial powers, namely Protestant England and Holland. The author of *Antangil* could not have been better versed in geography, it seems; and it was not in sport that he

or she came up with the name "Antangil." Rather, the author borrowed the name of an existing bay in northeast Madagascar. The learned toponymy that complements his or her map expertly mixes Indian and Amerindian roots to create a linguistically hybrid universe, a kind of verbal utopia located midway between Brahmin India and the America of Peru and Brazil. And the riches of this fabulous kingdom are not synonymous with the playful and somewhat childish pleasure of counting. Rather, they set forth a program of exploitation and trade.

Religious heterodoxy and deviance from established systems are the forebears of future utopias. More's *Utopia*, founded within the frame of declamation, sought to establish an ideal republic founded on the laws of reason and nature. After *Antangil*, however, utopian man no longer inhabited the edge but made his home on the margins. He ceased being the Catholic humanist, standing at the threshold of the Reformation to look beyond it or, on the other side of the tennis court, the one who projected the real dream of an evangelical society into a magical garden or the blueprint of an ideal city. The paths that would open henceforth into utopia, and Protestant utopias in particular, would emerge as both more desperate and more radical: they would include the exile's search for asylum on foreign continents and the self-imposed construction of compensatory universes by the shunned and marginalized.

In the first instance, the utopian dynamic found its way into the colonial projects that flourished around the time of the revocation of the Edict of Nantes, when persecuted French Protestants, looking for a refuge, obeyed the biblical injunction to flee "perverted Babylon" and to found a New Jerusalem that conformed to the Evangelical ideal. Along similar lines, we find colonial tracts urging Huguenots to come and settle the Carolinas,[50] or again, in 1689, the project of Henri Duquesne (eldest son of the admiral) "to found the Island of Eden," in reality Bourbon Island, known today as Réunion. Beginning in the 1650s, the massive settlements of nonconformist Protestant colonies in North America – Mennonites in Delaware, Quakers in Pennsylvania, the Moravian Brotherhood – were, as Jean-Michel Racault has noted, part of the same impulse.[51] Henri Duquesne's project was doomed to terrible failure, although it did produce the idyll of Rodrigues, recounted by François Le Guat, who with seven companions was stranded for two years on the smallest of the Mascareignes Islands with its miraculously preserved flora and fauna. Utopia then turned to the Robinsonade; Le Guat's "true tale" may have been a source for Daniel Defoe's famous work. The detailed economic and social plan Duquesne envisaged for his ideal society was eventually restored to a simpler Adamic universe in a land of milk and honey where the prey offered itself up to the hunter.[52] And so the elitist utopia was supplanted by a primitive one, which in turn gave way to a pastoral world inspired by Honoré d'Urfé's *L'Astrée*; this progression is not unlike the one undergone a century and a half earlier by a Huguenot minority on a remote Brazilian island during the brief experiment of French Antarctica (1555–60). The cobbler and future minister Jean de Léry related how, after a few months of difficult cohabitation with Villegagnon, the Catholic head of the colony, he and his brethren chose savagery and its freedoms over civilization and its servitude and joined their lot to that of the Indian cannibals of the region.[53]

The other path opened to reformist utopia by *Antangil* is one of marginality and rupture. Calvinism had already been modified and even challenged in *Antangil*; the primacy that was given to good deeds was a major departure that sought to restore trust in fellow human beings and in the world and, consequently, legitimized the tutelary role of the clergy. But this utopia still registers as a collective project. While it may stray at the level of dogma, it is, nonetheless, firmly rooted in Protestant projects of colonial expansion and completely subscribes to the dream of refuge in a distant land. As the century draws to a close, everything will change with the appearance of Foigny and Vairasse d'Allais. Under cover of a return to nature, utopia will henceforth elicit models that will be impossible to apply in reality. The model, increasingly distorted, will culminate in the disturbingly unnatural world of Foigny's Hermaphrodites. In due course, the new counter-utopias will come full circle to the archipelago of monsters in Rabelais's Fourth Book, and then *Gulliver's Travels* will appear, to reinvest the utopian model with a striking and unprecedented topicality.

Crisis Utopias of the Reformation

Utopias and Counter-utopias of the Classical Age: Foigny, Vairasse d'Allais, Tyssot de Patot
The Edict of Fontainebleau, revoking the Edict of Nantes in 1685, launched the long century during which Protestantism was legally banned in France.

The reformed community found itself displaced; it had entered its desert, so to speak, and utopia became one of the means to counter a scandalous history, by making the Reformation a non-place. In *Les Entretiens des voyageurs sur la mer*, published in 1715, the minister Gédéon Flournois points to the unsteady bridge of a ship at sea as the only place left for free expression. In the same book, which combines fiction with controversy, we encounter a solitary Protestant, ingeniously borrowed from the Catholic tradition of holy seclusion, who has cloistered himself in a grotto to live in accordance with his conscience and far from the society of others.[54]

In truth, utopias often preceded fact: Gabriel de Foigny's *La Terre Australe connue* dates from 1676 and Denis Vairasse d'Allais's *L'histoire des Sévarambes* was published between 1678 and 1679. Only Tyssot de Patot's *Les Voyages et aventures de Jacques Massé* came later: predated to coincide with the millenarianism of 1710, the book was actually published between 1714 and 1717. It is the least original of the three; in it, utopia proper is consigned to a limited space – fittingly located on the Australian hemisphere, somewhere in the vicinity of the as-yet-undiscovered Kerguelen – where an ideal republic unfolds its methodical geometry on a rigorously flat landscape that recalls the polders of Holland.[55]

According to Raymond Trousson,[56] the compensatory claim is nowhere more apparent than in the case of Denis Vairasse d'Allais (or Veiras d'Alès), an obscure soldier and clientless lawyer, using the anagram Sévarias to announce himself to the world as a brilliant legislator and founder of utopias. *Histoire des Sévarambes* is the most accomplished of all romantic utopias. Its skillful balance of fictional statistics and the imaginary journey make it a paradigmatic example of a "narrative utopia," to use Jean-Michel Racault's term. The work is organized into five sections: the first relates an ill-fated seafaring adventure that culminates in shipwreck on *Terra Australis* and a Robinsonian scenario; the second part includes the usual anecdotes of utopian tourism and describes how Siden (anagram of Denis) and his companions came to live among the Sévarambes for fifteen years; the ensuing three sections are entirely devoted to the history and mores of the Sévarambes. Sévarais, the civilizing hero of the narrative, hails from Persia, adheres to the Parsee faith, and worships fire and the Sun. He founds a "heliocratic" monarchy in *Terra Australis*, of which he is only the vice-king and the great priest, like Moses among the Hebrews or Calvin, the Lieutenant of God in the Republic of Geneva.

Apart from its reference to such illustrious fore-bears, this form of rule seeks to address the great political preoccupation of the day "by instituting a government that excludes tyranny but does not forego stability and power."[57] In a certain sense, this *heliocracy* is a compromise between freedom of conscience and the prestige of the Sun King. And, for good measure and all around happiness, private property is abolished, and hereditary nobility dispensed with too.

As had already been the case in *Antangil*, here, too, religion figures prominently. This time we are not simply presented with the tenets of an ideal religion; the book begins its discussion of faith by invoking a counter-example. It seems an imposter had preceded the happy religious reform brought about by Sévarais; Stroukaras-Omigas, a miracle-worker and healer, had, at an earlier date, founded a solar religion, but his cult was founded on false miracles that are strangely reminiscent of those performed by Moses and Jesus. This false prophet claimed to have been fathered by the Sun, and he surrounded himself first with apostles who sang his praises and then with a corrupt and profit-hungry clergy. Sévarais countered his predecessor's lies with a cult that centered around a reasonable Trinity com-posed of the Sovereign God Khodimbas, also known as The Great Being and inaccessible to mortals, as well as a subordinate God, the Sun, who was seen as "a salutary conduit through which all the blessings and benefactions of the Great Being who sustains us flow to us," and finally, a goddess of the homeland. The invisible God is reminiscent of Pachacamac in ancient Peru, and the cult of the homeland was inspired by Sparta, Athens, and Rome.

The religious pastiche that was already appar-ent in *Antangil* is substantiated by Vairasse d'Allais, a great reader and a fervent compiler of utopias, who cannot pass on the opportunity to mention (so as to immediately distance his work from theirs) "Plato's *Republic*, Thomas More's *Utopia*, or the *New Atlantis* of Lord Chancellor Bacon." This pastiche is further confirmed by the presence of a minority Christian sect living among the tolerant Sévarambes. The so-called Giovannites, named after their founder Giovanni, a Venetian who had been governor of Sévarias, practice Holy Commu-nion like the Calvinists, but deny the Trinity and the eternal divinity of the Son of God, making them Arians or Socinians; but this does not mean that they do not also believe in "almost everything that is believed by the Roman Church, such as Purgatory, the prayer for the dead, the invocation

of the saints, the merit of good deeds," and revere the Pope as the true successor of Saint Peter.

These contradictions, not to say inconsisten-cies, are bewildering to say the least. They attest, from *Antangil* onward, to utopia's tendency to temper Calvinism and to a formidable wave of uniformity. All rites and beliefs are equal. Diverse religious dogmas are seen as interchangeable approximations of the truth, and as such can be combined in varying proportions. What lies behind Vairasse d'Allais's thinking, as Trousson has suggest-ed, is in all probability the materialism with which the philosopher Scromenas brings his argument to a close. The deism of the Sévarambes does not offer serious reasons for life – it is simply the most sensi-ble and tolerable of religions.

A similar anthropological pessimism was already evident in Gabriel de Foigny's *La Terre Australe connue*, published at a false address in Geneva in 1676 and reissued, with major cuts, in 1692.[58] Foigny, who was even more marginal than Vairasse d'Allais, went from being a Franciscan monk to a heterodox Protestant before returning to Catholicism shortly before he died. This lifelong dissident had been influenced by Isaac La Peyrère's *Préadamites* and would in turn influence the fourth and last of *Gulliver's Travels*.[59] His impossible search for a peaceful haven would take Jacques Sadeur, the hero of *Terre Australe connue*, broken in body and spirit and pursued by an inexplicable curse, into imaginary realms far beyond the confines of the known world. His odyssey ends with his suicide by drowning shortly after he reaches the port of Livorno.

Sadeur had spent thirty-two years of his turbulent life among the hermaphrodite peoples of *Terra Australis*, who reproduced themselves through a mysterious parthenogenesis. Blood and sperm were notably absent from the procreative functions, which, furthermore, they viewed with utmost repugnance. Their aversion was so pronounced that at the mere mention of their "beginnings"[60] they would quickly volunteer that children grew inside them in the same way that fruits grow on trees. Even though they did not cover their bodies, their nakedness did not stir up desire, and their genitalia, which were smaller than the norm, were not very noticeable. During pregnancy, their habitually flat stomachs swelled almost imperceptibly, and even though both sexes were present in their bodies, these exhibited very few apertures or protuber-ances. Their bodies were perfect and perfectly closed. The female part of their organism did not produce "the monthly discharge common to women when not pregnant."[61] And their male half was completely unmoved by the sight of "brethren" with rounded and vermillion teats.

Their dietary practices show a similar restraint and restriction. Their appetites were so frugal that they barely produced any waste; a week could elapse before they produced their insignificant stool. They subsisted solely on a diet of fruits and scoffed at cooking as an unnatural practice; the little they did eat was in hiding, as if the activity itself was shameful. As, in fact, it was – because man "should abstain as much as he is able." As for nourishing themselves, "they steal away and eat in private."[62] All in all, they despised all activities that reminded them of their animal nature. Their particular aversion to the consumption of meat was a case in point. This aversion was motivated by a spiraling fear of contagion; the inevitable outcome of such a practice would lead them to devour their own kind. They held that "animal flesh is similar to that of men, and eating the former could lead to eating the latter."[63] *Terra Australis* purged itself of blood.

Purged from the center, blood flowed to the frontiers, where it was spilled in torrents. The wars they fought there spared neither women nor children nor the elderly; in keeping with an oft-repeated practice of the Old Testament, they celebrated their victories over the enemy by slaying all life including livestock. This recurring extermination of intruders on its peripheries is the paradoxical price this utopia must pay to safeguard itself from its own animality and to preserve its oblivion of the demands of the flesh. The "whole men" who inhabited this utopia were, in fact, demigods whose imperviousness to old age and disease drove them to kill themselves from boredom. This "humanity without sin and consequently, without salvation," to use Jean-Michel Racault's phrase,[64] forcibly pushed the vestiges of sacrificial thinking outside its own territory. Thus, we witness a parody of the Eucharist taking place in Ausicant or Oscamt, an island in a neighboring archipelago, where Jacques Sadeur, on his return from the Australian continent, was captured, stripped of his clothing, and bound to a thirty-foot-high scaffold. His wrists and thighs were pierced, and the priests drank his blood while the crowd cheered. His imminent sacrifice was interrupted in the nick of time by the extremely fortuitous landing of a party of French corsairs.

By virtue of its aversion to flesh and ingestion, *Terra Australis* categorically falls under the sign of vomiting – or of "anthropemy" as Claude Lévi-Strauss would say.[65] It rejects, exterminates, and

burns all things that come from elsewhere. Oscamt, on the other hand, follows an anthropophagic regimen. It embraces the intruder and welcomes him into its innermost flesh. If we choose to read *La Terre Australe connue* as a theological allegory, we can easily discern an "image of Geneva's rigorous Calvinism"[66] in the first society it depicts and a clear allusion to Catholicism in the second one. The first model is bent, through the prism of fiction, toward a deism without ritual or sacrament, where each individual may pray to the divinity in accordance with individual spiritual and moral needs; the second model reveals a bloody and theatrical religion in which sacrifice is literally enacted for all to see. In its contempt for the body and its needs, the informal, silent cult reflects a Protestant sensibility.[67] The ritual excess and the grand sacrificial spectacle that exalts the carnal body before consuming it is an equally transparent allusion to the pomp and ritual of the Catholic Church during the Counter-Reformation.

In this transposition of his own historical situation, caught between Rome and Geneva, Gabriel de Foigny sets his hero on a course that mirrors his own painful fate – the trials and tribulations of a defrocked Franciscan monk who converted to Calvinism, a marginalized and rebellious figure in all respects, an unrelenting object of scandal and reprobation, who returned to die, after being cast out of Geneva for misconduct, in a convent in Savoie. But the scope of such an account must be expanded: between a religion that, confused by reason, expressed in the very name of nature a visceral horror of nature,[68] and another religion that bowed to excess and tottered on the brink of savagery, there was no choice at all.

Utopia as Imposter:
George Psalmanazar's Formosa Island
The individual known as George Psalmanazar, in all likelihood a Huguenot who fled France in the aftermath of the revocation of the Edict of Nantes, takes us on a voyage that is no less somber.[69] But rather than follow Foigny's example and have a hypothetical *Terra Australis*, replete with its geography, flora and fauna, and hermaphroditic peoples, emerge out of the ocean, he chose instead the beautiful and luxuriant Formosa island, familiar to all since the Renaissance, and proceeded to reinvent it. This strategy proved extremely successful; not only did he camouflage the fictional character of his endeavor, he even managed to have his hero and narrator live to tell the story. He was taken at his

word and used his imaginary account to secure for himself fame and a brilliant career that even included a Formosa Chair at Oxford University.

First published in London in 1704, *An Historical and Geographical Description of Formosa* is, in effect, one of the most famous hoaxes in travel literature.[70] This minutely detailed depiction transplanted the bloody ceremonies of the Aztec religion to a Far Eastern theocratic and cannibalistic society, thereby critiquing the energetic missionary efforts of Jesuits in that part of the world. The idolatry practiced by the Formosans had the ricochet effect of stigmatizing the Catholic concepts of sacrifice and Holy Mass. While his work was well received in London, where his *apologia* for Anglicanism was appreciated, George Psalmanazar was denounced as an imposter by the French Jesuits. Yet apart from their protestations, the account of this pseudo-Japanese expert went generally unchallenged for thirty years.

Formosa, in fact, tests the furthest limits of utopia; whereas it claims to be a real place, it is not a utopia in the strict sense of the term – it can be located on the map, and has a name and clearly defined contours. The book includes the country's main statistics, a map of the China Sea, a complete alphabet (which includes Greek and Hebrew characters), a grammar, drawings of a currency stamped with curious hieroglyphs, and a dress code that designates sex and social rank.

What is most striking about this work is its ability to convey a feeling of familiarity that makes even the most far-fetched incidents seem believable. The accounts of human sacrifices on Formosa contradicted the information that had been brought back by travelers up to that time. The purported magnitude of these slaughters simply defies common sense. And yet, such horror was not entirely alien; it was at the heart of the Catholic sacrament of the Eucharist as it had been spontaneously interpreted and cordially detested by Protestants. The Formosan utopia gave to this rite a spectacular dimension that was all the more scandalous for being perpetrated calmly in the neighboring countries of southern Europe, where the Roman Church had absolute dominion.

Every year, at least eighteen thousand male children perished as sacrificial victims on Formosa. There had certainly been precedents, the narrator informs us, for the bloody theocracy found on Formosa, and these among the greatest civilizations known to man, no less – the Greeks, the Romans, the Israelites. The risk of extinction posed to the nation by this sacrificial excess was circumvented through polygamy, a practice that ensured abundant progeny. Furthermore, the number eighteen thousand was not strictly enforced: the "positive law" that commanded it was not "followed to the letter."

The ritual is described with technical precision. The sacrifices could last for hours, as victims were lined up to have their throats cut and their hearts ripped out for good measure. There were no cries or tears or vain convulsions; the profound silence was broken only by the prayers of the officiating priests. These were followed by sacred hymns accompanied by flutes, kettledrums, and "other Instruments of Musick playing all the while."[71] The victim's flesh was chopped into little pieces and boiled in its own blood; it was then distributed among the faithful. The priests dexterously skewered the nuggets of manflesh that they offered in turn to the assembled men, women, and children over the age of nine, who approached the altar one by one and respectfully took the consecrated meat directly from the priests' hands; then they knelt on the ground and ate the morsel.

This is where the process of "sociological revolution" – which would, in time, receive the ultimate seal of approval from Montesquieu[72] – enters the picture. The observer of the Formosan rites remains unperturbed by these purportedly familiar ceremonies. On the other hand, he feels it his duty to enlighten his European readers through comparisons that strike him as appropriate; the after-shock of these connections will help to expose the strangeness of the most widely accepted local practices. To this end, we encounter ambiguous formulations such as "a kind of Communion" used in reference to the cannibalistic rituals of the Formosans.

An allegorical reading is consistently encouraged by the ensuing accounts of Formosan ceremonies and further fostered by footnotes addressed to the reader. Consequently, the Great Priest, whose privilege it is to rip out the hearts of children, has a mitre very much like a bishop's, and the "Cloth of a Violet-colour" which he wears looks like the scapular "such as are commonly us'd by the *Capuchines* in the *Romish* Church." Later on, the Great Priest's footwear will prompt comparisons to the sandals of the Capuchin order.[73]

Whereas the first part of the book stigmatizes Catholicism through an exotic aside, the second continues this condemnation through the complementary arguments of the narrative. George Psalmanazar so impressed a Jesuit priest with his intelligence that he was taken from the island and sent to Europe to be instructed in Catholicism. But despite his familiarity with spilt blood and the ingestion of human flesh, he was deeply repulsed by the dogma of transubstantiation. To escape the Inquisition, he fled to Cologne, where he made the acquaintance of Lutherans and learned of their concept of consubstantiation; he found it no less shocking than "Roman Transubstantiation." He did eventually find Calvinism more to his liking; lest we forget, the "real" Psalmanazar was in all likelihood a Huguenot, in defiance of the Edict.

Our Formosan hero proceeds to consult a Reform minister but shies away from the latter's adherence to the principle of absolute predestination. Disappointed yet again, he wanders from one faith to the next until he finds himself in the Low Countries, where he joyfully embraces Anglicanism, the only doctrine, in his view, that concurs with natural religion and the only one that is in harmony with the primitive Church.

When all is said and done, the Formosan fable relies on a luminous simplicity. The enigma presented as a geographic riddle is resolved in an edifying tale that culminates in a highly moral sentiment. In the aftermath of the revocation of the Edict of Nantes, such a testimonial constitutes a weighty argument in the struggle against the Roman Church and rising intolerance.

At around the same time, Daniel Defoe's Robinson Crusoe will reach a somewhat similar Pharisaic conclusion in his *Serious Reflections*. After an adventurous life of trials and tribulations, the colonizer of the Island of Despair will arrive at the comforting, and soon to become accepted, opinion that:

Nor will it be denied . . . that even among Christians, those who are more reformed, and farther and farther christianized, are still in proportion rendered more humane; more soft and tender; and we do find, without being partial to ourselves, that even the Protestant countries are much distinguished in the humanity and softness of their tempers: the meek, merciful disposition extends more among Protestants than among the Papists, as I could very particularly demonstrate from history and experience.[74]

Such a mark of approval no doubt pleased the Anglican readers of the *Serious Reflections* as much as it would have the readers of *Formosa*, but where did Psalmanazar really stand? The cannibal allegory, after all, could also be understood in another way. There is no denying that Catholicism is an anthro-

pophagy, but is not the principle of absolute predestination promoted by Calvin and his disciples equally "monstrous"? Is it not as "monstrous" as the dogma of transubstantiation is "absurd"? On the occasion of a public dispute in Ecluse, in the Low Countries, the Formosan who had balked at baptism had the presence of mind to counter the outrage his interlocutors had expressed on learning about the practice of sacrificing children by saying that a God who "create[s] Men on purpose to make them eternally miserable, and to condemn them to this Misery before they are born," is "infinitely more cruel."[75] The lesson is that the symbol may be even more terrible than the reality. In their opposition to the Pope, the Calvinists did their best to reform and purify their religion to distance it from its original sacrificial constraints.[76] Be that as it may, they did not succeed in ridding it of the terror that haunts the human soul.

On his return from the counter-utopia of Formosa, the sage Psalmanazar, in keeping with the pattern documented several times in this study, opts for the religious golden mean, the path of compromise and reason. This hybrid solution attests to the author's genius for pastiche, a genius that is equally attested to by the overall implausibility of the island he created. It is only fitting that the imposter's lesson should have been an imposture. The choice of Anglicanism was well suited to the task of convincing his audience of the authenticity of his stance. But this proxy authenticity was a trick, a false truth, much like the allegorical geography that served as both the pretext and evidence for his case. *Formosa*, therefore, beyond the short-term service it supplied to the Reformation and enemies of the Jesuits, may very well have been Psalmanazar's ingenious way of thumbing his nose at the Reformation and at religion in all its forms.

Translated by Nadia Benabid

Notes

1 Karl Mannheim, *Ideology and Utopia: An Introduction to the Sociology of Knowledge*, trans. Louis Wirth and Edward Shils; with a preface by Louis Wirth (London and New York: Routledge, 1991). Cited by Jean-Michel Racault, *L'Utopie narrative en Angleterre et en France, 1675–1761* (Oxford: The Voltaire Foundation, at the Taylor Institution, 1991), 11.

2 Jean Wirth, *Luther: Etude d'histoire religieuse* (Geneva: Droz, 1981), 49.

3 Quoted in Norman Rufus Colin Cohn, *The Pursuit of the Millennium: Revolutionary Millenarians and Mystical Anarchists of the Middle Ages* (London: Maurice Temple Smith Ltd., 1970), 248.

4 Ibid., 245–46.

5 Wirth, 50.

6 Ibid., 74.

7 Cohn, 272.

8 On this distinction, see Racault, 7–19.

9 See Patrick Dandrey, *L'Eloge paradoxal: De Gorgias à Molière* (Paris: Presses Universitaires de France, 1997), especially the chapter devoted to the "Paradoxical Montaigne," 137–73.

10 For excellent examples of declamation, see Pascal Quignard, *Albucius*, trans. Bruce Boone (Venice, Calif.: Lapis Press, 1992), 12. This work, in which fifty-three fictional premises lead to fifty-three novels that are as rigorously logical as they are implausible, offers excellent examples of declamation.

11 See especially Andre Tournon, *Montaigne: La glose et l'essai* (Lyon: Presses Universitaires de Lyon, 1983), 203–28.

12 Michel de Montaigne, "Of Friendship," Book I, Chapter 28, in *The Complete Essays of Montaigne*, trans. Donald M. Frame (Stanford, Calif.: Stanford University Press, 1958), 135. See Jean Lafond, "Le Discours de la Servitude volontaire de la Boétie et la rhétorique de la déclamation," in *Mélanges sur la littérature de la Renaissance à la mémoire de V.-L. Saulnier* (Geneva: Droz, 1984), 736. For a comparative study of La Servitude and "Of Cannibals," see Frank Lestringant, *Cannibals: The Discovery and Representation of the Cannibal from Columbus to Jules Verne*, trans. Rosemary Morris (Cambridge, England: Polity Press, 1997), 106–10.

13 Ibid., 144.

14 Montaigne, Book I, Chapter 31, 150–59.

15 Jacques Chomarat, *Grammaire et rhétorique chez Erasme*, 2 vols. (Paris: Les Belles Lettres, 1981), 2: 935.

16 Ibid., 2: 940.

17 Desiderius Erasmus, *The Praise of Folly*, in *The Praise of Folly and Other Writings: A New Translation with Critical Commentary*, chosen, trans., and ed. Robert M. Adams (New York: Norton, 1989), Chapter VIII, 10–11.

18 Lafond, 740.

19 Raymond Ruyer, *L'Utopie et les utopies* (Paris: Presses Universitaires de France, 1950), 9.

20 André Thevet, *Le Grand Insulaire et Pilotage, ca. 1588* (Paris, Bibliothèque nationale de France, Manuscrits, français, 15452, f. 6r).

21 See Claude Lévi-Strauss, *The Story of Lynx*, trans. Catherine Tihanyi (Chicago: University of Chicago Press, 1995), 217. "The wise person finds intellectual and moral hygiene in the lucid management of this schizophrenia."

22 Luis de Matos, "L'Utopia de Thomas More et l'expansion portugaise," Chapter VIII (pp. 382–422) in his *L'Expansion portugaise dans la littérature latine de la Renaissance* (Lisbon: Fundação Calouste Gulbenkian, 1991).

23 Francis Bacon, *The Advancement of Learning* (1605), in *Francis Bacon*, ed. Brian Vickers. *The Oxford Authors* (Oxford and New York: Oxford University Press, 1996).

24 The most thorough commentary is that of Erich Auerbach, *Mimesis: The Representation of Reality in Western Literature*, trans. Willard R. Trask (Princeton, N.J.: Princeton University Press, 1953).

25 François Rabelais, *Gargantua and Pantagruel*, trans. Burton Raffel (New York: Norton, 1990), Book 2, Chapter 2, 139.

26 Rabelais, Book 1, Chapter 52, 115.

27 Rabelais, Book 4, Chapter 57, 497 and 498. On this chapter, see Terence Cave, "Transformations d'un topos utopique: Gaster et le rocher de vertu," *Etudes rabelaisiennes* 21 (1988): 319–25.

28 Paris, Bibliothèque nationale de France, Estampes, Qb 1 (1585): wood engraving, colored stencil, 370 x 475 mm. On this document, see Philip Benedict, "Of Marmites and Martyrs: Images and Polemics in the Wars of Religion," pp. 109–37 in *The French Renaissance in Prints from the Bibliothèque Nationale de France* (Los Angeles: Grunwald Center for the Graphic Arts, University of California, Los Angeles, 1994). Complemented by Frank Lestringant, "Le Cannibale et la Marmite," *Bulletin du Bibliophile* (1996; no 1): 82–107.

29 Jean-Baptiste Trento and Pierre Eskrich, *Histoire de la Mappe-Monde Papistique: En laquelle est déclaré tout ce qui est contenu et pourtraict en la grande Table, ou Carte de la Mappe-Monde. Composée par M. Frangidelphe Escorche-Messes* (Geneva: Brifaud Chassediables [François Perrin]), 1567. Whereas copies of the *Histoire* are widely available, there are only three copies of the map itself, the *Mappe-Monde nouvelle papistique*. I consulted the one at the British Library (c. 160.c.7). Ms. K. Szykula kindly forwarded me a reproduction of the assembled and colored copy owned by Wroclaw University in Poland. A third copy is said to be at the Sonderhausen Museum in Germany. See Dror Wahrman, "From Imaginary Drama to Dramatized Imagery: The Mappe-Monde nouvelle papistique, 1566–1567," *Journal of the Warburg and Courtauld Institute* 54 (1991): 188, note 4. This copy is also colored. The two copies that were in Berlin before the war have apparently been lost. See also Frank Lestringant, "Une cartographie iconoclaste: La 'Mappe-Monde Nouvelle Papistique' de P. Eskrich et J.-B. Trento," pp. 99–120 in *Géographie du monde au Moyen Age et à la Renaissance*, ed. Monique Pelletier (Paris: Editions du C.T.H.S., 1990).

30 Rabelais, Book 5, Chapter 3, 532.

31 Bernard Palissy, *Recette véritable: 1563*, ed. Frank Lestringant and Christian Barataud (Paris: Macula, 1996), 68.

32 For this grand metaphor of the "book of nature," see Ernst Robert Curtius, *European Literature and the Latin Middle Ages*, trans. Willard R. Trask (New York: Pantheon Books, 1953), 319–26.

33 See my "Preface" to Palissy, *Recette véritable*, 42.

34 Eugenio Battisti, *L'Antirinascimento. Con un appendice di testi inediti* (Milan: Garzanti, 1989).

35 Jacques Perret, *Des fortifications et Artifices: Architecture et perspective* (Paris: Iaques Perret, 1601). In addition to the copy at the Bibliothèque nationale de France (Rés. V. 410), compiled haphazardly and missing several plates, including the one for the twenty-three-sided city, I have consulted the one at the Bibliothèque de l'Institut de France (Rés. Folio N. 160), which is properly mounted and lets one follow the progression of plates, starting with the "quadratur" citadel and ending with the "great and excellent edifice with two farmyards." Other copies have been reported by Bruna Conconi (see next note) at the Bibliothèque du Génie (Génie B-b fol. 13) and, incomplete, at the Bibliothèque de la Société de l'histoire du protestanisme français (in-fol. 396).

179

•

Utopia and the Reformation

36 This series of observations were inspired by the work of Bruna Conconi, "Il Salmo e il Compasso: Ovvero gli artifici di un inventore Riformato," *Studi di Letteratura francese* (vol. 20, Cinquecento visionario tra Italia e Francia) (Florence: L. S. Olschki, 1992), 411–36.

37 Perret, f. G2.

38 Saint Augustine, *The City of God Against the Pagans*, trans. George E. McCracken et al. (Cambridge, Mass.: Harvard University Press; London: W. Heinemann, 1957–72), Book XV, Chapter v: "Primus itaque fuit terrenae civitatis conditor fratricida: nam suum fratrem civem civitatis aeternae in hac terra peregrinantem invidentia victus occidit."

39 See *Les Frontières religieuses en Europe du XVe au XVIIe siècle. Actes du XXXIe colloque international d'études humanistes*, ed. Robert Sauzet (Paris: J. Vrin, 1992).

40 Perret, f. K.

41 *Histoire du grand et admirable royaume d'Antangil. Incogneu jusques à présent à tous Historiens et Cosmographes: composé de six vingts Provinces très-belles et très-fertiles. Avec la description d'icelui, et de sa police nom-pareille, tant civile que militaire. De l'instruction de la jeunesse. Et de la Religion. Le tout compris en cinqs livres* (Saumur: T. Portau, 1616). Reissued as *La Première Utopie française. Le Royaume d'Antangil (inconnu jusqu'à présent), réimprimé sur l'unique édition de Saumur, 1616, annotated by Frédéric Lachèvre* (La Roche-sur-Yon: Impr. Centrale de l'Ouest; Paris: La Connaissance, 1933).

42 Identification proposed by Alexandre Cioranescu, "Le Royaume d'Antangil et son auteur," *Studi Francesi* 7, no. 19 (January–April 1963): 17–25.

43 Lancelot-Voisin de La Popelinière, *Les Trois Mondes* (Paris: Pierre l'Huillier, 1582); critical edition, *Lès Trois Mondes*, ed. Anne-Marie Beaulieu (Geneva: Librairie Droz, 1997). Also see Frank Lestringant, *Le Huguenot et le sauvage: L'Amérique et la controverse coloniale, en France, au temps des guerres de Religion: 1555–1589* (Paris: Aux Amateurs de Livres, 1990), 226–34 and 257–61.

44 *La Première Utopie française*, I, II, p. 30.

45 Ibid., I, IV, p. 33.

46 Ibid., I, VII, p. 37.

47 Ibid., V, II, p. 124.

48 As noted by Bernard Reymond in "Les Styles architecturaux du protestantisme: un survol du problème," *Etudes théologiques et religieuses* 68, no. 4 (1993): 507–35, esp. 516, the reformed temple is not exactly a structure like all others, and its differences will become more pronounced as the centuries progress. It is modelled on the structure (rectangular, oval, or octagonal) that scholarly reconstructions attributed to the Temple of Solomon; hence the name with which the reformed chose to designate their place of worship. See also, in the same issue of *Etudes théologiques et religieuses*, Paul Tillich, "L'Architecture protestante contemporaine," 499–506, and Isabelle Grellier, "Les bâtiments d'église, une question théologique," 537–56.

49 *La Première Utopie française*, V, VIII, 132–33.

50 See on this point the works of B. Van Ruymbeke, especially his dissertation, *L' Emigration huguenote en Caroline du Sud sous le régime des Seigneurs Propriétaires* (Paris: Université de Paris III, 1995).

51 Jean-Michel Racault, introduction to François Le Guat, *Voyage et aventures de François Leguat et de ses compagnons en deux îles désertes des Indes orientales (1690–1698) . . . suivi de Recueil de quelques mémoires servant d'instruction pour l'établissement de l'île d'Éden par Henri Duquesne (1689)* (Paris: Editions de Paris, 1995), 16.

52 On this adventure, see Racault, *L'Utopie narrative*, 63–74.

53 Jean de Léry, *Histoire d'un voyage faict en la terre du Bresil* (Geneva: Antoine Chuppin, 1580); translated as *History of a Voyage to the Land of Brazil, otherwise called America*, trans. Janet Whatley (Berkeley: University of California Press, 1990).

54 Gédéon Flournois, *Les Entretiens des voyageurs sur la mer* (Cologne: P. Marteau, 1715).

55 Racault, *L'Utopie narrative*, 395–405.

56 Raymond Trousson, preface to Denis Vairasse d'Allais, *Histoire des Sévarambes* (Geneva: Slatkine, 1979), viii.

57 Ibid., xvi.

58 Gabriel de Foigny, *La Terre Australe connue* (Geneva: Jacques Vernevil, 1676); translated as *The Southern Land, Known*, trans. and ed. David Fausett (Syracuse, N.Y.: Syracuse University Press, 1993).

59 The profound kinship between Foigny and Swift has been brought to light by Racault, *L'Utopie narrative*, 594–95.

60 Foigny, *The Southern Land, Known*, Chapter 7, 76.

61 Ibid., 77.

62 Ibid., 79.

63 Ibid., Chapter 10, 102.

64 Racault, *L'Utopie narrative*, 513.

65 Claude Lévi-Strauss, *Tristes Tropiques*, trans. John and Doreen Weightman (New York: Modern Library, 1997), 473. "[F]rom the Greek émein, to vomit."

66 Racault, *L'Utopie narrative*, 509.

67 Gustave Lanson's observation in this regard is completely justified. See M. T. Bovetti-Pichetto, "Gabriel de Foigny, utopista et libertino," in *Studi sull'utopia*, ed. Luigi Firpo (Florence: L. Olschki, 1977), 388.

68 I concur in the formula of Henri Coulet, *Le Roman jusqu'à la Révolution* (Paris: A. Colin, 1967), 1: 283: "These natural beings are in truth horrified by nature, they see her as sullying and disgraceful, as sin itself."

69 See Frank Lestringant, "Travels in Eucharistia: Formosa and Ireland from George Psalmanazar to Jonathan Swift," *Yale French Studies*, no. 86 (1994): 109–25. For a different reading of the character and the work, see Tzvetan Todorov, *The Morals of History*, trans. Alyson Waters (Minneapolis: University of Minnesota Press, 1995), 93–99.

70 On the character, of French origin, and the sources for this work, see Percy G. Adams, *Travelers and Travel Liars, 1660–1800* (Berkeley: University of California Press, 1962), 93–97. And by the same author, *Travel Literature and the Evolution of the Novel* (Lexington: University Press of Kentucky, 1983), 71 and 108. In his later years, Psalmanazar became friends with Samuel Johnson.

71 George Psalmanazar, *An Historical and Geographical Description of Formosa*, 2nd ed. (London: Printed for M. Wotton [etc.], 1705), Book I, Chapter 7, 34.

72 On the concept of "sociological revolution," see Roger Caillois's preface to Montesquieu, *Oeuvres complètes*, 2 vols. (Paris: Gallimard, 1949–51), 1: v. See G. May, "Sens unique et double sens: Réflexions sur les voyages imaginaires," *Le Diogène*, no. 152 (October–December 1990): 3–21.

73 Psalmanazar, Book I, Chapter 16, 63.

74 Daniel Defoe, *Serious Reflections of Robinson Crusoe, With His Vision of the Angelic World*, Vol. 3 of *The Life and Adventures of Robinson Crusoe, of York, Mariner* (London: Printed at the Logographic Press; and sold by J. Walter, 1790), Chapter IV, 129–30.

75 Psalmanazar, Book II, 207.

76 I address this problem in *Une sainte horreur, ou, le Voyage en Eucharistie: XVIe–XVIIe siècle* (Paris: Presses Universitaires de France, 1996).

Gregory Claeys and Lyman Tower Sargent

On the Frontiers of Utopia: Satires and Robinsonades

IN 1719, Daniel Defoe published *The Life and Strange Surprizing Adventures of Robinson Crusoe, of York, Mariner*, better known as *Robinson Crusoe*. In the first of its three volumes (the others are little known), Defoe described the experience of a shipwrecked sailor who establishes himself on an island using tools, including firearms, that he managed to bring ashore from the wreck. It is possible to argue at great length about *Robinson Crusoe* and whether or not it should be called a utopia. The crux of the question seems to us to be whether or not a solitary utopia is possible. Certainly Crusoe does not think so, and while the arrival of Friday helps, it is not sufficient to change the situation. While it might be possible to construct a solitary utopia, Defoe did not do so.

Most people appear to be first introduced to *Robinson Crusoe* in a children's version or a film; these versions have generally heightened the potentially utopian aspects of Crusoe's island and, after the shipwreck and the first few days, have downplayed Crusoe's continuing unhappiness. This has led some to believe that Defoe presented an idealized state of nature as a contrast to civilization. This is what most of Defoe's imitators did, but it is not what Defoe did. First, Crusoe spends most of his early days on the island retrieving as much as he can of the civilization that the wrecked ship still contains. Second, he survives only because he man-

ages to bring substantial stores and tools – the essence of civilization – to the island from the ship. Third, Crusoe is miserably unhappy most of his time on the island. Even though when finally rescued he is a bit ambivalent about leaving and, in a later work, returns to visit the colony that has been established on the island, he is not content while there. He survives and, in most senses, prospers only through the tools of civilization, and for all its weaknesses, that civilization is better than life alone or with only one other person.

Still, *Robinson Crusoe* gave rise to a genre of literature we call the Robinsonade (even though there were, as always, earlier models), which was for a time extremely popular, particularly in German; the most famous German Robinsonade is the book known as *Die Insel Felsenberg* (1731) by Johann Gottfried Schnabel. Among these works are some which are utopias.

The earliest Robinsonade predated *Robinson Crusoe* by some six hundred years. *Hayy Ibn Yaqzan* by Ibn Tufayl dates from twelfth-century Granada and might have been known by Defoe because English translations were published regularly from 1671 to 1710. *Hayy Ibn Yaqzan* is best thought of as a philosophical novel and traces the life through to adulthood of a man abandoned as an infant on an island. A very similar work was

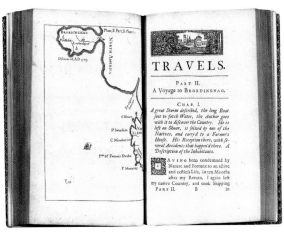

*The Ideal Society
of the Houyhnhnms*

[Jonathan Swift]
***Travels into several Remote Nations of the World. In Four Parts. By Lemuel Gulliver* [pseud.]**
London: Printed for Beng. Motte, 1726
NYPL, Rare Books Division

Straddling many literary genres, including travel narrative, political satire, and fiction, *Gulliver's Travels* invites its readers on a journey through, among other places, the kingdoms of Lilliput, Brobdingnag, Laputa, and Houyhnhnmland, pointing out the virtues and

vices of each strange new place and contrasting them with the England of Swift's day. Among the Houyhnhnms, a society of horses for whom reason is the guiding principle, Gulliver believes he has found the ideal society. Because of his resemblance to the Yahoos (a group of human-like animals governed only by their passions and detested by the Houyhnhnms), Gulliver is forced to leave and returns to England. This map of Brobdingnag locates this fictional country off the coast of what is now the state of Washington.

Brobdingnagians and Lilliputians

Jonathan Swift
***A Voyage to Brobdingnag
made by Lemuel Gulliver
in the year 1702 and
A Voyage to Lilliput by
Dr. Lemuel Gulliver 1699***
New York: The Limited
Editions Club, 1950
NYPL, Rare Books Division

Book designer Bruce Rogers
seems to have had his
Brobdingnagian and Lilliputian
readers in mind when he
created this modern edition
of the first two books of
Gulliver's Travels.

published in England in 1736. *The History of Autonous* by John Kirkby was later republished containing a utopia as *The Capacity and Extent of the Human Understanding* (1745).

Among the most influential of the Robinsonades was *Der schweizerische Robinson* [*The Swiss Family Robinson*] (1812–13) by Johann David Wyss. Constantly reprinted and translated, mostly as a book for children, and made into many films, *Der schweizerische Robinson* is the Robinsonade as utopia, presenting a family escaping the corruption of Europe to create a better life for themselves on an isolated island.

Versions of Defoe's tale have been published regularly from the eighteenth century to the present. Twentieth-century examples include *Vendredi* [*Friday*] (1985) by Michel Tournier and *Foe* (1986) by the South African writer J. M. Coetzee.

The Robinsonade, utopian or not, is a reflection of a worldview based on the various voyages of exploration. The world is a vast place with many unexplored, perhaps empty, perhaps eutopian islands left to discover. Therefore, one of the typical utopian forms includes a shipwreck and the accidental discovery of an isolated island inhabited by a people who are better, in at least some ways, than those landing on the island. This form, which increasingly had difficulty in achieving verisimilitude, lasted well into the twentieth century.

Gulliver and the Problem of Reason

Gulliver's Travels (1726) by Jonathan Swift is the basis for another subgenre of utopian literature, the Gulliveriana. The first books of *Gulliver's Travels* are satires on various aspects of contemporary culture, although there is a certain amount of disagreement over precisely what is being satirized. None of these books presented a eutopia. It might be possible to argue about whether or not Brobdingnag could be considered a eutopia, but there seems to be no good reason for doing so. Parts of the third book, particularly Laputa, might be considered dystopian but none are developed much beyond rather pointed satire. The eutopia is left for the fourth book, describing the island of the Houyhnhnms, a race of rational horses. Although there is considerable disagreement among critics, one point that Swift may have been making is that a wholly rational being cannot be human. The Houyhnhnms are rational by nature. As Swift said, "As these noble *Houyhnhnms* are endowed by Nature with a general Disposition to all Virtues, and have no Conceptions or Ideas of what is evil in a rational Creature; so their grand Maxim is, to cultivate *Reason*, and to be wholly governed by it. Neither is *Reason* among them a Point problematical as with us, where Men can argue with Plausibility on both Sides of a Question; but strikes you with immediate Conviction; as it must needs do where it is not mingled, obscured, or discoloured by Passion and Interest."[1] These rational beings

Island Paradise

The story of Robinson Crusoe is a glorification of self-reliance, hard work, piety, and common sense. Crusoe, shipwrecked on an island for twenty-eight years, created a small island paradise where he was master over all of nature and "wanted nothing but what [he] had, and had nothing but what [he] wanted."

The frontispiece of Part 1 shows him standing with guns salvaged from the shipwreck, while the map at the beginning of Part 3 depicts the island.

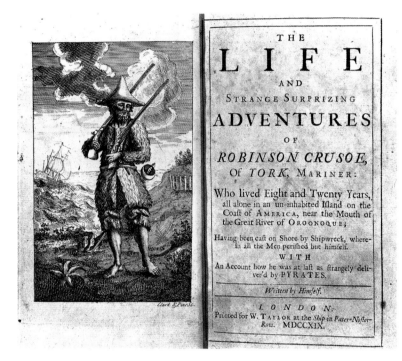

left

[Daniel Defoe]
The Life and Strange Surprizing Adventures of Robinson Crusoe, of York, Mariner: Who lived Eight and Twenty Years, all alone in an un-inhabited Island on the Coast of America, near the Mouth of the Great River of Oroonoque; Having been cast on Shore by Shipwreck, where-in all the Men perished but himself. With An Account how he was at last as strangely deliver'd by Pyrates. Written by Himself
London: Printed for W. Taylor, 1719
NYPL, Henry W. and Albert A. Berg Collection of English and American Literature

below

[Daniel Defoe]
Serious Reflections during the Life and Surprising Adventures of Robinson Crusoe: with his Vision of the Angelick World. Written by Himself
London: Printed for W. Taylor, 1720
NYPL, Henry W. and Albert A. Berg Collection of English and American Literature

have a language that has no word for lying or falsehood. The closest the Houyhnhnms can come is to speak of someone as having "*said the thing which was not.*"[2] Swift repeatedly points out the ways in which rationality eliminates unnecessary words for the Houyhnhnms. In addition to words for duplicity and for both emotion and business in marriage, words like "power," "government," "war," "law," and "punishment" are not found in the language. As Swift noted, "their Language doth not abound in Variety of Words, because their Wants and Passions are fewer than among us."[3]

The Houyhnhnms are devoid of sexual desire because "when the Matron *Houyhnhnms* have produced one of each Sex, they no longer accompany with their Consorts, except they lose one of their Issue by some Casualty. . . ."[4] In addition, "Courtship, Love, Presents, Joyntures, Settlements, have no place in their Thoughts; or Terms whereby to express them in their Language. The young Couple meet and are joined, merely because it is the Determination of their Parents and Friends: It is what they see done every Day; and they look upon it as one of the necessary Actions in a reasonable Being. But the Violation of Marriage, or any other Unchastity, was never heard of. . . ."[5]

Swift also noted that "Friendship and *Benevolence* are the two principal Virtues among the *Houyhnhnms*; and these not confined to particular Objects, but universal to the whole Race. For, a Stranger from the remotest Part, is equally treated with the nearest Neighbour, and where-ever he goes, looks upon himself as at home."[6]

Although Swift had Gulliver stress the bestiality of the Yahoos (humans) and the humaneness of the Houyhnhnms, the picture developed by this brief glance at the characteristics of the Houyhnhnms must raise some questions regarding Swift's intentions. Such a picture reinforces the notion that a purely rational creature cannot be human, but some utopians have in fact argued for purely rational human beings. Reflecting this, many anti-utopians have castigated the entire utopian enterprise as trying to dehumanize all humankind precisely because the anti-utopians contend that utopians propose a purely rational life.

Swift was certainly doing more than one thing with his horses. First, he was making the point about reason. Second, the Houyhnhnms are admirable creatures, and, of course, even more so in contrast with the grossness of the Yahoos. Therefore, Swift appears to suggest that it might be a good thing to emulate the Houyhnhnms in some

respect. Third, the contrast with the Yahoos does point to some of the reasons for Swift's seeming misanthropy; the Yahoos may be caricatures, but like all good caricatures, they exaggerate only characteristics that are present.

Thus, Swift does not appear to have held up either the Yahoos or the Houyhnhnms as completely worthy of emulation. The Yahoos are, unfortunately, human; the Houyhnhnms are horses. Certain human characteristics may be held in the gross form of the Yahoos (who come straight from medieval tales of the wild man) but to be totally rational would be inhuman.

Gulliver's Travels has produced a voluminous literature of imitators, although in many cases the imitation is limited to the use of the name Lemuel Gulliver. The imitations have continued well into the twentieth century, with *The Mistress of Lilliput* (1999) by Alison Fell being the most recent.

The best known of the Gulliveriana is probably *Nicolai Klimii iter subterraneum* (1741) by Ludvig Holberg, but Holberg, like most of the imitators of Swift, fails to be as subtle as Swift in his commentary. The points of the caricatures tend to be obvious and leave us with none of the doubts regarding meaning that we have with Swift.

Notes

1 Jonathan Swift, *Gulliver's Travels*, ed. Paul Turner. The World's Classics (Oxford and New York: Oxford University Press, 1991), 272–73.

2 Ibid., 237.

3 Ibid., 244.

4 Ibid., 274.

5 Ibid.

6 Ibid., 273.

See pp. 189, 188, 197.

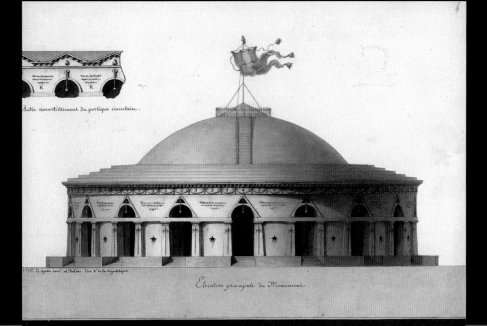

Autre amortissement du portique circulaire.

Élévation principale du Monument.

Développement des lunettes C.

Intérieur du lieu des Assemblées.

Utopia and Revolutions

Utopianism and the American Revolution

Lyman Tower Sargent

THE AMERICAN Revolution is still thought of primarily as a political revolution, as opposed to the supposedly more far-reaching social revolution in France and the later Communist revolutions in countries like Russia, China, and Cuba. While it is true that the American Revolution has been read as narrowly focused on ridding the country of the British, and it is true that many Americans who held positions of power before the revolution were also in power after the revolution, there were significant and deeply rooted changes in American society that make it possible to talk about the "radicalism" and "utopianism" of the American Revolution.

Historically the key document in the revolution is the Declaration of Independence (1776), written by Thomas Jefferson and revised by the Continental Congress. Closely modeled on *The Second Treatise of Government* (published 1690) by John Locke, the Declaration of Independence uses the social contract theory as presented by Locke to argue that government is based on the consent of the people and that such consent can reasonably be withdrawn when one of the contracting parties (here, the British) violates the contract. Thus, much of the Declaration is taken up with a detailed list of the ways in which the British have broken the contract, thereby justifying the revolution.

Jefferson's initial draft of the Declaration included one significant criticism that was deleted by the Congress, a criticism of slavery. Such criticism was not acceptable to the Southern states, and the controversy illustrates central tensions in American attitudes that have persisted throughout American history, about the nature of equality and the extent to which rights should be accessible to all.

Still, the ringing words of the Declaration "that all men are created equal; that they are endowed by their Creator with certain unalienable ["inalienable" in Jefferson's draft] rights; that among these are life, liberty, and the pursuit of happiness [modifying Locke's "life, liberty, and property"]" establish two

of the main themes of American utopianism: equality and rights. The former was manifested in movements to eliminate the property qualification for voting, to abolish slavery, and to eliminate limitations on voting based on race and gender, and, in the twentieth century, by attempts during the Civil Rights Movement and since to make these realities. The latter theme is illustrated by the fact that most of these movements for equality were expressed as movements to grant rights. Americans have, since the Declaration, tended to define equality as an equality of rights.

As many historians have noted, another major theme of the American Revolution was the tension between virtue and corruption. Most of the political theorists of the revolutionary period, like John Adams, Jefferson, and Tom Paine, believed that human beings were capable of being virtuous citizens, but that they were also corruptible, usually by power. The theorists differed on how to solve the problem: Jefferson and Paine leaned toward strong limitations on power, such as annual elections or the expiration of all laws after a specified period. Adams wanted to ensure that the least corruptible got into office and were able to stay there, albeit with various checks to limit them in case they were too weak. Both Adams and Jefferson believed that a system of education should be established to identify and assist "the natural aristocracy" who should become the leaders. As a result, Jefferson founded the University of Virginia. All these devices were intended to ensure that society was capable of both creating virtuous citizens and limiting the possibility of corruption. Such devices were meant to make for not only a good government but also the best life for all citizens.

Some took the desire for virtue a few steps further. Benjamin Franklin recorded in his *Autobiography* (1791 in an incomplete version) that he had "conceiv'd the bold and arduous project of arriving at moral perfection" and specified thirteen virtues that he believed "necessary or desirable." He then placed these virtues in the order in which he would attempt to achieve them (from "temperance" to "humility") and tested his success daily. Franklin's *Poor Richard's Almanac* (1732–57) was one of his attempts to provide moral instruction to the people

The Signers of the Declaration of Independence

This famous scene, with its accompanying key, was painted
by John Trumbull between 1786 and 1820. Trumbull consulted
extensively with Thomas Jefferson and John Adams to correctly
portray the scene of June 28, 1776, when Jefferson submitted
his draft of the Declaration of Independence to John Hancock,
President of the Continental Congress. The image depicts forty-
eight of the signers of the Declaration, thirty-six of them painted
from life. The painting had numerous incarnations: it was reproduced life-size on the walls of the Capitol rotunda in Washington,
D.C.; it was engraved in 1823 by Asher B. Durand; and in 1896,
it was reproduced on a U.S. postage stamp.

Although Durand is better known as a painter, his long career
as an engraver was launched with this scene. The large size of
the print made it difficult to sell, but its artistic quality ensured
Durand's success for many years.

**Asher B. Durand
after John Trumbull**
*The Declaration of
Independence of the
United States of America*
Engraving, 1823
NYPL, Miriam and Ira D. Wallach
Division of Art, Prints and
Photographs

**Asher B. Durand
after John Trumbull**
*Key to The Declaration
of Independence of the
United States of America*
Engraving, [1823]
NYPL, Miriam and Ira D. Wallach
Division of Art, Prints and
Photographs

A Declaration by the Representatives of the UNITED STATES OF AMERICA in General Congress assembled.

When in the course of human events it becomes necessary for one people to dissolve the political bands which have connected them with another, and to assume among the powers of the earth the separate and equal station to which the laws of nature & of nature's god entitle them, a decent respect to the opinions of mankind requires that they should declare the causes which impel them to the separation.

We hold these truths to be self-evident; that all men are created equal; that they are endowed by their Creator with inherent & inalienable rights; that among these are life, liberty, & the pursuit of happiness; that to secure these rights, governments are instituted among men, deriving their just powers from the consent of the governed; that whenever any form of government becomes destructive of these ends, it is the right of the people to alter or to abolish it and to institute new government, laying it's foundation on such principles & organising it's powers in such form as to them shall seem most likely to effect their safety & happiness. prudence indeed will dictate that governments long established should not be changed for light & transient causes. and accordingly all experience hath shewn that mankind are more disposed to suffer while evils are sufferable, _____ themselves by abolishing the forms they are accustomed. but when a long train of abuses & usurpations, begun at a distinguished period & pursuing invariably the same object, evinces a design to reduce them under absolute despotism, it is their right, it is their duty, to throw off such government & to provide new guards for their future security. such has been the patient sufferance of these colonies; & such is now the necessity which constrains them to expunge their former systems of government. the history of the present king of Great Britain is a history of unremitting injuries & usurpations, among which appears no solitary fact to contradict the uniform tenor of the rest; but all have in direct object the establishment of an absolute tyranny over these states. to prove this let facts be submitted to a candid world, for the truth of which we pledge a faith yet unsullied by falsehood

He has refused his assent to laws the most wholesome & necessary for the public good:

he has forbidden his governors to pass laws of immediate & pressing importance, unless suspended in their operation till his assent should be obtained; & when so suspended he has neglected utterly to attend to them:

he has refused to pass other laws for the accommodation of large districts of people, unless those people would relinquish the right of representation in the legislature, a right inestimable to them & formidable to tyrants only:

Manuscript Copy of the Declaration of Independence

**Thomas Jefferson
The Declaration of Independence**
Philadelphia, July 1776
NYPL, Manuscripts and Archives Division

In June 1776, Thomas Jefferson was appointed by the Second Continental Congress to draft an eloquent statement declaring the independence of the British colonies in North America from the Crown. Drawing on the Virginia Bill of Rights, state and local declarations of independence, and the philosophers of the Enlightenment, Jefferson finished his draft in only two days. The entire Congress then met to edit the document (Jefferson characterized their work as mutilation), which was ratified on July 4. Among the deleted passages was a long condemnation of slavery. In the days following ratification, Jefferson made five copies of his original draft, underlining those passages that Congress had expunged, and sent the copies to five friends. This is one of three known surviving copies.

of the colonies, who he believed needed this assistance to become virtuous citizens.

Hence, it is clear that the American Revolution was expected to transform the lives of the people, not just change who governed them. The first Continental Congress (1774) did not just discuss relations with Britain, it banned such activities as racing horses and the theater.[1]

The New Constitution

J. P. Elven after H. Singleton
Washington Giving the Laws to America
Etching and engraving, ca. 1800
NYPL, Miriam and Ira D. Wallach
Division of Art, Prints and
Photographs

Combining Classical and biblical references, this image shows George Washington as Caesar, holding a stone tablet labeled "The American Constitution" in the manner of Moses holding the Ten Commandments.

Some Utopian Aspects of the French Revolution

Roland Schaer

Very early on, French revolutionaries were aware of being actors in a historic rupture that would open up a new era. Sentiment ran high beginning in the summer of 1789, after the taking of the Bastille, over the surrender of privileges and the Declaration of the Rights of Man; it took more radical forms after the fall of the monarchy and the proclamation of the Republic at the end of the summer of 1792. Now, this awareness of rupture, of historical swing, can be understood in various ways. For Condorcet, the revolutionary moment is certainly an episode of extreme density, a veritable acceleration of history, but it still belongs to the long process of continuous progress of the human spirit. In presenting his *Rapport et Projet de décret sur l'organisation générale de l'instruction publique* [*Report and Plan for a Decree on the General Organization of Public Instruction*] to the National Assembly on April 21, 1792, he added: "I long considered these views as dreams that could only be realized in an indeterminate future, and in a world in which I no longer exist. A happy event has suddenly opened enormous scope for the hopes of the human species; a single instant has put the distance of a century between today's man and tomorrow's." As we can see, while utopia put itself, like a dream, on the horizon of history, which was now about human perfectibility, the revolution had achieved an abrupt contraction of time, making happen in the present what had been far away in time. With Robespierre, the reading of the revolutionary process is quite different: it is no longer just a major moment in history, but a rupture so radical that it implied breaking with heritage and then founding from scratch the basic structures of human culture. His references to Rousseau feed the theme of *regeneration*, of the institution of a totally unprecedented age in which virtue triumphs – in short, the advent of a "new man" torn out of history. The revolution is ground zero.

Nevertheless, beyond this difference in opinion, and even if the utopian references of each vary – Robespierre refers to Rousseau, but also to the Salente of Fénelon's *Les Aventures de Télémaque* [*Adventures of Telemachus*], while Condorcet, in particular in the posthumous fragment on Atlantis, clearly belongs among the heirs of Francis Bacon – both had the feeling that utopia, precipitated by

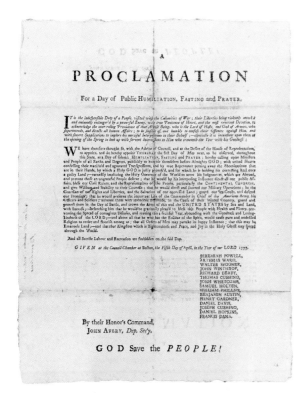

The Encouragement of Virtue

Massachusetts Bay Council
A Proclamation for a Day of
Public Humiliation, Fasting
and Prayer
Boston: [Benjamin Edes], 1777
NYPL, Rare Books Division

This proclamation, issued by
the Massachusetts Bay Council, asks the colonists to set
aside May 1, 1777, as a day
of "solemn humiliation, fasting
and prayer" in order to gain
God's "merciful interposition
on their behalf" during the
American Revolution; at least
four other days of thanksgiving or fasting were declared
that year. Such proclamations
had been issued in Massachusetts since the first Puritan

settlements were established
there in the seventeenth
century, and it was deemed
appropriate during the Revolutionary period to remind
the colonists of the divine
providence that had originally
brought them to America, and
to encourage the virtue that
would be necessary to prepare the new colonies for a
Republican government and
to prepare an upstanding
citizenry to sustain it. At
this time, the line "God Save
the People" replaced the
earlier "God Save the King";
later broadsides replaced
"People" with "America,"
the "American States," or
the "United States."

events, had passed from the kingdom of the imaginary to that of history; it was no longer merely a
program to be put into operation, but the latent
content of the hopes of a people on the move,
which put them at the top of the agenda.

We cannot review here all the utopian aspects
of the revolutionary process in France in the last
years of the eighteenth century. We will touch on
only two: the advent of national sovereignty, and
the attempts to "rationalize space" and above all
to "revolutionize time."

The Sovereign Nation

We must ask ourselves three questions.

1 What is the Third Estate? Everything.
2 What has it been until now in the political
order? *Nothing.*
3 What does it want to be? Something.[2]

It was in these terms, in *Qu'est-ce que le Tiers Etat*
[*What Is the Third Estate?*], a brochure that appeared
in January 1789, several weeks before the elections
to the Estates General took place, that Emmanuel
Joseph Sieyès announced the entry of the Third
Estate onto the political stage. The process that
would see its deputies proclaim successively the

National and then Constitutive Assemblies is contained within his text: the Third Estate is right to
identify itself with the whole Nation, since it is
composed of the active and productive elements of
the community; and any sovereignty has its source
only in the Nation, which comes first; therefore,
excluded until then from the "political order," the
Third Estate has complete legitimacy to "constitute" it. "The nation," wrote Sieyès, "is prior to
everything. It is the source of everything. Its will
is always legal; indeed it is the law itself."[3] By right,
the ensemble of citizens, now an ensemble of free
wills, finds itself projected into the position of
being the absolute origin of the law, that is to say,
into the position of Sovereign. Hence the citizen
utopia, wherein each person is defined as a member
of the body politic.

Political life will confront this utopia with the
real exercise of political power, particularly a power
that will remain both centralized, in a striking continuity between Jacobinism and absolute monarchy,
and yet delegated: "A democracy," writes Robespierre,
"is a state where the sovereign people, guided by laws
of their own making, do for themselves everything
that they can do well, and by means of delegates
everything that they cannot do for themselves."[4]

But as Rousseau had seen in *Du Contrat Social*
[*The Social Contract*], the very utopia of national

Hope for Change

Engravings symbolizing a new wave of hope for change, reconciliation, and concord were widely distributed in France at the end of the eighteenth century. These two engravings suggest the people's weariness of inequality before the law, particularly with regard to taxation, whose weight fell entirely on them; the caption for the male version observes: "Messrs Clergymen and Nobles not only paid nothing but also were granted graces, pensions that drained the State, and the Unhappy farmer could barely provide for his own subsistence." In 1788, when French financial director Jacques Necker denounced the exclusion "from public life of a whole class of men united to the prosperity of the State" and when Louis XVI granted to the Third Estate, or the common people, as many deputies as were granted to the nobility and the clergy combined, the political force of the people began to emerge.

A faut esperer q'eu s'jeu la finira ben tôt. Un païsant portant un Prélat, et un Noble
Colored etching, [1789]
BNF, Département des Estampes et de la Photographie

A faut esperer qu'eu se jeu la Finira bentot
Colored etching, [1789]
BNF, Département des Estampes et de la Photographie

The Rights of Man

Niquet le Jeune
*Déclaration des droits de
l'homme et du citoyen,
décrétés par l'Assemblée
Nationale dans les séances
des 20, 21, 23, 24 et 26 août
1789, acceptée par le Roi*
Paris: chez l'Epine, 1789
Colored etching
BNF, Département des Estampes
et de la Photographie

In this engraving, a young
woman presents the recent
French *Declaration of the
Rights of Man* to a child
dressed in a military uniform
who holds her hand. Behind
her, a joyous group dances
around a liberty pole topped by
a Phrygian cap. The text is
propped against a palm tree,
which symbolizes wealth. At
the left, a man, representing
feudal rights, lies prostrate
under a dead tree that has been
struck by a bolt of lightning.

A Declaration of Rights

**"Droits de l'homme et du
citoyen"**
**In *Collection complète des
tableaux historiques de la
Révolution Française***
Paris: Chez Auber . . . de l'im-
primerie de Pierre Didot l'ainé, an
XI de la République Française, 1802
NYPL, General Research Division

On August 26, 1789, the
National Assembly declared
liberty, equality, and property
as "natural" and "inviolable"
rights of man. Printed
versions of the *Declaration
of the Rights of Man* made
use of prose, images, and
verse to inform citizens about
the underlying principles
of the new regime; this example depicts the Declaration
as heavenly tablets of the
law, in an allusion to the Ten
Commandments.

sovereignty contains an intrinsic difficulty: its unity. If sovereignty belongs to the nation, and if it is thereby "one, indivisible, inalienable, and imprescriptible,"[5] how does the multitude of disparate wills become the general will, a unified expression of this originating subject? Beyond the theoretical debates and constitutional quarrels, one of the answers to this question is found in the motif of the revolutionary festival, which here finds its raison d'être: in the impassioned mood of the festival, particular interests dissolve into a higher unity in which the Nation is realized. It is in festive fusion that the subject-Nation finds a concrete form of existence. Rousseau, contrasting the festival with the theater, as the leisure activity of a free people compared to that of a submissive community, had already indicated the meaning of this "spectacle" in which each person is an "actor," in which mutual sympathy realizes the unity of a people:

But let us not adopt these exclusive entertainments which close up a small number of people in melancholy fashion in a gloomy cavern, which keep them fearful and immobile in silence and inaction. . . . No, happy peoples, these are not your festivals. It is in the open air, under the sky, that you ought to gather and give yourselves to the sweet sentiment of your happiness. . . . [L]et the sun illuminate your innocent entertainments; you will constitute one yourselves, the worthiest it can illuminate. . . . What will be shown in them? Nothing, if you please. . . . Plant a stake crowned with flowers in the middle of a square; gather the people together there, and you will have a festival. Do better yet; let the spectators become an entertainment to themselves; make them actors themselves; do it so that each sees and loves himself in the others so that all will be better united.[6]

Like an echo, Robespierre in the Year II takes up the same theme, deducing from Rousseau's analysis the regenerative function of the festival:

Assemble men together and you will make them better; for men assembled together will seek to please each other, and thus will only be able to please each other by those qualities which make them estimable. Give a great moral and political motive to their meeting and the love of what is right will enter their hearts along with the sentiment of pleasure; for men do not meet together without pleasure.

    Man is the greatest object that exists in nature; and the most magnificent of all spectacles is that of a great people assembled. . . . A system of well-organized national festivals would be at once the most gentle of fraternal ties and the most powerful means of regeneration.[7]

Regeneration, which establishes the regime of virtue, is the precondition of national unity, and the festival is one of the paths to its realization.

To Rationalize Space and Revolutionize Time

From the beginning, an awareness of having inaugurated a new time led revolutionaries to add to the "prognostications of the vulgar era" new denominations for the calendar; thus the year 1789 was called "Year I of Liberty." But it was with the fall of the monarchy and the proclamation of the Republic, on September 22, 1792, that public acts were officially dated as "Year I of the Republic" and that a profound reform of the calendar got under way. Fabre d'Eglantine said, "We could not go on reckoning the years during which we were oppressed by kings as part of our lifetime."[8] Utopia here consists of erasing the traces of the time before, the "symbols of despotism and superstition" (as revolutionary vandalism will do) in order to institute, by an act of public will, a new origin of history. The idea of regeneration commanded the revolution to attack the deep structures of the culture inherited from the Ancien Régime. In this sense, the reform of the calendar belongs alongside the new administrative divisions, the regulation of weights and measures and of national education (beyond, precisely, public instruction), but also with the projects for instituting a universal language (anticipated by the prohibition of dialects, which the Abbé Gregoire saw as the precondition of Enlightenment "communication" on a national scale) in a set of founding arrangements that it is justified to call utopian, even if some proved lasting while others remained chimeras.

    In the first place, this meant giving body to national unity by suppressing inherited disparities, so that the Nation, rationalized, becomes transparent to itself; second, it meant, often in the same gesture, de-Christianizing and assuring the triumphant advent of Reason and Nature. The year will begin – miracle of history – with the autumn equinox, a day on which equality belongs to nature; the decimal system will supplant, in the measurement of time, biblical references to the seven days of creation; the names of months and festivals will consecrate the renunciation of superstition and the universalizing recognition of natural phenomena.

    For the revolutionaries of the Year II, the advent of a regenerated people will come about through the remaking of what we might call the "symbolic," the ordinary tools of life, the landmarks of time and space, that bear history within themselves and that mobilize, well beyond discourse, the sensibility and imagination of each person. "The Revolution," explained Gilbert Romme, "has requenched French souls; it forms them each day to Republican virtues. Time opens a new book of history; and in its new march, majestic and simple like equality, it should engrave with a new chisel the annals of a regenerated France."⁹ If the counting of time must begin anew, it is because utopia, through the regeneration of the people, now enters into history.

One could discuss why reforms bearing on space were successful while those bearing on time failed. It remains the case that the attempt to "revolutionize time," that attempt at a radical break in the processes of transmission that ordinarily socialize individuals through the appropriation of their heritage, is the extreme form of revolutionary utopia: that of a society that each day wants to found itself anew by taking itself as its own origin.

Translated by Susan Emanuel

1 See Ann Fairfax Withington, *Toward a More Perfect Union: Virtue and the Formation of American Republics* (New York: Oxford University Press, 1991) for a discussion of these and other attempts to change behavior during the revolutionary period.

2 Emmanuel Joseph Sieyès, *What Is the Third Estate?*, trans. M. Blondel; ed. S. E. Finer (New York: Praeger, 1963), 51–52.

3 Ibid., 124.

4 Maximilien Robespierre, *Rapport sur les principes de morale politique qui doivent guider la Convention nationale dans l'administration intérieure de la République, fait au nom du Comité de salut public, le 18 [sic] pluviôse, l'an 2e de la République [February 5, 1794]* (Paris: Imprimerie nationale, n.d.), quoted in *The French Revolution*, ed. Paul H. Beik (New York: Walker and Company, 1971), 279.

5 *The French Constitution* (1791), Title I, Article 1, in *The French Revolution: Introductory Documents*, ed. Donald I. Wright (St. Lucia, Queensland: University of Queensland Press, 1974), 7.

6 Jean-Jacques Rousseau, *Politics and the Arts: Letter to M. d'Alembert on the Theatre*, trans. with notes and intro. by Allan Bloom (Glencoe, Ill.: Free Press, 1960), 125–26.

7 Maximilien Robespierre, *Rapport fait au nom du Comité de salut public, par Maximilien Robespierre, sur les rapports des idées religieuses & morales avec les principes républicains, & sur les fêtes nationales: séance du 18 floréal, l'an second de la République française une & indivisible*, delivered in Paris, May 7, 1794, quoted in *The French Revolution*, 310–11.

8 P.F.N. Fabre d'Eglantine, quoted in J. M. Thompson, *Leaders of the French Revolution* (Oxford and New York: Basil Blackwell, 1988), 156.

9 Gilbert Romme, *Rapport sur l'ère de la République* (Paris: Imprimerie nationale, [1793?]).

Project for a Local Assembly

Jean-Jacques Lequeu was a visionary architect and an eccentric. By virtue of his faith in science and his religious eclecticism, he was a man of his time, but left little mark on it. Although he conceived several projects inspired by the Revolution and designed for a new era, he never brought any to fruition.

left
Jean-Jacques Lequeu
Monument destiné à l'exercice de la Souveraineté du Peuple en Assemblées primaires . . .
Watercolor drawing, June 24, 1793
BNF, Département des Estampes et de la Photographie

opposite
Jean-Jacques Lequeu
Elévation principale du Monument. Intérieur du lieu des Assemblées
Watercolor drawing, [1793]
BNF, Département des Estampes et de la Photographie

Autre amortissement du portique circulaire.

Elevation principale du Monument.

Développement des lunettes C.

Interieur du lieu des Assemblées.

An Ideal Egalitarian Plan

Chassis figuratif du territoire de la France partagé en divisions égales entre elles conformément au rapport du comité de Constitution fait à l'Assemblée Nationale le mardi 25 septembre 1789 sur l'établissement des bases de la représentation proportionnelle
Engraving with holograph annotations in color, 1789
Paris, Archives nationales

In 1789, the National Assembly decreed that France should be rearranged into new administrative units. The legend on this idealized proposal for the new France reads: "This first draft, ideally regular, will be accompanied, without delay, by the map of France drawn up in accordance with this new organizational plan for a representative administration and government as soon as the National Assembly has fixed the administrative districts of departments, communes, and cantons, by deviating as little as possible from the former borders that were formed naturally by rivers, mountains, and by the ease of communications."

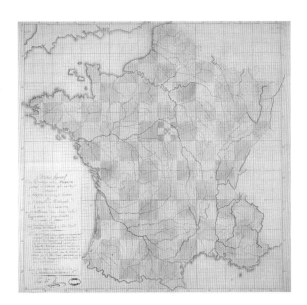

The Map of the New Regime

Carte de la France divisée en départements et districts vérifiée au Comité de la Constitution dediée et présentée à l'Assemblée nationale, au roi et à M. le dauphin, par les Auteurs de l'Atlas National de France
Hand-colored engraving, 1790
NYPL, Map Division

In 1790, the National Assembly redrew the map of France. The overlapping and intersecting administrative districts, toll zones, and judicial and religious units of the Old Regime were replaced by a single, unified set of administrative units that divided the former provinces of France into eighty-three departments, each comprising district and communes. The cartouche on this map of the new France shows a man displaying a copy of the Constitution.

Rationalizing Time

M.-P. Vallet
CALENDRIER NATIONAL cal-culé pour 30 ans et présenté à la Convention nationale Le 31 décembre 1792
Paris: chez la Citoyenne Lesclapart
. . . et à la Convention nationale,
[1793]
Etching
BNF, Département des Estampes et de la Photographie

This large piece, designed to be posted publicly, uses revolutionary iconography: the *Declaration of the Rights of*

Man (1793 version), the list of departments accompanied by administrative and demograph-ic information, the calendar with the former names of the months and days, as well as religious festivals, saints, plan-ets, signs of the zodiac, etc. In addition, at the edges there are two banners, each held by a cherub, one describing the "Idea of France under the Ancien Régime," the other listing the "Celebrated Days of the French Revolution."

Rationalizing Measurement

Nouveaux poids en fer et en cuivre
Colored engraving, 1800–1801
Musée des arts et métiers –
CNAM – PARIS

This table corresponds to instructions concerning weights and measures as rewritten between floréal, Year IX, and brumaire, Year X (May to November 1801). It is a response to the government's concern for increasing aware-ness and knowledge of the new weights and measures and for standardizing the fabrication of the tools used in the new system. Between 1799 and 1805, to familiarize the public with the use of the new measurements, a large number of color engravings were widely distributed. Similar pedagogical campaigns have been conducted in France for more recent admin-istrative changes, such as the introduction of the "new franc," of a new telephone numbering system, and, most recently, of the Euro.

RIGHTS OF MAN:

BEING AN

ANSWER TO MR. BURKE'S ATTACK

ON THE

FRENCH REVOLUTION.

BY

THOMAS PAINE,

SECRETARY FOR FOREIGN AFFAIRS TO CONGRESS IN THE
AMERICAN WAR, AND
AUTHOR OF THE WORK INTITLED *"COMMON SENSE."*

LONDON:
PRINTED FOR J. S. JORDAN, No. 166. FLEET-STREET.
MDCCXCI.

*Liberty, is the Right and Happiness of all,
for all by Nature are equal and free, and
no one can without the utmost injustice become
the Slave of his like.*
Inscribed on the Athenian Statue of Liberty

Pub: as the act directs, Apr. 9, 1795, by W. Hodgson, Newgate.

In Defense of the Revolution

Thomas Paine
***Rights of Man: being an
answer to Mr. Burke's attack
on the French Revolution***
London: Printed for J. S. Jordan,
1791
NYPL, General Research Division

This response to Edmund
Burke's *Reflections on the
Revolution in France* contains
a spirited defense of republican government and a vicious
attack on the privileges of
the aristocracy. Thomas Paine
offers proposals for a better
government and argues for
a strong social program to
combat poverty, illiteracy, and
inequality of all kinds, all to
be financed by a progressive
income tax. Paine's book was
extremely popular (there were
eight editions in 1791), but it
was considered revolutionary
and dangerous, and was
banned after Paine was found
guilty of seditious libel.

A Commonwealth of Reason

William Hodgson
***The Commonwealth
of Reason***
London: Printed for and sold
by the author, 1795
NYPL, General Research Division

This plan for a new form of
government, complete with a
Constitution, draws heavily
from the ideals of the French
Revolution. Among other
proposals, William Hodgson
envisions a secular society
characterized by political,
social, and economic equality
for all, religious tolerance,
free education for all children
ages four through fourteen,
no capital punishment, and
no lawyers.

Fin-de-siècle Landscapes Against a Background of Ruins

IN THE year 1800, at the end of the eighteenth century, the word "utopia" conjured up a field of ruins.

In 1797, after a seemingly endless trial, the longest in the history of the French Revolution, the journalist François-Noël ("Gracchus") Babeuf was sentenced to death, bungled a suicide attempt, and was guillotined. The "Conspiracy of Equals" he had led was a desperate attempt to combine political nostalgia with a social dream. This small militant band had set out to overturn the Directory, reinstate revolutionary dictatorship in the mold of the Year II, and found an egalitarian and collectivist society.

Fifty accomplices were sentenced together with Babeuf. The Conspiracy drew its members from the dismantled sans-culottes movement and the terrorist personnel of the Year II. Vengeance was the dominant passion of the Thermidorean period. The Equals were recruited from among the victims of the Thermidorean reprisals, who, after years spent stagnating in prison, burned to take, in their turn, revenge on the vengeful. The Revolution, which at the outset had propelled their political mission and awakened their zeal, giving them their first dizzying taste of power, was later to exclude them, relegating them to a social and political marginality. As a matter of course they felt betrayed: if the Revolution had failed to keep its promises and resulted in a regime in which the nobility had simply been replaced by rich men and politicians, it was only because it had been led astray. To the great detriment of direct action by the people, the democratic imperative had simply been reduced to a succession of electoral episodes. It fell to advanced patriots, therefore, to rescue the revolution and bring it to safe harbor. In the pursuit of their goals, the Equals resorted to terror as part and parcel of the social dream: the systematic repression of treacherous leaders would give the people access to "true equality" and "general happiness."

The young Babeuf had been won over, even before the Revolution began, by writings on the renewal of the human race and the means by which its happiness could be secured. Time and again, in the course of his trial, he cited passages from Morelly's *Code de la nature* (attributed to Diderot at the time) and from Rousseau's *Discours sur les origines de l'inégalité*. Social inequality and the division and appropriation of wealth were at the heart of all evil. For justice and general happiness to flourish and widespread privation to cease, society had to be collectivized, private property abolished, and wealth equally redistributed. Was not the Revolutionary army a case study of the feasibility of such a plan in communal living? Had not the Republic assembled hundreds of thousands of citizen-soldiers, whose livelihood and welfare were guaranteed by the State and who were, to a man, worthy representatives of the Nation and participants in an exemplary, virtuous, and heroic community? While the Conspiracy of Equals never did make it off the drawing board (it was so heavily infiltrated and subjected to surveillance by the police that it was summarily dismantled before any of its projected actions could be carried out), the Directory did not pass up the opportunity to exploit the group for its own propagandistic ends – to further compromise the concept of an egalitarian utopia, fuel social fears, and spread the notion that "anarchy" destabilizes the very foundations of society and foreshadows the bloody resurgence of terrorist power.

The coup d'état of 18 brumaire (November 9, 1799) marked the end of democracy and consigned civic utopia to oblivion. After 1789, the revolutionary imaginary had accorded a select place to representations of the yet-to-be-built city of the future. These multiple and diverse projections paid particular attention to the image of the ideal "citizen," the emblematic figure of both democratic space and the revolutionary process. Reborn, the Nation was to be a community of enlightened citizens, fully aware of their rights and duties, capable of making choices for the public welfare, and willing to sacrifice themselves to advance the Nation. The Nation, for its part, had the self-imposed duty to use its public educational system to mold present and future generations into citizens.

A citizen is first and foremost a free individual who benefits fully from inalienable rights, namely those that pertain to the safety of his person and possessions and to freedom of thought and expression. Any government whatsoever that threatens these rights is despotic and illegitimate. The fact remains, however, that the freedom of the citizenry is not limited to individual rights; it includes further dimensions. A citizen is also, and more to the point, an integral part of a sovereign people who participates fully in the formation and exercise of that sovereign will. Involvement in public life and political action, therefore, is part of a citizen's duty; one can only be a citizen side by side with other citizens, acting in solidarity to promote equality and social justice. A citizen, furthermore, affirms the Nation against all declared and undeclared enemies as well as against all nefarious conspiracies. Many and various though they may be, all revolutionary models of citizenship place great value on political and civic duty and implicate the individual in the public sphere. The understanding of civic duty, however, can take diverse forms, as illustrated by the Jacobin and Liberal models. Whereas one insisted on the preeminence of the public interest and the identification of the individual with the Nation, on the centralizing and formative role of the State, on revolutionary zeal and militancy, the other emphasized the autonomy of the individual and diversity of opinion as conditions of freedom in the forming of public opinion and in the operations of representational institutions and the freedoms of the press and electoral suffrage.

Condorcet's pedagogical and political writings, especially his *Esquisse d'un tableau historique des progrès de l'esprit humain*, posthumously published in 1795, contain the most complete and rationalist account of a civic utopia. The new city, heir to the achievements of the Enlightenment, is defined by civic reason. The citizen is at once a political and cultural construction; whereas democracy makes cultural demands, education has a democratic mission. In contrast to previous generations bred by prejudice and despotism, the citizen is the new man who cannot be expected to emerge spontaneously from the revolutionary turmoil, but whose evolution will be effected by the Republican Nation's self-imposed, lengthy pedagogical regimen.

In the last years of the Directory, civic utopia was greatly misused. Orchestration of it was in the hands of a power that lacked legitimacy and whose civic appeals registered as empty rhetoric. The coups d'état and electoral fraud not only undermined the legitimacy of established power, they also discredited the Republican institutions themselves. After 18 brumaire, the consular regime remained formally a republic and, for a time, the title of *citoyen* continued to be de rigueur for all official transactions. As the new power became increasingly authoritarian, however, it soon dispensed with civic utopia, a confused idea that could only get in

the way. The idea of the State was the only element of Republican public spiritedness that Bonaparte deemed worthy of recycling. The country after the Revolution was in dire need of public order, not political activism. The gains of the Revolution amounted to the right of ownership, to the guarantee of personal safety and equality in the eyes of the law; everything else was nonsense and chimeras. The leader and the Nation communed without benefit of intermediaries; the providential man, rising above abstract legalities, embodied both his will and destiny. The Nation did not in the least aspire to change; quite the contrary, it had had its fill of upheaval. A lasting peace and the restoration of historical continuity, the reconciliation of Old and New France, were more pressing aspirations.

After the Revolution, it seemed as if the whole utopian paradigm – uniting in a single discourse the admiration of modernity, the will to rationalize public life, and confidence in man's perfectibility – had exhausted its resources. The "best-seller" that launched the new century was not a utopian text but the *Génie du christianisme*. The book's resounding success was certainly due in part to the concordat and the Church's reentry into public life. Aside from exalting the beauties of Christianity and forcefully affirming the return of things religious, however, Chateaubriand also answered to another deep need by calling for a return to tradition. He reached beyond revolutionary rupture to reestablish continuities; contrasted the long term to the explosive period of the troubles; praised traditional time-honored values over the pernicious taste for innovation; defended an intimacy with the eternal and the certitudes of faith against tortured, critical reasoning. Forecasting the future is an abstract, chimerical, and sterile exercise; man, deprived of memory, can only grope blindly and lose his way in life; a nation that is faithful to its past recovers its vital resources. Coming in the wake of the eighteenth century, the century of Voltaire and skeptical modernity, the new century looped back to attach itself to the seventeenth century, the era of Racine and Bossuet, of faith and national grandeur. From the vantage of historical perspective, one era was in decline while the other was elevated to the heavens.

This sketchy tableau, in the melancholy and nostalgic style that was all the rage in the late eighteenth century, with its affinities for a dark palette and the twilight hour, needs to be completed, nuanced, and relativized. The perception of any landscape, and of historical and cultural ones in particular, is greatly determined by the viewer's position, the distance, and the attention paid to each detail as well as to the overall composition. Time distances. The further we stray from the eighteenth century, the less its end seems like a finish line, and the more it looks like a bridge connecting the shores of time. Babeuf's conspiracy marked the union between utopia and revolutionary action and, in so doing, heralded the advent of revolutionaries, those new political actors who would people the nineteenth century. The Revolution did not end on 18 Brumaire; it reached beyond the Napoleonic episode to impose itself as a model for radical social change, while republicanism continued to plumb civic utopia for its sources. Cultivating nostalgia was another way of mourning the past; Chateaubriand, following the sinuous paths of which only he knew the secrets, turned his defense of tradition into an irrefutable argument for a system of representation, individual freedoms, and political modernity.

AT THE end of the twentieth century, the cultural and ideological landscape is again littered with utopian ruins. While fin-de-siècles may succeed one another, they do not resemble each other; beyond the analogies, essential differences emerge.

As the totalitarian regimes collapsed, their future-exalting utopias came crashing down with them. After the Fascist and Nazi utopias were checked by the end of World War II, the implosion of the Soviet empire tolled the death knell of the Communist utopia. The collapse of regimes claiming to have secured the future by dint of the logic of history would reinforce distrust of utopias, those chimeras of every stripe and color. As this century of unreason and murderous madness draws to its painful end, utopia occupies a very uncertain status. The Liberalism that prevailed after the Cold War scarcely favors the utopian imagination. The distinguishing marks of Liberal ideology are, in fact, its misgivings about political voluntarism and global social projects in any guise. Liberal societies, flexible and pragmatic by definition, exclude the possibility of a planned future: theirs is a temporal mode that attaches a very high value to the present. With the proviso of allowing individuals to further their own interests freely while mutually respecting the rights of others, in the framework of the legally constituted state, social agents, operating much like the "invisible hand" of the market economy, ensure the equitable redistribution of wealth and status according to individual performance. This game of social promotion, by and large open-ended, produces a strong social

adhesion to the system. Public powers are responsible for preserving conditions that favor the continuance of the system and that correct, should the need arise, the negative social effects of its deficiencies. The future, like the pursuit of happiness (another inalienable individual right), is above all else a personal affair. Usually, the state lurks behind the social constructions that are called upon to manage the future; the number of its interventions and regulations invariably takes on a totalitarian cast. Formerly, in the nineteenth century, the increasing value placed on the present was joined to a certain productivist ideology and to a belief in the civilizing mission of progress; industrial advances and technological innovations would purportedly give rise to meaning and moral values; from one era to the next, the increasingly more efficient free societies would carry civilization forward, and in so doing they would set themselves on a path of constant betterment. Relieved of this ideological baggage, liberalism today usually adapts itself to economic trends projected for the short or middle term.

The decrease in the value placed on the future is further reinforced by the emergence of consumer society. The consumer is prevailed upon to hurry and take as much advantage as possible of the goods and services the market has to offer; advertising campaigns whet his desires, urge immediate gratification, and persuade the consumer not to put off until tomorrow buying what can be had today. The great abundance of products and the unrelenting pace of the *new and improved* lead to an increased succession of needs: earlier models are soon made obsolete by fashion, and technological progress creates new and unprecedented needs. The consumer lives in an eternal, immediate present. For its part, the computer revolution has transformed utopian visions and imaginary historical scenarios, past and future, into a myriad of everyday consumer products. The utopian imaginary has already absorbed many consequences of this ongoing mutation.

Utopia has always cultivated its secret links with the playful and fantastic. Thomas More's seminal account of an imaginary voyage to a theretofore undiscovered land is a notable case in point – an intellectual and erudite flight of fancy that consists in deciphering a utopian toponymy. Hence Amaurotum, the capital city of Utopia, corresponds to Mirage City; the river Anydrus is the Waterless river; and the text's key term, Utopia, refers at one and the same time to a nowhere place and a place of happiness.

Fantastic literature, in turn, also cultivates links to utopia. Science fiction, for example, brings the utopian and fantastic together: travels in time and space lead to the discovery of strange worlds, of extraterrestrial civilizations no less. Given their extraordinary knowledge and technologies, these imaginary societies must confront the moral and social consequences of soaring scientific and technological progress. The information revolution has radically changed representations of otherness in the domains of play and virtual realities: interactive games free each player to equip, create, and destroy virtual civilizations and empires, to reenact ancient battles and to invent new ones. The marketplace and the World Wide Web offer us the best and the worst of everything – games that stifle and games that stimulate the social imagination. Only the playful dimension of the utopian imaginary is retained by this virtual reductionism, however.

The year that marks the end of a century also marks the beginning of another. No epoch delivers the secrets of its becoming from its beginning. History's selection of one scenario to the exclusion of all others makes these secrets all the more impenetrable. With every change of tack, History abandons other possibilities, for which it remains forever in our debt.

Translated by Nadia Benabid

The Universal Republic

Frédéric Sorrieu
République universelle, démocratique et sociale. Le pacte
Paris: Imprimerie Lemercier, 1848
Lithograph, hand-colored with gouache, 1848
Musée Carnavalet, Paris

The 1848 uprising in France reverberated across Europe, to such an extent that one can speak of "the revolutions of 1848." The liberation movements saw this conjunction of events as a signal for the establishment of a "Universal Republic." The allegorical homage symbolized here by the statue of Christ combines faith, internationalism, political optimism, and historical references. From the sky, Christ blesses the rediscovered fraternity of human beings, made concrete in a long procession that mingles nations, social classes, genders, and ages. Citizens, recognizable by their traditional costumes, parade before a tree of liberty under their respective flags and form a human chain that nothing seems able to break – at least not the power of monarchs, whose decline is recalled by the attributes of royalty strewn on the ground.

Frédéric Sorrieu
Le Jugement de Dieu / Le Prologue
Paris: Imprimerie Lemercier, 1848
Lithograph, hand-colored with gouache, 1848
Musée Carnavalet, Paris

The calm determination of people resolved to govern themselves contrasts with the fear and panic instilled in the defeated sovereigns. It is divine power, through the intercession of its angels, that disperses today's princes and destroys their feudal castles, just as in the past it had condemned their predecessors, among them Louis XVI and Napoléon I, to the flames of hell. The artist has forcefully expressed the idea of '48: an essential linking of political will and religious belief – in other words, a conviction that Progress and Providence complement each other.

Gregory Claeys

Socialism and Utopia

SOCIALISM, AND more particularly communism, is the characteristic form that utopian aspirations have assumed in the modern world. That is to say, if we can agree that utopianism, as contrasted with the literary utopian tradition, constitutes the desire for a society greatly improved[1] over that of the present, in which the regulation of production and property relations is a crucial basis of social order, then socialism has been the principal form such desires have taken in the nineteenth and twentieth centuries. The appeal of socialism has lain chiefly in the fact that its chief competitor, radical republicanism, or democracy, seemingly failed in the nineteenth century to solve the problem of poverty by leaving, under a system of private property, political power in the hands of the wealthy, the sole alternative for socialists being recourse to the utopian program of community of property in one variation or another. From the early nineteenth century onward, the constant point of reference for socialists was thus the United States, so widely heralded as a working-class paradise only decades earlier, but increasingly derided by socialists (for instance, in the chief Owenite literary utopia, John Francis Bray's *A Voyage to Utopia,* 1842) as tolerating a rapacious and unscrupulous financial aristocracy no less exploitative than the hereditary peerages or their new capitalist counterparts of old Europe.

Historiography, Theory, Definition

Initially consciously linked to the utopian literary tradition of Thomas More, socialism after Marx came usually to reject the label of "utopian," and instead to proclaim the historical inevitability of the collapse of capitalism. Consequently the historiography of socialism usually, but tendentiously, distinguishes between an early or "utopian" phase of the socialist movement, dominated by Robert Owen in Britain, by the French thinkers Charles Fourier and Etienne Cabet, and the followers of Henri de Saint-Simon, and in Germany by Moses Hess, Wilhelm Weitling, and others; and a later, "scientific" phase dominated by Marx. This distinction originates in the *Manifesto of the Communist Party* (1848) of Marx and Engels, and more especially in Engels's later recasting of it in *Anti-Dühring,* and the essay published from it subsequently under the title *Socialism: Utopian and Scientific.* The distinction was initially driven politically by a desire to separate the Marxian program from that of other theoretical schools active at the time of the 1848 revolutions. It also functioned to distance Marx and Engels from the failures of the early socialists, whose small-scale communities, notably the Queenwood or Harmony community in Britain, which collapsed in 1845, seemed in their "failure, disastrous and complete, as one observer put it, utterly to discourage one generation and likely to intimidate another." Nonetheless, the Marxian distinction between "utopian" and "scientific" socialism not only played down, by seeming to deny entirely, the utopian element in Marxism, it also caricatured the early socialist writers, whom it disparaged chiefly for three reasons: (1) for seeing the proletariat merely as a passive "suffering mass," rather than the active agent of revolution; (2) for believing that society could or should be transformed by propaganda and experiments only, rather than revolution; (3) for refusing to believe that the needs of social development lay in the economic development of capitalism.

I have contended elsewhere that these assertions, which are in some respect a conscious caricature of early socialism, are essentially false.[2] Many early socialists, like the Chartist leaders James Bronterre O'Brien and William Lovett in Britain, or the Cabetists in France, saw the struggle for the franchise as a means to socialist ends, though they rarely counselled revolutionary transformation as such. Robert Owen and most of his followers adopted a theory of economic immiseration, the centralization of capital, and recurrent commercial crises to argue that the existing economic system would usher in its own collapse. They also saw the advent of industrialization as ensuring a higher standard of living for the working classes, and contended thus that socialism could not have been introduced in any earlier historical period. The early socialists, particularly in Britain, were also well aware of the same historical scheme that underpinned Marx and Engels's account of the materialist conception of history in 1845–46, drawn from Adam Smith, Adam Ferguson, and the other leading writers of the Scottish Enlightenment. Their vision was thus much less ahistorical than is often assumed. The differences between Marxian and earlier forms of socialism thus lie less in these areas than in the moral and quasi-religious form and emphasis of many early socialists, and in other aspects of political and economic theory, of which more anon.

Socialism, then, can be described as "utopian" in four main senses (barring the common-language definition of "impossible" or "unworldly"): (1) in the sense of continuity with the program and ideals of More's *Utopia;* (2) in the chronological sense of "early" or "pre-Marxian"; (3) in the possession of some set of characteristics making its realization less likely than other forms of socialism; (4) in any essentialist presumption that it can tap or strengthen a "social" or "communal" basis in human nature that has been somehow eroded or repressed by the development of civilization.

The Origins of Socialism

In some respects, taking the first of these latter definitions, socialism was clearly and consciously based upon the "classical" utopian ideal from the Spartan state (notably as described by Plutarch) through Plato's *Republic* and More's *Utopia,* insofar as community of property, or the holding of goods in common, has proven the most distinctive attribute of the "utopian" program, and was certainly recognized as such by the late eighteenth century.[3]

A teleological reading of this type can be misleading, however. Many literary utopians, whatever lip service they may pay to Thomas More, have not envisioned communal property-holding as the basis of social order. Moreover, and more importantly, many early as well as later forms of socialism have urged experimentation with a variety of forms of property organization and management, rather than insisting on one model. Again, the predominance of the Marxian model in the later nineteenth and twentieth centuries must not be allowed to obscure essential variations in the socialist tradition. Nonetheless, other distinctive features of Spartan life, such as the rearing of children in common, and the abolition of many forms of exchange and money, remain recurrent themes in most forms of nineteenth-century socialism.

Though socialism is specifically the result of the course assumed by the French Revolution, its roots also lie in republicanism and in religiously motivated schemes for the relief of the poor in the late seventeenth and eighteenth centuries, such as the plan for housing the poor in monastery-like buildings proposed by the Quaker John Bellers in

1696. Republican writers had since the Renaissance revival of classical letters emphasized that the end of government was the common good of all, notably the freedom of citizens from arbitrary government. The rage of constitutionalist speculation that begins with the American and French revolutions took monarchical and aristocratic privilege as its chief targets, and the virtues of citizenship as their antidote. We are less likely today to see these as "utopian." But in a historical context, the ideas of democracy, popular sovereignty, and the restraint of tyranny are remarkable, and went well beyond what might reasonably be expected of political order generally, the more so since the scope now proposed was the nation-state, rather than the small-scale classical Greek *polis.* (Here it is worth recalling the recurrent, compulsive appeal of classicism, and particularly the image of the Athenian *polis,* for writers as diverse as Hegel, Nietzsche, and Matthew Arnold throughout the nineteenth century.)

We tend today, thus, to forget that at the end of the eighteenth century, democracy as such was "utopian" insofar as classical, medieval, and early modern political thought invariably regarded popular sovereignty as an unstable and temporary form of rule bound to end in tyranny and the reestablishment of hereditary kingship or aristocratic government. One of the most prominent doctrines of the revolutionary period, the idea of natural rights, also had several utopian dimensions, notably in its invocation of an original "state of nature" in which such rights had been granted and then enjoyed (or violated); and then in the explosive idea of formal human equality (of master and servant or slave, man and woman, peer and commoner), which has come to dominate the civic ethos of the twentieth century. The desire of creating a methodical, rationalist uniform system of equality, and exporting it to the less fortunate, was applied in the revolutionary period to clothing, language, calendars, national and provincial organization, money, and forms of address as well as to constitutions and forms of law. The desire to make all things new, to sweep away vestiges of feudal privilege but also to impose rational and scientific order on the world, is a characteristically modernist ideal, and one that is often situated closer to a Baconian than a Morean vision.

The age of Enlightenment, whose hostility to superstition and clericism did so much to popularize this rationalism, spawned a variety of utopian schemes, both theoretically, in plans for model constitutions such as David Hume's essay on the "Idea of a Perfect Commonwealth" (1752) and in proposals for European peace, notably by Kant; and in practical experiments, especially in the colonies of the New World, which were often religious in orientation and often included, at least at the beginning, a measure of community of property, as did the early colonies of Virginia and Massachusetts.[4] The radical impulse of the eighteenth century, as manifested in the thought of Rousseau and in British popular radicalism, however, was chiefly concerned with individual and civil liberty, and sought a balanced constitution as the means of achieving this. The most extreme form of democratic sentiment, rare in this period, was the utopian element in republicanism, often linked to primitive, and especially puritan, Christianity, which sought much more substantial social equality, often through economic regulation and sometimes by limiting trade and especially property in land through the classical mechanism of an agrarian law. In Britain such ideas were popularized early in this period by James Harrington's *Oceana* (1656), and later by works such as James Burgh's *Account . . . of the Cessares* (1764), in which sumptuary restrictions, notably on clothing, also ensure both greater social uniformity and the inhibition of consumption. (This theme is echoed in the sumptuary regulations of the first American utopia, John Lithgow's *Equality – A Political Romance,* 1802, where no variation of dress or "equipage" was allowed.)

Though the American Revolution was clearly driven in part by the greater social equality of the colonies, as pamphlets like Thomas Paine's *Common Sense* (1776) indicate, proposals for the abolition of ranks as such were rare, the abolition of a hereditary monarchy and titled aristocracy being seen as sufficiently idealistic. The French Revolution and the movements and debates to which it gave rise, however, pushed this egalitarian impulse in a more extreme direction. Lacking the safety valve of unlimited free land, it also invited speculation about the division of existing landed estates. One of the principal causes of the French Revolution had been the failure of state regulation of the grain trade, with a consequent sharp rise in food prices during the 1770s and 1780s. The prospect of further regulation of these markets, and even of commerce generally, in the interests both of economic justice and social order, necessarily followed. Some utopian writers of the revolutionary era, such as Thomas Northmore, in *Memoirs of Planetes* (1795), remain implacably hostile to luxury, and the association of primitivism with civic and personal virtue remains a pronounced theme throughout this period. In France, the Revolution also produced its own revolutionary egalitarian, "Gracchus" Babeuf (1760–1797), whose "Conspiracy of Equals," which planned to overthrow the Directory in 1796 and institute a division of land among the peasantry, was the forerunner for most secret, conspiratorial revolutionary societies of the early nineteenth century. Most of the leading revolutionaries and their intellectual allies, however, were hostile to the notion of an agrarian law, though Thomas Paine, for instance, included a mild variation on the theme in the form of a scheme of progressive taxation on large landed estates in his *Rights of Man,* part two (1792).

For most participants, what the French Revolution promised was not the arcadian commune, close to the state of nature, which the poets Coleridge and Southey planned for their "pantisocracy" on the banks of the Susquehanna, not thus the renunciation of civilization, but the wider extension of its benefits, and the supplanting of a society based on privilege by one based on merit, secured by political democracy. Wedded to the enticing promise of political equality by 1830 was the equally alluring image of industrial opulence, which the increasingly popular science of political economy assured would become universal if doctrines of free trade were universally implemented. What industrialization and urbanization brought the working classes, however, was often low wages, recurrent bouts of unemployment, and unpleasant and dangerous working conditions in the new factories. Disillusionment with both capitalism and industry, and a nostalgic affection for a life on the land, which for most urban dwellers until the late nineteenth century was a recent memory, play a major role in shaping the horizons and expectations of early socialism.

The origins of nineteenth-century socialism lie thus in two elements of the revolutionary experience: the growth of poverty and hunger under the *ancien régime;* and the failure of the revolution itself to introduce democracy and political stability. Commercial liberalism seemed increasingly not to favor the poor; the politics of revolution had brought Bonapartism rather than democracy. Socialism would found its originality, and cement its identity, on the claim to solve both of these problems.

Communitarianism
Three schools dominate early nineteenth-century socialism: Owenism, Fourierism, and Saint-Simonism.[5]

Robert Owen (1771–1858) gained renown as an immensely successful cotton spinner, whose factory at New Lanark near Glasgow, though never a utopian or socialist community, also became a noted experiment in the improvement of working conditions, infant education, and social order generally, guided by Owen's famous principle that the characters of mankind were "formed for them, not by them." It was when Owen failed, after repeated efforts, to persuade fellow manufacturers to extend such regulations elsewhere in the rapidly expanding factory system that he began to propose a much more dramatic solution to the problems of national poverty and unemployment. Though the term "socialism" would only gain currency slowly from the mid-1820s onward, Owen from 1817 proposed that the unemployed poor be housed in "co-operative communities" of up to about 2,500 individuals, who would work for their common benefit, by sharing their produce in common; being freed of the evil influences of the competitive system, they would introduce a "new moral world." (And the language of millenarianism would often thereafter accompany Owenite pronouncements.)

Owen was well aware, as were his early follow-ers like George Mudie and John Minter Morgan, that the literary utopian tradition and the ideals of Platonic republicanism, as well as the plans of religious reformers like Bellers, had anticipated these plans. (Owen was acquainted with Godwin personally, and doubtless knew that the *Enquiry concerning Political Justice* referred to Swift's *Gulli-ver's Travels*, Burke's *Vindication of Natural Society*, and similar works.) Most of the early socialist writers rejected the liberal, Smithian principle that a narrow division of labor was the essential prerequisite for economic progress, and dismissed suggestions that large-scale urbanization inevitably accompanied the enclosure of common agricultural lands and extension of the factory system. Instead they proposed a routine of varied agricultural and manufacturing activity, with sufficient free time for both leisure and education.

The early socialists did not, however, insist on one uniform solution to the problem of property-holding. Partially to attract wealthy investors, the French writer Charles Fourier (1772–1837), the son of a prosperous Besançon merchant family, agreed that anarchic competition, and the profits of "para-sitic" merchants and middlemen, were the chief causes of working-class poverty. Fourier is distinc-tive in the generous, indulgent, and epicurean, rather than Spartan or stoical emphasis, given in his vision of the future and of human nature. In

Fourier's phalansteries, work, as well as the rest of life, was to be organized according to the grand psychological principle, first outlined in the *Theory of the Four Movements* (1808), of "passionate attrac-tion," whereby the passions rather than reason were to be harnessed to ensure the maximum gratifica-tion of sexual, social, and other instinctual desires, and the commensurability of aptitudes with socially necessary labor. (A sexual "minimum" of pleasure equivalent to a minimum wage was to be estab-lished.) Labor itself would be organized according to the principle of "attractive association" in "com-pound groups," with the aim being that "attractive labor" would make work as free, and as interesting, as possible. Individuals would rotate tasks up to eight times daily, work no longer than two hours at any job, and have as many as forty activities in all. A typical day would involve five meals, attending a concert, visiting the library, hunting, fishing, and cultivation, with manufacturing occupying no more than one-quarter of the total labor. Some creative forms of competition would be permitted, and a differential reward agreed upon for tasks of true drudgery. The results of work were to be divided between capital (four-twelfths), labor (five-twelfths), and talent (three-twelfths), without any "general community of goods," though Fourier hoped that "the spirit of societary or compound property" would nevertheless prevail.

Nor were all the early socialists exclusively devoted to small-scale communities. The French nobleman Henri de Saint-Simon (1760–1825) achieved fame through his incisive analysis of the newly emerging industrial society, and his insistence that the "industrialists" (by which he meant all use-ful laborers) should seize power, if need be by force. Thereafter society would be organized meritocrati-cally, through social and industrial institutions, with scientific power replacing older forms of spiritual and military authority, and the vastly more produc-tive and efficient "industrial system" supplanting earlier forms of "parliamentary system." European nation-states in turn would become subordinate to a new European parliament. These ideas were car-ried forward in the 1830s and 1840s by Saint-Simon's more socialistic followers, notably Olinde Rodrigues, Barthélemy Prosper Enfantin, Gustave d'Eichthal, Michel Chevalier, Saint-Amand Bazard, and Philippe Buchez, who established a quasi-reli-gious sect that emphasized the delights of free love, spiritual rebirth, and artistic creativity. Of consider-able importance from the early 1830s until late nineteenth-century France, Saint-Simonism did

New Society, New Man

John Minter Morgan was a wealthy philanthropist and follower of Robert Owen. The author of a number of books supporting Owen's schemes, his main contribution was to inspire those who wished to reconcile Christian beliefs with Owen's social theories. Owen had spoken out sharply against Christianity, and most particularly against the doctrine of Original Sin, although he did encourage religious tolerance among his followers. Morgan argued that the goals of Christianity and Owenism were the same, so one ought to ignore any theoretical or dogmatic difficulties between them. Eventually, Morgan was to start his own organization, the Church of England Self-Supporting Village Society, which advocated a Christian Owenite community.

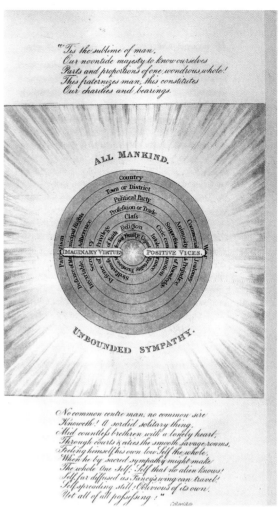

John Minter Morgan
Hampden in the Nineteenth Century; or, Colloquies on the Errors and Improvement of Society, **vol. 2**
London: Edward Moxon, 1834
NYPL, General Research Division

In 1799, Robert Owen purchased the cotton spinning mills of New Lanark, Scotland, and shortly thereafter began his first experiment in instituting his ideas of social and labor reform. Although Owen paid lower wages than most of the surrounding factories, his employees, whose number fluctuated between 1,400 and 1,500, enjoyed low-rent housing, free medical care, low-cost education, reduced prices on food and other household supplies, and free access to social and recre-

ational facilities, gardens, and parks. Owen's efforts at social reform also included a steady reduction in the number of working hours (from twelve to ten and a half per day) and his refusal to employ any children under the age of ten. New Lanark's guest book reveals that the model factory community received almost 20,000 visitors between 1815 and 1825.

While Owen's experiment at New Lanark was a success on many levels, he did not believe it was the ideal community in which to establish his "New Moral World." In 1824, he purchased the community of Harmony, Indiana, and 900 of his followers moved there the following year to start over.

John Minter Morgan
Hampden in the Nineteenth Century; or, Colloquies on the Errors and Improvement of Society, **vol. 1**
London: Edward Moxon, 1834
NYPL, General Research Division

This diagram expresses Morgan's theories on "the variety of impediments which restrain the exercise of that love and universal brotherhood enjoined in the New Testament." The seven rings relate to seven areas in which man may succumb to vices and to those vices that are often mistaken for virtues. These fourteen vices impede man's progress toward "unbounded sympathy" for the community of "all mankind." Of particular interest is the second ring, Religion, which warns of the dangers of both Intolerance and Steadfastness of Faith.

*The Community
of New Harmony*

**The Co-operative Magazine
and Monthly Herald, no. 1
(January 1826)**
London: Knight and Lacey
NYPL, Rare Books Division

In 1824, Robert Owen pur-
chased 20,000 acres and a
small settlement in Indiana
from the Harmonists, a religious community who had
moved back to Pennsylvania.
The following year, 900 of
Owen's followers immigrated
to the town, renamed New
Harmony, which provided a
substantial prefabricated infrastructure for Owen's communal experiment, with its many
and varied industries, including mills, a textile factory, a
tanning yard, orchards, vineyards, and almost 2,000 acres
of arable land. This illustration
shows Owen's grand vision
for a parallelogram-shaped,
self-contained community
of buildings designed by the

architect Stedman Whitwell.
Set on a platform, the design
centered on a greenhouse.
Houses made up the four
sides, with schools and
"conversation rooms" at
the corners. Other buildings
housed communal facilities
for dining and other activities.
Although the edifice was
never built, a six-foot-square
model of it toured the United
States, and was displayed at
the White House.

The New Harmony communi-
ty never achieved the success
imagined by Owen; disorgani-
zation and bad management
led to its demise in 1828.
By then, most of the settlers
had left for offshoot Owenite
communities or for other
groups such as the Shakers,
or had set out on their own;
those who stayed at New
Harmony eventually divided
up the land and worked it

privately. Nevertheless, New
Harmony had a lasting impact,
both through some of its residents who started other communities and through the influence on the American school
system of Owen's educational
ideas. Owen's son, one of the
first Senators from Indiana, was
active in the anti-slavery movement and introduced the bill that
established the Smithsonian
Institution in Washington, D.C.

*The Co-operative Magazine
and Monthly Herald*, one of
a series of Owenite publications, was the leading vehicle
for the dissemination of
Owen's ideas from 1826 to
1830. Its purpose was to provide reports from the Owenite
communities and societies
in America and Europe and
to foster "full and free discussion to the cause of truth"
about Owen's social theories.

An Innovative Education

M. Egerton
Airy Nothings; or, Scraps and Naughts, and Odd-Cum-Shorts; in a Circumbendibus Hop, Step, and Jump. By Olio Rigmaroll
London: Pyall and Hunt, 1825
NYPL, The Carl H. Pforzheimer Collection of Shelley and His Circle

Owen's Institution Established for the Formation of Character, which opened at New Lanark in 1816, provided a nursery and school for children up to the age of ten (when they could start working) as well as classes for adults. For Owen, education was the element most essential to effect social reform; he based all his theories on the idea that "character is universally formed *for* and not *by* the individual."

Dancing, singing, playing, and other activity-centered learning were at the heart of his radical educational principles. He abhorred book learning and rote memorization, and forbade any artificial reward or punishment for the students. Owen believed that the goal of education was to teach people the consequences of their conduct and in doing so to reveal to them that the well-being of the community was a necessary prerequisite to individual happiness. Rather than punishing people for stealing, lying, and other bad behavior, Owen believed that a proper education about the widespread consequences of those actions could prevent them from occurring in the first place.

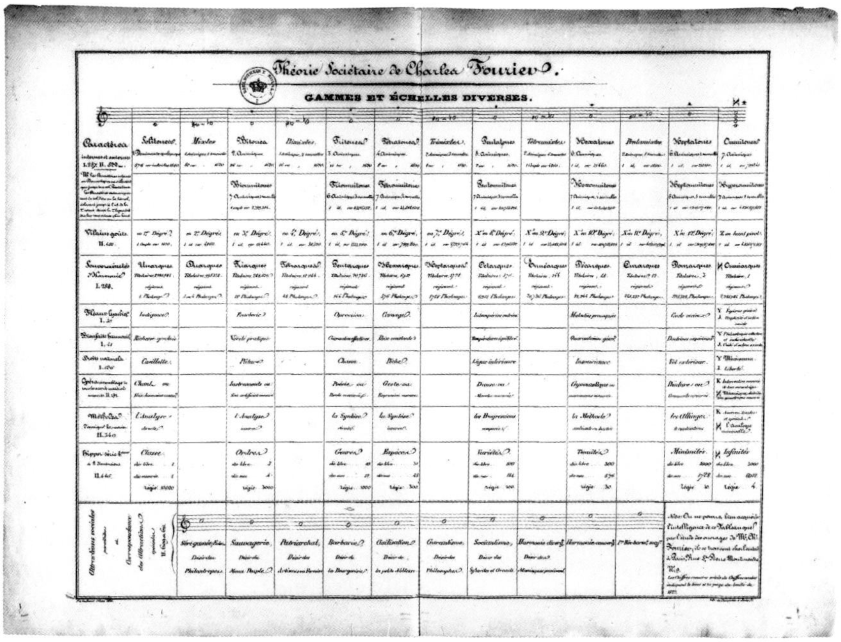

Fourier's Classifications of the Passions

top

Charles Fourier
Théorie sociétaire de Charles Fourier: gammes et échelles diverses
Nantes: P. A. Guilbaud, 1836
Lithograph
BNF, Département Littérature et Art

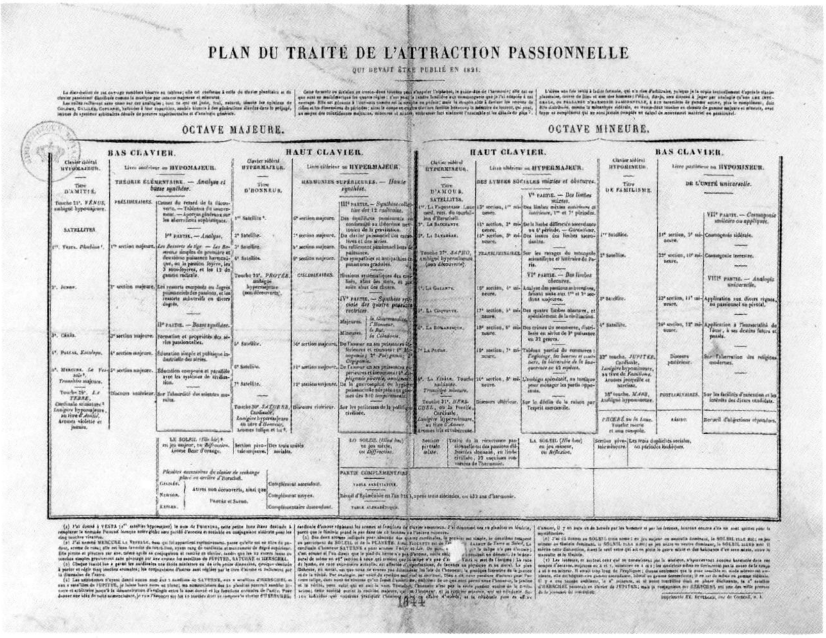

bottom

Charles Fourier
Plan du traité de l'attraction passionnelle
Paris: E. Duverger, [1844]
BNF, Département Philosophie, Histoire, Sciences de l'Homme

In the Phalansteries of French socialist writer Charles Fourier, work, as well as the rest of life, was to be organized according to the grand psychological principle of "passionate attraction," whereby the passions rather than reason were to be harnessed to ensure the maximum gratification of sexual, social, and other instinctual desires. These tables are devices for decoding the secret correspondences between the physical, biological, psychic, and social worlds; through the use of analogies, they also attempt to reveal the permanence of these relationships. But these austere, scientific schemes cannot encompass Fourier's abundant imagination. For Fourier, finding "the new social world" meant discovering the preexisting providential harmony that allows society to be organized so that individual tastes blossom naturally. His disciple Victor Considérant is true to Fourier's theories in the formula "Each man is a note in the great concert."

Similarly, the analogy between "planetary keyboard and passional keyboard arranged as in music by major and minor octaves" is one of the other keys that Fourier offers. For example, he reveals a continuous gradation "in titles of love," between the "faquiresse," the "bacchante," the "bayadere," and, at the bottom of the ladder, the "romantic," the "prude," and, finally, the "faithful." In keeping with his lavish spirit, Fourier intermingles these maniacal taxonomies of desire with his particular *bêtes noires*: "crimes of commerce" and "aberration of modern religions."

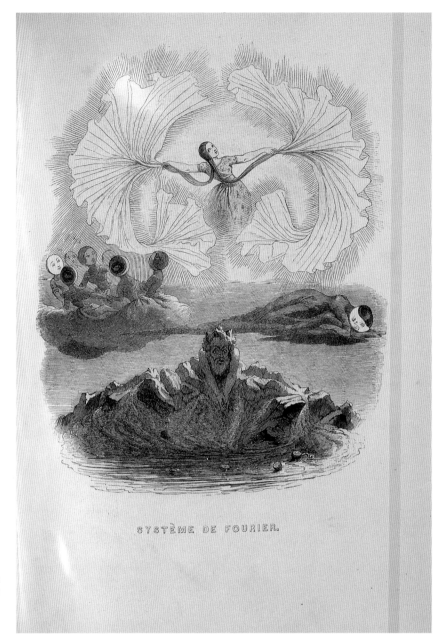

SYSTÈME DE FOURIER.

A Magical World

Grandville (pseud. of Jean-Ignace-Isidore Gérard) *Un Autre Monde: transformations, visions, incarnations . . . et autres choses*
Paris: H. Fournier, 1844
NYPL, Miriam and Ira D. Wallach Division of Art, Prints and Photographs

Nothing provided greater inspiration to the talent of Grandville than the fanciful work of Fourier. Indeed, the conjunction of the rapid expansion of European utopian thought in the 1840s, the perseverance of followers of the "Phalanstery School," and the public's attraction to Fourier's original ideas made his work fashionable shortly after Fourier's death in 1837. Many satiric artists took cruel advantage of Fourier's extravagant predictions; others, like Grandville, were clearly seduced by the dreamlike atmosphere that pervades his worldview. This drawing, which accompanies a text by Taxile Delord, depicts the "butterfly" or "dilettante," the passion that invites one to "steal from pleasure to pleasure."

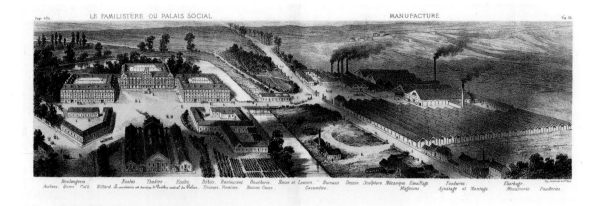

*The Familistère: A Phalanstery
for Workers' Families*

Jean-Baptiste André Godin
Solutions sociales
Paris: A. Le Chevalier, 1871
BNF, Bibliothèque de l'Arsenal

Fourier's lifelong search for a "capitalist" willing to invest in his Phalanstery was unsuccessful, and so, apart from some quickly aborted projects, the Phalanstery remained only a beautiful dream. In 1859, inspired by the Fourierist ideas of his youth, Jean-Baptiste André Godin, an industrialist who had made his fortune in the fabrication of cast-iron stoves, undertook the creation of a social palace at Guise. This bird's-eye view of the Familistère presents not only the buildings that had actually been constructed (living spaces, cooperative stores, school, and theater) but also future projects (the right wing, which Godin reserved for himself, and the buildings surrounding it). The design itself shows no evidence of social innovation, and while it provides great comfort for the factory worker, especially given the miserable conditions of the time, the plan indicates a retreat from Fourier's ambitions: rather than integrating the majority of activities under a single roof, which was the original plan of the Phalanstery, the Familistère returns to a classic functional organization.

*Fourierism and the
Revolutionaries of 1848*

H. Fugère
Organisation du travail par la fondation d'une commune modèle d'après la théorie de Ch. Fourier
Paris: Imprimerie de Wittersheim, [1848]
BNF, Département Philosophie, Histoire, Sciences de l'Homme

With the creation of the newspaper *La Phalange* in 1836, a period of intense activity began among Fourier's disciples. The most important of these efforts was the publication of doctrinal texts for the common man, issued by *La Phalange* itself, by the Phalanstery bookstore, or by the society bookstore. Independent disciples sometimes took it upon themselves to spread the doctrine; this 1848 lithograph, published by the Lyonnais engraver Fugère, advocates the creation of a "model commune" based on Fourier's theories. Although the general attributes have stayed the same, the substitution of the term "commune" for that of "Phalanx" shows signs of the evolution of Fourier's system and indicates attempts to merge with the socialist or democratic trends of the Revolution of 1848.

Light and Health

**Postcard views of
Godin's Familistère,
Guise, ca. 1905–8**
BNF, Département des
Estampes et de la Photographie

At the beginning of the twentieth century, the red brick buildings of the Familistère had been a part of the landscape at Guise for more than a generation. The architectural organization attests to preoccupations with good hygiene. Godin wanted spaces that were "wide open, in which the air purified itself through contact with the vegetation." On the interior, "the light that shines everywhere in the living quarters, in the courtyards, the stairwells, signifies the intellectual and moral progress of the generations who will give birth to the new social enlightenment." The vast central courtyard was illuminated by a skylight, and at each level a gallery surrounded the apartments. This arrangement provided shelter from bad weather, Fourier's great fear. On a more disturbing note, this plan recalls Jeremy Bentham's prison design, the Panopticon. Indeed, by Godin's own admission: "The principal fact of the order at the Familistère is that the life of each person there is revealed." The cozy comfort of these residences, which greatly contrasts with the unhealthiness of most workers' housing of the time, testifies to the abandonment of the most subversive aspects of the Phalanstery.

The Example of Saint-Simonism

Les Saint-Simoniens dans leur maison de Ménilmontant: description des travaux des Saint-Simoniens, leurs différens emplois selon ce que chacun d'eux est capable de faire, et l'histoire de Saint-Simon, depuis sa naissance jusqu'à sa mort, ses aventures en France, dans les pays étrangers, et la grande dispute concernant ce que veulent les Saint-Simoniens

Paris: Setier, [1832]
Lithograph
BNF, Réserve des Livres Rares

In 1832, after a period of intense intellectual activity marked by much divisiveness, the Saint-Simonian Barthélemy Prosper (Père) Enfantin and forty of his disciples came together to construct this large building at Ménilmontant, on the then-rural outskirts of Paris. Louis Reybaud reported on their occupations: "They organized the work by categories; they made groups of shovellers, wheelbarrow pushers, earth packers, and, so that the job would be less harsh, they accompanied it with hymns composed by a member of the community." Although the Saint-Simonians produced less propaganda during this period than previously, placards promulgating the example of their lifestyle and the rudiments of their doctrine were still distributed widely. Although there were a few converts, it was generally only mocking curiosity that attracted Parisians to the spectacle of these ostentatious, eccentric reformers.

Père Enfantin's vest
BNF, Bibliothèque de l'Arsenal,
fonds Enfantin

Within the liturgy of Saint-Simonism, clothing played an important role. "White is the color of love, red that of work, blue violet, that of faith." Thus, their blue violet leotard, short skirt, patent leather belt, red cap, white twill pants, and handkerchief knotted around the neck harmonized with their long hair and Eastern-inspired mustaches and beards.

On June 6, 1831, during the retreat to Ménilmontant, Père Enfantin presided over an outdoor ceremony in which his followers "took the habit." The romantic character of the occasion, in which the "Family" gathered in concentric circles around the "Father," was accentuated by a violent storm.

Because the vests buttoned up the back, members of the community could not dress themselves without help from others, which symbolized fraternity. To signify individual responsibility, the name of each of the Saint-Simonians was inscribed on his or her vest in large letters. On this vest, which belonged to Enfantin, one can read "Le Père" ("The Father").

Sketch by a Disciple

Joseph Machereau
Untitled pen-and-ink drawing,
ca. 1833
BNF, Bibliothèque de l'Arsenal,
fonds Enfantin

When free from manual labor, Enfantin's disciples devoted themselves to doctrinal analysis. Numerous manuscripts testify to their feverish speculations, especially *Le Livre nouveau* [*The New Book*], a synthesis that resulted from a collaboration between Enfantin and Michel Chevalier, who later became known as an economist. Whereas his "brothers" debated the conceptual bases of a "new life," Joseph Machereau drew sketches like this one. Later, having left, like Enfantin, for the Orient, he settled in Cairo, where he converted to Islam and married an Egyptian.

much to popularize notions of cultural as well as industrial malaise, and their potential of being supplanted by a new system of familial, social, industrial, and political organization. (Saint-Simon's own secretary, Auguste Comte, would formalize these ideals of progress in a new system of sociological analysis.) Partially through its religious emphasis on, and search for, a new Female Messiah, Saint-Simonism like Owenism also gave an important role to women, and demanded the extension of the franchise to women at the time of the revolution of 1830. Much contemporary feminist writing in this period, until the 1860s, when the women's suffrage movement begins, is thus linked to these socialist movements.

The main schools of early socialism were thus not exclusively concerned with or committed to "community" as the sole context in which the ideal life could be lived, though this was certainly the case for Owen and Fourier themselves. In Britain, and on the Continent among the Saint-Simonians

in particular, many of the most influential early economic writers, notably the economists William Thompson and John Gray, envisioned a substantial degree of national economic planning and the organization of production. This indicates perhaps the most important division among the pre-Marxian writers: that over the question of luxury. Many early socialists inherited a Spartan, puritan bias against both indolence and refinement, and in addition believed that the production of luxury goods for the rich entailed greater labor for the poor. In order to make more free time available for the poor, to avoid the corrupting temptations of luxury, and the inequalities that the possession of such goods introduced, they proposed regulations to curtail or abolish the production of and trade in rare and costly items. Other socialists, however, rejected this view. The British political economist John Gray is an interesting case in point: having rejected luxury in his *Essay on Human Happiness* (1825), Gray came to believe that any restriction on needs, and division

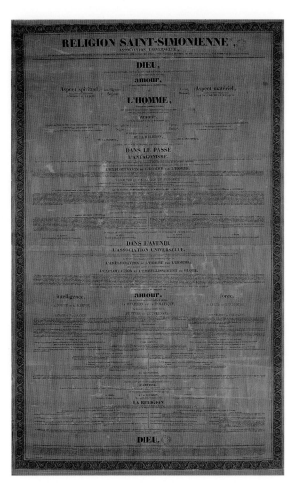

A New Religious Creed

Religion Saint-Simonienne
Roll, ca. 1831
BNF, Bibliothèque de l'Arsenal,
fonds Enfantin

The "New Christianity" conceived by Saint-Simon in his later years is a strange composite: he wanted to combine a material mastery of the universe founded on scientific rationality with a spirituality that would both legitimate and invigorate it. Completely transfiguring Christian dogmas but not abolishing them, this religion coincided with the economic boom – with its mechanization, major building projects, and the unification of the world into a single unit – of which Saint-Simon himself had seen only the start or merely prophesied as imminent. The faith that underlay this religion was also a powerful motivating force for enterprise.

Satirizing Utopian Ideas

Bertall [Albert d'Arnould]
La Foire aux idées, dessinée par Bertall, professeur de prothèse comique
Pen lithograph from *Journal pour rire*, no. 37 (October 1848)
BNF, Département des Estampes et de la Photographie

The effervescence and variety of ideas ignited in Paris during the first months of 1848 are represented here in a spirited but very partisan way by the illustrator Bertall. Depicted as carnival barkers, the great contemporary figures of utopian and socialist thought outdo each other in rhetorical eloquence before an astonished audience. These so-called social reformers propose remedies to the most pronounced evils of society. At the left, Etienne Cabet flaunts a map of Icaria, whose capital the illustrator has maliciously placed in Charenton, at that time the seat of the major insane asylum in France. Next come Pierre Leroux, who had just been elected deputy and whose disheveled hair is met with ridicule; Louis Blanc, a short-lived member of the provisional government; and Pierre-Joseph Proudhon, who is infatuated with his own ideas – each in his way sings the praises of socialist solutions. At the right, flanked by a one-man band (very possibly the publicist Samuel-François Girard), whose emanations are doubtless not what Fourier intended with his dreams of harmony, Victor Considérant seriously propounds one of the most extravagant aspects of Fourier's theory: the future biological mutation of humans. The artist also takes pleasure in including quests for "social prosthetics" and the quackery of toothsellers, which was the specialty of a certain Fattet – bringing to mind the expression, "lying through one's teeth." Thus, Bertall's satiric drawing was directed at defenders of the status quo, who were shocked by social critics, denounced their contradictions with relish, and reacted vigorously against all utopias, in which they wanted to see only illusions.

between "natural" and "artificial" needs or wants, was false in theory, if not impossible to uphold in practice. From his *The Social System* (1832) onward, Gray thus argued for a managed, centralized system of production in which, while basic needs had the highest priority, no restriction on production as such was proposed. It was this type of scheme that Marx and Engels would adopt, thus renouncing any association of socialism with a monastic or Spartan, moralizing rejection of refinement. Thenceforth the Athenian model of the expanding commercial republic would predominate over the Spartan model of restricted desire in socialism. A similar contrast can be seen in the antagonism between the future ideals of Edward Bellamy and William Morris, discussed below. But the abandonment of any form of ascetic renunciation also implied in principle the willingness to relinquish giving education and cultural advancement the highest priority. (This theme would reemerge in twentieth-century utopias like B. F. Skinner's *Walden Two.*)

Nonetheless, it was the idealized small-town and even arcadian vision of "Community" that captured the imagination of many early socialists. "Community" was a respite from excessive urbanization and industrialization, from the life of slums and factories that would come for so many to epitomize the century. But it was much more besides. In cooperative communities, no police forces were to be required, since the vastly greater force of public opinion operating on a restricted scale would, it was widely assumed, suffice to regulate moral conduct through mutual supervision, with all living, as More had expressed it in *Utopia,* in "full view" of one another. (Social and psychological transparency remains a quintessentially utopian quality, as opaqueness similarly remains a recurrently attractive aspect of modern urban life for many escaping the weight of traditional society.) Expressions of selfish individualism would be further curtailed by the education of children in common, and by an extension of the familial ideal to the community itself. Women in Owenite communities were to have freedom of divorce and, in principle, equal rights with men. Communitarian schemes also frequently involved calls for a near-mathematical similarity of housing, dress, meals, and work, in the name of social justice and equality. Sometimes counterbalancing mechanisms were introduced: in Cabet's Icaria, for instance, the length, timing, and content of meals are regulated, but the "republican restaurant" varied its menus daily so as to ensure variety amid uniformity.

Most forms of early socialism relied on variations of traditional Christian themes to give the communal and fraternal priority over the individual. After a devastating attack in 1817 on the priesthood, which he believed was a principal obstacle to progress through its emphasis on original sin, Owen came by 1830 to recast his necessitarian philosophy as a "new religion," with a muted, deistical respect for the supreme being wedded to a scheme for rational social improvement. At the height of the Owenite movement (1839–45), though its meeting places were called "Halls of Science," the chief Owenite organization, the Association of All Classes of All Nations, was also termed the University Community Society of Rational Religionists, with traveling lecturers called "Social Missionaries," and a scheme of organization that many thought was indebted to Methodism. The Saint-Simonian religion, similarly, took its cue from the demand in Saint-Simon's *Nouveau Christianisme* (1825) that religion be devoted to satisfying the needs of the poor. Etienne Cabet, too, gave great prominence to the Christian basis of communism, as did the German tailor Wilhelm Weitling, whose *Mankind as It Is and as It Should Be* (1838), *The Poor Sinner's Gospel,* and other works, forcibly drove home the Christian origins of socialistic egalitarianism.

Most nineteenth-century communitarians (Marx included) were explicitly hostile to "politics," and suggested or described its disappearance in the future ideal society. Commonly – this is the great Saint-Simonian theme – "politics" is simply subordinated under "production," the great political divisions of the past being presumed to have been mere epiphenomenal reflections of the chief class divisions of the period (a view echoed by Owen and Marx). Some writers, such as Owen, solve the problem of politics in the Platonic or Morean vein, by instituting a system of rule by elders, or gerontocracy. More often, socialists preferred that decision-making be simply left in the hands of the majority. Sometimes more complex arrangements are described, as in Morris's *News from Nowhere,* where, while "politics" no longer exists, a delicate harmony between minority and majority opinion prevails in which majoritarian tyranny is avoided by a reluctance to ride roughshod over opinions held by substantial minorities. Most communitarian socialists assumed that the unit of government would be no larger than the parish (the central unit for Thomas Spence and William Godwin a generation earlier), and thus thought some harmonious scheme of social and political organization could be devised. For Owen, whose scheme of communitarian government was the most fully articulated, this was based on the principle of age, with each person passing successively through eight age groups that would replace the existing class system, being successively educated, laboring, supervising others, and governing the community and its relations with other communities. Morally, "community" was also meant to function as an extension of the "social" ideal, combating the selfish individualism of the "old society," abolishing such divisive elements as the love of accumulation, rank, privilege, and domination, and replacing these with the "social" emphasis of the pursuit of the communal good. Politically, the evils of contested elections, partisanship, and division of interest would be avoided by ensuring that the right of government was in principle universal, but vested in those possessing the greatest experience. This ambiguity concerning, and sometimes opposition toward, simple democratic procedures would be a recurrent theme in many later forms of socialism.[6]

The heyday of communitarianism was from the mid-1820s until the late 1840s. In the United States, the most important early socialist community of the 1820s was at New Harmony, Indiana, bought from George Rapp and expanded by Owen's followers between 1824 and 1838. For this brief period, however, New Harmony was a center of intellectual, cultural, and scientific life on the frontier, before internal divisions, and poor planning and choice of members on Owen's part, tore it asunder. Similar problems were to plague other community experiments, few of which lasted longer than a year or two. In France, a few Fourierist phalansteries were attempted in France, notably at Condé-sur-Vesgres (1833) and Citeaux (1841), though these were disavowed by Fourier himself, who insisted on absolute conformity to his own plans and models. In Britain, Owenite communities were founded at Orbiston, Manea Fen, and elsewhere, and at urban sites in London and Edinburgh. In the mid-1830s, developing a new strategy to attract wider working-class support, Owen flirted with trade unionism and labor exchanges, where artisans traded produce directly without the need for shopkeepers as middlemen. The culmination of communitarianism in England, and symbolically the most important Owenite experiment, was the Queenwood or Harmony colony at Hampshire, which began in 1839 and lasted until 1845.[7] This was accompanied by the construction of an elaborate network of local Owenite branches, which often built "Halls

of Science" where teas and lectures were held. Some fifty of these existed by the early 1840s, chiefly in the industrial midlands, with as many as ten thousand people attending Sunday functions. Queenwood itself was constructed of the most lavish materials, befitting the aesthetic as well as moral promise held out by socialism. This expense, along with the poor agricultural land of the site, finally bankrupted the movement. Communitarianism would never again be a serious option for socialists, though a pronounced anti-urban bias was evident in later writers like William Morris. Instead, the principle of association was simply extended to joint-stock enterprise as such, with workers' control and ownership defining the "socialist utopias," as Charles Bray put it in 1844.[8]

Marx and Engels
It has always been controversial to assert that Marxian socialism after 1848, or (following Althusser and other theorists of the intellectual "break" that followed the discovery of the "materialist conception of history") after the composition of the *German Ideology* in 1845–46, should also be termed "utopian."[9] In the preceding period, of course, both Marx and Engels converted to communism, Engels first via Moses Hess, and then by Owen's followers in Manchester. Marx, more philosophically, was led inexorably toward communism through his first incursions into the critique of political economy. In the "Paris Manuscripts" of 1844, he realized that the problem of alienated labor could not be solved without the abolition of private property, which most divisively prevented mankind's "species being" or communal essence (the category is owed to Feuerbach) from being expressed naturally and fully. Both Marx and Engels clearly accepted the gist of the early socialists' criticisms of capitalism and the effects of the division of labor on the working classes. In the most famous "utopian" pronouncement of the early writings, jointly composed in *The German Ideology* and clearly indebted to Fourier, they agreed that variation and rotation of task alone provided the basis for a rich, full human life, one in which it would be possible to engage in hunting in the morning, fishing in the afternoon, rearing cattle in the evening, and criticism after dinner, without as such ever becoming hunter, fisherman, herdsman, or critic.

At the same time, however, Marx was critical of much of the early socialist inheritance. He was unwilling to assign to a specific class of "educators" the task he felt Owen had given them, of remaking

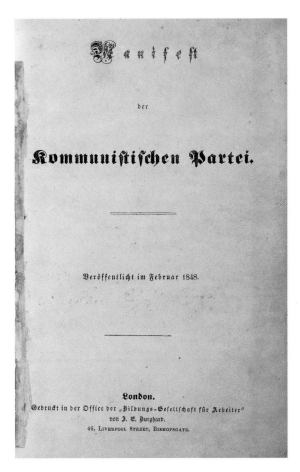

The Communist Manifesto

**Karl Marx and
Friedrich Engels**
***Manifest der
Communistischen Partei***
London: Gedruckt in der Office
der "Bildungs-Gesellschaft für
Arbeiter," von J. C. Burghard, 1848
Houghton Library,
Harvard University

The *Communist Manifesto*
established the platform of
the Communist party and
proclaimed the inevitability
and desirability of a full-scale
overthrow of nineteenth-
century industrial capitalism
by the working class. The
abolition of private property
was the stated ultimate goal
of the party. Calling for a
unified working-class revolt,
the pamphlet ends with a
rousing call to action: "The
proletarians have nothing to
lose but their chains. They
have a world to win. Workers
of all countries, unite!"

the character of the working classes. (See the
third "Thesis on Feuerbach," on Owen, concerning
the tendency of the materialist doctrine of
circumstances to divide society into two parts,
one of which was necessarily superior to the other.)
Instead, Marx's "revolutionizing practice" was
now to solve the problem of educating the working
classes and rendering them fit to rule. Revolution
was now necessary, thus, not only because "the
ruling class cannot be overthrown in any other
way, but also because the class overthrowing it
can only in a revolution succeed in ridding itself
of the muck of ages and become fitted to found
society anew," a theme that would arise in later
theorists of the "cleansing" effects of violence,
such as Sorel and Fanon. Yet Marx and Engels too
were as reliant on the notion of a revolutionary
science as Owen had been on his "social science,"
and the notion of the inherent superiority of the
professional revolutionary, not too distant from
the Platonic ideal of the philosopher-king, would
be closely associated with later forms of Marxism,
and especially Marxism-Leninism.

Marx and Engels were also initially sympathetic to communitarian speculation of various types,
and as late as the *Manifesto of the Communist Party*
considered as appropriate plans to redistribute the
congested working-class population in "palaces"
in the countryside of a Fourierist and Owenite type.
Such proposals, however, as well as the priority
of overcoming economic specialization, largely
disappear from the later works of both Marx and
Engels, which programmatically differ little from
the scheme of nationalization and centralized
economic management outlined in the *Manifesto*.
Moreover, any priority given to superseding narrow
economic specialization in Marxism tends to give
way in the later nineteenth century to the provision
of a maximum productivity in order to raise the
standard of living of the working classes. Schemes
of rotation of task and variation of employment
thereafter are rarely discussed.

The "utopian" element in Marxism, then,
might lie in any or all of the following assumptions:
(1) that human behavior or "nature" might improve
dramatically following the revolutionary recon-

struction of society, particularly in the direction of recapturing any supposed social "essence" in human nature; (2) that the coercive apparatus of state, army, and police might be dramatically reduced in the future as a result (the state for Marx was to "wither away" once the eventual stage of "communist society" had been reached); (3) that a limited range of improvements in behavior, possible in a small-scale community, and often inspired by religious motives, might be transferred to a national scale and motivated by a secular ideology; (4) that national, centralized economic planning was viable; (5) that rotation of employment might be combined with a plan for large-scale collectivization on a national scale.

It should be noted that, from the perspective of the early socialists, Marxism is in at least one fundamental sense *more utopian* than the communitarian schools, for it accepted the logic of behavioral improvements while making two unacceptable assumptions: that revolution as such would aid in remaking working-class behavior; and that improvements possible on a small scale could be transferred to the nation state.

The Response of J. S. Mill

While much of liberalism is consciously anti-utopian in the sense of building any progressive improvement in civilization upon slow, steady, modest economic development based on a system of competition and private property, the revolutions of 1848 provoked one of the leading nineteenth-century liberals, John Stuart Mill, to react more sympathetically to Owenite and Fourierist communitarianism.

In revisions in the second and third editions of his *Principles of Political Economy,* first published in 1848, Mill broke firmly from the tradition of Smith, Ricardo, Bentham, and his father, James Mill, in suggesting that the division of profits between capitalist and worker might be dramatically equalized through cooperative ownership and industrial management. Mill, like Owen and to a lesser extent Marx and Engels, was clearly driven primarily by the notion that capitalist industrialization produced an inferior type of human being. His own "utopia," as he had put it in 1845, was "that of raising the labourer from a receiver of hire to the opposition of being, in some sort, a partner in

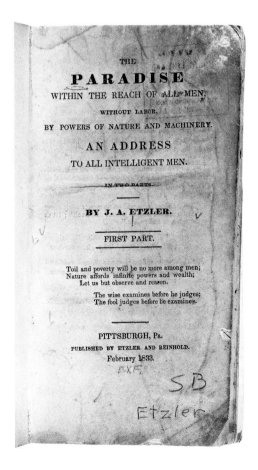

An American "New Eden"

J[ohn] A[dolphus] Etzler
The Paradise Within the Reach of All Men, Without Labor, by Powers of Nature and Machinery: An Address to All Intelligent Men
Pittsburgh, Penn.:
Etzler and Reinhold, 1833
NYPL, General Research Division

"I promise to show the means for creating a paradise within ten years, where every thing desirable for human life may be had for every man in superabundance, without labor, without pay; where the whole face of nature is changed into the most beautiful form of which it may be capable; where man may live in the most magnificent palaces, in all imaginable refinements of luxury, in the most delightful gardens; where he may accomplish, without his labor, in one year more than hitherto could be done in thousands of years. . . . He may lead a life of continual happiness, of enjoyments unknown yet, he may free himself from almost all the evils that afflict

mankind, except death, and even put death far beyond the common period of human life, and finally render it less afflicting: mankind may thus live in, and enjoy a new world far superior to our present, and raise themselves to a far higher scale of beings."

Upholding parallel faiths in man's ability to reason and in the potential of future technology, and strongly influenced by the organizational formulas of Fourier, John Adolphus Etzler dreamed of an American "New Eden" where man could dominate and domesticate nature with the help of machines yet to be invented; *The Paradise Within the Reach of All Men* was the first of four books he wrote on the subject. In the 1840s, he attempted to bring his ideals to life by establishing a community in Venezuela; it ultimately disbanded due to dissension within the group, disease, and the everyday hardships of life in the jungle.

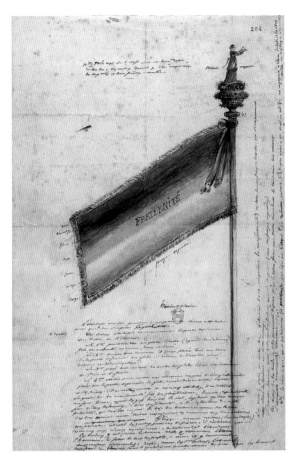

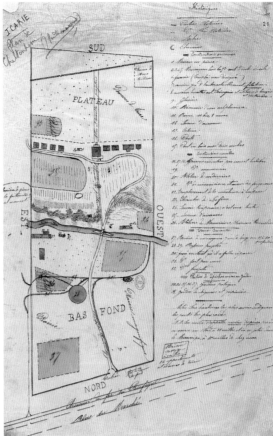

Icarian Communities

Icarian flag
Drawing, ca. 1848
BNF, Département des Manuscrits

Plan of Cheltenham
Drawing, ca. 1848
BNF, Département des Manuscrits

Etienne Cabet's Icaria was more successful on paper than in practice. In 1847, his "Let's Go to Icaria," a rousing article in the magazine *Populaire*, called for the new Icarians to head for the New World the following year. The Icarians were unable to assure the expansion of their communities, the first of which was founded in Texas and the second in Illinois, largely because of Cabet's authoritarianism. His desire to spread his ideas by example was never realized, although a few isolated experiments survived until the end of the century: the Cheltenham, Missouri, settlement lasted until 1864; the Corning, Iowa, community lasted, with some interruptions, until 1895.

it."[10] By the third edition of the *Principles* (1852), this was specified more precisely: The form of association that, if mankind continued to improve, must be expected in the end to predominate is "the association of the labourers themselves on terms of equality, collectively owning the capital with which they carry on their operations, and working under managers elected and removeable by themselves."

Beyond this, Mill went so far as to argue that a "stationary state" – the bugbear of no growth or development so feared by the classical economists – far from being a condition to be avoided, might well permit the shifting of social priorities toward moral and intellectual development and the elimination of that "trampling, crushing, elbowing, and treading on each other's heels, which form the existing type of social life," with no further expansion of population or production. This conception, the progenitor of all "green" or ecological ideals of the "steady state" economy in the late twentieth century, was virtually ignored by later nineteenth century liberals, but remains of great importance today.

Developments After 1848
Communitarianism after 1848 was chiefly an American phenomenon.[11] Both established and new religious foundations, such as the Amana community in Iowa, founded in 1855, and itself the offspring of a Buffalo, New York, community begun in 1842, retained considerable vitality, and usually far greater longevity, than secular efforts. (Amana, reorganized on a joint-stock basis and famous for the production of household appliances, still claimed six hundred members in the late 1970s, while Amish and Mennonite communities still persist in some numbers.) In the United States, early religious foundations like the Rappists and Shakers were joined by the 1830s and 1840s by colonies of Separatists, Transcendentalists, Millenarists, and others. Following the decline of Owenism, a number of Fourierist communities were created under the leadership of Albert Brisbane, Parke Godwin, and Horace Greeley, including, among some twenty-eight communes, the North American Phalanx and the Clermont Phalanx.[12] Another Fourierist effort in Texas, established in 1852, was led by one of Fourier's chief followers, Victor Considérant. Etienne Cabet (1788–1856), whose *Voyage en Icarie* (1840) spawned one of the most impressive communistical movements in nineteenth-century France, led several hundred socialists to New Orleans in 1848–49, and purchased the old Mormon settlement at Nauvoo, Illinois, which under his guidance grew to some 1,800 persons before splitting under severe internal strains in 1856.[13] Cabet's great principle, "fraternity," aimed to maximize equality and popular democracy by providing education and work in common, and rewarding labor on the principle adopted by Marx, "To each according to his needs, from each according to his powers." Though some colonies were in the eastern states (in New England, Transcendentalism helped to underpin the Brook Farm experiment, while late Jewish agricultural settlements existed in New Jersey), most sought cheaper land on the frontier. Various colonies of other European socialists enjoyed a brief existence, such as that of the Weitlingians at Communia in Iowa, while the followers of the German-American inventor John Adolphus Etzler emigrated further still, to South America. As the century progressed, colonies were founded in the West. Mystical communes emerged at Fountaingrove and elsewhere; Theosophical communities were developed; a belated Icarian effort, Icaria Speranza, was founded in California in 1881; and many other communes were established in the West and Northwest.

Perhaps the best-known late nineteenth-century American community was that founded by John Humphrey Noyes at Oneida, New York, lasting from 1848 to 1881. Oneida was distinguished less by its property arrangements than by Noyes's group marriage ideals, which involved the regulation of sexual intercourse by the community and, coincidentally, the fathering of a substantial number of children by various mothers by Noyes himself.[14] It also included an institutionalized system of weekly "mutual criticism" designed to suppress authoritarian tendencies and, like many forms of early socialism, was underpinned by Christian religious beliefs, without which, Noyes insisted, socialism could never be practicable.

In Europe, communitarian socialism was throughout the nineteenth century displaced by revolutionary socialism, which aimed to reorganize the nation-state, and by a melange of schemes derived from various strands of socialist economic criticism. The revolutions of 1848 gave a tremendous impetus to socialist speculation, while marking at the same time a watershed in socialist theory, and the transition from communitarianism to statist and other forms of socialism. The ideas of Owen and Fourier now seemed too little relevant to changing events. Instead, those of Marx, and of such other revolutionary socialists as Auguste Blanqui (1805–1881), whose followers would play a prominent role in the workers' uprising that created

A. *Ecole*
b. *Ecole (Ecole des filles)*
c. *Ecole (Ecole des garçons)*
D. *Ecuries des bœufs.*

Etablissement provisoire à Nauvoo,

(*ancien couvent des Mormons, dans l'Illinois, Etats-Unis*)

de la colonie Icarienne arrivée le 15 Mars 1849.

E. *Bon lieu doré*
F. *Ecots à porcs.*
G. *Refectoire*
H. *Ecuries des chevaux.*

The Icarian Colony of Nauvoo

**Etablissement provisoire
à Nauvoo (ancien couvent
des Mormons, dans
l'Illinois, Etats-Unis) de la
colonie Icarienne arrivée
le 15 mars 1849**
Pen, ink, and watercolor on paper,
ca. 1850s
NYPL, Miriam and Ira D. Wallach
Division of Art, Prints and
Photographs

After the failure of Etienne
Cabet's settlement in Texas,
he relocated 275 of his followers to the town of Nauvoo,
Illinois, in 1849, a year after
it was abandoned by the Mormons. In the center are the
ruins of the old Mormon Temple building, which had been
destroyed by fire, and which
Cabet had planned to reconstruct for use as a school. He
was thwarted in this intention
when the Temple was hit with
a tornado and demolished
beyond repair; the limestone
blocks were recovered from

the ruins and used to construct a new schoolhouse,
at left. Education was very
important to Cabet, and
members of the community
received free schooling from
age four until adulthood.

The refectory, on the right,
was one of the first buildings
constructed by the Icarians.
The ground floor contained a
dining room that seated 400
and a stage on which theatrical
and musical productions
were frequently presented.
The walls were festooned with
painted words and phrases
that reinforced Cabet's ideas:
Fraternity, Equality, Unity, and
the like. Upstairs were living
quarters. Other buildings
in the community included a
distillery (all working men
in the community started the
day with a shot of whiskey),
a flour mill, a sawmill, a shop
housing a printing press, and
a large library.

The Shakers

Nathaniel Currier
Shakers Near Lebanon
Lithograph, n.d.
NYPL, Miriam and Ira D. Wallach
Division of Art, Prints and
Photographs

Dancing, whirling, singing, clapping, marching, and other physically expressive means of worship were central to the United Society of Believers in Christ's Second Appearing, and such activities led to their being popularly called Shakers. The ecstatic state induced by their dancing encouraged direct communication from the spirits of ancestors, especially Mother Ann Lee, the founder of the Shakers, who died in 1784. An eyewitness account by Charles Nordhoff in 1875 described the type of dance shown here: "In their marching and dancing they hold their hands before them, and make a motion as of gathering something to themselves: this is called gathering a blessing. In like manner, when any brother or sister asks for their prayers and sympathy, they, reversing their hands, push towards him that which he asks." Shakers were not entirely closed off from the outside world: they hired laborers to work their fields, they sold their seeds and other products in local towns, and they allowed outsiders to visit and stay in their communities. Here, the woman in the red dress, on the left, is clearly a visitor to the Shaker community.

Messages from the Spirit World

[Polly Ann (Jane) Reed]
"The Word of the Holy Heavenly Father To a Child of his Love"
Ink on paper, [Mount Lebanon, N.Y.], April 14, 1844
NYPL, Manuscripts and Archives Division

In the 1840s and 1850s, an estimated 1,320 "spirit drawings" were created by the Shakers; fewer than 200, most of them from the Mount Lebanon, New York, community, survive today in public and private collections. Depicting religious and secular symbols and shapes, they contained messages from the spirit world, communicated to a Shaker in an ecstatic state. The wording is both in English and in "Indian writing," which was thought to be the direct result of spirit possession. Many drawings contain messages thought to have been directly transferred from Mother Ann Lee, from Jesus, and from other spiritual "parents" or ancestors. They were often given as gifts to other members of the community and seem to have been part of an effort to connect the growing new populations of Shakers with their predecessors.

On the morning of June 2, 1844, the members of the Shaker Community at Mount Lebanon entered their meeting house and found paper hearts laid out on the table. For each member of the community, there was a heart containing a spiritual blessing. This one was made by Polly Read, a tailor in the community, who made many of the gift hearts in April 1844.

the Paris Commune (1870–71), were widely popularized for the first time. Much better known during the revolution itself were the proposals of the French socialist Louis Blanc (1811–1882), who became a member of the Provisional Government following the February revolution. Blanc's *The Organization of Labor* (1839) advocated the state establishment of workshops controlled by their employees as a means to achieve a form of socialism devoted not to absolute equality, but to the just reward of labor. Like most socialist proposals of the period, it thus shifted away from the notion of voluntarily begun, small-scale experiments, and toward nationally organized, public initiatives.

In Britain, following the collapse of Owenism, many socialists immigrated to the New World. Others took up Rochdale-style retail cooperation as a lesser, but more dependable, alternative to the "new moral world," and derided as utopian the notion that any fundamental change in human character would have to precede a more just social order. Owenite economics remained influential chiefly through the adaptation of their chief themes in John Ruskin's *Unto This Last* (1862), which was enormously influential on New Liberal writers such as John Hobson, and on socialists, from the 1880s until World War I. (Ruskin's own colony, the Guild of St. George, did not prosper.) In Britain, the statist, interventionist ideals of Thomas Carlyle, dubbed "feudal socialism" by Marx and Engels, continued to be of influence, and popularized the idea that "industrial armies" might be created in which lifetime employment could be guaranteed in return for the acceptance of an ethos of professional devotion to work on the part of the employed.

By the late nineteenth century, the notion of a planned and organized economy had become the most commonly accepted definition of socialism. That this ought to be the *beau ideal* of socialism was not uncontested, however. William Morris's *News from Nowhere* (1890), for instance, was written specifically against the enormously influential *Looking Backward* (1888), by the American Edward Bellamy. Where Bellamy described a centrally planned economy and the state guarantee of nurture, education, and a comfortable maintenance from cradle to grave through centrally organized credit and the management of society, Morris, who in such matters admired the anarchist writers more than Marx, was explicitly hostile to centralization, and left even the regulation of markets and exchange to the vague determination of "custom" and established practice. Rather than life being

organized around the system of production and consumption, the latter was to be subordinated to the higher realms of aesthetic and cultural experience. Much inspired by Ruskin, Morris famously described his leading passion as a hatred of modern civilization, and did much to popularize a medieval ethos in manners and style, through his firm, Morris and Company, and the Arts and Crafts Movement. The appeal to the pre-industrial past would remain a recurrent theme within British socialism until World War II (for instance, in the early writings of Orwell). But while *News from Nowhere* remains the best-known nineteenth-century socialist literary utopia, its glorification of the medieval found few sympathizers in the mainstream, increasingly Marxian world of the Second International.

Divisions over the question of how centralized and hierarchical the revolutionary movement should be were to become pronounced in the second half of the nineteenth century, and were fuelled by the growing popularity of anarchism. Individualist communities were established in Britain under the influence of the Russian anarchists Tolstoy and Kropotkin and of Edward Carpenter (The Fellowship of the New Life), and in France (the Free Society at Vaux; the colony at Aiglemont). In France, too, the mutualist anarchism of Pierre-Joseph Proudhon (1809–1865), which proposed that property be left in the hands of the primary producer, whether peasant or artisan, proved very popular. (See *What Is Property*, 1840.) Proudhonist ideas attained popularity among Russian and Spanish popularists, and in the syndicalist wing of the trade union movement. Equally critical of centralized communism were other anarchists, notably Mikhail Bakunin (1814–1876), who proved to be Marx's primary antagonist in the First International, and who insisted that Marx's dictatorial personal style heralded a future dictatorship of intellectuals over the workers' movement, and of German socialists over European labor in general. From the constructive, rather than the critical, viewpoint, the anarchist schemes of Peter Kropotkin (1842–1921) proved more influential in the late nineteenth and early twentieth centuries.

Collectivism and the Conquest of Liberalism

The most important turning point in modern social theory lay in the decades between 1880 and World War I, when liberalism and conservatism alike moved in a sharply collectivist direction, partially in response to the threat of socialism from below, and laid the foundations of modern welfare states. Though undiluted collectivism of the Marxist-

Stereoscopic Views of a
Shaker Community

In the second half of the nineteenth century, the Shakers allowed themselves and their communities to be photographed extensively, often in the hope of promoting their communities and attracting new converts; stereoscopic views were an extremely popular form of information and entertainment at that time, and the Shakers sold sets of them along with seeds and homemade products. These views, made by Willis G. C. Kimball, depict the community of Canterbury, New Hampshire. Founded in 1792, Canterbury became relatively prosperous, especially in the nineteenth and twentieth centuries. Members engaged in diverse pursuits such as farming, livestock, weaving, broom making, and washing machine production, and they welcomed many visitors during the summers. The last resident of the Canterbury community died in 1992, and today, like other former Shaker communities, Canterbury is a popular tourist attraction (the only remaining active Shaker community is at Sabbathday Lake, Maine).

The stereoscopic views illustrated here are from The New York Public Library's Robert N. Dennis Collection of Stereoscopic Views.

Willis G. C. Kimball
*Church Family from
the Office*
Concord, N.H.:
W.G.C. Kimball, [1865?–85?]
Stereoscopic view
NYPL, Miriam and Ira D. Wallach
Division of Art, Prints and
Photographs

Each Shaker community was divided into "families" or groups of thirty to one hundred people who had entered the community around the same time. The Canterbury community had three families, and this stereoscopic view shows the buildings of one of them, the Church Family.

Willis G. C. Kimball
Group of Shakers
Concord, N.H.: W.G.C. Kimball,
[1865?–85?]
Stereoscopic view
NYPL, Miriam and Ira D. Wallach
Division of Art, Prints and
Photographs

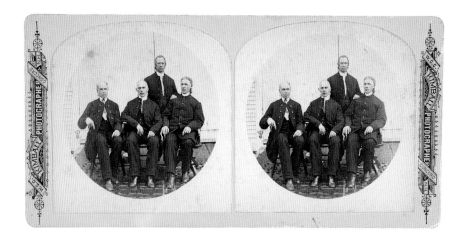

A Mormon Town

Dorothea Lange
[Untitled], from the series
Southern Utah –
Mormon Towns
Silver gelatin print, 1953
NYPL, Miriam and Ira D. Wallach
Division of Art, Prints and
Photographs

This photograph was taken by
Dorothea Lange in 1953 for a
story on Southern Utah towns
in *Life* magazine. It was never
published, and the town is
unidentified. Mormon colonization of the West was highly
organized and systematic,
following a prescribed pattern
for establishing a town. Often
the first building constructed
was for a temple and a school,
and, as in Salt Lake City, it
provided the center around
which uniformly sized housing
lots were demarcated.

Zion in Utah

A[ndrew] J[oseph] Russell
Great Mormon Tabernacle
1868, Plate 50 in *The Great West
Illustrated* Vol. 4 (New York: Union
Pacific Railroad Company, 1869)
Albumen print (black and white)
on letterpress mount
NYPL, Miriam and Ira D. Wallach
Division of Art, Prints and
Photographs

The Mormons, also called
the Church of Jesus Christ
of Latter Day Saints, believed
that in these "latter days"
before the second coming,
it was necessary to construct
a holy city to be Jerusalem's
equivalent in the Western
Hemisphere. Believing that
this city, named Zion, should
be modeled on the Celestial
Jerusalem, founder Joseph
Smith designed a city on a
grid pattern, with the communal temples and storehouses
at the center surrounded
by wide streets and uniformly
sized residential lots for
private houses and gardens.
One always knows where
one is in relation to the
temple as all the streets are
named for their distance and
direction from the Temple
(such as Fourth East Street).
Brigham Young, Smith's successor, brought the Mormons
from Illinois to the Salt Lake
area and established the city
there.

While the Temple is the
central sacred space for the
Mormons, the Tabernacle has
always served as the main
social and cultural center,
hosting conferences from
the moment it could accommodate an audience. Built
between 1865 and 1875, it
measures 250 feet by 150
feet, and the dome is held up
entirely by wooden pegs and
rawhide thongs.

Views of Oneida

Like many utopian groups, the Perfectionists believed that their social ideals should be reflected and supported by the architecture of their community. When John Noyes and his followers arrived in Oneida from Vermont, they lived in wooden buildings that were included in their land purchase. Initially, the Oneidans hoped to make their living from horticulture, and they built numerous frame buildings and designed orchards and gardens that reflected this pastoral ideal. By 1859, they had abandoned their hope for agricultural self-sufficiency and begun to look to their manufacturing enterprises for income; they had also abandoned their ideas about creating an Eden-like garden and begun to construct a series of brick buildings around a central courtyard. The interiors of the buildings were designed to house a growing population and reflected the dual needs of communal and solitary activities. Private bedrooms were grouped around or near public parlors, and the central building housed a large hall with a stage for community meetings and entertainment. While satellite communities of Perfectionists existed in Wallingford, Connecticut; Newark, New Jersey; Putney and Cambridge, Vermont; and Manlius, New York, Oneida remained the central community.

[View of the Oneida Community]
[N.p., 1865?–75?]
Stereoscopic view
NYPL, Miriam and Ira D. Wallach Division of Art, Prints and Photographs

This is a view of the new complex from the south, showing the South Wing, which housed the children's area, bedrooms, parlors, and a large hall with a stage. Parlors were used for socializing and for the practice of "mutual criticism." Viewed as a means to achieve perfection, mutual criticism required a member of the community to come before a committee that would discuss the strengths and weaknesses of the member's character.

D. E. Smith
[View of the Oneida Community]
Community, N.Y., [1865?–75?]
Stereoscopic view
NYPL, Miriam and Ira D. Wallach Division of Art, Prints and Photographs

This is a view of the community from the east.

This view shows the front
lawn of the "Mansion
House," the central building
of the Oneida community. In
the early 1870s, the community was experiencing a peak
in population, in part because
of stirpicultural (or selective
breeding) experiments and in
part because of the prosperity
that resulted from successful
enterprises in the production
of steel traps, silk thread, and
fruit preserves. This prosperity
would continue throughout
the decade. By 1881, dis-
agreements over leadership
and widespread criticism from
the outside world over the
practice of Complex Marriage
led to the dissolution of the
community and the formation
of a joint stock corporation to
manage the businesses. One
of their enterprises, the manufacture of silver and stainless
steel dinnerware, remains a
successful company today.

The Oneida community
practiced what they believed
was complete "Bible
Communism," sharing not
only possessions and products, but also people. Their
system of Complex Marriage
discouraged monogamy,
which was considered selfish
and possessive, and the raising of children was considered
the responsibility of the entire
community. From shortly after
birth, children were housed
in a separate building and
raised by a group of nurses
and teachers. This system,

the Perfectionists believed,
produced better-behaved
children and allowed new
mothers time for educational
and social pursuits.

Between 1869 and 1878,
Noyes enlisted one hundred
men and women in the com-
munity for his experiments
in "stirpiculture" or selective
breeding. Since procreation
was the desired way to
increase membership in the
community (rather than to
bring in new members),
Noyes thought he could
create a new generation of
better inhabitants by pairing
together the most "robust"
members of the community.
His experiments resulted
in fifty-eight children born
to eighty-one parents.

Leninist sort, with complete centralized economic planning, fell into disfavor at the end of the twentieth century, this mixture of liberalism and socialism, in most respects equidistant from the "pure" ideological types of each belief, has proven enormously popular, and is the predominant form of government among developed nations. It dates from various efforts to contend with the crises of poverty and unemployment of the 1880s, and from the willingness to adapt socialist ideas to the creation of dual, statist and private, economies. Guarantees of unemployment and disability benefits, education and medical care, and old age pensions, which derived from existing socialist demands (in Britain, for instance, notably by the prominent New Liberal writer John Hobson), were now gradually provided by legislation, but secured through schemes of progressive taxation rather than communal or collective ownership of the means of production as such. The early years of the Soviet revolution included some mixtures of private and state ownership and management, too, though the predominant model after the mid-1920s was to be wholesale collectivization and centralized planning along the lines first suggested in the *Communist Manifesto*. Mainstream European socialism and Social Democracy, however, blended increasingly with collectivist forms of liberalism throughout this period.

The notion of a compromise between liberalism and socialism was in some respects a consciously anti-utopian choice by some types of socialists. With reference to means, Fabian socialism, for instance, abjured revolution in favor of a gradualist "permeation" of existing political institutions, as did German Social Democracy in embracing the ballot box rather than the bayonet. Yet another prominent Fabian, H. G. Wells, used the utopian literary device to popularize socialist ideals in works like *A Modern Utopia* (1905), and became his era's leading prophet of a new, rational economic order, and, eventually, of the idea of world government. Most of the socialists of this era, like Wells, welcomed the Soviet experiment, despite Marx's warnings, mitigated to some degree in his private correspondence, that Russia would have to pass through a bourgeois, capitalist stage prior to any possible movement toward socialism. Many, however, became antagonistic toward Stalinism in the 1930s and, like Orwell, began to perceive a generalized onslaught on individuality and nonconformity as the legacy of the less tolerant forms of nineteenth-century socialism.

The Socialist Utopia:
Some Unanswered Questions

Nineteenth-century socialism was firmly rooted in the notion that human character could be

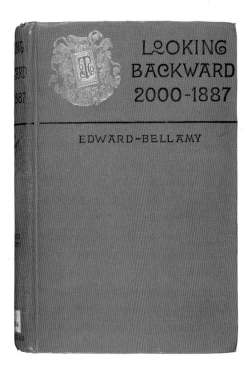

Standing Straight Before God

Edward Bellamy
***Looking Backward,
2000–1887***
Boston: Ticknor and Company,
1888
NYPL, General Research Division

Since its initial publication in 1888, Edward Bellamy's most famous work has never been out of print. *Looking Backward* is the story of a man, Julien West, who sleeps for 113 years and then awakens in an idealized Boston in the year 2000. He describes a "vivid dream-world, in that glorious city, with its homes of simple comfort and its gorgeous public palaces . . . faces unmarred by arrogance or servility, by envy or greed, by anxious care or feverish ambition, and stately forms of men and women who had never known fear of a fellow man or

depended on his favor, but always, in the words of that sermon which still rang in my ears, had 'stood up straight before God.'" In this completely classless society, all men and women work at jobs that are equal in prestige and salary, eat in common restaurants, and shop in government-owned stores. Full access to education, medicine, and financial assistance leads to a society in which poverty, disease, and crime are virtually unknown. In a dream, West returns to the Boston of his own time, where his story of this wondrous future city and his condemnation of his own society are considered the ravings of a madman. Happily for him, he awakens in the Boston of 2000, where he remains.

improved if the environment were first altered so as to accentuate only the higher or more moral aspects of behavior. The advance of science, especially the advent of psychology and the application of Darwinism to humanity, gave a much stronger impetus to the view that an original human nature existed which, if perhaps not fallen in the Christian sense, nonetheless was far less malleable than socialists suggested. Society could no longer therefore be made at will, like an architectural edifice; it had an organic existence, a history and biology, which were independent of the will of even the most determined legislators. Much less, given the individualist and competitive emphases of both psychology and Social Darwinism, could human nature be bent in an overwhelmingly altruist direction, or returned to a state of pristine sociability. Various forms of socialism attempted to come to terms with Social Darwinism, even to wed eugenics to a socialist worldview, though this was to be developed much further by German fascism.

If socialism could be said to be "utopian" in two *negative* senses (as opposed to the neutral or positive sense of building on the literary utopian tradition), then the first is the insistence on the *fundamental*, as opposed to the temporary or partial, malleability of human nature. The second is the belief that production can be organized rationally, planned centrally, and distributed justly according to need and the principles of justice, on a scale that is national, even international, rather than communal in scope. Since the collapse of the Soviet Union, it has been a commonplace, following Hayek and others, to assert that such complex calculations could never in principle have been achieved, and that the distributive mechanism provided by the market, whatever its wasteful shortcomings and injustices, is inevitable. This is the principal objection now levelled against Marxian economics, but it is frequently deployed to contend that socialism as such is untenable. And if communitarianism on any other than a very small scale has also proven unattractive to the majority, such arguments seem dismissive of the viability of nineteenth-century socialism as such.

Nonetheless, as we have seen, this is to take too limited a view of socialism. Between anti-centralist communitarianism and wholly centralist Marxism there lay a variety of mixtures of collectivist ideals, sometimes termed socialist, sometimes "New Liberal," which have proven remarkably popular and resilient. These involve, to a substantial degree, the same guarantees of social and economic security, if not of full employment, which are associated with the utopian tradition as a whole, but without the degree of economic planning associated with Marxism, or the social equality and uniformity frequently commended by the early

The Paris Commune

W. Alexis
Je veux être libre! . . . C'est mon droit et je me défends
[Paris]: Duclaux, [1871?]
Lithograph
NYPL, Miriam and Ira D. Wallach Division of Art, Prints and Photographs

In the wake of France's defeat in the Franco-Prussian War, the citizens of Paris staged a violent rebellion, founded in large part on their fear of a return to a monarchy. As a result, the Parisians elected their own government and established the Paris Commune in March 1871. Led by a loose assembly of socialists and revolutionaries, the Commune called for the use of the Revolutionary calendar, the abolishing of religion, and better working conditions. At the end of May 1871, government troops, seeking to quash the insurgents of Paris, entered an undefended section of the city and for one week attacked the barricades erected by the Parisian people. At the end of the week, 20,000 insurgents were dead, 38,000 more had been arrested, and 7,000 had been deported. Although the Paris Commune lasted only two months, Karl Marx saw it as the first real attempt by the proletariat to rise up against the bourgeoisie.

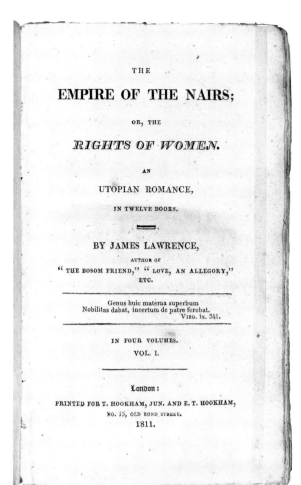

James Lawrence
***The Empire of the Nairs;
or, The Rights of Women.
An Utopian Romance,
in twelve books***
London: Printed for T. Hookham,
Jun. and E. T. Hookham, 1811
NYPL, The Carl H. Pforzheimer
Collection of Shelley and His Circle

In his introduction, James
Lawrence explains, "This
work was designed to shew
the possibility of a nation's
reaching the highest civilization without marriage." Based
on a society in India, and
heavily influenced by the ideas
of Mary Wollstonecraft and
William Godwin, the society
he describes is a matrilineal
one where men fight wars,
and women own property,
raise children, and hold power.
Paternity is unimportant, and
free love is encouraged.

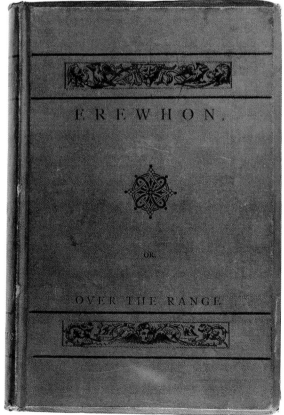

The City of Nowhere

[Samuel Butler]
***Erewhon; or, Over the
Range***
London: Trübner, 1872
NYPL, Henry W. and
Albert A. Berg Collection of
English and American Literature

Samuel Butler's *Erewhon*
(an anagram of "nowhere")
describes a dystopian city
where people seem happy
and tolerant and open, but
in fact, behind this hypocritical
facade, they suffer from
all the human weaknesses.
A nation of Luddites, they
abhor technology and classify
themselves by horsepower.
The protagonist finally
escapes the city of Erewhon
by means of a hot air balloon.

NEWS FROM NOWHERE OR AN EPOCH OF REST. CHAPTER I. DISCUSSION AND BED.

UP at the League, says a friend, there had been one night a brisk conversational discussion, as to what would happen on the Morrow of the Revolution, finally shading off into a vigorous statement by various friends, of their views on the future of the fully-developed new society. SAYS our friend: Considering the subject, the discussion was good-tempered; for those present, being used to public meetings & after-lecture debates, if they did not listen to each other's opinions, which could scarcely be expected of them, at all events did not always attempt to speak all together, as is the custom of people in ordinary polite society when conversing

THIS IS THE PICTURE OF THE OLD HOUSE BY THE THAMES TO WHICH THE PEOPLE OF THIS STORY WENT HEREAFTER FOLLOWS THE BOOK ITSELF WHICH IS CALLED NEWS FROM NOWHERE OR AN EPOCH OF REST & IS WRITTEN BY WILLIAM MORRIS.

Work as Creativity

William Morris
News from Nowhere;
or, An Epoch of Rest.
Being Some Chapters
from a Utopian Romance
Hammersmith: The Kelmscott
Press, 1892
NYPL, Rare Books Division

In William Morris's utopian novel, a man named William Guest awakens one morning after a troubled sleep to find himself in a world completely unlike the industrial London of the nineteenth century, where he fell asleep. As he explores this clean, prosperous place, he discovers a society of youthful people who are happy, energetic, free from want, and, most important, engaged in work for the pure

pleasure of serving others and expressing their own creativity. Morris's "Nowhere" reflects his own socialist and anti-industrialist points of view and depicts a post-revolutionary society free of class division, formal education, governmental structures, money, poverty, crime, and industrial pollution.

This edition of *News from Nowhere* was printed by Morris at his Kelmscott Press in Hammersmith, England, and reflects Morris's highly decorative style of book design. The frontispiece depicts Kelmscott Manor, where Morris lived and where the character of William Guest finds himself at the end of his adventures.

a

*William Morris's Workshops
at Merton Abbey*

Edmund Hort New
Proofs on woodcut to illustrate
The Life of William Morris by
J. W. Mackail (London, 1899)
The Pierpont Morgan Library,
New York

**a. *Merton Abbey Mill
Pond with Weaving and
Painting Sheds***

**b. *Merton Abbey Glass
Painting Sheds from
Dyehouse***

**c. *Merton Abbey Chintz
Printing Room***

William Morris's work as an
author and designer reflected
his aesthetic and philosophical
beliefs. He valued handmade
objects and favored pre-industrial methods of production.
His workshops at Merton
Abbey, where, in 1881, he
established facilities for dye-
making, textile printing and
weaving, and glass painting,
were designed to provide a
pleasant environment that promoted equality and creativity
among the employees. These
scenes – proofs for illustrations in J. W. Mackail's important biography of Morris –
show some of the working
areas at Merton Abbey.

b

c

The Libertarian Golden Age

Paul Signac
Au temps d'harmonie
Color lithograph, 1895–96
BNF, Département des Estampes
et de la Photographie

This idyllic image of a libertarian utopia was inspired by the
artist Paul Signac's anarchist
ideas. He initially entitled it
"In the time of anarchy," then
added a subtitle, taken from
Saint-Simon, to clarify the allegorical meaning: "The golden
age of mankind is not behind,
but before us." This is one
of seven known proofs of a
print reproduction; the monumental painting itself hangs
in Montreuil's City Hall.

utopians, which have an undoubted tendency to suppress individuality. Such doctrinal compromises have also entailed renouncing substantial concerns for the moral improvement of humanity, or conscious genetic manipulation of the species, or the abolition of "politics," since class systems remain in place in such mixed economies.

The enormous appeal of socialism in the twentieth century indicates not merely the persistent vitality of the utopian ideal, but the explosive rise in expectations, and the progressive appeal of egalitarian systems, which fuel it. The legacy of nineteenth-century socialism at the end of the twentieth century lies less in communitarianism, however, than in ecological efforts to restrain the growth of production and population in order to assure the survival of the species, an idea which, in modern terms, dates from the socialist writers of the 1820s and 1830s. The Green utopia notably mirrors the tensions of nineteenth-century socialism, too: whether to aim for systems of restricted, local and small-scale production or to focus on the nation-state; whether to attempt to supersede national sovereignty by some form of world government; whether to give the often-unpopular restraint of needs a high priority; and how to deal with the population problem effectively. Finally, there lingers at the end of the twentieth century another vestige of Enlightenment cosmopolitan utopianism that passed into socialism in the nineteenth century: the proposal for world government, based probably on the United Nations, and superseding to an unprecedented degree national sovereignty in matters of international order and humanitarian aid.

Notes

1 Not a "perfect" society, as is often suggested; the concept is essentially theological. There is some crime and disorder in virtually all utopias, including More's.

2 See my *Citizens and Saints: Politics and Anti-Politics in Early British Socialism* (Cambridge, England: Cambridge University Press, 1989).

3 See, for instance, the linkage of More to Owen in Robert Southey's *Sir Thomas More, or Colloquies on . . . Society* (London: John Murray, 1829).

4 See my *Utopias of the British Enlightenment* (Cambridge, England: Cambridge University Press, 1991), for this and further examples.

5 See generally W.H.G. Armytage, *Heavens Below: Utopian Experiments in England 1560–1900* (London: Routledge and Kegan Paul, 1961).

6 A survey of the problem of politics in early socialism is Keith Taylor, *The Political Ideas of the Utopian Socialists* (London and Totowa, N.J.: Frank Case, 1982).

7 Its history is now told in Edward Royle, *Robert Owen and the Commencement of the Millennium: A Study of the Harmony Community* (Manchester: Manchester University Press, 1998).

8 Charles Bray, *The Philosophy of Necessity*, 2nd ed. (London: Longman, Green, Longman & Roberts, 1863), 374–412.

9 For a summary of the arguments, see Vincent Geoghegan, *Utopianism and Marxism* (London: Methuen, 1987).

10 John Stuart Mill, *Dissertations and Discussions*, 4 vols. (London: Longmans, Green, Reader and Dyer, 1862), 2: 210.

11 The most recent survey is Robert Fogerty, *American Communes and Utopian Movements 1860–1914* (Chicago: University of Chicago Press, 1990).

12 See Carl Guarneri, *The Utopian Alternative: Fourierism in Nineteenth-Century America* (Ithaca, N.Y.: Cornell University Press, 1991).

13 Two studies of the movement are Christopher Johnson, *Utopian Communism in France: Cabet and the Icarians, 1839–1851* (Ithaca, N.Y.: Cornell University Press, 1974), and Robert Sutton, *Les Icariens: The Utopian Dream in Europe and America* (Urbana: University of Illinois Press, 1994).

14 The theme generally is treated in Raymond Lee Muncy, *Sex and Marriage in Utopian Communities in Nineteenth Century America* (London: Penguin Books, 1975).

Utopia and Nineteenth-century French Literature

BETWEEN THE fervent desire for realization that drives political utopias and the disregard for reality that pervades a number of literary utopias, all gradations can be found. While social reform may not have figured prominently for most nineteenth-century men of letters,[1] the fact remains that they lived in times that were singularly marked by the concomitant rise of novel political ideas and of an unprecedented evolution in the sciences and, to a greater degree, in technology. Consequently, most nineteenth-century literary works that qualify as utopian can be situated at the crossroads of politics and techno-science: either because they express a firm faith in a better future that will integrate technological advances and revolutions into a revitalized political framework, or because they hold out little hope for a future they fear will be ruled by the technological climate, the tyrannical demands of the political structure, or a combination of the two. A typology of nineteenth-century literary utopias would have to take stock of the many, and often overlooked, authentically utopian works (songs, manifestoes, digressions that have slipped from the author's pen) whose importance rivals that of certain novels; while the novels themselves, were we to limit ourselves to them, present a corpus that is far too vast and heterogeneous for a significant conclusion to be reached. We shall limit ourselves, therefore, for the purposes of this study to taking our cue from a handful of authors whose positions with regard to the technological and social orders of the future can generally be qualified as alternatively confident, doubtful, or defiant in the face of the future's capacity to ensure freedom and happiness.

Belief in the Radiant Future

To the degree that "utopia" is admissible as a literary genre, in the nineteenth century that genre was to undergo a fundamental modification: the alternate worlds it proposed were less and less "*elsewhere*" and increasingly in a "*time to come*." By virtue of its new ties to time, rather than to space, utopia set the stage for *uchronia*, long before Charles Renouvier had come up with the neologism, thereby facilitating literature's ideology of progress.

Félix Bodin was no doubt under the influence of a brand of Saint-Simonian optimism when, in

Le Roman de l'avenir (1834), he imagined that the world at the end of the twentieth century would still be divided into States but that these would be administered by international institutions run by learned men. The idea of a radiant future persisted throughout a century every single decade of which was to produce an illustrative novel: hence, Georges Pellerin, in *Le Monde dans deux mille ans* (1878), saw supreme authority exercised, in the interest of general welfare, by an international congress of all nations;[2] ten years later, Neulif's *L'Uthopie contemporaine, notes de voyages* described an irenic world; Albert Quantin, writing *En plein vol, vision d'avenir* (1913) on the eve of the worldwide conflict of World War I, transported his reader to the year 2001 and a world in which progress had yet again engendered happiness.

In 1896, Gabriel de Tarde, who was one of the most prestigious sociologists of the late nineteenth century and who was chosen over Henri Bergson by the Collège de France in 1900,[3] published, in the *Revue internationale de sociologie*, his *Fragment d'histoire future*, a charming, fanciful piece in much the same vein as his 1892 *Les géants chauves*, which had appeared in the *Revue bleue*. Both allegories have lessons to impart: "the fulness of peace . . . the almost gratuitous abundance of every kind of wealth" promised in the first text were widely spouted by the novelists of the day. More original by far are the "certain leaven of discord" and "relaxation of our morals"[4] that he forecast for the new humanity. While the number of nineteenth-century novelists who contested the idea of progress was small to begin with, the number of those who, before Tarde, envisaged the possibility of a social retrogression was even smaller. The second tale, set in 1992, is no more encouraging: a society that has managed to manipulate biology to create a race of geniuses (the bald giants) has to face the dire consequences of its untrammeled excess. The future may very well be radiant, Tarde seems to be saying in these undoubtedly rich narratives, which deserve much closer analysis, but it is intrinsically doomed to instability all the same. In Tarde's work, we find one of the major articulations in the renewal of a genre whose schemes were so often bound by convention. On the eve of the twentieth century, the new doubt that had insinuated itself into the minds of many had less to do with the consequences of a technological progress that by and large had delivered on its promise (which, incidentally, drove novelists to ever-increasing feats of the imagination as today's chimera turned into tomorrow's reality), and more to do with society's ability to adapt to new rules. Even a novelist like Jules Verne, the chief prophet of Promethean science, was not exempt from such concerns.

The preceding gloss should not distract us from the great number of nineteenth-century novelists who without qualms used science and in turn were used by it, to mutual advantage. A statistical account of their work, and more so of its reception, would clearly demonstrate their prevalence. Paschal Grousset, for example, comparable in talent to Jules Verne though his politics could not have been more dissimilar (he was successively a Communard, a deportee to New Caledonia, and a socialist deputy for Paris), writing under the pen name André Laurie produced quite a few adventure novels of utopian bent, among them the rather successful 1889 *De New York à Brest en sept heures*. Leaving aside the controversy surrounding the number of books published under the name Jules Verne that are attributed to Grousset,[5] it is, nonetheless, useful to point out the association of both authors with that category of writers who were well versed in technology and had the ability to introduce this knowledge to a captive audience of adolescent readers.[6] What is more, Grousset embodied the double persona of utopian novelist and social utopian; at the age of twenty-five, in 1869, he had written *Le Rêve d'un irréconciliable*, which took issue with Bonapartist politics.

Science illustrated by fiction (it would be anachronistic to speak of science fiction proper) emerges as the domain of numerous popular authors. As a general rule, they are responsible for a body of work that comprises works of pure vulgarization[7] as well as novels in which they give their imagination a freer rein; of their works, only the latter can be said to pertain to the utopian spirit. The indefatigable popularizer Camille Flammarion was the undisputed central figure among them; in his work, the astronomer endures in the persona of the writer whose concourse with imaginary worlds steers him toward the anticipation of astronautics. In his novels *Uranie* [*Urania*] (1889), *La Fin du monde* (1894), and *Stella* (1897), society has attained human perfection. The second novel, for example, goes well beyond the scope of its title: set twenty thousand years hence, the novel allows ample time for

society to have improved itself and for man to have achieved his physical and mental perfection. A long phase of self-refinement is all that awaits man in the civilization of the future, that voluptuous era to come — Flammarion is not exactly forthcoming with the details. After all, he is not Fourier.

Prior to Flammarion, belief in science had found its chronicler in Samuel Henry Berthoud, who in "L'an deux mille huit cent soixante-cinq," the final chapter of *L'Homme depuis cinq mille ans* (1865), played up the importance of new inventions in a world that functioned by means of and for the sake of science. The neologism "epistemocracy" adequately describes the limitless political power conferred on science by the believers whose embrace of this new genre coincided, by and large, with an emphatic rejection of religion.

Under the category of "extraordinary scientific voyages," we find collaborative works by Georges Le Faure and Henri de Graffigny that despite their more modest intellectual ambitions are not without literary merit. The four volumes that comprise their *Aventures extraordinaires d'un savant russe* (1889–96) are particularly noteworthy for their evocation of other worlds: these texts are extremely representative of an attitude toward technology that was shared by the ruling classes and the masses alike.

This synthesis between knowledge and technological and moral progress, which was generally accompanied by a Christian spirituality, at least in the early part of the century, and which culminated in the hopes of 1848, was perhaps most aptly portrayed in the Pellerin painting that was gleefully described by Flaubert as "the Republic, or Progress, or Civilization, in the person of Jesus Christ driving a railway engine."[8]

Political Militants

The apparent evasiveness with which supporters of scientific progress treat the subject of society's future organization follows from a consensus that this somewhat secondary matter will take care of itself. Political militants, on the other hand, imagine the future as a time of perfect equilibrium between social change and scientific progress bolstered by widespread popular support. The central debate that occupied late nineteenth-century socialist movements, which sought to establish the relevance of a specifically utopian aspect to the revolutionary struggle, resulted in an almost unanimous rejection (and not just on the part of Marxists) of "utopian socialism." Literary works were not exempted from this dismissal, as any revival of utopian scenarios was bound to undermine the mass movement by diverting it from the struggle at hand. Marx had already stated that the "working class . . . have no ready-made utopias to introduce *par décret du peuple*"[9] and that it was futile to write "recipes . . . for the cook-shops of the future."[10] This position no doubt accounts for the marked reticence that characterized socialist attitudes toward utopian fiction for almost the entire latter half of the nineteenth century, and for the favored status given to works of economics and politics. For example, "Conjuration chez les Atlantes" by the reformist Benoît Malon, published in the *Almanach du peuple* in 1874 and never reprinted, counts for little beside his five-volume *Histoire du socialisme* (1882–86). Later, another socialist, Ernest Tarbouriech, author of *La Cité future, essai d'une utopie scientifique* (1902), felt obliged to include an introductory chapter in which he sought to justify his reliance on the utopian paradigm. This work, too, as the title clearly states, is not a novel but an essay. In fact, it is a rather abstract intellectual exercise in which Tarbouriech the militant humors Tarbouriech the jurist by essentially allowing him to legislate in a vacuum and to regulate an economy administered down to the last detail. For the record, we cite two additional texts of the same ilk: *Lois collectivistes pour l'an 19. . .*, by Georges Dazet (1907), and *Projet de code socialiste* (1908–12) by Lucien Deslinières.[11] This silence was not broken until the last decade of the century, when socialist authors again allowed their activism to spill over into the writing of fictions that imagined the future; in 1890, Alain Le Drimeur published *La Cité future*; Auguste Chirac's *Si . . . étude sociale d'après-demain* followed in 1893. This revival can perhaps be explained by the success of the translations of Bellamy's *Looking Backward* that were published around this time. Or perhaps not, as renewed interest really took off with the 1897 publication of an early version of Charles Péguy's *De la cité socialiste* in *Revue socialiste* and of *Chez nos petit-fils* by the old Communard Eugène Fournière, which appeared in 1900.

Travail* (1901), one of the last novels by Emile Zola, certainly pertains to the socialist sphere, if only because of the manifest influence of Fourierism as interpreted by Pierre Leroux. Set in a futurist twentieth-century France, *Travail* lacks the power of Zola's other novels. To be sure, it is difficult to tell the story of happiness in full swing. Like *Fécondité* (1899) and *Vérité* (1903), also part of the unfinished cycle entitled *Les Quatre Evangiles*, *Travail* fails because it describes a world that is more unreal than fictional.

The panorama of works of the imagination inspired by political thought would be incomplete if we did not include, alongside the socialist works, those that rose out of the libertarian movement, which incidentally had a knack for expressing itself with vigor and originality. In London, Ernest Coeurderoy published two works of undeniable utopian character, *Hurrah !!! ou la révolution par les cosaques* (1854) and *Jours d'exil* (1854–55), a collection of futurist scenarios, narratives, and political observations. Joseph Déjacque, also writing from exile, in New York, published *L'Humanisphère* (1858–59) serially in *Le Libertaire, journal du movement social*; he devotes an entire chapter to the description of a society that has severed all ties to Authority. Louise Michel's *Le Monde Nouveau* (1888) has a similar approach, which attaches greater importance to human development than to technological advances, which are considered little more than means to an end. Jean Grave addressed his first book, *Les Aventures de Nono* (1901), to children, then followed it with a book for adolescents, *Terre libre* (1908); the later book revived the scenario of a shipwreck followed by new beginnings for a colony stranded on a desert island.[12] An analogous theme is developed in *Le Nouvel Adam* (1910), a work that probably should be attributed to Michel Verne rather than to his father, Jules, in which a handful of people, survivors of a catastrophe, create a society built on new premises. These anarchist works are singularly given to imprecision, a natural by-product of the concern for individual freedoms, which contrasts with the obsessive equality of socialist texts that, despite intentions to the contrary, ends up stifling the societies of the future.

Uchronia

While the motivations that prompt the creation of utopias are for the most part apparent, the same does not hold for *uchronias*. Are the authors of the latter, one wonders, drawn by the purity of the literary exercise, by the supreme fictitiousness of telling the story of things that have not happened? Or is it a wish to highlight the contingencies that burden history that attracts them to apocryphal accounts "of the development of European civilization as it was not but could have been," as the philosopher Charles Renouvier put it in the subtitle of his 1876 *Uchronie*? He may very well have invented the word, now a mainstay of the vocabulary, but not the idea. Even if we disregard the seventeenth century, we will still find that Renouvier was preempted by the likes of Delisle de Sales (*Ma République*, 1791) and Louis Geoffroy (*Napoléon et la conquête du monde, 1812 à 1832*, 1836). These works, together with many other kindred ones, overlap in their effort to remove history from causality and to free societies from the necessities that engender them. Verging on the Leibnizian idea of "contingent futures," these forays into what could have been put us in mind of the "palace of the fates" where there are "representations not only of that which happens but also of all that which is possible," in such a way as to impart the knowledge of "what would happen if any particular possibility should attain unto existence."[13]

The popularity of a genre that aimed to reconcile narrative with history, by returning to it and reinventing it *a posteriori*, just as utopia sought to direct its course *a priori*, is also largely due to the nineteenth century's deep-rootedness in history and especially to its reliance on it as a model for the analysis of societies. The genre also points to a shift from a fiction that sees itself, to varying degrees, as either programmatic or counter-progammatic, to a fiction that is aware of itself as a double fiction: the prospect of an ideal society falls away in favor of a society that is perpetually other.

Toward a Counter-utopia

The utopian literary genre is well suited to the literary game of conjecture. As a result, the nineteenth century abounds with texts meant as pure entertainment and devoid of critical content; these works fall outside the limits of the present discussion, which is restricted to those authors who took an explicit position with regard to the representations of possible futures. Moreover, the parameters of the genre are ill-defined and overlap with those of the imaginary adventure voyage.

On the other hand, there emerged as early as the July Monarchy a school of thought that vigorously contested the idea of a future in which socialism and technocracy would be joined. Charles Nodier is one of the most emblematic figures of these new "right-wing utopias."[14] In three narratives in which sarcasm and a lively style are perfectly attuned (*Hurlubleu* and *Léviathan-le-Long* in 1833, *Voyage pittoresque et industriel dans le Paraguay-Roux et la Palingénésie australe* in 1835), he contests the progressive illusions of the day[15] as well as the optimism that Pierre-Simon Ballanche had championed in *La Ville des expiations* (1832). Emile Souvestre's far more ambitious work, *Le Monde tel qu'il sera* (1845), also belongs to this tradition. Despite its obvious flaws, this prescient cautionary tale about the dangers of mechanization, thought control, and the inhumanity of a society obsessed with material possessions is the undisputed matrix of all the "great modern anti-utopias."[16] We are meant to

take as ironic its promise that "man shall rest, his work taken on by his creatures, as the proletariat will be a thing of the past and all social problems resolved in universal happiness and wealth." If Emile Souvestre stands out in this gallery of "grumblers about the future," it is not because of the quality of his writing, which is in fact rather poor, but because of the themes he brings into play; the future, industrial as expected, is not at all appealing, although less because of its loathsome political system (the "Republic of United Interests," with its excessive insistence on specialization, is hardly a happy place) than because of the subjugation to machines that this specialization implies. As early as 1845, a novelist had come forward to denounce a future "in which man would be enslaved by the machine and self-interest would replace love."

Counterrevolutionary, reactionary, and aristocratic circles make up the first ranks of this denunciation; their disapproval has more than a little to do with the alleged egalitarianism of this so-called future. It is hardly an accident, therefore, that in the next generation the two masterpieces based on these ideas are the work of aristocrats. *Ignis* (1883), the only novel written by Count Didier de Chouzy, offers a lively account of the misfortunes that befall a society that relies exclusively on technology to solve all its problems. Perhaps inspired by the "steam-powered slaves" conceived by Théophile Gautier thirty-five years earlier,[17] Chouzy's "athmophites," the human machines that are the paradigm for all the robots that will overrun twentieth-century science fiction, give us cause for alarm. In *L'Eve future* (1886), Count Auguste Villiers de L'Isle-Adam was, for his part, more than happy to pessimistically warn against the dire consequences of Edison's discoveries, at a time when many of his contemporaries could see only their possible benefits.[18] Beyond the theme of the automaton betrothed to a perpetual future, this rich but difficult novel must also be singled out for its magical power.

It would not take long for the critique of a technological society — which at first had been associated with an elitist mentality — to sweep society as a whole. By the turn of the century, among both Republicans and Democrats, the critical readiness had had its effect. And it is here that rigid classifications reveal their limits, as when a single author expresses divergent opionions about the future. Thus, we can justifiably classify the Anatole France of *Sur la pierre blanche* [*The White Stone*] (1903) as a utopian optimist: in this book,

Le Lawn-Tennis.

L'Agent Aviateur.

In the Year 2000

Villemard
En l'an 2000
N.p.: Villemard impr., 1910
Chromolithographs
BNF, Département des Estampes
et de la Photographie

These vignettes, and others in
the same series, were probably
meant to accompany food products. Displayed in groups of a
dozen comic sketches each, they
show inventions designed to
improve daily life alongside others
devoted to science or exploration.
Curiously, the fashion in clothes
remains that of the Belle Epoque!

Les Petits Dénicheurs d'Aiglons.

Les Pompiers aériens.

Sur la Route de Londres (Pas-de-Calais).

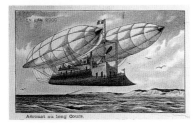

Aéronat au long Cours.

Un Sauvetage.

L'Avenue de l'Opéra.

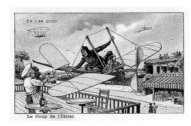

Le Coup de l'Étrier.

Sentinelle avancée en Hélicoptère.

Chantier de Construction électrique.

Le Train électrique Paris-Pékin.

Une Fête des Fleurs.

Le Barbier nouveau Jeu.

Madame à sa Toilette.

Un Dîner chimique.

which takes place circa 2270, the world is saved from war and poverty by technology. But in *Ile des Pingouins* [*Penguin Island*] (1908), France paints an altogether less appealing picture; the novel's final book, "Future Times," unequivocally condemns a society founded on the acquisition of material wealth and is a forerunner of the counter-utopia. Undoubtedly, this writer, who would be plunged even deeper into pessimism by the barbarous spectacle of World War I, represented an attitude that was widespread in European society.

Jules Verne, in the last twenty years of his life, would experience a similar progression. His early utopias did indeed exalt the utter glory of science: *Les Cinq Cents Millions de la Bégum* [*The Five Hundred Millions of the Begum*] (1879), for example, in which Franceville, a city devoted to happiness, and Stahlstadt, a military-industrial creation of German imperialism, are locked in Manichean opposition, or *Mathias Sandorf* (1885), in which the protagonist's private island is home to a scientific colony. But later, disenchantment would take over; Verne scholars point to 1886 and the appearance of the malefic *Robur-le-Conquérant* as the turning point.[19] Even when we exclude the texts whose attribution is contested (*L'Etonnante Aventure de la Mission Barsac*, posthumously published in 1914, or the aforementioned *L'Eternel Adam*), we can see the steady encroachment of doubt into Verne's work.

There has yet to be a bibliography of those minor works included in anthologies or published in the daily press: quite forgotten today, these works nonetheless have much to reveal about the spirit of the times.[20] Well before the century's close, these works exhibit a growing distrust of scientific feats. The playwright and novelist Ernest d'Hervilly is typical of this trend; in the short piece "Josuah Electricmann" (published in *Timbale d'histoire à la Parisienne*, 1883), he derides and caricatures the many useless operations that can be performed thanks to a "network of conductor cables that are connected to every telegraphic station on the globe" and to a *scribographe* or "mechanical secretary," which, incidentally, is not all that different from today's personal computer. His tone, not in the least accusatory, is one of amused irony in the face of the spectacle of a science-besotted modernity. Charles Cros plays with a similar comic impulse when he describes "electric currents capable of producing talent in the most obtuse minds," feeding into the editorial offices of the *Journal de l'avenir*.[21] The social critique takes a more acerbic turn when talent threatens to become "proportionate to wealth."

The Hostility Toward the Promised Future

We now turn to the newly rediscovered author and artist Albert Robida, whose relationship to the present discussion has several aspects. Beyond his predictions of how technology would regulate daily life (*Le Vingtième Siècle*, 1883; *Le Vingtième Siècle. La vie électrique*, 1892), Robida described collateral social transformations with extraordinary foresight and incisive irony. His clear-sightedness had him warning against the imminent risks of an arms race in *La Guerre au XXe siècle* (1883),[22] and of the fragility of an armistice incapable of securing everlasting peace in *L'Ingénieur von Satanas* (1919). His ability to coax comedy out of extremely serious situations and the humor that consistently runs through his writing should not blind us to his critical stance, which was the exception in those very conformist times. Long before anyone else, for example, he warned against environmental damage and chemical hazards.[23] His eloquence was not limited to his own output, as he produced many illustrations for the works of others, Octave Uzanne's *La Locomotion future* (1905), for example, and Pierre Giffard's *La Guerre infernale* (1908).

During the Belle Epoque, the reservations about, not to say the radical questioning of, the uses to which science was being put were frequently expressed in novels: in the work of the physician André Couvreur, for example, who would later create a kindred spirit to H. G. Wells's Dr. Moreau, the character of the mad scientist Professor Tornada, and who warned against the excesses of science in his *Caresco, surhomme, ou le Voyage en Eucrasie, conte humain* (1904). There was also the very grave magistrate Eugène Mouton, who used the pseudonym Mérinos, and wrote the caustic "La fin du monde" (in *Nouvelles et fantaisies humoristiques*, 1872), in which widespread public education leads to an excess of production, consumption, and heat, resulting in the "spontaneous combustion of the Earth and all its inhabitants."[24]

Daniel Halévy's *L'Histoire de quatre ans, 1997–2001*, on the other hand, functions less as a warning about the dangers of techno-science and more as "a meditation on the direction of social evolution" and a "reflection on the indispensable ethical dimension of a 'true' socialism,"[25] which to all appearances seems to have every reason to fear material abundance and social levelling.

WHAT CONCLUSIONS can we reach as we near the end of this brief overview, in which great names (and great works) have been deliberately placed alongside figures whose fame has all but disappeared? In the first place, literature in the nineteenth century, more so than in any other era, bore witness to the controversies of its day. The civilization of the Belle Epoque experienced and described itself as ephemeral: technological excess and social fragmentation and war conspired to challenge its foundations. We further note that very few works went beyond the theme of science in action, be it to celebrate, disparage, or dispute; a distinction can thus be made between strictly utopian narratives and adventure stories that deemed science a suitable and enlivening addition to their narratives and invoked utopian themes only as secondary devices. And finally, only ill-defined boundaries divided the utopian narrative from related genres that addressed the future, some of which came into their own in the next century as futuristic science, science fiction, and social or political forecasts. As yesterday's expectations became reality, with its attendant undesirable aspects, utopia, at the beginning of the twentieth century, had lost much of its appeal. The novelists' utopias on paper merely anticipated by a few years the disenchantment of society as a whole.

Translated by Nadia Benabid

Notes

1 The opposite is not always true, at least in the case of Charles Fourier, who interspersed his work with exquisitely crafted psychological portraits describing the behavior of this or that Harmonian. His ability to endow his characters with depth helped him avoid the habitual pitfall of utopias, in which characters lack all originality and are mere foils for the doctrines they serve.

2 See Georges Minois, *Histoire de l'avenir: des prophètes à la prospective* (Paris: Fayard, 1996), 506.

3 On Gabriel de Tarde, see Pierre Favre, *Naissances de la science politique en France, 1870–1914* (Paris: Fayard, 1989), 145–69.

4 Gabriel de Tarde, *Fragment d'histoire future*, trans. by Cloudseley Brereton as *Underground Man*; with a preface by H. G. Wells (London: Duckworth, 1905), reprinted in *The Quest for Utopia: An Anthology of Imaginary Societies*, ed. Glenn Negley and J. Max Patrick (New York: Henry Schuman, 1952), 194 and 206.

5 Francis Lacassin, "Le communard qui écrivit trois romans de Jules Verne," *Europe* (November–December 1978): 94–105.

6 See Xavier Noël, "Hetzel et André Laurie," *Un éditeur et son siècle, Pierre-Jules Hetzel, 1814–1886* (Saint-Sébastien: ACL éd. Société Crocus, 1988), 107–15.

7 See *La science pour tous*, catalogue for the exhibition at the Musée d'Orsay, 1994, ed. Bruno Béguet, Marilyn Cantor, and Ségolène Le Men (Paris: Réunion des Musées Nationaux, 1994).

8 Gustave Flaubert, *L'Education sentimentale [A Sentimental Education]* (1869), Part 3, Chapter 1, quoted in Eugen Weber, *France, Fin de Siècle* (Cambridge, Mass.: Belknap Press of Harvard University Press, 1986), 70.

9 Karl Marx, *Der Bürgerkrieg in Frankreich*, trans. as *The Civil War in France*, in *Later Political Writings*, ed. and trans. Terrell Carver (Cambridge, England, and New York: Cambridge University Press, 1996), 188.

10 Karl Marx, "Postface" to the 2nd ed. of *Das Kapital*, trans. as *Capital: A Critique of Political Economy*, trans. Ben Fowkes, 3 vols. (New York: Vintage Books, 1977–81), 1: 99.

11 See Madeleine Rebérioux, "La littérature socialisante et la représentation du futur en France au tournant du siècle," pp. 408–21 in *Histoire sociale, sensibilités collectives et mentalités: Mélanges Robert Mandrou* (Paris: Presses universitaires de France, 1985).

12 See Raymond Trousson, "L'utopie anarchiste de Jean Grave," pp. 221–32 in his *D'utopie et d'utopistes* (Paris: L'Harmattan, 1998).

13 Gottfried Wilhelm Leibniz, *Theodicy: Essays on the Goodness of God, the Freedom of Man, and the Origin of Evil*, trans. E. M. Huggard; ed. with an intro. by Austin Farrer (New Haven, Conn.: Yale University Press, 1952), Part III, section 414, 370–71.

14 See Jean-Claude Drouin, "Les utopies de droite au lendemain de la Révolution de 1830," pp. 199–211 in *Romantisme et politique, 1815–1851: Colloque de l'Ecole normale supérieur de Saint-Cloud, 1966* (Paris: A. Colin, 1969).

15 See Raymond Trousson, "Charles Nodier et le voyage imaginaire," *Francofonia* (Cádiz), no. 2 (1993): 197–211.

16 See Raymond Trousson, "Emile Souvestre et *Le monde tel qu'il sera*," pp. 179–92 in *D'utopie et utopistes*.

17 In his "La république de l'avenir," *Le Journal*, July 28, 1848; quoted in Robert Snell, *Théophile Gautier: A Romantic Critic of the Visual Arts* (Oxford: Clarendon Press; New York: Oxford University Press, 1982), 188.

18 See Jacques Noiray, *Le Romancier et la machine: l'image de la machine dans le roman français, 1850–1900*, vol. II: *Jules Verne, Villiers de L'Isle-Adam* (Paris: J. Corti, 1982).

19 See Herbert R. Lottman, *Jules Verne: An Explanatory Biography* (New York: St. Martin's Press, 1996), 255.

20 There is, however, an anthology of some of these pieces: Monique Lebailly, ed., *La Science-fiction avant la SF: anthologie de l'imaginaire scientifique français du romantisme à la pataphysique* (Paris: L'Instant, 1989).

21 In his *Le Tout-Paris des Hydrophathes*, May 23, 1880; revised version published in *La Chat noir*, March 13, 1886.

22 Reissued by Henri Béraldi (Paris: Dorbon-aîné, 1916) under the title *Un caricaturiste prophète: la guerre telle qu'elle est, prévue par A. Robida il y a trente-trois ans.*

23 See Bernard Cazes, *Histoire des futurs: les figures de l'avenir, de saint Augustin au XXIe siècle* (Paris: Seghers, 1986), 101.

24 Quoted in Pierre Versins, *Encyclopédie de l'utopie, des voyages extraordinaires et de la science fiction* (Lausanne: L'Age d'homme, 1972), 330.

25 See Raymond Trousson, "L'utopie prolétarienne de Daniel Halévy," pp. 209–19 in *D'utopie et d'utopistes*.

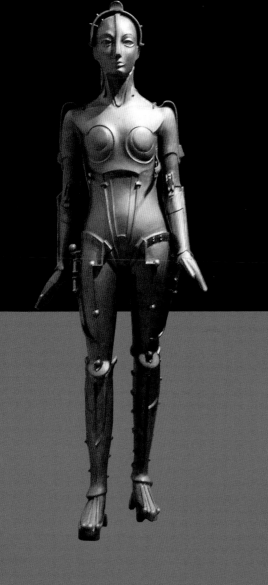

See pp. 283, 327, 287.

Utopia and Anti-Utopia in the Twentieth Century

The Form of Utopia

THE STRENGTH of utopia has always lain in its literary form. Various other forms – utopian social theory, millenarianism, the experimental community – can for a time substitute for the literary utopia; but if it languishes for too long, so too does utopia. The question of utopia in the twentieth century therefore turns on the fate of the literary utopia.

Recall what happened in the nineteenth century. It opened with the blaze of the French Revolution, and the idea that humans were now able to construct the good society not just in the air but on the ground, in real societies with real people. Writers such as Saint-Simon, Fourier, Owen, and Comte elaborated schemes for the perfection of humanity. Social science was to provide the theoretical tools for the construction of the new world; socialism was to be its practical form.

What room in all this was there for utopia? In the writing of the socialists, especially the Marxists, utopia was consigned to the dustbin of history, as the wish-fulfillment of ages that could only dream of the good society. Now nineteenth-century science, nineteenth-century technology, and the power of the common people were delivering up what could only exist in the imagination of former times. "I do not write cook-books for the kitchens of the future," was Marx's crushing riposte to requests that he provide a detailed portrait of the future Communist society.

In the face of this, the literary utopia went into abeyance. A form of writing that had flourished throughout Europe in the wake of Thomas More's *Utopia* (1516), reaching something of a climax in the eighteenth century, virtually disappeared in the first half of the nineteenth century. Utopian social theory, and the experimental utopian community, not the literary utopia, became all the rage.

The failure of revolutionary politics, and the obstinate refusal of socialism to realize itself in any other way than as isolated experimental communities, might well have spelled the end of the whole utopian project. But it was socialism itself that led the renaissance of the literary utopia. Despite the strictures of its founders, later socialists became only too well aware of the need to provide "speaking pictures" of the socialist future if socialism were to break out of the coterie of intellectuals and appeal to ordinary people. Socialism needed its "religion," and the socialist utopia was to be its bible. From the 1880s to the early years of the twentieth century, a striking series of works,

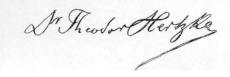

A Garden for Every House

Theodor Hertzka
Freiland: Ein soziales
Zufunstbild von
Theodor Hertzka
Dresden and Leipzig: E. Pierson's
Verlag, [1892]
NYPL, General Research Division

Inspired by the theories of Karl Marx and Friedrich Engels, the Austrian economist Theodor

Hertzka imagined a classless society controlled by a central administration. A direct response to the physical drudgery that Hertzka saw as part of the Industrial Revolution, *Freiland* proposes long vacations, work suited to the specific temperament of each person, and gardens for every house.

mostly of a socialist character, renewed the literary utopia and kept alive the hope of a socialist future. Key among these was the utopia *Looking Backward* (1888) by the American Edward Bellamy. The enormous success of Bellamy's book both showed the appeal of this kind of thinking and stimulated a large number of works by way of imitation, criticism, or refutation. Among these were Theodor Hertzka's *Freeland* (1890), William Morris's *News from Nowhere* (1890) – an indignant retort to Bellamy's version of socialism – and H. G. Wells's *A Modern Utopia* (1905). Together these ensured that not just the socialist vision but the literary form of utopia would be carried into the twentieth century.[1]

What makes the literary utopia superior to other ways of promoting the good society? Why were Bellamy's *Looking Backward* and Morris's *News from Nowhere*, whose theoretical pretensions are modest by comparison with Marx's *Capital* or even the *Communist Manifesto*, nevertheless infinitely more successful than those works in turning men and women toward socialism? There are the obvious attractions of a story over abstract analysis. But Bertrand de Jouvenel makes the additional point that utopia allows us to make a more honest test of theory than do merely abstract formulations, however profound. The utopian mode of persuasion is "to paint pleasing pictures of daily life," such that we are impelled to want to make the world that is thus portrayed. He considers this feature to be so essential to utopian writing that he is prepared to argue that "the designation of 'Utopia' should be denied to any exposition of a 'New Model' of Society which is bereft of pictures concerning daily life." But this mode is not merely concerned with persuasion, it is also a method of analysis. Unlike the abstract theoretician, who asks us to accept as it were on trust that the desirable consequences will follow from the application of the relevant theoretical principles – that happiness will, indeed, follow upon the "expropriation of the expropriators," for instance – the utopian writer is under an obligation to present a fully developed and detailed picture of the happy world that is expected to result from the application of particular principles. We see people at work and at play, at home and in the public spaces of society, in their personal and in their political lives. We experience, through involvement with characters and events, as well as through the description of the scenes and settings of everyday life, a "good day" in the new society. We can therefore judge of both the plausibility and the desirability of the life so presented.[2] Does Bellamy's form of socialism attract

us, or Morris's? Which is more likely to follow from the fundamental act of the abolition of private property, seen by both alike as the source of the disorder and discontents of modern society? While in the end this may come down to a matter of temperament, both Bellamy and Morris in their very way of depicting the future society give us the materials by which to judge the likely outcome of their socialist principles, and the extent to which we may feel we want to live in their societies.

It is these qualities of the literary utopia that make it the benchmark for the fate of utopia as such. However vivid and original the speculations of the theorist might be, unless he or she "fixes" it in the mind of the reader by presenting it in the form of a portrait of a living society, the chances are that the vision of the good or future society will lose its force. We remember Bellamy's and Morris's and Wells's worlds when the ideas of the socialists have become hazy or blurred. They may all draw upon the same storehouse of general ideas, but their manner of representing them is quite different. The *Fabian Essays* or the Erfurt Program of the German Social Democratic Party are not *Looking Backward* or *A Modern Utopia*.

The same is true of the other face of utopia, the anti-utopia. No theory of totalitarianism, no conscientious warning of scientific hubris or the technological threat, has stamped itself on the twentieth-century imagination as has *Nineteen Eighty-four* or *Brave New World*. As much as utopia, anti-utopia needs the literary imagination to proclaim its message. Here, too, the nineteenth century points the way. The revival of the literary utopia was accompanied by a powerful resurgence of its alter ego, the dystopia or anti-utopia. Richard Jefferies's apocalyptic *After London* (1885) was followed by several anti-utopias commenting critically on the utopian hopes of Bellamy, Morris, and others. Prominent among these were Ignatius Donnelly's *Caesar's Column* (1890), Eugene Richter's *Pictures of a Socialistic Future* (1893), and Jack London's *The Iron Heel* (1907). At the same time there was a fresh outpouring of the Gothic imagination that fed the modern anti-utopia some of its enduring archetypes, in such works as Robert Louis Stevenson's *Strange Case of Dr. Jekyll and Mr. Hyde* (1886), Oscar Wilde's *The Picture of Dorian Gray* (1891), H. G. Wells's *The Island of Doctor Moreau* (1896), and Bram Stoker's *Dracula* (1897).

The contest of utopia and anti-utopia was undoubtedly good for the health of both. Response followed challenge, becoming itself a fresh challenge that demanded further response. Nor was this simply a question of utopia's being matched by anti-utopia. Since one man's utopia could be another man's nightmare, the pattern of challenge and response could take place within the utopian tradition itself. *Looking Backward* provoked *News from Nowhere*, which in turn provoked *A Modern Utopia*.[3] What George Orwell called "the chain of utopias" was strengthened with every addition of a link, whether this took strictly a utopian or an anti-utopian form.

The nineteenth-century story is important not simply because these works of its last years set the terms for much of the twentieth-century debate of future possibilities. It also establishes the pattern of utopia and anti-utopia, and the conditions for their mutual flourishing. Utopia and anti-utopia support each other; they are two sides of the same literary genre. They gain sustenance from each other's energy and power. The one paints the future in glowing tones; the other colors it black. But the imagination of whole societies and the techniques of representing them in all their particularities are features that they share in common. Both deal in perfected societies, the only difference being whether they attach a plus or a minus sign. The fate of utopia in the twentieth century turns partly on the extent to which this dialectic of utopia and anti-utopia continues.

Wells: Utopia and Anti-Utopia

In this dialectic, H. G. Wells is critical. He straddles the late nineteenth-century revival of utopia and its apparent demise in the first half of the twentieth century. As one of the inventors of science fiction (a genre that increasingly absorbed utopia), a world-famous writer, and a thinker and publicist who played some part in the founding of both the League of Nations and the United Nations, he can justly claim to be not just the witness but one of the principal contributors to the evolving story of the hopes and fears of twentieth-century Western society.

Quixotically but resolutely, Wells swam against the tide. Though a socialist, in his early years he refused to side with such fellow-socialists as Bellamy and Morris in picturing mankind's future in glowing terms. Quite to the contrary, he occupied himself with providing devastating critiques of socialist visions and hopes, their faith in science and the proletariat. In his first major work, *The Time Machine* (1895), he portrayed a future society in which the class war has led to a grotesque parody of socialism. In a sense the Morlocks, the underworld tenders of the machines, do rule, in that they

terrorize and prey on the effete upper-world aristocracy of the Eloi. But these brutalized barbaric cannibals, the lineal descendants of the proletariat of old, can in no way be seen as the carriers of a higher form of civilization. Leaving this world, the time traveler journeys farther into the future, until finally he witnesses the death of the planet, as the sun dulls and darkness covers the earth. This is a fitting finale to a tale that has poured scorn on all hopes of future happiness – for, we are told, the time traveler "thought but cheerlessly of the Advancement of Mankind, and saw in the growing pile of civilization only a foolish heaping that must inevitably fall back upon and destroy its makers in the end."

Others of Wells's stories of these times sounded the same note of somber warning. *The Island of Doctor Moreau* (1896) and *The Invisible Man* (1897) questioned the hope placed in science and the scientists, with their depiction of scientists as perverted and power-mad intellectuals who put science to cruel and inhuman ends. *The War of the Worlds* (1898) and *The First Men in the Moon* (1901) also warned against the hypertrophy of the merely rational and scientific. The Martians of the first and the Selenites of the second are all brain and no feeling, and the consequence is power without compassion and efficiency without purpose.

But already in these later stories the utopian Wells is emerging from his anti-utopian shadow. The scientist Cavor admires the way Selenite science and technology have abolished waste and want, along with war and political strife. The Martians, the author of *The War of the Worlds* speculates, may be showing humankind the image of its own future, in which it accomplishes "the suppression of the animal side of the organism by the intelligence." In the resistance to the Martians has arisen "the conception of the commonweal of mankind," the common unity of the human race that must at some time – as Wells was later to hold – find expression in the World State. The tone of these novels is still critical and minatory. Neither the Martians nor the Selenites can be true utopian exemplars. But Wells is clearly feeling his way toward the utopian conception that was to dominate his later writing.

This burst upon the world in the form first of an exercise in social prophecy, *Anticipations* (1901) and later, in more formal utopian mode, in *A Modern Utopia* (1905). The latter delineated the main features of the Wellsian utopia: a World State founded upon science and under the benevolent direction of scientists.[4] It is a socialist world because for Wells, science and socialism were two

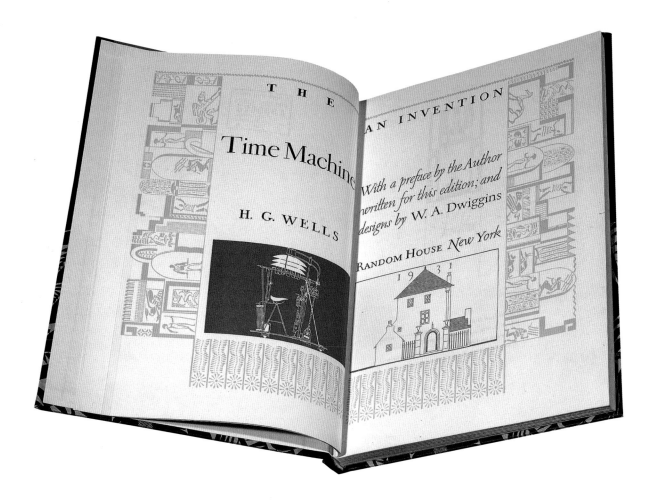

A Dystopian Vision

H. G. Wells
The Time Machine:
An Invention
New York: Random House, 1931
NYPL, Rare Books Division

In this novel, first published in 1895, H. G. Wells's time traveler visits the year 802,701 using a time machine that he has invented. One artist's rendering of this contraption is shown on the title page of this 1931 edition. Wells's vision of a dystopian future warns against continued industrialization and exploitation of the working class. The traveler continues on into the future, only to find in the year 30,000,000 that all life has disappeared from the surface of the earth, leaving only a barren landscape. An advocate for the working classes, and an outspoken critic of war and technology, Wells incorporated his social views into much of his fiction and nonfiction. In addition to *The Time Machine*, he is best known for *The Invisible Man* (1897), *The War of the Worlds* (1898), *A Modern Utopia* (1905), and *The Shape of Things to Come* (1933).

sides of the same coin: "just as science aims at a common organized body of knowledge, to which all its servants contribute, and in which they share, so Socialism insists upon its ideal of an organized social order which every man serves and by which every man benefits." But the informing spirit is clearly science, and *A Modern Utopia* contains one of Wells's most celebrated paeans to science:

The plain message physical science has for the world at large is this, that were our political and social and moral devices only as well contrived to their ends as a lino-type machine, an antiseptic operating plant, or an electric tram-car, there need now at the present moment be no appreciable toil in the world, and only the smallest fraction of the pain, the fear, and the anxiety that now makes human life so doubtful in its value.

For the rest of his long life, in novels and tracts, Wells tirelessly propagated this vision of a World State guided by the scientific outlook. The pattern of the stories was usually the same: a natural or man-made catastrophe destroys the old order on earth, allowing those who remain painfully to put together the structures of a lasting new world order. In *Men Like Gods* (1923), it is the civilization of another planet that earthlings are directed to as the utopian model; in *The Shape of Things to Come* (1933), it is earth itself that goes through a series of cataclysmic convulsions resulting finally in the establishment of the World State. In the real world of politics, Wells put his hopes first in the League of Nations, as the germ of the World State. Its abject failure in the 1930s did not prevent him from contributing, in the last years of his life, to the work that led to the founding of another incipient world-state, the United Nations. It is a remarkable story of dedication to the utopian ideal. If utopia remained alive in the first half of the twentieth century, it did so largely through the powerful presence of H. G. Wells.

Dystopian Times?

Wells was one reason why anti-utopia did not overwhelm utopia, as many have thought it did, and as the way of the world seemed to suggest was the only possible outcome. It is true that the utopian Wells moved increasingly against the temper of the times, just as in his earlier anti-utopian phase he stood out against the mood of socialist optimism. For literary intellectuals and humanists in particular, World War I, the rise of Fascism, the descent of Soviet communism into Stalinism, the failure of Western

capitalism in the 1930s: all these were mocking commentaries on utopian hopes. The more fitting responses seemed to be the crushing indictment of industrial civilization in the works of D. H. Lawrence, the icy pessimism of T. S. Eliot's *The Waste Land* (1922), and the flight from the modern in the poetry of William Butler Yeats and Ezra Pound. So far as utopia itself was concerned, the dominant mood and mode seemed to be unequivocally dystopian. It was not the Wellsian utopia but, in the first half of the century, the anti-utopia that seemed to capture the public imagination. We read the fate of utopia in this period through such powerful and influential anti-utopias as Evgenii Zamiatin's *We* (1924), Aldous Huxley's *Brave New World* (1932), and George Orwell's *Nineteen Eighty-four* (1949).

But we should remember two things. First, as Zamiatin himself pointed out in some sparkling essays on Wells, it was Wells himself who supplied many of the themes and suggested many of the features of the twentieth-century anti-utopia.[5] Zamiatin's own anti-utopia, *We*, with its autocratic world-state ruled by the Benefactor and his Guardians, is clearly indebted to Wells's "A Story of the Days to Come" (1899) and *When the Sleeper Wakes* (1899). Huxley's *Brave New World* similarly draws on the graded hierarchy of the Selenite civilization *of The First Men in the Moon;* and Orwell considered Wells's influence to be so pervasive in the early twentieth century that it would certainly not have surprised him to be told that the ground-plan of *Nineteen Eighty-four* can be found in a number of early Wells stories, notably *When the Sleeper Wakes.*[6]

The second point is that even when Wells was the target rather than the inspiration of the anti-utopia, it clearly implied that he was worth attacking, that his influence was indeed thought to be so dominating as well as pernicious that the anti-utopian writer felt the need to answer him. E. M. Forster's anti-utopian fable, "When the Machine Stops" (1909), an account of a dehumanized machine civilization based on a world state, was described by its author as "a counterblast to one of the heavens of H. G. Wells." For Huxley it was clear that Wells was the enemy. *Brave New World,* he said, was "a novel about the future on the horror of the Wellsian utopia and a revolt against it." Orwell too inveighed against Wells's influence, cruelly speaking in *The Road to Wigan Pier* (1937) of "the by now familiar Wellsian utopia, aptly caricatured in *Brave New World,* the paradise of little fat men." During World War II he went so far as to see Hitler's National Socialist state as the perverted but clearly recognizable offspring of Wells's scientific utopia; and in *Nineteen Eighty-four* he completed the case against Wells by presenting his own nightmare vision of the world-state – a picture no less powerful and frightening for owing many of its key images and ideas to Wells's own earlier novels.

As with the nineteenth century, we see the importance of the dialogue between utopia and anti-utopia, even if the dialogue becomes on occasion an unseemly shouting match. Utopia survived, even in such unpropitious circumstances, partly because it became the object of a fierce struggle. As before, utopia and anti-utopia sustained each other. Moreover, the anti-utopia does not emerge out of nothing. It draws its energies, to a good extent, from the strength of utopia. It is possible that utopia could thrive without the stimulus of anti-utopia, but it is impossible for the anti-utopia to do so on its own. Its life-blood is its utopian antagonist. The force of Huxley's and Orwell's anti-utopias is the measure of the continuing vitality of utopia.

The evidence, partly from the very presence and urgency of these anti-utopias, is that utopia maintained a strong showing in the first half of the twentieth century, and that in this Wells's contribution was critical. This suggests that we should reconsider the traditional view that utopia died in the twentieth century, that it simply could not stand up to the battering that it received from the enormities of twentieth-century history.[7] We read the history of utopia in the first half of the twentieth century too much through the prism of *Brave New World* and *Nineteen Eighty-four*. This chimes well with the received view of the shock administered to Western ideas of progress and reason by the horrors of the trench warfare of World War I, the Nazi attempt at genocide, the purges and gulags of Stalinist Russia, the atomic bombardment of Hiroshima. Unquestionably these provided rich fuel for the anti-utopia. But so too did the continuing presence of the utopia, in both literary and nonliterary forms. Utopian writing has always turned as much on the utopian tradition itself as on the events of the always non-utopian world. In the first half of the twentieth century, the anti-utopia confronted and drew sustenance from its traditional other face, the utopia.

Utopia for Dystopian Times
The predominance of the themes and images of anti-utopia in the standard accounts of twentieth-century developments hides and suppresses many other features that are apparent as soon as they are brought to mind. We remember, thanks to Huxley, test-tube babies, life-time conditioning, mindless conformity, the feelies, and *soma*; thanks to Orwell, we also remember Big Brother, the Thought Police, round-the-clock surveillance, and the corruptions and degradation of language in the modern totalitarian state.[8] In that sense the anti-utopian imagery of Huxley and Orwell clearly seems more persuasive, to a later age at least, than the utopian pictures of *A Modern Utopia* or *The Shape of Things to Come*.

But why have we forgotten Ebenezer Howard's Garden City, Frank Lloyd Wright's Broadacre City, and Le Corbusier's Radiant City? Why have we forgotten the whole movement in architecture and town planning in the first half of our century that sustained the Wellsian faith in science and reason?[9] If the literary utopia did not inspire the imagination or command the attention as it had in an earlier time, its leading ideas found plenty of support in other forms and disciplines. Many of them too were expressed in the utopian mode, though for various reasons their authors eschewed the literary utopia. Ebenezer Howard was indeed directly inspired by Bellamy's *Looking Backward* and, paradoxical as it sometimes seems, much of the work of the Bauhaus and of other pioneers of modern design was indebted to the utopian ideas and practical example of that great utopian, William Morris.[10] But even if there are no great literary utopias in the manner of Campanella's *City of the Sun* (1623), with its depiction of the ideal city of the Renaissance, the high priests of modern architecture and urbanism produced strikingly utopian works in such writings as Howard's *Garden Cities of Tomorrow* (1902) and Le Corbusier's *La Ville Radieuse* (1935). All renounced nostalgic or neo-romantic views of the city and the countryside with strong declarations of faith in industrialism and the capacity of modern science, technology, and rational planning to make fit habitations for humanity.

Even stronger support for the Wellsian utopia was to be found in another quarter: the "science and society" movement that developed in the 1920s and 1930s around such British scientists and mathematicians as J.B.S. Haldane, Lancelot Hogben, J. D. Bernal, Joseph Needham, and Hyman Levy.[11] While the literary intellectuals were wringing their hands in despair, these scientists, together with their counterparts on the Continent and in America, were confidently looking to science for the realization of mankind's age-old dreams of freedom, peace, and plenty. In *Daedalus, or Science and the Future* (1924), Haldane aspired to outbid Wells –

"the very mention of the future suggests him" – in imagining the dizzying heights to which science could raise mankind. Haldane's far-reaching projection of a world transformed by the applications of science was in its turn outbid by J. D. Bernal's dazzling *The World, the Flesh and the Devil* (1929), the most sparkling and provocative of the products of the science and society movement. In this work Bernal confronted "the three enemies of the Rational Soul" and sought to rout them once and for all with science. Physics would tame "the massive, unintelligent forces of nature"; biology would cure the problems of the human body; and psychology would control man's "desires and fears, his imagination and stupidities." But this modest prospectus gives little clue to the lengths to which Bernal was prepared to put the scientific imagination. Physics enables mankind to colonize the planets and to turn the stars into "efficient heat engines"; biology enables humans to get rid of their inefficient bodies and to experiment with forms of life such as "dual or multiple organisms," leading eventually to a complete "dematerialization" and spiritualization of humanity in which the human intelligence takes control of all life forms in the universe, while "psychology" is interpreted, in a somewhat Machiavellian way, as a scheme whereby scientists as the nucleus of a new disembodied species take over the direction of the universe and, ensconced in their "celestial spheres," treat the remnants of the old unreconstructed humanity on earth as "a human zoo," "a zoo so intelligently managed that its inhabitants are not aware that they are there merely for the purposes of observation and experiment."

Bernal's extraordinary and extravagant vision was all of a piece with the confidence with which the scientists confronted the future. Rather like the socialists of the early nineteenth century, they felt that the time for literary utopias was past: science could deliver utopia in real life and in real time. But their scientific speculations were couched in a manner only one remove from utopia. *The World, the Flesh and the Devil* could easily have been presented as a formal utopia – indeed, it did no more than continue the spirit and intent of Wells's *A Modern Utopia*. The closeness of these two forms was made manifest when Aldous Huxley combined elements of both works – together with other contributions from the scientists – and turned them against their authors in his anti-science anti-utopia *Brave New World*.

Wells was even more evidently present in another form that kept alive the spirit of utopia: the new genre of science fiction. Science fiction is too vast and heterogeneous a field, and to some extent too restricted in its appeal, to carry the cause of either utopia or anti-utopia on its own. At any one time one might find scores of examples of both without being clear in what way either was being advanced or held back. Utopias and anti-utopias really have to break through the genre of science fiction, as Wells's *A Modern Utopia*, Huxley's *Brave New World*, and Orwell's *Nineteen Eighty-four* did, to command wide public attention. But that does not mean that science fiction cannot contribute its own measure, in its own way, to the fate of utopia. And here it is clear that the genre that Wells pioneered and did so much to promote returned the compliment by being for much of its earliest years an ardent supporter of the Wellsian philosophy. Both the two leading science fiction magazines, Hugo Gernsback's *Amazing Stories* (launched in the United States in 1926) and *Astounding Stories* (started in 1930), throughout the Depression and war years maintained a resolutely optimistic stance, portraying societies on earth and on distant planets in which science and technology have performed miracles of economic advancement and social engineering. Right up to the end of World War II – when the dropping of the atom bomb gave it pause for thought – technological utopianism was the dominant strain in science fiction.[12]

Technology in the optimistic vein was also the hallmark of the Technocracy movement that flourished on both sides of the Atlantic, but especially in America, in the interwar period. Inspired by Thorstein Veblen's idea of a "Soviet of Technicians," the movement adopted the conventional aim of the scientific utopia, of banishing want and waste through science and technology. Its principal literary statement, Harold Loeb's *Life in a Technocracy: What It Might be Like* (1933), made clear the derivativeness of Technocracy's ideas and its dependence on earlier forms of technological utopianism, especially that of Bellamy. But as with science fiction, this popular form of faith in science, held as it was by an influential group of scientists and engineers, gave added strength to the scientific utopia. Something similar can be said, but in a looser way, of the great world's fairs of the 1930s in various American cities, culminating in the World of Tomorrow fair in New York in 1939. These were based on the real achievements of industrial designers such as Raymond Loewy and Norman Bel Geddes, and reflected their technological optimism. The fairs, with their vivid futuristic urban panoramas, aspired to promote the idea that technology was on the point of realizing utopia – the World of Tomorrow actually set the date at 1960.[13]

There is one further thing to be said about popular utopianism in the first half of the twentieth century. The dystopian temper of the times has often been noted. But precisely the gloomy tenor of world events might give rise to a counter-movement of culture to lighten the oppressiveness. Such, at any rate, seems the reasonable interpretation of the heady and hedonistic "Jazz Age" of the 1920s, the crowds that flocked to the fantastically decorated and ornate picture palaces to see films that took them out of their everyday lives and made them forget their cares, and the success of such old-fashioned, Shangri-La utopias as James Hilton's *Lost Horizon* (1933). People were in need of dreams, and Hollywood and other purveyors of mass culture were there to provide them in abundance. We may call it escapism, and certainly it was no substitute for the serious presentation of utopia in literary form (briefly, because it presented utopia in too accessible and easily acquired a form – as quickly forgotten as enjoyed). But along with other forms of popular utopianism it undoubtedly contributed in some measure to keeping alive the utopian spirit.

Finally, it is important to stress an often over-looked aspect of the utopian story in the earlier part of the century. We are accustomed to see the defor-mations of Fascism and Communism as central to the assault on utopia – as, indeed, the building blocks of such anti-utopias as *We* and *Nineteen Eighty-four*. There is no need to deny that, in essence. But we should also remember that, in conception at least, these were utopian schemes. It may be more difficult to see this in the case of Fascism – *Mein Kampf* is not easily read as a utopia – but even here the utopi-an elements are apparent in Mussolini's grandiose projects for a redesigned Rome and Albert Speer's plans for an architectural expression of the spirit of Fascism in Berlin and elsewhere. Fascist philosophy celebrated the body and the modern machine, aiming to make the former work with the strength and efficiency of the latter (Leni Riefenstahl's 1938 film *Olympia* lyrically celebrates this, as much as her *Triumph of the Will*, a 1934 documentary about the Nuremberg Rallies, celebrates the power of collective emotion and striving). At the same time, especially in its Nazi variety, it contained strong elements of nature-worship, looking to the fields, forests, and mountains to regenerate the soul of modern man. Out of this contradictory mix was fashioned a fascist utopia that had an appeal well beyond the confines of its Italian and German heartlands.[14]

With communism or socialism the utopian dimension is clearer – we could almost say, unavoid-able. Socialism was *the* utopia of the nineteenth century; and its disfigurement in twentieth-century social experiments never entirely removed the utopian promise. This was paradoxically even truer of the greatest experiment of all, Soviet communism. It is obvious that the excesses of Stalinism and the many other ways in which Soviet communism failed to live up to its self-professed principles supplied some of the central ingredients of the anti-utopia (Orwell's *Animal Farm* [1945] proclaimed this even more than his *Nineteen Eighty-four;* an equally brilliant rendering, though not formally an anti-utopia, was Arthur Koestler's *Dark-ness at Noon* [1940]). But at the same time, what was just as important for many people was the fact that the Soviet Union existed at all, that socialism was being attempted on the grandest scale, and not in some small Third World country but in the largest country in the world, not far from the center of Europe. The young Arthur Koestler was only one of many intellectuals who thought that "the new star of Bethlehem had risen in the East"; for André Gide the Soviet Union was "a land where I imag-ined Utopia was in the process of becoming reali-ty."[15] Both Koestler and Gide later became famous recanters; but it would be a mistake to see in this disillusionment of certain celebrated intellectuals a general abandonment of faith in the socialist utopia. So long as the Soviet Union remained in being, so long as socialism maintained an actual existence in some real societies, the hope remained that the defects and deficiencies of socialist prac-tice could be remedied at some point in the future. Only when the Soviet Union faltered and fell were these hopes threatened at their very foundation.

In 1948, the year in which Orwell wrote his *Nineteen Eighty-four*, the American psychologist B. F. Skinner produced his *Walden Two*. It was provoca-tive and revealing in almost equal degrees. It was provocative in that, in a world struggling to emerge from the devastation of World War II and trying to come to terms with the revelations of the Nazi and Stalinist horrors, Skinner proposed a utopia that seemed to borrow to an uncomfortable extent from some of the practices of those very societies that had perpetrated those atrocities. This utopia of "behavioral engineering" proclaimed a confidence in science, and in the ability of scientific experts to manipulate and re-shape human behvior, that was strongly reminiscent of fascist and communist principles. Aldous Huxley, in *Brave New World*, had already produced a damning satire on behavioral conditioning as the solution to individual and social ills; now here was Skinner cheerfully taking up the challenge and throwing behaviorism straight back in Huxley's face.[16]

But *Walden Two* was significant for other reasons than this flying in the face of the anti-utopia. We are accustomed to dwelling on the somber aspects of the post-1945 world. The apocalyptic scenes, in Dresden, Hamburg, Berlin, that ended World War II; the dropping of the atomic bombs on Hiroshima and Nagasaki; the massive expulsion and resettlement of peoples in Central and Eastern Europe; the devastated European economies; the beginnings of the Cold War: these were not, it seems, propitious times for utopia. *Nineteen Eighty-four* was surely their appropriate image; even more perhaps Aldous Huxley's savage post-holocaust anti-utopia *Ape and Essence* (1948).

But out of World War II came the United Nations, and the germ of the European Community. To restore the European economies came the Marshall Plan. Democracy was established in Germany and Japan. In Britain a new Labour Government aspired to lay the foundations for a new kind of welfare society, and elsewhere in Europe socialist parties, buoyed by the prestige of the Soviet Union, seemed poised to take the initiative. At the same time, a powerful United States stood as a check against the imperial ambitions of the Soviet Union, in Europe and elsewhere in the world. In the *kibbutzim* of the newly instituted state of Israel, the religious philosopher Martin Buber, in his influential *Paths in Utopia* (1949), discerned a renewal of the communitarian tradition of the utopian socialism of Owen and Fourier, and offered it to the world as an alternative to Soviet communism. Utopia – in other words, the imagination of the good society – was not wholly out of keeping with the times. *Walden Two* was not such an aberration, any more than was Robert Graves's pastoral utopia of the same time, *Seven Days in New Crete* (1949). As earlier in the century, utopia accompanied anti-utopia and remained its necessary partner as well as natural antagonist. This pattern was to persist in the second half of the century as well. But the new thing was the changing position of the literary utopia – and therefore a new condition of utopia.

Utopianism Without Utopia?

The pattern of utopian thought in the second half of the twentieth century seems to be as follows. There is a strong revival of utopianism – in popular writing, in social theory, even in certain forms of politics. At the same time, there is no continuation or revival of the literary utopia – not, at any rate, in a form that commands a wide or general audience. Put another way, there is no Wells for the second part of the century. This means that, compared with the first part, and despite the greater degree of optimism generally prevalent, utopia is weaker and its fate less certain than at any other time in the century – perhaps in any other century.

The peculiarity of this situation needs to be noted. There have been periods in the past when the literary utopia weakened or almost disappeared – the early nineteenth century, we have suggested, was one of them. Utopia has been sustained in those lean periods by other forms of utopianism – utopian social theory and the experimental community being common substitutes. But generally the literary utopia has revived and in the process reinvigorated the utopian tradition. It is almost as if without the literary utopia there would be no striking images, no concrete pictures, by which to remember and fix in the mind the utopian vision. What would utopia be like in the first half of the twentieth century without Wells's Samurai and the World State? What comparable images are there for the second half of the century? Nor has the anti-utopia been much more persuasive. There is really nothing – bar stale repetitions – to put beside Huxley's decanted babies and Orwell's Big Brother.

Why this should be so we will consider later. The first thing to remark is the powerful groundswell of optimism that swept over Western nations in the 1950s and 1960s. Typically this took the form – as in the first half of the nineteenth century – of the repudiation of utopias, as obsolete and fanciful devices. "The age of utopias is past. An age of realism has taken its place. . . ." So declared the authors of *Industrialism and Industrial Man* (1960), a widely read and much-quoted work of social science. But in the same breath they went on to resurrect utopia in a new form: as the whole system of industrialism and industrial society. Industrial civilization itself, it seemed, could be the fit object of utopian strivings. In the twentieth century, they proclaimed, industrialism as developed by Western societies had become "the goal of mankind and the essence of national aspiration."[17]

In the decades following World War II, there were many statements of this kind. Ideological conflicts, it was claimed, were now obsolete. Whether a society took a socialist or a capitalist form was not in the end a matter of great moment. What mattered was that both forms were industrial: that is, that they were dedicated to economic growth and to the fullest realization of the potentialities of science and technology. The old bogeys of the anti-utopia, the fears bred by science and technology, were blown away, at least for the time. It was the scientists, said Sir Charles Snow in *The Two Cultures and the Scientific Revolution* (1959), who "had the future in their bones." Literary intellectuals were "natural Luddites" whose complaints about industrial civilization had to be seen for the feeble and self-indulgent whinings that they were. It was the titans of MIT and the Soviet Academy of Sciences who were ending want in the world and putting men into space.

This strong echo of the "science and society" movement of the 1920s and 1930s found a parallel in the rehabilitation of two of the principal enemies of utopia, Darwin and Freud. Darwin – despite the misunderstandings or misrepresentations of some of his followers – had shown evolution to be blind and utterly lacking in moral principle. Freud had pitted the forces of the "death instinct" (Thanatos) against those of the "life instinct" (Eros), and the whole of his social philosophy showed civilization to be the weakest and most vulnerable of defenses against the destructive impulses of the unconscious. Together, Darwin and Freud presented the most serious obstacle to any idea of progress; together theirs were the discordant voices that threatened to drown forever what Freud contemptuously called "lullabies about Heaven."[18]

In the 1950s, biologists such as Sir Julian Huxley, confounding the views of his eminent grandfather Thomas Henry Huxley and his brother Aldous (not to mention his own earlier work), sought to rescue Darwin from the pessimists and to see in him the apostle of progress. Far from evolution being – as Julian Huxley himself had once put it – a "series of blind alleys," it was now seen as a cosmic process leading to a general increase in the all-around efficiency, organizational complexity, and intelligence of living matter. Evolution demonstrated that "progress is inevitable as a general fact."[19] Such a conclusion was also presented by an ambitious work that synthesized Christian theology and evolutionary biology: Pierre Teilhard de Chardin's *The Phenomenon of Man* (1959), fittingly introduced to the English-speaking world by Huxley. In Chardin's account, evolution culminates in the advent of human consciousness and the ascent to the "noosphere," the sphere of pure mind in which bodily existence disappears and the noo-

sphere, like Hegel's Spirit, "closes in upon itself." With this transcendental vision we reach the "Omega point" of all life and all matter, a resolution of all the conflict and disharmony that has been the universal story thus far.

Darwin having been pointed in the right progressive direction, it was Freud's turn. This was the accomplishment largely of a brilliant school of "Freudo-Marxists," starting with Wilhelm Reich and continuing with Erich Fromm and Herbert Marcuse. What they attempted to show was that Freud's pessimism was based on an over-biologized view of the instincts, that what he thought of in particular as possessive or aggressive instincts were fundamentally the implants of society, specifically of capitalist society. They were not therefore insurmountable obstacles to the achievement of a peaceful and harmonious socialist society. In works such as *Eros and Civilization* (1955), *One Dimensional Man* (1964), and *An Essay on Liberation* (1969), Marcuse proposed the transformation of the libidinal instincts into forces for cooperative production and the creation of aesthetic objects. Society itself would become "a work of art." Given the right social and political changes, the "pleasure principle" could overcome the recalcitrant "reality principle," Eros tame Thanatos.[20]

Marcuse was one of the heroes of the "counterculture" of the 1960s, and here too utopian currents flowed freely. The criticism of industrial society was converted into a vision that differed from traditional socialist alternatives in the emphasis put on play and the pleasures of procreation.[21] The problem, as the sixties radicals saw it, was not production but the uses of production: its concentration in mind-numbing and body-stunting consumerism. In the "May Events" of Paris, 1968 – the high point of the student radicalism of the 1960s – the French students mixed Karl Marx with Groucho Marx, Freud with Fourier, de Sade with Dali and the Surrealists to produce a heady utopia that turned the traditional socialist program on its head and proclaimed the preeminence of spontaneity and the power of imaginative thought. The graffiti that covered the walls of Paris in these months were replete with these utopian sentiments: "Be realistic – demand the impossible"; "All power to the imagination"; "It's the dream that's real."

Ecotopia
Utopian as the sixties were, they produced no striking literary utopia. The works that caught the public imagination were works of cultural and social criti-

cism, especially as popularized in such celebratory accounts as Charles Reich's *The Greening of America* (1970). Literature as such remained in a grimly dystopian mood. The successes of these years were novels such as William Golding's *Lord of the Flies* (1954) and Anthony Burgess's *A Clockwork Orange* (1962), both of which dealt with the potential for violence and savagery inherent in the human condition. Science fiction too was chiefly full of foreboding, as it had been since Hiroshima. Under the slogan of the writer J. G. Ballard, "the only true alien planet is earth," science fiction writers portrayed worlds devastated by overpopulation and ecological catastrophe. Journeys into space increasingly ended in hell, especially the inner hell of the psyche.[22]

But out of anti-utopian science fiction, out of the social criticism of the counter-culture, a new utopia was in the making. A new view of society appeared, drawing on the abundant recent critique of technology, economic growth, capitalism, and consumerism. This was the ecological utopia or "ecotopia," a vision of society organized along ecological lines. Ecology – along with feminism – was the main inheritor of sixties radicalism; in the 1970s and 1980s, it was the driving force of alternative accounts of modern society. Overwhelmingly, as was the fashion, most of these accounts were expressed in scientific and social-scientific terms, even when these carried messages of urgency and high drama. Such were Paul Ehrlich's *The Population Bomb* (1968), the Club of Rome's *Limits to Growth* (1972), *The Ecologist* magazine's "Blueprint for Survival" (1972), and Fred Hirsch's *Social Limits to Growth* (1977).

But the ecotopia, unlike the countercultural critique, also achieved literary form. The great model here was William Morris's arcadian *News from Nowhere* (1890), an ecotopia before the name and to a good extent before its time. More immediately, and symbolically in many ways more important, there was the genial utopia of the aging Aldous Huxley, *Island* (1962). In this reversal of his anti-utopian *Brave New World*, Huxley deployed many of the ingredients of his former satire, such as drugs and scientific conditioning, to present a portrait of a gentle, ecologically conscious society that has married Western science with Eastern religion. Electricity plus Buddhism equals the good society, say the Palinese. Western science gives the means; Eastern philosophy shapes the ends, in the direction of a nonaggressive, cooperative, ecologically balanced society.

Non-Western philosophy of a more immediately available kind – drawn in this case from the native Indians of North America – was partly the inspiration behind Ernest Callenbach's *Ecotopia* (1975), the literary utopia from America's West Coast that seems to have given the ecotopia its name, though in most other respects it drew on standard ecological ideas. Ecotopia, a breakaway republic of the U.S. Pacific Northwest, incorporates the "small is beautiful" philosophy of the economist E. F. Schumacher together with recycling technologies and the careful, quasi-religious, attitude to the environment advocated by "deep" ecologists. There is much fun and frolicking in saunas and steam baths: the Ecotopians have been able to reduce the work week to twenty hours and take their leisure and pleasure seriously, in good Californian style. But the most important thing is the love and respect of nature. Here Ecotopians borrow much from the tribal lore of the Indians. The visitor Will Weston notes in his diary:

Some Ecotopian articles – clothing and baskets and personal ornamentation – perhaps directly Indian in inspiration. But what matters most is the aspiration to live in balance with nature, "walk lightly on the land," treat the earth as mother. No surprise that to such a morality most industrial processes, work schedules, and products are suspect! Who would use an earthmover on his own mother?

North American Indian culture was also an important influence – through her father, the anthropologist Alfred Kroeber – on Ursula K. Le Guin's *The Dispossessed* (1974), the most complex and interesting of the contemporary ecotopias. But there is no simple primitivism here, nor indeed any simple utopianism. The use of the science fiction mode allows Le Guin to complicate the presentation of utopia. She describes two contrasting civilizations on two planets – Urras, a thinly disguised Earth that has entered the high technological phase, and Anarres, formerly a mining colony of Urras, which has gone its own way and become a largely self-sufficient community organized on anarchistic and ecological principles. Urras is rich and beautiful but marked by inequality and exploitation. Anarres is arid and materially poor but rich in its egalitarian and cooperative spirit. Le Guin does not remain impartial between the two. She clearly favors Anarres, and at the end her protagonist Shevek, the physicist who moves between the two cultures, chooses to return to Anarres despite the tempting offers made to him on Urras. He has seen the poverty and misery on Urras, he has been caught up in a failed rebellion, and he reflects:

There is no freedom. It is a box – Urras is a box, a package, with all the beautiful wrapping of blue sky and meadows and forests and great cities. And you open the box and, what is inside it? A black cellar full of dust, and a dead man.

But Le Guin does not wish us to be comfortable with this choice. She originally subtitled her story "An Ambiguous Utopia," and ambiguity, or perhaps more properly ambivalence, is its hallmark. Anarres is not all good, and Urras not all bad. The former is bleak and inhospitable, and its revolution has reached an only too predictable point of doctrinaire rigidity that is inhibiting the research of scientists such as Shevek. On Urras, for its part, Shevek feels a liberating sense of ease and opulence, and is attracted by its respect for privacy and the opportunities it offers for the exercise of individual initiative and talent. The line between utopia and anti-utopia is blurred; the possibility seems to exist for utopia to degenerate into anti-utopia and, correspondingly, for anti-utopia to modulate into utopia. This ambivalence is perhaps a fair reflection of the state of ecotopia. For some it is the only future, if we are to escape the trap of vanishing resources and a spoilt and polluted world; for others, it threatens an authoritarian and conformist order, perhaps even some kind of "eco-fascist" regime.

Feminist Utopias

The Dispossessed is almost as much a feminist utopia as it is – or contains – an ecotopia. The revolutionary founder of Anarres is a female prophet, Odo, and Anarres is scrupulously egalitarian between the sexes. The ecotopia overlaps the feminist utopia, just as the feminist utopia almost unconsciously, it seems, adopts an ecological perspective. Since both ecology and feminism share common roots in the culture of the 1960s – and even further back – this is hardly surprising. But it seems worth adding a note on the feminist utopia, as perhaps the most thriving form of utopia at the present time.

It was perhaps inevitable that women should take to utopia. Where else would they be free and equal? No known society in history has allowed them material or symbolic equality with men. Even in past utopias they have been firmly subordinated to men. One of the earliest feminist utopias was indeed a spirited response to the portrayal of women in Bellamy's *Looking Backward*. In *Herland* (1915), Charlotte Perkins Gilman redressed the balance in her presentation of a gentle matriarchal society in which men have been abolished and women give birth in an ecstatic act of parthenogenesis.

Gilman's example seems to have been infectious. Among more recent feminist utopias, the utopian society of Whileaway in Joanna Russ's *The Female Man* (1975) also gets on happily without men; while in Sally Gearhart's *The Wanderground* (1978), men are masters in their mechanized cities but in the countryside they are helpless in the face of women who have established all-female communities and have developed the powers of telepathy, telekinesis, and even flight. Men are present, as equals, in Marge Piercy's *Woman on the Edge of Time* (1976), but her future society has borrowed *Brave New World* techniques of laboratory reproduction, thereby not merely freeing women from childbirth but allowing men to experience the joys and cares of motherhood along with the women ("We all became mothers. Every child has three.").

The energy that has inspired these visions has also, in characteristic fashion, stimulated their opposite: the feminist anti-utopia. In Margaret Atwood's *The Handmaid's Tale* (1985), women are enslaved to men, either as decorative spouses or as simple breeding machines. The anti-utopia, here as in general, tends to take the form of an intensification and projection of currently existing patterns. Hence the feminist utopia often contains an explicit anti-utopia to highlight the present position of women (thus reverting to the older pattern, found in More's *Utopia* as well as Swift's *Gulliver's Travels*, in which utopia and anti-utopia appear in the same work). Russ's *The Female Man* plays with four alternative futures for women, at least two of which are dystopias of sexual inequality and female degradation. *Woman on the Edge of Time* also includes a glimpse of an alternative future: a paranoid, power-mad world of gross inequality and exploitation, in which women, continually remodelled by cosmetic surgery, exist simply as paid whores for the men. And in *The Dispossessed* the egalitarian position of women on Anarres is contrasted with their conventional role on Urras as the dependents and playthings of men.[23]

The feminist utopia is one of the indications that the literary utopia is far from dead. Women writers – rather more than men – have explored its potential with force and imagination. Doris Lessing in her sequence *Canopus in Argus: Archives* (1979–83) is an outstanding recent example of a writer who has turned to the utopian tradition, in its science-fiction guise, to explore possible future worlds. But the fate of Lessing's work is instructive. Unlike her earlier novels, such as *The Golden Notebook* (1962), *Canopus* has been relegated to the science-fiction shelves of bookshops and libraries, and attracted a correspondingly restricted readership. This has in general been the fate of most utopian writing in the latter part of the twentieth century. Utopia has been "ghettoized." For the most part it has been absorbed in the mass popular genre of science fiction, where it gets an enthusiastic but generally undiscerning readership, but is largely ignored by critics and the public at large. When it breaks out of this circle, as it does occasionally with the ecotopia and the feminist utopia, it once more tends to speak to restricted and specialized constituencies. *The Female Man* and *Woman on the Edge of Time* are welcomed by feminists and their sympathizers, and energetically discussed among them; *Ecotopia* has a devoted following among ecological groups. But it would be no surprise to find that many educated people in Britain and America had never heard of them, nor would they feel particularly ashamed of their ignorance if such works were brought to their attention.[24] It is difficult to imagine such a situation, in their own times and even since, with *A Modern Utopia* or *Brave New World* or *Nineteen Eighty-four.* "Speaking pictures" of the future, whether in the positive or negative vein, are out of fashion. Utopia has lost its audience.

Utopia at the End of the Twentieth Century

Utopia did not die in the twentieth century, despite frequent pronouncements to this effect. Wells alone would have been sufficient to keep it alive in the first half of the century. But in the second half it faltered, or was at best chanelled in particular directions, toward specialized constituencies. There was, as we have seen, plenty of utopianism. But it remained largely in the realm of social and cultural theory – as indeed did its faithful partner, anti-utopia – rather than being expressed in the classic form of the literary utopia. If the argument of this essay is correct, this poses a problem for utopia, and its future health. What can we say about its condition in the closing years of the twentieth century, and at the opening of a new century and, indeed, a new millennium? Has the millennial pull worked in its favor?

Some novelties were certainly evident as the century drew to a close. The outstanding event has been the fall of the Soviet Union and the dissolu-

tion of communist regimes practically everywhere (China and Cuba, with North Korea and Vietnam, remain the principal exceptions so far). The significance of this for utopia can hardly be exaggerated. Whatever the feeling about the Soviet Union, its existence suggested the possibility of an alternative to the capitalist system of the West. It was an alternative couched in the terms and imprinted with the promise of socialism, the great utopia of the nineteenth and twentieth centuries. Never mind that for many socialists the Soviet Union was socialist in name only: there can be great power in a name.

The death of the Soviet Union has therefore suggested to many the end not just of socialism as a hopeful and viable project, but the end of utopia itself. Once more, as at several earlier points in this century, intellectuals – especially those in the former communist countries – have pronounced the death of utopia. But the world cannot, it seems, live without some image of utopia, for one direct consequence of the fall of communism has been the elevation of the liberal market society of the West to utopian status. In one of the most-publicized statements of this kind, the American thinker Francis Fukuyama pronounced "the end of history," by which he meant the end of all ideological contest in the world. This was not because all systems had ceased to have an appeal, but because one of them, the system of liberal capitalist society, had shown its clear superiority and announced itself, finally and decisively, as "the end-point of mankind's evolution." Liberal capitalism *was* utopia; a system that for much of its history had been tolerated and promoted as the least bad we might devise now found itself recast as the goal of human history, the embodiment of all of humanity's hopes and desires.[25]

Fukuyama's ebullient reworking of an old Hegelian idea certainly chimed with the hopes of many people in the former communist countries, although it may have been more Californian consumerism than liberal democracy that represented some kind of utopia to them. Their disappointments in the event have led not so much to disenchantment with the goal as to a sober recognition that for them at least it may be a long time in coming. But to others Fukuyama's pronouncement appeared to be not only an offensive piece of Western triumphalism but a serious misreading of what lay ahead. Blinded by the socialist challenge, Fukuyama failed to see that there were far more profound threats to the Western way of life than Soviet communism – which, after all, was a variety of modernity and was indeed founded on a Western ideology. In a powerful contribution to the public debate in the wake of communism's demise, the American political scientist Samuel Huntington argued that far from history's coming to an end, it was about to restart with a vengeance. In the rise especially of religious fundamentalism in various parts of the world, Huntington discerned the still persisting and in many ways accentuated "fault lines" dividing the world's great civilizations. Communism may have gone, but there was still Islam, now massively resurgent; and Russia remained the center of an Orthodox civilization that in many respects differed from the societies of Western Christianity. The future would be marked not by the worldwide victory of Fukuyama's "universal homogeneous state" but by a disorderly and potentially violent "clash of civilizations."[26]

The end of the millennium sees a confused picture. Apocalypse wars with optimism, utopianism with an acute sense that a "new world disorder" is upon us.[27] Perhaps that is why it seems to have been so difficult for anyone to produce a convincing utopia *or* anti-utopia in traditional literary form. The break-up of communism has not produced the clarity that some had earlier hoped it would; a world with only one superpower, far from having a stabilizing effect, seems instead to have set off a chain reaction of violent conflicts, many of them of an ethnic kind. The shape of the future world order remains cloudy and uncertain.

And yet there are opportunities, and reason enough, for utopia. More than at any other time in this century, the world seems to be struggling toward some kind of world government, with the United Nations the as yet uncertain but increasingly tested prototype. Visions of an "international civil society" and a "cosmopolitan democracy" have appeared in recent years, suggesting that while these are still only in the making and remain largely in ideal form, there are enough indications to make their realization more than wishful thinking.[28] Economic and technological "globalization," on an unprecedented scale, add to this sense that a new world order is struggling to be born. Wells would have been in his element: there are better prospects now for his "World-State" than at any time during his lifetime. The absence of an end-of-the-century Wells underscores the obvious point that social opportunity is not enough; creativity and imagination are also necessary ingredients of utopia.

In no other sphere does this pressure toward utopia show itself more than in that of electronic communication. While politically the world still remains a world of nation states, and even economically "globalization" is still patchy and uneven, in culture and communication the world is fast becoming one. Satellites and fiber-optic cable, computers and the World Wide Web, global media networks and corporations, have linked the world in one integrated information and communication grid. We are, many theorists tell us, in an Age of Information, one that marks off our age as decisively as the nineteenth-century industrial revolution separated us from the old agrarian world.[29] Once more, Wells, with his idea of the encyclopedic "World Brain" and the "world-wide House of Salomon," would have felt at home. Once more, unlike Wells, no one seems willing to step forward and clothe the idea in utopia's vivid colors.

It is not that the opportunities have not been exploited in other forms and ways. The very idea of the "Information Society" is replete with utopianism. Few of its exponents have been able to avoid a euphoric sense that the new possibilities opened up by the gigantic advances in information and communication will resolve most of our age-old problems of scarcity, ignorance, and inequality. The term "computopia" itself has been coined to express the wonderful world that the manifold applications of the computer are bringing into being. There has been much optimism around the idea of the "virtual community," the re-creation of a new "electronic agora" through the agency of the world-wide democracy of the Internet.[30] Some imaginative science fiction has developed to explore the idea of "cyberspace" and "virtual reality," though where this has overlapped with utopian concerns it has generally taken dystopian form, as in William Gibson's *Neuromancer* (1984).[31]

What has not been attempted, any more than with the idea of a new world society or world state, is a full-fledged utopian representation of the information age and the information society – this despite the abundance of resources available to any would-be utopist. It suggests that utopia does not have the appeal or command the attention that it once did – that the imaginative depiction of the good society is thought either misplaced or impossible. Utopianism, yes; and there are innumerable outlets, ranging from academic social theory to the popular culture of film and television, for its expression. But for the distinctive form of the literary utopia, as invented by Thomas More and practiced for more than three centuries, there no longer seems much call.

The End of Utopia?

We have seen that this is a condition that developed steadily throughout the second half of the twentieth century. There has been no successor to Wells, none even to Huxley or Orwell. Anti-utopia has fared almost as badly as utopia, though some novelists and science-fiction writers have drawn upon its modes and techniques to conjure up their particular nightmare visions of the future. Here they have continued in that vein of pessimism and nostalgia for past life that has characterized the literary intelligentsia for most of this century. In the high culture, at least, success usually turns more on pouring icy waters on our hopes than on raising them.

The fate of the novel itself might offer some explanation of utopia's plight. Utopia rose and fell with the novel. It was itself in its origins a kind of novel – a narrative of adventures in strange lands – and it was sustained by all the techniques later developed by the eighteenth- and nineteenth-century novel. The classic novel – the novel of Balzac, Dickens, and Tolstoy – took the whole of society as its object. It was panoramic in the way that utopia too aspired to comprehend the whole of social life. Not so the twentieth-century novel, the novel of Joyce, Woolf, and Kafka. The novel of our times has retreated to private worlds, to that "inner space" to which the best science fiction also takes us. Psychology or psychoanalysis are its tools, not sociology or political science. Such a literary climate is profoundly hostile to utopia, which has always dwelt in the bracing spaces of politics and society.

Or is the decline of utopia to do with the decline of religion, specifically the decline of Christian belief, as some have suggested?[32] It is true that though utopia is a secular form, Christian ideas of paradise and the millennium have provided it with some of its imagery and much of its emotional charge. If, as the utopian thinker Ernst Bloch believed, utopia is inextricably bound up with "the principle of hope,"[33] then declining faith in religion might well undermine the wellsprings of utopia as well, since it is religion that has sustained the hope of the world. Against this, there is the obvious point that religion, even Christian religion, has not declined to the extent predicted by both its friends and enemies in the nineteenth century, and can even be said to be experiencing a marked revival today. More importantly, much of the emotional as well as the intellectual structure of Christianity passed over into secular social philosophies, such as Marxism, so that the principle of hope was carried on their shoulders into the twentieth century.

More to the point might be the declining faith in those secular philosophies themselves. When philosophers announce the "end of grand narratives," when it is said that there is no philosophical basis for Enlightenment beliefs in Truth, Reason, Science, and Progress, it is hard to see how utopia, which tends to believe in most of those things, can survive. Fortunately, such "postmodern" theories, in their strict form at least, are believed in by only a handful of intellectuals, and most people, including intellectuals, do not appear to be unduly influenced by them in their everyday lives. But this is a different matter from saying that secular philosophies still retain a hold on the imagination of the people, at least in the manner and to the extent that they once did. Clearly they do not. The decline of socialism is only the most spectacular instance of the change. There is abundant evidence, from the political life of most Western nations, not only that people have little faith in politicians (that is hardly new) but that they also give little credibility to political ideologies and political programs. Politics is reduced in their eyes to horse-trading and careerism; at best it offers better or worse teams of managers. This is not so much postmodernist skepticism and irony as it is a resigned sense of disappointment at the failure of ideologies to deliver what they promise. In any case, it is clearly not the stuff of utopia, or even of anti-utopia on any meaningful scale.

If this is an accurate perception of current realities, it suggests an "end of history" in a more profound sense than that intended by Fukuyama. Even liberal capitalism here loses its gloss. All aspirations toward the good society appear illusory. We might even say, with Jean Baudrillard, that we cannot even talk of the "end" of history, since that suggests some sort of consummation. History can now "only turn around or repeat itself."[34] What one gets is endless recycling of the past, endless recovery and restoration. The millennium ends not with a bang but a whimper.

Karl Mannheim, a great student of utopias, thought that the elimination of the "reality-transcending power of utopia" would mean "the decay of the human will": "With the relinquishment of utopias, man would lose his will to shape history and therewith his ability to understand it."[35] Even East European intellectuals, such as Czeslaw Milosz and Milan Simecka, who, feeling it has been tried on them, are passionately aware of the dangers of utopia, warn against the rejection of all visions along with that of Marxism. A world without utopias, says Simecka, "would be a world without social hope, a world of resignation to the status quo and the devalued slogans of everyday political life."³⁶ To inveigh against the disappearance of utopias when the conditions for their creation may have all but vanished might seem vain. But perhaps that is not the point. Utopia can probably take care of itself, in the long run at least. It is unlikely that so long as the human race continues the "principle of hope" will ever entirely disappear. Utopia will be reborn, even if in forms that we cannot anticipate. What seems important today is to understand why it is so difficult for us to contemplate utopia, and the consequences of failing to do so. That by itself might play some part in recovering this historic vehicle of mankind's hopes and desires.

1 See on this Krishan Kumar, *Utopia and Anti-Utopia in Modern Times* (Oxford: Basil Blackwell, 1987), Chapter 2. It is probably correct to say that the revival of the literary utopia was inspired by a work that was not itself a formal utopia but that did not scorn a utopian picturing of the socialist future: August Bebel's *Woman in the Past, Present and Future* (1879; 2nd ed. 1883). A similar accompaniment to the revival of the literary utopia can be found in writings that, though not formal utopias, have a distinctly utopian cast, such as Oscar Wilde's *The Soul of Man Under Socialism* (1891) and Ebenezer Howard's *Tomorrow* (1898).

2 See Bertrand de Jouvenel, "Utopia for Practical Purposes," in Frank E. Manuel, ed., *Utopias and Utopian Thought* (London: Souvenir Press, 1973), 221–23.

3 For this "chain of utopias," see the introductions to my editions of *News from Nowhere* (Cambridge, England: Cambridge University Press, 1995) and *A Modern Utopia* (London: Dent and Sons, 1994).

4 For a full discussion of the Wellsian utopia, see my *Utopia and Anti-Utopia in Modern Times*, Chapter 6.

5 See especially "H. G. Wells" (1922), in *A Soviet Heretic: Essays by Yevgeny Zamyatin*, trans. and ed. Mirra Ginsburg (Chicago and London: University of Chicago Press, 1970).

6 The best study of all this is Mark R. Hillegas, *The Future as Nightmare: H. G. Wells and the Anti-Utopians* (New York: Oxford University Press, 1967).

7 See, for example, Chad Walsh, *From Utopia to Nightmare* (London: Geoffrey Bles, 1962).

8 I discuss these features of *Brave New World* and *Nineteen Eighty-four* in *Utopia and Anti-Utopia in Modern Times*, Chapters 7 and 8.

9 See on this Robert Fishman, *Urban Utopias of the Twentieth Century* (Cambridge, Mass.: MIT Press, 1982) and Peter Hall, *Cities of Tomorrow* (Oxford: Basil Blackwell, 1988).

10 See Nikolaus Pevsner, *Pioneers of Modern Design: From William Morris to Walter Gropius* (London: Penguin Books, 1975).

11 See on this movement Gary Werskey, *The Visible College* (London: Allen and Unwin, 1978); for their works, see my *Utopia and Anti-Utopia in Modern Times*, 230–42.

12 See, for example, Robert Scholes and Eric S. Rabkin, *Science Fiction: History, Science, Vision* (New York: Oxford University Press, 1977), 26–42.

13 On Technocracy and associated movements, see Howard P. Segal, *Technological Utopianism in American Culture* (Chicago: University of Chicago Press, 1985); on the world's fairs, see Robert W. Rydell, *World of Fairs: The Century-of-Progress Expositions* (Chicago: University of Chicago Press, 1993).

14 The utopian aspects of Fascism are well brought out in Zeev Sternhell, "Fascist Ideology," in Walter Laqueur, ed., *Fascism: A Reader's Guide* (Harmondsworth: Penguin Books, 1979).

15 For the utopian hopes placed in the Soviet Union, see Richard Crossman, ed., *The God That Failed: Six Studies in Communism* (London: Hamish Hamilton, 1950).

16 For the reaction to Skinner, and the general character of *Walden Two*, see my *Utopia and Anti-Utopia in Modern Times*, Chapter 9.

17 Clark Kerr and others, *Industrialism and Industrial Man*, 2nd ed. (Harmondsworth: Penguin Books, 1973), 81, 264–65.

18 Sigmund Freud, *Civilization and Its Discontents* (1930; London: Hogarth Press, 1963), 59.

19 Julian Huxley, *Evolution in Action* (London: Chatto and Windus, 1953), 113.

20 For further discussion of Marcuse and the "Freudo-Marxists," see my *Utopia and Anti-Utopia in Modern Times*, 393–402.

21 See Theodore Roszak, *The Making of a Counter Culture: Reflections on the Technocratic Society and Its Youthful Opposition* (Garden City, N.Y.: Doubleday, 1969).

22 For the science fiction of these years, see Kingsley Amis, *New Maps of Hell* (London: Gollancz, 1961) and Patrick Parrinder, ed., *Science Fiction: A Critical Guide* (London: Longman, 1979).

23 For further discussion of the feminist utopia, see Tom Moylan, *Demand the Impossible: Science Fiction and the Utopian Imagination* (New York and London: Methuen, 1986) and Frances Bartkowski, *Feminist Utopias* (Lincoln: University of Nebraska Press, 1989).

24 The one work of this kind that seems to have broken out of the ghetto is Ursula Le Guin's *The Dispossessed*. See, for instance, the appreciation in Raymond Williams, "Utopia and Science Fiction," in his *Problems in Materialism and Culture* (London: Verso, 1980).

25 See Francis Fukuyama, *The End of History and the Last Man* (New York: The Free Press, 1992). For a discussion see my "The End of Socialism? The End of Utopia? The End of History?," in Krishan Kumar and Stephen Bann, eds., *Utopias and the Millennium* (London: Reaktion Books, 1993).

26 See Samuel P. Huntington, *The Clash of Civilizations and the Remaking of the World Order* (New York: Touchstone Books, 1997). Analogous views were expressed by Benjamin R. Barber, *Jihad vs. McWorld* (New York: Ballantine Books, 1996), and Mark Juergensmeyer, *The New Cold War? Religious Nationalism Confronts the Secular State* (Berkeley: University of California Press, 1993).

27 See further my "Apocalypse, Millennium and Utopia Today," in Malcolm Bull, ed., *Apocalypse Theory and the Ends of the World* (Oxford: Blackwell, 1995).

28 For an example see Daniele Archibugi and David Held, eds., *Cosmopolitan Democracy: An Agenda for a New World Order* (Cambridge, England: Polity Press, 1995).

29 The best statement of this view is Manuel Castells, *The Information Age: Economy, Society and Culture*. 3 vols. (Oxford and Malden, Mass.: Blackwell, 1996–98).

30 See Howard Rheingold, *The Virtual Community: Finding Connection in a Computerised World* (London: Secker and Warburg, 1994).

31 For a discussion of the idea of the information society, see my *From Post-Industrial to Post-Modern Society* (Oxford and Cambridge, Mass.: Blackwell, 1995), Chapter 2.

32 See, for example, Frank and Fritzie Manuel, *Utopian Thought in the Western World* (Cambridge, Mass.: Harvard University Press, 1979), 801 ff.

33 See Ernst Bloch, *The Principle of Hope*, trans. Neville Plaice, Stephen Plaice, and Paul Knight. 3 vols. (Oxford: Basil Blackwell, 1986; Cambridge, Mass.: MIT Press, 1986); see also Ruth Levitas, *The Concept of Utopia* (Hemel Hempstead: Philip Allan, 1990), especially 83–105.

34 Jean Baudrillard, *The Illusion of the End*, trans. Chris Turner (Cambridge, England: Polity Press, 1994), 103.

35 Karl Mannheim, *Ideology and Utopia* (1936; London: Routledge and Kegan Paul, 1960), 236.

36 Milan Simecka, "A World with Utopias or Without Them?," in Peter Alexander and Roger Gill, eds., *Utopias* (London: Duckworth, 1984), 175. For Milosz, see my "Apocalypse, Millennium and Utopia Today," 219–20.

Yaacov Oved

Communal Movements in the Twentieth Century

THE ASPIRATION to an ideal society fulfilled in communes is a phenomenon that has been part of the Western world since ancient times and has mainly occurred in the past in schismatic groups like the Essenes, Christian monks, and heretic and Protestant sects. Since the sixteenth century, this aspiration has also found inspiration in utopian literature. The nineteenth century saw utopian socialism join the trend, and the expanse of the New World was fertile soil from which scores of different communal communities sprang. It was, however, not until the twentieth century that millions of people all over the world took part in various forms of communal life, some voluntarily and others as a result of compulsion, some for short periods and others for life. Their social origins were varied: there were poor farmers and people from the wealthy middle classes, intellectuals, idealists, visionaries, seekers, and escapists. This was the communes' most fruitful century; from its early years, large communal movements, which expanded over the years, were in existence. The twentieth century saw the uninterrupted appearance of various forms of communalism; not a decade passed without the appearance of new communes. While in previous centuries the phenomenon of communalism was limited to isolated, closed communities mainly in the United States, the twentieth century saw extensive waves of communes in numerous countries, on every continent, which left their mark on large populations.

At the beginning of the twentieth century, there were only a few communes, the main concentration of which were in the United States. The most notable of these were the Hutterites, an Anabaptist communal sect that is the oldest of its kind, having been founded in the sixteenth century in central Europe. In 1874, its members immigrated to the United States and settled in the Midwest; by the beginning of the twentieth century, the sect had a dozen colonies with a total population of some two thousand. As the century progressed, the sect expanded significantly and today, on the threshold of the twenty-first century, has a membership of some forty thousand in four hundred communes in the United States and Canada.

In the second decade of the twentieth century, immediately after the outbreak of the Russian

Revolution, hundreds of communes appeared simultaneously all over Russia. These communes had their historical background in the rural *mir*, but there were also communes of a different type that had appeared among the "old believers" sects at the end of the nineteenth century. In addition, some anarchists and disciples of Tolstoy lived a communal life apart from outside society. The postrevolution communes constituted a previously unknown phenomenon. In the initial stage, the revolutionary regime indulged the communes although it had some reservations regarding their spontaneous-anarchist characteristics. The economic decline that occurred in the "war communism" years impelled many workers to leave the cities for the villages, where "committees of the poor" had expropriated lands for the starving workers; on some of these lands, communes were established.

In the 20s, a few dozen foreign communes were founded by returned Russian émigrés and by foreign radicals and communists who had gone to Russia for ideological reasons. The majority of these were Americans who went to Russia to become part of the building of a communist society, equipped with both agricultural equipment and revolutionary consciousness. The members of these communes, who were motivated by ideology, established stable communes in which they diligently pursued a cooperative approach to production and consumption. The introduction of the New Economic Policy brought with it a less tolerant attitude toward the communes on the part of the regime, with the political leadership intentionally halting the existing communes' development and preventing the establishment of new ones. Unemployment in the cities dropped, and the incentive of unpaid work in the communes gradually diminished in those circles that had been economically motivated to take it. As a result, between 1921 and 1925 the number of existing communes was cut by half, and any incentive for new segments of the population to join them also lessened. Large numbers of members left the existing communes, in which prevailing economic weakness found expression in internal tension, struggles, and strife. Between 1925 and 1929, another change in economic policy led to an increase in the number of communes. However, this rise was dramatically halted in 1930 as a result of Stalin's forced collectivization policy, and those living in communes were forced to move over to the *kolkhoz* system, which put an end to their voluntary communal principles. Numerous communes were brutally and cruelly dismantled. The collectivization of 1930 became a movement to destroy all the communes established in the 20s, and only a few managed to survive until the eve of World War II. In general terms it can be said that in the 30s, the communes of the USSR were a fleeting phenomenon, but it should still be noted that despite hostility from the communist regime, several of them existed for some fifteen years.

Two communal movements established in the 1920s showed stability and persisted throughout the century. In 1920, the Bruderhof commune was established in Germany by a group of young Anabaptists and remained there until the rise to power of the Nazis. The commune was expelled from Germany in 1937 and moved to England, but was forced to leave during World War II because of local hostility toward its German members, who immigrated to Paraguay. From the 1950s onward, they moved their settlements to the United States and Great Britain while diligently maintaining their communal way of life. At the end of the twentieth century, this movement numbered some 2,500 souls living in seven economically and socially stable flourishing communes.

In the mid-1920s, the cornerstone was laid for the establishment of the kibbutz movements in the Land of Israel. This followed the establishment of the first *kvutza*, Degania, in 1909, and the consequent appearance of additional cooperative settlements. The kibbutz movement has been in existence ever since; as the century drew to a close, it numbered some 125,000 souls living in 277 settlements. Its founders were young Jewish idealists who sought to establish agricultural communes inspired by national ideals and the Zionist-socialist vision. The essence of this was the creation of a Jewish working class and the establishment of a new society based upon the foundations of social justice under the historic circumstances of modern Jewish national revival. This vision motivated the founders to establish large communes, called "kibbutzim," and to become integrated into the infrastructure of the new society then being formed in the Land of Israel, which was still called "Palestine."

The vast majority of the kibbutzim were secular communities, but in the 30s a small stream of religious kibbutzim were formed. From a historical standpoint, all the kibbutzim and their movements had some common basic principles: agricultural

settlement, self-labor, full partnership in the ownership of their production and consumption assets, equality, mutual economic support, and democratic self-management. Despite the great similarity in their basic principles, at their inception the streams differed in their interpretation of socialism, their approach to the size of the kibbutz, and the integration of agriculture and light and heavy industry in their economy. Two typical models of the kibbutz community were formed: the smaller, more intimate *kvutza* and the bigger, growing kibbutz, which was open to wide absorption. Over the years, the lines of distinction between the kibbutz streams have become blurred, in both the settlements' structure – they have all integrated industry with agriculture – and in the structure of their society, which in all the kibbutzim has become heterogeneous, multigenerational, and open to absorption. Until the establishment of the State of Israel, the kibbutzim played a central role in the political and social life of the Jewish community of Palestine, and they continued to do so in the State's early years. The dominant values of the kibbutz also stood at the center of Israeli society's ideologies. The kibbutzim gained great esteem and also preferential treatment in the allocation of national funds because of their fidelity to the national missions they undertook. This preferential treatment was terminated during the 1970s when a right wing government came to power in Israel and with the strengthening of materialistic and individualistic trends in Israeli society.

In the second half of the 1930s, there were two great waves of cooperative communities. On July 19, 1936, with the outbreak of the civil war in Spain, a social revolution began. Collective organizations called *colectividades*, whose activists were anarchists, appeared in villages in a number of the republic's regions. During the summer of 1936, these initiatives spread throughout the districts held by the republicans. The majority of the *colectividades* established in the first five weeks following the outbreak of civil war were located in the province of Aragon, and the movement later spread to Catalonia, Levante, Andalusia, and Castilla. The winter of 1936–37 was the apogee of this process: the number of agricultural collectives reached some two thousand, with approximately one million citizens – a phenomenon most impressive in its scope.

The *colectividades* were not only an economic enterprise but also aspired to form a new society. One expression of this was the abolition of the use of money wherever anarcho-communist–inspired collectives were formed. From September 1936,

Communal Upbringing

**Nursery school teacher,
Kibbutz in Yizreel Valley**
Photograph, 1936
Yad Tabenkin Archives (Research
Center of the United Kibbutz
Movement, Israel)

Communal education in
the kibbutz is based on the
principle of comprehensive
responsibility of the community to its children. In the early
years of the kibbutzim, it was
customary for children to live
apart from their parents, in
communal living quarters.
During the day, the children
were cared for by trained
nurses and teachers; in the
evening, they spent leisure
time with their parents. But
in the 1990s, significant
changes occurred, as com-
munal living quarters for the
children gave way to family
sleeping arrangements.
The children's houses have
become day-care centers,
and the children now sleep
in their parents' apartments.

Kibbutz

Eliahu Cohen
Kibbutz Ashdot Ya'akov
Photograph, 1936
Yad Tabenkin Archives (Research
Center of the United Kibbutz
Movement, Israel)

Kibbutz Ahdot Ya'akov is a
Jewish communal settlement
founded in the Jordan Valley
in 1935 by members of youth
pioneer groups who had
emigrated from Poland, Latvia,
and Germany. Today, the
population numbers 550. The
main economic endeavors
are fruit groves (avocados,
bananas, olives), a cowshed,
poultry, and plastics. An
art gallery in the settlement
is named for two brothers
who were born in the kibbutz
and died in the wars.

During the 1946 War of
Independence and the years
that followed, this kibbutz
faced the challenges of a
border settlement. After the
Jordanian-Israeli peace treaty,
it became an important link
for peaceful relations.

they introduced family wages as a step in their program to fulfill the communal principle of "to each according to his needs." Another cooperative sphere common to all these communities was collective organization of work. All were subject to strict labor discipline, and the system of direct democracy was adopted, with the sovereignty of the general meeting above all. Despite the war effort, which placed a heavy burden on the collectives, their members found time for social and educational activities. The majority of the collectives provided education for boys and girls up to the age of fifteen. Schools became an integral part of the rural landscape in the collectivization areas. The collectives also played a pioneering role in the fostering of health and welfare services for their members and for the surrounding area.

But it quickly became clear that the collectives faced numerous obstacles. The political parties that formed the ruling coalition in the republic were not sympathetic to the *colectividades*, and the bitterest opposition came from the communists because of global political considerations and from fear of radicalization of the revolution in the villages. Once the communists had consolidated their position in the government of the republic, they embarked on a wave of persecution of the anarchist collectives in Aragon. On the other hand, after the first year the *colectividades* began to show signs of internal weakening. The majority of them instituted a wage scale that was determined by social usefulness, profession, and office. Gaps between the poor and wealthier collectives also became apparent. The longer the communities held on, the more distanced from reality the vision of the founders became. Although the vision was not completely fulfilled, the agricultural achievements attained, and most particularly the way the communities faced up to the challenge of establishing new societal cells, gave elements of constructivism to the revolution in Spain that set it apart from other revolutions of its generation.

In October 1936, the foundations were laid in Mexico for cooperative agricultural settlements called *ejidos colectivos*, as part of the agrarian reform instituted by President Lázaro Cárdenas (1934–40). These settlements were mainly voluntary associations of farmers who were given land for joint cultivation while participating in a cooperative community that offered management of production and consumption, mutual economic support, and education. The first *ejidos colectivos* were in the Laguna district of the state of Durango and Coahila in central Mexico, and they were followed by *ejidos*

in other districts of Mexican states; by 1939, there were some eight hundred settlements.

The characteristics of the *ejido colectivo* were: (1) land was jointly owned and cultivated and was not divided into small units; (2) accumulated capital and credit were both under the supervision of the *ejido*; (3) the members placed themselves at the disposal of the *ejido* for work in production; (4) the joint produce and fruits of the collective labor belonged to the society, and its distribution for consumption was on the basis of contribution. In 1936, the Banco Nacional de Credito Ejidal was founded to provide credit for the *ejidos*; it was not only their only source of credit but also played a role in advancing the vocational skills of the members of the *ejidos* by organizing professional training courses for them. The first years of the *ejidos*' existence showed a sharp rise in the standard of living, reflected in a number of areas: for example, a medical service was organized, and there were great developments in education. More schools were opened in better buildings and with better teaching staffs.

The end of Cárdenas's term of office brought a change in agrarian policy. Emphasis shifted to fostering private agriculture, and the *ejido colectivo* was neglected. At the same time, weakening factors were at work within the *ejidos*: the appearance of bureaucracy and corruption caused a gradual decline during the following years. The *ejido colectivo* enjoyed a short period of rejuvenation in the 1970s during the presidency of Luis Echeverria, but it was not enough to extricate it from the deep crisis that had beset it.

After World War II, a search for ways of communalism began in various corners of the world. In postwar Europe, cooperative groups of various kinds were formed: communes appeared in Holland, Great Britain, Germany, the Scandinavian countries, and France where the Boimondau cooperative working groups were established. During the same period, the foundations were laid in Great Britain for the Camphill movement, which established therapeutic communities, according to Rudolf Steiner's principles of anthroposophy, for mentally impaired young people. This movement had been founded in Austria in 1938 by Dr. Karl König, who after the German annexation escaped to Scotland where he founded educational institutions that gradually became a global network of communities that today has ninety settlements. In Africa, too, a local esoteric Christian sect founded a commune known as *Aiyetoro* in southwest Nigeria; it existed until 1968. But the greatest concentration of communes during this period was in the United States. There were the long-established Hutterite colonies as well as a number of communes founded in the 30s. Of the new communes that appeared in the United States after World War II, the majority were pacifist in nature and decided, in 1952, to become the "Fellowship of Intentional Communities" (FIC). By 1954, this fellowship numbered nine communitarian groups whose members pooled their property and work.

Two distinct trends were at work in the Fellowship groups: on the one hand, the individualism that characterized conscientious objector pacifists who rejected authoritarianism, and on the other a trend toward fostering communal integration.

Of all the Fellowship groups, only Koinonia in Georgia survived as an independent community. This commune was founded in 1942 by Clarence Jordan, a Southern Baptist preacher. Jordan took pains to build an interracial commune in which whites and blacks could live together, but in this regard he encountered problems from the surrounding racist population of the southern state. In the 1950s, Koinonia established contacts with the FIC communes and the Hutterites, and these helped the community to withstand racist attacks by its neighbors and the Ku Klux Klan. Although the commune went into decline after Clarence Jordan's death in 1969, the community continued to play a role in the advancement of inexpensive housing for blacks and other deprived populations.

The 50s saw a communal awakening in Asia, too. In the summer of 1958, thousands of communes appeared in China. Their scope was large and their characteristics different from those of any communes in the West; as they were initiated by government policy, they constitute a special chapter in the history of modern communes. The decision to establish these communes was made by the Chinese Communist party leadership at Mao Tse-tung's instigation. The objective was to advance the cause of communism among millions of farmers in a "great leap forward" and allow for the recruitment of the masses for infrastructure and development projects.

By the end of 1958, on some twenty-four thousand "people's communes," hundreds of thousands of farmers were engaged in agriculture, industry, commerce, education, and public works. The "people's communes" were built in local sub-units numbering some 450–500 people. These groups constituted the basic nucleus of the communes, and it was in them that the everyday work was done. The communes' leaders compelled their members to transfer their private property, land, plantations,

etc., to the commune; in return, they were paid according to their needs. In the majority of these communes, food was provided free in public dining halls that were also designed to free women from the burden of housework. Children's houses were established to release mothers for productive work and thus foster Communist education.

By the beginning of 1959, less than a year after the beginning of the "great leap forward," it had become clear that communism was not germinating among the communes' farmers, so the Communist party leadership began a slow, pragmatic withdrawal from its full and immediate communalization policy for all spheres of life. Over their lifetime, the communes underwent changes in both production and consumption principles. During the "Cultural Revolution," there was an unsuccessful attempt to reinforce collectivism; afterwards, communalism weakened gradually until it disappeared completely by the mid-70s.

In 1958, the Yamagishi Kai commune movement was founded in Japan. Its founder and spiritual leader was Miyozo Yamagishi, an Osakan chicken farmer whose philosophy contained a mixture of Marxism, anarchism, and Chinese philosophy. This movement was successful both economically and in terms of attracting members; by the 1990s, some five thousand people were living in its communes in Japan, Korea, Switzerland, Germany, Thailand, Australia, Brazil, and the United States. To join this movement, an applicant must participate in doctrinal seminars. Then the initiate transfers all his assets to the commune, which in return provides for all his needs and guarantees lifetime social security. Those joining the commune come from varying social strata; among them are many from the wealthy middle class, who seek to drop out of the materialistic rat race that so typifies Japanese society. This is a secular commune with no binding religious belief. The members' social attitude is egalitarian, and work is a focal point of their lives. They produce for their own consumption and also market agricultural produce.

The biggest and most significant wave in the history of twentieth-century communes began in the United States in the 60s. Its influence quickly spread beyond the boundaries of the U.S., reaching Europe, Australia, and New Zealand, and marking the beginning of the globalization of modern communalism. This wave had its origins in the protest movements involving young people and students in the United States and Europe. This generation had grown up during a period of radical awakening: it witnessed the civil rights struggle in the United

States, was shocked by the wave of political assassinations, and was active in the battle against the war in Vietnam. These traumatic events all motivated idealistic, middle-class young people to rebel against the bourgeois society in which they had been raised. Their objective was not partial reform, but rather the reconstruction of society. Amid the agitation and rebellion there arose a spiritual quest that laid the foundations for a counterculture, which propounded an alternative system of values and critical positions against the bourgeois way of life, industrial society, bureaucracy, competitiveness, consumption, careerism, and alienating work. These people favored the ideals of world peace and brotherhood, spontaneity, freedom, naturalism, sexual permissiveness, and drug use to achieve cosmic consciousness.

The "hippies" typified this culture. The countercultural hippie ethic raised the banner of "dropping out" as a means of protest against the status quo. A great many hippies expressed their protest and their aspiration to create an alternative society by establishing communes. They had a naïve approach to human nature; they believed that if people were taken out of traditional American society and culture and placed in an alternative humanistic system, they would change and adapt to a new type of social life. The basic ethos of these communes was therefore openness – anyone could join.

In the early years, the Haight-Ashbury district of San Francisco was the most active center of hippie activity. Later came a move to rural areas, among other things because of the availability of cheap land in isolated areas and the possibility of withdrawing from society into an exclusive community. Large concentrations of rural hippie communes were formed in a number of states, first California, then Oregon and Washington, and then other areas in the East and Southwest. The biggest concentration on the East Coast was in New England, particularly Vermont, where the communes were also a focal point for social and political change in their areas. In the Southwest, New Mexico and Colorado were prominent hippie commune centers.

The majority of the 60s communes, both rural and urban, were short-lived, vanishing after only a year or two. Their members were not only idealists but also marginal individuals who sought refuge from society. Those who joined came from different backgrounds, had different motives, and did not always agree on lifestyle choices. An example of such disagreement is the debate over drug use and sexual permissiveness, which were initially accepted

and later rejected. In general, these communes had neither a clear ideology that could provide them with a stable doctrinal belief nor a theoretical and practical philosophy on ways to organize an alternative society. It is therefore hardly surprising that so many fell apart after only a short time.

Accepted opinion holds that the communes of the 60s failed, and if the criterion for success is the duration of their existence, then that is true. But if the communes are viewed as a catalyst to an experiment in reorganizing society, then they can be seen as having made an important contribution to their generation. Moreover, the impact of the communes of the 60s remains in the consciousness of younger generations in America and other countries, even after the majority have been dismantled. And along with the thousands of short-lived communes, several dozens of the 60s communes have demonstrated stability and staying power, surviving up to today.

The late 60s also saw the beginning of a search for spiritual meaning by many young people, which brought dozens of new religious communes in its wake. Together with them, in 1967–68, came widespread agitation by tens of thousands of young people on the West Coast, known as "Jesus freaks," which spawned communal movements that displayed a talent for prolonged existence. One of these was Children of God, in whose colonies a communal way of life was directed by an authoritarian hierarchy of leaders. Broad expansion in 1972 led to the establishment of dozens of communal colonies. The authorities became suspicious of the group, and police surveillance began. A 1974 report accused the leaders of abduction, brainwashing, violence, sexual permissiveness, and tax evasion; as a result, members began to move from country to country as fugitives. Between 1973 and 1975, the majority moved to Europe, Latin America, and Australia, and in 1977 they began living in family groups, changed their name, and became The Family. The change of name indicated a change of image designed to remove the stigma from the group and to help it become socially acceptable. Under these circumstances, The Family was able to return to the United States and live there undisturbed.

Another movement that appeared in these circles was the Shiloh Youth Revival Center, which existed from 1968 to 1989. Founded in California, the movement later transferred its headquarters to Oregon. In its first years the movement opened rural communities and urban "Shiloh Houses" that were open to all and provided food and shelter. In all their communities, communal property was a means to an end, which was Christian evangelism. Beset by an economic and social crisis in 1978, the movement sank into debt and was sued by the Internal Revenue Service for back taxes. Most of its assets were subsequently mortgaged, and in 1989 Shiloh was dissolved.

Among the reasons for the collapse of so many of these communes are the authoritarian regime that prevailed in them and the submission of members to the will of manipulative leaders. It should be noted that the communes created an atmosphere in which such manipulation could take place and opened the door to widespread corruption.

One cannot ignore the horrifying instances of violence and crime that have occurred in a number of groups that lived as communes. The Manson Family, which was involved in the mass murder of seven people, and the People's Temple sect, whose members committed mass suicide in Jonestown, Guyana, are but two notable examples. Other communes were involved in incidents that aroused much hostility, contention, and even attacks by outside society. There have been court trials of communes presented as cults in which brainwashing, abduction, sexual license, and child abuse were alleged. For a time these phenomena cast a stigma on the term "commune"; although in the majority of cases the allegations were rebutted and the charges dropped, the stigma remained.

In the 60s, spiritual searches for mystical meaning also spawned sects with links to Oriental religions. This trend began in 1965, when U.S. immigration laws regarding immigrants from the East were relaxed; the flow of immigrants that ensued included a number of charismatic religious leaders. Within a short time, these leaders gathered followers around them. These sects attracted young people from the counterculture because they offered a new kind of spiritual-religious experience that contained mystical elements. Some of these religious leaders founded relatively stable communal movements.

The most famous of these was the International Society of Krishna Consciousness ("Hare Krishna"), which began in 1965 with the arrival in New York from Calcutta of its founder, Swami Prabhupada. During its first decade in the West, it became a world movement with several thousand believers. The movement's central nucleus lived a communal life in both cities and rural settlements. By the 1980s, it had a core of five thousand believers in the United States and a further ten thousand in other countries.

The 70s saw the rapid spread of communes in the United States and numerous other countries throughout the world. Their philosophical roots and spiritual sources encompassed worlds as different and distant from one another as anarchism and Buddhism. Also during this period, the communes' founders were joined by spiritual, syncretistic streams of New Age disciples who combined mystical sources from Oriental religions with Western beliefs. During the 70s and 80s, millions of disciples were involved in these spiritual movements; some of them believed that the "Age of Aquarius" was nigh and that they must prepare for it by forming communities with a lifestyle appropriate to the age. Their choice of cooperation and solidarity over competitiveness and antagonistic individualism found its best expression in communes that emphasized nurturing the individual's inner spiritual world through meditation. The long-awaited global change was expected to occur through the adoption of this kind of lifestyle, and the accepted belief was that if such communities proliferated, the coming of the New Age would be accelerated. The communal sector of this movement did not last long; it began to diminish in size in the 90s when it became clear that no significant change was about to take place in the world, and that the Age of Aquarius was not on the horizon.

The most notable of the communes that adopted the New Age way is Findhorn in Scotland. It began in the early 60s when a small group of young hippies gathered on the northwest coast of Scotland to live under the spiritual leadership of Peter and Eileen Caddy. In 1971 they were joined by an American, David Spangler, under whose influence the community became a spiritual center of the New Age and a "University of Light" that showed the way to the Age of Aquarius. Although the community underwent numerous changes in its communal system, it has continued to function as a spiritual center that holds courses and congresses in which tens of thousands of people have participated over the years.

The spread of communes throughout the world during these years is also connected to the rapid development of communications media – the press, radio, and television. Through them, local events were given wide coverage even in distant regions. A notable example of this was the 1973 "Aquarius Festival" in Nimbin, Australia, in which some ten thousand young Australians participated. As a result of media coverage, a great wave of communes were founded, from small urban communes to territorial communal communities that sought to foster cooperative cells with an alternative ecological and technological lifestyle. In recent years, tens of thousands of Australians have become involved in the alternative lifestyle movement, but only a small number still actually live in communes. In the 70s in Great Britain and continental Europe, too, various kinds of communes appeared that were similar to those in the United States. These were years of consolidation for the various modern commune streams and years of growth for communalism all over the world, but after only a few years the tide turned.

The change occurred in the 80s: Reaganism in the United States, Thatcherism in Britain, and the collapse of communism in Eastern Europe created a conservative, anti-utopian climate. During these years, attacks by local authorities also played a part in the withdrawal from the communal way of life in the majority of communes founded in the 70s. Yet it should be noted that in addition to these external factors, there were also numerous internal ones. Cumulative personal fatigue resulted from intensive activity and the pressure of communal living arrangements. Some, who had come to the communes to find refuge and a remedy for their personal woes, left the communes once these issues had been resolved. Finally, after two decades of a hard life with no prospects for improvement, the 60s enthusiasm for creating an alternative society began to wane; in its place arose the temptation of returning to personal careers in the society they had abandoned.

But despite the alienated and hostile economic atmosphere of the 80s, some older communes continued, and new ones appeared at the beginning of the twentieth century's final decade. Furthermore, thousands of cooperative communities with a wide variety of beliefs and a broader form of cooperation than had been known in the past existed worldwide during these years. They ranged from the older religious conservative Hutterite and Bruderhof communes, through spiritually motivated groups founded by the "new religions," to various types of secular communes. A large number of these had their origins in the waves of the 60s and 70s, while scores of other cooperative communities, both secular and religious, have been established in more recent years.

The majority of the 90s communes are different from their predecessors. The utopian element in them has diminished while the pragmatic-realistic approach has grown, and it is this realism that gives them a greater degree of stability and opens the lines of communication with the surrounding community. Most of them are interested in fostering intercommunal relations and have established communications networks and federations. A noteworthy example of this is the revival of the 1950s Fellowship for Intentional Community, which now brings together communities with cooperative elements, such as joint ownership of land, buildings, and assets, partial communes, cooperative residence groups, as well as communities of self-employed people united by their desire for a cooperative lifestyle. A popular subject among these communities is alternative ecology and technology. There are also communities whose objective is improved quality of life; their members seek to establish for themselves isolated islands where they can provide for their needs through a simple, tranquil, and pastoral lifestyle.

In the 1990s, there has been an apparent waning of integrative communalism. Wide-ranging change is apparent in both the newer and long-established communes. At the root of such change is a trend toward broadening the freedom of the individual and his or her economic independence. The *Zeitgeist* extols the balanced combination of individualism and social solidarity while seeking ways to employ cooperative elements in the framework of autonomous communities. The result is the maintaining of pluralistic cooperative arrangements, often within the same community. It should be noted that these trends have not yet penetrated the older religious communes of the Hutterites and the Bruderhof, but they do affect, to varying degrees, all the rest.

In the kibbutz movement in Israel, there is a bitter internal struggle between those who advocate change in order to better adapt to the outside world because they lack confidence in the kibbutz's ability to maintain communal life, and the believers in the commune who are seeking ways to adopt the lessons of the new era to reinforce the communal foundations. This has led to two trends in the kibbutz movement. On the one hand are kibbutzim that have made far-reaching changes and diminished the applicability of communal principles; on the other are the majority of kibbutzim, which seek to increaase individual freedom in the areas of earnings and consumption, yet still preserve the elements of the commune. It appears that despite the changes and the variety of forms of cooperation, at the end of the twentieth century the kibbutz movement is still the most widespread secular communal movement.

WE HAVE noted here the variety of twentieth-century communes. Many of them had short-lived, episodic existences, only a few lasted for any length of time, and others, such as the Hutterites, the Bruderhof, and the kibbutz movement, have a history dating from the beginning of the century or even earlier. Some traveled the long road without change; although the majority underwent significant changes during their history, these, too, usually remained loyal to the principles of economic and spiritual cooperation. The histories of the communes include some riveting stories of the lives of idealists and world reformers. Among the millions who have experienced communal life, tens of thousands are still alive and some maintain a communal lifestyle to this day. Among the many who left, there are those who regret years "wasted" on a hopeless social experiment, but others look back on the commune with a certain nostalgia as the most significant chapter of their lives, one that enriched them with experiences and spiritual assets.

In conclusion, it must be said that overall, even at the time the communes were at their zenith, they were no more than a few isolated cells in general society. This considered, we must ask the following question: Can we note a contribution to humanity in general that derives from the communes' experience, apart from that made in the circles in which they lived? There is no simple answer, and the pros and cons must be carefully considered. On the debit side, the small numbers and isolation that characterize the communes, which are selective social cells, limit their general social contribution. But to their credit, the communal experience and lifestyle have and do constitute social laboratories in which the possibility that human beings can live cooperatively in voluntary communities with no private property is realistically examined. Their achievements have revealed ways of living together, while their failures have shown the limitations of the communal lifestyle. Their experience shows that this lifestyle is not suitable for the masses and that a basic condition for the stability of alternative social cells is religious belief, a social or national vision that gives content and meaning to the survival efforts of the exclusive way of life. At the same time, the continuing existence of communal movements throughout the twentieth century, the fact that they were undeterred by the failures of earlier communes and the collapse of communist regimes that purported to establish a new society by governmental means, indicates the deep human need to search for ways to live cooperatively in voluntary communities. It also points to the endless potential for attaining this utopia in a modern society, even as we move into the third millennium.

Communities Directory. Langley, Wash.: Fellowship for Intentional Community, 1996.

Dolgoff, Sam. *The Anarchist Collectives.* Montreal: Black Rose, 1974.

Eckstein, Salomón. *El Ejido Colectivo en México.* México: Fondo de Cultura Ecónomica, 1978.

Fairfield, Richard. *Communes U.S.A.: A Personal Tour.* Baltimore, Md.: Penguin, 1972.

Hall, John R. *The Ways Out: Utopian Communal Groups in an Age of Babylon.* Boston: Routledge and Kegan Paul, 1978.

Hostetler, John. *Hutterite Society.* Baltimore, Md.: Johns Hopkins University Press, 1974.

Melville, Keith. *Communes in the Counter Culture: Origins, Theories, Styles of Life.* New York: William Morrow, 1972.

Metcalf, Bill. *From Utopian Dreaming to Communal Reality: Cooperative Lifestyles in Australia.* Sydney, Australia: University of New South Wales Press, 1995.

Miller, Timothy. *The Quest for Utopia in 20th-Century America.* Syracuse, N.Y.: Syracuse University Press, 1998.

Near, Henry. *The Kibbutz Movement: A History.* Vols. 1 and 2. New York: Oxford University Press, 1997.

Oved, Yaacov. *The Witness of the Brothers: A History of the Bruderhof.* New Brunswick, N.J.: Transaction Books, 1996.

Richardson, James; Mary White Stewart; and Robert B. Simmonds. *Organized Miracles: A Study of Contemporary, Youth, Communal, Fundamentalist Organization.* New Brunswick, N.J.: Transaction Books, 1978.

Stites, Richard. *Revolutionary Dreams.* New York: Oxford University Press, 1989.

Wesson, R. G. *Soviet Communes.* New Brunswick, N.J.: Rutgers University Press, 1963.

Zicklin, Gilbert. *Countercultural Communes: A Sociological Perspective.* Westport, Conn.: Greenwood Press,

Roland Schaer

Utopia and Twentieth-century Avant-gardes

Redemptive Violence

"WE WILL glorify war – the world's only hygiene."[1]
Some may explain Marinetti's claim, made in the
first Futurist Manifesto and published in *Le Figaro*
on February 20, 1909, as the bombast of a writer
in keen need of scandal. Indeed, his phrasing bears
the hallmark of an inspired agitator. But above
and beyond its provocative form, the declaration
expresses the undeniable fervor for confrontation
as well as the desire for apocalypse that were so
characteristic of the beginning of the century, a
time that witnessed the advent of a common language that joined political and artistic avant-gardes
in their shared conviction that only a destructive
and violent showdown would succeed in freeing
the future from the past. At an end was a vision of
history in which progress proceeds by continuous
accumulation, along a royal road toward the enrichment of tradition. The time had come for a relentless antagonism between the future and the past;
the new, a value in and of itself, could come forth
in all its radical purity only from the destruction
of the old, in a violent break that would separate
the old world from the one that was clamoring
to be born. War was the necessary and welcome
fulfillment of this rupture.

Futurist attacks on "passéists," "that vast
cohort of enemies" that needed to be "torn to
pieces and overthrown," were on the rise. Like
Marinetti, who raised the rallying cry for an
"abolition of the past," Apollinaire, in the July 1913
manifesto *L'Anti-tradition futuriste: manifeste-synthèse*,
based his whole aesthetic on the destruction of
the formal tradition. And he added: "no regrets."[2]

War was embraced, therefore, as an absolute
means of regeneration, as the total mobilization of
the convulsive forces that would bring the past to an
end, as a conflagration of simultaneously destructive
and creative powers. "War? . . . Very well, yes; It's
our only hope, our reason for living, our only desire!
. . . Yes, war! Against you, for dying too slowly, and
against all the dead for cluttering our roads!"[3] This
artistic gesture to liquidate the past is also a political
act, a provocative intervention to exacerbate tensions and hasten the longed-for explosion.

Our search for the matrix of the Futurist
discourse leads us straight to the threshold of anarchism; aside from the avant-garde's fascination
with the exalted figure of the bomb planter, there
is also the striking affinity for Georges Sorel's
Réflexions sur la violence, first published in 1906 in *Le
Mouvement socialiste* and later in book form in 1908.
Sorel, a reader of Marx and Nietzsche, held mass
violence, in its essential expression in the general
strike, as the very moment of regeneration, and as
the only war machine equal to tackling the entropy
that was the deadly consequence of democracy and
economism; violence was the necessary condition
for the advent of the New Man. And despite Lenin's
harsh criticism of Sorel, the latter's faith in the liberating properties of violence is irrevocably linked
to the development of Leninism between 1905
and 1917, particularly with regard to its affirmation,
against the reformist wing of the workers' movement, of an inevitable confrontation between the
masses and the bourgeois State.

Given that violence was to be the path to future
epiphany, the creative and destructive gestures were
so closely allied that it is all but impossible to tell
them apart; the face of utopia, the profile of the new
world, tended to model itself on the forms required
for the destruction of the old. In "Die totale Mobilmachung," an extraordinary essay published in 1930,
Ernst Jünger reassessed the significance of World
War I: "Perhaps we can best identify the special
nature of this great catastrophe by the assertion that
in it, the genius of war was penetrated by the spirit
of progress. This was not only the case for the fight-
ing among the different countries; it was also true
for the civil war that gathered a rich second harvest
in many of them." Jünger proceeded to show how
the industrial mobilization required by the war
economy furnishes a model for another, more powerful kind of mobilization, namely the enlisting of
each individual as a worker in the global order of a
world that is ruled by the quasi-metaphysical
demands of technological rationality. "With a plea-
sure-tinged horror, we sense that here, not a single
atom is not in motion – that we are profoundly
inscribed in this raging process. Total Mobilization
is far less consummated than it consummates itself;
in war and peace, it expresses the secret and inex-
orable claim to which our life in the age of masses
and machines subjects us. It thus turns out that each

individual life becomes, ever more unambiguously, the life of a worker."[4] The war effort, represented in the all-encompassing image of a community bent on victory, made the merger between society and the State tangible, prefiguring and announcing future productivist utopias.

Mechanical Life

Let us return to the Futurists. In an astounding statement, Marinetti was to make an appeal for "a militarized revolution of gears."[5] The "magnificence of the world," he claimed, "has been enriched by a new beauty, *the beauty of speed*."[6] Beginning at that moment and continuing in the years that followed, there arose a cult to the Dionysian powers of the machine, to the roaring splendor of the racing car "more beautiful than the *Victory of Samothrace*,"[7] to the "holiness of wheels and rails,"[8] to "those places inhabited by the divine" – trains, bridges, and tunnels – to "modern, pulsating cities" and "battlefields."[9]

This fanatic support for a mechanized existence was far more than a salute to the promise of greater abundance and comfort dangled by industry and technology, as had been the case at the World's Fairs that had charted the paths of progress. It came rather closer to a complete upheaval of aesthetic values, a rupturing of the sensibilities that helped

establish, according to the "magic word" coined by Umberto Boccioni, "modernolatry."[10] Here, speed, the product of the formidable energies that impel and propel machines, is the dominant symbol of this new world, the chief deity of modernity.

Speed = synthesis of every courage in action. Aggressive and warlike.

Slowness = analysis of every stagnant prudence. Passive and pacifistic.

Speed = scorn of obstacles, desire for the new and unexplored. Modernity, hygiene.

Slowness = arrest, ecstacy, immobile adoration of obstacles, nostalgia for the already seen, idealization of exhaustion and rest, pessimism about the unexplored.[11]

Speed brought distant things closer, made instant synthesis possible. Speed was the sign of frenetic mobility, of danger, of a desire for the new; it sustained the lyricism of the intensely lived life.

"As Futurists, we call for the Machine to overcome its practical functionality and ascend to the spiritual and disinterested life of Art, so as to become a sublime muse."[12] In addition to

Words in Freedom

Filippo Tommaso Marinetti
Zang tumb tuuum: Adria-nopoli ottobre 1912: parole in libertà
Milan: Edizioni futuriste di "Poesia," 1914 (Milan: Stab. Tipo-litografico A. Taveggia)
NYPL, Spencer Collection

The Italian writer Filippo Marinetti, in his "Manifesto tecnico della letteratura Futurista" ["Technical Manifesto on Futurist Literature"] of 1912, declared the libera-tion of words from traditional grammar and syntax. Along with other Italian and Russian Futurists, he used typography to give poems pictorial and other expressive qualities, often choosing words for their sound alone. A note in *Zang tumb tuuum* explains that it is illustrated with various typographical devices, including "Synchronic map of sounds, noises, colors, images, odors, hopes, desires, energies, nostalgias. . . ."

Fortunato Depero
Depero futurista, 1913–1927
Milan and Paris:
Edizioni della Dinamo-Azari, [1927]
NYPL, Spencer Collection

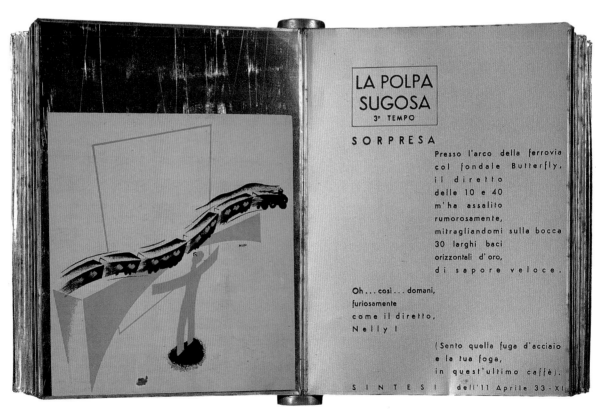

Tullio d'Albisola
L'anguria lirica: lungo
poema passionale
Rome: Edizioni futuriste di Poesia,
[1933?] (Savone: Lito-Latta)
NYPL, Spencer Collection

Metallic Futurist Books

The book was one of the Futurists' favorite objects of subversive invention. Focusing on the materiality of the book as object, they readily applied to books the aesthetic of the machine that they had extolled elsewhere.

In 1927, Fortunato Depero published an album for which his publisher, Azari, proposed a "dynamo binding" in which the pages were held together by bolts. Depero referred to this as the "bolted machinic edition."

The first book printed on tin pages, Filippo Tommaso Marinetti's *Parole in Libertà* [*Words in Liberty*], was published in 1932 by Marinetti with graphic assistance from Tullio d'Albisola. Presented in a tin case, the book was made in collaboration with the firm Nosenzo, a manufacturer of tin cans in Savone.

In 1934, d'Albisola, a ceramist, sculptor, graphic designer, and poet, published a long poem, illustrated by Munari, called *L'anguria lirica* [*The Lyrical Watermelon*], also printed on tin pages. These works exalted what Giovanni Lista called "the ephemeral character of the new materials which correspond to modern techniques of advertising, consumption, and fast sports (the airplane and the automobile)."

above and below

Filippo Tommaso Marinetti
Parole in libertà futuriste
Rome: Edizioni futuriste
di Poesia, 1932
Stedelijk Museum, Amsterdam

The Machine as "Subject"

Fernand Léger
Elément mécanique
Oil on canvas, 1924
Musée national d'Art
moderne, Paris

In the aftermath of World
War I, the "cult of the object"
(painting freed from its
"subject") and the growing
fascination with machines
gave rise to Léger's interest
in the mechanical world. "The
beautiful machine," he wrote,
"is the beautiful modern
subject." A few years later,
Le Corbusier would note in
his *Cahiers d'art* that "this
was the point at which Léger,
having completed his mechanical canvasses, was to pursue
his discovery of the modern
world and feel his potential
to participate as a painter in
the great current, increasingly
more pervasive, of contemporary architecture: innumerable
new objects have emerged
under the sign of this new
spirit; the overall production
of this era severs us from
the past and projects us
into an imminent cycle. . . .
For years now, he and [Blaise]
Cendrars have been on a
great bender in that postwar
world, breathing in the smells
of a new Spring."

being a symbol of human creativity, the Machine also emerged as a creature unto itself, capable, as though it were some kind of "metallic animal," of re-mobilizing instinctive powers and multiple primitive energies; the machine was a principle of identification whose intensity is disclosed by Futurism. This principle of identification was in actuality twofold and emerged as one of the major motifs of the twentieth century's utopian imagination: man as machine, and the human machine.

"We are irresistibly attracted to the clear-cut and precise mechanical ideal. Gear mechanisms purify our eyes of the fog of uncertainty. All things are cutting, aristocratic, distinct. We feel mechanically. We feel we are made of steel. Let us therefore be inspired machines!"[13] This motif of the metallic or iron man, trotted out at every turn during the 1930s, bespoke the exalted mimetic stance toward the mechanical universe.

And then, emerging like a mirror image, the figure of the robot was introduced; the genius technician in Villiers de Lisle-Adam's 1886 *L'Eve future* was the first to announce this creature's advent; subsequently, in 1921, Karel Čapek gave the creature a name in his play *R.U.R.* In 1926, Fritz Lang staged a complex game of hate, tension, and love between masters, slaves, and man-eating machines in his film *Metropolis*. Here, the robot assumed the character of a beautiful female mediator in order to harness that character to the forces of evil.

Abstraction – Construction

As is well known, shortly after 1910, Russian avant-garde movements became heavily influenced by Futurism. In 1913, Kazimir Malevich collaborated — with Kruchenykh, who wrote the libretto, and Matiushin, who composed the music — in the creation of a very unusual opera. "*Victory over the Sun* is a vast lyrical rodomontade and the details and overall action of the plot are extremely difficult to grasp. A host of futurist and reactionary characters taken from all environments and periods of history file on and off and confront each other around the sun, which is the emblem of old-world conservatism."[14] Having vanquished the moonlight, the Futurists confront the sun in a gesture of ultimate defiance against the supreme source of natural light. Malevich designed the costumes and sets. And while the costume designs drew on Futurist themes, unprecedented and purely geometric motifs appeared on the stage curtain; some were the square forms placed at the center of a square background that would come to characterize the

post-1915 style Malevich called "suprematism."

Malevich's most brilliant disciple, El Lissitzky, was to come back to this opera in the early 1920s, when, as part of an experimental scenographic work, he designed a group of hyper-geometric figurines representing the play's characters.

In his December 1915 exhibit, entitled *0.10 Last Futurist Exhibition*, Malevich showed his *Black Square*: "I have been transfigured in the zero of forms and have emerged beyond 0.1. Considering that Cubo-Futurism has fulfilled its objectives, I now move to Suprematism, to new painterly realism, to non-figurative creation."[15] This

Metropolis

Walter Schulze-Mittendorf
***Metropolis* Robot**
Resin, painted silver, Paris, 1970
Collection Cinémathèque
française–musée du Cinéma, Paris

For the museum established in 1972 by Henri Langlois, founder of the French Cinémathèque, Walter Schulze-Mittendorf, Fritz Lang's scenic designer, created this exact replica of the robot from Lang's 1926 film *Metropolis* (Lang had already donated nearly all of his archive to Langlois). For more than twenty years, until the museum closed in 1997, the robot, which represented the character of Maria (played by Brigitte Helm in the film), was among the greatest treasures of the Musée du Cinéma Henri-Langlois.

Invention of the Word "Robot"

Karel Čapek
***R.U.R. (Rossum's Universal
Robots). A Fantastic
Melodrama,* translated by
Paul Selver**
Garden City, N.Y.: Doubleday,
Page & Company, 1923
NYPL, Slavic and Baltic Division

The word "robot," derived
from the Czech word *robota*,
meaning drudgery or statutory
labor, was used for the
first time in this play by Karel
Čapek. First published
in Czech in 1921, *R.U.R.
(Rossum's Universal Robots)*
was translated into English
in 1923 and enjoyed success
that year on the stage in
both New York and London.

Set on an island where robots
are manufactured on assembly lines, the play provides
a critical look at the use of
machines to replace human
labor and also acts as a
warning against genetic
manipulation. Rossum's Universal Robots are identical to
human beings but lack a soul
and emotions, which makes
them more efficient and less
expensive than human workers. The robots eventually
revolt, killing all but one of
the humans, and then dis-
cover that they are unable to
reproduce themselves. The
play ends on a note of hope
when two of the robots,
who had been modified in an
experiment before the revolt,
fall in love with each other.

pronouncement marks one of Abstraction's many
births. Malevich believed that he had won the right
to work in pure forms that owed nothing to imitation, in the realm not only of natural objects but,
in a wider sense, of inanimate ones as well. Having
used Cubism and Futurism to undertake the deconstruction of this world of objects, Malevich now
embarked on its abolition: the world that lay before
him was entirely made up of pure intuitive forms,
so to speak: of those elements in the construction
of a consciousness that directly pertain to the
human subject and achieve their visibility in the
purely pictorial figure. Malevich and his friends
spoke at this time of a "world without objects" as
the only living world.

In the months that followed, Malevich painted
what he called "suprematist constructions." While
these two-dimensional floating geometric forms
still qualified as canvas paintings, they had no real
right side up and had left density behind in order
to exist in a cosmic space free of gravitational references. These objects from nowhere resurfaced, this
time in a three-dimensional form, at the beginning
of the 1920s, and went by the name of "Planits."
"The globe is simply a lump of intuitive wisdom
that must run over the paths of the infinite."[16] If
we take the artist at his word, he settled on the
term "suprematism" (which, incidentally, does not
have a Russian root) because it means "dominance."

A mere two years after the *Black Square* exhibit,
the avant-garde that had embraced Abstraction
crossed paths with the formidable revolutionary

movement that was sweeping Russia. The
encounter of these two trajectories was undoubtedly one of the most significant moments in the
history of twentieth-century utopia.

By 1918, in keeping with the prevailing mood of
revolutionary effervescence, the *svomas*, open ate-
liers, which took the place of the traditional schools
and academies, had already been established. In
1919, the movement gained momentum and Malevich found himself setting out for a teaching post in
the city of Vitebsk, where with friends he founded
the Vitebsk Unovis,[17] the first school devoted
solely to modern art, the following year. Here is
an excerpt from the rallying cry of the creative
committee of Unovis:

Youths of the West, the East and the South, go towards
the red pole of the new earth, since that is where burns
the flag of the new art. For action, votes and movement
we call not only on those responsible for the arts, but also
upon our comrades – the smiths, fitters, braziers, concrete
pourers, foundry men, carpenters, machinists, aviators,
stone cutters, miners, textile workers, tailors, dressmakers
and all who make useful things in the world at large so that
under the common flag of the UNOVIS we may together
dress the earth in clothes of new shape and purpose.[18]

As with many militant texts from the 1920s, what
we see here is a call for artists to merge with the
mobilized free proletariat. The themes that were
set forth by most Western avant-gardes in the last
years of the teens are also echoed here, namely the

Suprematist Composition

Kazimir Severinovich Malevich
Suprematist Painting
Oil on canvas, 1915
Stedelijk Museum, Amsterdam

In 1915, Malevich crossed the threshold into nonfigurative painting – the art "without an object" that he called Suprematism. What he strove for was the achievement of an "essence, of the pictorial form *per se*," no longer "outfitted by the shape of a given object." He saw Suprematism as the outgrowth of two earlier movements that had paved the way for it; while Cubism had deconstructed the object, Futurism had privileged dynamic energy. "The dynamism of painting is only a rebellion that induces the emergence of the pictorial mass of objects toward autarkic forms that designate nothing." In 1920, he would note that "Suprematism, in its historical evolution, underwent three phases: black, color, and white. In every period its development fell under the conventional sign of the flat surface which, we could say, expressed the designs of future volumes." The cosmic dimension he attributed to plastic creation dates from this time: "Each constructed Suprematist body shall be integrated into a natural organization in keeping with physical nature and will, in and of itself, form a new satellite."

Overleaf

Victory over the Sun

El Lissitzky
Die plastische Gestaltung der elektro-mechanischen Schau Sieg über die Sonne
Hanover: Leunis and Chapman, 1923
Color engravings
Stedelijk Museum, Amsterdam

The First Congress of the eulogists of Russia's Future met in July 1913 at the composer Matiushin's *dacha* in Finland. The poet Kruchenykh presided over the Congress, and Malevich served as its Secretary. A resolution declared Vladimir Mayakovsky's *Tragedy* and the opera *Victory over the Sun* as "dramatic exemplars for the Man of the Future." In December of that year, the opera was performed on four consecutive evenings at Saint Petersburg's Luna Park. Malevich's designs for some of the costumes and for the stage curtain introduced the monochromatic square that over the next two years would become the emblem of Suprematism.

In the early 1920s, El Lissitzky came up with the idea for a scenic device that would make it possible to present, in public spaces, spectacles orchestrated by a central operator who could command a variety of systems for sound, light, and movement. To put the idea into practice, a new production of *Victory over the Sun* was planned, and it was for that production that Lissitzky designed various geometric figurines, in the abstract style he called "Proun" (an acronym for the Russian words meaning "Projects affirming the new in art") to play the parts of the opera's characters. "The sun, an expression of the energies of the old world, is uprooted from the sky and thrown to the ground by modern man who has created his own sources of energy by dint of his technological superiority." Lissitzky's vision remained unrealized, but two of his engravings, from a portfolio of ten, are reproduced on the following pages.

El Lissitzky
[*Victory Over the Sun*]
Troublemaker

El Lissitzky
[*Victory Over the Sun*]
New Man

Poet of the Revolution

Vladimir Mayakovsky
***Groznyi smekh: okna
ROSTA [Menacing Laughter:
The Windows of ROSTA]***
Moscow and Leningrad: Gos. izd-vo
Khudozhestvennoi lit-ry, 1932
NYPL, Slavic and Baltic Division

The Russian Futurists, including the poet and artist Vladimir
Mayakovsky, sought to put
their art at the service of the
Bolshevik Revolution. From
1919, Mayakovsky worked
for ROSTA (the Russian
Telegraphy Agency) in
Moscow, creating large propaganda posters to display in
shop windows; each poster
paired a humorous rhyming
text with a matching image.
*Menacing Laughter: The Win-
dows of ROSTA*, a collection
of his poetry based on themes
reflected in the ROSTA
posters, was designed by
Varvara Stepanova, one of
the principal founders of the
Russian Constructivist movement, which embraced the
principle of "the organic entry
of art into life." The caption
for her graphic image of the
Red Army is from a poem
by Mayakovsky.

tenets on which the Bauhaus was founded in 1919: tearing down the boundaries between the fine and applied arts, putting artists in the service of industrial design and, in a larger sense, of "societal imperatives," while at the same time restoring architecture, as a principle of the constructivist project, to its status as a driving force among disciplines.

But for Malevich these texts said something further: the movement that brought about Suprematist Abstraction joined forces with the social and political revolution at the precise moment it called upon all producers to create a new world covered exclusively with the products of human labor, a world devoid of legacies and established models, composed of abstract forms that are not derivative and are, as a result, elemental and capable of standing in for the four elements that are the unadulterated components of all natural things. The revolutionary upheaval gave meaning to artistic rebellion; the construction of a materially new world became something more than a metaphor. It was no longer a matter of infusing artistic milieus with revolutionary activism or of finding politically appropriate directions for art. Rather, it was a utopia in the true sense of the word; this entire undertaking, which began with the new century (with Cézanne, according to Malevich), had set itself the task of toppling the figurative representation of tangible materiality and had succeeded in making it vanish in an apocalyptic surge of new forms that came from nowhere to reveal the true newness of the world that had yet to be built.

It would not take long for Malevich to abandon painting on canvas to devote himself entirely to what he called "Architektons," a form he considered to be the true artistic summit of architecture – a preservation, salvaging, and prolongation of the immense effort of abstraction, an extreme rupture with the natural world that had brought him to this point. Hence the "Planits" and the "Architektons" of the 1920s, the abstract structures, flying cities, and white constructions that could belong only to the future.

The undertaking was heavy with contradictions: between abstraction and utility, and between pure poetic creation and application to the social or propagandistic project. This contradiction would crisscross the history of constructivism up to the disaster of the 1930s.

1 Filippo Tommaso Marinetti, "The Founding and Manifesto of Futurism," in *Marinetti: Selected Writings*, ed. with intro. R. W. Flint; trans. R. W. Flint and Arthur A. Coppotelli (New York: Farrar, Straus and Giroux, 1972), 42.

2 Guillaume Apollinaire, *L'Anti-tradition futuriste: manifeste-synthèse* (Milan: Direction du mouvement futuriste, 1913); reprinted in Giovanni Lista, *Futurisme: Manifestes, proclamations, documents* (Lausanne: L'Age d'homme, 1974), 122–24.

3 Filippo Tommaso Marinetti, "Let's Murder the Moonshine," in *Marinetti: Selected Writings*, 45.

4 Ernst Jünger, "Die Totale Mobilmachung," trans. as "Total Mobilization" by Joel Golb and Richard Wolin in *The Heidegger Controversy: A Critical Reader*, ed. Richard Wolin (New York: Columbia University Press, 1991), 123, 128.

5 Filippo Tommaso Marinetti, *La nouvelle religion-morale de la Vitesse*, May 11, 1916; expanded ed. September 11, 1922; reprinted in Lista, 366–70; quotation on 369. The 1916 version is reprinted in *Marinetti: Selected Writings* as "The New Religion-Morality of Speed," 94–96.

6 Marinetti, "The New Religion-Morality of Speed," 94.

7 Marinetti, "The Founding and Manifesto of Futurism," 41.

8 Marinetti, "The New Religion-Morality of Speed," 96.

9 Marinetti, *La nouvelle religion-morale de la Vitesse*, 368.

10 See Enrico Prampolini, Ivo Pannaggi, and Vinicio Paladini, "L'Art méchanique," January 11, 1923; reprinted in Lista, 221–24.

11 Marinetti, "The New Religion-Morality of Speed," 95–96.

12 Prampolini, et al., 223.

13 Ibid., 222.

14 Serge Fauchereau, *Malevich*, trans. Alan Swan (London: Academy Editions, 1992), 17.

15 Kazimir Malevich, "From Cubism and Futurism to Suprematism: The New Realism in Painting," quoted in Fauchereau, 20–21. On the *0.10 Last Futurist Exhibition*, see Jean-Claude Marcadé, *L'Avant Garde Russe, 1907–1927* (Paris: Flammarion, 1995), 140 ff.

16 Kazimir Malevich, "On New Systems in Art," in *Essays on Art*, ed. Troels Andersen; trans. Xenia Glowacki-Prus and Arnold McMillin; 2 vols. (London: Rapp & Whiting; Chester Springs, Penn.: Dufour Editions Inc., 1969), 1:104.

17 "Unovis" is an acronym for "uchilishche novovo iskusstva," meaning affirmation (or affirmers) of the new art. See Fauchereau, 28.

18 Kazimir Malevich, "UNOVIS – The Champions of New Art," quoted in Fauchereau, 29.

**Kornell Zelinski and
Ilie Selvinski, eds.
*Biznes: sbornik
literaturnogo tsentra
konstruktivistov* [*Business:
A Collection of the Literary
Center of Constructivists*]**
Moscow, 1929
Cover illustration by Aleksandr
Rodchenko
NYPL, Slavic and Baltic Division

Published, as the subtitle
says, by the Constructivists'
literary center, this anthology
illustrates the ideas of Zelinski,
one of the organizers and
"leaders" of the Constructivist
group. *Business* argues that
the Soviet Union could benefit
from American know-how
in order to modernize itself.
America represents a reservoir
of ideas and a set of tools
without which "not even
a barn can be constructed."
The cover (eyeglasses
against skyscrapers) is a photomontage usually attributed
to Aleksandr Rodchenko,
but sometimes to Solomon
Benediktovich Telingater.

***Vlast' Sovetov za desiat'
let 1917-1927* [*The Power
of the Soviets During the
Ten Years 1917–1927*]**
Leningrad: Izd. "Krasnoi gazety,"
1927
NYPL, Slavic and Baltic Division

This typical propaganda
pamphlet extolling the achievements of the Soviet government during the decade after
the Russian Revolution is
illustrated with reproductions
of work by several contemporary artists, including the
painter, theatrical designer,
and ceramist Natan Isaevich
Al'tman, portraitist Boris
Mikhailovich Kustodiev,
Ukrainian artist Mykola
Samokysh, and the noted
painter of revolutionary themes
Isaak Izrailevich Brodskii.
The cover design, portraits of
Lenin, and various ornaments
are original contributions
by Suprematist graphic artist
Sergei Chekhonin, whose
agitprop ceramics decoration
is shown opposite.

The Moscow Art Theatre

Carlo Gozzi
Printsessa Turandot . . .
Moscow and Petrograd:
Gosizdat, [1923]
Cover illustration by
Ignatii Nivinskii
NYPL, Slavic and Baltic Division

This book documents the staging of Carlo Gozzi's Chinese fairy tale, *Turandot, Princess of China*, by the director Yevgeny Vakhtangov at the Third Studio of the Moscow Art Theatre in 1922. In this production, Vakhtangov sought to transcend the gap between pre-revolutionary naturalism and the avant-garde with a brilliant theatricality based on commedia dell'arte techniques of bold gesture and vivid color. The theatrical experimentation of the Soviet post-revolutionary period came to an end when Stalin came to power in 1932.

The Soviet Empire

Sergei Vasilevich Chekhonin
State-manufactured
porcelain plate
Illustrated in *S. Chekhonin*, by
A. M. Efros and N. Punin (Moscow
and Leningrad: State Publishing
House of the R.S.F.S.R., [1924])
NYPL, Slavic and Baltic Division

This plate, inscribed "There will be no end to the Kingdom of Workers and Peasants" (parodying the Lord's Prayer, perhaps), is an example of "mass agitational porcelain," or Socialist propaganda applied, with ironic effect, to a luxury object. Its designer, Sergei Chekhonin, was artistic director of the State Porcelain Factory in Petrograd in 1918–23 and 1925–27, and produced his porcelain plates and bowls with revolutionary slogans on a mass scale from 1923 to 1925 in Volkhov. Because he adapted the techniques of the earlier Imperial Porcelain Factory to the purposes of agitprop – combining such features as gold engraving with Suprematist geometrical simplicity – his followers called his style "Soviet Empire."

Constructivist Photomontages

**Iu Iurii Libedinskii
and Gustav Klutsis
Photomontages**
From *Zavtra* [*Tomorrow*]
(Moscow and Leningrad:
Molodia gvardia, 1924)
Stedelijk Museum, Amsterdam

Majestic Machines

Lewis Wickes Hine
Man and Micrometer
Silver gelatin print, New York, 1920
NYPL, Miriam and Ira D. Wallach
Division of Art, Prints and
Photographs

This photograph comes from
a series of "work portraits"
made by the documentary
photographer Lewis Wickes
Hine between 1920 and
1940. Unlike Hine's previous
documentary projects,
which exposed the harsh
experiences of the American
immigrant at home and at
work, this new series set
out to honor the relationship
between man and machine.
Hine viewed the machine
as a tool to ease the burdens
of America's labor force,
and these photographs show
his unique ability to capture
the power of the majestic
machines unleashed by the
dominant hands of the men
who used them.

Bauhaus Photography

In 1919, the painter, photographer, set designer, typographer, and designer Laszlo Moholy-Nagy left Hungary, first for Vienna and then for Berlin where he joined the faculty at the Bauhaus and became involved in the Dadaist movement. The rise of fascism led to his emigration from Germany in 1935, first to London and then, in 1937, to Chicago, where he organized and directed the New Bauhaus (later the Institute of Design of the Illinois Institute of Technology).

His photographic work explores new perspectives through the use of high and low angles (see *View from the Berlin Radio Tower in Winter*). He also used photomontage – Fotoplastiks in his terminology (see *Between Heaven and Earth [Look Before You Leap]*). He saw photography as a new and independent art form that had evolved through technological advances and was subject to its own laws; photography was the expression of what he termed *The New Vision* in a theoretical work published in 1929. The photographs shown here are exact reprints of the original images published by the Heiner Friedrich Gallery in Munich in 1973.

Laszlo Moholy-Nagy
Blick von Radioturm Berlin
[**View from the Berlin**
Radio Tower in Winter]
Photograph, 1928
BNF, Département des Estampes
et de la Photographie

Laszlo Moholy-Nagy
Hinter Gottes Rücken I
[*Between Heaven and Earth*
(*Look Before You Leap*)]
Photomontage, 1925
BNF, Département des Estampes
et de la Photographie

The Propaganda Poster in the 1930s

Gustav Klutsis
Pod znamenem Lenina za
sotsialisticheskoe stroitelstvo
[For the Building of Socialism
Under Lenin's Banner]
Mixed media, 1930
Stedelijk Museum, Amsterdam

Gustav Klutsis
Na shturm – 3go goda
piatiletki [On the Attack –
The 3rd Year of the
5-year Plan
Lithograph, 1930
Stedelijk Museum, Amsterdam

Gustav Klutsis
*SSSR – udarnaia brigada
miprovogo proletariata
[SSSR – The Leading Brigade
of the World Proletariat]*
Lithograph, 1931
Stedelijk Museum, Amsterdam

Valentina Kulagina
*Mezhdunarodnyi den
robotnits [International
Women Workers' Day]*
Lithograph, 1930
Stedelijk Museum, Amsterdam

Ruth Eaton

Architecture and Urbanism: The Faces of Utopia

"Oh Satan, my youngest born . . . thy work is Eternal Death with mills and Ovens and Cauldrons." The premonitory words of the English poet Blake were cried out in a virtual wilderness amid the initial enthusiasm that embraced the rapid development of industrialization in the late eighteenth and early nineteenth centuries. Cities grew at breakneck speed at this time, with London's population topping the million mark in 1811, that of Paris some thirty years later. Living and working conditions in these huge agglomerations proved miserable for the majority. Pollution, overcrowding, disease, poverty: these were the realities recorded in social commentaries such as Sir Frederick Eden's first sociological survey, *The State of the Poor* (1797), or Friedrich Engels's *The Condition of the Working Class in England* (1844). The echoes of Blake's words began to resonate as the promises of liberty, equality, fraternity, and greater riches for all faded. Writers such as Eugène Sue, Victor Hugo, Emile Zola, and Charles Dickens added their voices to the outcry, portraying the plight of the urban poor in fiction.

Such were the hellish conditions against which utopianism was to do battle in the industrialized world. Architects, too occupied, perhaps, with mastering the engineering feats of the age, tended to leave it to others – and one thinks particularly of reformers such as Fourier or Owen – to carry the utopian torch at this time. The frameworks proposed by those that Marx dubbed "utopian socialists" to house their societies took the forms of the phalanstery, Stedman Whitwell's design for "New Harmony" and such "social palaces of the future,"[1] imagined amid the invigorating countryside. Toward the end of the nineteenth and during the twentieth century, however, the architects (and non-architects particularly concerned by spatial conditions) entered the fray. Some, often inspired by – though not simply reproducing – a time long past, sought to create a sort of pre- or postindustrial environment in which the values of community reigned, craftsmanship was appreciated, and urban units maintained a relatively modest scale (their groupings of population numbering in the thousands). An increasing majority, keen to take advantage of every new sign of material progress in the conviction that this offered the path to social

perfection, envisaged industrialized ideal worlds on a huge scale in which the organization and the form of the physical surroundings would be determined by the logic of the production process.

In his foreword to the Kelmscott Press edition of *Utopia*, William Morris appreciated and shared More's nostalgic regret at the loss of many of the values of the Middle Ages: "Doubtless the *Utopia* is a necessary part of a Socialist's library; yet it seems to me that its value as a book for the study of sociology is rather historic than prophetic, and that we Socialists should look upon it as a link between the surviving communism of the Middle Ages (become hopeless in More's time and doomed to be soon wholly effaced by the advancing wave of Commercial Bureaucracy), and the hopeful and practical progressive movement of to-day. In fact I think More must be looked upon rather as the last of the old than the first of the new."[2] Morris sought, in *News from Nowhere*, to create a compelling picture of the communist world that he envisaged, reconciling his admiration for Marx with that for John Ruskin, whose idealization of the medieval world had in turn been anticipated by A.W.N. Pugin. In Morris's postrevolutionary, anti-industrial England of 2102, the state has become redundant and withered away, work is pleasure, individuals are free, and the centuries-old process of rural exodus has been reversed so that the differences between the city and the countryside have diminished as the respective populations have leveled out. Old Hammond explains: "This is how we stand. England was once a country of clearings amongst the woods and wastes, with a few towns interspersed, which were fortresses for the feudal army, markets for the folk, gathering places for the craftsmen. It then became a country of huge and foul workshops and fouler gambling-dens, surrounded by an ill-kept, poverty-stricken farm, pillaged by the masters of the workshops. It is now a garden, where nothing is wasted and nothing is spoilt, with the necessary dwellings, sheds, and workshops scattered up and down the country, all trim and neat and pretty."[3] The historical and luxuriant heart of London, small towns, villages, and woodlands dotted by idyllic houses comprise the face of his future England.

The dreams of Ruskin, Morris, and others were to find a practical formulation in 1898 when

SCHNEE
GLETSCHER
GLAS

Die Aufführung ist gewiss ungeheuer schwer und opfervoll, aber nicht unmöglich; "Man verlangt so selten von den Menschen das Unmögliche." (Goethe)

10

Alpine Architecture

Bruno Taut
Alpine Architektur
[Vienna]: Hagen, 1919.
NYPL, Miriam and Ira D. Wallach
Division of Art, Prints and
Photographs

Bruno Taut was a leading figure in the expressionist movement in architecture that emerged in Germany at the end of World War I. In this portfolio, he gives free rein to his dreams of brilliant glass cathedrals clinging to mountain peaks. He believed that participating in so monumental a project as the transformation of a mountain range would absorb human energies and reverse man's propensity for aggression by leading him to universal brotherhood. The cathedral as a symbol of reconciliation appeared in another work the same year, *Die Stadtkrone*, in which Taut imagined a society guided by a new supra-socialist or nonpolitically socialist religion, housed in modest dwellings gathered around a distinguished crystal building.

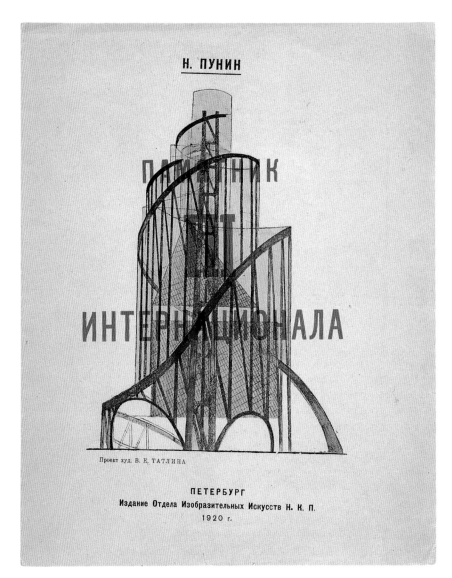

Н. ПУНИН

ПАМЯТНИК III ИНТЕРНАЦИОНАЛА

Проект худ. В. Е. ТАТЛИНА

ПЕТЕРБУРГ
Издание Отдела Изобразительных Искусств Н. К. П.
1920 г.

Monument to the
Third International,
A Project by V. E. Tatlin

Nikolai Nikolaevich Punin
Pamiatnik III Internatsionala
[*Monument to the*
***Third International*]**
St. Petersburg:
Izo-Narkompros, 1920
Collection Martin-Malburet

The principles adopted by
Tatlin, a champion of Constructivism, in his propagandistic architectural project
for a Monument to the Third
International are set forth in
this brochure by Nikolai Punin.
A synthesis of architecture,
painting, and sculpture, this
monument, which was never
realized, was to have stood
328 feet higher than the Eiffel
Tower, and its design deliberately incorporated industrial
materials, with an emphasis
on glass and steel.

Ebenezer Howard, an English autodidact stenographer, borrowed £50 to publish *To-morrow: A Peaceful Path to Real Reform*, a description of his "invention," the garden city.[4] In this highly influential work, he quoted Ruskin's call, made some thirty years earlier, for the restoration of existing houses and the building of more, "strongly, beautifully, and in groups of limited extent kept in proportion to their streams and wall around so that there be no festering and wretched suburb anywhere, but clean and busy street within and open country without, with a belt of beautiful garden and orchard round the walls so that from any part of the city perfectly fresh air and grass and sight of far horizon might be reachable in a few minutes' walk. That is the final aim."[5] Marked also by the writings of Henry George, Peter Kropotkin, and Edward Bellamy, Howard recalled that after reading *Looking Backward*: "I went into some of the crowded parts of London, and as I passed through the narrow dark streets, saw the wretched dwellings in which the majority of the people lived, observed on every hand the manifestations of a self-seeking order of society, and reflected on the absolute unsoundness of our economic system, there came to me an overpowering sense of the quite temporary nature of nearly all I saw, and of its entire unsuitability for the working life of the new order – the order of justice, unity and friendliness."[6] His aim was a fairer redistribution of land, and his garden cities were to be established initially through the support of philanthropists setting up nonprofit companies, raising money by issuing bonds, purchasing the land, and building the transport, water, and power infrastructures. Rising land and rental income was expected to pay the interest upon and buy back the bonds and make substantial improvements to the town. Clusters of garden cities of 30,000–32,000 inhabitants, each – in contrast to More's plan – of a different design, would be linked to one another and to a larger Centre City by a circular canal (later changed to a rapid-transit system) to make up the Social City. His schematic model was accompanied by his important proviso that "Of course, no actual plan for the laying out of the town can be presented until an estate has been selected."[7] The world's first garden city was shortly to be built at Letchworth in England upon a design by Barry Parker and Raymond Unwin. Clearly a product of the nineteenth century, Howard's concept was to have an enormous impact on twentieth-century urbanism, even though his ideas were frequently compromised and his term often employed incorrectly for the ever-sprawling garden suburb.

Despite having its origins in the prewar period, the backcloth of German Expressionism is essentially that of the aftermath of the great war, Germany's own attempted revolution of 1918, unemployment, inflation, and the collapse of the building industry. It shared Morris's passions for medieval architecture, fine craftsmanship, and a pride and satisfaction in work. Bruno Taut, in *Die Stadtkrone* (1919) and *Die Auflösung der Städte* (1920), revealed his distaste for the arachnid city where the property speculator is king, depicted so forcefully by George Grosz, and called instead for a reinvestment of the countryside with the creation of new low-density garden cities. In *Alpine Architecture* (1919), he dreamt of a monumental scheme to create shining glass cathedrals amid the mountain ranges, transforming them into havens of peace where national conflict is transcended. Light, synonymous with right, plays a major role as in most utopian schemes, filtered here through innumerable colored glass panels, and the cathedral suggests reconciliation, a symbol to be found again in Fritz Lang's *Metropolis* (1926). Among the members of the *Gläserne Kette* ("glass chain"), Taut's secret circle which corresponded about the nature of the perfect future city, was Walter Gropius, first director of the Bauhaus. The early utopian ambition and expressionist origins of the school are evident in the words of its manifesto, *Programm des Staatlichen Bauhauses in Weimar* (1919): "Let us form a new guild of craftsmen, without those arrogant class divisions which have insolently erected a wall separating artists from craftsmen. Let us desire, envisage and create together a new guild, the guild of the future, which will be everything in a single form – architecture and sculpture and painting, which will rise aloft from the hands of a million craftsmen as the crystal symbol of a new faith to come."

Morris's work was directly influenced by his reading of and reaction against Edward Bellamy's *Looking Backward* with its bureaucratic society in which monopoly capitalism has given rise to the corporate state working for the benefit of all. Ruskin, Morris, and Howard all envisaged worlds in which the machine and the automobile had little if any place, whereas Bellamy's environment of the year 2000 is highly mechanized and urbanized. While H. G. Wells alerted attention to their potential dangers, most artists and architects perceived the avalanche of new inventions as the very expression of the continuing march of progress, and optimism regarding the impending benefits thereof remained a powerful sentiment. Even those who

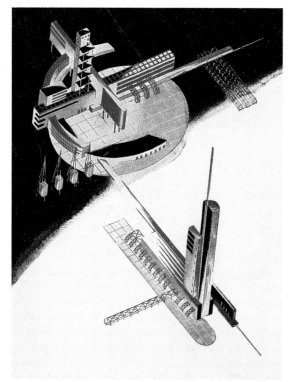

Cities of the Future

Iakov Georgievich Chernikhov
Arkhitekturnye fantazii [Architectural Fantasies]
Leningrad, 1933
Collection Martin-Malburet

Russian Futurist, Constructivist, and Suprematist theories are clearly illustrated in the work of the prolific architect Iakov Chernikhov, whose more than 17,000 drawings have earned him the well-deserved nickname the "Russian Piranesi." His three most important publications appeared a few years after these movements had reached their peak: *Osnovy sovremennoi arkhitekturny [Fundamentals of Contemporary Architecture]* in 1930, *Konstruktsiia arkhitekturnykh i mashinnykh form [Construction of Architectural and Machine Forms]* in 1931, and *Arkhitekturnye fantazii [Architectural Fantasies]* in 1933. Relying on geometry's basic forms – the square, the circle, and the rectangle – *Arkhitekturnye fantazii* is a project encompassing an entire series of designs, simultaneously typical and idealized, for skyscrapers, factories, and cities. The powerful influence of the machine – Chernikhov saw it as the symbol of the dynamic energy of the twentieth century – is felt not only in the movement these drawings suggest but also in the models he seeks to identify.

decried the sufferings to which the early phases of industrialization had subjected humankind often felt convinced that it alone offered the path to a better world as long as it was harnessed correctly in its later phases. The many "-isms" that characterized the artistic world in the early decades of the twentieth century engendered as many different visions of an urban setting appropriate to a world whose total break with the past had been rendered so obvious by World War I and the revolutionary events in Germany and Russia. Almost all of these early avant-garde "-isms" rejoiced in the avalanche of technological advances. By the outbreak of World War II, most of them had succumbed to the bulldozer effect of the most powerful "-ism" of them all: Functionalism and the significantly named International Style,[8] architecture's most outstanding reflection of the obsession with industrial production and efficiency.

Architectural drawings, by their inevitable staticity, fail to convey the urban vision of the Italian Futurists as convincingly as Umberto Boccioni's paintings, such as *La Città che sale* (1910). "Take up your pickaxes, your axes and hammers and wreck, wreck the venerable cities pitilessly!" clamored F. T. Marinetti in the first Futurist manifesto.[9] Theirs was to be a world of aggression, militarism, patriotism, speed, and technology with highly mechanized, multileveled cities undergoing incessant demolition and reconstruction, clearly suggested by the scaffolding in the background of Boccioni's work. Marinetti, in his novel *Gli Indomabili* (1922), went even further, transforming them into elusive entities, constantly moving like the sea, composed of hitherto unknown, vaporous materials. The futurists mocked the usual rigidity of utopia, turning it inside out, for here it became a process of perpetual metamorphosis in a manner that anticipates some of the movements of the 1950-60s.

Revolutionary Russia was inebriated with a utopian optimism about the dawning age, one which, breaking completely with the backwardness and social inequalities of the past, would be future-oriented, rich in state-of-the-art technology. This still predominantly rural country would be liberated by Bolshevism and industrialization, marching hand in hand. The enthusiasm touched every aspect of life. Artists, thrilled by the prospect of new horizons, cast their bourgeois easels aside and descended into the streets. Once more the city walls spoke out as Lenin instigated his monumental propaganda plan (1918), inspired by Tommaso Campanella's *City of the Sun* (1623), for the erection of hundreds

of statues and plaques bearing Marxist inscriptions. The Vesnin brothers defined the role of the architect: "A new era in the history of mankind had begun, and everything that impeded the development of the new life had been swept away by the impetuous wave of the Revolution. Architects were confronted with the task, as it applied to the realm of architecture, of marching in step with the builders of the new life, . . . through the realistic reflection and organization of the new living processes."[10] The new world was typified by Tatlin's Monument to the Third International (1919), whose model was paraded through the streets. The huge transparent structure would have been comprised of an iron spiral framework on an asymmetrical axis with internal revolving glass bodies housing congress facilities, a news center, and all the latest in technical prowess. It was even to include a system for projecting texts onto the sky in cloudy weather! "My monument," he explained, "is a symbol of the epoch. Unifying in it artistic and utilitarian forms, I created a kind of synthesis of art with life."[11] The skies indeed became the limit, and while Tatlin was soon to design his 'plane called the Letatlin, Alexander Lavinsky imagined a city in the air (1923) and George Krutikov a floating apartment block (1928). The future metropole of the early years after the revolution would be multileveled, mechanized, replete with lifts, rotating billboards, escalators, cranes, and so forth. Alexei Gastev had already set one of the scenes before the revolution: In *Express: A Siberian Fantasy*, Siberia is highly industrialized, super-urbanized, with geometrically shaped megapoles called Steel City or Energy City stretching far above and below the ground. The ultimate quest is the joining of Russia and America; not surprisingly so, since, for utopia, an island is second best only to an entire planet. Tatlin's tower was designed to move, as were the numerous projects for buildings or sets such as Liubov Popova and Aleksandr Vesnin's design for Vsevolod Meyerhold's mass pageant "Struggle and Victory of the Soviets" (1921), complete with its "City of the Future." Their movement was that of the machine, symbol of that aspired-to modernity, and while Meyerhold's actors gestured Biomechanically on their constructivist stage sets, Lenin embraced Taylorism under the name of *NOT/ Nauchnaia organizatsiia truda* ("the scientific organization of labor"), Gastev sought to train people to work like automatons, and Kerzhentsev hoped to make them live like them too. Zamiatin in his anti-utopia, *We* (1924), which influenced George

Orwell so deeply, mocked Gastevism and also the excessive urbanizing tendencies he noted around him. Zamiatin's city has become the massive parody thereof, United State, a giant conglomeration of blue cubic buildings and geometric shapes.

As every aspect of life became subject to an organization as strict and effective as that in a factory run by Ford, how could the architects do otherwise than to apply the same methods to building? Moisei Ginzburg advocated the use of the most up-to-date materials and techniques in conjunction with his very own "functional" method whereby every element of the users' requirements and movements must be scientifically analyzed in order to establish the separate functions that a building must fulfill and to assess its optimal arrangement. This would enable the creation of architectonic prototypes that could be economically mass-produced using standardized components. Prototypes became the rage. El Lissitzky's *Prouns* (signifying "projects affirming the new in art") proposed idealized design solutions for typical instances (the bridge, the intersection . . .), Kazimir Malevich's *Planits* drawings and his *Architectonics*, *Ornaments*, and *Monuments* models sought to express the quintessence of a new universal Suprematist order, and the highly prolific Iakov Chernikhov analyzed general concepts such as space, harmony, and functionality and applied a system of geometrically based spatial organization to building types. In 1921, El Lissitzky moved to Berlin, taking his theories with him.

During the course of the 1920s, the early Expressionist orientation of the Bauhaus gave way to Functionalism and a progressive *rapprochement* with heavy industry. Among the ideal cities designed at this time, those of Ludwig Hilberseimer, who later joined the teaching staff there, pointed the direction, from the beginning of the decade, that town planning was to take. For Hilberseimer, rational, modernist conglomerations should take the problem of circulation as their point of departure, be divided into functions, and be planned according to basic geometrical principles upon an orthogonal grid. He designed two ideal projects devoid of site but also suggested razing much of Berlin to implant his basic concept thereupon. One was for a series of residential satellite towns, each with a population of 125,000 and made up of seventy-eight long, rectangular blocks, surrounding a central city. The other, for a city of towers, was rejected by its own creator in the 1960s when Hilberseimer lamented that it resembled a necropolis. Before producing the second design,

he had visited Le Corbusier in Paris where he had seen the latter's drawings for the *Ville contemporaine de trois millions d'habitants*.

Although many, such as Richard Neutra, author of "Rush City," were working in an apparently similar vein, few people went so far as Le Corbusier in compiling complete schemes to transform both the urban and the social scenes almost beyond recognition. For the Swiss theoretician, the first global conflict had created a *tabula rasa* for a great new age that would be classical and orderly in accordance with scientifically established rules of harmony in tune with the universe. "There is a new spirit," he wrote in 1920; "it is a spirit of construction and synthesis guided by a clear conception . . . A GREAT EPOCH HAS BEGUN."[12] The new standardized, mass-manufactured world required a centralized industrial stucture, a military-style organization, and the equivalent of a general at its head. Administration would become all-important and party politics an irrelevance. The central point of his contemporary city is not a palace or a church but an enormous intersection, indicating the importance of transportation and communication in his scheme. It is surrounded by twenty-four sixty-story skyscrapers that make up the business district. These are in turn encircled by the luxurious towers destined as residences for the captains of industry, finance, and politics and the leading intellectuals of this bureaucratic and hierarchical new world; blue-collar workers are to be housed in garden apartments in the satellite towns on the outskirts. Disappointed at his inability to find backing in business quarters for his *Plan Voisin*, a scheme based on his Contemporary City whereby a vast area on Paris's right bank would be replaced by eighteen skyscrapers, Le Corbusier sought, in vain, a political leader who could effect the "complete system, coherent, just and indisputable."[13] This system was elaborated in his scheme for the Radiant City, a geometrically laid-out home to a syndicalist world in which social class distinctions are eliminated, as reflected in the fact that citizens are no longer segregated but all reside in high-rise *unités* containing residential, sports, cultural, educational, and social facilities.

Hilberseimer made reference to Letchworth and Welwyn garden cities with regard to his satellite city project, which reveals the cross-references and the complexities encountered when one tries to categorize the output of this period in any way. Le Corbusier's sources of inspiration were numerous but included Tony Garnier's design for a zoned,

An Industrial City

Tony Garnier
Une Cité industrielle. Etude
pour la construction des
villes
2nd ed. Paris: C. Massin, 1939
NYPL, General Research Division

When Tony Garnier submitted
a series of drawings to the
Ecole des Beaux Arts in Paris
in 1901 and 1904 (he was
then living at the Villa Medici
in Rome), he broke with tradition. In the years that followed, he elaborated on this
project, which formed the
basis of this book, *Une Cité
industrielle* [*An Industrial City*],
first published in 1919. One
can see within it an architectural transcription of Emile
Zola's novel *Travail* (1901). In
his city, Garnier undertakes to
shelter a radically new society
where the land is common
property. Despite this, the
city's formal structure, as the
book's title suggests, is organized on a functional plan
imposed by the industrial
world. The principle of dividing
a city into sectors and eliminating streets would appear
soon thereafter, in the drawings of Le Corbusier.

Piercing the Sky

Lewis Wickes Hine
***Empire State Building
Construction***
Silver gelatin print, New York, 1931
NYPL, Miriam and Ira D. Wallach
Division of Art, Prints and
Photographs

Photographer Lewis Hine,
best known for his depictions
of American immigrants at
home and at work, was hired
to photograph the Empire
State Building during its construction in 1930 and 1931. To
document many phases of the
project and to gain the best
vantage points, Hine often put
himself in the same precarious positions as the workers,
or swung out in a specially
designed basket. His pho-
tographs capture the dizzying
elation of piercing the sky
with what was, until 1972, the
tallest building in the world.
New York was becoming a
metropolis of vertical splendor
where the sky was truly no
longer the limit.

Berenice Abbott
Henry Street, looking west from Market Street, November 29, 1935
Silver gelatin print, New York, 1935
NYPL, Miriam and Ira D. Wallach
Division of Art, Prints and
Photographs

From 1935 to 1939, Berenice
Abbott worked for the Federal
Art Project photographing
New York City's rapidly changing landscape, a project she
had been interested in since
the early 1930s. The result,
Changing New York, is her
best-known series of pho-
tographs. Bringing a mod-
ernist sensibility to her subject, she portrays a city
moving from the horizontal to
the vertical plane. In this
image, the brilliant skyscrapers rise like a new Jerusalem
over the Lower East Side.

The Metropolis of the Future

Hugh Ferriss
The Metropolis of Tomorrow
New York: Ives Washburn, 1929
NYPL, Miriam and Ira D. Wallach
Division of Art, Prints and
Photographs

Although an architectural
draftsman by profession,
Hugh Ferriss is considered
one of the greatest architects,
artists, urban planners, and
visionaries of the twentieth
century. His expertise in all
these areas is evident in his
1929 book, *The Metropolis of
Tomorrow*. The drawings it
contains, prepared in 1925,
creatively address his fascination with the New York City
zoning law of 1916. Imposing
severe design restrictions on
new skyscrapers, the law
required setbacks in buildings
over a certain height so that
more light and air would reach
city streets. Ferriss viewed
this new law as an inspiration

rather than a restriction, and
drew a series of majestic,
imaginary buildings that
demonstrated the potential for
new design possibilities. *The
Metropolis of Tomorrow* contains renderings of skyscrapers that had been built in conformity with the new law,
such as the Chrysler Building,
as well as proposals for Ferriss's city of the future.

This bird's-eye view shows the
three centers of the city dedicated to business, art, and science. Between these vertical
complexes lie low, residential
buildings with rooftop gardens
or swimming pools. When
viewed from above, Ferriss
states, "the first confirmed
impression of the city is thus
of a wide plain, not lacking in
vegetation, from which rise, at
considerable intervals, tower-
ing mountain peaks."

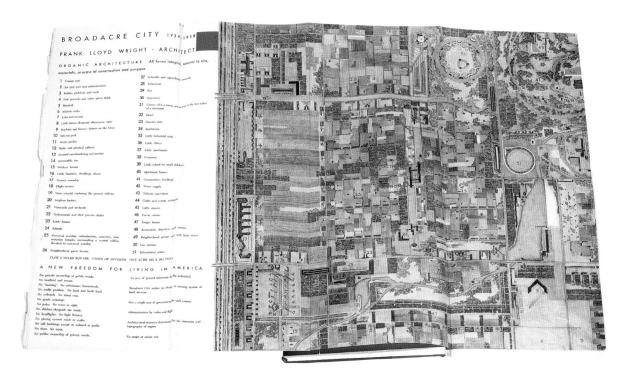

Broadacre City

Frank Lloyd Wright
The Living City

New York: Horizon Press, 1958
NYPL, Miriam and Ira D. Wallach
Division of Art, Prints and
Photographs

Frank Lloyd Wright worked
many years on a project for a
new city called Broadacre City.
He published his ideas on this
subject in *The Disappearing
City* in 1932, as well as in *The
Living City* (1958), published
when he was nearly ninety
years old. Comparing the town
plans of his era to a "section
of a fibrous tumor," he wanted
to represent the city of the
future, convinced that the
transformation of the physical
environment would give birth
to a new civilization. Broadacre City shatters the model
of the traditional city: each
family owns and lives on
at least one acre per person.
This proposal originates in
traditional American values:
individualism, the pioneering
spirit, and a sensitivity to
the bounty of nature, traits
that have been adapted
to the demands of a world
dominated by the airplane
and the automobile.

A Radiant Tomorrow

Bird's Eye View of Democracity
Silver gelatin print, New York, before 1939
NYPL, Manuscripts and Archives Division

The New York World's Fair of
1939–40 presented numerous positive visions of a radiant World of
Tomorrow. Coming at the end of the
Great Depression and on the eve of
America's involvement in World War
II, the fair celebrated democracy,
prosperity, consumerism, and faith
in technology, and it gave visitors
hope for a better, all-American
future. The central buildings of the
fair were the Trylon and Perisphere;
the latter contained a diorama of
"Democracity," a city plan designed
by Henry Dreyfuss, which promised
a happy future of ease and prosperity. Mimicking the design of the fair
itself, Democracity was built as a
semi-circular collection of buildings
for work and leisure; this photograph shows the designer's model
for the diorama. When the Trylon
and Perisphere were demolished at
the end of the fair, the 4,000 tons of
steel that had been used in their
construction were sent to munitions
factories as scrap metal for wartime
production needs.

standardized, and ornament-free Industrial city
that had been imagined as home to a radically new
society in 1899-1901, sent to the Ecole des Beaux-
Arts in Paris from Rome in 1901 and published
as *Une Cité industrielle. Etude pour la construction des
villes* in 1917. Garnier had been directly inspired
by Zola's novel *Travail* (1901), in turn influenced by
Fourier, but had most probably also read *News from
Nowhere, Looking Backward*, and Anatole France's
Sur la pierre blanche (1903). It is important to recall
that the schemes of Hilberseimer and Le Corbusier,
however horrendous they may appear to us now,
were attempts to procure a healthier, materially
more comfortable, and hence "happier" way of
living. They integrated into their schemes certain
features shared by the garden city movement, and
both Fourierism and the medieval Carthusian
monastery at Ema in Italy influenced Le Corbusier.

In 1932, Stalin closed the lid definitively on
the enthusiasm of informal art groups of the early
postrevolutionary years by decreeing their dissolution, proclaiming Soviet Socialist Realism as the
only acceptable artistic style, and gathering archi-

tects within the Union of Soviet Architects. The
Bauhaus was closed down in 1933. Le Corbusier
flirted with the totalitarian governments of both
Russia and Italy in his quest to see his ideal cities
realized, and dedicated his book *La Ville Radieuse*
(1935) quite simply "To Authority." Authoritarian
leaders were deaf to his call, however. Mussolini
preferred the monumental and classical schemes
that sang the glories of ancient Rome. Hitler's
favors went to Albert Speer, whose megalomaniacal
ambitions for Berlin were halted by World War II.
Nazism perfected another planning reflection of
its own dystopia, a horrendous example of political,
military, and functional efficiency, in cities of mass
extermination such as Auschwitz.

From America emerged the theories of
Taylor and Ford, which were to have so enormous
an impact upon architectural and urban design.
In America, with its skyscrapers and its many other
symbols of modernity, the new, better world of
the future would be achieved not through the organization of social relations but through material
progress. The country's technological prowess

Geodesic Dome

[Aerial view of the World's Fair Pavilion]
Silver gelatin print, New York,
[1964]
NYPL, Manuscripts and Archives
Division

Developed in the late 1940s
and early 1950s, geodesic
domes were R. Buckminster
Fuller's answer to the problems of modern architecture. A
visionary architect who sought
to "do more with less," Fuller
designed a lightweight, inexpensive, efficient alternative
to the square building. The
domes are very light, extremely strong, energy efficient, and
offer a limitless variety of possible floor plans, making them
ideally suited for housing. They
have also been widely used to
cover sports stadiums and as
protective shelters for sensitive scientific equipment in the
Arctic. Shown here is Fuller's
World's Fair Pavilion for the
New York World's Fair of
1964–65. The dome of the
pavilion is still standing in
Flushing, New York, and currently houses an aviary.

Futurama

**Aquascooter and Under-
water Hotel in a scene
from Futurama "Ride into
Tomorrow"**
Silver gelatin print, New York,
August 30, 1964
NYPL, Manuscripts and Archives
Division

At the New York World's Fair
of 1964–65, most of the exhibitions were sponsored by
major industrial, scientific, and
automotive companies of the
time, promoting one of the
themes of the fair: "Man's
achievements on a shrinking
globe in an expanding universe." As it had at the
World's Fair of 1939–40, General Motors sponsored a ride

called "Futurama" that
predicted transportation and
urban development trends
of the future (specifically,
the year 2064). Most had to
do with creating usable space
from earthly environments
formerly seen as hostile
to human development.
In addition to predicting the
efficient clearing of major
tracts of forest for the building
of superhighways and the
development of the desert
for agricultural cultivation,
"Futurama II" predicted
that humans would develop
colonies on the ocean floor.
Shown here is an underwater
hotel, at which guests arrived
in "aquascooters."

COTTAGE HOMES

Cottage Homes are quaint and friendly, similar to homes in the small town where I grew up.

Our cycling outings take a while, because we see so many friends along the way.

Disney's Celebration

Celebration Realty, Inc.
Memory Book, Celebration, Florida
Sales prospectus, 1990s
©The Celebration Company

"I don't believe there's a challenge anywhere in the world that's more important to people everywhere than finding solutions to the problems of our communities."
– Walt Disney

Billed as a "community built on a foundation of cornerstones: Community, Education, Health, Technology, and a Sense of Place," the town of Celebration, Florida, was developed in the 1990s by The Celebration Company, part of The Walt Disney Company's Imagineering group. It was conceived as a small southeastern town (anticipated population, 12,000–15,000) with pre-1940s architecture. The houses, recreational facilities, downtown area, municipal buildings, and office park were designed by some of the most prominent architects and architectural firms of the time, including Robert A. M. Stern Architects, Jaquelin Robertson of Cooper Robertson & Partners, Michael Graves Architect, and Philip Johnson, Ritchie & Fiore Architects. With an emphasis on creating a traditional small-town community with all the conveniences of modern technology, this planned town was designed to encourage interaction between neighbors through large front porches on every house, wide sidewalks and services well within walking distance, a hospital, a school, and a central business district. Its strict rules on architecture and landscaping have been hailed by some as the answer to modern town planning and criticized by others as an attempt by the Walt Disney Company to control the lives of the residents.

certainly provided an ongoing source of passion on both sides of the Atlantic in the early twentieth century, and cities like New York became symbols of its triumph along with that of capitalism. When New York threatened to become too dark because of the straight upward development of skyscrapers, the Zoning Laws of 1916 sought to remedy the situation by obliging them to rise in tiers; it is this that Hugh Ferriss was coming to grips with both rationally and aesthetically in his haunting drawings for *The Metropolis of Tomorrow* (1929). The ideas and drawings of architects like Charles R. Lamb, relating to similar issues, were quickly taken up by the science fiction press, and one thinks, for example, of the Julian Krupa image entitled *Cities of Tomorrow* that appeared on the back cover of *Amazing Stories* in August 1939. Industry was the driving force of society, and industrial designers like Raymond Loewy or Norman Bel Geddes became glamorous stars, streamlining and packaging the mass-produced items that would assuredly bring happiness to all. R. Buckminster Fuller designed his dynamic, efficient 4-D Utility Unit, later re-named the Dymaxion House (1927), which was intended to provide cheap housing for the masses and to be dropped into the countryside by zeppelin. Exhibitions, such as the Century of Progress Exhibition in Chicago (1933) or the New York World's Fair (initially called "The Fair of the Future") of 1939, provided major industry-sponsored platforms for exploring the not-so-distant or so-different future. The aim of the latter was to "stress the vastly increased opportunity and the developed mechanical means which this twentieth century has brought to the masses for better living and accompanying human happiness."[14] Accompanying something already under way, not creating something quite new. The New York fair included the General Motors Futurama exhibition, which transported visitors above a giant model of an urbanism dominated by the automobile. However, it also presented Henry Dreyfuss's "Democracity" exhibition of a "perfectly integrated future metropolis" that portrayed a less technological vision of the future, a distorted reading of Howard's garden city, with a cultural and business center surrounded by a green belt and commuter suburbs beyond.

Frank Lloyd Wright went further, seeking social change in his conception of Broadacre City even though it was one that embraced modern technology and particularly the private car and 'plane. His highly personal scheme stands apart from the others we have encountered, but it seems firmly rooted in the American pioneering traditions, emphasizing the independence of the individual. Like Howard and like Soria y Mata, inventor of the linear city concept in Spain in the 1880s,[15] he too sought to replace the industrial megapolis, he too sought to eliminate the rich/poor divide, and he too was influenced by the ideas of Henry George. He proposed shattering the city by creating an endless series of at least one-acre homesteads across the land, thus sharing property and ensuring democracy in a manner that recalls Jefferson's views (discussed above in my essay on pp. 119–31). "Broadacre City," proclaimed Wright, "is everywhere or nowhere. It is the country come alive as a great city."[16] In the nineteenth century, Marx, who opposed his "utopian" label to his own scientific method, though generally reluctant to depict the physical environment he envisaged for his communist world, had ventured to suggest that it would witness the suppression of the distinction between town and country. A fairly risk-free speculation, one could argue speciously, in view of the extreme contrast between the two at the time, but Frank Lloyd Wright, like Ebenezer Howard and many others we have encountered, tried in his own original way to achieve just that.

The first half of the century, increasingly obsessed with factory-style productivity, efficiency, and organization, had seen Functionalism become the dominant ideology among architects. The various ideas that had been tossed about in the early decades had failed to compete in the long run with the arguments expressed so convincingly in the *Charte d'Athènes*. The period after World War II, with its pressing need for economical mass housing, provided an opportunity for many of the ideas of the Functionalists to be realized in numerous rows of zoned, standardized blocks and towers. France, from the construction of the large Sarcelles estate in the suburbs of Paris in 1955, was a particularly avid consumer of this housing of urgency, physically more comfortable, without a doubt, than the living conditions in the shanty towns and other miserable lodgings that it replaced but nonetheless highly criticizable by comparison with what might have been realized in their stead.

Nonetheless, the iron grip of the modern movement was to be brought into question as part of a general reaction against the rigidity and the excessive domination of authority. Artists and architects sought to be the midwives of a process of liberation in a number of projects that privileged nomadism, metamorphosis, and the individual's right to determine his or her own immediate environment. Many of the visionary urban schemes of the 1950s and 1960s took the form of huge, skeletal megastructures comprised of the most up-to-date, lightweight, tensile materials that could supply the basic infrastructural services and into which commercial, residential, office, or other units could be plugged or unplugged at will. The autonomy of these elements was developed to varying degrees, in some cases to such an extent that the megastructure became virtually redundant. Other projects explored the idea of entire cities, or parts thereof, literally getting up and moving from one location to another, like a traveling circus. Many of these designs, while seeking to throw off the straitjacket of Functionalism in favor of maximum individual choice and flexibility, betrayed a continuingly optimistic, and unrealistic, belief in the benefits of technology and the march of progress. They encouraged a euphoric throw-away lifestyle – similar to that suggested in Richard Hamilton's pop art painting of 1956 of an interior overflowing with consumer goods, *Just what is it that makes today's homes so different, so appealing* – which has since proven ecologically unacceptable. They assumed, too, that the free time that would be procured by increasing mechanization would procure a better way of life for all, rather than generating the social exclusion that we have since witnessed.

The group known as the International Situationists (1957–72) was one of the most active in this liberating movement and indeed played a catalytic role in the uprisings of 1968 in France. At its founding conference, its leading protagonist, Guy-Ernest Debord, proclaimed: "We believe, above all, that the world must be changed. We want the most liberating transformation possible of both society and of the life in which we find ourselves incarcerated. . . . We must construct new ambiances that are simultaneously the product and the instrument of new modes of behavior."[17] They proposed a heterogeneous series of *unités d'ambiance*, the key element in their unitary urbanism, in preference to the increasing unification and homogenization from which the modern city, the space of late capitalism, the "society of spectacle" as Debord defined it, was suffering. Practising *dérive* (drifting), they accumulated data about the atmosphere of different parts of the city to compile psychogeographical maps, a new form of cartography, which indicates the strength of their belief in the determinant effect of the built environment upon human behavior.[18] The series of models and drawings entitled *New*

Babylon, by Constant Nieuwenhuys (known as Constant) who referred to it as "a different city for a Different Life," was the closest the International Situationists got to projecting an ideal city, to depicting the everyday spaces that would both reflect and induce the desires of *homo ludens*.[19] Constant's space is labyrinthine, indicative of the infinite number of possibilities with which each and every space and moment is pregnant. Already in his painting *Ode à l'Odéon* (1969), in memory of the Odéon's central role in the revolts of May 1968, the labyrinth is present. His lightweight megastructure in *New Babylon* would be laid out in a dense, multileveled, modifiable manner in order to encourage play, social interaction, and the *dérive* amid an explosive and unpredictable cocktail of transient ambiances.

Archigram, a combination of the words "architecture" and "telegram," was the name of a magazine produced in England from 1961 to 1974 but also that of the group of people responsible for its creation: Warren Chalk, Peter Cook, Dennis Crompton, David Greene, Ron Herron, and Mike Webb. They produced a number of design ideas about the city of the future in projects with self-explanatory titles such as Plug-in City, Living City, Walking City, and Control and Choice, distinguishing between structure and infill as "hardware" and "software." Progressively, the individual unit gained importance: the Living Pod, the Cushicle, and the Suitaloon were all increasingly spacesuit-inspired autonomous homes. Another megastructuralist, Yona Friedman, developed a series of Spatial city schemes from 1958 in which huge, lightweight structures that inhabitants could fill in or not according to their requirements were to be built above the ground, thus leaving the space below free for vegetation and historic monuments. Suitable for all conditions and climates, these were suggested for sites as diverse as Paris or Tunis, and his giant bridge cities, initially just intended to cross the Channel, were to link up all five continents by 1963-64. Thereafter, Friedman's work took on an interesting new direction, a natural progression (like that of the Archigram team but in a different, low-tech way) from his desire to empower the inhabitant by reducing the static urban infrastructure to a strict minimum, for he became increasingly involved in autoconstruction in the developing world. Paolo Soleri, an Italian architect active primarily in America, though still working with megastructures, was one of the first people to seek responses to the growing environmental problems.

The word he invented, *Arcology*, combining "architecture" and "ecology," indicates his concern and covered a number of his projects. Among these, Arcosanti, now under construction, is intended to group together 5,000 people in a high-density solar-powered structure occupying 14 acres on a site of 3,000 devoted primarily to agriculture. His arcologies are intended to eradicate problems such as crime and ethnic segregation, and his belief in the important influence of the built environment upon the social one is clearly stated: "A social pattern is influenced, if not directed, by the physical pattern that shelters it."[20]

The majority of the projects we have mentioned presented their critique of Functionalism in a positive utopian manner by proposing alternatives; indeed, examples of projects that take an anti-utopian stance are extremely rare in the architectural field (where three-dimensional realization is the ultimate aim). An exception to this is the work of the Italian group Superstudio, founded by Adolfo Natalini and Cristiano Toraldo di Francia in 1966. They caricatured the modernists and on occasion the megastructuralists too in projects such as the Continuous Monument, 12 Ideal Cities, the 2,000-ton city, and Vita, Educazione, Cerimonia, Amore, Morte, crushing individuals beneath heavy ceilings and covering the planet with terrifying grid networks of walls that showed a total disrespect for any natural or man-made preexisting elements.

From the ideal city designs produced in Quattrocento Italy and Thomas More's *Utopia* in early sixteenth-century England, Western culture has demonstrated a penchant for projecting the forms that the ideal city, and the ideal society, might take. Riding high on the confident belief that these could be worked out like the orderly mathematical formulae of a Luca Pacioli, this contradicted the incessant change and essential chaos that make up the very nature of the real city in all its complexity. Working from the illusory premise that society and the city could be similarly formulated, those ideal city designs, be they envisaged on the scale of More's island with its fifty-four almost identical towns or of the whole planet, sought to avoid or eliminate external influences through natural or man-made barriers or the achievement of world domination. The horrors witnessed in the twentieth century with the realization of so-called utopias on an unprecedented scale leading to an estimated twenty-five million dead in the name of nazism, one hundred million in that of communism,[21] seem to justify the current mistrust of utopia. But are we

right to recoil before utopia? Its ability to provoke improvement upon the real world by portraying appealing pictures of alternatives remains as vitally important and necessary as ever. Should we not instead demand that utopia, whose capacity to adapt has been proven in the past, change a little or that we modify our attitude thereto, abandoning its universal ambition in acceptance of the fact that one model cannot suit the myriad of conditions that make up the world. The planet may be shrinking due to recent advances in information technology, but the existence of this potentially all-encompassing global network (which still touches only a very small proportion of the six billion population) should contribute not to the annihilation of local differences but to a greater tolerance thereof. To the question "What does today's utopia look like?" there must be no one answer. The only viable approach must embrace a multitude of context-friendly utopias.

Notes

1 The words are those of J.-B.-A. Godin, who created the Familistère on the borders of Guise in northern France, in *Solutions Sociales* (1871): "Since it is impossible to make a palace of the cottage or hovel of every working family, we have aimed to place the worker's dwelling in a palace: the Familistère, indeed, is nothing less than that: it is the social palace of the future."

2 William Morris, Foreword to *Utopia* by Thomas More (Hammersmith: Kelmscott Press, 1893).

3 *News from Nowhere or An Epoch of Rest, being some chapters from a Utopian Romance* was serialized in the Socialist League's newspaper, the *Commonweal*, between January 11 and October 4, 1890, and published in Boston in book form in 1890 (revised London, 1891). The quotation is from *News from Nowhere and Selected Writings and Designs*, ed. with an introduction by Asa Briggs (Harmondsworth: Penguin, 1986), 245.

4 Ebenezer Howard, *To-morrow: A Peaceful Path to Real Reform* (London: Swan Sonnenschein, 1898); the second edition was published under the title *Garden Cities of To-morrow* in 1902. For a full discussion of the utopian schemes of Ebenezer Howard, Le Corbusier, and Frank Lloyd Wright, see Robert Fishman, *Urban Utopias in the Twentieth Century: Ebenezer Howard, Frank Lloyd Wright, and Le Corbusier* (New York: Basic Books, 1977).

5 John Ruskin in a lecture delivered in 1868, "The Mystery of Life and Its Arts"; quoted in Michael H. Lang, *Designing Utopia: John Ruskin's Urban Vision for Britain and America* (Montreal: Black Rose Books, 1999), 41.

6 Ebenezer Howard, "Spiritual Influences Toward Social Progress," in *Light*, April 30, 1910; quoted in Robert Beevers, *The Garden City Utopia: A Critical Biography of Ebenezer Howard* (New York: St. Martin's Press, 1988), 27.

7 Quoted in Walter L. Creese, *The Search for Environment: The Garden City, Before and After* (New Haven: Yale University Press, 1966), 206.

8 *The International Style*, a name that betrays the movement's universal ambitions, was derived from the title of the first architectural exhibition, curated by Philip Johnson and Henry Russell Hitchcock, at New York's Museum of Modern Art in 1932.

9 Marinetti, "Manifesto of Futurism," published in *Le Figaro*, 1909; quoted from Umbro Apollonio, ed., *Futurist Manifestos* (London: Thames and Hudson, 1973), 24.

10 Aleksandr A. and Viktor A. Vesnin, "Tvorcheskie otchety" ["Creative accounts"], in *Arkhitektura SSSR*, no. 4 (1935): 40.

11 Vladimir Evgrafovich Tatlin, quoted in Christina Lodder, *Russian Constructivism* (New Haven: Yale University Press, 1983), 277.

12 Le Corbusier, first issue of *L'Esprit nouveau* (1920).

13 Le Corbusier, *La ville radieuse* (Boulogne-sur-Seine: Editions de l'architecture aujourd'hui, 1935), 181.

14 Quoted in Helen A. Harrison, ed., *Dawn of a New Day: The New York World's Fair, 1939/40* (New York: New York University Press, 1980), 4.

15 In 1882, in the newspaper *El Progreso*, Soria y Mata exposed his scheme to "ruralize the town and urbanize the country" by creating "a single street of 500 meters' width and of the length that may be necessary – such will be the city of the future, whose extremities could be Cadiz and St. Petersburg, or Peking and Brussels." This was the linear city, designed to permit a new, equitable distribution of land. In the 1890s, Soria set up a limited company to realize his scheme, but only 5 kilometers of an intended 55-kilometer-long railway encircling the city of Madrid was built due to economic constraints and difficulties of land expropriation. It was to influence a number of twentieth-century schemes, reemerging, for example, in Soviet Russia in the 1930s. Soria was influenced by the doctrines of the American economist Henry George as indeed was Ebenezer Howard.

16 Frank Lloyd Wright and Baker Brownell, *Architecture and Modern Life* (New York: Harper & Brothers, 1937).

17 G.-E. Debord, "Rapport sur la construction des situations et sur les conditions de l'organisation et de l'action de la tendence situationniste internationale," reprinted in Gérard Berreby, ed., *Documents relatifs à la fondation de l'Internationale Situationniste 1948–1957* (Paris: Editions Allia, 1985), 607–19.

18 Debord defined the new science of psychogeography, a Situationist neologism, as "the study of the precise laws and the exact effects of the geographic environment, built or unbuilt, in terms of its direct influence on the affective behavior of individuals" in "Introduction à une critique de la géographie urbaine" in *Les lèvres nues* 6 (September 1955), reprinted in Berreby, 288.

19 Constant, "Une autre ville pour une autre vie," *Internationale Situationniste* 3 (December 1959), quoted in Thomas Y. Levin, "Geopolitics of Hibernation: The Drift of Situationist Urbanism," in Liberto Andreotti and Xavier Costa, eds., *Situationists: Art, Politics, Urbanism* (Barcelona: Museu d'Art Contemporani de Barcelona, 1996), 126.

20 Paolo Soleri, in *Art in America* (May–June 1979): 67.

21 Stéphane Courtois et al., *Le livre noir du communisme* (Paris: R. Laffont, 1997), 8 and 20.

Frédéric Rouvillois

Utopia and Totalitarianism

AT A cursory level, it may seem shocking, almost scandalous, to bring together terms like utopia and totalitarianism. The term utopia, as it is generally understood, implies an appealing but impossible ideal, a generous chimera. If our understanding of utopia were to rest merely on the conjunction of sympathy and frivolity, then our investigation need go no further. Totalitarianism seems to produce a similar phenomenon in reverse; horrific evidence to stop us in our tracks, as though the manifestation of horror were reason enough to exempt us from studying the logic of its roots and genesis. Viewed superficially, therefore, utopia is a sadly inaccessible boon and totalitarianism a distressingly real evil – it would appear, therefore, that utopia is the exact antithesis of totalitarianism.

Despite the convenience of its symmetry, such a formula soon proves untenable. The vulgar definition of utopia is both flimsy and irrelevant; if we are to qualify any unattainable goal, in any domain, as utopian, then the term can legitimately be applied across the board. Its general application deprives it of meaning, and the word consequently becomes nothing more than an uncertain and temporary judgment based on subjective values. Such a gauge would be unequal to the task of accounting for self-proclaimed utopian works. If we were to keep within these bounds, then even explicit utopias would in the end be no more "utopian" than any other project.

To avoid absurd conclusions such as these, we must refer to the sources, or rather the source – Thomas More's *Utopia*,[1] the founding text that invented and launched the word and its attendant current of thought. The work, instantly acclaimed upon its 1516 publication, describes an ideal republic that is the happy creation of inhabitants guided solely by virtue and reason. The play on words that is embedded in the work's title is a key to the text: *utopia* is both the nonexistent place and the benevolent *eutopia*. If this republic is nowhere to be found, it is precisely because it is perfect and because such perfection has yet to be achieved in the here and now. At the core of the book, we find perfection assimilated to a political order that has evolved out of the will and actions of human beings.

As attested to by the countless authors and thinkers who have revived and reclaimed utopia, posterity has understood More's vision in terms of this assimilation. The 1795 edition of the *Dictionnaire de l'Académie française* concurs; it defines utopia as a noun that refers to "a plan of an imaginary government in which all things are perfectly ordered for the common good."

To seriously posit utopia against totalitarianism, we must first arm ourselves with this definition, the only historically and theoretically pertinent one, and with the body of work associated with it. As we narrow the evidence that links these two phenomena, the scandalous incongruity mentioned above will begin to seem less improbable.

On the one hand, the most blatant utopias, with their obsession to rehabilitate man and condemn him to happiness, do indeed reveal traits that we habitually attribute to totalitarian systems. On the other hand, totalitarian systems – Fascism, Nazism, Stalinist or Chinese Socialism – even when they don't acknowledge the connection, invariably remind us of utopias, whose goals, mottoes, and means they appropriate.

The proximity is too frequent to be accidental. Utopia and totalitarianism are both engaged in a mirroring game, tirelessly sending the same image back and forth as if utopia were nothing more than the premonition of totalitarianism and totalitarianism the tragic execution of the utopian dream. Only the distance that separates a dream from its realization seems to stand between the two.

Utopia: Premonition of Totalitarianism

Utopias do not all forecast totalitarian regimes to the same degree. Their central theme, the erection of the perfect polis by human beings, is subject to infinite permutations and as such capable of a widely varying range. The differences are of less importance to us, however, than the similarities – the unifying traits that qualify them as utopias. It is precisely because of their utopian aims that they are harbingers of totalitarianism – by virtue of their Promethean project to make a tabula rasa of the past and to install the reign of the new self.

The Bolshevik Revolution

R.S.F.S.R.
1e maia 1920 goda
[*May 1, 1920*]
Poster, photomechanical, 1920
NYPL, Miriam and Ira D. Wallach
Division of Art, Prints and
Photographs

In this poster celebrating the
Bolshevik revolution of 1917,
workers and peasants, men
and women, triumphantly
trample symbols of the imperial power of the overthrown
Romanov dynasty.

The Unmaking of Society

"You have stripped off the old self . . . and have
clothed yourself with the new self":[2] transposed
onto the temporal order, this teaching of Saint
Paul's is at the very heart of utopia. In this case, to
strip off the old self means to rid man of those
things that keep him from "full being," the things
that make him selfish, apathetic, and unhappy.
Hence, the specific social practices and the intermediary bodies that bar the way of redemptive
intervention must be destroyed.

Bolstered by arguments culled from Plato's
Republic, utopias take special aim at the family; viewing family as the product of nature and chance, they
proceed to dismiss it on those very same grounds.

Paternity is the first object of attack. "Father-
hood and reason are not mutually implicit,"[3]
observes one of the inhabitants of *Caléjava*. And
as humanity is characterized by reason, then to

submit to the father pertains more to the realm
of "beast than [of] man."[4]

The "word *father* is unknown"[5] in Foigny's *Terre
Australe*. For Campanella's Solarians, the physical
entity itself disappears: man is no more than an
anonymous forebear, whose sole value is in the
utilitarian pursuit of the best possible, healthiest,
and most beautiful progeny.[6] Though the mother
may temporarily be accorded a more eminent role,
her status is likewise greatly diminished after the
birth; leaving children, who "belong not so much
to their parents as to the public,"[7] in her care
is unthinkable. Once they are weaned, infants
become adoptees, "children of the state."[8]

"It is not mere chance that determines the
name of a person," but rational criteria.[9] When
the family name disappears entirely as it does in
Anatole France's "federation of peoples," where
only first names are needed since family has been

displaced by the social community, it comes as
no surprise.[10] This trend eventually reaches its full
expression in *L'Isle des hommes raisonnables*, where
proper names are completely replaced by numbers.[11]

Opacity in any form is prohibited; all places
and all relationships are subject to surveillance and
the law. The ban on private property, the aversion
to secrecy and amusements, the abolition of family
and boundaries, are all driven by this single-minded
obsession with transparency.

These ideals find a corresponding embodiment
in a State that is all powerful and bent only on
securing and perpetuating them. Paradoxically, this
utopian state is everywhere and nowhere, a nameless
and faceless analogue to Orwell's Big Brother, who
is both everybody and nobody. Hannah Arendt saw
this "rule of nobody," manifested here in a culture of
denunciation, as a clear-cut symptom of totalitarianism. In More's Utopia, "nowhere is there any license
to waste time, nowhere any pretext to evade work.
. . . On the contrary, being under the eyes of all, people are bound"[12] to carry out their assigned duties.
"Nowhere else," one of Cabet's Icarians claims, "are
the police so numerous, because . . . all our citizens
are required to oversee the law, to enforce it and
report any criminal offense they witness."[13]

Such a pervasive and menacing authority heeds
only its own will: "When power is united to reason,"

wrote Castel de Saint-Pierre, "it will never prove . . .
too despotic."[14] In its pursuit of perfection, the totalitarian State exacts a license to lie, corrupt, violate,
and terrorize. Fontenelle's Ajaoïens, for example,
begin by enslaving the "somewhat indolent peoples"
that inhabit the island where they choose to settle.
Later, when the number of slaves strikes them as
excessive, they slaughter them in cold blood, sparing
only two thousand men, nubile women, and little
girls. They also decide to limit the number of births
in the future in a way that will avoid "superfluity"
and be proportionate to and regulated by the need
to replenish the work force.[15] A similar logic must
have served to goad Jean-Baptiste Carrier, the insti-
gator of the late eighteenth-century drownings
at Nantes, into action: "I am ready to sacrifice all
mankind to my beloved Republic."[16]

In utopia, the higher the stakes (the installation of Man at the summit of a regained Paradise),
the more imperious the Reasons of State become.

Remaking Man
Stripped of the loyalties that had shrouded him,
the individual stands alone against a State that can
finally embark on his renewal. This process, like
all others, colludes with the creation of the ideal
polis: the perfection of the whole must imperiously
correspond to that of its parts.

This correspondence is at the very essence of the project: the old self was wrapped up in its desires and selfish interests; the new self must learn to renounce the "me" and identify with the "us" in order to be born.

The utopian drive to monitor intimacy is motivated precisely by the desire to eliminate any gaps that may exist between individual and collective freedoms. Utopias never tire of reiterating that the citizen's body belongs to the collective. Sexuality, as is to be expected, is subjected to a particularly strict code. In More's *Utopia*, for example, transgressors are condemned to eternal abstinence. While the punishment is less extreme in Campanella, the code is more fastidious: the choice of mate, and the place, day, and even the exact hour of coupling, are left to the "rational" discretion of the authorities. Anatole France's utopians go so far as to dream that they "may some day reach the point of creating neutrals, and produce female workers, as in the case of bees."[17]

The perfect polis clashes with the rebellious and perturbing potentialities of desire itself. Thus, among Campanella's Solarians, "only loving friendship, rather than concupiscent ardor, is recognized";[18] and Paul Adam's Malais are rehabilitated through satiety in weekly public orgies in which the "communism of erotic sensations"[19] results in the successful neutralization of sexuality.

Education also figures importantly in the utopian project, and underlying the concerted effort toward pedagogical perfection is the expectation that it will make all other forms of control superfluous. Until this perfection is achieved, however, a prescriptive code aptly prevails as one of the most efficient modalities of education. Through subservience to a law that is everywhere evident, one begins to spontaneously submit (as in self-criticism), to accept punishment as a just desert for having failed in one's duty: it is thus that the Sever-ambians "are early trained to strict observance of their laws. It comes naturally to them, and then it is also a matter of free and deliberate choice, as they grow old enough to reflect and find that their laws are just and reasonable."[20]

When one wants only what one is supposed to want, strict obedience and freedom coincide. The freedom one enjoys must satisfy utopia's subservience to a collective and unanimous totality, like that at the Abbey of Thélème, where if anyone said, "'Let's drink,' everyone drank. If he or she said, 'Let's play,' they all played. If he or she said, 'Let's go and have fun in the meadows,' there they all went."[21]

Totally reconciled to himself and to his kind, the new self thus fulfills yet another biblical prediction: "Your eyes will be opened, and you will be like God, knowing good and evil" (Genesis 3: 5). In this instance, to be "in some way gods"[22] means to leave one's animal nature behind to become more fully human. Anatole France, like Engels before him, foresaw the future in similar terms: "[Life] will be ordered, reasoned and harmonious,"[23] when "we completely emerge from primeval barbarism and set up on earth, in succession to bestial rule, which is the rule of war, the human rule, the rule of justice [and peace]."[24]

The break with bestial origins, a quintessential pursuit of the utopian project, takes on a particularly spectacular guise in Foigny's hermaphroditic Australian race of consummately whole beings. The hermaphrodite is, in effect, the embodiment of plenitude regained, a fusion of the sexes that obviates differences. From a utopian perspective, in which equality, unanimity, and uniformity are simply modes of unity and the instruments for its perpetuation, the hermaphrodite represents the paragon of humanity. He is both a complete and a total being; he is a symbol of the aspiration to be delivered from desire and its trammels and in so doing to attain the ultimate liberation from animality. Foigny's man is also a vegetarian and an ascetic, has never known sleep or illness, and dies only by his own volition (provided he has authorization to do so).

Utopia's hygienic compulsion, its aversion to odors and filth and, by extension, to all recalcitrant forms of nature – forests and swamps – grows out of a similar tendency. The new self merits a leveled, smooth, and transparent environment that fully displays the demiurgic powers of its designer.

"There is nowhere in the world a more excellent people nor a happier commonwealth."[25] But such happiness is untenable. This transparent but sealed-off world, whose absolute internal cohesion is a symbolic consequence of its rupture with the outside world, despises difference and all things that may challenge its perfection. Utopia prohibits both contamination and flight; whereas gaining entry to its sanctum is all but impossible, one can leave it only by decree. In Anatole France's admonition, "Take heed, Comrades . . . you have condemned yourselves to be honest men in perpetuity."[26]

In this closed space, where each one is "universally informed upon and a universal informer,"[27] we are, as one of Paul Adam's Malais acknowledges, "the perpetual object of a watchful eye. But this does not bother us. No one has anything to hide."[28]

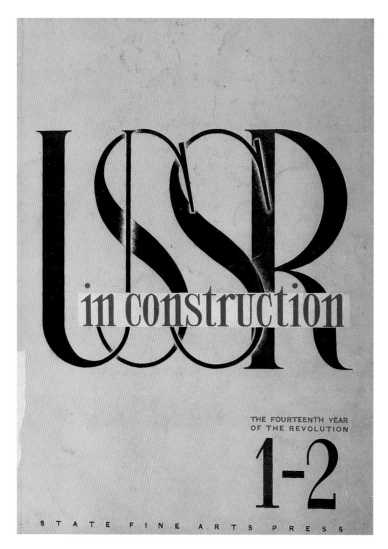

EVERY PHYSICAL CULTURIST

above and opposite

The Art of Propaganda

**U.S.S.R. in Construction.
A monthly illustrated magazine published in Russian,
English, German and French**
Moscow: The State Publishing
Union of R.S.F.S.R., 1930–41
NYPL, Slavic and Baltic Division

Published between 1930 and
1941 in Russian, English, German, French, and, eventually,
Spanish, *U.S.S.R. in Construction* was a major propaganda
tool for the Soviet Union
under Stalin. Articles and photographs by highly esteemed
writers and artists showed

the major construction projects undertaken by Stalin
to bring the U.S.S.R. onto the
world stage as an important
industrial power. Many issues
featured a single theme,
such as the electrification of
the country, athletics, or the
building of the canal from
the White Sea to the Baltic.
Elaborate foldouts and
photomontages were part
of the innovative design
and layout by such well-
known artists as Aleksandr
Rodchenko, El Lissitzky,
and Boris Ignatovich.

The images on the facing
page are from a 1934 issue
devoted to labor communes
for juveniles in need of rehabilitation. The first images
in the issue, they provide a
before-and-after demonstration of the radical change
the communes could achieve.
The caption remarks that
"The first was taken by our
photographer in 1922. It is
typical of the homeless waifs
of these years. The second
is also a former waif but now
a young communard."

No one, indeed, as deviants are eliminated or institutionalized, and the disabled and the elderly warehoused in outlying zones, so that only perfect uniformity holds sway and there is nothing to distinguish one person from the next. By the same token, nothing binds them to one another except their membership in the Whole and their obedience to the Law. "The sweetness of losing oneself in a whole that is greater than our respective parts"[29] is insufficient to the task of overriding the melancholy, the formless "anxiety"[30] experienced by the inhabitants of the ideal city. Obligatory happiness breeds a vertiginous boredom, a solitude that is most acute on the Holy Days that come to punctuate a daily life in which nothing much happens anymore.

Utopia, therefore, emerges as the site of perpetual inversion: unanimity becomes isolation, freedom alienation, and transparency emptiness, and total humanization engenders robots and monsters. "In the deadened eyes of the Utopians, we see only . . . the endlessly multiplying reflection of an identical Other."[31]

By virtue of its enthronement of duplicity and double-speak, utopia emerges as a premonition of totalitarianism and its institutionalized schizophrenia.

Totalitarianism: Utopia Fulfilled

Claude Lefort's definition of totalitarianism as "a society instituted without divisions that assumes command over its organization, is self-reflexive in all its parts, and permeated by the same project throughout"[32] could easily apply to utopia. Similarly, totalitarian discourse is steadfast in its appropriation of utopian ends as well as of the means it envisions as necessary for their attainment.

The Order of Endings
Perfection constitutes the very essence of the utopian project: it is to be an acquired perfection that can always be improved upon and must be defended at all times to ensure its longevity, eternity being the principal corollary of perfection. Totalitarian doctrines follow suit: they too want to put an end to adversity, and to history.

Like utopia, totalitarianism seems obsessed with unity; all human misfortune is the result of division, separation, and difference. It comes as no surprise, therefore, that totalitarianism should have appropriated the Tolstoyan maxim "that social improvement could be achieved only when all members of society had achieved perfection."[33]

In Communist society, which can only be established when man no longer lives "in the midst of egoism,"[34] all divisions will be done away with, as will the differences between classes and nations, the gap between rulers and ruled, the conflict between man and nature, the division of labor and the "stunting of man" it brings about.[35]

More profoundly, writes Henri Lefebvre, "communism . . . is defined . . . as the transcendence of the alienation and the internal conflicts of the individual. Even in early versions, the new self sets itself a similar course."[36] All barriers must give way to general emancipation. The resulting world, anticipated with certainty, will be, according to Fidel Castro, "a world of good men . . ., generous, . . . a large, extended family in which every man and woman will have not one but millions of brothers and sisters, millions of children, millions of fathers and mothers."[37] And, furthermore, "the integral development of each citizen within a [harmonious] society" will result.[38]

But if the future is to be radiant and happiness absolute, then the fear of death, the ultimate separation, must also be abolished. Totalitarianism, like utopia, purports to have triumphed over the anguish of time and the accidents of history. The new era it announces will be everlasting, and the new self can confidently expect a smooth and reassuring future wherein his supremacy will only be confirmed.

To begin with, the establishment of the new system is described as a "second birth,"[39] as the advent of a new day with no ties to the past. As André Wurmser has pointed out, October 1917 was not a crowning moment but a "point of departure" for

the end of the prehistory of humanity, which at last had become humane. Even the sans-culottes had invented a new calendar according to which the first year of the republic was the year one. In a similar way the Christian Church established its calendar by which we still tick off days and months. So let November 7 become both the birth of a new world and the holiday of the new year.[40]

Invocations of the Jacobin Revolution are to be expected – its radicalism was not limited, as in the case of Fascism, to resetting the clock of human history at zero; it reinvented the names, rhythms, and even measures of time in a sweeping gesture that simultaneously announced both the freedom and omnipotence of the new self.

The Gulag

**[Labor camp prisoners
at work, 1936–37]**
Photographs, n.p., 1936–37
NYPL, Slavic and Baltic Division

Depicting workers at one of
the Soviet Ministry of Foreign
Affairs camps in the winter of
1936–37, these images convey the reality of life behind
the propaganda of the Soviet
Union. At the camp, called
Falangi #7, prisoners were
"encouraged" to mine the
riches of the Northern Russian
forest. On the verso of many
of these images, a clear hand
in ink describes the people
and the work photographed in
this bleak environment.

But the principal feature is that the new era will last for eternity. "Our revolution," said Hitler, "is a new stage or, rather, the final stage in an evolution which will end by abolishing history."[41] An even earlier statement by Moeller Van Den Bruck asserted that "We are thinking of the Germany . . . of an eternal present."[42] These statements go beyond rhetoric; it is in this context of the "thousand-year Reich" that Nazism developed its program and priorities. Nazi policies of eugenics and euthanasia, for example, were founded on the premise that the "passing pain of a century can and will redeem millenniums from sufferings,"[43] and that the "state must act as the guardian of a millennial future in the face of which the wishes and the selfishness of the individual must appear as nothing and submit."[44] Hence, "at last the best of humanity, having achieved possession of this earth, will have a free path for activity in domains which will lie partly above and partly outside it,"[45] and will regain forever "the paradise which he had made for himself."[46]

Marxist systems, in turn, describe the advent of Communism as signalling the end of humanity's prehistory and the beginning of its true history; a history, according to Engels, that will no longer dominate human beings, but which will be "the result of his own free action . . . with full consciousness, [he will] make his own history."[47] In a similar vein, Mao wrote, "When human society advances to the point where classes and states are eliminated, there will be no more wars, counter-revolutionary or revolutionary, unjust or just; that will be the era of perpetual peace for mankind."[48] Alongside these

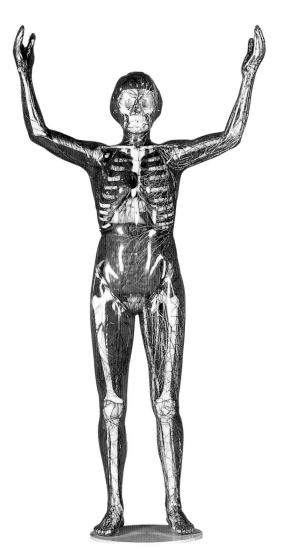

The Transparent Human

Franz Tschakert
Glass Woman
Replica, 1980
Deutsches Hygiene-Museum, Dresden

The first world exposition on hygiene (Dresden, 1911), attended by over five million visitors, is indicative of the rise in the late nineteenth century of widespread movements throughout Europe to educate the public on health and hygiene. In the 1920s, hygiene and eugenics were to become increasingly associated; campaigns, exhibits, and museums promoted the idea that an individual with a healthy lifestyle "contributed to the well-being of the nation," and as early as 1926, the Deutsches Hygiene-Museum claimed that "the single most important public health duty of a nation was the preservation of its genetic heritage."

In 1930, shortly after the museum opened, Dresden hosted a second world exposition on hygiene, at which the *Glass Man*, created by the model builder Franz Tscharkert, caused an immediate sensation; the use of a new material had made possible the three-dimensional reproduction of human anatomy and physiology in their entirety. "Spectators passed through a kind of light grid to enter a hall that was plunged in semi-darkness. Leaving the hectic streets behind, they entered a vast cathedral-like space where a large dark blue curtain was side-lit by hidden light sources. The spectators descended a few stairs and came face to face with a circular pedestal on which stood a three-dimensional human model of the internal anatomy. . . . When the hall was completely dark, the organs, starting with the heart, would light up one after the other while a melodious prerecorded voice gave precise explanations; spectators were fascinated by this 'illuminated' reconstruction of the human body."

The glass statue in Dresden, representing man both as a masterpiece and as a model of unitary and hierarchical organization, gave rise to the numerous reproductions, of both the male and female, that were displayed in almost all the great exhibitions of the 1930s, most notably in Paris in 1937 and in New York in 1939.

The Nazi Ideal

The Central Propaganda Office of the Nazi Party produced posters like these once a week, posting them in meeting halls, on bulletin boards, and in other public places. Featuring inspirational quotations from some of the major figures in the party, they served to reinforce the anti-Semitic, anti-Communist, and political messages of the Nazis.

Bauern und Soldaten stehen Hand in Hand zusammen, um dem Volke sein täglich Brot zu geben und dem Reiche seine Freiheit zu sichern [Farmers and soldiers stand hand in hand together to give the people their daily bread and to safeguard freedom for the Reich. – Dr. Goebbels]
Munich: Wochenspruch der NSDAP, Herausgeber Reichspropagandaleitung, Zentralverlag der NSDAP, No. 41, October 5–11, 1941
NYPL, Rare Books Division

Juden waren es, die den Marxismus erfanden, Juden sind es, die mit ihm seit Jahrzehnten die Welt zu revolutionieren versuchen [It was the Jews who invented Marxism. It is the Jews who, for decades, have used Marxism to endeavor to revolutionize the world. – Dr. Goebbels]
Munich: Wochenspruch der NSDAP, Herausgeber Reichspropagandaleitung, Zentralverlag der NSDAP, No. 40, September 28–October 4, 1941
NYPL, Rare Books Division

a

Gods of the Stadium

Leni Riefenstahl
Schönheit im Olympischen
Kampf [Beauty in the
Olympic Struggle]
Berlin: Im Deutschen Verlag, [1937]
NYPL, Miriam and Ira D. Wallach
Division of Art, Prints and
Photographs

a. "Free exercises in the
stadium"

b. "Youth on the Maifeld"

c. "Olympic winner in the
twelve events Schwartz-
mann – Germany"

In 1936, Leni Riefenstahl was
commissioned by the International Olympic Committee
and Olympic official Carl Diem
to produce and direct a film
commemorating the 1936
Summer Games in Berlin.
The result, *Olympia* (1938),
released in two parts, *Fest der
Völker [Festival of the People]*
and *Fest der Schönheit [Festi-
val of Beauty]*, was a glorification of the "beauty of Olympic
competition." In 1937, stills
from the film, along with
photographs taken by Riefenstahl and other photographers,
were reproduced in a book;
these stills are from the second part of the film.

b

c

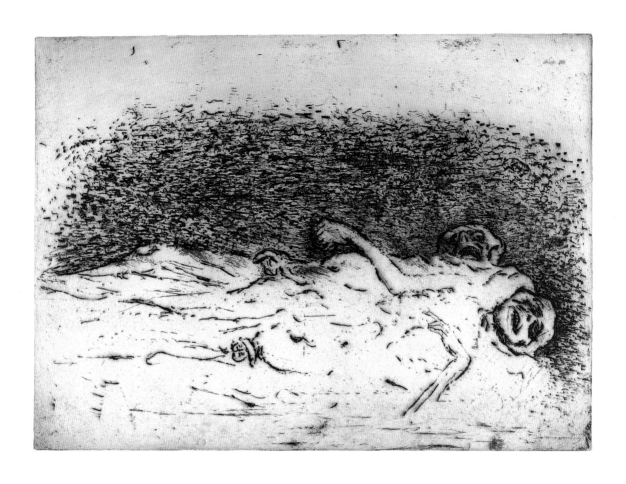

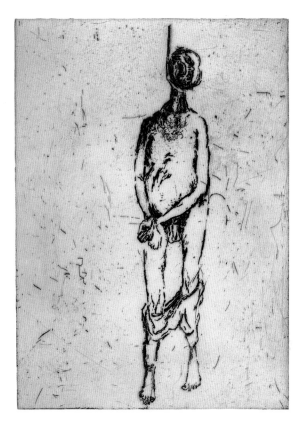

Dachau

Zoran Music
Nous ne sommes
pas les derniers
Paris: Editions Lacourière
Frélaut, 1985
Etchings
BNF, Département des Estampes
et de la Photographie

"Comrades, I am the last,"
a prisoner had cried out as he
was hanged just prior to the
liberation of Auschwitz. "We
are not the last," answered
Zoran Music, choosing that
title for the 1970 exhibition
of his drawings, paintings,
and etchings at the Galerie

de France in Paris. In
1944–45, as a political deportee to Dachau, Music had
secretly made two hundred
drawings, of which he saved
thirty-five sheets. After his
release, the artist tried to
erase the horror from his
memory. Dream imagery,
poetry, *joie de vivre*, "silent
happiness" infused his work.
But around 1969, the past
reemerged, to be expressed
in a cycle of sixteen engravings, entitled *We are not the
last*, created between 1970
(the first etchings) and 1975
(the last drypoints).

one can place Moeller van den Bruck's claim that "The thought of enduring peace is in very truth the thought of the Third Empire."[49] As it happens, it also pertains to utopias and cemeteries.

Plans and Means

The introduction of the new self, which will "storm the heavens"[50] and earth, justifies all means, especially those that utopia suggests, like purifying men and bringing them together.

If totalitarian doctrines claim to embrace man in his totality, it is because they are, by definition, founded on an ideology of totality; if some trace of the old self were to remain, if some part were to escape redemption, then everything would be corrupted and irremediably and irretrievably condemned. Here, utopia's obsession with transparency becomes a will to purification, a purification that Hitler believed would "be extended to nearly all fields."[51]

The purification of society means first and foremost the elimination of all those who do not fit the new definition of human being. The definition does not include the men of the past, or aliens, or the "subhuman," but this does not mean that these groups are analogous. Whereas some must be destroyed as a class until such time as their "re-education" can be effected, others are to be eliminated on the basis of personal identity, and these must be ousted or slaughtered. But in the end, all are anathema to an ideal of homogeneity that sanctions extermination of the other as a matter of principle, according to modalities that are ultimately analogous in their monstrosity.

That accomplished, the individual himself must be purified by making him accede to a superior morality. Vice is only a remnant of the old self and its refusal to submit to the totality. "The totalitarian State will make no difference between law and morality,"[52] said Hitler as Robespierre had said before him and as Stalin and Mao would say after him. The "universal happiness"[53] of the crystal city will fall only to a virtuous and renewed humanity.

The new self's virtue is characterized by its rejection of selfishness – "base and cruel, which isolates a man from his fellows."[54] For the task of achieving such "forgetting of the self," there are no measures that equal the quintessentially utopian formulas of communal living. Canteens and dormitories, the wholesale takeover of daily life, the practice of organized and collective leisure activities, are all characteristic of totalitarian regimes, in which from morning to night, from birth until

death, the individual must be kept from isolation, which is tantamount to withdrawal and is fraught with danger. All adversity is the result of schism, and human beings must at all costs live in mental as well as physical unity and communion. For this reason, totalitarian regimes pay particular attention to festivals, with their heightened emphasis on union. Had not Robespierre proclaimed, "Assemble men together and you will make them better" and added, "A system of well-organized national festivals would be at once the most gentle of fraternal ties and the most powerful means of regeneration."[55] It is a question of being, but above all of acting, thinking, feeling with and like others, and of loving and hating identically. One for all and all for one: the more men are together, the more easily they will give up their desires and interests and identities, all things that distinguish them from the totality, and the more they will come to resemble the new self they must become.

The Dream and Its Achievement

The appearance of the deliberate and necessary closeness between utopia and totalitarianism and the regularity, much too frequent to be coincidental, with which the first seems to give way to the second, leave us no choice but to question the significance of this association.

Whereas all totalitarian regimes distance themselves from the misnamed utopias of general discourse and challenge the utopianism of dreamers, they also, as a rule, consciously and deliberately ally themselves with any one of a number of specific utopias. Socialist States have never hesitated to claim and pay homage to the great regenerative and revolutionary utopias as naive, albeit brilliant, precursors. In 1913, predating the creation of Fascism by only a few years, Mussolini launched the journal *Utopia*, "in homage to the labor and martyrdom of one of the earliest pioneers of Socialism."[56] And, implicit though they may be, the allusions to Plato's *Republic* in Hitler's *Mein Kampf* are neither subtle nor scant.[57]

The fact remains, however, that beyond conscious comparisons and banal imitations, a true kinship permeates all totalitarian systems in their consistent effort to enthrone the new self in its eternal reign over conquered nature. Utopias are all akin insofar as their inherent project is the construction of an ideal city that is impervious to division, time, and evil. In the end, after we dismiss superficial particularities, the kinship between utopia and totalitarianism is revealed as a perfect fit: both aspire to the absolute and in both cases the ends justify the means. "All utopias are totalitarian," said Léo Moulin.[58] And, conversely, all totalitarian states are fundamentally utopian. By way of absurd corroboration, we need only think that if Hitler had not risen to power, then *Mein Kampf* would have been nothing more than an (atrocious and oppressive) utopia; and if Campanella *had* risen to power, the implementation of the City of the Sun would have brought about the most terrifying instance of pre-modern totalitarianism.

Fundamentally, utopia and totalitarianism share a similar conception of man, nature, and history. They understand history as a necessary and perpetual progress[59] with conscious, rational man as its principal actor and propelling force. He has been cast as an eternal "Prometheus,"[60] a figure endowed by totalitarian states and utopias with all the traits of the all-powerful Worker who little by little transforms the world. "[A] world changed over and planned and built afresh,"[61] writes the utopist Wells, speaking of Lenin as the "dreamer in the Kremlin," a world made in the image of its re-creator.

And what we see beyond the common project of seeing "the kingdom of heaven fulfilled at last upon earth"[62] is a similar wish, inherently linking utopia and totalitarianism, to put man in God's place, even if he must endure all the torments of hell to reach it.

Translated by Nadia Benabid

1 Thomas More, *Utopia*, ed. Edward Surtz (New Haven, Conn., and London: Yale University Press, 1964). All quotations are from this edition.

2 Colossians 3: 9–10.

3 Claude Gilbert, *Histoire de Caléjava, ou de l'isle des hommes raisonnables*, (n.p., 1700), 129.

4 Gabriel de Foigny, *The Southern Land, Known*, trans. and ed. David Fausett (Syracuse, N.Y.: Syracuse University Press, 1993), 53. Foigny's work was first published as *La Terre Australe connue* (Geneva: Jacques Vernevil, 1676).

5 Ibid., 54.

6 See Tommaso Campanella, *The City of the Sun*, trans. with introd. and notes by Daniel J. Donno (Berkeley: University of California Press, 1981), 53 ff.

7 François de Salignac de La Mothe-Fénelon, *Telemachus, Son of Ulysses*, ed. and trans. Patrick Riley (Cambridge, England, and New York: Cambridge University Press, 1994), 194.

8 Denis Vairasse d'Allais, *Histoire des Sévarambes*, excerpted and trans. by Frank E. Manuel and Fritzie P. Manuel in their *French Utopias: An Anthology of Ideal Societies* (New York: Free Press, 1966), 54.

9 Campanella, 59.

10 Anatole France, *The White Stone*, trans. by Charles C. Roche (London: John Lane; New York: John Lane Company, 1910), 197.

11 Gilbert, 166.

12 More, 82–83.

13 Etienne Cabet, *Voyage en Icarie*, quoted in Léo Moulin, "Structure des utopies politiques," *Etudes* (March 1995): 354.

14 Charles Irénée Castel de Saint-Pierre, *Ouvrajes de politique* (Rotterdam: J.-D. Beman; Paris: Briasson, 1733–40), 3: 203–4.

15 M. de Fontenelle, *La République des philosophes; or, Histoire des Ajaoiens* (Geneva, 1768), 92–95.

16 Quoted in Jacques Dupâquier, "Le précédent oublié," *Catholica* (Paris), no. 59 (1998): 37.

17 France, *The White Stone*, 226.

18 Campanella, 63. See also *L'Utopie*, with introd., selection, and commentaries by Frédéric Rouvillois (Paris: Flammarion, 1998).

19 Paul Adam, *La Cité prochaine, lettres de Malaisie* (Paris: Bibliothèque des auteurs modernes, 1908), 93.

20 Allais, in *French Utopias*, 53. See also Campanella, 97–101; Adolf Hitler, *Mein Kampf*, trans. Ralph Manheim (Boston: Houghton Mifflin, c1943), 249–50.

21 François Rabelais, *Gargantua and Pantagruel*, trans. Burton Raffel (New York: Norton, 1990), Book I, Chapter 57 ("How the Men and Women of Thélème Governed Their Lives"), 124.

22 Gilbert, 57.

23 Anatole France, "A Speech Delivered at the Festival Held in Honour of Diderot, Friend of the People, in the Salle Wagram on the 30th July, 1900," in *The Unrisen Dawn: Speeches and Addresses*, trans. J. Lewis May (London: John Lane, 1928), 40.

24 France, "An Address Delivered at the Annual Festival of the 'Soirées Ouvrières' of Montreuil-sous-Bois on 7th January, 1900," in *The Unrisen Dawn*, 17.

25 More, 102.

26 France, "A Speech Delivered at the Inaugural Celebrations of 'L'Emancipatrice,' the Communist Printing Works, on the 12th May, 1901," in *The Unrisen Dawn*, 48.

27 Moulin, 355.

28 Adam, 60.

29 Ibid., 244.

30 Ibid., 34.

31 Raymond Trousson, introduction to *Requiem pour l'utopie?: Tendances autodestructives du paradigme utopique: mélanges*, coordinated by Carmelina Imbroscio (Pisa: Libreria Goliardica, 1986), 15–16.

32 Claude Lefort, *L'invention démocratique: Les limites de la domination totalitaire* (Paris: Fayard, 1981), 98.

33 André Wurmser, "The USSR Is One Hundred Years Old," in *The Year 2017: Past, Present, and Future*, trans. from the Russian by A. Shkarovsky; ed. S. Kotlobye and L. Tetskaya (Moscow: Novosti Press Agency, 1968), 77.

34 Fidel Castro, "Communism Will Be Abundance Without Egoism: On Intellectual Property" (delivered April 29, 1967, "Year of Heroic Viet Nam"), in *Fidel Castro Speaks*, ed. Martin Kenner and James Petras (New York: Grove Press, 1969), 244.

35 Friedrich Engels, *Anti-Dühring: Herr Eugen Dühring's Revolution in Science*, 3rd ed. (Moscow: Foreign Languages Publishing House, 1962), 401.

36 Henri Lefebvre, *Le Marxisme*, 16th ed. (Paris: Presses Universitaires de France, 1974), 59.

37 Fidel Castro, *Citations de Fidel Castro*, selected by Henri de la Vega and Raphaël Sorin (Paris: Editions du Seuil, 1968), 91. See also Campanella, 39-41.

38 Ibid., 123.

39 William Morris, *News from Nowhere or An Epoch of Rest, being some chapters from a Utopian Romance* (1890), in *News from Nowhere and Selected Writings and Designs*, ed. with intro. by Asa Briggs (Harmondsworth: Penguin, 1986), 298. See also Hitler, 405–6.

40 Wurmser, 75.

41 Quoted in Louis Pauwels and Jacques Bergier, *The Morning of the Magicians*, trans. Rollo Myers (New York: Stein and Day, 1964), 195.

42 Arthur Moeller van den Bruck, *Das dritte Reich*, trans. (condensed) as *Germany's Third Empire*, trans. E. O. Lorimer; intro. Mary Agnes Hamilton (London: George Allen & Unwin, 1934), 264.

43 Hitler, 255.

44 Ibid., 404.

45 Ibid., 383–84.

46 Ibid., 296.

47 Engels, 388–89.

48 Mao Tse-tung, "Problems of Strategy in China's Revolutionary War" (December 1936), quoted in *The Thoughts of Chairman Mao Tse-tung* (London: A Gibbs, 1967), 45. See also Castro, *Citations de Fidel Castro*, 89.

49 Moeller van den Bruck, 258. See also Hitler, 287–88 and 396.

50 Hitler, 408.

51 Ibid., 255.

52 Adolf Hitler, Speech to the Tagung of German jurists, October 3, 1933, in *The Speeches of Adolf Hitler, April 1922–August 1939*, ed. Norman H. Baynes (New York: Howard Fertig, 1969), 523. See also Henri Barbusse, *Stalin: A New World Seen Through One Man*, trans. Vyvyan Holland (New York: The Macmillan Company, 1935), and Castro, *Citations de Fidel Castro*, 128.

53 Maximilien Robespierre, *Rapport sur les principes de morale politique qui doivent guider la Convention nationale dans l'administration intérieure de la République, fait au nom du Comité de salut public, le 18 [sic] pluviôse, l'an 2e de la République [February 5, 1794]* (Paris: Imprimerie nationale, n.d.), quoted in *The French Revolution*, ed. Paul H. Beik (New York: Walker and Company, 1971), 279.

54 Maximilien Robespierre, *Rapport fait un nom du Comité de salut public, par Maximilien Robespierre, sur les rapports des idées religieuses & morales avec les principes républicains, et sur les fêtes nationales. Séance du 18 floréal, l'an second de la République française une & indivisible [May 7, 1794]* (Paris: Imprimerie nationale, 1794), quoted in *The French Revolution*, 302.

55 Ibid., 310–11.

56 Benito Mussolini, "Al largo!," *Utopia* 1 (November 22, 1913): 1.

57 Hitler, 432–33, 446–47, and 448–49.

58 Moulin, 357.

59 Frédéric Rouvillois, *L'invention du progrès: Aux origines de la pensée totalitaire: (1680–1730)* (Paris: Kimé, 1996), 423 ff.

60 The Aryan "is the Prometheus of mankind" (Hitler, 290).

61 H. G. Wells, *Russia in the Shadows* (New York: George H. Doran, 1921), 162.

62 Emile Zola, *Labor*, a translation of *Travail* (New York and London: Harper & Brothers, 1901), 588.

Utopia and the Late Twentieth Century: A View from North America

FROM THE perspective of utopianism, the twentieth century has been a dialectic between utopia/good place and dystopia/bad place. The period from World War I to 2000 includes the establishment of Communist governments throughout the world and the overthrow of many of them in the late 1980s, the Great Depression of the 1930s and a cycle of "boom-and-bust" economies, the rise of fascism and National Socialism and their defeat and recent resurrection, World War II, the rejection of colonialism and numerous wars related to that rejection, the "killing fields" of Cambodia/Kampuchea, the establishment of welfare systems in both capitalist and socialist countries and the reaction against them in the 1980s and 90s, the Islamic revival, the Sixties with its explicit resurgence of utopian aspirations (including, in the United States, the Civil Rights Movement that had begun in the 1950s), the rebirth of the communal movement, and the growth of feminism. And, with the coming of the year 2000, there has been a rebirth, mostly in North America, of millenarianism.

The twentieth century is frequently thought of as an age of ideology rather than utopia, but the reality is more complex. The beginning of the century saw the continuance of the resurgence of utopian writing stimulated by *Looking Backward* (1888) by Edward Bellamy, but that is best thought of as a reflection of the end of the nineteenth century and the hopes engendered by the turn of the century.

In the United States, Bellamy had temporarily made socialism respectable as Nationalism; during the early years of the century, others insisted on its respectability and desirability. According to these writers, capitalism had run its course while producing horrifying conditions for the vast majority of the populace. Capitalism, which prides itself on the efficiency of the market, was shown to be both incredibly corrupt and very inefficient, even on its own terms. Therefore, socialist utopias were produced at a great rate during the height of American capitalism. They give one the feeling both that their authors believed deeply in socialism and that they believed that anything would be better than capitalism. The best-known author of such eutopias was Upton Sinclair, whose *Prince Hagen* (1903) showed the financial destruction of the world and a revolt

against the capitalists. This was followed by *The Industrial Republic* (1907), a standard socialist eutopia, and then *The Millennium* (1929; written in 1907), a dystopia of capitalism.

In addition to the socialist eutopias, one important prewar dystopia was published in the United States; *The Iron Heel* (1907) by Jack London was clearly the best of the American dystopias for some time to come. *The Iron Heel*, a dystopia of capitalism modeled on *The Communist Manifesto*, shows the various stages of capitalism as described by Marx and Engels. The capitalists suppress the workers while there are ever more extreme fluctuations in the economic system. This leads to a bloody revolution. The dystopia that is capitalism and the revolution are the main story of *The Iron Heel*. Hope is held out at the end that a better society will be created.

The most important writer of utopias in the early part of the century was H. G. Wells, but even in his earliest novels Wells gave a mixed message about the future by presenting both positive and negative images. His earliest works – *The Time Machine* (1895), "A Story of the Days to Come" (1899), *When the Sleeper Wakes* (1899), and *The First Men in the Moon* (serialized 1900–1901) – are dystopian. But Wells enters a hopeful period, and during this period he seems to think that it is really possible to bring about wholesale change and produce a better future and does not include his, or at least as many of his, usual caveats. This period falls roughly between his two greatest eutopias, *A Modern Utopia* (serialized 1904–5) and *Men Like Gods* (serialized 1922–23), and includes *The World Set Free* (serialized 1913–14). During this period, Wells neither seems as impatient as usual nor sounds as desperate as he did before and will again. For example, in *Mankind in the Making* (1903), he writes, "the serious aspect of our private lives, the general aspect of all our social and co-operative undertakings, is to prepare as well as we possibly can a succeeding generation, which shall prepare still more capably for still better generations to follow."[1]

The intellectual turn of the century was World War I and the successful Bolshevik revolution in Russia. While World War I produced a widespread loss of hope, the Russian Revolution produced hope followed, for many, by rapid disillusionment.

For others the hope remained, but the disillusionment combined with the hopelessness produced by the war led to the creation of the modern dystopia, its first manifestation being *We* by Evgenii Zamiatin/Yevgeny Zamyatin, an explicit attack on Soviet communism but also satirizing the time management systems developed by industrial capitalism. Two other exceptional dystopias followed: *Brave New World* (1932) by Aldous Huxley, an attack on the consumption ethos of capitalism, and *Nineteen Eighty-four* (1949) by George Orwell (born Eric Blair), a general attack on totalitarianism. Huxley reinforced the negative message by publishing a "Foreword" to the 1946 edition of his book and *Brave New World Revisited* in 1958, in which he argued that the dystopia described in *Brave New World* was approaching much faster than he had expected. These three dystopias gained sufficient recognition that many people came to believe that the eutopia had disappeared. While this is far from the case, it is true that neither popular nor scholarly commentary paid much attention to the eutopia from World War I to the 1960s.

There were obviously good reasons for focusing on the dystopia, rather than the eutopia. As mentioned above, a century of almost constant war, one major depression and a recurring boom-and-bust cycle, the loss of colonies and the resultant need for many nations to rearrange their self-perception, the concentration camps and gulags, the "killing fields" of Cambodia, and so on and so on illustrate that the twentieth century deserves its reputation as the dystopian century.

In the United States, the period known as the McCarthy Era – named after Senator Joseph McCarthy, the focal point of the hunt for real and imagined subversives in American life – was the peak of the anti-Communist crusade that dominated the dystopian dreams of a generation. Many novels were published depicting a Soviet-dominated future as a means to rally people to the cause. Groups like the Minutemen armed themselves to withstand the expected invasion. Measures like "The Communist Control Act of 1954" (68 Stat. 775 [1954]) were passed to limit the rights of individuals and groups thought to be sympathetic to Communism. The John Birch Society was formed to identify such people (Chief Justice of the Supreme Court Earl Warren was a major target) and to provide a cadre of people throughout both the economic and political systems to offset the Communist threat. Together with many of the other organizations formed at the time, the John Birch Society is still active.

But, for all the horrors, for many people the twentieth century was also, at least at times, one of hope. While many dystopias were written about collectivism, so were many eutopias.

The Twentieth-century Dialectic Between Eutopia and Dystopia

The eutopian hopes of social movements have been brought into being as dystopias and then overthrown by the belief in a new eutopia. The most obvious case is communism, in which the dream of a classless society – reflected in many literary eutopias and satirized in many literary dystopias – is actualized in authoritarian regimes that are overthrown in part based on the belief in the eutopia of the free market. In addition, National Socialism and the movements for rights for the poor, women, and racial, sexual, and ethnic minorities have produced both eutopias and dystopias.

The communal movement, which had never entirely disappeared (the kibbutz movement in Israel began in the 1920s), was revived in the twentieth century. Until the revival of the Sixties, these communities were frequently called "utopian" communities. Today they are mostly called intentional communities, but many members of these communities explicitly connect them to utopianism, and a number of communities (such as Twin Oaks and East Wind in the United States and Los Horcones in Mexico) explicitly drew their inspiration from *Walden Two* (1948) by B. F. Skinner. All three are still in existence, and Twin Oaks is over thirty years old.

The Sixties

The one period in which a positive view of the future seemed to dominate was the period we call the Sixties (roughly 1965–75). Many of the movements and issues initially brought forth during the Sixties are still on the political map, although often in significantly different forms.

The closest that the United States has come to having a meaningful left was the so-called New Left of the Sixties. The New Left advocated a system of decentralized, participatory democracy that was spelled out in the "Port Huron Statement" of 1962:

We would replace power rooted in possession, privilege, or circumstance by power and uniqueness rooted in love, reflectiveness, reason, and creativity. As a social system we seek the establishment of a democracy of individual participation, governed by two central aims: that the individual share in those social decisions determining the quality and direction of his life; that society be organized to encourage independence in men and provide the media for their common participation.[2]

The symbolic year of the Sixties was 1968. While '68 is less of a symbol in the United States than in France, it was still important there. In the latter part of the century, a divergence occurs because the effects of the Sixties are very different in France and the U.S. France came to the brink of revolution and backed off. Since then it has oscillated between the center-right and the center-left, while trying to deal with a growing challenge from the far right. The United States came nowhere near revolution, but the combined effects of Vietnam, the Civil Rights Movement, the assassinations of John F. and Robert F. Kennedy, Martin Luther King, Jr., and Malcolm X (born Malcolm Little), among others, produced profound changes in the country together with an ongoing backlash against those changes. Some of the backlash uses themes very similar to that of the far right in France. The United States has not had a serious left whereas France has had one.

The New Left was briefly influential but split into factions when both African Americans and women came to resent the dominance of white men and when tactical disputes and struggles for power among the white men divided the movement. Many New Left activists migrated to more narrowly focused movements: initially, the antiwar movement; later, the anti-nuclear weapons and power movements; and then various aspects of the environmental movement. Other activists became involved in the political process, either running for office, working on campaigns for candidates or issues, or working in some capacity within the bureaucracy. Some brought their earlier utopianism with them; others lost it.

The popular French wall painting, translated in North America as "Be Realistic, Demand the Impossible," is a fitting symbol of the period and its connection to utopianism, the impossible. In the United States, the most explicit statement of the call to integrate utopia into political life was Martin Luther King, Jr.'s "I Have a Dream" speech of 1963. Harking back to the Declaration of Independence, King said, "I have a dream that one day this nation will rise up and live out the true meaning of its creed: 'We hold these truths to be self-evident: that all men are created equal.'" King's speech was the utopian high point in the struggle of an oppressed minority for the rights supposedly guaranteed them in the U.S. Constitution.

There was a significant revival of the positive utopia (see the essay by Kumar in this volume, pp.

251–67) and a resurgence of communal experimentation (see the essay by Oved in this volume, pp. 268–77). The Sixties were brought about by a reaction against the 1950s and the war in Vietnam and by the birth control pill and LSD, but politically they were a continuation of movements that emerged in the 50s. The U.S. Civil Rights Movement, and the abortive revolts against the Soviet Union, beginning in the German Democratic Republic (East Germany) in 1953 followed by Hungary in 1956, helped create the politics of the Sixties. Both these movements reached their peak in the Sixties, as did the student rebellion. In 1968, both the anti-Soviet movement (particularly around the Soviet invasion of Czechoslovakia that year) and the student movement (particularly in France) came to a peak.

The Frankfurt School, and particularly Herbert Marcuse, contributed much to the intellectual analysis of and support for the various movements. Marcuse's *Essay on Liberation* (1969) is often treated as a utopia.

There was a deep divide in the Sixties between political activism and withdrawal into drugs, sex, and/or rural communes. While some communes, mostly but not entirely urban, served as "safe houses" for activists, many activists vilified those who retreated to the countryside, and most of those who joined communes stressed that they wanted their utopia *now* and were not interested in working to free others at some future date.

The people who came to be known as hippies descended from the beatniks or beats (from "beatific"), the dropouts of the 1950s. The beats are best known through *On the Road* (1957) by Jack Kerouac. The long poem *Howl* (1956) by Allen Ginsberg shows the rage and despair at America as dystopia that led to so many dropping out. Kerouac's less well-known novel *The Dharma Bums* (1958), and *Beat Zen, Square Zen, and Zen* (1959) by Alan Watts, reflect the centrality of Oriental religion to the beat ethos and illustrate that there was a positive side to the beats. For example, the poet Gary Snyder, one of the central characters in *The Dharma Bums*, became a leading figure in the environmental movement.

The beats saw America primarily as a dystopia that was probably incapable of improvement and responded by retreating into sex, drugs, and religion. The hippies saw America as possibly irretrievably dystopian but responded either by working to overthrow the dystopia by revolutionary action or by withdrawing into a rapidly growing communal movement.

Stranger in a Strange Land (1961; uncut edition first published in 1991) by Robert A. Heinlein was

"I have a dream"

The march on Washington, D.C., in August 1963 marked the climax of the Civil Rights movement in America. Officially called the "1963 March on Washington for Jobs and Freedom," the demonstration was organized to support the United States Civil Rights Act, which Congress was debating at the time. The Act was signed the following year by President Lyndon B. Johnson.

From the steps of the Lincoln Memorial, Dr. Martin Luther King, Jr., addressed the racially mixed crowd of 250,000 people with his "I Have a Dream" speech, proclaiming: "I have a dream that one day this nation will rise up and live out the true meaning of its creed: 'We hold these truths to be self-evident, that all men are created equal.'" Widely televised and printed in newspapers nationwide, the speech quickly became one of the most famous in American history.

Bert Miles
[Bird's-eye view of the
March on Washington,
D.C., 1963]
Silver gelatin print, 1963
NYPL, Schomburg Center for
Research in Black Culture,
Photographs and Prints Division

**Bert Miles
[Martin Luther King, Jr.,
speaking at the March on
Washington, D.C., 1963]**
Silver gelatin print, 1963
NYPL, Schomburg Center for
Research in Black Culture,
Photographs and Prints Division

the eutopia most reflective of hippie values. In *Stranger*, Heinlein stresses the revolutionary potential of a freed sexuality that, while primarily heterosexual, crosses genders and includes all ages. He also emphasizes the desirability of communal living.

While it is impossible to assign priority precisely, one of the first North American communes, and certainly the best known of the early communities, was Drop City, founded in Colorado in 1965 by a group of young artists interested in Oriental religion and psychedelic drugs. But it later became the symbolic "open" community, leaderless and welcoming all comers. It lasted until 1973. Hundreds, perhaps thousands, of communities followed, and many thousands of young Americans spent at least part of their youth in such a community. Quite a few of the communities founded during this period still exist. Of these, Twin Oaks in Virginia is the best known.

A number of communities were founded with the stated intent of pushing the limits of sexual relations. The best known was the Kerista community in San Francisco, which practiced a form of group marriage that encouraged each individual to have sexual relations with all members of a defined subgroup on a set, rotating basis. An offshoot of Kerista still exists.

The concern with sexual freedom found in both the fiction and the communities was a reflection of the "sexual revolution" brought about largely by the ready availability of birth control, particularly the birth control pill, which, for the first time, clearly gave women the power to control pregnancy.

Over time, the negative aspects of this revolution, combined with AIDS and a growing concern with technological solutions to problems (the pill and other manufactured birth control devices), diminished the impact of the sexual revolution, but at present it appears fair to say that sexual relations have changed permanently. In addition, the easy availability of birth control methods brought the hope that it might be possible to control the boom in worldwide population that produced many dystopian visions of overcrowded future earths. One of the best of these, *Stand on Zanzibar* (1968) by John Brunner, depicts the utter inability of both natural and social systems to cope with the rapidity of population growth. While such dystopias are currently published less frequently, the problem has not gone away, and in the 1990s there appeared to be a resurgence of concern with the issue.

Even though many communities remain, the hippies gradually faded from the scene, having contributed significantly to mid-twentieth-century utopianism. One movement in which the hippies' ideas have been perpetuated, in combination with various popular therapy systems, is the New Age. While the hippies were clearly focused on community, and although there are some New Age communes (Findhorn in Scotland is the best known), the New Age stresses personal transformation.

Feminism

Some women, initially energized by the publication in France in 1949 of *Le Deuxième Sexe* (published in English in 1952 as *The Second Sex*) by Simone de Beauvoir and *The Feminine Mystique* (1963) by Betty Friedan and disgusted by their treatment within the radical movements of the time, became aware that they were also denied equality. The resulting feminist movement has produced the strongest current of late-twentieth-century utopianism. One of the most important aspects of the early women's movement was the establishment of "consciousness-raising" groups, small groups of women who met throughout Europe and North America to discuss their situations. Besides teaching them that they shared things they had not expected, these groups created communities of women who became and have remained active socially and politically.

In North America, the most important utopian novels produced by feminism have been *The Left Hand of Darkness* (1969), *The Dispossessed* (1974), and *Always Coming Home* (1985) by Ursula K. Le Guin, *The Female Man* (1975) by Joanna Russ, *Woman on the Edge of Time* (1976) by Marge Piercy, and *The Handmaid's Tale* (1985) by the Canadian author Margaret Atwood. With the exception of *The Handmaid's Tale*, which is a dystopia, these novels are examples of a new type of utopia, most often called the "critical utopia," which presents a society that has both positive and negative features.

For a time, the critical utopia became the norm, at least among the best utopian literature, and more recently a similar complexity is being seen in the dystopia. For example, *He, She and It* (1991; U.K. edition as *Body of Glass* [1992]) by Marge Piercy presents a dystopia that still manages to include at least two eutopian enclaves.

The recognition of discrimination throughout American society against African Americans, women, Hispanics, and gay men and lesbians led to both the realization of a dystopian reality and the desire for a eutopian future encompassing an equality that recognizes differences. This issue has dominated the last part of the twentieth century and continues to be the focus of debates on how to create a truly multicultural society. Of course, there are many who oppose such a utopia and see it as a dystopia to be avoided. In utopian literature, the best-known author dealing with these issues is Samuel R. Delany, an African American homosexual whose novels *Dhalgren* (1975) and *Triton* (1976) are examples of the critical utopia.[3]

Anarchism

Another result of 1968 was the revival of anarchism. The black flag of anarchism was carried through the streets of Paris during the demonstrations there, and the Situationists in France and the Kabouters in the Netherlands both drew explicit connections between their ideas and anarchism. In North America, a peculiarly American version of anarchism, anarcho-capitalism, was given a modern voice by Ayn Rand (born Alissa Rosenbaum), particularly in *Atlas Shrugged* (1957). Followers of Rand were active in the early political career of Ronald Reagan, and the Chairman of the Federal Reserve and arguably one of the most powerful men in the United States, Alan Greenspan, was a supporter. *Anarchy, State and Utopia* (1974) by Robert Nozick is the most intellectually rigorous statement of anarcho-capitalism and refers to Rand's inspiration.

Anarchism in the dominant collectivist tradition was restated in the United States by Ursula K. Le Guin in her story "The Day Before the Revolution" (1974), which served as an introduction to her novel *The Dispossessed: An Ambiguous Utopia* (1974), which presents a flawed but definitely utopian anarchist society. Peter Kropotkin and Emma Goldman were Le Guin's direct inspiration.

Other writers, particularly feminists, also published descriptions of anarchist societies;[4] Le Guin and Marge Piercy were the most important of these writers.

Technology

For most people, the most important changes in their lives, negative and positive, in the twentieth century have been brought about by technology.[5] From the automobile to the computer, birth control to population growth, pollution to the green movement, the daily lives of people have been influenced by technological change and attempts to both enhance and counter the impact of such changes. And utopianism has played a role in both supporting the desirability of technology and criticizing its effects.

The split over technology can be represented within feminist utopianism. In Marge Piercy's *Woman on the Edge of Time*, children are born in "brooders" to free women from pregnancy, and men are adapted to breastfeed. She says,

"It was part of women's long revolution. When we were breaking all the old hierarchies. Finally there was that one thing we had to give up too, the only power we ever had, in turn for no more power for anyone. The original production: the power to give birth. 'Cause as long as we were biologically enchained, we'd never be equal. And males would never be humanized to be loving and tender. So we all became mothers. To break the nuclear bonding."[6]

These words are among the most controversial parts of the novel.

Alternatively, *The Kin of Ata Are Waiting for You* (1976; originally published as *The Comforter* [1971]) by Dorothy Bryant presents a society with no technology. Ata is an agricultural society controlled by the people's dreams and is among the least technological of modern feminist utopias.

Environmentalism

Even the book that gave the environmental utopia its name, *Ecotopia* (1975) by Ernest Callenbach, used technology within its environmentally focused society. A good example is the train that the protagonist travels on after he first enters Ecotopia.

I went down to my train. It looked more like a wingless airplane than a train. At first I thought I had gotten into an unfinished car – there were no seats: The floor was covered with thick spongy carpet, and divided into compartments by knee-high partitions; a few passengers were sprawled on large baglike leather cushions that lay scattered about. One elderly man had taken a blanket from a pile at one end of the car, and laid down for a nap. Some of the others, realizing from my confusion that I was a foreigner, showed me where to stow my bag and told me how to obtain refreshments from the steward in the next car. I sat down on one of the pillows, realizing that there would be a good view from the huge windows that came down to about six inches from the floor. . . .

By the time you notice you are underway in an Ecotopian train, you feel virtually no movement at all. Since it operates by magnetic suspension and propulsion, there is no rumble of wheels or whine or vibration. People talk, there is the clink of glasses and teacups, some passengers wave to friends on the platform. In a moment the train seems literally to be flying along the ground, though it is actually a few inches above a trough-shaped guideway.[7]

Terra Nueva

Donald E. Janzen
Terra Nueva CoHousing
Oceano, California (San Luis Obispo
County), July 21, 1999
Photograph, color print made from
slide
Donald E. Janzen Collection

Terra Nueva CoHousing is a
cluster of twenty-seven solar-
powered housing units built
around a common house and
gardens. A combination of private and public spaces, it was
founded in 1988 with the
intent to create a stronger
sense of community and connection between neighbors
than traditional housing plans
allow. It is open to anyone
willing to make the commitment to the CoHousing
lifestyle. Community decisions
are made by consensus at
weekly business meetings,
and smaller committees meet
regularly about more specific
topics including community
social life, legal matters, and
outreach.

Palace of Gold

Donald E. Janzen
New Vrindaban
Moundsville, West Virginia
(Marshall County), October 1, 1994
Photograph, color print made from
slide
Donald E. Janzen Collection

This temple, the "Palace of
Gold," stands at the center of
a community of Hare Krishnas
in West Virginia called New
Vrindaban. Constructed over a
seven-year period by devotees
who also created the paintings, marble work, and stained
glass that occur throughout, it
is dedicated to the founder of
the Hare Krishnas, A. C. Bhak-
tivedanta, also called Swami
Prabhupada.

The Hare Krishnas, formally
known as the International
Society for Krishna Consciousness, have numerous temples
and communities around the
world. Each temple community is self-supporting and self-
governing. Hare Krishnas (the
name derives from the community's mantra, meaning
"Oh Lord Krishna") wear
Hindu dress and practice
devotional yoga (bhakti-yoga)
and ritual chanting to achieve
spiritual purification. Religious
enthusiasm is encouraged and
members must follow strict
rules against gambling, extra-
marital sexual relations, eating
meat, fish, and eggs, and
intoxicants of all kinds, including drugs, alcohol, coffee, tea,
and cigarettes.

Walden Two

Donald E. Janzen
Twin Oaks
West Virginia, March 2000
Photograph, color print made from
slide
Donald E. Janzen Collection

Twin Oaks is an intentional
community of about eighty
people living on 456 acres of
farm and forest land in rural
Virginia. One of the longest-
lived and most prominent
intentional communities in the
United States, Twin Oaks was
founded in 1967 on the principles expounded in B. F. Skinner's novel, *Walden Two*
(1948). Skinner imagined a
community where behavior
was conditioned and sound
social structures would
encourage a smoothly functioning society. Many of his
proposals have been adopted
with some modifications. For
example, Twin Oaks residents
have created an economy
based on labor credits rather
than money. Members choose
their schedules and types of
work and accrue credits based
on the number of hours they
work. Possible jobs include
income-producing activities,
like hammock making and
book indexing, and jobs that
keep the community running
smoothly, such as childcare,
cooking, and farm chores. The
community is run as a democracy, with rotating planners,
managers, and committees,
and all community decisions
are voted upon, including
issues such as the admission
of new members, and
whether members may have
or adopt children. Cooperation,
sharing, nonviolence, equality,
tolerance, and ecology are the
stated values of Twin Oaks.

Familyism

Donald E. Janzen
Padanaram Settlement
Williams, Indiana (Lawrence
County), May 23, 1992
Photograph, color print made from
slide
Donald E. Janzen Collection

Padanaram is a spiritual,
agricultural community of two
hundred people living on 2,400
acres in rural Indiana. Founded
in 1966, the community practices "familyism," in which
small nuclear families live
separately within the larger
communal family, share three
meals a day, and work together as equals doing household
chores, farming, weaving,
and sawmilling. Once a week
there is a communal "rap"
session as well as a communal worship. Members of
Padanaram adhere to five
principles: "(1) As one would
that others do, do unto them.
(2) Hold all things in common,
count nothing one's own.
(3) Distribution to each according to the need. (4) Of one
who has much, much is
required. (5) One that won't
work, shall not eat."

Trains are generally considered to be more environmentally friendly than cars and appear in a number of environmental eutopias, but saying that ignores the fact that trains must be produced and that the manufacture of trains is not environmentally friendly.

A better example of an environmentally concerned utopia is Piercy's *Woman on the Edge of Time*. To the protagonist Connie Ramos, the society seems primitive. "She saw . . . a river, little no account buildings, strange structures like long-legged birds with sails that turned in the wind, a few large terracotta and yellow buildings and one blue dome, irregular buildings, none bigger than a supermarket in her day, an ordinary supermarket in any shopping plaza. The bird objects were the tallest things around and they were scarcely higher than some of the pine trees she could see. A few lumpy free-form structures with green vines."[8]

The "bird objects" are windmills. The future has as part of its past a few of our disasters, nuclear and otherwise. The world is still recovering from our farming methods and our pollution. No one in the future would ask another person to go down into mines to get coal or metals. Human life and health are more important than what the mines could provide and substitutes will just have to be found or the resources done without.

The stress on technological solutions has most recently been expressed in the Mars trilogy – *Red Mars* (1993), *Green Mars* (1994), and *Blue Mars* (1996) – by Kim Stanley Robinson, in which the planet Mars is terraformed to make it livable by humans and a eutopia is created in the process. The technology required for this positive result is most often used these days to produce a negative result. A supplementary volume, *The Martians* (1999), includes "The Martian Constitution," which includes restrictions on the extent of terraforming and states that "The primal state of Mars shall have legal consideration. . . ."[9] Thus, one of the most technological of recent eutopias is also sensitive to the environment of the place it is transforming.

Intentional Communities and Environmentalism – Communitarians have responded to environmental issues by developing the eco-village movement, currently headquartered in Germany.[10] The idea behind the eco-village movement is to create small communities (or even areas within large cities) that are sensitive to the ecology of the area and environmentally sustainable.

Environmental Politics – In North America, the environmental movement has taken a different approach than in Europe. Most North American environmentalism is quite conservative by European standards, and because the U.S. political system discourages new political parties, no explicitly green political party has been formed.

But Greenpeace was initially established in 1971 in Canada; followers of the Norwegian philosopher Arne Naess, who coined the term "Deep Ecology," have created a direct action group with anarchist elements called Earth First!; and Murray Bookchin is a leading theorist of environmentalism and a well-known anarchist theorist. Thus, a small but active radical wing of environmentalism does exist in North America, and these radical activists are explicitly utopian. Most recently, the North American animal rights movement has begun to copy the direct action tactics of the British movement. The advocates of Deep Ecology and animal rights argue for a complete revolution in attitude, saying that human beings must be thought of as equal partners in the biosphere with animals and plants and that humans should not be privileged in any way. Whether this particular vision is eutopian or dystopian is open to debate.

Theodore J. Kaczynski, known as the "Unabomber," published a manifesto in which he said, "The Industrial Revolution and its consequences have been a disaster for the human race." He advocated a revolution "to overthrow not governments but the economic and technological basis of the present society."[11] Kaczynski represents a neo-Luddite response to modern technology that, while backward looking, is clearly utopian.

Aspects of Contemporary Utopianism
Turn-of-the-Century Millenarianism – The coming of the millennium produced a religious revival of sorts, and this revival produced both negative and positive responses. Many believers expected that the world would come to an end at the end of 1999, and they have written books describing the coming of the Antichrist and the troubles that will follow.[12] Some religious communities also looked forward to the coming end of the world and planned for the turmoil around the end.

Israel expelled a number of groups who were visiting the country in expectation of the Second Coming. In the United States, the Federal Bureau of Investigation (FBI) warned cities to expect attempts at social disruption at the end of the century.

The Utopianism of the Far Right – While the right usually criticizes the left for its utopian aspirations, the last part of the century saw explicit utopianism from the far right.[13] The most famous novel of the right in America is *The Turner Diaries* (1978) by William L. Pierce writing as Andrew Macdonald. It is a depiction of a future race war in the United States and is thus mostly dystopian, but there is, from the author's perspective, a eutopian ending after the victory of the white race. The extreme right in America sees *The Turner Diaries* as its *Mein Kampf*. A number of extremist groups have established communes, most notably The Aryan Nations in Idaho. In these communities, of which there are dozens throughout the United States, members are able to practice their beliefs with minimal outside interference.

Y2K – We now know that the so-called Y2K problem has not produced the catastrophe and resulting dystopia that many expected. Some people joined or created isolated, self-sufficient communes to avoid the disaster some believed would follow the collapse of the world's computer network and the power failures and even nuclear explosions they expected would follow.

The Internet as Utopia – In contrast to those who expected the worldwide computer system to bring about the end of civilization, there are many who see the Internet and the World Wide Web as providing the basis of a utopian future. At one level, the utopian potential of the Internet is seen in its ability to re-create "town meetings" in which people from the entire community can discuss issues and vote directly on them, supplanting representative government. On November 8, 1999, the President of the United States answered questions over the Internet from anyone who logged on during the time period. At a much broader level, the Internet's utopian potential is seen in the possibility of creating community across geography, race, gender, age, etc., among those online. The capacities of computer networks have thus far been used as much for dystopian crime, sexual harassment, and the sponsorship of hate as for community-building, thus illustrating the continued utopian and dystopian potential of technology.

Conclusion

So far I have identified approximately 360 utopias (eutopias, dystopias, utopian satires, and critical utopias and dystopias) published by U.S. authors from 1990 to 1999. Preliminary analysis of the literature suggests that religion is one of the main themes of these works, particularly the ones published by the more obscure publishers. A few describe the eutopian visions of the far right. A number describe eutopian visions from a gay male perspective; these works are a recent addition to the many lesbian

eutopias published during the period. Communes exist reflecting all these positions.

Thus, it is clear that as we begin the new millennium, utopianism is not merely alive and well but flourishing. The symbolic year 2000 has probably added slightly but not significantly to the production of utopias, but the number of communes has not changed in any major way. Roughly the same number are being created or disappearing as in the past; there are currently at least 1,500 communes in the United States, and certainly that many more in other countries. These phenomena and the other expressions of utopianism suggest that humanity's penchant to dream of better and worse lives and to act on those dreams, which has been so much a part of our history, will be around for another exhibition in the year 3000.

Notes

1 H. G. Wells, *Mankind in the Making* (London: Chapman & Hall, 1903), 20.

2 Students for a Democratic Society, *The Port Huron Statement*, Appendix in James Miller, *"Democracy Is in the Street": From Port Huron to the Siege of Chicago* (Cambridge, Mass.: Harvard University Press, 1994), 333.

3 On the critical utopia, see Tom Moylan, *Demand the Impossible* (London: Methuen, 1986).

4 See my "A New Anarchism: Social and Political Ideas in Some Recent Feminist Eutopias," pp. 3–33 in *Women and Utopia: Critical Interpretations*, ed. Marleen Barr and Nicholas D. Smith (Lanham, Md.: University Press of America, 1983).

5 On technology and American utopianism and the beginning of the century, see Howard P. Segal, *Technological Utopianism in American Culture* (Chicago: University of Chicago Press, 1985).

6 Marge Piercy, *Woman on the Edge of Time* (London: Women's Pres, 1979), 105.

7 Ernest Callenbach, *Ecotopia* (Berkeley, Calif.: Banyan Tree Books, 1975), 7–8.

8 Piercy, 68.

9 Kim Stanley Robinson, *The Martians* (New York: Bantam Books, 1999), 231.

10 See Barbro Grindheim and Declan Kennedy, eds., *Directory of Eco-villages in Europe* (Steyerberg, Germany: Global Eco-village Network (GEN)–Europe, 1998).

11 An excerpt can be found in Lyman Tower Sargent, ed., *Political Thought in the United States: A Documentary History* (New York: New York University Press, 1997), 427–28.

12 See, for example, Marlin Maddoux, *The Seal of Gaia: A Novel of the Antichrist* (Nashville, Tenn.: Word Publishing, 1998).

13 See Lyman Tower Sargent, ed., *Extremism in America: A Reader* (New York: New York University Press, 1995) for documents from a variety of far right and left groups.

 343

Utopia and the Late Twentieth Century: A View from North America

Summer of Love

The photographs on these pages were taken between 1965 and 1967 in the Haight-Ashbury neighborhood of San Francisco, near Golden Gate Park. For fifteen months, photographer Gene Anthony captured the celebratory air of the hippie community and its flower children by documenting the be-ins, concerts, happenings, neighborhood fairs, festivals, and street life. Together, his photographs create a portrait of a time when drugs, music, free love, meditation, vegetarianism, and radical activism were the paths to enlightenment, everything in modern society was up for questioning, and anything could be accomplished with enough love. These photographs were eventually published in a 1980 book, *The Summer of Love: Haight-Ashbury at Its Highest.*

The album cover at the lower right is typical of the psychedelic art of this period.

Gene Anthony
***A gathering of people
in the panhandle***
Silver gelatin print,
[San Francisco, 1965–67?]
California Historical Society,
Photography Collection

above

Gene Anthony
***Two 1960s youths whose
appearance typifies
the hippie movement***
Silver gelatin print,
[San Francisco, 1965–67?]
California Historical Society,
Photography Collection

above right

Gene Anthony
***A laughing youth with
painted face frolics
at the Human Be-In***
Silver gelatin print,
[San Francisco, January 14, 1967]
California Historical Society,
Photography Collection

Inner Utopia

Cream
Disraeli Gears
Atco, 1967
Cover design by Martin Sharp
The New York Public Library
for the Performing Arts,
Rodgers & Hammerstein
Archives of Recorded Sound

Françoise Choay

Utopia and the Philosophical Status of Constructed Space

UTOPIA, A proper noun coined by Thomas More and launched by him into the universe of the printed word in 1516, met with an immediate and extraordinary popularity. Before the end of the sixteenth century, the proper noun had passed into common usage and had come to designate a specific literary genre, its paradigm provided by More's book.

For nearly five hundred years, the word has followed a tortuous course, along which, by countless approximate associations and analogies, its contours have been altered, assuming new and frequently rather vague social, futuristic, and oneiric connotations. Yet such semantic variations and the aleatory life of languages do not suffice to account for the vitality of the term "utopia" nor for the periodic revivals of utopian literature at certain critical junctures of Western history – at the end of the eighteenth century, as well as at the beginning and at the end of the nineteenth – nor for the renewed interest the notion of utopia has provoked in the year 2000, to which the present exhibition, mounted jointly by the Bibliothèque nationale de France and The New York Public Library, attests.

I propose to show here that the utopian project is more topical than ever, as much by its conception of space as by the logic generating that conception: two dimensions that I shall attempt to locate within a general anthropological context. And More's seminal text will serve as the starting point for my presentation and discussion of contemporary problems.

Thomas More and Space

Whenever More mentions his book in his correspondence, he refers to it as "my Utopia," and in the course of successive editions and translations, all that has remained of the original lengthy title[1] is the name of the island. This name, derived from the Greek *topos* ("place"), is qualified by the prefix *U*-, understood by More as a contraction of the negating *ou*- ("non-place") and as the adjective *eu*- ("good-" or "right-place"). Space therefore has been designated as the book's subject from the start, albeit in an antinomic form. And this shortened title becomes emblematic, for as we shall see, space and antinomy establish the dynamic of the text.

Before proceeding, let us for the record briefly review the work's form and themes. In a circum-stantial narrative, More describes his diplomatic mission to Flanders, his encounter with an unknown traveler, Raphael Hythlodaeus, and his long exchange with the latter concerning politics and English society, in the company of the humanist Peter Giles. It is in the course of this allegedly factual account, with its arsenal of semantic and formal devices, that More describes the island of Utopia and the model society inhabiting it.

Yet this model society, as Raphael has discovered and describes it, does not come out of nowhere: on the one hand, it is inseparable from a radical and uncompromising critique of an existing society – in this case England, of which it constitutes the antithesis; on the other hand, the functioning of its institutions depends on the establishment of a model constructed space. In other words, an existing society under criticism, a model society, and a model space are the three interdependent terms that constitute the utopian genre. If a critical approach generates the conception of Utopia, constructed space is the instrument of its realization, and of the transformation of a vicious society into a virtuous one. The spatial model (which, as we discover around the middle of the description of the island, was long ago conceived by a certain Utopus) is presented to the reader from the start, before the institutions it served to establish and stabilize. Raphael describes "in order, the terrain, the rivers, the *cities*, the inhabitants, the traditions, the customs, the laws."[2]

The priority given to this spatial configuration emphasizes the importance More assigns it in the functioning of human societies. Of course Plato, in *Laws* and *Critias*, had already attributed to constructed space the stabilizing role of *pharmakon*[3] in the foundation of colonies and of new societies. But given its discredited status with regard to the ontological truth of the world of ideas, Plato evokes the spatial configuration only as a complementary means, after the institutions it might support. Thomas More, on the contrary and for the first time, proclaims the efficiency and real value of a model constructed space, that of the cities of Utopia, such space becoming the very pivot of his essay.

Yet the status of this space is less simple than it appears. In the traveler's eyes, its uniformity and its standardization contrast from the first with the particularity and the diversity of the island's natural space, the original form of which – the rugged and craggy coastal perimeter, as well as the hilly terrain – permits the reader to recognize it as a version of England. In contrast, the cities of Utopia, uniformly 24 miles apart, are identical in layout and limited size, as well as in the standardized configuration of their streets, staircases, temples, and houses. "The person who knows one of the cities will know them all."[4] This urban configuration permits no extraordinary or whimsical feature. Rationalized and subject to geometry, its function is to ensure the equality of all the cities, to compel each citizen to occupy his own place and to play his part within the community, assuring and reminding everyone at all times of the operation of those domestic, economic, and religious institutions that establish social coherence. At first sight there is no relation between Utopia's physical geography and the space its inhabitants have constructed under the direction of Utopus. Constructed space is superimposed upon natural space, negating the latter's differences and extending the isotropic arrangement of its surface: a grid that offers a certain prefiguration of today's technological networks which blanket territories with an absolute disregard for cultural, natural, and local features.

A closer reading of Raphael's description shows that there is, occasionally, a surreptitious link, only faintly suggested and immediately occulted, which seems to contradict the absolute autonomy of the two kinds of space: the plan of the capital, Amaurotum, is not a perfect square but "almost perfect"; its surrounding wall is not continuous, because of its geographical position, and certain sophisticated hydraulic devices have been required by the conformation of the terrain.

In More's Utopia, the role of constructed space counterpoints that of time. As it happens, the perfection of model space eliminates temporality in favor of a quasi-eternity. Spatial configuration not only ensures the identical reproduction of institutional functioning; it consecrates the permanent presence of utopian society in a transparency everywhere evident, proceeding through the winding streets from the syphogrant's table to the temple's interior. Constant maintenance and repair also guarantee the permanence of the spatial grid, safeguarding it from any alteration.

But this non-history, the constant instantaneity of this motionless society, is not given from the start. It is the consequence of a radical transformation achieved only in the course of time, within a certain history. The *deus ex machina* to which it must

be imputed, according to the archives of Utopia, is the heroic statesman and builder who gave his name to the island: Utopus. It was he who, as a result of an unprecedented project and of enormous labor, separated the territory from the mainland of which it was once a part, and on this island achieved the modern plan of Utopia. Utopus's creative time cannot be separated from technological progress, entirely absent from the island according to Hythlodaeus's descriptions of it. Just as the invention of the compass and the perfection of the caravel enabled Raphael to cross the seas and discover an unknown world and society, and just as the invention of the printing press allows him to communicate his discovery to the known world, so it was Utopus's mastery of technology that permitted him to create an artificial island and to equip it with complex hydraulic works.

Evidently space and time are deployed in More's text according to homologous and interrelated modalities. The two superimposed, autonomous, and unconnected spaces correspond to two antinomic relations with time: on the one hand, immersion in a mundane and historical time and, on the other hand, a break with time, the historical epoch in which Utopus performed his labors having no more relation to utopian eternity than Utopia's local landscape has with its isotropic urban configuration. Similarly, the island still presents the aleatory and unavowed traces of an organic time and of a certain history: Utopus has left to his successors the task – to him, inessential – of decorating cities and houses, and the memory lingers of the huts that preceded the present-day comfortable dwellings.

Utopia as Mythic Form

The foregoing analysis attests to the founding role More attributed to constructed space in the institutionalization of human societies. Since antiquity, in a tradition extending from Lucretius and Ovid to Vitruvius, etiological narratives had traced the origins of architecture and of building to those of society, until Alberti splendidly inverted their relationship and proposed building as the origin and cause of the state of society.[5] Thomas More, however, is less concerned by the etiology of constructed space than by its corrective or orthopedic power. Yet, contrary to Plato (to the degree that these authors can be compared at all), More does not conceive this power as restoring an ancient and lost social order, but rather as establishing an unprecedented new order.

At the same time, it becomes apparent that the theme of the spatial model is inscribed in a text marked by the antinomy its title proclaims. In them, More posits and multiplies antinomies: life within time and life outside of time, individual freedom and conformity to the norm, innovation and tradition, inauguration and replication. More does not attempt to transcend these antinomies by seeking middle terms: he resolves them by intervention of the hero Utopus and of his quasi-magical plan, which simultaneously establishes a radical change and radically blocks its further development. The text of *Utopia* operates in the same way and performs the same function as myth according to Claude Lévi-Strauss's definition:[6] it is a means of symbolically resolving antinomies, contradictions, or unthinkable and unmanageable conflicts by enclosing them in the foliated structure of a narrative. In this instance such a structure is most apparent in the grand *mise-en-scène* of Raphael's description of Utopia, but it also underlies this description, though in a masked fashion, in a kind of counterpoint.[7] However, unlike an authentic myth, always transmitted orally in the form of an anonymous narrative, this utopia is inscribed in the very material confines of a book, assumed in the first person by More himself, who signs it with his own name. It is a pseudo-mythic form, then, one which, by a further contradiction, refuses to speak its name.

In order to understand why and how Thomas More came to elaborate this analogon of myth, we must restore his enterprise to the destabilized and destabilizing context of his epoch, when the institutions of medieval society are everywhere jeopardized by the opening-up of the natural world, the birth of the physical sciences, the discovery of the relativity of cultures, the extension of individual liberty, at the same time that technological power and effectiveness are being elaborated and, due in large part to the development of spatial instruments, reaching a previously unimaginable level. Utopus's plan allows More to function simultaneously within the range of the future and of the past, to acknowledge the advent of a new world experienced with all its attendant fascination and scandal, and still to preserve social solidarity and the institutional reproduction of tradition. By the mediation of his plan, Utopus incarnates the freedom and technological possibilities of the developing modern world even as he blocks its unpredictability.

Yet Utopus's solution remains symbolic, confined as it is within the image-system of myth. The surreptitious anomalies noted previously in utopian space and time have the value of Freudian slips: they indicate the desire and fugitive recognition of a real and constructed articulation between past and future, earth and human artifice, individual liberty and the law.

Does the book-bound nature of utopian solutions deprive them of any value, of any social and political effectiveness? Such was the position of Louis Marin.[8] The magical quality More attributes to a model space as a legitimation of an institutional functioning strikes me, on the contrary, as a consciousness that is prerequisite to any political engagement. Utopia's spatial configuration takes the place of a lost referent. And far from being the instrument of a manipulative and policing "power," as Foucault suggests, such a spatial device designates, by symbolically awarding itself the transcendent power of the law, its very erasure.

Chesterton remarks somewhere that More "was the founder of all Utopias, but he used Utopia as what it really is, a playground," because his "Utopia was partly a joke."[9] This judgment must be qualified. Nothing is more serious than what is at stake in Utopia's mythic dimensions; it is their vocation to enunciate unformulable or insoluble problems. And just as myth is assumed, transformed, even mutilated by oral transmission from generation to generation, from individual utterance to new enunciation, so the (mythic) textual genre More created has been assumed, transformed, and often falsified by successive generations of authors whom the history of Western societies has confronted with similar questions and problems.[10]

Hence true utopias have continued to be written, advancing the same three structural terms: (1) critique of a society, (2) model space, and (3) model society, all of which define the content of the Morean paradigm, as well as, quite frequently, its textual organization. It is not a coincidence that utopias have thrived especially during epochs of great upheaval in Western civilization, in particular at the end of the eighteenth century.

But in the course of the nineteenth century, the new destitution of cities, the alteration of ancestral environments, as well as the ideal of efficiency and "economism" promoted by the industrial project produce a hypertrophy of the spatial model and, for the first time, its projection into reality. Robert Owen's "New Harmony" and Fourier's "Phalanstery" are destined to be constructed and replicated many times over, but both fictions and antinomies disappear from these "achievable" utopias. By an irony of fate, when Marx condemns, in the name of revolutionary realism, those utopian socialists aiming to construct the spatial model of the new society, it is he who remains faithful to the logic of utopia, as Raymond Williams has demonstrated.[11] Actually, the last major utopia, strictly speaking, of the nineteenth century is William Morris's *News from Nowhere* (1890). After Morris, utopia disappears from literature. Its remains are henceforth annexed by urbanism, which, except for Ebenezer Howard's Garden City,[12] will not sustain the project of a society. Progressive urbanism not only abandons utopia's plan but also eliminates its societal vision; or rather, urbanism's actually constructed spatial model will impose, in a quite totalitarian fashion, a technological order. Le Corbusier's texts on urbanism give the full measure of this impoverishment.

Utopia in the Twenty-first Century

Has the transition to an electronic era, together with the post-1950s technological advances that have revolutionized the entirety of Western mental practice and behavior and thereby constituted the threshold of a new civilization, afforded the utopian project a renewed vitality? It would appear that in the second half of the twentieth century, the fate of utopia as a textual genre was sealed: a demise to be related to the weakening of political thought and the decline of the notion of the State in advanced industrial societies, where the market economy and its rationalizations have laid siege to and indeed conquered the site of a reflexive foundation reduced to the snares of sociologism. Furthermore, the "technotopias" – those false utopias characterized by the associations of elements (2) and (3) – which flourished between 1950 and 1970 have subsequently vanished. Texts and images like those of Nicolas Schöffer, Yona Friedman, and Iannis Xenakis are nowadays tinged with archaism without ever having had an impact on the process of urbanization. This is because, in their time, when technology reigns supreme, its progress has been so accelerated as to outdistance specialists and users alike, so that no measure of anticipation can hope to compete.

Yet the new technological mastery over the natural and human milieu has constituted, in the spirit of 1968, the theme of a literature that claims a utopian filiation: these texts offer a militant social dimension in which the constructed context represents an essential element. They proceed, in the main, from the Situationist Internationale (with its marked social concerns) and from the English group Archigram and its sympathizers (with their marked spatial concerns). The title of a long article that appeared in the weekly *New Society* in 1969, signed by Reyner Banham, Paul Barker, Peter Hall, and Cedric Price, sets the tone of the controversy: "Non plan, an experiment in freedom."[13] For these authors, such planning as Utopus proposed and as urbanists have continued to understand it has now become obsolete: all it could offer would be a context ill-adapted to human needs, activities, and desires, one that would be rendered chronically anachronistic by the speed of sociocultural change and the staggering freedoms of the "cybernetic revolution."[14] Under such conditions, the real problem facing the developers is how to enable the individual to determine the establishment that will best safeguard his liberties and his liberty within a generalized transformation and mobility. That such an article and others in the same vein might be read as utopian is readily accounted for by their subversive style, their uncompromising critique of advanced industrial society, and their virulent opposition to urbanism, a discipline whose supposedly scientific knowledge was undisputed at the time. Nonetheless, these were veritable anti-utopias. As a matter of fact, the *New Society* article denies constructed space any founding vocation: far from being in the service of a lasting transformation of society-as-subject, such space becomes an instrument serving to promote the freedom of the individual-as-subject. The antinomies that establish the utopian dynamics have no currency in the *New Society* article or in other related texts. "Non plan" unreservedly welcomes, in its conflictual complexity, the real world, both cultural and natural, to which More's Utopia was related only by means of its social critique. When the authors of "Non plan" describe the society they advocate and anticipate, they might be describing our own, which they could foresee in the forms of an unchanged life context. This is why, despite the role they assign to an isotropic space, such exercises propose only a mock-utopia from which they strictly exclude the founding project, the symbolic character, and any and all allegiance to myth.

It is nonetheless interesting to specify the nature and uses of this new technological space, which will henceforth occupy a hegemonic role in our planet's organization. Since the 1960s, in fact, the forms of local development that traditionally shaped rural and urban milieus have tended to disappear: the logic of articulation and contextualization, which linked their constructed elements among themselves and with their natural environment, has ceased to function. To put it another way, we are witnessing the erasure of local constructed context, on a human scale, which we may well credit with the vocation of sustaining the permanent recasting of social practices and institutions. The great technological networks (of the transmission of fluids, high-speed transportation, telecommunications), which mobilize in the service of their connective logic all the advances of technics and technologies, and especially all forms of electronic assistance, have turned entire territories, and then the whole planet, into an immense isotropic space. After the fashion of the old Morean grid, they tend to do away with local determinations imposed by physical geography as well as by urban and rural history; they serve to promote an unprecedented freedom, and impose a rigorous normalization. Yet such similarities are actually illusory, for our networked spaces are inscribed not in a symbolic realm but in a real one. Furthermore, their prosthetic effectiveness, with the freedoms it affords to individuals, is counterbalanced by their globalization, i.e., a planetary normalization or conditioning imposed, without being either desired or assumed, upon the totality of individual behaviors.

The consecration of this process of delocalization then appears as a utopia only in the negative sense (*ou-topos*) of the Morean neologism: a society whose functioning is rid of any allegiance to a local physical space. And is this not, in fact, what telecommunications networks and the Internet promise to deliver? Do not the eulogists of cyberspace credit it with the power to create a direct and immediate link between all members of human society: the very one that united the members of the small communities invented by Fénelon in *Télémaque* and by Rousseau in *La Nouvelle Héloïse*? Melvin Webber was among the first to state that the immateriality of the new forms and of the new networks of telecommunications would definitively eliminate the role of local space in the constitution and functioning of human communities.[15] Yet the metaphorical designation of *cyberspace* given to this non-space is merely a deception, indicating as if in mockery the inescapable role of place. The only community in which cybernauts participate is that of personal interest and, in the guise of immediate contact "in real time," their exchanges are reduced to an instrumental relation, quasi-disembodied and mediated by any number of computer screens. The individual freedom dispensed by cyberspace networks can no longer be informed nor transformed by the double presence of the natural world and the constructed world together with the living corporeality of other humans.

Without seeking to define within the context of a general anthropology the connection of society as an institution with local, natural, and cultural space,

as well as with the bodies of the human animals that evolve within it, we should still have to ask ourselves if global society today is not heading toward a one-dimensional prosthetic space that will retain only the epiphenomenal character of natural space and traditional constructed configurations. Such a hypothesis seems to be refuted by the scope and the popularity now enjoyed, the world over, by campaigns for the preservation of the natural environment and of historical and traditional constructed sites. Yet we must be careful. Do not such practices come down to no more than a mass museumification? And are they not also inscribed in a worldwide process of normalization? Are they not, in the hands of the cultural industry, supported by the world banks and other international institutions that propose nothing but global development and conceive of space only in terms of prosthesis, economy, norms, and statistics?

As a matter of fact, while the disintegration of cities and the urbanization of the countryside was accelerating, a multidisciplinary investigation was coming into being concerning the nature and the role of spaces constructed and articulated on a local scale. Maurice Le Lannou was one of the leading figures in this effort.[16] Starting with a critical reflection on the practices of the so-called historic heritage, I myself have in an earlier work attempted to discuss the anthropogenetic vocation of such spaces as well as their compatibility with technological networks.[17]

But heightened awareness of the consequences of the delocalization of our globalized societies has not been confined to the theoretical field alone. New efforts are being made to reappropriate the scale of local development; such attempts – few in number and difficult to pursue – have achieved concrete and effective results in "developing" countries like Brazil,[18] for example, as well as in certain "developed" countries where the trace of traditional socio-spatial organization has survived despite globalization and in reaction to it. A very recently centralized State organization and a strong local identity, maintained over a long period by a "constellation" of small and middle-size cities, dating back to antiquity and closely linked to a well-structured countryside, have made Italy in this regard a privileged territory among the other European nations. The experiment I shall now describe brings us back to the question of utopia – its protagonists themselves dubbed it "a concrete utopia,"[19] adopting, though with a different meaning, the expression of Ernst Bloch.

An Italian Utopia

Launched in the late 1980s, this experiment has been implemented in key metropolitan regions[20] throughout northern and southern Italy by a team of multidisciplinary university laboratories coordinated by Professor Alberto Magnaghi.[21]

The entire undertaking is based on the in-depth, unstinting, critical assessment of damages to the region brought about by globalization – in other words, by the (successful) integration of the regions in question into a free global economy and into the planetary technical networks. It is not so much a matter of denouncing specific ecological disasters (the gradual destruction of the famous hydraulic network of the Po Valley as a consequence of the automobile industry, for example) as of showing how deterritorialization tends toward the complete erad-ication of the national historic heritage through the long process of anthropisation (rural and urban sites as social and practical activities) and exposing the new poverty specific to the late twentieth century.

Whence, according to the project's initiators and their chief theoretician, Magnaghi, the necessity of a radical reversal of the situation. There is no ques-tion of defensive ecology nor of heritage conserva-tion; nor of an equilibrium sought between the global and the local ("the glocal"), which would subordinate the latter to the imperatives of the former. Local development and reterritorialization are necessary as "a strategic alternative to global development."

The great innovation of this initiative is the assertion that the natural heritage and the local cultural one (included together in the concept of "territorial heritage") cannot be conceived in static terms – that is, as property to be protected as such – but as indissociable from a totality of activities and behaviors that give them meaning: there can be no preservation of the local natural and con-structed heritage without the social practices that are united with them and correspond to their scale and differences, without a local economy associat-ing micro-agriculture and artisanal micro-industry, autonomous labor, and various services coupled with nonmercantile activities. But such an inversion or subversion of the worldwide process of develop-ment does not thereby signify archaism or nostal-gia. There is no question of the inhabitants turning their backs on reality and on history and taking up a position outside of or apart from the technological networks. The effectiveness of the latter is fully acknowledged; only their hegemony is contested. In other words, their prosthetic function becomes sec-ondary. It is subordinated to the creation of another space and a different society. Magnaghi sums this up in a formula, "globalization from below": instead of the local values being destroyed or conditioned by the imperatives of a worldwide market society and of competition subject to decisions and powers from elsewhere, it is starting from an endogenous project, consisting of local forces, attached to exter-nal networks, subordinating them to local needs.

The subversive effectiveness of such a project implies that all local inhabitants be involved in it, regardless of origin, without privileging local roots: it mobilizes "new farmers, producers and consumers, on behalf of a 'creole' society consisting of ethnic and émigré groups that do not necessarily identify themselves with the local residents." Hence, while rejecting exogenous planning, the Italian initiative demystifies the anti-utopia of "Non plan" and substi-tutes for the splintering of its individual projects a common project, one that reinstates the social bond and "revives the social image-repertoire."

Such a regional integration of metropolitan areas and rural spaces suggests the possibility of an Ecopolis,[22] consisting of a constellation of communi-ties restructured, assembled, and redefined within their own spatial limits and yet closely united by means of the most active instruments of technology.

For the purposes of my present discussion, this summary of the work of Magnaghi and his associates is schematic at best. Still, the reader will have under-stood the distance maintained from the utopian project by this experiment, in the service of a local cultural space (disregarded by More and his succes-sors) and inscribed within a temporality excluded by the symbolic dimension of utopian plans.

Yet in the very first lines of the article we have quoted, Magnaghi refers to utopia and claims an affiliation with it. Utopian traces are evident in the deployment of "utopian image-repertoire," above all in the strategic scenario bolstering an experi-ment "not constructed for purposes of its immedi-ate application by current decision-makers, but to serve potential actors."[23] The analysis of these ele-ments in Magnaghi's enterprise which still derive, explicitly or otherwise, from the Morean genre onstitutes a kind of experiment that helps us under-stand better the fate of utopia, its limits, but also its share of immortality.

The Truth of Utopia

Let us return to the ternary structure of utopia.

Unlike other penetrating critics of globaliza-tion (Riccardo Petrella, for example),[24] the initiators of Ecopolis have preserved the dynamic function and the anthropogenetic aims of the Morean critique. This radical social auto-critique institutes a process of auto-creation, rooted today as yesterday in Western modernity, whether in the Europe of the early sixteenth century, proclaiming for the first time its vocation to master and to transform the world, or on the worldwide stage of the late twentieth century, proclaiming globalization.

On the other hand, the antinomies that the model society of utopia was called upon to solve show their age and no longer seem pertinent to us. Or at least we have learned to conceive of and experience them in the theoretical wake of the sciences of nature and man, utilizing the concepts of philosophical and juridical reflection and in a struggle with a secularized world brutally confronting us with the dialectics of freedom and power, of nature and culture, of memory and forgetting.

In other words, rational analysis seems capable, to some degree at least, of short-circuiting the symbolic function of utopia, whence the syntagm of "concrete utopia." The inventors of Ecopolis assume, in effect, the weight and determinations of the totality of a given local space, as well as the creative dimension of time. Hence their project is based on an inventory of the territorial heritage represented and analyzed in its historical dynamic by means of unprecedented methods and technologies,[25] and it unifies heterogeneous actors animated by conflictual tensions. Loyalty to the long duration of the past and the openness to the unforeseeable are simultaneously affirmed, a coexistence which, in Magnaghi's text, acquires the name "sustainable ecological and human auto-development."

The function of the utopian symbolic resolution is thus transferred to regulatory notions which, by an interplay of extrapolations, integrate the imaginary with the real, binding the projected to the given, the local to the global, the latent to the dominant. The concepts of local society ("an idea to be empowered and not a heritage to preserve"), of local identity, of new municipal power, the kinds of schemes on the frontiers of the conceivable and the projectable, lead to a "culture of the limit" that strongly resembles a new avatar of utopia.

More's model space calls for the same readjustments today. The project of Ecopolis is, of course, similarly conditioned by an action on space and by the establishment of a spatial model. We soon realize, however, that what is involved here is a model-process and, above all, local space, which plays no part in Utopia where, as we have seen, it is introduced only by the author's inadvertence.

The fact remains that neither More nor his successors, until the second half of the nineteenth century, were concerned by the status of a local space the existence of which was not yet threatened. The notions of urban and rural heritage would not emerge and would not be named until the moment when the gradual dissolution of their referents would raise a problem. The question of the link, which, in "places," unites natural space and cultural space, was not inscribed in the utopian problematics.

Doubtless this link was manifest, as the ancient Tuscan language attests, over some three centuries. From the fourteenth to the sixteenth century, that language designated the city by the name of *terra*, emphasizing the fact that the institution of society is rooted in the earth, where the speaking animal is bound to the world of nature and of life. It is no accident that in his treatise on the institution of the family,[26] Alberti so often relied on the word "*terra*" in the sense of "city": later he would clarify this usage as a direct reference to the nodal function of the earth in Book I of *De re aedificatoria*,[27] in which he states the earth's consubstantial relation to building in the context of what today we would call a general anthropology.[28] Half a century later, More's reflection focuses on the corrective function of constructed space with respect to a Western identity of whose fluctuation and vulnerability he has a premonition. The shared perspective of anthropogenesis makes the two visions complementary: the theorists of concrete utopia can affirm in their turn today that "the earth and its resources, in fact, have a strategic role in the society of the future."[29]

Furthermore, when he condemns the dispersion of structures and circumscribes the cities of Utopia within precise and reduced limits, More symbolically launches a hypothesis as to the dimensions of the political; a hypothesis that remains open and urgent at the hour of globalization with its parade of abstractions; a hypothesis that, as a good utopian, Magnaghi has used for his own purposes.

As our societies enter a world in which the West's prosthetic vocation seems pledged to one-dimensionality, Utopia still remains a living entity. It still beckons us to the subversion of a radical social critique and to the revalorization of an anthropogenetic space. And finally it reminds us of the antinomic condition of human beings, obliging us to explore that condition further in its ineluctable depths.

Translated by Richard Howard

Notes

1 *Libellus vere aureus nec minus salutaris quam festivus de optimo reip[ublicae] statu, de[que] nova Insula Utopia.*

2 Thomas More, *Utopia*, ed. Edward Surtz (New Haven, Conn., and London: Yale University Press, 1964), 56, italics mine. All quotations are from this edition.

3 See Jacques Derrida, "La pharmacie de Platon" in his *La Dissémination* (Paris: Le Seuil, 1972), and my discussion of utopia in *La Règle et le modèle* (Paris: Le Seuil, 1980), 184.

4 *Utopia*, 63.

5 Leon Battista Alberti, *De re aedificatoria*, trans. and ed. Giovanni Orlandi as *L'architettura* (Milan: Il Polifilo, 1966), Prologue, 9. Alberti's work was first published in 1485 (Florence: Nicolò di Lorenzo Alemano).

6 See his *Anthropologie structurale*, vols. I and II (Paris: Plon, 1958, 1973) as well as *Le Cru et le cuit* (Paris: Plon, 1964).

7 *La Règle et le modèle*, Chapter II, 192 ff.

8 *Utopiques, jeux d'espaces* (Paris: Editions de Minuit, 1973).

9 Quoted in E. E. Reynolds, *Thomas More and Erasmus* (London: Burns & Oates, 1965), 120.

10 See *La Règle et le modèle*, Chapter II, 192 ff.

11 *The Country and the City* (New York: Oxford University Press, 1973; London: Chatto and Windus, 1973).

12 See his *Garden Cities of To-morrow (Being the Second Edition of "To-morrow: A Peaceful Path to Real Reform")* (London: Swan Sonnenschein & Co., Ltd., 1902).

13 In *New Society*, March 20, 1969.

14 "The cybernetic revolution makes our traditional planning technologically and intellectually obsolete . . . the word planning itself should be scrapped." Ibid.

15 "The Urban Place and the Non Place Urban Realm," in *Explorations into Urban Structure* (Philadelphia: University of Pennsylvania Press, 1964).

16 See his *Le Déménagement du territoire, rêveries d'un géographe* (Paris: Le Seuil, 1967).

17 *L'Allégorie du patrimoine* (Paris: Le Seuil, 1992), and "Une nutation à l'oeuvre" in *De la ville à la mégalopole* (Paris: Ministère de l'Equipment, Centre de prospective et de veille scientifique, 1998).

18 See L. Kroll, "Curutiba" in *A+*, 1999.

19 Alberto Magnaghi, "Per una costellazione di città solidali," *Ecopolis, Rivista critica di ecologia territoriale* (October–December 1998), 26.

20 Milan, Florence, Venice, Turin, Bologna, Rome, Bari, and Palermo.

21 He is Chair of Territorial Planning of the Department of Architecture at Florence; director of the "Progettazione ecologica degli insediamenti" laboratory; and the national coordinator of the "Per uno sviluppo locale autosostenibile: teorie, metodi e esperienze" project, launched by the Italian Ministry of Universities and Scientific and Technological Studies (MURST). See especially Alberto Magnaghi, ed., *Il territorio dell'abitare: lo sviluppo locale come alternativa strategica* (Milan: Franco Angeli, 1990), and "Il patrimonio territoriale: un codice genetico per lo sviluppo locale autosotenibile" in *Il territorio degli abitanti. Società locali e autosostenibilità* (Milan: Dunod, 1998).

22 See Magnaghi, "Per una costellazione." This article includes a valuable bibliography.

23 Ibid., 27.

24 Riccardo Petrella, *Le Bien commun, éloge de la solidarité* (Brussels: Labord, 1996).

25 See the Atlases presented in the fascicles of *Rappresentare i luoghi* (Florence: Alinea).

26 *I libri della famiglia*, new edition by F. Furlan (Turin: Einaudi, 1994).

27 *De re aedificatoria*, Chapters II and III, 21–23 and 25–33.

28 See Françoise Choay, "L'architecture d'aujourd'hui au miroir du *De re aedificatoria*," *Albertiana* I (Florence: Olschki, 1998).

29 In ANCI Toscana, *Agricoltura e territorio: un laboratorio per lo sviluppo sostenibile della Toscana. Un manifesto* (Florence: Edizioni Centro A-Zeta, 1996), 14.

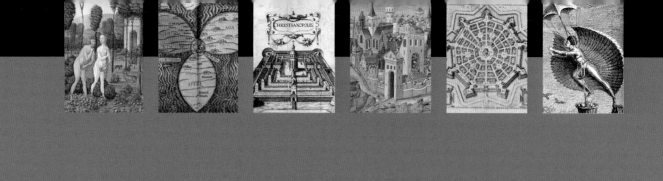

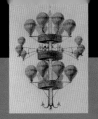

Symbolic Collapse: Utopia Challenged by Its Representations

"The true harmony of the soul can only be experienced in surroundings whose shapes, volumes, colors, etc., offer to the senses a reflection of the soul's loftiest thoughts, feelings, and impulses"; Rudolf Steiner's statement appeared in *Luzifer-Gnosis*, no. 33, published in 1907. The notion of the embodied ideal, however, runs counter to a philosophical understanding of the world that holds up "appearance" and dismisses profound "invisible" values. Concrete actualizations of utopia, therefore, are bound to guarantee its dissolution. For the same reason, the decision to build the Goetheanum in Dornach, Switzerland, and to assign a discrete material and spiritual order to an earthly place was not at all in keeping with the dominant tendency of utopian aims.

From the moment we broach the problem of utopian representation, we are led to the tacit conflict inherent in such a configuration, the questions it raises with respect to the Platonic definition of "reflection," which is wedded to image, and its implicit patent betrayal of figured reality. Utopia, that "nowhere land," that imaginary realm where universal happiness has been secured through ideal rule, is, on the face of it, resistant to iconographic (and *a fortiori* material) fixity in all its forms. Accordingly, utopia has gravitated, from its Morean beginnings, toward the more prolific (fluid, shifting) extrapolations that are specific to abstract images. Utopia has first and foremost been textual. It is told, not seen; it is "Nowhere," like the Poland of Alfred Jarry's *Ubu Roi*.

And yet, from very early on, utopian works have been complemented by illustrations, and societies (like Steiner's Anthroposophists later) have insisted on developing visible material universes that would correspond to their ways of looking at the world and organizing life. In this context, we cannot fail to recall monasticism's invariable urge to distance itself from settled society and to select a residence in accordance with a singular reading of the universe. It is in this way that utopia becomes material, invents its habitations and mores. Even when it is oneiric, Utopia elicits tangible visualizations.

What are these visualizations? Do they lend themselves to classification? And how reliable are the labels – the vague and interchangeable "utopic," "utopist," "utopian" – when they are indiscriminately applied to representations of radically different realities? And what are such "realities" made of? Is there not a fundamental difference between utopian writings and societies that want to found ideal governments *hic et nunc*? Some have taken the strict definition of utopia to mean the exclusion of all materiality. Pushed to its extremes, the argument allows us to posit utopia's nonfigurative essence and to sustain utopia's ties to its genesis in a book, in a written text. The book, by virtue of its basal function of interpreting signs and transposing them into an imaginary construct, can be deemed the ultimate utopian instrument.

We must, like the proverbial seer, sacrifice sight for insight; such is the paradox of a multitude of visions. As a matter of fact, though, the first edition of Thomas More's *Utopia*, printed in Belgium in 1516, was illustrated. Utopia may have been mistrustful of description, but it nonetheless invoked a visual realm whose powerful oneiric resonance prompted abstract representations that prepared the way for material ones. Do these images drawn from utopia's miscellany of genres and its wide-ranging and exhaustive scope conform to a particular cast? Do they augment narrative? How plausible is the notion of "iconographic betrayal"? At issue here, in short, is the entire illustrative undertaking.

The Closed Circle

The circle is utopia's first figure. The utopian island is round and closed, doubly hemmed in by water and walls. Utopia stands apart. It protects itself from the world. It is an enclosure for secret societies.

Plato, in *Laws*, had already described a similar model city: "Temples should be built all round the marketplace and on high ground round the perimeter of the city, for purposes of protection and sanitation."[1] Similarly, Thomas More's city "is surrounded by a high and broad wall."[2] Utopia's initial configuration, like its description, insists on a "contour." One could hardly fault its design for proselytism; at no time does it presume to be a beacon, an outward-beckoning light. Rather, it is a sealed hearth, cowering from intrusion and destruction behind its barricaded doors. Utopia imagines

itself as a place adrift – a place ruled by the moon, the moon when it is full, and not by the sun. These qualities are further reinforced by its island attributes. We know of course that in the first wood engraving inspired by More's work (p. 3), the distant coastlines seem inhabited. The assumption here is that Utopia is located somewhere within the confines of the known world. There are even a pair of sailing ships (the vessels of all nations) to attest to its trading practices. But its innermost recesses are twice sealed, doubly girdled by water and walls. A crescent-shaped river introduces an anthropomorphic element that corroborates our initial supposition. Utopia takes on the aspect of a human brain. Such an assertion, as we know, pertains to a nonmimetic figurative representation; rather than serving realism, these analogical operations seek to replace one reality by another through their manipulation of evocative plastic forms.

Immured behind its protective skull, the island of Utopia thus becomes the nucleus of a thought that is insulated from the adjacent turmoil. And despite its peripheral placement, Utopia presents itself as the epicenter of truth. Utopia proves incapable of ever resolving the dilemma of cloistered marginality envisaged as a vital center. By refusing propagation, it protects an idea that is curtailed but pure. Utopia is "surrounded." Consequently, it embodies a principle of disjunction; its reflexes are sectarian. It is the citadel of reason.

Hence, we are not surprised that utopian representations systematically have recourse to geometry. The objective here is not to reproduce nature, but to propose an idealized version that has been recast, tamed, and ordered by the human hand. What better way to capture this absolute and eternally expected and expectant universe than in the perfection of the circle, the feminine roundness, the metaphorical womb of all life awash in amniotic fluid, forever protected and preserved from the outside world? Utopia, in this sense, is embryonic, a retreat to original purity and to a prelapsarian world, before the screams and the

separation. Its wish is never to be born, never to succumb to time.

This tacit stifling of the call to existence is at the crux of utopian representation. The salient difference between the Belgian illustration and the subsequent Basel version clearly bears this out. The later illustration (p. 105) literally rejoins the island to the contemporaneous world. Leafy garlands reel it in closer to shore, and the churches that have cropped up throughout the area proclaim it as a Christian land. The human figures (Thomas More among them) who occupy the foreground look on from the opposite shore, discussing the easiest and fastest way to approach the island by boat. This Utopia is cautiously laden with contemporaneous preoccupations.

By contrast, the circle, when used in reference to an Ovidean or Edenic universe, for example, suggests Christendom's consummate – thus atemporal – perfection. The circle also appears as the figure of choice associated with Earthly Paradise in the *Livre des Propriétés des choses* (1479–80), the French translation of Bartholomaeus Anglicus's *De proprietatibus rerum* (1220–40). Rivers, implicitly internal, are another fixture of this topography; they are cut off from the sea and its protective, distancing waters. The loss of ideal perfection, stemming from the monotheistic Old Testament, was forever to leave its mark on the West.

The globe is yet another extension of the initial model; it too corroborates the principle of circumscription – the closed "orb," the sphere. Utopia is a solid; it is the virtual projection of a map. It expresses an improbable conjunction, imagines a planet's isolation in the universe. In Tommaso Campanella's *Civitas Solis* [*The City of the Sun*], concentric circles guard the inner core. The situationist Constant would be the first to use this figure as a prevailing model for urban planning. Nothing less than the ideal configuration of the world is at stake.

Architecture emerges as the means by which immutability takes on a material shape. Rebuilt around 125 by Hadrian, the Roman Pantheon,

whose monumental dome was seemingly doubled in size by the receding coffered ceiling pierced by an oculus, its sole opening to the light, had quashed the individual by flaunting all human scale. Etienne-Louis Boullée, in 1784, saw Newton's Cenotaph as a perfect sphere (pp. 128–29). Jean-Jacques Lequeu's design for a monument to the sovereignty of the people (pp. 196–97) is topped by a dome (much like R. Buckminster Fuller's later geodesic domes [p. 310]), and Claude-Nicolas Ledoux's perspective view of the City of Chaux (p. 127) resurrects Plato's circular structure.

In the twentieth century, concentric circles, domes, and spheres characterized the architecture of the totalitarian regimes of the 1930s. Is a reductionist cosmogony truly at issue here? Or are we simply witnessing a pragmatic effort to domesticate the world? Either way, the symbolic thrust of this vision is a system that is closed, fixed, and eternal – a system, in short, that is emphatically apart, guarded, and self-reflexive. Repetition attests to the figure's meaningfulness. It emerges as a metaphorical shorthand that can skirt all ancillary explanations, and compensate for descriptive gaps in the texts. Processions of athletes unfurl like human corollas, like the orderly bloom of collective happiness; the advancing columns fill the collective space with a microcosm of the "totality" that is posited as the cardinal measure, the enlightened reprieve, the inner radiance at the end of the tunnel.

Symbolically, the circle invariably refers to inner realms. By definition tautological, the circle is mute on the subject of utopia. In fact, it has nothing to impart; its very minimalism enables it to accommodate those things that fall outside time and reappraisal. Because it is a celestial intrusion on the terrestrial, it cannot be fathomed by human beings who are in turn subject to an order they cannot fathom. Monumental architecture, by virtue of its suprahuman dimension, perfectly expresses this disproportionate perfection. The circle and the sphere are self-sufficient entities signaling a full stop.

While their implicit reductionism may seem eminently unsuitable to utopian figures, it would be a mistake to dismiss them on such grounds. Their limitations are not without import; in fact, they are the astute expression of a circumscribed universe. Utopia is not a dream; it is not the imagination run wild, or the search for fantastic tropical forests. Rather, it seeks an absolute perfection devoid of human beings. Utopia is the geometer's stone. It is serial music. And humanity must reconcile itself to the place to which it has been consigned by the oculus.

In the first pictorial representation of Thomas More's island, we can see a similar principle of disembodiment. The map, the plan, the spatial projection are all tools equal to the task of rendering the idea graphically. The circle is instated as a utopian logotype upheld by the citizens. Any representation of them, once their utilitarian function has been established, is unnecessary, superfluous.

Utopian aims are unlikely to find a more beautiful expression than they do here, where the expectation as well as its imperfect implementation are reflected at the same time. Indeed, except for those infinitely repeated orderly processions, temporal intrusions upon this architecture that result from events in adjacent regions invariably introduce disorder. One must never disrupt a circle, a beehive, a termites' nest, where each and all have a proper place.

The Square of Equality

In the 1511 edition of Vitruvius's *De architectura*, illustrated by Giovanni Giocondo, the circle and the square, the most-often-repeated figures of utopian representation, appear in conjunction. While the circle or the sphere, even when accompanied by concentric waves, assumes the perfect uniqueness of its kernel, the square contains other squares; it assumes division and multiplication. And the same holds for its avatar, the rectangle.

Visually, the square expresses equality. It is a box-like compartment. While it is numerically

determined, it takes into account only a single, repeated number. It is not the numerical encoding of a suitable alternation o/1 but the recurring multiplication of a perfect module. A similarly repetitive grid was used in the creation of new orthogonal cities in the seventeenth century (Washington, D.C., and Versailles, after which it was modelled). Philadelphia's 1682 ordinance sought to rationalize space by imposing a checkerboard plan (p. 125). Such plans are ruled by repetition and similarity. They also direct us to reconsider the links among geometry, architecture, and utopia. Utopia's proposed construction of an ideal society, best expressed in a nature that has been remedied by the "perfecting" intervention of the human hand, essentially relies on "unobservable" mathematical propositions. It stands to reason, therefore, that the architecture of the ancients, with its affirmation of the formal elements of the circle and the straight line, should have found favor among those who wished to give form to an idea.

The objective is not so much the creation of new forms, nor artistic inventiveness, as it is transposition, to translate into architecture the idea of a perfect society. To side with those who ill-advisedly seek to rally inventive plastic artists (Bernini in the Baroque period or Gaudi in the twentieth century) to the utopian camp, or with those who express dismay at the "paucity," the banality, and the dullness of executed utopian projects, is to miss the point entirely. Utopia, in essence, always proffers a solution for the end of time and a model that is to remain resolutely conceptual. In the world it has set apart for itself, volumes are governed by a theoretical order.

Hence utopia is the antithesis of "fantasy." To put it plainly, there is an entrenched gap between what is commonly understood as utopian – the dream, the imaginary construct, the surrealist non sequitur – and what are in fact the implemented or projected visions of societies with utopian aims; societies, that is, that vow to take on the end of history, to attain the ultimate outcome and the dis-

solution of the future. Utopia pits itself against evolutionary principles; it is the antipode of Darwinism.

The multiplied square expresses a rather similar ambition. Given that its operative principle is cloning, it stands in direct opposition to the principle of the differentiation of the species and the singularity of each organism. Its use of repetition suggests the purportedly harmonious structures of the insect world (the beehive being a frequent metaphor), artificial structures built in defiance of a thriving vegetation. Utopian figuration relies entirely on the principle of boxed "comprehensive similarity" and not at all on individual "comprehensive difference." Implicit in the pursuit of a society where all share and share alike and where everyone's lot is made the same through standardized repetition is the advent of the last threshold of progress, the abolition of all elsewheres, of all difference, and all domination.

In view of this, it is important to note the striking similarity of the plans for ideal cities inspired by Robert Owen, Jean-Baptiste André Godin, and Charles Fourier. The Familistère at Guise (p. 213), for example, uses repeated modules in the design of a collective displaying a rectangular uniformity. Mathematics held sway as French revolutionaries embarked on a project, worthy of the cult of Reason, to regulate time. The metric system gave rise to an architecture for the masses. A similar impetus would later give rise to the vast, complex structures of the 1930s, whether they were inspired by American industrial architecture and skyscrapers, by the Bauhaus, or by Communist or Fascist societies. The idioms of repetition, of troops of soldiers in uniform, of parades and geometric human formations are all expressions of the collective in which the cloned individual is simultaneously negated and yet indispensable to the chain (a single missing link will disrupt the overall composition).

Totalitarian models draw on the structure of military camps. As demonstrated by the architectural historian Jean-Louis Cohen, even deportation camps were modelled after utopian cities. Such

361

Symbolic Collapse: Utopia Challenged by Its Representations

constructs are always couched in the methodical repetition of an invariable unit, and at least at the level of structure, the ideal city and ideal servility are difficult to tell apart. In 1527, Albrecht Dürer designed a perfect city in accordance with the orthogonal plan (p. 121). In 1717, Robert Montgomery followed suit with his plan for the new colony of South Carolina (p. 126), as Father Manuel Paramás was later to draw up plans for a mission in Paraguay, and the industrialist William Hesketh Lever was to create Port Sunlight for his workers in Liverpool. In every single instance, squares and rectangles prevailed – neatly aligned and repeated ad nauseam inside bigger squares and rectangles. The operating principle here is of the world in "totality," of a closed world as expressed by Testi's famous 1932 poster, in which everyone wears Mussolini's face. The sum total amounts to unity.

Moreover, this horizontal agglomeration begins to be intermittently replaced by a vertical one. As long as the right angle and equidistance are respected, repetition, in any direction, comes to symbolize infinite perfection. The square is never alone; a kind of spatial eugenics is at work, ensuring its reproduction. As in George Orwell, freedom is servitude. René Clair's film *A nous la liberté* (1931) and, later, Charlie Chaplin's *Modern Times* (1936) clearly express the paradox of Taylorism: its attempts to establish equality (in the workforce) resulted in the standardization of robotic human mechanisms. Marcel L'Herbier's *L'inhumaine* (1924), and somewhat more ambiguously Fritz Lang's *Metropolis* (1926), also invoke these avatars of the modernist utopia. But the constructed collective habitat was far and away the most steadfast exponent of the square and rectangle's implicit rhetoric of equality.

Utopia's deliberate abolition of difference is abetted by these measures. The individuals it addresses are molded to the collective image, and the end of history, it seems, presupposes the end of behavioral diversity. Every possible and terrible conception of servitude is contained in those

repeated squares. What we have here is indicative not only of utopia's symbolic collapse but also of its bloody failures in the field.

The Diagonal of Perpetual Motion

Even in a perfect world, the idea of the "journey," with its undercurrent of far-reaching aspirations, cannot be disregarded. Whereas the ideal, as shown above, may rely on static principles to express its insurpassable perfection, the ways and byways that led to Utopia's shores cannot be ignored. No run-of-the-mill expedition this, but a taking leave of high ground to navigate the high seas with their promise of adventure and exploration and odyssey. This change from one element to another is necessary for those who set their sights on an unknown land, on Utopia, city of the "farthest point," *terra incognita*.

Seafaring vessels cross in the distance. The new continents that were uncovered during the Renaissance (by Magellan and Christopher Columbus) give credence to the belief in a vast expanse of peaceful and plentiful lands. Let us recall that More's narrator, Raphael Hythlodaeus, accompanied Amerigo Vespucci on his voyage to Brazil. The seafaring vessel essentially became synonymous with the dream of uncovering new lands; in fact, it became such an eloquent metaphor for Edenic mania that in Watteau's *L'embarquement pour Cythère* [*Embarkation for Cythera*], a simple mast signals imminent departure for the embracing couples who indulge in one last frolic before tearing themselves away from earthbound pleasures to set sail for celestial bliss.

Such images of difficult departure are a prevailing motif of the twentieth century. While the discovery of new territories is no longer at issue, the new redemptive societies are called upon to foster a radical shift from the old order to the new. The word "revolution," although, curiously, it is rooted in the idea of a "return," itself suggests such ruptures and becomes synonymous with upheaval – an upheaval that is brought about by motion that

proceeds from left to right, in keeping with Western textual practice, and from bottom to top as befits Western symbolic constructs (terrestrial/celestial; conquered/conqueror; dominated/dominating), in an oblique diagonal that runs from the bottom left to the upper right; this ascending transversal becomes a permanent fixture of the imagery of revolutionary discontinuities. It depicts the violent passage to a new order; it is a salute to the liberating upsurge.

The Futurist Luigi Russolo's great 1911 composition, *La Rivolta* [*The Revolt*] perfectly expresses this mystique of motion and rupture. Its impact persisted during the period between the two world wars; after its first manifestations in the works of Futurists and Russian Constructivists, it was adopted by both the right and left as the figure of choice to represent the undivided masses. In *New Planet*, a 1921 painting by the Russian Konstantin Fedorovich Iuon, men raise their arms toward red beams that converge into a diagonal as they soar toward the scarlet constellations. The diagonal's destabilizing momentum becomes a systematic element in the composition of advertising posters, magazine photography, and illustrated political propaganda. Everyone seems to want a piece of this action; no one seems deterred by its association with falling bodies, with the Apocalypse, with the very collapse of the world as seen in the German Expressionist film *The Cabinet of Dr. Caligari* (1920). This collapse of the world as it had been gives way to the construction of the new city of nightmares and of dreams: the broken pane of cubism exploding reality into smithereens gives way to the trenchant arrow's upward sweep. Vladimir Ivanovich Kozlinskii's 1919 *The Sailor* is defiantly pitched toward the future. The ideology of speed, of departure and transit, takes up residence. In Mikhail Matiushin's synthetic statement, *Movement in Space* (1917–18), the canvas is brushed with parallel bands of color that move from left to right and from the bottom up.

El Lissitzky's famous 1919 canvas *Beat the Whites with the Red Edge* reveals more complexity.

The ubiquitous diagonal is most certainly present – the red corner suggests that the bayonet, following the usual left-to-right thrust, has left the enemy prostrate. The circle of white is pierced to the quick by the sharp angle of the motion. A similar rhetoric prevails in the propagandistic ephemera constructed for use in parades, in the design of stage sets, and even in the cinematic aesthetic of Dziga Vertov and Sergei Eisenstein. The spirals in Vladimir Tatlin's *Monument to the Third International* (1919) soar at a sheer angle toward the sky (p. 300). This headlong spatial dynamic informs the design of everything from the oceanliners and locomotives in the poster designs of A. M. Cassandre to motor cars (the 1925 poster *Peugeot accélération*, for example) to the lithographs designed by Paul Colin, notably that for the 1927 *Bal Nègre*. The onward march toward the ideal had settled on a course. In the East, a similar motif was at work in the montages of the Stenberg brothers' 1928 *Symphony of a Great City*.

This skyward ascent to an undepicted but implicit and hoped-for paradise was even appropriated by the artists of Fascist Italy and Nazi Germany. Here, the obliqueness of the image is emphatically reinforced by the low angle of the point of view (in, for example, Gino Boccasile's *Mostra nazionale dello Sport* {*National Sports Exhibition*}, Milan, 1935). The visual progression toward the transfiguring properties of a superior essence has been systematized. It avoids descriptions of happiness and is bent only on recruitment and training. It designates the right "path to follow." Sporting events, with their orderly mass formations, emerge as an appropriate arena for professing the ideology of new beginnings. Aleksandr Rodchenko, in 1932, took photographs at an angle of the "morning exercises" that brought participants closer to the radiant future. In the 1924 photograph he took of Lili Brik for an advertising photomontage, her V-shaped mouth is ostensibly alerting the masses to her hopes for the future. Similar examples of 1930s photomontage abound in the journal *USSR in Construction*. But what is the

famous World War I soldier by Abel Faivre doing on one of the most widely circulated posters of the war, *On les aura!* [*We'll get them!*], in 1916?

The revolutionary volition to destroy the old order is no longer only a journey to a new and distant land, to an island utopia that is isolated, withdrawn, closed off, and shielded from the world. Destruction has become part and parcel of resurrection. Already in 1925, Ludwig Hohlwein had drawn diagonal banners soaring toward the sky for German president Paul von Hindenburg. In 1939, Hein Neuner incorporated a similar line in his configuration of the young Nazi, the Führer, and the invisible "absolute." The consistent use of the low angle suggested an impending lift-off, a leaving behind of the prosaic earth for a celestial "beyond" where it is generally assumed aspirations reside. Viewers are thus visually suctioned upward, subjected to visual "aspiration." For twenty years (until the end of World War II), every kind of commercial diffusion of images was put to use to draw those viewers in.

A theory of rupture entails a more precise delineation of the workings of departure. Countless icons suggest that this voyage is in fact a passage between an old and a new world. Neither world is depicted; rather, it is the collective transit that is shown. A rushing column of men falls in behind the leader; they head for the front; they advance toward victory. The inherent subservience to speed that we find in these representations (pp. 296–97) is fitting, practical even, for a world that deems itself "modern." These headlong images dodge several pitfalls; while they skirt reminders of the shameful past, they also avoid the stasis of effortlessly achieved happiness and the difficult and abstract visualization of the insurmountable totality. The diagonal provides utopia with a figure that is at once anchored in a terrestrial reality and endowed with superior abilities of mobilization: a signpost to the path of escape from a reality that has been challenged. Happiness is found by enlisting in the column and offering oneself up to the collective all.

Perpetual exploration. Sacrifice. Delivery from the daily round of betrayal comes with obedience and abnegation. But what of the viability and legitimacy of the Ideal? That is a subject these images never address.

The Truth of the Naked Body

So how do human beings figure in all this? They appear to be glaringly absent from the representations of idyllic societies that promise eternal happiness. Perhaps utopia is nothing more than a schematic outline, a geometric idea that charts the contours of a blank territory, an infrastructure without inhabitants. Does the visibility of the latter occur only when their bodies have been triggered into motion by orderly aspirations toward happiness?

Nevertheless, utopians do figure in the city of happiness. In Christine de Pisan's fifteenth-century *Book of the City of Ladies*, both virtue and innocence are portrayed. The "savage" had to be discovered before the stereotype of "truth" could enter the picture; this truth, linked to the nakedness of a human body that did not clad itself in the artifice of social trappings though its indulgence in ornaments (body paint, jewels, scarification), was prominently depicted. Theodore de Bry's engraving, after Jacques Le Moyne, for de Bry's *America*, Part 2 (1591), sets women at their domestic chores against extravagantly adorned European soldiers across from the Native council of the Timucuan (p. 146). The soldiers' presence serves to interject the feelings of horror, pity, and derision that the mores of these uncivilized "others" elicit. It also serves to offset the wholesomeness of a lost innocence.

Here, to no one's surprise, are the innocent predecessors of Jean-Jacques Rousseau's "noble savage," untouched by the corruption of progress. Here is natural man laid bare like an ancient deity, like Truth emerging from a well. While these images may seek to justify territorial and religious conquest by insisting in part on the nonhumanity, the bestiality, and the cruelty of this figure, they are

also fascinated by the figure's inherent innocence and communion with an inviolate, and hence abundant, nature. This is precisely the subject of *La Cuccagna: Descrittione des gran paese de cuccagna dove chi piu dorme piu guadagna* (p. 74), an engraving depicting a country that is suffused with a desire for communion with a primal and generous nature.

In the 1715 illustrated Leyden edition of Thomas More's *Utopia*, the society's generalized sameness and simplicity of dress are repeatedly stressed (p. 102). "The Prince was only distinguished from other citizens by his extreme affability. His Majesty carried in one hand a handful of wheat to indicate that he understood his first duty was to nourish his subjects." Visually, a link is established between the riches of nature and the paring down of attire. Bridal couples are brought together naked to avoid "their agreeing ill together if something afterwards gives them offense."³ The equality of their overall condition is further emphasized by the communal life they share. We are especially struck by how the "savages" in these drawings are undifferentiated and always function in groups, like ants or bees.

All selfishness and individualized behavior must be obliterated from the society. The lone utopian is impossible to imagine. Like the savage, he is faceless. All utopians look alike. Equality spreads by osmosis. The quest for Beauty here, much as it was for the ancients (according to Winckelmann), is a function of Virtue. This means that even when the physiognomy in question is described – as is the case with the engraving showing the signing of the U.S. Declaration of Independence (p. 188) – it is the repetition of a stance that is emphasized; differences are glossed over and it is the bare solemnity of a collective consensus that is physically figured. On November 10, 1793, the French Revolution adopted a similar aesthetic to represent the cult of Reason, and when J. J. Grandville got his hands on "Fourier's system," he drew a bevy of women with identical moon-shaped heads (p. 214).

The lost paradise in Bernardin de Saint-Pierre's *Paul et Virginie* (1788) is also cast from the same mold: the smooth figures of Adam and Eve are stand-ins for all of humanity. The clothing of the Saint-Simonians, especially as worn by Père Enfantin (p. 218), yet again echoes the sobriety and purity of life before artifice. Utopia, in effect, never manages to rid itself of its Judeo-Christian message. It distances itself from Eastern representations of a world contained within a cosmogonic space where a dialogue between Heaven and Earth is possible. Rather, the Garden of Eden represents a sublimated nature that preceded the Flood and not a new mapping of the eternal universe.

The utopian does not belong to the world of carnival and imaginary rupture with the established order. Rather, he is the austere servant of a collective law that extols the virtue of a return to an original purity linked with nature. From a visual point of view, the utopian is reactionary; lacking individualistic ornamental and behavioral features, he obstinately insists on the inherent barrenness of "true" appearance.

The naked body, which is the prerogative of pagan goddesses as well as savages, signifies equality of condition. When Paul Signac, influenced by anarchist ideas, painted *Au Temps d'Harmonie* [*In the Time of Harmony*] ("The golden age of mankind is not behind, but before us") in 1895, he depicted a society that mixed work and leisure in the protective lap of a radiant nature (p. 239). Everyone is simply clad, the men are barechested, women bathe naked in the distance. Activities take place in groups, and some are even dancing a farandole in the shade of a tree. Some years later, in 1904, Henri Matisse, working from Signac's home in St. Tropez, painted *Luxe, calme et volupté*, following it up with *Le Bonheur de vivre* [*The Joy of Life*] (1905–6) in which naked figures burgeon out of the maternal space of a verdant and aquatic landscape. Despite Signac's insistence on the promise of the future, the nostalgia for a "Golden Age" is impossible to circumvent here: not for the heyday of industrial hustle and bustle but for earlier times when the innocent savage existed in ancestral communion

with the generous forms of a pristine, virginal landscape. A similar agrarian nostalgia, a similar Marian allusion, is at work in twentieth-century French political propaganda; whereas for Philippe Pétain, in 1941, it was Bernard Villemot's little village cozied up around its church (*Patrie – Suivez-moi, gardez votre confiance en la France éternelle*), for François Mitterand, in 1981, it would be Jacques Séguéla's campaign slogan, "La force tranquille" ["The quiet force"].

What else do the standardized militants of the 1930s reveal? Theirs is a battle to establish a new order by destroying an old order that has failed, and to do so in the name of happiness and the new innocence associated with the truth of the body communing with nature. While technology (factories, tractors, locomotives) is glorified, men and women, unadorned and pure as pioneers, are clones allied in a collective smile at life's reconciliation with the body – a redundancy of robots (as in Fritz Lang's *Metropolis* [p. 283] or the works of Karel Čapek [p. 284]) streaming out of a square structure. Sportsmanship, the exploration of virgin lands, and nudism all comply with an ideology that counteracts the corruption of power and money by a return to the original purity. Virtue pitted against interest, and the Hero against the merchant. In addition to exemplary motherhood, the role of women grows to encompass the new athleticism that is at the vanguard of the battle to secure the eternal youth that is held up as a model.

Eternal youth is also one of the tenets of the postwar baby boomers. Are the communitarian models of the 1960s really all that different, we ask? Granting that physical fitness and the cult of discipline were hardly the rule and that Paul Lafargue's cherished right to laziness was much more congenial, the return to nature, the shedding of clothing, the hirsute nakedness, the functioning in circles and groups, the herd instinct, and unisex clothing are de facto similarities between the two periods. Activists in the feminist, African American, and gay and lesbian movements all contest their exclusion from "white male bourgeois society" by asserting their Beauty and their right to autonomy. Even though drug use, the refusal to work, and wanderlust may have produced behaviors and representations that were original (and often set to music), it seems that as the desire to build a utopian society increases, so, too, does its "retroactive" filiation.

Militant revolutionary practices, at any rate, are consistently associated with a form of austerity that is overtly and directly linked to previous periods. Only individual splits and collective creative experiences (music and theater groups, happenings) or a handful of phases – Berkeley, Berlin, May–June '68 in France – introduce those truly imaginative representations identified as "countercultural." But on the whole, communitarianism presupposes the discipline of organized utopians, and in some instances, category-specific qualifications have to be met before access to its circles can be gained. Ingenious architectures (New Babylon by the situationist Constant, the Archigram projects, Ernest Callenbach's Ecotopia) are often the exception, although it cannot be denied that their recycling of materials, their brazen reinvention, and their unruly frescoes mark the territory. But the pursuit of puritan egalitarianism in an unspoiled, natural setting (ecology) leads to expurgation, to the search for a stripped "essence" (religious at times), and to the cult of innocence associated with the noble savage's break with social conventions (inexorably linked to "progress"), which goes so far as to refute hygiene and medicine.

The utopian is thus figured as the true agent of Virtue. Even as he constructs an alternate present and prepares the way for a radiant future, he is motivated by nostalgia and a desire to regain a lost Golden Age. This supposed return, this hunger for the future, is in fact put to the test by immemorial and abundant Nature. The ideals of beauty form a circle in a glen, they are all of a kind, all innocent. The future is reactionary.

Resisting Representation or Representing Resistance to Reality?

In the course of this much too hasty overview, we have shown the great degree to which utopian representations (with some leeway for overlapping expressions, as clear-cut distinctions are difficult) have generated synthetic images. Apparently, the vague outlines of a society at the end of history are best expressed enigmatically, by a perfect symbol. Utopia is thus delivered from temporality and saved from the trap that would violate its principle.

Indeed, to describe quotidian details would be effectively to relegate this culminating vision of history to the realm of the accidental, of the imponderable, of human failings – in other words, of evolution. Only the semantic compactness of a circle, of repeating squares, of the diagonal, and of the naked body in a sylvan setting can avoid the lapses of narrative. The image in this context has nothing to tell; it introduces another kind of chronology, namely contemplation. Counter-utopias, it should be noted, are to the contrary built entirely on precision and narrative. They dwell on every nightmarish detail; they multiply the vistas of anguish and cataclysm. They insist on revealing the particular histories of *identified* individuals. They privilege the anecdote to introduce the quotidian, to give a sense of the daily horror.

Such a visual lacuna reveals – by virtue of its gap – utopia's inhumanity, in fact its disregard for all natural laws despite its seemingly straightforward and benevolent figurations of nature, of sunlit springs and summers when bodies inhale the salubrious air in unison. The illustrators of utopia, as we have seen, resolved the problem of representing it by resorting to an impressionistic and chronologically stagnant reductionism. As a result, utopian narrative found itself transplanted into tautological symbols.

Is this surprising? After all, utopia arose out of a textual projection; it is borne by abstract images. At the risk of betrayal, icons, conveying condensed and codified versions, are flashed like I.D. cards.

The utopian utterance never loses its primacy – even when the *modus vivendi* is announced daily, as was the case with the murals of prints and placards posted by the Paris Commune (promoting the "Central Committee of the Women's Union," the "Barricade Commission," and so on). The word prevails. It leaves to the image an illustrative function, for the image-makers know better than to rely on haphazard description, and instead opt for metaphors. The utter failure of fulfilled and unfulfilled utopias is thus visually revealed as totalitarianism.

While utopia is most certainly imagined, it does not pertain in the least to the realm of the imaginary. By seeking to bring history to a standstill, it denies the future. Its laws are sealed. The static Paradise it proposes and its recurrent insistence on a reactionary return to a mythical and communitarian Golden Age (Garden of Eden) could not be further from the dream, from the invention. So perhaps the issue is less one of the difficulty of representing utopia, given that utopia seems to have found its emblematic modules, and more one of identifying the ways in which these modules reveal a symbolic failure that translates into defeat in practice. By severing itself from the idea of transformation and invention, utopia uses narratives and images to construct static and sealed societies. As such, it radically distances itself from its oneiric significance in everyday language.

Even though André Breton wrote an *Ode à Charles Fourier* in 1945 in which he proclaimed his "unreasoned belief in the movement towards an edenic future" as a necessary "lever," he considered it "proven that the betterment of human fate can be effected only very slowly and fitfully by means of down-to-earth demands and cold calculations."[4] His vision of Fourier is based on fantasy, collage, the shock of icons and derision. Fourier is "absorbed" in a transcendental aspiration. Breton wants to see him as the prophet of a dream world, not as the accountant of a space that has been checkerboarded by intangible dictates.

An "edenic future"? Is utopia truly synonymous with "hope"? Such seems to be the case, especially in the twentieth century when the "movement toward" took precedence over the "arrival at." Paradoxically, utopia's most salient representation turns out to be, not the closed, protective circle, or the grid with its egalitarian squares, or even the alleged return to truth and mythical innocence, but the diagonal of perpetual motion – the signpost to the worst catastrophes. By leaving behind static and totalitarian illusion to associate itself instead to the imaginary dream, it becomes an invention of a fleeting and "perpetually overtaken" future.

If we abide by this new definition, then the true representation of utopia would follow from the total absence of the image (to avoid fixity), or in a multiplicity of views that would announce the return of Chronos, hence metamorphosis. This "lever" would release analogy and transfiguration, and a double symbolic failure, with its implicit bloodied and desperate avatars, would be averted. Both the resistance *to* the real and the resistance *of* the real would be resurrected. It would reinstate narrative and free it to reassess the journey, to entertain second thoughts, and to move toward becoming. Then the fleeting aspects of collective desire, of curious pleasures, and of stimulating illusions would appear. Each step would lead from the apparent image to the encountered imaginary.

Translated by Nadia Benabid

Notes

1 Plato, *Laws*, Book VI, 778 c, in *Complete Works*, ed., with introduction and notes, by John M. Cooper; associate ed. D. S. Hutchinson (Indianapolis: Hackett Publishing Co., 1997), 1451.

2 Thomas More, *Utopia*, ed. Edward Surtz (New Haven, Conn., and London: Yale University Press, 1964), 65.

3 Ibid., 110.

4 André Breton, *Ode to Charles Fourier*, trans. Kenneth White (London: Cape Goliard Press, 1969), 61.

Utopian Literature: A Selective Bibliography

Denis Bruckmann, Laurent Portes, and Lyman Tower Sargent

This chronological bibliography has been compiled in part from the following sources: Arthur O. Lewis, *Utopian Literature in The Pennsylvania State University Libraries: A Selected Bibliography* (University Park: Pennsylvania State University Libraries, 1984); Glenn Negley, *Utopian Literature: A Bibliography with a Supplementary Listing of Works Influential in Utopian Thought* (Lawrence: Regents Press of Kansas, 1978); Lyman Tower Sargent, *British and American Utopian Literature, 1516–1985: An Annotated, Chronological Bibliography* (New York: Garland, 1988), plus unpublished supplements; Raymond Trousson, *Voyage au pays de nulle part: histoire littéraire de la pensée utopique* (Brussels: Université de Bruxelles, 1975); Pierre Versins, *Encyclopédie de l'utopie des voyages extraordinaires et de la science fiction* (Lausanne: L'Age d'homme, 1972); and Michael Winter, *Compendium Utopiarum: Typologie und Bibliographie literarischer Utopien*, Vol. 1: *Von der Antike bis zur deutschen Frühaufklarung.* Repertorium zur deutschen Literaturgeschichte, vol. 8 (Stuttgart, Germany: J. B. Metzler, 1978). In addition, Professors Raffaella Baccolini, Carol Farley Kessler, Lise Leibacher-Ouvrard, Arthur O. Lewis, Timothy Miller, and Kenneth M. Roemer made suggestions.

1516 More, Thomas. *Libellus vere aureus nec minus salutaris quam festivus de optimo reip[ublicae] statu, deq[ue] noua Insula Vtopia.* [Louvain, Belgium]: Arte Theodorice Martini. In English: *Utopia.* Ed. and trans. George M. Logan and Robert M. Adams. Cambridge, England: Cambridge University Press, 1989. Ed., with introduction and notes, Edward Surtz, S.J. New Haven, Conn.: Yale University Press, 1964.

1521 Eberlin von Günzburg, Johann. *New Statuten die Psitacus gebracht hat uss dem Land Wolfaria welche beträffendt Reformierung geystlichen stand. . . . Der X Bundtgnosz und Ein newe Ordnüng weltlichs standts des Psitacus anzeigt hat in Wolfaria beschriben. Der XI Bundtgnosz.* Basel: Pamphile Gegenbach.

1525 Müntzer, Thomas. *Etwa Pfarrer zu Altstat.* Regensburg: Paul Kohl.

1527 Guevara, Antonio de. *Libro aureo de Marco Aurelio, emperador y eloquentissimo orator, nuovamente impresso.* Valladolid: N. Thierri.

1532 [Rabelais, François]. *Les Grandes y inestimables cronicques du grant y énorme géant Gargantua, contenant sa généalogie, la grandeur et force de son corps. Aussi les merveilleux faictz d'armes qu'il fist pour le roy Artus, comme verrez cy après. Imprimé nouvellement.* By Alcofribas Nasier [pseud.]. Lyon: A. D.

1552 Doni, Antonio Francesco. *I Mondi del Doni. . . .* Vinegia: F. Marcolini.

1553 Patrizi, Francesco. *La Citta Felice.* Venice: G. Griffio.

1555 Stiblin, Gaspar. *Coropædia, sive de Moribus et vita virginum sacrarum . . . Ejusdem de Eudæmonensium republica commentariolus.* Basel: for J. Oporinum.

1579 Nicholas, Thomas. *A Pleasant dialogue betweene a lady called Listra, and a pilgrim, concerning the government and common weale of the great province of Crangalor.* London: J. Charlewood.

1580 Agostini, Lodovico. *La Repubblica immaginaria di Ludivico Agostini.* Turin: L. Firpo.

1590 Sidney, Sir Philip. *The Countesse of Pembrokes Arcadia.* London: W. Ponsonbie.

1600 Floyd, Thomas. *The Picture of a perfit Common Wealth, describing as well the offices of princes and inferiour magistrats over their subjects, as also the duties of subjects towards their governours.* London: S.Stafford.

1605 Artus, Thomas, sieur d'Embry. *Les Hermaphrodites.* N.p.

1605 [Hall, Joseph]. *Mundus alter et idem, sive Terra australis antehac semper incognita, longis itineribus peregrini academici nuperrime lustrata.* London, H. Lownes. In English: *The Discovery of A New World or A Description of the South Indies, Hetherto Unknowne.* By An English Mercury [pseud.]. [London]: Imprinted by G. Eld for Ed. Blount and W. Barrett, [1609]. New translation as *Another World and Yet the Same: Bishop Joseph Hall's Mundus Alter et Idem.* Trans. and ed. John Millar Wands. New Haven, Conn.: Yale University Press, 1981.

1609 La Vega, Garcilaso de, El Inca. *Primera parte de los commentarios reales, que tratan del origen de los Yncas.* Lisbon: P. Crasbeeck.

1611 Shakespeare, William. *The Tempest* Mr William Shakespeares Comedies, histories and tragedies. First published in 1623: London: I. Jaggard and E. Blount.

1614 Boccalini, Trajano. *De' Ragguagli di Parnaso, di Trajano Boccalini . . . centuria prima.* Milan: G. B. Bidelli.

1616 *Histoire du grand et admirable Royaume d'Antangil incogneu jusques a present à tous historiens et cosmographes. . . . Le tout compris en cinq livres, par J. D. M. G. T.* Saumur: T. Maire.

1619 Andreae, Johann Valentin. *Reipublicae Chistianopolitanæ descriptio.* Strasbourg: Héritier de L. Zetner.

1621 [Burton, Robert]. ["An Utopia of Mine Owne"]. "Democritus Iunior to the Reader." Pp. 56–61 in his *The Anatomy of Melancholy, What It is. With all the Kindes, Causes, Symptomes, Prognostickes and Severall Cures of It. In Three Maine Partitions with their seuereii Sections Members and Subsections. Philosophically, Medicinally, Historically, Opened and Cut Up.* By Democritus Iunior [pseud.]. Oxford: Printed by Iohn Lichfield and Iames Short, for Henry Cripps, 1621. Over the various editions, this section tripled in size. Critical ed. as *The Anatomy of Melancholy.* Ed. Thomas C. Faulkner, Nicolas K. Kessling, and Rhonda L. Blair. 3 vols. Oxford: Clarendon Press, 1989–94, 1: 85–103.

1621 Zuccolo, Lodivico. *Considerationi politiche e morali.* Venice: M. Ginami.

1623 Campanella, Tommaso. *Politicae Civitas Solis Idea Reipublicae Philosophicae.* Appendix to Part 4 of *Realis Philosophiae Epilogisticae.* Frankfurt, 1623. In English (in bilingual ed.): Trans. Daniel J. Donno. Berkeley: University of California Press, 1981. Also trans. A. M. Elliott and R. Millner. London: Journeyman Press, 1981.

1625 La Pierre, Jean de. *Le Grand Empire de l'un et l'autre monde divisé en trois royaumes: le royaume des aveugles, des borgnes et des clair-voyants.* Paris: D. Moreau.

1627 [Bacon, Francis]. *New Atlantis, A Worke unfinished.* Added to *Sylva sylvarium or a Naturall Historie. In Ten Centuries.* London: Printed by J[ohn] H[aviland] and Augustine Mathewes] for William Lee.

1634 Kepler, Johann. *Somnium, seu Opus posthumum de astronomia lunari.* n.p.

1638 [Godwin, Francis]. *The Man in the Moone; or A Discourse of a Voyage Thither.* By Domingo Gonsales [pseud.]. London: Printed by John Norton.

1640 Sgualdi, abbate Vicenzo. *Republica di Lesbo, overo della Ragione di Stato in un dominio aristocratico.* Bologna: N. Tebaldini.

1641 [Plattes, Gabriel]. *A Description of the famous Kingdom of Macaria; shewing its excellent Government, wherein the Inhabitants live in great Prosperity, Health, and Happiness; the King obeyed, the Nobles honoured, and all good Men respected; Vice punished, and Virtue rewarded. An Example to other Nations: In a Dialogue between a Scholar and a Traveller.* London: Printed for Francis Constable.

1648 [Gott, Samuel]. *Novae solymae. Libri Sex.* Londini: Typis Johannis Legati. Republished as *Novae Solymae Libri Sex; Sivi Institutio Christiani. 1. De Pueritia. 2. De Creatione Mundi. 3. De Juventute. 4. De Peccato. 5. De Virile Aetate. 6. De Redemptione Hominis. Cujus Opus, Studio Cur Tantum Quaeries Inani? Qui Legatis, Et Frueris, Feceris Esse Tuum.* London: Typis Johannis Legati, 1649. Second ed. as *Nova Solyma. The Ideal City, or Jerusalem Regained. An Anonymous Romance Written in the Time of Charles I. Now First Drawn from Obscurity, and Attributed to the Illustrious John Milton.* Edited by Rev. Walter Begley. 2 vols. London: John Murray, 1902.

1650 Scudéry, Madeleine de. *Histoire de Sapho,* in *Artamène ou le Grand Cyrus.* Paris: Courbé (2nd ed.).

1652 Winstanley, Gerrard. *The Law of Freedom in a Platform: Or, True Magis-*

tracy Restored. Humbly presented to Oliver Cromwel, General of the Commonwealths Army in England, Scotland, and Ireland. And to all Englishmen my brethren whether in Church-fellowship, or not in Church-fellowship, both sorts walking as they conceive according to the Order of The Gospel: and from them to all the Nations in the World. Wherin is Declared, What is Kingly Government, and what is Common-wealths Government. London: Printed for the author.

1655 [Cavendish, Margaret]. Lady M[argaret] of Newcastle. "The Inventory of Judgements Commonwealth, the Author cares not in what World it is established." Pp. 205–12 in her The Worlds Olio. London: Printed for J. Martin Allestrye, 1655. 2nd ed. London: A. Maxwell, 1671, 399–412.

1656 Harrington, James. The Common-Wealth of Oceana. London: Livewell Chapman.

1657 Cyrano de Bergerac, Savinien de. Histoire comique contenant les états et empires de la Lune. Paris: C. de Sercy. In English: Cyrano de Bergerac's Voyages to the Moon and the Sun. Trans. and notes by Richard Aldington, intro. by John Wells. London: Folio Society, 1991.

1659 Baxter, Richard. A Holy Commonwealth, or Political Aphorisms, Opening the true Principles of Government: For The Healing of the Mistakes, and Resolving the Doubts, that most endanger and trouble ENGLAND at this time: (if yet there may be hope.) And directing the desires of sober Christians that long to see the Kingdoms of this world, become the Kingdoms of the Lord, and of his Christ. London: Printed for Thomas Underhill and Francis Taylor. Modern ed.: Ed. William Lamont. Cambridge, England: Cambridge University Press, 1994.

1659 Eliot, John. The Christian Commonwealth: Or, The Civil Policy of the Rising Kingdom of Jesus Christ. Written Before the Interruption of the Government. London: Printed for Livewell Chapman.

1659 [Plockhoy, Pieter]. A Way Propounded to Make the poor in these and other Nations happy. By bringing together a fit suitable and well qualified people unto one Household-government, or little-Commonwealth, Wherein every one may keep his propriety, and be imployed in some work or other, as he shall be fit, without being oppressed. Being the way not only to rid these and other nations from idle, evil and disorderly persons, but also from all such that have sought and found out many inventions to live upon the labour of others. Whereunto is also annexed an invitation to the Society, or little Commonwealth. By Peter Cornelius, Van-Zurik-Zee [pseud.]. London: Printed for G.C.

1659 Pure, Michel de. Epigone, histoire du siècle futur. . . . Paris: P. Lamy.

1660 H., R., Esquire. New Atlantis. Begun by the Lord Verulam, Viscount St. Albans: and Continued by R. H. Esquire. Wherein is set forth a Platform of Monarchical Government. With A Pleasant intermixture of divers rare Inventions, and wholsom customs, fit to be introduced into all Kingdoms, States, and Common-Wealths. London: Printed for John Crooke.

1665 Zieglschmid, A.J.F. Die älteste Chronik des hutterischen Brüder. First published in 1943: Ithaca, N.Y.: The Cayuga Press.

1666 [Cavendish, Margaret], Duchess of Newcastle. The Description of a New World, Called the Blazing World. Part IV (separately paged) of her Observations Upon Experimental Philosophy. London: Printed by J. Maxwell. First separate publication: London: Printed by A. Maxwell, 1668.

1668 [Neville, Henry]. The Isle of Pines, or, a late Discovery of a fourth Island near Terra Australis, Incognita, by Henry Cornelius Van Sloetten [pseud.]. Wherein is contained, A True Relation of certain English persons, who in Queen Elizabeths time, making a Voyage to the East Indies were cast away, and wracked near to the Coast of Terra Australis, Incognita, and all drowned, except one Man and four Women. And now lately Anno Dom. 1667. a Dutch Ship making a Voyage to the East Indies, driven by foul weather there, by chance have found their Posterity, (speaking good English) to amount (as they suppose) to ten or twelve thousand persons. The whole Relàtion (written, and left by the Man himself a little before his death, and delivered to the Dutch by his Grandchild) is here annexed with the Longitude and Latitude of the Island, the scituation and felicity thereof, with other matter observable. London: Printed for Allen Banks and Charles Harper.

1669 Le Grand, Antonii. Scydromedia seu sermo, quem Alphonsus de la Vida Habuit Coram Comite de Falmouth, De Monarchia. London: n.p.

1669 Grimmelshausen, Hans Jakob Christoph von. Simplicissimus. Nuremberg: W. E. Felsecker.

1675 Barnes, Joshua. Gerania: A New Discovery of a Little sort of People Anciently Discoursed of, called Pygmies. With a lively Description Of their Stature, Habit, Manners, Buildings, Knowledge, and Government, being very delightful and profitable. London: Printed by W. G. for Obadia Blagrave.

1675 Vairasse, Denis. The History of the Sevarites or Sevarambi; a Nation inhabiting part of the third Continent, Commonly called, Terra Australis Incognitae. With an Account of their admirable Government, Religion, Customs, and Language. Written By one Captain Siden [pseud.]. A worthy Person, Who, together with many others, was Cast upon those Coasts, and lived many Years in that Country. [Translated by A. Roberts]. London: Printed for Henry Brome. The Second Part more wonderful and delightful than the First is added after Country, 1679. First published in French as L'Histoire [Histoire, Conclusion de l'Histoire] des Sevarambes, peuples [sic] qui habitent une partie du troisième continent communément appellé [sic] la Terre australe. Paris: C. Barbin, 1677.

1676 Foigny, Gabriel de. La Terre australe connue, c'est-à-dire la description de ce pays inconnu jusqu'ici, de ses mœurs et de ses coutumes, par Mr Sadeur. . . . Vannes [Geneva]: J. Verneuil. In English: The Southern Land, Known. Trans. and ed. David Fausett. Syracuse, N.Y.: Syracuse University Press, 1993.

1681 Fleury, Claude. Les Mœurs des Isrëalites. Paris: Veuve G. Clouzier.

1686 Fontenelle, Bernard Le Bovier de. Entretiens sur la pluralité des mondes. Paris: Veuve C. Blageart.

1686 Fontenelle, Bernard Le Bovier de. Relation de l'Ile de Bornéo, in Pierre Bayle, Nouvelles de la République des lettres, janvier 1686.

1689 L'Epy, M. Heliogenes de. A Voyage into Tartary. Containing a Curious Description of that Country, with part of Greece and Turky; the Manners, Opinions, and Religion of the Inhabitants therein; with some other Incidents. London: Printed by T. Hodgkin.

1693 [Lee, Francis]. Antiquity Reviv'd or the Government of a Certain island Antiently Called Astreada, In Reference to Religion, Policy, War, and Peace. Some hundreds of Years Before the Coming of Christ. London: n.p.

1694 [Astell, Mary]. A Serious Proposal To the Ladies; For the Advancement of their true and greatest Interest. By A Lover of Her Sex [pseud.]. London: Printed for K. Wilkin.

1696 The Free State of Noland. London: Printed for J. Whitlock. 18 pp. 2nd ed. as The Free State of Noland: or, The Frame and Constitution of that Happy, Noble, Powerful, and Glorious State. In which all Sorts and Degrees of People find their Condition Better'd. London: Printed for D. Brown, 1701. 61 pp.

1698 An Essay Concerning Adepts: or, A Resolution of this Inquiry, How it cometh to pass that Adepts, if there are any in the World, are no more Beneficial to Mankind than they have been known hitherto to be, and whether there could be no way to Encourage them to Communicate themselves. With some Resolutions concerning the Principles of the Adeptists; And a Model, Practicable, and Easy, of living in Community. By A Philadept [pseud.]. London: Printed by J. Mayos.

1699 Fénelon, François de Salignac de La Mothe. *Suite du quatrième livre de l'Odyssée d'Homère ou les Avantures de Télémaque, fils d'Ulysse.* Paris: Veuve Barbin. Modern ed. in English: *Telemachus, Son of Ulysses.* Ed. and trans. Patrick Riley. Cambridge, England: Cambridge University Press, 1994.

1699 *Der Wohleingerichte Staat.* Leipzig: n.p.

1700 Gilbert, Claude. *Histoire de Calejava ou de l'isle des hommes raisonnables, avec le paralele de leur morale et du christianisme.* [Printed at Dijon].

1703 Russen, David of Hythe. *Iter Lunare: or, A Voyage to the Moon. Containing Some Consideration on the Nature of that Planet. The Possibility of getting thither. With other Pleasant Conceits about the Inhabitants, their Manners and Customs.* London: Printed for J. Nutt.

1706 Lesconvel, Pierre de. *Nouvelle relation du voyage du prince de Montberaud dans l'isle de Naudely.* Mérinde [Paris or Liège?]: Innocent Démocrite.

1708 Psalmanaazaar [also spelled Psalmanazar], George [pseud.]. *An Historical and Geographical Description of Formosa, an Island Subject to the Emperor of Japan. Giving an Account of the Religion, Customs, Manners, &c. of the Inhabitants. Together with a Relation of what happen'd to the Author in his Travels; particularly his Conferences with the Jesuits, and others,*

in several Parts of Europe. Also the History and Reasons of his Conversion to Christianity, with his Objections against it (in defence of Paganism) and their Answers. To which is prefix'd, A Preface in Vindication of himself from the Reflections of a Jesuit lately come from China, with an Account of what passed between them.* London: Printed for Dan. Brown, G. Strahan, and W. Davis, and Fran. Coggan.

1708 Smeeks, Hendrick. *Beschryvnge van het magtig koningryk Krinke Kesmes.* Amsterdam. In English: *The Mighty Kingdom of Kinke Kesmes (1708).* Presented by David Fausett. Trans. Robert-H. Leek. Amsterdam: Rodopi, 1995.

1710 Tyssot de Patot, Simon. *Voyages et avantures de Jaques Massé.* Cologne [La Haye]: Jaques Kainkus. In English: *The Travels and Adventures of James Massey.* London, 1733.

1711 Lefebvre, François. *Relation du voyage de l'isle d'Eutopie.* Delft: H. Van Rhin.

1715 [Morgan, Joseph]. *The History of the Kingdom of Basaruah, Containing A Relation of the most Memorable Transactions, Revolutions and Heroick Exploits in that Kingdom, from the first Foundation thereof unto this present time. Collected from the most Antient Records of that Country, and translated into our Language, not only for Delight, but for the abundant Instruction that may be learned therefrom, in these Remote Parts. Written in Discharge of the Trust reposed in the Author by his Majesty, for the Discovery of Foreign things.* By a Traveller in Basaruah [pseud.]. Boston: n.p. [actually New York: Bradford]. Reprinted as *The History of the Kingdom of Basaruah, and Three Unpublished Letters.* Ed. Richard Schlatter. Cambridge, Mass.: Harvard

University Press, 1946.

1719 [Defoe, Daniel]. *The Life and Strange Surprizing Adventures of Robinson Crusoe, of York, Mariner: Who lived eight and twenty Years all alone in an un-inhabited Island on the Coast of America, near the Mouth of the Great River of Oroonoque; Having been cast on Shore by Ship wreck, where-in all the Men perished but himself. With An Account of how he was at last strangely deliver'd by pyrates. Written by Himself.* London: Printed for W. Taylor.

1720 Tyssot de Patot, Simon. *La Vie, les aventures et le voyage de Groënland du Révérend Père Cordelier Pierre de Mésange. . . . .* Amsterdam: E. Roger.

1721 Montesquieu, Charles-Louis de Secondat, baron de La Brède et de. *Lettres persanes.* Cologne: P. Marteau.

1723 Sinold von Schütz, Philipp Balthasar. *Die Glüseeligate Insul.* Leipzig: n.p.

1726 [Swift, Jonathan]. *Travels into several Remote Nations of the World. In Four Parts.* By Lemuel Gulliver [pseud.]. 2 vols. London: Printed for Beng. Motte.

1727 Brunt, Captain Samuel. *A Voyage to Cacklogallinia with a Description of the Religion, Policy, Customs and Manners of that Country.* London: Printed by J. Watson. Reprinted, New York: The Facsimile Text Society, 1940.

1730 Desfontaines, Pierre-François Guyot. *Le Nouveau Gulliver ou Voyage de Jean Gulliver, fils du capitaine Gulliver. . . .* Paris: Veuve Clouzier.

1731 Prévost, abbé Antoine-François. *Le Philosophe anglois ou Histoire de Monsieur Cleveland, fils naturel de Cromwell.* Paris: F. Didot.

1731 [Schnabel, Johann Gottfried]. *Die Insel Felsenburg.* By Gisander [pseud.]. Nordhausen: J. H. Gross.

1731 Terrasson, abbé Jean. *Sethos, histoire, ou Vie tirée des monumens anecdotes de l'ancienne Egypte, traduite d'un manuscrit grec.* Paris: J. Guérin.

1734 Mouhy, Charles de Fieux, chevalier de. *Lamekis ou les Voyages extraordinaires d'un Egyptien dans la terre intérieure avec la découverte de l'isle des Silphides.* Paris: L. Dupuis. Reprinted in *Voyages imaginaires*, 1787.

1734 Rustaing de Saint-Jory, Louis. *Les Femmes militaires, relation historique d'une île nouvellement découverte.* Paris: C. Simon.

1737 [Berington (sometimes spelled Berrington), Simon]. *The Memoirs of Sigʳ Guadentio di Lucca [pseud.]: Taken from his Confession and Examination before the Fathers of the Inquisition at Bologna in Italy. Making a Discovery of an Unknown Country in the midst of the Vast Deserts of Africa, as Ancient, Populous, and Civilized, as the Chinese. With an Account of their Antiquity, Origine, Religion, Customs, Polity, &c. and the Manner how they got first over those vast Deserts. Interspers'd with several most suprizing and curious Incidents. Copied from the original Manuscript kept in St. Mark's Library at Venice: With Critical Notes of the Learned Signor Rhedi, late Library-Keeper of the said Library. To which is prefix'd, a Letter of the Secretary of the Inquisition, to the same Signor Rhedi, giving an Account of the Manner and Causes of his being seized. Faithfully Translated from the Italian, by E. T. Gent* [written in English]. London: Printed for T. Cooper.

1741 Holberg, Ludwig. *Nicolai Klimii Iter subterraneum.* Copenhagen and Leipzig: J. Preus. In English: *Journey of Niels Klim to the World Underground.* Ed. James I. McNelis, Jr. Lincoln: University of

Nebraska Press, 1960.

1745 [Kirkby, John]. *The Capacity and Extent of the Human Understanding; Exemplified In the Extraordinary Case of Automathes; A Young Nobleman, Who was Accidentally left in his Infancy, upon a desolate Island, and continued Nineteen Years in that solitary State, separated from all Human Society. A Narrative Abounding with many surprizing Occurrences, both Useful and Entertaining to the Reader.* London: Printed for R. Manby and H. Shute Cox.

1749 Seriman, Zaccaria. *Viaggi di Enrico Wanton alle Terre Incognite Australi, ed al Paese delle Scimmie.* Venice: Giovanni Tagier.

1749 Tiphaigne de La Roche, Charles-François. *L'Amour dévoilé ou le systême des simpathistes, où l'on explique l'origine de l'amour, des inclinations, des simpathies, des aversions, des antipathies, etc.* N.p.

1751 Coyer, abbé Gabriel-François. *Découverte de l'Isle frivole, augmentée de l'Année merveilleuse ou les hommes-femmes.* La Haye: J. Swart.

1751 [Paltock, Robert]. *The Life and Adventures of Peter Wilkins A Cornish Man: Relating particularly, His Shipwreck near the South Pole; his wonderful Passage thro' a subterraneous Cavern into a kind of new World; his there meeting with a Gawry or flying woman, whose life he preserv'd, and afterwards married her; his extraordinary Conveyance to the Country of Glums and Gawrys, or Men and Woman that fly. Likewise a Description of this strange Country, with the Laws, Customs, and Manners of its Inhabitants, and the Author's remarkable Transactions among them. Taken from his own Mouth, in his Passage to England from off Cape Horn in America, in the ship Hector. With an*

INTRODUCTION, giving an Account of the surprizing Manner of his coming on board that Vessel, and his Death on landing at Plymouth in the Year 1739. Illustrated with several CUTS, clearly and distinctly representing the Structure and Mechanism of the Wings of the Glums and Gawrys, and the Manner in which they use them either to swim or fly. London: J. Robinson and R. Dodsley.

1752 Maubert de Gouvest, Jean-Henri. *Lettres iroquoises*. Irocopolis: chez les Vénérables.

1752 Stanislaw Leszczyn-ski, Stanislas I, King of Poland. *Entretien d'un européen avec un insulaire du Royaume de Dumocala.*

1752 Voltaire, François Marie Arouet de. *Micromégas*. London [Paris]: Lambert.

1753 Morelly. *Naufrage des isles flottantes ou Basiliade du célèbre Pilpai, poème héroïque traduit de l'indien*. Messine [Paris]: Une société de libraires.

1753 [Smith, William]. *A General Idea of the College of Mirania; with a sketch of the Method of Teaching Science and Religion, in the several classes and some account of rise, establishment and build-ings. Address'd more immediately to the consid-eration of the trustees nominated, by the Legisla-ture, to receive proposals etc. relating to the estab-lishment of a college in the province of New York*. New York: Printed by J. Parker and W. Weyman.

1755 Morelly. *Code de la nature ou le Véritable esprit de ses lois de tout temps négligé ou méconnu*. N.p.

1755 *Voyages curieux d'un philadelphe dans des pays nouvellement découverts*. La Haye: aux dépens de la compagnie.

1755 *A Voyage to the World in the Centre of the Earth. Giving an account of the manners, customs, laws, government and religion of the inhabitants. Their Persons and Habits described: With several other Particulars. In which is introduced, The History of an Inhabitant of the Air, Written by Himself. With some account of the planetary worlds*. London: Printed for S. Crowder and H. Woodgate.

1759 Voltaire, François Marie Arouet, dit. *Candide ou l'Optimisme*. Geneva: Cramer. In English: *Candid: or, All for the Best*. London: Printed for J. Nourse, 1759. Modern ed.: *Voltaire's Candide: A Bilingual Edition*. Trans. and ed. Peter Gay. New York: St. Martin's Press, 1963.

1759 Johnson, Samuel. *The Prince of Abissinia. A Tale*. London: R. and J. Dodsley. Also known as *The History of Rasselas, Prince of Abissinia. A Tale*. London: Harrison and Com-pany, 1787; and *Rasselas, Prince of Abissinia: A Tale*. London: Printed for Joseph Wennman, 1787.

1760 Tiphaigne de La Roche, Charles-François. *Giphantie*. Babylone [Paris]: Durand.

1761 Tiphaigne de La Roche, Charles-François. *L'empire des Zaziris sur les humains ou la Zazirocratie*. Pékin [Paris]: Dsmgtlfpqxz.

1762 Deschamps, Dom Léger-Marie, O.S.B. *Le Vrai Système ou le Mot de l'énigme métaphysique et morale*. First published in 1939: Paris: Droz. The date of 1762 was assigned by Raymond Trousson.

1762 Rousseau, Jean-Jacques. *Du contrat social ou Principes du droit politique*. Amsterdam: M. M. Rey.

1762 [Scott, Mrs. Sarah Robinson]. *A Description o f Millenium Hall, And the Country Adjacent: Together with the Character of the Inhabitants, And such Historical Anecdotes and Reflections, As May excite in the Reader proper Sentiments of Humanity, and lead the Mind to the Love of Virtue. By a Gentleman on his Travels* [pseud.]. London: Printed for J. Newbery.

1763 *The Reign of George VI 1900–1925*. London: Printed for W. Nicholl. Reprinted, London: Corn-market Reprints, 1972.

1764 [Burgh, James]. *An Account of the First Settlement, Laws, Form of Government, and Police, of the Cessares, a People of South America: In Nine Letters, from Mr. Vander Neck* [pseud.], *one of the Senators of that Nation, to his Friend in Holland. With Notes by the Editor*. Lon-don: Printed for J. Payne.

1765 Tiphaigne de La Roche, Charles-François. *Histoire des Galligènes ou Mémoires de Duncan*. Paris: Veuve Durand.

1768 Coyer, abbé Gabriel-François. *Chinki, histoire cochinchinoise qui peut servir à d'autres pays*. London: n.p.

1768 Fontenelle, Bernard Le Bovierde, and S. Van Doelvelt. *La République des philosophes ou Histoire des Ajaoiens*. Geneva: n.p.

1769 *Private Letters from an American in England to his Friends in America*. London: Printed for J. Almon. Reprinted as *Antici-pation, or The Voyage of an American to England in the Year 1899, in a series of letters, humourously describing the supposed situation of this Kingdom at that Period*. London: Print-ed for W. Lane, 1781.

1769 Restif de La Bre-tonne, Nicolas-Edme. *Le Pornographe ou Idées d'un honnête homme sur un projet de réglement pour les prostituées, propre à prévenir les malheurs qu'occasionne le publi-cisme des femmes, avec des notes historiques et justificatives*. London: J. Nourse.

1770 or 1771 Diderot, Denis. *Supplément au Voyage de Bougainville ou Dialogue entre A et B sur l'inconvénient d'attacher des idées morales à cer-taines actions physiques qui n'en comportent pas*. First published in 1921: Paris: Ed. de la Nouvelle Revue française.

1771 Mercier, Louis Sébastien. *L'An deux mille quatre cent quarante, rêve s'il en fût jamais*. London [probably Lausanne]. In English: *Memoirs of the Year Two Thousand Five Hundred*. Trans. W. Hoop-er. London: Printed for G. Robinson, 1772; Philadel-phia: Printed by Thomas Dobson, 1795.

1772 Haller, Albrecht von. *Usong, eine morgenländis-che Geschichte in vier Büchern*. Bern: Verlag der neuen Buchhandlung.

1777 Restif de La Bre-tonne, Nicolas-Edme. *Les Gynographes ou Idées de deux honnêtes femmes sur un projet de règlement proposé à toute l'Europe pour mettre les femmes à leur place et opérer le bonheur des deux sexes, avec notes historiques et justificatives*. La Haye: Gosse et Pinet.

1778 [Elliott, John, sup-posed author]. *The Travels of Hildebrand Bowman, Esquire, Into Carnovirria, Taupiniera, Olfactaria, and Auditante, in New-Zealand; in the Island of Bonhommi-ca, and in the powerful Kingdom of Luxo-volupto, on the Great Southern Continent. Written by Him-self; Who went on shore in the Adventure's large Cut-ter, at Queen Charlotte's Sound New Zealand, the fatal 17th of December 1773; and escaped being cut off, and devoured, with the rest of the Boat's crew, by happening to be a-shooting in the woods; where he was afterwards unfortunately left behind by the Adventure. By Hildebrand Bowman* [pseud.]. London: Printed for W. Strahan; and T. Cadell.

1781 Restif de La Bre-tonne, Nicolas-Edme. *La Découverte australe par un homme volant ou le Dédale français, nouvelle très philosophique, suivie de la lettre d'un singe.* . . . Paris: Veuve Duchesne.

1782 Restif de La Bre-tonne, Nicolas-Edme. *L'Andrographe ou Idées d'un honnête homme sur un projet de règlement proposé à toutes les nations de l'Europe pour opérer une réforme générale des mœurs, et, par elle, le bonheur du genre humain*. La Haye: Gosse et Pinet.

1782 [Spence, Thomas]. *A Supplement to the History of Robinson Crusoe, Being the History of Crusonia, or Robinson Crusoe's Island, Down to the Pre-sent Time. Copied from a letter sent by Mr. Wishit, Captain of the Good-Intent, to an intelligent Friend in England, after being in a Storm in May, 1781 driven out of his course to the Said Island. Published by the said Gentleman, for the agreeable Perusal of Robinson Crusoe's Friends of all Sizes*. New ed. Newcastle upon Tyne, England: T. Saint.

1784 Grivel, Guillaume. *L'Isle inconnue ou Mémoires du chevalier Des Gastines, recueillis et publiés par M. Grivel*. Paris: B. Le Franq. In *Voyages imaginaires*, 1787.

1784 [Restif de La Bretonne, Nicolas-Edme]. *Les Contemporaines ou Avantures des plus jolies femmes de l'âge présent, recueillies par N* [pseud.], vol. II: *Les Associés*. Paris: Veuve Duchesne (2nd ed.).

1787 Casanova di Seingalt, Giacomo Girolamo. *Icosaméron ou Histoire d'Edouard et d'Elisabeth qui passèrent quatre-vingts-un ans chez les Mégamicres, habitans aborigènes du Protocosme dans l'intérieur de notre globe*. Prague: Ecole nor-male. In English: *Casano-va's "Icosameron."* . . . Trans. Rachel Zurer. New York: Jenna Press, 1986.

1787 Heinse, Wilhelm. *Ardinghello und die Glückseeligen Inseln.*. . . . Lemgo: Meyer.

1787 *Voyages imaginaires, songes, visions et romans*

cabalistiques ornés de figures. Amsterdam and Paris: Cuchet, then Panckoucke, 36 vols. published up to 1789.

1791 Beffroy de Reigny, Louis-Abel, called Cousin Jacques. *Nicodème dans la lune ou la Révolution pacifique, folie en prose et en 3 actes, mêlée d'ariettes et de vaudevilles. . . .* Paris: Froullé.

1791 Bentham, Jeremy. *Panopticon; or, The inspection-house: containing the idea of a new principle of construction applicable to any sort of establishment, in which persons of any description are to be kept under inspection. . . .* London: T. Payne.

1791 Mirabeau, Honoré-Gabriel de Riquetti, comte de. *Catéchisme de la Constitution, à l'usage des habitans de la campagne, par un député de l'Assemblée nationale.* N.p.

1791 Paine, Thomas. *Rights of man, being an answer to Mr Burke's attack on the French Revolution.* London: J. S. Jordan.

1791 Volney, Constantin François Chasseboeuf, comte de. *Les Ruines ou Méditation sur les révolutions des empires.* Paris: Desenne.

1792 Fokke Simonsz, Arend. *Het toekomend Jaar 3000.* Amsterdam: Fokke Simonsz.

1792 Le Mercier de La Rivière, Pierre-Paul-François-Joachim-Henri. *L'Heureuse Nation ou Relations du gouvernement des Féliciens, peuple souverainement libre sous l'empire absolu de ses loix. . . .* Paris: Buisson.

1792 Le Sueur, Théodore. *Idées sur l'espèce de gouvernement populaire qui pourrait convenir à un pays de l'étendue et de la population de la France, essai présenté à la Convention nationale, par un citoyen.* Paris: Mayer.

1792 Wollstonecraft, Mary. *A Vindication of the rights of woman, with strictures on political and moral sub-*

jects. London: J. Johnson.

1793 Aratus. *A Voyage to the Moon strongly recommended to all lovers of real freedom.* London.

1793 Cloots, Anacharsis. *Bases constitutionnelles de la République du genre humain.* Paris: Imprimerie nationale.

1793 Godwin, William. *An Enquiry Concerning Political Justice, and its influence on general virtue and happiness.* 2 vols. London: Printed for G.G.J. and J. Robinson.

1795 Condorcet, Jean-Antoine-Nicolas de Caritat, marquis de. *Esquisse d'un tableau historique des progrès de l'esprit humain.* Paris: Agasse.

1795 Hodgson, William. *The Commonwealth of reason.* London: H. D. Symonds.

1795 Kant, Immanuel. *Zum ewigen Frieden, ein philosophischer Entwurf.* Königsberg: F. Nicovius. In English: *Perpetual Peace.* Trans., with an introduction, by Lewis White Beck. New York: Liberal Arts Press, 1957.

1795 [Northmore, Thomas]. *Memoirs of Planetes, or a Sketch of the Laws and Manners of Makar.* By Phileleutherus Devoniensis [pseud.]. London: Printed by Vaughan Griffiths.

1795 Sade, Donatien-Alphonse-François. *Aline et Valcour ou le roman philosophique.* Paris: Veuve Girouard.

1795 Sade, Donatien-Alphonse-François. *La Philosophie dans le boudoir, ouvrage posthume de l'auteur de Justine.* London.

1796 [Whitmore, W.; sometimes ascribed to H. Whitmore]. *Modern Gulliver's Travels. Lilliput: Being A New Journey to that Celebrated Island. Containing a Faithful Account of the Manners, Character, Customs, Religion, Laws, Politics, Revenue, Taxes, Learning, General Progress in Arts and Sciences, Dress,*

Amusements, and Gallantry of Those Famous Little People. From the Year 1702 (when they were first discovered and visited by Captain Lemuel Gulliver, the Father of the Compiler of this Work), to the present Aera 1796. By Lemuel Gulliver, Jun. [pseud.]. London: Printed for T. Chapman.

1798 Restif de La Bretonne, Nicolas-Edme. *L'Anti-Justine ou les Délices de l'amour.* Paris: Veuve Girouard.

1800 Say, Jean-Baptiste. *Olbie ou éssai sur les moyens de réformer les mœurs d'une nation.* Paris: Deterville.

1802 [Lithgow, John]. "Equality – A Political Romance." *The Temple of Reason* 2, nos. 17–23 (May 22–July 3, 1802). Reprinted as *Equality; or, A History of Lithconia.* Philadelphia: Liberal Union, 1827; and Boston: Published by J. P. Mendum, 1863. Also published as *Equality, A History of Lithconia.* Philadelphia: The Prime Press, 1947.

1803 Gallet, Pierre. *Voyage d'un habitant de la Lune à Paris à la fin du XVIIIe siècle.* Paris: Levrault.

1805 Grainville, Jean-Baptiste Cousin de. *Le Dernier Homme.* Paris: Deterville (posthumously published).

1808 Fourier, Charles. *Théorie des quatre mouvements et des destinées générales. Prospectus et annonce de la découverte.* Leipzig [Lyon: M. Rustand]. In English: *The Theory of the Four Movements.* Ed. Gareth Stedman Jones and Ian Patterson. Trans. Ian Patterson. Cambridge, England: Cambridge University Press, 1996.

1808 Jaunez-Sponville, Pierre-Ignace, and Nicolas Bugnet. *La Philosophie du Ruvarebohni, pays dont la découverte semble d'un grand intérêt pour l'homme. . . .* [Paris]: Impr. de Le Normant.

1810 Mosneron de Launay, Jean-Baptiste. *Le Vallon*

aérien ou Relation d'un voyage d'un aéronaute dans un pays inconnu. Paris: J. Chaumeret.

1810 Voss, Julius von. *Ini, ein Roman aus dem 21. Jahrhundert.* Berlin: K. F. Amelang.

1811 Lawrence, James. *The Empire of the Nairs; or, The Rights of Women. An Eutopian Romance.* 4 vols. in 2. London: Printed for T. Hookham and E. T. Hookham.

1812 Wyss, Johann. *Der schweizerische Robinson oder der schiffbrüchige Schweizer-Prediger und seiner Familie.* Zurich: Orell. Modern ed. in English: *The Swiss Family Robinson.* Ed., with an introduction, by John Seelye. New York: Oxford University Press, 1991.

1813 [Owen, Robert]. *A New View of Society; or, Essays on the Principle of the Formation of the Human Character, and the Application of the Principle to Practice. By One of His Majesty's Justices of Peace for the Country of Lanark* [pseud.]. London: Printed for Cadell and Davies, by Richard Taylor and Co.

1814 Saint-Simon, Claude-Henri de, and Augustin Thierry. *De la réorganisation de la société européenne ou De la nécessité et des moyens de rassembler les peuples de l'Europe en un seul corps politique, en conservant à chacun son indépendance nationale.* Paris: A. Egron.

Ca. 1816 Fourier, Charles. *Le Nouveau Monde amoureux.* First French publication in 1999: Ed., with notes and introduction, by Simone Debout-Oleszkiewicz. Paris: Stock. In English: published in part in *The Utopian Vision of Charles Fourier.* Trans. and ed. Jonathan Beecher and Richard Bienvenu. Boston: Beacon Press, 1971.

1820 [Ellis, G. A.]. *New Britain. A Narrative of a Journey, by Mr. Ellis, To a*

Country So Called By Its Inhabitants, Discovered in the Vast Plain of the Missouri, in North America, and Inhabited by a People of British Origin, Who Live Under an Equitable System of Society, Productive of Peculiar Independence and Happiness. Also, Some Account of Their Constitution, Laws, Institutions, Customs and Philosophical Opinions: Together With a Brief Sketch of Their History from the Time of Their Departure from Great Britain. London: Printed for W. Simpkin and R. Marshall.

1826 Morgan, John Minter. *Revolt of the Bees.* London: Longman, Rees, Orme, Brown, and Green.

1827 [Tucker, George]. *A Voyage to the Moon: With Some Account of the Manners and Customs, Science and Philosophy, of the People of Morosofia, and Other Lunarians.* By Joseph Atterley [pseud.]. New York: Elam Bliss.

1828 Buonarroti, Philippe. *Conspiration pour l'égalité, dite de Babeuf, suivi du procès auquel elle donna lieu et des pièces justificatives, etc., etc.* Brussels: Librairie romantique.

1828 [Disraeli, Benjamin]. *The Voyage of Captain Popanilla.* London: Henry Colburn; Philadelphia: Carey, Lea and Carey.

1829 Fourier, Charles. *Le Nouveau Monde industriel et sociétaire ou Invention du procédé d'industrie attrayante et naturelle distribuée en séries passionnées.* Paris: Bossange père.

1832 Ballanche, Pierre-Simon. *La Ville des expiations.* Paris: A. Pinard.

1833 Etzler, J[ohn] A[dol]phus]. *The Paradise within Reach of All Men, without Labour, by Powers of Nature and Machinery.* 2 parts. Pittsburgh, Pa.: Etzler and Reinhold.

1834 Bodin, Félix. *Le Roman de l'avenir.* Paris: Lecointe et Pougin.

1836 [Griffith, Mary]. "Three Hundred Years

Hence." Pp. 9–92 in her *Camperdown; or, News from Our Neighborhood: Being Sketches*. By the Author of "Our Neighborhood" [pseud.]. Philadelphia: Carey, Lea and Blanchard, 1836. Reprinted as *Three Hundred Years Hence*. Philadelphia: Prime Press, 1950.

1837 [Whately, Richard]. *Account of an Expedition to the Interior of New Holland*. Ed. Lady Mary Fox. London: Richard Bentley.

1838 Considérant, Victor. *Destinée sociale*. Paris: bureau de "La Phalange."

1840 Brisbane, Albert. *Social Destiny of Man: or, Association and Reorganization of Industry*. Philadelphia: C. F. Stollmeyer. Reprinted, New York: Augustus M. Kelley, 1969.

1840 Cabet, Etienne. *Voyage et aventures de Lord William Carisdall en Icarie*. Paris: H. Souverain. As *Voyage en Icarie*. Paris: au bureau du *Populaire*, 1840. In English: *Journey to Icaria*. Syracuse, N.Y.: Syracuse University Press, 2000 (forthcoming).

1840 Proudhon, Pierre-Joseph. *Qu'est-ce que la propriété? ou Recherches sur le principe du droit et du gouvernement. Premier mémoire*. Paris: J.-F. Brocard. In English: *What Is Property? An Inquiry into the Principle of Right and of Government*. 2 vols. in 1. Trans. Benjamin R. Tucker. London: William Reeves, n.d.

1841 Etzler, J[ohn] A[dolphus]. *The New World or Mechanical System, To Perform the Labours of Man and Beast by Inanimate Powers, That Cost Nothing, for Producing and Preparing the Substance of Life*. Philadelphia: C. F. Stollmeyer.

1842 Weitling, Wilhelm. *Garantien der Harmonie und Freiheit*. Vivis: im Verlage des Verfassers.

1846 Melville, Herman. *Narrative of a Four Month's Residence Among the Natives of a Valley of the Marquesas Islands; or,*

A Peep at Polynesian Life. London: John Murray. Reprinted as *Typee; or, A Narrative of a Four Month's Residence Among the Natives of a Valley of the Marquesas Islands; or, A Peep at Polynesian Life*. London: John Murray, 1847.

1846 Sand, George. *Le Péché de M. Antoine*. Brussels: A. Lebègue et Sacré fils.

1846 Souvestre, Emile. *Le Monde tel qu'il sera*. Illustré par MM. Bertall, O. Penguilly et St-Germain. Paris: W. Coquebert.

1847 [Cooper, James Fenimore]. *The Crater; or, Vulcan's Peak. A Tale of the Pacific*. 2 vols. New York: Burgess, Stringer and Company. U.K. ed. as *Mark's Reef; or, The Crater. A Tale of the Pacific*. 3 vols. London: Richard Bentley. Reprinted as *The Crater or Vulcan's Peak*. Edited by Thomas Philbrick. Cambridge, Mass.: The Belknap Press of Harvard University Press, 1962.

1848 Leroux, Pierre. *Projet d'une constitution démocratique et sociale, fondée sur la loi même de la vie, et donnant, par une organisation véritable de l'état, la possibilité de détruire à jamais la monarchie, l'aristocratie, l'anarchie, et le moyen infaillible d'organiser le travail national sans blesser sa liberté; présenté à l'Assemblée nationale par un de ses membres, le citoyen Pierre Leroux*. Paris: G. Sandré.

1848 Marx, Karl, and Friedrich Engels. *Manifest der Kommunistischen Partei*. N.p. In English: *The Communist Manifesto: A Modern Edition*. Introduction by Eric Hobsbawm. London and New York: Verso, 1998.

1848 Mill, John Stuart. *Principles of political economy, with some of their applications to social philosophy*. London: J. W. Parker.

1852 Berlioz, Hector. *Euphonia ou la Ville*

musicale, in *Les Soirées de l'orchestre*. Paris: Michel Lévy frères.

1852 Hawthorne, Nathaniel. *The Blithedale Romance*. Boston: Ticknor, Reed and Fields.

1854 Pemberton, Robert. *The Happy Colony. Dedicated to the Workmen of Great Britain*. London: Saunders and Otley. Reprinted, New York: Garland, 1985.

1858 Dejacque, Joseph. *L'Humanisphère*, published in *Le Libertaire, journal du mouvement social* (New York), June 1858–August 1859.

1864 [Blanchard, Calvin]. *The Art of Real Pleasure: That New Pleasure, for which An Imperial Reward Was Offered*. New York: Calvin Blanchard. Reprinted, New York: Arno Press, 1971.

1865 Fournel, Victor. *Paris nouveau et Paris futur*. Paris: J. Lecoffre.

1865 Mettais, Hippolyte. *L'An 5865 ou Paris dans 4000 ans*. Paris: Librairie centrale.

1869 Grousset, Paschal. *Le Rêve d'un irréconciliable*. Paris: Madre.

1869 Moilin, Tony. *Paris en l'an 2000*. Paris: l'auteur.

1871 [Bulwer-Lytton, Edward]. *The Coming Race*. Edinburgh: William Blackwood. Also published as *Vril. The Power of the Coming Race*. Blauvelt, N.Y.: Rudolf Steiner Publications, 1972; and as *The Coming Race*. Santa Barbara, Calif.: Woodbridge Press Pub. Co., 1979; and Stroud, England: Alan Sutton, 1995.

1872 [Butler, Samuel]. *Erewhon; or, Over the Range*. London: Trübner.

1874 Malon, Benoît. *Une conjuration chez les Atlantes*, published in the *Almanach du peuple* (Paris).

1876 Renouvier, Charles. *Uchronie: l'utopie dans l'histoire, esquisse historique apocryphe du développement de la civilisation européenne tel qu'il n'a pas été, tel qu'il aurait*

pu être. Paris: bureau de la Critique philosophique.

1876 Richardson, Benjamin Ward. *Hygeia: A City of Health*. London: Macmillan. Reprinted, New York: Garland, 1985.

1878 Pellerin, Georges. *Le Monde dans deux mille ans*. Paris: E. Dentu.

1879 Verne, Jules. *Les Cinq Cents Millions de la Bégum*. Paris: J. Hetzel. In English: *The 500 Millions of the Begum*. New York: G. Munro, 1879.

1880 Dooner, P[ierton] W. *Last Days of the Republic*. San Francisco: Alta California Publishing Company.

1880–81 [Lane, Mary E. (Bradley)]. *Mizora: A Prophecy. A Mss. Found Among the Private Papers of the Princess Vera Zarovitch* [pseud.]. *Being a true and faithful account of her Journey to the Interior of the Earth, with a careful description of the Country and its Inhabitants, their Customs, Manners and Government. Written by Herself*. New York: G. W. Dillingham, 1889. Reprinted as *Mizora: A Prophecy*. Boston: Gregg Press, 1975; and as *Mizora: A World of Women*. Lincoln: University of Nebraska Press, 1999. Originally published as "Narrative of Vera Zarovitch" in the *Cincinnati Commercial* (November 6, 1880–February 5, 1881).

1881–82 [Trollope, Anthony]. "The Fixed Period." *Blackwoods Edinburgh Magazine* 130–131 (October 1881–March 1882). Republished in 2 vols. London: William Blackwood and Sons, 1882. Reprinted, ed. R. H. Super. Ann Arbor: University of Michigan Press, 1990.

1883 Robida, Albert. *Un caricaturiste prophète. La guerre telle qu'elle était prévue par A. Robida il y a trente-trois ans*. First published in 1916: Paris: Dorbon aîné.

1883 Robida, Albert. *Le Vingtième Siècle, roman d'une parisienne d'après-demain*. Paris: G. Decaux. Text and drawings by

A. Robida.

1884 Gronlund, Laurence. *The Coöperative Commonwealth in its Outlines. An Exposition of Modern Socialism*. Boston: Lee and Shepard. Reprinted, Cambridge, Mass.: Belknap Press, 1965.

1885 Jefferies, Richard. *After London; or, Wild England*. London: Cassell and Company. Reprinted, Oxford: Oxford University Press, 1980.

1886 Villiers de L'Isle-Adam, Auguste de. *L'Eve future*. Paris: M. de Brunhoff. In English: *Eve of the Future Eden*. Trans. Marilyn Gaddis Rose. Lawrence, Kans.: Coronado Press, 1981.

1887 [Hudson, William Henry]. *A Crystal Age*. London: T. F. Unwin.

1888 Bellamy, Edward. *Looking Backward: 2000–1887*. Boston: Ticknor and Company.

1888 Boussenard, Louis. *Les Secrets de Monsieur Synthèse*. Paris: C. Marpon et E. Flammarion.

1888 Hale, Edward Everett. *How They Lived in Hampton: A Study of Practical Christianity Applied in the Manufacture of Woollens*. Boston: J. Stilman Smith & Co. Reprinted without the subtitle, New York: Arno Press, 1971.

1888 Michel, Louise. *Le Monde nouveau*. Paris: E. Dentu.

1889 [Clemens, Samuel Langhorne]. *A Connecticut Yankee in King Arthur's Court*. By Mark Twain [pseud.]. New York: Charles L. Webster. Reprinted, Oxford: Oxford University Press, 1996. U.K. ed. as *A Yankee at the Court of King Arthur*. London: Chatto & Windus, 1889. Critical ed., ed. Bernard L. Stein. Berkeley: Published for the Iowa Center for Textual Studies by University of California Press, 1979.

1889 Flammarion, Camille. *Uranie*. Paris: C. Marpon et E. Flammarion.

1889 [Grousset, Paschal]. *De New-York à Brest*

en sept heures. By André Laurie [pseud.]. Paris: J. Hetzel.

1890 [Donnelly, Ignatius]. *Caesar's Column: A Story of the Twentieth Century.* By Edmund Boisgilbert, M.D. [pseud.]. Chicago: F. J. Schulte and Company. New ed., ed. Walter B. Rideout. Cambridge, Mass.: Belknap Press, 1960.

1890 Hertzka, Theodor. *Freiland, ein sociales Zukunftsbild.* Leipzig: Duncker & Humblot. In English: *Freeland, A Social Anticipation.* Trans. Arthur Ransom. London: Chatto & Windus, 1891.

1890 Morris, William. *News from Nowhere; or, An Epoch of Rest. Being Some Chapters from a Utopian Romance.* Boston: Roberts Bros. (unauthorized ed.). First authorized book ed.: Reeves & Turner, 1891. Reprinted, London: Kelmscott Press, 1892.

1891 Jerome, Jerome K. "The New Utopia." Pp. 261–79 in his *Diary of a Pilgrimage (And Six Essays).* Bristol, England: J. W. Arrowsmith.

1891 Richter, Eugen. *Sozialdemokratische Zukunftsbilder. Frei nach Bebel.* Berlin: Verlag Fortschritt. In English: *Pictures of the Socialistic Future (freely adapted from Bebel).* Trans. Henry Wright,. London: Swan Sonnenschein, 1893.

1891 Thomas, Chauncey. *The Crystal Button; or, Adventures of Paul Prognosis in the Forty-Ninth Century.* Ed. George Houghton. Boston: Houghton, Mifflin.

1892 Robida, Albert. *Le Vingtième Siècle, la vie électrique.* Paris: Librairie illustrée. Text and drawings by A. Robida.

1893 Gillette, King Camp. *Human Drift.* Boston: New Era Publishing Company.

1893 Olerich, Henry. *A Cityless and Countryless World: An Outline of Practical Co-operative Individualism.* Holstein, Iowa: Gilmore and Olerich. Reprinted, New York:

Arno Press, 1971.

1894 Flammarion, Camille. *La Fin du monde.* Paris: E. Flammarion.

1894 Howells, William Dean. *The Traveler from Altruria.* New York: Harper and Bros.

1895 Wells, H[erbert] G[eorge]. *The Time Machine: An Invention* [subtitle later dropped]. London: William Heinemann. Reprinted, ed. Michael Moorcock. London: Everyman, 1993. Revised centennial ed., ed. John Lawton. London: Everyman, 1995. Differing text in New York: Henry Holt, 1895.

1896 Tarde, Gabriel. *Fragment d'histoire future.* Paris: V. Giard et E. Brière. In English: *Underground Man.* Trans. Cloudesley Brereton. Westport, Conn.: Hyperion Press, 1974.

1896–97 Sheldon, Charles M[onroe]. *In His Steps. "What Would Jesus Do?"* Chicago: Advance Publishing Company, [1897]. Serialized in *Advance* (November 5, 1896–June 3, 1897).

1897 Bellamy, Edward. *Equality.* New York: D. Appleton.

1897 [Caryl, Charles W.]. *New Era. Presenting the Plans for the New Era Union To Help Develop and Utilize the Best Resources of this Country. Also to Employ the Best Skill There Is Available to Realize the Highest Degree of Prosperity for All Who Will Help To Attain It. Based on Practical and Successful Business Methods.* Denver, Colo.: Author. Reprinted, New York: Arno Press, 1971.

1897 Lasswitz, Kurd. *Auf zwei Planeten, Roman in zwei Büchern.* Leipzig: B. Elischer Nachfolger. In English: *Two Planets. Auf zwei Planeten.* Abridged by Erich Lasswitz. Trans. Hans H. Rudnick. New York: Popular Library, 1971.

1897 Mantegazza, Paolo. *L'anno 3000, un sogno.* Milan: fratelli Treves.

1898 Adam, Paul. *Lettres de Malaisie, roman. . . .*

Paris: G. Grès.

1898 Howard, E[benezer]. *To-Morrow: A Peaceful Path to Real Reform.* London: Swan Sonnenschein. Better known as *Garden Cities of To-Morrow (Being the Second Edition of "To-Morrow: A Peaceful Path to Real Reform").* London: Swan Sonnenschein, 1902.

1899 Griggs, Sutton E[lbert]. *Imperium in Imperio.* Cincinnati, Ohio: Editor Publishing Company. Reprinted, New York: Arno Press, 1969. The first known eutopia by an African American.

1899 Kropotkin, Petr. *Fields, factories and workshops; or, Industry combined with Agriculture and Brain Work with Manual Work.* Boston: Houghton, Mifflin and Co. Reprinted as *Fields, factories and workshops tomorrow.* Ed. Colin Ward. London: Allen & Unwin, 1974.

1899 Wells, H[erbert] G[eorge]. *When the Sleeper Wakes.* [Cover adds *A Story of the Years to Come*]. New York: Harper & Bros. Reprinted, ed. John Lawton. London: Everyman, 1994. Later ed. entitled *The Sleeper Wakes.* London: Thomas Nelson, 1910. Esperanto ed.: *La Dormanto Vekigás.* Trans. A. Frank. London: Esperanto Pub. Co., 1929.

1900 Peck, Bradford. *The World a Department Store. A Story of Life Under a Coöperative System.* Lewiston, Maine: Bradford Peck. Reprinted, New York: Arno Press, 1971.

1901 Butler, Samuel. *Erewhon Revisited twenty years later, both by the original discoverer and his son.* London: G. Richards.

1901 Grave, Jean. *Les Aventures de Nono. . . .* Paris: P.-V. Stock.

1901 Thirion, Emile. *Neustria, utopie individualiste.* Paris: Frischbacher.

1901 Zola, Emile. *Travail.* Paris: E. Fasquelle. In English: *Labor.* New York and London: Harper & Bros., 1901.

1902 Herzl, Theodor.

Altneuland. Berlin: H. Seemann Nachfolger. In English: *Oldnewland.* Trans. Lotta Levensohn. New York: Bloch, 1941.

1902 Tarbouriech, Ernest. *La Cité future, essai d'une utopie scientifique.* Paris: P.-V. Stock.

1902 Wooldridge, C[harles] W[illiam]. *Perfecting the Earth: A Piece of Possible History.* Cleveland, Ohio: Utopia Publishing Company.

1903 [Brown, John Macmillan]. *Limanora. The Island of Progress.* By Godfrey Sweven [pseud.]. New York: G. P. Putnam's Sons. 2nd ed. London: Humphrey Milford, Oxford University Press, 1931.

1903 Halévy, Daniel. *Histoire de quatre ans, 1997–2001.* Paris: Cahiers de la Quinzaine.

1904 Chesterton, G[ilbert] K[eith]. *The Napoleon on Notting Hill.* London: John Lane. Reprinted, Oxford: Oxford University Press, 1994.

1904–5 Wells, H[erbert] G[eorge]. *A Modern Utopia.* London: Chapman and Hall, 1905. U.S. ed. New York: Scribner's, 1905. Reprinted, Lincoln: University of Nebraska Press, 1967. Reprinted, ed. Krishan Kumar. London: Everyman, 1994. Originally published in *The Fortnightly Review* (October 1904–April 1905).

1905 France, Anatole. *Sur la pierre blanche.* Paris: C. Lévy. In English: *The White Stone.* Trans. Charles E. Roche. London: John Lane, 1910.

1906–7 Blatchford, Robert. *The Sorcery Shop; an Impossible Romance.* London: The Clarion Press, [1907]. Originally published in *The Clarion* (November 19, 1906–March 22, 1907).

1907 Howells, William Dean. *Through the Eye of the Needle; A Romance with an Introduction.* New York: Harper and Bros.

1907 London, Jack. *The Iron Heel.* New York: Macmillan. Reprinted, New York: Sagamore Press, 1957; London: Arco, 1966;

and London: Journeyman Press, 1974.

1907 Newte, Horace W. C. *The Master Beast; Being a True Account of the Ruthless Tyranny Inflicted on the British People by Socialism A.D. 1888–2020.* London: Rebman Ltd. Another ed. as *The Red Rosette.* London: Holden & Hardingham, [1913]. 2nd ed. as *The Red Fury: Britain Under Bolshevism.* London: Holden & Hardingham, Ltd., [1919].

1908 France, Anatole. *L'Ile des pingouins.* Paris: C. Lévy. In English: *Penguin Island.* Trans. A. W. Evans. New York: Blue Ribbon Books, 1909.

1908 Grave, Jean. *Terre libre.* Paris: Librairie des temps nouveaux.

1911 Kellermann, Bernhard. *Der Tunnel.* Berlin: S. Fischer.

1911 Renard, Maurice. *Le Péril bleu.* Paris: L. Michaud.

1911 Saunders, W. J. *Kalomera; The Story of a Remarkable Community.* London: Elliot Stock.

1915 [Gilman, Charlotte Perkins]. "Herland." *The Forerunner* 6 (January–December 1915). Republished, New York: Pantheon Books, 1979.

1918 Gregory, Owen. *Meccania. The Super-State.* London: Methuen.

1919 Benoit, Pierre. *L'Atlantide.* Paris: Albin Michel.

1919 Cram, Ralph Adams. *Walled Towns.* Boston: Marshall Jones Co. Reprinted, Seattle, Wash.: Entropy Conservationists, n.d.

1920 Poisson, Ernest. *La République coopérative.* Paris: Grasset.

1920 Taut, Bruno. *Die Auflösung der Städte oder Die Erde eine gute Wohnung oder auch Der Weg zur Alpinen Architektur.* Hagen: Folkwang-Verlag.

1921 Čapek, Karel. *R. U. R. (Rossum's Universal Robots).* Prague: Aventinum.

1921 Masson, Emile. *Utopie des îles bien-*

heureuses dans le Pacifique en l'an 1980. Paris: F. Rieder.

1921 Shaw, George Bernard. *Back to Methuselah; A Metabiological Pentateuch.* New York: Brentano's.

1922 [Hammill, Mary Cicely]. *Theodore Savage; A Story of the Past or the Future.* By Cicely Hamilton [pseud.]. London: Leonard Parsons. Revised as *Lest Ye Die.* London: Jonathan Cape, 1928.

1922–23 Wells, H[erbert] G[eorge]. *Men Like Gods.* London: Cassell, 1923. Originally published in *The Westminster Gazette* (December 5, 1922– January 17, 1923).

1923 Tolstoy, Aleksey. *Aelita.* Moscow: n.p. In English: *Aelita.* Trans. Antonina W. Bouis. New York: Macmillan; London: Collier Macmillan, 1981.

1924 Döblin, Alfred. *Berge, Meere und Giganten.* Berlin: S. Fischer.

1924 Hauptmann, Gerhart. *Der Insel der Grossen Mutter oder Das Wunder von Ile des Dames.* Berlin: S. Fischer. In English: *The Island of the Great Mother.* Trans. Willa and Edwin Muir. New York, 1925.

1924 Zamiatin, Evgenii. *We.* Trans. Gregory Zilboorg. New York: E. P. Dutton. First publication was in English.

1925 Harbou, Thea von. *Metropolis.* Berlin: A. Scherl. In English: *Metropolis.* Norfolk, Va.: Donning Co., 1988.

1925 Madariaga, Salvador de. *La Jirafa sagrada.* Madrid: Espasa-Calpe. In English: *The Sacred Giraffe; Being the Second Volume of the Posthumous Works of Julio Arceval* [pseud.]. New York: Harper and Bros., 1925.

1926 *Amazing Stories* founded by Hugo Gernsback.

1926 Chesterton, G[ilbert] K[eith]. *The Return of Don Quixote.* New York: Dodd, Mead; London: Chatto and Windus, 1927.

1927 Maurois, André. *Voy-age au pays des Articoles.* Paris: J. Schiffrin (with engravings by A. Alexeieff). In English: *A Voyage to the Island of Articoles.* Trans. David Garnett. New York: D. Appleton & Co., 1929.

1928 Jouglet, René. *Voyage à la République des Piles.* Paris: Grasset (7th ed.).

1929 Ferriss, Hugh. *The Metropolis of Tomorrow.* New York: Ives Washburn.

1930 *Astounding Stories* founded by Harry Bates.

1930 Duhamel, Georges. *Scènes de la vie future.* Paris: Mercure de France. In English: *America: the Menace. Scenes from the Life of the Future.* Trans. Charles Minar Thompson. London, 1931; Boston: Houghton Mifflin, 1931.

1930 Stapledon, [William] Olaf. *Last and First Men: A Story of the Near and Far Future.* London: Methuen.

1930 Vassos, John, and Ruth Vassos. *Ultimo: An Imaginative Narration of Life Under the Earth.* New York: E. P. Dutton.

1931 Bordewijk, Ferdinand. *Blokken.* Gravenhage: Nijgh en van Ditmar.

1932 Huxley, Aldous. *Brave New World.* Garden City, N.Y.: Doubleday, Doran.

1932 Leacock, Stephen [Butler]. *Afternoons in Utopia: Tales of the New Time.* London: John Lane, The Bodley Head; New York: Dodd, Mead, 1932.

1932 Wright, S[ydney] Fowler. *The New Gods Lead.* London: Jarrolds. Enlarged as *The Throne of Saturn.* Sauk City, Iowa: Arkham House, 1949.

1933 Hilton, James. *Lost Horizon.* New York: William Morrow & Co.

1933 Wells, H[erbert] G[eorge]. *The Shape of Things to Come: The Ultimate Revolution.* London: Hutchinson; New York: Macmillan, 1933.

1935 Lewis, Sinclair. *It Can't Happen Here.* New York: Doubleday Doran. Reprinted, New York: Dell, 1961. The U.K. ed. (Lon-don: Jonathan Cape, 1935) includes a publisher's note saying that while the title *It Can't Happen in America* was considered, it was felt that the circumstances fit the U.K. also.

1935 Read, Herbert. *The Green Child: A Romance.* London: William Heine-mann. Reprinted without the subtitle, London: Grey Walls Press, 1945 with illustrations by Felix Kelley; London: Eyre & Spottiswoode, 1947; Harmondsworth, England: Penguin, 1969; and New York: New Directions, n.d.

1937 [Burdekin, Katherine Penelope]. *Swastika Night.* By Murray Constantine [pseud.]. London: Victor Gollancz. Reprinted, under the author's real name, Old Westbury, N.Y.: The Feminist Press, 1985.

1937 [Wilkinson, Iris Guiver]. *Wednesday's Children.* By Robin Hyde [pseud.]. London: Hurst & Blackett. Reprinted, Auckland, New Zealand: New Women's Press, 1989; and Dunedin, New Zealand: University of Otago Press, 1993.

1938 Lewis, C[live] S[taples]. *Out of the Silent Planet.* London: John Lane, The Bodley Head. Reprinted, New York: Scribner Classics, 1996. First volume of a trilogy.

1938 Rand, Ayn. *Anthem.* London: Cassell. First US ed. Los Angeles: Pamphle-teers, 1946. U.S. reprint, New York: New American Library, n.d. U.K. reprint, London: Cassell, 1953. Expanded 50th anniversary ed., New York: Dutton, 1995, using the 1946 ed. and including Rand's marked-up 1938 ed. show-ing the extensive revisions.

1941 Borges, Jorge Luis. *La Biblioteca de Babel,* in *El Jardín de senderos que se bifurcan.* Buenos Aires: Sur.

1942 Hesse, Hermann. *Das Glasperlenspiel.* Zurich: Fretz und Was-muth. In English: *Magister Ludi.* Trans. Mervyn Savill. New York: Ungar, 1949.

1942 Lewis, C[live] S[taples]. *Perelandra.* London: John Lane, The Bodley Head. Reprinted, New York: Scribner Clas-sics, 1996. Reprinted as *Voyage to Venus.* London: Pan, 1953. Second volume of a trilogy.

1942 Samuel, Viscount [Herbert Louis]. *An Unknown Land.* London: George Allen and Unwin.

1942 Wright, Austin Tappan. *Islandia.* New York: Farrar & Rinehart.

1945 *Anticipations* founded in Brussels. The first science fiction magazine in French.

1945 Koestler, Arthur. *Twilight Bar: An Escapade in Four Acts.* London: Jonathan Cape. Originally written in 1933 and lost.

1945 Lewis, C[live] S[taples]. *That Hideous Strength, A Modern Fairy Tale for Grown Ups.* London: John Lane, The Bodley Head. Reprinted, New York: Scribner Classics, 1996. Abridged as *The Tortured Planet.* New York: Avon, 1958. Final volume of a trilogy.

1945 Orwell, George [pseud. of Eric Blair]. *Animal Farm; A Fairy Story.* London: Secker & Warburg. First illustrated ed., with illustrations by Joy Batchelor and John Halas: London: Secker and Warburg, 1954. 50th Anniversary Ed. with illus-trations by Ralph Stead-man. New York: Harcourt Brace & Co., 1995.

1946 Werfel, Franz. *Stern der Ungeborenen.* Frank-furt: S. Fischer. In English: *Star of the Unborn.* Trans. Gustave O. Arlt. New York, 1946.

1947 Buber, Martin. *Netiv-ot be-utopyah.* Tel-Aviv: Am oved. In English: *Paths in Utopia.* Trans. R.F.C. Hull. London: Routledge & Kegan Paul, 1949. U.S. ed.: New York: Macmillan, 1950. Reprinted, Boston: Beacon, 1958.

1947 [Eldershaw, Flora Sydney Patricia, and Marjorie Faith Barnard]. *Tomorrow and Tomorrow.* By M. Barnard Eldershaw [pseud.]. Melbourne, Australia: Georgian House. Reprinted, London: Phoenix Press in Associa-tion with Georgian House Melbourne, 1948. "Uncen-sored edition": London: Virago, 1983.

1947 Goodman, Percival, and Paul Goodman. *Communitas: Ways of Livelihood and Means of Life.* Chicago: University of Chicago Press. 2nd ed. New York: Vintage Books, 1960. Reprinted, New York: Columbia University Press, 1990.

1948 Skinner, B[urrhus] F[rederick]. *Walden Two.* New York: Macmillan. Reissued with new introduction (pp. v–xvi) by Skinner, "Walden Two Revisited." New York: Macmillan, 1976.

1949 Graves, Robert. *Watch the North Wind Rise.* New York: Creative Age Press. U.K. ed.: *Seven Days in New Crete.* London: Cassell. Reprinted under the U.K. title: Oxford: Oxford University Press, 1983.

1949 Huxley, Aldous. *Ape and Essence.* New York: Harper. Reprinted, New York: Bantam, 1958; London: Flamingo, 1994.

1949 Jünger, Ernst. *Heliopolis: Rückblick auf eine Stadt.* Tübingen: Heliopolis-Verlag.

1949 George Orwell [pseud. of Eric Blair]. *Nineteen Eighty-four.* Lon-don: Secker & Warburg. Edition *With a Critical Intro-duction and Annotations by Bernard Crick.* Oxford: Clarendon Press, 1984. See also *Nineteen Eighty-four: The Facsimile of the Extant Manuscript.* Edited by Peter Davison. San Diego, Calif.: Harcourt Brace Jovanovich; Weston, Mass.: M & S Press, 1984.

1949 Stewart, George. *Earth Abides.* New York: Random House.

1949 Williamson, Jack. *The Humanoids.* New York: Simon & Schuster.

1950 Bradbury, Ray. *The Martian Chronicles.* Garden City, N.Y.: Doubleday.

U.K. ed. with variations as *The Silver Locusts*. London: Rupert Hart-Davis, 1951. Garden City, N.Y.: Doubleday, 1973 ed. includes notes on the stories that were brought together to form the basis of the novel. Fortieth anniversary ed.: New York: Doubleday, 1990.

1950 *Galaxy, Science Fiction* founded by Horace L. Gold.

1952 Daumal, René. *Le Mont analogue*. Paris: Gallimard. In English: *Mount Analogue: A Novel of Symbolically Authentic Non-Euclidean Adventures in Mountain Climbing*. Trans. Roger Shattuck. New York: Pantheon, 1959.

1952 Pohl, Frederik, and C[yril] M. Kornbluth. *The Space Merchants*. New York: Ballantine, 1953. Originally published as "Gravy Planet," *Galaxy* (June–August 1952).

1952 Vonnegut, Kurt, Jr. *Player Piano*. New York: Charles Scribner's Sons. Also entitled *Utopia 14*. New York: Bantam, 1954.

1953 Blish, James. *A Case of Conscience*. New York: Ballantine, 1958. Originally published in *If* (September 1953).

1953 Bradbury, Ray. *Fahrenheit 451*. New York: Ballantine. A special limited ed. was bound in Johns-Manville Quintera (asbestos). 40th anniversary ed.: New York: Simon & Schuster, 1993.

1953 Clarke, Arthur C. *Childhood's End*. New York: Ballantine. The London: Pan, 1990 ed. has a revised first chapter and a new "Foreword" [i–iv] by Clarke.

1953 *Fiction* founded and edited by Maurice Renault. Originally the French ed. of *The Magazine of Fantasy and Science* but later became independent.

1953 Hergé. *Objectif lune*. Tournai: Casterman.

1953 Waugh, Evelyn. *Love Among the Ruins; A Romance of the Near Future*. London: Chapman and Hall.

1954 Golding, William. *Lord of the Flies*. London: Faber & Faber.

1955–59 Bloch, Ernst. *Das Prinzip Hoffnung*. 3 vols. Berlin: Aufbau-Verlag. In English: *The Principle of Hope*. Trans. Neville Plaice, Stephen Plaice, and Paul Knight. 3 vols. Oxford: Basil Blackwell, 1986.

1957 Jünger, Ernst. *Gläserne Bienen*. Stuttgart: E. Klett. In English: *The Glass Bees*. Trans. Louise Bogan and Elizabeth Mayer. New York: Noonday Press, 1966.

1957 Rand, Ayn. *Atlas Shrugged*. New York: Random House.

1958 Huxley, Aldous. *Brave New World Revisited*. New York: Harper.

1959 Burroughs, William S. *The Naked Lunch*. Paris: Olympia. As *Naked Lunch*. New York: Grove, 1962. Reprinted, New York: Grove Weidenfeld, 1992. U.K. ed. as *The Naked Lunch*. London: Calder and Boyars, 1964.

1960 Miller, Walter M., Jr. *A Canticle for Leibowitz*. Philadelphia: J. B. Lippincott. Reprinted, Boston: Gregg Press, 1975. U.K. ed.: London: Weidenfeld & Nicolson, 1960.

1961 Heinlein, Robert A[nson]. *Stranger in a Strange Land*. New York: G. P. Putnam's Sons. Uncut ed. New York: Ace/Putnam, 1991.

1962 Burgess, Anthony. *Clockwork Orange*. London: Heinemann. U.S. ed. with significant differences: New York: W. W. Norton, 1963.

1962 Huxley, Aldous. *Island*. New York: Harper & Row. Reprinted, London: Flamingo, 1994.

1963 Martel, Suzanne. *Quatre Montréalais en l'an 3000*. Montreal: Ed. du Jour. Published also as *Surréal 3000*. Montreal: Heritage, 1980. In English: *The City Under Ground*. Trans. Norah Smaridge. New York: Viking Press, 1964; and Toronto: Douglas & McIntyre, 1982.

1963 Vonnegut, Kurt, Jr. *Cat's Cradle*. New York: Holt, Rinehart & Winston.

1964 Havel, Vaclav. *Zahradni slavnost*. Prague: Orbis. In English: *The Garden Party*, trans. Vera Blackwell. In Vaclav Havel, *Selected Plays. 1963–83*. London and Boston: Faber and Faber, 1992.

1965 Havel, Vaclav. *Vyrozumeni*. Reinbeck bei Hamburg: Rowohlt Verlag. In English: *The Memorandum*, trans. Vera Blackwell. In Vaclav Havel, *Selected Plays. 1963–83*. London and Boston: Faber and Faber, 1992.

1966 Rimmer, Robert. *The Harrad Experiment*. Los Angeles: Sherburne Press.

1967 Tournier, Michel. *Vendredi ou les Limbes du Pacifique*. Paris: Gallimard. In English: *Friday*. Trans. Norman Denny. Garden City, N.Y.: Doubleday, 1969.

1968 Brunner, John [Kilian Houston]. *Stand on Zanzibar*. Garden City, N.Y.: Doubleday.

1969 Fuller, R[ichard] Buckminster. *Utopia or Oblivion. The Prospects for Humanity*. New York: Bantam.

1969 Le Guin, Ursula K. *The Left Hand of Darkness*. New York: Ace. Also New York: Walker and Co., 1969. The 25th anniversary ed. (New York: Walker, 1994) contains an important "Afterword" and appendixes.

1969 Soleri, Paoli. *Arcology: The City in the Image of Man*. Cambridge, Mass.: MIT Press, 1969.

1969 Wittig, Monique. *Les Guérillères*. Paris: Ed. de Minuit. In English: *Les Guérillères*. Trans. David Le Vay. Boston: Beacon, 1971.

1970 Brown, James Cooke. *The Troika Incident. A Tetralogue in Two Parts*. Garden City, N.Y.: Doubleday.

1970 Frame, Janet. *Intensive Care*. New York: George Braziller. Reprinted, Wellington, New Zealand: A. H. & A. W. Reed, 1971; and London: W. H. Allen, 1971.

1970 Levin, Ira. *This Perfect Day*. New York: Random House.

1971 Boulle, Pierre. *Les Jeux de l'esprit*. Paris: Julliard.

1971 Bryant, Dorothy. *The Comforter*. San Francisco: Moon Books. Republished as *The Kin of Ata Are Waiting For You*. Berkeley, Calif.: Moon Books; New York: Random House, 1976. Reprinted, Berkeley, Calif.: Moon Books; New York: Random House, 1997.

1971 Fairfield, Richard, ed. *Modern Man In Search of Utopia*. San Francisco: Alternatives Foundation.

1971 Houriet, Robert. *Getting Back Together*. New York: Coward, McCann & Geoghegan.

1971 Percy, Walker. *Love in the Ruins*. New York: Farrar, Straus, & Giroux. U.K. ed.: London: Eyre & Spottiswoode.

1971 Silverberg, Robert. *The World Inside*. Garden City, N.Y.: Doubleday.

1972 Brunner, John [Kilian Houston]. *The Sheep Look Up*. New York: Harper & Row.

1972 Calvino, Italo. *Le Città invisibili*. Turin: Einaudi. In English: *Invisible Cities*. Trans. William Weaver. New York: Harcourt Brace Jovanovich, 1974.

1972 Carter, Angela. *The Infernal Desire Machines of Doctor Hoffman*. London: Rupert Hart-Davis. U.S. ed. as *The War of Dreams*. New York: Harcourt Brace Jovanovich, 1974.

1972 Druillet, Philippe. *Les Six Voyages de Lone Sloane*. Paris: Dargaud.

1972 Merle, Robert. *Malevil*. Paris: Gallimard. In English: *Malevil*. Trans. Derek Coltman. New York: Simon and Schuster, 1973.

1972 Rochefort, Christiane. *Archaos ou le Jardin Etincelant*. Paris: Grasset.

1973 Kinkade, Kat[hleen]. *A Walden Two Experiment: The First Five Years of Twin Oaks Community*. New York: William Morrow.

1973 Reynolds, [Dallas McCord]. *Looking Backward, From the Year 2000*. By Mack Reynolds [pseud.]. New York: Ace. U.K. ed.: Morley, West Yorkshire, England: Elmfield Press, 1976.

1974 Le Guin, Ursula K. *The Dispossessed: An Ambiguous Utopia*. New York: Harper & Row. Subtitle dropped in some later printings but then generally restored. Reprinted without subtitle, New York: Avon, 1975; reprinted with subtitle, New York: Harper, 1991.

1975 Callenbach, Ernest. *Ecotopia. The Notebooks and Reports of William Weston*. Berkeley, Calif.: Banyan Tree Books. Reprinted, New York: Bantam, 1977.

1975 Delany, Samuel R. *Dhalgren*. New York: Bantam. Reprinted, Hanover, N.H.: Wesleyan University Press, 1996.

1975 Perec, Georges. *W ou le Souvenir d'enfance*. Paris: Denoël. In English: *W Or the Memory of Childhood*. Trans. David Bellos. Boston: David R. Godine, 1988. U.K. ed.: London: Collins Harvill, 1988.

1975 Russ, Joanna. *The Female Man*. New York: Bantam Books.

1976 Bersianik, Louky. *L'Euguélionne*. Ottawa: Ed. de la Presse. In English: *The Euguelion*. Trans. Howard Scott. Montreal: Alter Ego Editions, 1996; and as *The Euguélionne*. Trans. Gerry Denis, Alson Hewitt, Donna Murray, and Martha O'Brien. Victoria, B.C., Canada: Press Porcépic, 1981.

1976 Curval, Philippe. *Cette Chère Humanité*. Paris: R. Laffont.

1976 Delany, Samuel R. *Triton*. New York: Bantam. Reprinted, Boston: G. K. Hall, 1977. Reprinted, as *Trouble on Triton: An Ambiguous Heterotopia*. Hanover, N.H.: Wesleyan University Press, 1996.

1976 Piercy, Marge. *Woman on the Edge of Time*. New York: Alfred

A. Knopf.
1977 Brantenberg, Gerd. *Egalias Døtre*. Oslo: Pax, 1977. In English: *Egalia's Daughters: A Satire of the Sexes*. Trans. Louis Mackay in cooperation with Gerd Brantenberg. Seattle: Seal Press, 1985.
1978 Charnas, Suzy McKee. *Motherlines*. New York: Berkley. U.K. ed.: London: Victor Gollancz, 1980.
1978 Gearhart, Sally Miller. *The Wanderground: Stories of the Hill Women*. Watertown, Mass.: Persephone Press.
1978 Stableford, Brian M[ichael]. *The City of the Sun*. New York: DAW.
1979 Wolf, Christa. *Kein Ort, Nirgends*. Darmstadt: Luchterhand. In English: *No Place on Earth*. Trans. Jan van Heurck. New York: Farrar, Straus, Giroux, 1982.
1979–83 Lessing, Doris. *Canopus in Argos: Archives*. 5 vols. New York: Alfred A. Knopf; London: Jonathan Cape.
1980 Hoban, Russell. *Riddley Walker*. London: Jonathan Cape. Expanded ed.. Indianapolis: Indiana University Press, 1998.
1981 Ireland, David [Neil]. *City of Women*. Ringwood, Victoria, Australia, and London: Allen Lane. Reprinted, Ringwood, Victoria, Australia: Penguin Books Australia, 1986.
1981 Vargas Llosa, Mario. *La Guerra del fin del mundo*. Barcelona: Seix Barral. In English: *The War of the End of the World*. Trans. Helen R. Lane. New York, 1984.
1983 Annestay, Jean, and Jean-François Jousson. *Moebius: la mémoire du futur*. Paris: Gentiane.
1983 Wolf, Christa. *Kassandra*. Darmstadt: Luchterhand. In English: *Cassandra*. Trans. Jan van Heurck. New York: Farrar, Straus, Giroux, 1984.
1984 Elgin, Suzette Haden. *Native Tongue*. New York: DAW.
1984 Gibson, William [Ford]. *Neuromancer*. New

York: Ace; London: Victor Gollancz, 1984. The 10th anniversary ed. (London: HarperCollins, 1994) has a short afterword by the author.
1985 Atwood, Margaret. *The Handmaid's Tale*. Toronto: McClelland and Stewart. U.S. ed.: Boston: Houghton Mifflin Co., 1986.
1985 Le Guin, Ursula K. *Always Coming Home*. New York: Harper & Row. Includes cassette of music and poetry.
1986 Slonczewski, Joan. *A Door into Ocean*. New York: Arbor House.
1987 Percy, Walker. *The Thanatos Syndrome*. New York: Farrar, Straus, Giroux.
1988 Acker, Kathy. *Empire of the Senseless*. New York: Grove Press.
1988 Brenton, Howard. *Greenland*. London: Methuen in association with the Royal Court Theatre.
1988 Gibson, William [Ford]. *Mona Lisa Overdrive*. London: Victor Gollancz; New York: Bantam, 1988.
1988 Peeters, Benoît, and François Schuiten. *Les Murailles de Samaris*. Paris: Casterman (first volume of the series *Les Cités obscures*).
1988 Tepper, Sheri S. *The Gate to Women's Country*. New York: Doubleday.
1989 Blais, Marie Claire. *L'Ange de la solitude*. Paris: Belfond. In English: *The Angel of Solitude*. Trans. Laura Hodes. Vancouver: Talonbooks, 1993.
1991 Piercy, Marge. *He, She and It*. New York: Alfred A. Knopf. U.K. ed. as *Body of Glass*. London: Michael Joseph, 1992.
1992 Vonarburg, Elisabeth. *Chroniques du pays des mères*. Montreal: Ed. Québec/Amérique. In English: *The Maerlande Chronicles*. Trans. Jane Brierley. Victoria, B.C., Canada: Beach Holme, 1992. U.S. ed. as *In the Mother's Land*. Trans. Jane Brierley. New York: Bantam, 1992.

1992 Woods, Lebbeus. *The New City*. New York: Simon & Schuster.
1993 Robinson, Kim Stanley. *Red Mars*. New York: Bantam.
1994 Robinson, Kim Stanley. *Green Mars*. New York: Bantam.
1994 Vonarburg, Elisabeth. *Les Voyageurs malgré eux*. Montreal: Ed. Québec/Amérique. In English: *Reluctant Voyagers*. Trans. Jane Brierley. Edmonton, Alberta, Canada: Tesseract Books, 1995.
1996 Robinson, Kim Stanley. *Blue Mars*. New York: Bantam; London: HarperCollins, 1996.
1998 Morrison, Toni. *Paradise*. New York: Alfred A. Knopf; London: Chatto & Windus, 1998.
1999 Fell, Alison. *The Mistress of Lilliput*. London: Doubleday.
1999 Robinson, Kim Stanley. *The Martians*. New York: Bantam; London: HarperCollins, 1999.
1999 Spinrad, Norman [Richard]. *Greenhouse Summer*. New York: TOR.
2000 *Communities Directory: A Guide to Intentional Communities and Cooperative Living 2000 Edition*. Rutledge, Mo.: Fellowship for Intentional Community, 2000.

Bibliography of Secondary Sources

Lyman Tower Sargent

Given the vastness of the topic, an exhaustive bibliography on the subject of utopia would be an immense undertaking. In the selective bibliography that follows, preference has been given to works published during the last thirty years, and to texts and collections of a general nature rather than those that address specific works or individual writers. Periodicals and conference publications devoted to this topic are listed, but their contents are not enumerated separately; therefore, this bibliography makes indirect reference to a great number of other texts. In addition, this bibliography does not systematically list all of the works cited in the footnotes and individual bibliographies that accompany the essays in this volume.

Works in the bibliography are listed under the following subject headings: bibliographies and anthologies, conference proceedings, general studies, chronological studies, and thematic studies; the latter two sections are broken down further into subsections. Within each section and subsection, the arrangement is alphabetical.

1. Bibliographies and Anthologies

Choay, Françoise. *L'Urbanisme, utopies et réalités: une anthologie*. Paris: Le Seuil, 1965; facsimile reprint, as part of the series "Points," Paris: Le Seuil, 1979.

Claeys, Gregory, and Lyman Tower Sargent. *The Utopia Reader*. New York: New York University Press, 1999.

Clarke, Ignatius Frederick. *Tale of the Future, from the Beginning to the Present Day: An Annotated Bibliography of those satires, ideal states, imaginary wars and invasions, coming catastrophes and end-of-the-world stories, political warnings and forecasts, inter-planetary voyages and scientific romances – all located in an imaginary future period – that have been published in the United Kingdom between 1644 and 1976*. 3rd edition, London: Library Association, 1978.

Lacassin, Francis, ed. *Voyages aux pays de nulle part* [a collection of texts]. Paris: R. Laffont, 1990.

Lewis, Arthur O. *Utopian Literature in The Pennsylvania State University Libraries: A Selected Bibliography*. University Park: Pennsylvania State University Libraries, 1984.

Negley, Glenn. *Utopian Literature: A Bibliography with a Supplementary Listing of Works Influential in Utopian Thought*. Lawrence: Regents Press of Kansas, 1977.

Rouvillois, Frédéric. *L'Utopie: introduction, choix de textes, commentaires, vade-mecum et bibliographie*. Paris: Flammarion, 1998.

Sargent, Lyman Tower. *British and American Utopian Literature, 1516–1985: An Annotated Chronological Bibliography*. New York and London: Garland, 1988.

Versins, Pierre. *Encyclopédie de l'utopie, des voyages extraordinaires et de la science-fiction*. Lausanne: L'Age d'homme, 1972.

Winter, Michael. *Compendium utopiarum: Typologie und Bibliographie literarischer Utopien*. Vol. I: *Von der Antike bis zur deutschen Frühaufklärung*. Stuttgart: J. B. Metzler, 1978.

2. Conference Proceedings

Alexander, Peter, and Roger Gill, eds. *Utopias*. London: Duckworth, 1984.

Baccolini, Raffaella; Vita Fortunati; and Nadia Minerva, eds. *Viaggi in utopia*. Ravenna: Longo, 1996.

Hudde, Hinrich, and Peter Kuon, eds. *De l'utopie à l'uchronie: formes, significations, fonctions: actes du colloque d'Erlangen, 16–18 octobre 1986*. Tübingen: G. Narr, 1988.

Kamenka, Eugene, ed. *Utopias: Papers from the Annual Symposium of the Australian Academy of the Humanities*. Melbourne, Australia: Oxford University Press, 1987.

Minerva, Nadia, ed. *Per una definizione dell'utopia: metodologie e discipline a confronto, actes du colloque international: Bagni di Lucca, 12–14 septembre 1990*. Introduction by Vita Fortunati and Nadia Minerva. Ravenna: Longo, 1992. Includes much in English.

Saccaro Del Buffa, Giuseppe, and Arthur O. Lewis, eds. *Utopia e modernità: teorie e prassi utopiche nell'età moderna e postmoderna*. Rome: Gangemi, 1989. Includes much in English.

Saccaro Del Buffa, Giuseppe, and Arthur O. Lewis, eds. *Utopie per gli anni ottanta: studi interdisciplinari sui temi, la storia, i progetti*. Rome: Gangemi, 1986. Includes much in English.

Utopian Studies 1. Edited by Gorman Beauchamp, Kenneth Roemer, and Nicholas D. Smith. Lanham, Md.: University Press of America, 1987.

Utopian Studies II. Edited by Michael S. Cummings and Nicholas D. Smith. Lanham, Md.: University Press of America, 1989.

Utopian Studies III. Edited by Michael S. Cummings and Nicholas D. Smith.

Lanham, Md.: University Press of America, 1991. Bound with *Utopian Studies IV*.

Utopian Studies IV. Edited by Lise Leibacher-Ouvrard and Nicholas D. Smith. Lanham, Md.: University Press of America, 1991. Bound with *Utopian Studies III*.

3. General Studies

Journals

Alternative Futures. Vol. 1, no. 1–vol. 4, no. 2–3 (Spring 1978–Spring/Summer 1981). Edited by Merritt Abrash and Alexandra Aldridge.

Utopian Studies: Journal of the Society for Utopian Studies. Vol. 1, no. 1– (1990–). Edited by Lyman Tower Sargent.

Books

Ahlefeld, Henricus ab. *Disputatio philosophica de fictis rebuspublicis. Quam divina favente gratia, praeside Georgio Paschio, Artis rationis, Philos. In Auditorio Majori publice defendet Henricus ab Ahlefeld, Esques Holsatus*. Kiloni: Typis Bartholdi Reutheri, Academ. Typogr., [1704]. Translated into German in Wolfgang Biesterfeld, "Ein früher Beitrag zu Begriff und Geschichte der Utopie. Heinrich von Ahlefeldts Disputatio philosophica de fictis rebuspublicis." *Archiv für Begriffsgeschichte* 16, no. 1 (1972): 28–47. The first known study.

Armytage, Walter Harry Green. *Heavens Below: Utopian Experiments in England, 1560–1960*. London: Routledge and Kegan Paul, 1961.

Berneri, Marie Louise. *Journey Through Utopia*. London: Routledge & Kegan Paul, 1950.

Bloch, Ernst. *Geist der Utopie*. Munich: Duncker & Humblot, 1918. *Faksimile der Ausgabe von 1918* as vol. 16 of his *Gesamtaus-*

gabe. Frankfurt am Main: Suhrkamp, 1971. *Bearbeitete Neuauftage der zweiten Fassang von 1923* as vol. 3 of *Gesamtausgabe*. Frankfurt am Main: Suhrkamp, 1975. Translated by Anthony Nassar as *The Spirit of Utopia*. Stanford, Calif.: Stanford University Press, 2000.

Bloch, Ernst. *Das Prinzip Hoffnung*. 3 vols. Berlin: Aufbau-Verlag, 1955–59; reprinted, as vol. 5 (2 volumes) of his *Gesamtausgabe*, Frankfurt am Main: Suhrkampf Verlag, n.d. Translated by Neville Plaice, Stephen Plaice, and Paul Knight as *The Principle of Hope*. 3 vols. Oxford: Basil Blackwell, 1986.

Bloch, Ernst. *The Utopian Function of Art and Literature: Selected Essays*. Translated by Jack Zipes and Frank Mecklenburg. Cambridge, Mass.: MIT Press, 1988.

Bloomfield, Paul. *Imaginary Worlds or The Evolution of Utopia*. London: Hamish Hamilton, 1932; reprinted, [Norwood, Pennsylvania]: Norwood Editions, 1976.

Buber, Martin. *Pfade in Utopia*. Heidelberg: Verlag Lambert Schneider, 1950. Translated by R.F.C. Hull as *Paths in Utopia*. London: Routledge & Kegan Paul, 1949; New York: Macmillan, 1950; reprinted, Boston: Beacon, 1958.

Cioran, E[mile] M[ichel]. *Histoire et utopie*. Paris: Gallimard, 1960. Translated by Richard Howard as *History and Utopia*. New York: Seaver Books, 1986.

Dupont, Victor. *L'Utopie et le roman utopique dans la littérature anglaise*. Dissertation, Université de Lyons. Cahors: A. Coueslant, 1941.

Elliott, Robert C. *The Shape of Utopia: Studies in a Literary Genre*. Chicago: University of Chicago Press, 1970.

Fortunati, Vita. *La Letteratura utopica inglese: morfologia e grammatica di un genere letterario*. Ravenna: Longo, 1979.

Geoghegan, Vincent. *Utopianism and Marxism*. London: Methuen, 1987.

Goodwin, Barbara, and Keith Taylor. *The Politics of Utopia: A Study in Theory and Practice*. London: Hutchinson, 1982.

Hansot, Elisabeth. *Perfection and Progress: Two Modes of Utopian Thought*. Cambridge, Mass.: MIT Press, 1974.

Hertzler, Joyce Oramel. *The History of Utopian Thought*. New York: Macmillan, 1923.

Hölscher, Lucian. "Utopie." In *Geschichteliche Grundbegriffe: Historisches Lexikon zur politisch-sozialen Sprache in Deutschland*. Edited by Otto Brunner, Werner Conze, and Reinhart Kosellock. 8 vols. Stuttgart: Klett-Cotta, 1990, 6: 733–88. Translated by Kirsten Petrak as "Utopie," with French quotations translated by Nancy Sloan Goldberg and Latin quotations translated by Annette Giesecke-Dunham, in *Utopian Studies* 7, no. 2 (1996): 1–65.

Kumar, Krishan. *Utopianism*. Milton Keynes, England: Open University Press; Minneapolis: University of Minnesota Press, 1991.

Levitas, Ruth. *The Concept of Utopia*. Hemel Hempstead, England: Philip Allan; Syracuse, N.Y.: Syracuse University Press, 1990.

Mannheim, Karl. *Ideologie und Utopie*. Bonn: F. Cohen, 1929. Translated by Louis Wirth and Edward Shils as *Ideology and Utopia: An Introduction to the Sociology of Knowledge*. New York: Harcourt, Brace & Co., [1936]; new edition, London: Routledge, 1991.

Manuel, Frank E., ed. *Utopias and Utopian Thought*. Boston: Beacon Press, 1967.

Manuel, Frank Edward, and Fritzie P. Manuel. *Utopian Thought in the Western World*. Cambridge, Mass.: Belknap Press of Harvard University Press, 1979.

Marin, Louis. *Utopiques: jeux d'espaces*. Paris: Minuit, 1973. Translated by Robert A. Vollrath as *Utopics: Spatial Play*. Atlantic Highlands, N.J.: Humanities Press, 1984.

Morton, A[rthur] L[eslie]. *The English Utopia*. London: Lawrence & Wishart, 1952.

Muchielli, Roger. *Le Mythe de la cité idéale*. Paris: PUF, 1960; facsimile reprint, Brionne: G. Monfort, 1982.

Mumford, Lewis. *The Story of Utopias*. New York: Boni and Liveright, 1922. New York: Viking Press, 1962, with a new "Preface" by the author.

Polak, Fred[erick] L. *De toekomst is verleden tijd*. Utrecht: W. de Haan, 1955. Translated by Elise Boulding as *The Image of the Future: Enlightening the Past, Orientating the Present, Forecasting the Future*. 2 vols. Leyden, The Netherlands: A. W. Sythoff; New York: Oceana Pub., 1961.

Racault, Jean-Michel. *L'Utopie narrative en France et en Angleterre de l'âge classique des Lumières, 1675–1761: étude de forme et de signification*. Geneva: Voltaire Foundation, 1991.

Ricoeur, Paul. *Lectures on Ideology and Utopia*. Edited by George H. Taylor. New York: Columbia University Press, 1986.

Servier, Jean. *Histoire de l'utopie*. Paris: Gallimard, 1967; revised edition, 1991.

Trousson, Raymond. *D'utopie et d'utopistes*. Paris: l'Harmattan, 1998.

Trousson, Raymond. *Voyages aux pays de nulle part: histoire littéraire de la pensée utopique*. Brussels: Université de Bruxelles, 1975; 3rd edition, revised and augmented, 1999.

Walsh, Chad. *From Utopia to Nightmare*. London: Geoffrey Bles, 1962. Earliest study of the dystopia.

4. Chronological Studies

Utopias from Antiquity to the Middle Ages

Baldry, H. C. *Ancient Utopias*. Southampton, England: University of Southampton, 1956.

Dawson, Doyne. *Cities of the Gods: Communist Utopias in Greek Thought*. New York and Oxford: Oxford University Press, 1992.

Delumeau, Jean. *Une histoire du paradis: le jardin des délices*. Paris: Fayard, 1992. Translated by Matthew O'Connell as *History of Paradise: The Garden of Eden in Myth and Tradition*. New York: Continuum, 1995.

Ferguson, John. *Utopias of the Classical World*. London: Thames and Hudson, 1975.

McGinn, Bernard. *Visions of the End: Apocalyptic Traditions in the Middle Ages*. New York: Columbia University Press, 1979.

Pardo, Isaac J. *Fuegos bajo el agua: la invención de utopia*. Caracas: Fundación Casa de Bello, 1983; reprinted, Caracas: Fundación Biblioteca Ayacucho, 1990.

Sixteenth-century Utopias

Eliav-Feldon, Miriam. *Realistic Utopias: The Ideal Imaginary Societies of the Renaissance, 1516–1630*. Oxford: Clarendon Press, 1982.

Hexter, J. H. *More's "Utopia": The Biography of an Idea*. Princeton, N.J.: Princeton University Press,

1952; reprinted, New York: Harper Torchbooks, 1965.

Leslie, Marina. *Renaissance Utopias and the Problem of History*. Ithaca, N.Y.: Cornell University Press, 1998.

Logan, George M. *The Meaning of More's "Utopia."* Princeton, N.J.: Princeton University Press, 1983.

Marc'Hadour, Germain. *L'Univers de Thomas More, chronologie critique de More, Erasme et leur époque (1477–1536)*. Paris: Vrin, 1963.

Prévost, André. *Thomas More (1478–1535) et la crise de la pensée européenne*. Paris: Mame, 1969.

Les Utopies de la Renaissance, colloque international (*Bruxelles, avril 1961*). Brussels and Paris: Presses universitaires de Bruxelles; PUF, 1963.

Seventeenth-century Utopias

Baczko, Bronislaw. *Lumières de l'utopie*. Paris: Payot, 1978. Translated by Judith L. Greenberg as *Utopian Lights: The Evolution of the Idea of Social Progress*. New York: Paragon House, 1989.

Becker, Carl L. *The Heavenly City of the Eighteenth Century Philosophers*. New Haven, Conn.: Yale University Press, 1932.

Boesky, Amy. *Founding Fictions: Utopias in Early Modern England*. Athens: University of Georgia Press, 1996.

Davis, J. C. *Utopia and the Ideal Society: A Study of English Utopian Writing 1516–1700*. Cambridge, England: Cambridge University Press, 1981.

Funke, Hans-Günter. "Utopie, Utopiste." In *Handbuch politisch-sozialer Grundbegriffe in Frankreich, 1680–1820*. Edited by Rolf Reichardt and Eberhard Schmitt in collabora-

tion with Gerd van den Heuvel and Anette Höfer. 11 vols. Munich: Oldenbourg, 1985–1991, 11: 6–104.

Leibacher-Ouvrard, Lise. *Libertinage et utopies sous le règne de Louis XIV*. Geneva: Droz, 1989.

Venturi, Franco. *Utopia and Reform in the Enlightenment*. Cambridge, England: Cambridge University Press, 1971.

Eighteenth-century Utopias

Baehr, Stephen. *The Paradise Myth in Eighteenth-century Russia: Utopian Patterns in Early Secular Russian Literature and Culture*. Stanford, Calif.: Stanford University Press, 1991.

Blaim, Artur. *Failed Dynamics: The English Robinsonade of the Eighteenth Century*. Lublin, Poland: Uniwersytet Marii Curie-Sklodowskiej Wydzial Humanistyczny, 1987.

Claeys, Gregory, ed. *Modern British utopias, 1700–1850*. 8 vols. (texts and introductions). London: Pickering & Chatto, 1997.

Claeys, Gregory, ed. *Utopias of the British Enlightenment*. Cambridge, England: Cambridge University Press, 1994.

Kenyon, Timothy. *Utopian Communism and Political Thought in Early Modern England*. London: Pinter Publishers, 1989.

Rees, Christine. *Utopian Imagination and Eighteenth-century Fiction*. London: Longman, 1996.

Rihs, Charles. *Les Philosophes utopistes: le mythe de la cité communautaire en France au XVIIIe siècle*. Paris: M. Rivière, 1970.

Van Wijngaarden, Nicolaas. *Les Odyssées philosophiques en France entre 1616 et 1789*. Haarlem: Vijbrief, 1932; reprinted, Geneva: Slatkine, 1982.

Yardeni, Myriam. *Utopie et révolte sous Louis XIV*. Paris: A.-G. Nizet, 1980.

Nineteenth-century Utopias

Alexandrian, Sarane. *Le Socialisme romantique*. Paris: Le Seuil, 1979.

Beecher, Jonathan. *Charles Fourier: The Visionary and His World*. Berkeley: University of California Press, 1986.

Claeys, Gregory. *Citizens and Saints: Politics and Anti-politics in Early British Socialism*. Cambridge, England: Cambridge University Press, 1989.

Claeys, Gregory. *Machinery, Money, and the Millennium: From Moral Economy to Socialism, 1815–1860*. Princeton, N.J.: Princeton University Press, 1987.

Claeys, Gregory, ed. *Selected Works of Robert Owen*. 4 vols. London: William Pickering, 1993.

Crétinon, Jean-François, and François-Marie Lacour. *Allons en Icarie: deux ouvriers viennois aux Etats-Unis en 1855*. Grenoble: Presses universitaires de Grenoble, 1980.

Dagognet, François. *Trois Philosophies revisitées: Saint-Simon, Proudhon, Fourier*. Hildesheim: Olms, 1997.

Desroche, Henri. *La Société festive: du fouriérisme écrit aux fouriérismes pratiqués*. Paris: Le Seuil, 1975.

Francis, Claude, and Fernande Gontier. *Partons pour Icarie: des Français en Utopie, une société idéale aux Etats-Unis en 1849*. Paris: Perrin, 1983.

Goodwin, Barbara. *Social Science and Utopia: Nineteenth-century Models of Social Harmony*. Hassocks, Sussex, England: Harvester Press, 1978.

Petitfils, Jean-Christian. *Les Socialismes utopiques*. Paris: PUF, 1977.

Petitfils, Jean-Christian. *La Vie quotidienne des communautés utopistes au XIXe siècle*. Paris: Hachette, 1982.

Taylor, Barbara. *Eve and the New Jerusalem: Socialism and Feminism in the Nineteenth Century*. London: Virago, 1983; New York: Pantheon Books, 1983; reprinted, Cambridge, Mass.: Harvard University Press, 1993.

Taylor, Keith. *The Political Ideas of the Utopian Socialists*. London: Frank Cass, 1982.

Walicki, Andrzej. *W kregu konserwatywnej utopii*. Warsaw: Panstwowe Wydawn. Naukowe, 1964. Translated by Hilda Andrews-Rusiecka as *The Slavophile Controversy: History of a Conservative Utopia in Nineteenth-century Russian Thought*. Oxford: Clarendon Press, 1975.

Zemel, Carol M. *Van Gogh's Progress: Utopia, Modernity, and Late Nineteenth-century Art*. Berkeley: University of California Press, 1997.

Twentieth-century Utopias

Gerber, Richard. *Utopian Fantasy: A Study of English Utopian Fiction Since the End of the Nineteenth Century*. London: Routledge & Kegan Paul, 1955; reprinted, with additions, New York: McGraw-Hill, 1973.

Greven-Borde, Hélène. *Formes du roman utopique en Grande-Bretagne 1918–1970*. Paris: PUF, 1984.

Hermand, Jost. *Der alte Traum vom neuen Reich: Volkische Utopien und Nationalsozialismus*. Frankfurt, Germany: Athenäum, 1988. Translated by Paul Levesque in collaboration with Stefan Soldovieri as *Old Dreams of a New Reich: Volkish Utopias and National Socialism*. Bloomington: Indiana University Press, 1992.

Kumar, Krishan. *Utopia and Anti-utopia in Modern Times*. Oxford: Basil Blackwell, 1987.

Moylan, Tom. *Demand the Impossible: Science Fiction and the Utopian Imagination*. London: Methuen, 1986.

5. Thematic Studies

American Communities

Bestor, Arthur Eugene, Jr. *Backwoods Utopias: The Sectarian and Owenite Phases of Communitarian Socialism in America, 1663–1829*. Philadelphia: University of Pennsylvania Press, 1950; 2nd enlarged edition, Philadelphia: University of Pennsylvania Press, 1970.

Creagh, Ronald. *Laboratoires de l'utopie: les communautés libertaires aux Etats-Unis*. Paris: Payot, 1983.

Dare, Philip. *American Communes to 1860: A Bibliography*. New York: Garland, 1990.

Fogarty, Robert S. *All Things New: American Communes and Utopian Movements 1860–1914*. Chicago: University of Chicago Press, 1990.

Fogarty, Robert S. *Dictionary of American Communal and Utopian History*. Westport, Conn., and London: Greenwood Press, 1980.

Miller, Timothy. *American Communes 1860–1960: A Bibliography*. New York: Garland, 1990.

Miller, Timothy. *The Quest for Utopia in Twentieth-century America. Volume I: 1900–1960*. Syracuse, N.Y.: Syracuse University Press, 1998.

Miller, Timothy. *The 60s Communes: Hippies and Beyond*. Syracuse, N.Y.: Syracuse University Press, 1999.

Pitzer, Donald E., ed. *America's Communal Utopias*. Chapel Hill: University of North Carolina Press, 1997.

Millenarianism

Barkun, Michael. *Disaster and the Millennium*. New Haven, Conn.: Yale University Press, 1974.

Barkun, Michael, ed. *Millennialism and Violence*. London: Frank Cass, 1996.

Cohn, Norman. *The Pursuit of the Millennium*. London: Secker & Warburg, 1957; 2nd edition, with the subtitle *Revolutionary Messianism in Medieval and Reformation Europe and Its Bearing on Modern Totalitarian Movements*, New York: Harper & Row, 1961.

Daniels, Ted. *Millennialism: An International Bibliography*. New York: Garland, 1992.

The Encyclopedia of Apocalypticism. Ed. Bernard McGinn, John J. Collins, and Stephen J. Stein. New York: Continuum, 1999.

Kumar, Krishan, and Stephen Bann, eds. *Utopias and the Millennium*. London: Reaktion Books, 1993.

Olson, Theodore. *Millennialism, Utopianism and Progress*. Toronto: University of Toronto Press, 1982.

Tuveson, Ernest Lee. *Millennium and Utopia: A Study in the Background of the Idea of Progress*. Berkeley: University of California Press, 1949.

Weber, Eugen. *Apocalypses: Prophecies, Cults, and Millennial Beliefs Through the Ages*. Cambridge, Mass.: Harvard University Press, 1999.

Feminist Utopianism

Albinski, Nan Bowman. *Women's Utopias in British and American Fiction*. London: Routledge, 1988.

Bammer, Angelika. *Partial Visions: Feminism and Utopianism in the 1970s*.

New York: Routledge, 1991.

Barr, Marleen S. *Feminist Fabulation: Space/Postmodern Fiction*. Iowa City: University of Iowa Press, 1992.

Barr, Marleen S. *Lost in Space: Probing Feminist Science Fiction and Beyond*. Chapel Hill: University of North Carolina Press, 1993.

Barr, Marleen S., ed. *Future Females: A Critical Anthology*. Bowling Green, Ohio: Bowling Green State University Popular Press, 1981.

Barr, Marleen S., ed. *Future Females, the Next Generation: New Voices and Velocities in Feminist Science Fiction Criticism*. Lanham, Md.: Rowman & Littlefield, 2000.

Barr, Marleen S., and Nicholas D. Smith, eds. *Women and Utopia: Critical Interpretations*. Lanham, Md.: University Press of America, 1983.

Bartkowski, Frances. *Feminist Utopias*. Lincoln: University of Nebraska Press, 1989.

Burwell, Jennifer. *Notes on Nowhere: Feminism, Utopian Logic, and Social Transformation*. Minneapolis: University of Minnesota Press, 1997.

Donawerth, Jane L., and Carol A. Kolmerten, eds. *Utopian and Science Fiction by Women: Worlds of Difference*. Syracuse, N.Y.: Syracuse University Press, 1994.

Jones, Libby Falk, and Sara Webster Goodwin, eds. *Feminism, Utopia, and Narrative*. Knoxville: University of Tennessee Press, 1990.

Kessler, Carol Farley, ed. *Daring to Dream: Utopian Stories by United States Women: 1836–1919*. London: Pandora Press, 1984; 2nd edition, as *Daring to Dream: Utopian Fiction by United States Women Before 1950*, Syracuse,

N.Y.: Syracuse University Press, 1995.

Sargisson, [Lucinda Mary] Lucy. *Contemporary Feminist Utopianism*. London: Routledge, 1996.

Utopian Literature in the United States

Bowman, Sylvia E., et al. *Edward Bellamy Abroad: An American Prophet's Influence*. New York: Twayne Publishers, 1962.

Heller, Arno; Walter Hölbing; and Waldemar Zacharasiewicz, eds. *Utopian Thought in American Literature: Untersuchungen zur literarischen Utopie und Dystopie in den USA*. Tübingen, Germany: Gunter Narr Verlag, 1988.

Lipow, Arthur. *Authoritarian Socialism in America: Edward Bellamy and the Nationalist Movement*. Berkeley: University of California Press, 1982.

Papanikolas, Zeese. *Trickster in the Land of Dreams*. Lincoln: University of Nebraska Press, 1995.

Parrington, Vernon Louis, Jr. *American Dreams: A Study of American Utopias*. 2nd edition. New York: Russell and Russell, 1964.

Patai, Daphne, ed. *Looking Backward, 1988–1888: Essays on Edward Bellamy*. Amherst: University of Massachusetts Press, 1988.

Pfaelzer, Jean. *The Utopian Novel in America 1888–1896: The Politics of Form*. Pittsburgh: University of Pittsburgh Press, 1984.

Rhodes, Harold V. *Utopia in American Political Thought*. Tucson: University of Arizona Press, 1967.

Roemer, Kenneth M. *The Obsolete Necessity: America in Utopian Writings, 1888–1900*. Kent, Ohio: Kent State University Press, 1976.

Roemer, Kenneth M., ed. *America as Utopia*. New York: Burt Franklin, 1981.

Rooney, Charles J., Jr. *Dreams and Visions: A Study of American Utopias, 1865–1917*. Westport, Conn.: Greenwood, 1985.

Segal, Howard P. *Technological Utopianism in American Culture*. Chicago: University of Chicago Press, 1985.

Utopia/Dystopia and Cinema

The lists that follow indicate some of the ways in which utopian themes have been interpreted by filmmakers, in both imaginative and nonfiction films. In no way meant to be definitive or comprehensive, they include suggestions from Barbara Bergeron, David Callahan, David Cronin, Marie Nesthus, Anne Skillion, and Joseph Yranski of The New York Public Library; Sylvie Dreyfus and Frédéric Ramires of the Bibliothèque nationale de France; and Lyman Tower Sargent and Anne Dressen.

Feature Films

1920
L'Atlantide [*Lost Atlantis*]. Jacques Feyder (France).

1924
Aelita [*Aelita: Queen of Mars*]. Yakov Protazanov (USSR).

1926
Metropolis. Fritz Lang (Germany)

1928
Potomok Chingis-Khana [*Storm Over Asia*]. Vsevolod Pudovkin (USSR)

1929
Novij Vavylon [*The New Babylon*]. Grigory Kosintsev and Leonid Trauberg (USSR)

Staroye i novoye [*The General Line, Old and New*]. Sergei Eisenstein (USSR)

1930
Zemlya [*Earth*]. Aleksandr Dovzhenko (USSR)

1932
Die Herrin von Atlantis [*The Mistress of Atlantis*]. G. W. Pabst (Germany)

1933
Island of Lost Souls. Erle C. Kenton (USA)

Zéro de conduit [*Zero for Conduct*]. Jean Vigo (France)

1934
Schastiye [*Happiness*]. Aleksandr Medvedkin (USSR)

1936
La Belle Equipe [*They Were Five*]. Julien Duvivier (France)

Modern Times. Charlie Chaplin (USA)

Things to Come. William Cameron Menzies (USA)

1937
Lost Horizon. Frank Capra (USA)

La Marseillaise. Jean Renoir (France)

1939
Gulliver's Travels (animated). Produced by Max Fleischer (USA)

The Wizard of Oz. Victor Fleming (USA)

1948
The Blue Lagoon. Frank Launder (UK)

1949
The Fountainhead. King Vidor (USA)

1950
Atoll K [*Utopia*]. Léo Joannon (France/Italy). With Laurel and Hardy.

1951
Plutopia. Charles A. Nichols (USA)

1954
Brigadoon. Vincente Minnelli (USA)

Robinson Crusoe. Luis Buñuel (USA)

1955
Animal Farm. Joy Batchelor and John Halas (UK)

1956
Nineteen Eighty-four. Michael Anderson (UK)

1958
Mon oncle. Jacques Tati (France)

1959
Green Mansions. Mel Ferrer (USA)

1960
The Time Machine. George Pal (USA)

1962
La Jetée. Chris Marker (France)

1963
Lord of the Flies. Peter Brook (UK)

1965
Alphaville. Jean-Luc Godard (France)

Sins of the Fleshapoids. Mike Kuchar (USA)

1966
Fahrenheit 451. François Truffaut (UK)

A Man for All Seasons. Fred Zinnemann (UK)

1968
Planet of the Apes. Franklin J. Schaffner (USA)

2001: A Space Odyssey. Stanley Kubrick (USA/UK)

Wild in the Streets. Barry Shear (USA)

1969
L'Enfant sauvage [*The Wild Child*]. François Truffaut (France)

If. Lindsay Anderson (UK)
Vladimir et Rosa. Jean-Luc Godard (France)

1971
A Clockwork Orange. Stanley Kubrick (USA)

Dark Spring. Ingemo Engström (Finland/RFA)

San Michele aveva un gallo [*St. Michael Had a Rooster*]. Paolo and Vittorio Taviani (Italy)

THX 1138. George Lucas (USA).

1972
L'An 01. Jacques Doillon and Alain Resnais (France)

Solaris. Andrei Tarkovsky (USSR)

1973
Lost Horizon. Charles Jarrott (USA)

Sleeper. Woody Allen (USA)

Soylent Green. Richard Fleisher (USA)

Westworld. Michael Crichton (USA)

Zardoz. John Boorman (USA)

1975
Allonsanfan. Paolo and Vittorio Taviani (Italy)

La Cécilia. Jean-Louis Comolli (France/Italy)

Rollerball. Norman Jewison (USA)

The Stepford Wives. Bryan Forbes (USA)

Winstanley. Kevin Brownlow and Andrew Mollo (UK)

1976
Jonah qui aura 25 ans en l'an 2000 [*Jonah Who Will Be 25 in the Year 2000*]. Alain Tanner (France)

Logan's Run. Michael Anderson (USA)

Utopia. Iradj Azimi (France)

1977
The Island of Dr. Moreau. Don Taylor (USA)

1978
Warlords of Atlantis. Kevin Connor (USA/UK/France)

1979
Falansterul [*The Phalanstery*]. Savel Stiopul (Romania)

Mad Max. George Miller (Australia)

Stalker. Andrei Tarkovsky (USSR)

1980
The Blue Lagoon. Randal Kleiser (USA)

A Idade da terra [*The Age of the Earth*]. Glauber Rocha (Brazil)

1981
Mad Max 2 [aka *The Road Warrior*]. George Miller (Australia)

1982
Android. Aaron Lipstadt (USA)

Blade Runner. Ridley Scott (USA)

1983
Born in Flames. Lizzie Borden (USA)

La Vie est un roman [*Life Is a Bed of Roses*]. Alain Resnais (France)

1984
Nineteen Eighty-four. Michael Radford (USA)

1985
Brazil. Terry Gilliam (USA)

Mad Max: Beyond Thunderdome. George Miller (Australia)

1987
The Last of England. Derek Jarman (UK)

1988
Crusoe. Caleb Deschanel (USA)

Saaraba [*Utopia*]. Amadou Saalum Seck (Senegal)

1990
Closet Land. Radha Bharadwaj (USA)

The Handmaid's Tale. Volker Schlöndorff (USA)

Lord of the Flies. Harry Hook (USA)

Total Recall. Paul Verhoeven (USA)

1991
The Rapture. Michael Tolkin (USA)

1992
Le Tombeau d'Alexandre [The Last Bolshevik]. Chris Marker (France)

1995
Twelve Monkeys. Terry Gilliam (USA)

Waterworld. Kevin Reynolds (USA)

1996
The Island of Dr. Moreau. John Frankenheimer (USA)

1997
Gattaca. Andrew Niccol (USA)

La Vie sur terre [Life on Earth]. Abderrahmane Sissake (USA)

1998
Utopia. James Benning (USA)

Documentaries

1922
Nanook of the North. Robert Flaherty (USA)

1926
Moana. Robert Flaherty (USA)

1927
Oktyabr [October: 10 Days That Shook the World]. Sergei Eisenstein (USSR)

1932
L'Idée [The Idea]. Berthold Bartosch (France)

1933
Architekturkongress. Laszlo Moholy-Nagy (Germany)

Triumph des Willens [Triumph of the Will]. Leni Riefenstahl (Germany)

1936
New Architecture at the London Zoo. Laszlo Moholy-Nagy (Germany)

1937
Spanish Earth. Joris Ivens (USA)

1938
Olympia. Leni Riefenstahl (Germany)

1949
La Vie commence demain [Life Begins Tomorrow]. Nicole Vedrès (France)

1953
Architecte maudit, Claude-Nicolas Ledoux. Pierre Kast (France)

1954
Salt of the Earth. Herbert Biberman (USA)

1959
The Old-Order Amish. Vincent R. Tortora (USA)

1963
City: Heaven and Hell. Produced by Ian Macneill (USA)

City and the Future. Produced by Ian Macneill (USA)

1966
It Happened Here. Kevin Brownlow and Andrew Mollo (UK)

1967
Summerhill. Dennis Miller (Canada)

1968
Les lycéens ont la parole. Pierre Zedine (France)

1970
Woodstock: Three Days of Peace and Music. Michael Wadleigh (USA)

1971
Le Train en marche [The Train Rolls On]. Chris Marker (France)

1974
The Shakers. Tom Davenport (USA)

1975
The Amish: A People of Preservation. John L. Ruth (USA)

Charles Fourier. Jean-Marie Berzosa (France)

1983
The Architecture of Frank Lloyd Wright. Barbara and Murray Grigor (UK/USA)

Roosevelt, New Jersey: Visions of Utopia. Richard Kroehling (USA)

Signals Through the Flames: The Story of the Living Theatre. Sheldon Rochlin and Maxine Harris (USA)

1984
Good Morning Mr. Orwell. Nam June Paik (USA)

The Shakers: Hands to Work, Heart to God. John Colby (USA)

2084. Chris Marker (France)

1985
The Amish: Not to Be Modern. Victoria Larimore and Michael Taylor (USA)

The Men Who Danced: The Story of Ted Shawn's Male Dancers, 1933–1940. Ron Honsa (USA)

1987
Le Corbusier. Jacques Barsac (France)

1988
Denishawn: The Contributions of America Dance Pioneers. Produced by Clarke Santee and Delia Gravel Santee (USA)

Living with the Living Theatre. Nam Jun Paik (USA)

1989
Undergångens Arkitektur [The Architecture of Doom]. Peter Cohen (Sweden)

1994
The Bauhaus in America. Judith Pearlman (USA)

Follow the Dirt Road: An Introduction to Intentional Communities in the 1990s. Produced by Monique Gauthier (USA)

1996
Expérience permanente: Laszlo Moholy-Nagy et le Bahaus. Jens Schmohl (Germany)

1997
Familistère de Godin. Philippe Spinau (France)

Familistère de Guise. Catherine Adda (France)

Hadès comme lecture utopique du xxe siècle. François Demuth (Belgium)

1998
Bauhaus, un mythe moderne. Karl Stutterheim and Niels Bolbrinker (Germany)

Une école pas comme les autres. Marina Goldovskaia (France/Russie)

The Shakers: I Don't Want to Be Remembered as a Chair. Produced by Jane Treays (UK)

DATE DUE
